"B.G Burkett's work has been used by police officers across the country. His expert testimony has put criminals in jail. *Stolen Valor* should be read by every law enforcement officer in America."

Jim Hughes,
Detective, Dallas Police Department

"War is hell, but what happened to us that we bought so many lies? Unfortunately, certain individuals expected posttraumatic stress in everyone who went to Vietnam. These psychological expectations, especially when supported by political conviction, resulted in some serious diagnostic errors. *Stolen Valor* reminds us to check reality."

Loren Pankratz, Ph.D.,
Clinical Professor, Oregon Health Services University

"Finally, a book which exposes these pathetic cowards for what they are: sociopathic con men feeding off the battlefield exploits of our true heroes."

Jack Trimarco,
Special Agent, FBI

"As Samuel Johnson said in 1778, 'Every man feels meanly of himself for not having been a soldier or not having been at sea. . . .' When it came to Vietnam, as *Stolen Valor* brilliantly portrays, some compensated by bad-mouthing those who did serve, while others stole the mantle of those who had. Must read for those who would understand Vietnam."

Colonel Harry G. Summers, Jr.,
author of Vietnam War Almanac,
and Editor, Vietnam magazine

STOLEN VALOR

STOLEN VALOR

How the Vietnam Generation Was Robbed
of Its Heroes and Its History

B. G. Burkett
Glenna Whitley

VERITY PRESS, INC.

DALLAS, TEXAS

VERITY PRESS, INC.
P.O. Box 50366
Dallas, Texas 75250
www.stolenvalor.com

Printed in Canada

02 01 00 99 98   5 4 3 2 1

Library of Congress Cataloging-in-Publication Data
ISBN 1–56530–284–2

Index by Michael C. Rossa
Book design by Mark McGarry
Set in Monotype Dante

To Bernie and Helen Burkett, who hoped and prayed that their son would return safely from Vietnam. And to the more than one million sets of parents of the Vietnam War whose prayers were not answered.

Contents

Preface

IN MARCH 1990, Susan McIntosh was found slain in the garage of her East Dallas home. Her husband, Dana, and a friend who worked for him had arrived in midmorning to pick up Susan's station wagon. It needed repairs before the McIntoshes were to leave for a trip to Washington, D.C., where one of Dana's companies had an office.

Dana screamed when he saw Susan lying on the concrete floor, stabbed thirty-three times. He scooped her up in his arms, ran to his Mercedes, and cradled her as the employee raced to a hospital emergency room. But she was already dead.

The homicide was shocking enough, but friends and family were even more stunned later that day to learn that Dana had been arrested and charged with his forty-two-year-old wife's murder.

Assigned to do a story about the case for *D Magazine*, where I was a staff writer, I began talking to friends of the McIntoshes, most of whom belonged to the same close-knit Sunday school class. The group went to movies, ate dinner, and played softball together. They insisted there was no way that Dana had committed the crime. Not only was he an accomplished businessman, Dana McIntosh, forty-four, also was a war hero—and more. "It couldn't be Dana," one friend said. "If Dana had killed her, she wouldn't have felt a thing. He was in Vietnam with the CIA. He wouldn't stab someone like that. He would do it real quiet, real quick."

Dana had often told friends of his combat experiences in Vietnam, where he served in the Army as an infantry platoon leader in 1969. Though his thick black hair was receding, and he had a slight paunch, his Vietnam experience still clung to him like an invisible suit. He still had a walk that was pure military (elbows out, thumbs down the seam of his pants).

When friends gathered in his study during social occasions, he would talk about his experiences as a second lieutenant in the elite Army Rangers. Though he had served in Vietnam for only four or five months, he had seen the worst of it. McIntosh claimed his many military medals, carefully framed and displayed in a glass case on a wall in their upper-middle-class home, attested to that heroism: two Silver Stars, three Bronze Star Medals for valor, a Purple Heart, and other awards making him the most highly decorated veteran in Texas other than Audie Murphy.

Dana's stories, though twenty years old, had lost none of their vivid detail. He talked about being wounded in Vietnam. He made it a point to see every movie made about the Vietnam experience and shared his impressions about their accuracy. Inevitably, during these sessions, Dana would lower his voice then confide that he had received no medals for his most dangerous work in Vietnam. "In fact," he told friends, "if I were caught, the U.S. government would deny they knew me." He had been with the CIA, he explained, and several times he had been dropped behind enemy lines on secret missions. He talked about the Phoenix Program, a secret strike group that assassinated leaders sympathetic to the Viet Cong. He said that while he was recovering from his wounds, he had helped bust a heroin smuggling ring in Taiwan that was bringing drugs to the United States in the coffins of dead GIs. "He told me he loved Vietnam," remembered one woman. "He would go back."

Dana's stories could be frightening. Several adults, hearing a speech he gave to a Methodist youth group about being dropped into Cambodia to assassinate civilians, became very upset. He always left the distinct impression that he was still doing covert work for the U.S. government. The fact that one of Dana's handful of companies had an office in Washington, D.C., where he kept an apartment and usually spent two nights a week, made it seem doubly believable. Perhaps Susan's murder was related to that work. Maybe somebody was taking revenge for Dana's covert activities.

His criminal defense attorney predicted that McIntosh would be acquitted, pointing out that the prosecutor could show no motive for Dana to kill Susan and no eyewitnesses or physical evidence linking him to the crime. His exemplary war service certainly would be brought in to show Dana's strong sense of honor and integrity. And surely the issue of McIntosh's years as a covert operative would be used to suggest the crime was revenge-related.

The only problem with this was McIntosh's weird behavior on the day of the murder. He had large scratches on his face and neck, and the friend who had driven him to the hospital and a nurse both reported seeing him with his dead wife's fingers in his mouth, as if he were trying to suck incriminating evidence from beneath her fingernails.

I began investigating McIntosh's background and filed a Freedom of Information Act request for the public portion of Dana K. McIntosh's military records with the National Personnel Records Center in St. Louis. Sure enough, the papers showed he was a war hero. Though he had served only a few months in Vietnam, the documents supported McIntosh's claims that he had been awarded two Silver Stars, three Bronze Stars, an Air Medal, and a handful of other decorations. Though not mentioned on the summary, one document indicated he had been wounded and received a Purple Heart.

Having never been in the military, I didn't understand some of the acronyms and abbreviations, and I wanted to know how to verify that McIntosh had been a covert operative. Word of mouth eventually led me to B. G. Burkett, who had been described to me as an amateur expert in acquiring and understanding military records. He agreed to examine McIntosh's military history for me.

Burkett explained that just because McIntosh had medals for valor framed on his wall didn't mean he had earned them. Since working to raise money for the Texas Vietnam Veterans Memorial, Burkett said he had run across numerous phonies who wore medals bought through catalogs or at flea markets. He also told me something that surprised me even more. Even though the records I received from the NPRC confirmed the decorations, that didn't necessarily prove they were legitimate. The only real proof were the signed and chronologically numbered general orders that awarded the decorations. The numbers were listed beside each acronym, but copies of the general orders were not included in the McIntosh packet. You had to go to the National Archives and other military sources to get them. So I flew to Washington and began digging.

By carefully cross-checking records, I discovered McIntosh had arrived in Vietnam in mid-September 1969 as a second lieutenant, rifle platoon leader, Company A, 4th Battalion, 9th Infantry, 25th Infantry Division. Most new arrivals in Vietnam received two weeks of "in-country" training before going out in the field. Since he had left Vietnam by mid-December, he served at most two-and-a-half months in combat.

My investigation showed that General Order 11936, listed on his file as awarding him a Bronze Star, actually gave Warrant Officer John Driscoll a Distinguished Flying Cross. General Order 15596, listed as awarding McIntosh a Silver Star, a medal given only for valor in combat, in reality gave soldier Larry Masters a Bronze Star for valor. General Order 1236, supposedly awarding McIntosh an Air Medal (given for twenty-five combat air assaults), was a number too low to be awarded in late 1969, when Dana saw combat. That GO actually awarded soldier Ray Black an Army Commendation Medal for valor.

Of the medals McIntosh claimed to have been awarded, the only one that seemed to be legitimate was the Vietnamese Gallantry Cross with Silver Star, a foreign decoration for an action on October 17, 1969. The Purple Heart was bogus. McIntosh didn't leave Vietnam because he was wounded; he was shipped to a military hospital in Japan because of a skin condition.

McIntosh had not become a member of the Army Rangers until he left Vietnam and returned to Texas. (As for covert operations, experts told me it was highly unlikely for someone with McIntosh's skills and length of service to be involved in such CIA operations.) There was one clue to how he had falsified his records: Between the time he was pulled from the field until he left Vietnam he had been assigned to administrative duties.

The truth is Dana McIntosh had created another persona, one more manly, more aggressive, more admirable, more successful. And his war record wasn't the only thing he had lied about. He claimed he was a CPA, held an engineering degree, and had earned an MBA (all false). Some of the companies he claimed he owned were in fact owned by others. Though he seemed to be very successful, his businesses had failed over the years. As a part of one business scheme, he had mortgaged his wife's portion of a family farm—and lost it.

My story, "Dr. Jekyll and Mr. McIntosh," ran in *D Magazine* in September 1990, six months before he went to trial. His war record, which earlier had appeared to be such a plus for his defense, was not raised during testimony. Dana McIntosh was convicted of his wife's murder and is now serving time in a Texas prison.

Burkett and I spoke on the phone frequently during this process, and it was evident that people like McIntosh infuriated him. He felt they were trading on the common stereotypes of the Vietnam War (covert operations, assassination of civilians) to pump themselves up, to compensate for failed lives. Though McIntosh had served briefly in the war zone, Burkett told me of other phonies who had never left the states—some had never even served in the military. He already had exposed some of them in the press.

What Burkett was telling me was astonishing. But even more interesting was the material he had gathered about Vietnam veterans as a group. His research into the myths and realities of Vietnam was fascinating, especially in that my understanding of the war had been entirely shaped by television and movies. The only time during my career that I had tried to write specifically about a Vietnam veteran was when working on a story about the homeless. The director of a shelter suggested I interview a Vietnam veteran who had become homeless after struggling with memories of the war. The interview ended abruptly when the "veteran," clearly mentally ill, dissolved into incoherence and abusive language. I never used that material, but it only reconfirmed what I thought I knew about Vietnam veterans. I believed the stereotypes that they were the "haunted generation," still troubled years after the war had ended.

Burkett and another writer had prepared a proposal for a book about his discoveries, so I tried to hook them up with an agent. At the time, I gave little thought to collaborating with Burkett myself. Though I was born on an Air Force base when my father served as a pilot in the mid-fifties (after Korea and before Vietnam), that was my only contact with military life.

It wasn't until 1994 that I actually met Jug Burkett face-to-face. Freelancing, I was looking for interesting stories and wondered what he was up to. He hadn't been able to interest a publisher in his book, but in the intervening years he had continued to gather material exposing more phonies. One had just been indicted on federal charges for wearing fraudulent medals, and a writer with *Reader's Digest* was working on a story about Burkett and his crusade.

I wrote a story about Burkett for *Texas Monthly*, which was followed by a segment on *20/20* with correspondent Tom Jarriel. Then in January 1995, Jug asked me to collaborate on *Stolen Valor*, for which I soon after wrote an outline and projected a nine-month effort to finish the project. Now, almost three years later, I can smile at how I underestimated the perseverance of the man and the vast amount of documentation he had collected.

In the beginning, Burkett brought me his research—boxes and boxes and boxes of books, videotapes, press clippings, studies from medical journals, and literally hundreds of military records. He was—and is—the most methodical, persistent, and creative investigative reporter I have ever met. Until we began to apply his research to a manuscript, I don't think we realized the tremendous scope of what he had discovered.

What he has taught me about military records and about examining not only my assumptions but also those of so-called "experts" has been enormous. He has also taught me a great deal about the need to be wary of the seduction of a "good story." As a journalist, I have always attempted to be fair and accurate, but the temptation to believe subjects who have sensational tales to tell is always there. We are rewarded by the market, by our peers, by professional advancement when our stories are juicy, outrageous, provocative. As this book makes clear, when it comes to the Vietnam War, far too many members of the press accept far too much at face value, a problem particularly acute for the daily press. While Burkett found many journalists willing to listen when they had printed a fake's story, a significant number dismissed him. Even after he told them how they could get the records themselves, they were not interested. Though I believe most journalists want to get it right, it was a depressing lesson to learn about my profession.

In the future, whenever I interview someone about their military service, especially those making claims about trauma, medals, decorations, or war crimes—I will request that they sign a form allowing me access to their complete military record. If they refuse, I will file a Freedom of Information Act request for the summary of their service and heavily discount any information they give me that cannot be verified independently. I believe anyone who claims "covert" actions or "secret missions" should be required to provide solid documentation of their service. I believe that if other reporters did the same, many of the phonies would reserve their war stories for the neighborhood bars.

In addition to thanking my husband, Peter, and my two sons, Eric and Andrew, for their patience while I was consumed with this project, I would like to thank Loren Pankratz and Richie Burns for their time and generosity in sharing information, and Michael Buckman, Ben Davis, and Wick Allison for their encouragement and feedback. Most of all, I would like to thank B.G. Burkett for trusting me with his material. His dedication to this project cost him a great deal both monetarily and personally. This is his story, and it's told in his voice. But *Stolen Valor* is the story of hundreds of thousands of Vietnam veterans who served their country honorably only to see their efforts and sacrifice denigrated and tarnished. I thank them for their willingness to serve, and I believe Burkett's work will stand as an important watershed in the understanding of the Vietnam War and its impact on those who fought it.

GLENNA WHITLEY
DALLAS, TEXAS

Acknowledgments

I suspect that many authors are like me—they never intended to be an author. All I hoped to do in the beginning was to perform a community service to the state of Texas and honor the men and women of my generation who gave their lives in Vietnam. I never expected to spend ten years researching a subject no one seemed to believe existed: the usurping of the good name of America's warriors who fought in Vietnam by individuals, by institutions, by government, by corporations, and by all manner of other organizations.

My own personal character flaws turned a curiosity into an obsession. I'm a natural-born skeptic and too dense to know when to quit. Often, I merely wanted to know if a news story or TV program was true. But after a few months, a pattern began to emerge. I was hooked. I could not put the subject down until I felt I knew the "whole story." I truly believe I have identified a social phenomenon that has occurred after every war, but became a particularly vile strain after the Vietnam War. Thousands of men lie, millions believe, and history is distorted. Since I have claimed the right of discovery, I have named this post-war occurrence the "Burkett Syndrome" (only half-jokingly).

When I decided the subject merited a book, I was confronted with reality: No major publisher thought my work worthy. And my meager writing skills were not going to bring glory to the subject.

Reinforced by my own motto of life—I don't know what I can't do until I do it—the obvious was to start my own publishing company and get a good writer to join me. No small matter when much of the literary world considered me a Don Quixote charging windmills. However, the gods blessed me when they sent Glenna Whitley across my path. Glenna and I had collaborated in the past, and she immediately perceived the implications of my work.

Glenna, who had been an investigative reporter for years, has a natural ability to grasp massive amounts of data and weave it into a great story. Glenna and I possess dissimilar but complementary skills. Fortunately, both our egos are at least secure enough that we never clashed over any of the turf. This allowed us to work smoothly long after we originally thought the book would be completed. Glenna, who has a full-time job, a husband, and two children, never wavered in her commitment to the project. Her skills as a writer are superb, and I have no doubt her peers will render the appropriate accolades when they review *Stolen Valor*. Glenna has performed not only a great service for me but to all those who believe in the truth, especially those who served in Vietnam. And to her husband, Peter, thank you for your patience, input, and encouragement.

No work like *Stolen Valor* is completed without help from dozens of individuals, each of whom had a significant impact on the outcome. I have listed them chronologically by category.

Much of my work involved the National Archives. I do not know how I could have maneuvered the complexities of this institution without the years of guidance by Paul Gray. He was always available and willing to give advice on the research. His knowledge of military subjects is amazing. He is truly one of those public servants who is a national treasure.

Dick Schrader, now deceased, and his able successor, Gary Hawn, for years skillfully guided me through the Marine Corps and Navy records system, an area where this old Army man would have been hopelessly lost.

Others at the National Archives who tirelessly answered my hundreds of inquiries include Rich Boylan, Peggy Adams, Cliff Amsler, Virginia Barrett, Ralph McCann, and Eric Voelz.

Dozens of journalists helped me with stories. Of special note: Doug Clark, Gene Mustain, L.B. Lyon, Jim Henderson, David Levy, Jeff Rubin, John MacCormack, Dean Takahashi, Bruce Tomaso, Howard Swindle, Bob St. John, Jeff South, Diane South, Marlowe Churchill, Susan Keating, Reed Irvine, Wayne Hall, Gil Reza, Don Driver, Michael Bicks, Greg Vistica, Ed Timms, Bryant Jordan, Richard Kolb, and Guy Aceto.

Many academics willingly shared their work with me: Guenter Lewy, Arnold Barnett, Dean Allard, William Scott, Ted Gittinger, Edward Marolda, Phoebe Spinrad, and Jim Reckner. Loren Pankratz was particularly helpful with information about posttraumatic stress disorder and the workings of the Department of Veterans Affairs.

By the very nature of this work, I often called on law enforcement for help: David Soldano, William Yetman, Robert Ressler, Jack Trimarco, Tom Cottone, Bob Rhodes, and Jerry Beall. Jim Hughes of the Dallas Police

Department and fellow Vietnam veteran often schooled me in the workings of the criminal justice system and taught me where to find invaluable records.

Several private investigators, some of whom are Vietnam veterans, were generous with their expertise: Carl Reich, Tommy Ponder, George Petrie, and Frank Thornton.

Within government, many guided this novice through their respective agencies: Sharon Cohany, Sally Satel, William Clark, Col. Gary Trinkle, and Judge Dick McConnell.

Several authors shared their work and research: Dale Andradé, Mark Moyar, Ed Murphy, Al Santoli, John Del Vecchio, Chuck Carlock, and Jim Webb.

Many military men, most of whom are Vietnam vets, shared their research, their stories, and their encouragement. Of special note: Hank Newkirk, Dan Cragg, Larry Bailey, Steve Sherman, Col. Harry Summers, Brad Bradfield, Harve Saal, Bob Brown, B.T. Collins, Ken Wallingford, Gen. Jack Singlaub, Gen. Barry McCaffrey, Hays Parks, Al Hemingway, Jack Wheeler, Tim Honsinger, Allen Clark, Jack Spey. Others include Jack Abraham, Pete Joannides, Mike Warziwiak, Robert Annenberg, Morris Worley, Everett Ireland, Gen. William Westmoreland, Mitchell Paige, Stan Sirmens, Larry Green, John Ripley, Bob Andrews, Clayton Scott, Mike Walsh, Gen. Duff Rice, Pat Carothers, Pete Bronstad, Charles Florczyk, Tom Baird, Bill Silva, Adm. Ray Smith, Chuck Melson, Fred Weber, and Gen. Bernard Trainor.

Friends, many of whom are Vietnam veterans, were always there for me: Paul Russell and Art Ruff fought the battle of the Texas Vietnam Veterans memorial to the end with me and then offered help and encouragement with the manuscript. Warren Hudson, Sky Page, Carl Yeckel Andy Beckey, Trent Hill, Rob Brooks, Betty Anderson, Wick Allison, and Gayle McNurlen always gave whatever help I requested and offered positive feedback when it was most often needed.

I have always felt a public list of the heroes of the Vietnam War would greatly diminish those claiming phony heroism. The government, however, has no such list. Through the efforts of Al Gleim, now deceased, the Distinguished Service Cross recipients are listed for the first time in an appendix to this book. The same is true of the list of Air Force Cross recipients. This list was compiled through years of research by Jeffrey Floyd. I am forever grateful for the work of these two truth seekers.

One of the gratifying results of working on this book was to realize there are many others who not only believe in the truth but also are willing to pursue it vigorously. Several individuals were willing to share expertise and research and to dedicate as many hours as I requested. Through the years of struggle, friendships have formed. In addition to Paul Gray of the National Archives, Malcolm McConnell of *Reader's Digest*, Richie Burns, and Cmdr. Frank Brown always offered their services and their encouragement. Malcolm, the author of numerous military books, not only emphasized the importance of our work but also helped outline and detail the entire project. Often, when we lost our way, he guided us back on track. Frank Brown may be the country's foremost expert on the Vietnam POW situation and was willing to share his research while never letting us forget the significance of our project. And Richie Burns never failed to rally me whenever any hint of weariness appeared even as he fought his own battle with cancer.

Richard Greenberg, a TV producer of national stature, always expressed confidence that our work had national and historic significance. Bill Thayer, one of the country's leading military experts, always helped whenever I asked. And Chris Ruddy, a print journalist who very early was willing to help me expose fraud, assured me that the pursuit of truth was important. To each and every one, thank you.

Lawyer Rob Hartmann, a fellow Vietnam veteran, not only offered friendship and encouragement but also gave countless legal hours keeping me out of trouble, including the years of travail with the Texas Vietnam Veterans Memorial. Attorney Don Templin generously reviewed the book and offered succinct comments and guidance. Jeff Becker and Jennifer Thoman also added their legal services and comments.

Mark Murphy, who patiently edited the book and endured my idiosyncrasies, made *Stolen Valor* all it could be. He's even suffered my ignorance and semiliteracy in good humor.

To those at Summit Publishing who often experienced my stubbornness (and probably my fanaticism), thank you: Len Oszustowicz, Jill Bertolet, Bill Scott, David Gavin, and Walter Kaudelka.

Barbara, my sister, was in college while I was in Vietnam. She not only prayed I would return unscathed but also flooded me with mail about the family and campus life. She threw herself with equal enthusiasm into the Texas Vietnam Veterans Memorial. Her countless days of effort received little public notice. Her hundreds of hours of work on *Stolen Valor* were not just for her big brother but because she believed in the cause. She was always on call to perform whatever dirty job was needed. I doubt if I could have persevered to completion if I had not been able to express my frustration and receive her soothing and invigorating counsel. I will always cherish her dedication to my all-consuming project.

Often, as I worked on the book, I thought of my parents, Bernie and Helen Burkett, now both deceased. Honesty and truth were core values they tried to impart to their children. I can only hope I display the same conviction as I try to pass on these values to their grandchildren. Maybe my parents can see in this book that at least some of their effort was not in vain.

For many authors, the completion of a book creates a sense of triumph and finality. I harbor no such illusion. The publication of this book is a declaration of war against deceit and falsehood. I have no doubt those who embrace such concepts are numerous and will respond.

B.G. BURKETT
DALLAS, TEXAS

Prologue

AT THE DINNER HOUR, the airport restaurant was half empty. I threw down my duffel bag, sat, and tried to catch the waitress's eye. "Miss, Miss," I said. The waitress, a woman in her thirties, was only a few feet away. But she pointedly ignored me and began waiting on people who had come in after me.

Finally a younger waitress came over. "Oh, don't mind her," she said. "She's got this antiwar thing. She won't serve anybody in uniform." The second waitress took my order, brought me the food, and I put the other woman's rudeness down to a personal quirk.

After eating, I sat at the gate and waited for the plane. When they called the flight, to my relief I was one of the last standbys who made it aboard.

After I found a seat, the man next to me said, "Oh, you're stationed at Fort Dix?"

"No, I just got home from Vietnam," I said.

"Oh, a big war hero?" announced a man across the aisle. He had obviously been on the plane from a previous leg, nipping at those little bottles of Jack Daniel's. "Hey, folks, we've been sitting here on the runway waiting for a big goddamn war hero." I grimaced but said nothing. It was May 1969. I had been back in the United States fewer than twenty-four hours after serving a tour of duty in Vietnam as an ordnance officer. First the waitress and now this.

The guy refused to let up. "Hey, bucko, you spent a year killing women and children," he said. "Make you feel like a big man, did it? You got your drugs with you, you fucking pothead?" The entire flight continued that way. For more than an hour, he constantly needled me. I knew if I decided to take the guy out, he was dead meat. But punching him would have confirmed all of his prejudices. I refused to do that.

What made me most angry was that no one on the plane said anything to him. The stewardess ignored him. None of the other passengers defended me. I felt like a pariah. If I had been a veteran of World War II, coming home after serving my country, somebody would have slugged the guy.

As I stood up in the aisle after the plane landed, the idiot continued his goading, his voice following me long after I walked off the plane. It aggravates me still. That personal insult was directed thousands of times in thousands of ways toward the men and women who served in Vietnam. In the decades after the war, the negative attitudes and assumptions of those times unfortunately became cemented in the American psyche.

Almost twenty years later, I got a glimpse of how the stereotypes had grown to epic proportions. In the spring of 1987, after I presided at a brief ceremony unveiling the granite tablets of the Texas Vietnam Veterans Memorial, a Dallas television reporter interviewed me about the effort to build the state monument.

"Let's get some comments from Vietnam veterans," she said, motioning to her cameraman. I directed her toward a dozen Dallas businessmen who had served in Vietnam. Dressed in suits and ties, they were answering questions from a few print reporters. Fit men in early middle age, they looked more like a gathering of business colleagues than men who had fought in the rice paddies and red clay hills of Vietnam twenty years earlier. Two had been prisoners of war in Hanoi, and a handful had received Silver Stars, Distinguished Flying Crosses, Purple Hearts, and other combat decorations. But the war had only been one episode in their productive lives. They came home and got on with the business of living.

"No, I mean *those* veterans," she insisted, gesturing toward a motley assortment of men wearing camouflage fatigues or various pieces of military uniforms with jeans and battered jungle boots.

As inevitably as sunrise and sunset, they appeared at every official function involving veterans. Some were involved with local veterans' centers; some were leaders in Texas veterans' groups. A few wore the distinctive headgear of the Green Berets. They pinned military medals and awards on their cammies and sewed patches from combat units on their faded boonie hats. Slovenly, tattered, a few had unkempt beards, and one wore a graying ponytail. They sported T-shirts emblazoned with slogans like "Death from the Sky" and flashy satin "R&R" jackets with an embroidered map of Vietnam on the back and unit insignia on the sleeves. Their cars bore bumper stickers touting the "Tonkin Gulf Yacht Club."

They often regaled nonvets with gruesome and horrifying descriptions of their experiences on the Vietnam battlefields. Or, breath reeking of booze, they whined about their mistreatment at the hands of the Veterans Administration, about their exposure to Agent Orange, about their nightmares of war. Invariably they became the focus of the press attention, irresistible magnets for reporters and photographers looking for a little gritty realism to add to their stories.

Their war stories were wildly improbable. Many of their tales of covert operations or heroic rescue missions were positively ludicrous. Their appearance and demeanor did not match that of men I knew who had served in the U.S. military, especially those in elite organizations like the Green Berets or Navy SEALs. Those men had too much pride to be seen in public unkempt, stinking of alcohol, wearing threadbare military garb decades after their discharge. Quietly, to satisfy my own curiosity, I had started to check out a few of those with the most outrageous stories. What I suspected all along was true.

"The likelihood is that those men are *not* Vietnam veterans," I blurted. "Why don't you talk to these guys? These are real Vietnam veterans." The reporter stopped in her tracks, taken aback. Not veterans? What was I talking about? She frowned in disbelief. *She thinks I'm nuts. Why would someone wear that garb if he weren't a Vietnam vet?* Disconcerted, she looked at her cameraman. "It's late," she said. "We've got enough. Let's get back to the station and file our story." She thanked me and beat a hasty retreat.

All TV reporters need exciting pictures for their stories, and the veterans in their suits were not as dramatic as the men in fatigues. But the problem involved something deeper. The successful, well-adjusted businessmen in the suits did not fit her—and the nation's—image of Vietnam veterans. The fellows in the ragtag fatigues—the scruffy losers—did.

Repeatedly, I tried to interest reporters in writing about the memorial only to be asked about homelessness or the supposedly widespread affliction of posttraumatic stress disorder (PTSD). Time and again I visited the office of a corporate leader or philanthropist and asked for a donation to the memorial only to be told: "Those losers? Why the hell should I support those drug addicts?"

Although I pointed out that many successful Dallas men, such as former Dallas Cowboys quarterback Roger Staubach, had served in Vietnam, to them, men like Staubach were the exceptions to the rule, the rare individuals who were not ruined by their war experiences. "Everybody" knew most soldiers who fought in Vietnam were reluctant draftees, poor minorities, or dumb cannon fodder not smart enough to avoid military service. When I told them that I—a stockbroker with undergraduate and graduate degrees from major universities—had voluntarily served in Vietnam, they looked at me in disbelief. "You?" one said. "That surprises me. You seem so normal." Another corporate executive looked right past me in his waiting room and asked his secretary, "Where's that Vietnam veteran who's here to see me?"

Exasperated after several of these experiences, I pointedly asked the president of one large company, "You mean I'm not a drunk or a drugged-out homeless guy in fatigues with a criminal record?" Chagrined, the man looked embarrassed but defended his opinion. "Well, aren't *most* Vietnam vets messed up?"

In the years following my return from military service in Vietnam in 1969, I watched the negative images portrayed in movies like *Apocalypse Now*, *The Deer Hunter*, or *Platoon*. I saw the stereotypes on bookshelves, in newspaper stories, on the TV news. By the eighties, more than two decades after the fighting ended, there were reputedly hundreds of thousands of homeless Vietnam vets, most suffering from PTSD. On top of that, they were said to suffer physical disabilities brought on by poisoning from the defoliant Agent Orange. The common refrain: More men had died by their own hand than had been killed during the decade duration of the war.

Still, the popular perception of Vietnam veterans as victims tortured by memories—drug-abusers, criminals, homeless bums, or psychotic losers—did not fit me or anybody I knew who had served in Vietnam, even those who had been horribly wounded or captured and tortured by the enemy. Certainly their lives were not always perfect, but most of their problems could not be attributed to their experiences in Vietnam. I brushed off the negative caricatures, thinking, That's not reality.

Only a few weeks into the fund-raising effort in 1986, the truth slapped me in the face: America accepted this pervasive stereotype, and it was constantly reinforced in a variety of ways. For agreeing to serve their country in Vietnam, an entire generation of veterans had been tainted with the labels of victim, loser, and moral degenerate. The men who had served in the military only twenty years earlier during World War II had received honor and respect for their efforts. Why had Vietnam been so different?

Over the next decade, answering that question became my passion, a quest that would lead me back to the Vietnam War in a way I could never have imagined. In ten years of research in the National Archives, filing hundreds of requests for military documents under the federal Freedom of Information Act, I discovered a massive distortion of history, a poisonous myth created by an entertainment industry so enamored of sensationalism that it had no qualms about presenting a false stereotype to generate profits, by a Department of Veterans Affairs as concerned with its own power base as America's war-wounded, by a legal system manipulated by unscrupulous attorneys motivated not by justice but by a need to win at all costs, by social welfare advocates and mental health professionals willing to support a lie to further their own agendas, and by print and television journalists unwilling to examine their own politics and preconceptions.

Americans think they know the truth about Vietnam veterans because they constantly see the traumatized men who fought the war portrayed in all their pathetic anguish in the nation's most prestigious media—*The New York Times*, the *Washington Post*, and the nightly network news. It never occurs to most of us to ask: Were these men really there?

But in this book, you'll read about phony Vietnam veterans who have fooled the nation's most prestigious investigative reporters. The murderer who deceived the *Boston Globe* and Mike Wallace, of *60 Minutes* fame, wangling early release from prison because his heroin addiction was "caused" by war trauma suffered in Vietnam. The bogus SEAL who pulled the wool over Dan Rather's eyes and became the centerpiece of an award-winning CBS documentary. The phony Green Beret who testified before a federal judge against members of a Mafia family and duped two savvy New York organized crime writers.

Liars and wannabes have absorbed the myth and now perpetuate it, aided and abetted by the VA, veterans advocates, and the mental health care industry. The price of this myth has been enormous—certainly for American taxpayers who have been bilked out of billions of dollars based on a myth—but especially for Vietnam veterans. In the final analysis, the true tragedy is the denigration of a generation of warriors who were among the finest America ever produced.

It is not my desire to refight the Vietnam War. But understanding why my search for the truth became an obsession makes more sense if I start at the beginning of the journey, with my own service in that war-torn corner of Southeast Asia that has so haunted our nation.

PART I

A Year in Vietnam

1

A Year in Vietnam

THE CARDIOLOGIST peered at the results of the electrocardiogram and raised an eyebrow. It was June 1966. At the induction center in Little Rock, Arkansas, where I had gone to enlist in the Army, another doctor had performed the usual physical and told me I had a heart murmur, and sent me to a heart specialist.

The specialist squinted at the test, then looked at me.

"Do you want to go in or don't you?" the cardiologist asked.

"Excuse me?" I said.

"Do you want to go in or not?" the doctor repeated. Without specifically saying so, he was letting me know that my heart murmur was not serious, but the defect could keep me out of the military. For a reluctant draftee, it was a get-out-of-jail-free card.

For most people, the Vietnam War was still just words on the evening news. Many men my age continued their college educations for the explicit purpose of maintaining student deferments. But as the son of a career Air Force officer, I considered serving in the military an important life experience.

"Oh, no, I do want to go," I said, already mentally committed. In fact, I realized in that moment how royally disappointed I would be if the Army rejected me. "Okay, you pass," the doctor said.

There were many times in the next few months when I second-guessed that decision.

They Were My Heroes
Joining the armed forces was something I had known I would do all my life. Reared among the Warriors—the men who fought and won World War II

—my heroes were not sports figures like Mickey Mantle and Willie Mays but the fighter pilots who had blasted the Luftwaffe out of· the sky. My father was a Canadian citizen who in 1942 joined the United States military under a program that allowed a limited number of citizens of allied countries to join the U.S. armed services as officers. Bernard J. Burkett never had to face combat during World War II. After becoming a naturalized U.S. citizen, he made the military a career and reached the rank of full colonel in the Air Force. Eventually, we lived on military bases in Florida, California, Louisiana, Kentucky, Newfoundland, Mississippi, Arkansas, Virginia, Alabama, Bermuda—literally throughout North America.

Life on a military base was structured around ceremony: flag raisings and flag lowerings, unit parades, and promotions. Each night, a bugler played "retreat," and the base abruptly came to a standstill. People stopped walking and faced the direction of the headquarters' flagpole, saluting or putting their hands over their hearts. Even drivers leaving the base got out of their cars, stood at attention, and saluted. This daily routine reinforced a deep sense of respect for America as well as an understanding that the military was the guardian of the freedoms enjoyed by the civilian population.

Base life also imbued residents with an awareness of mortality. Individuals on a military base know that in the event of a conflict, troops could be sent overseas without advance warning. His job (and now, in many cases, her job), is to go to war, perhaps returning in a box. Even during peacetime, that undercurrent of anxiety pervaded an air base. Throughout my childhood, planes occasionally crashed, killing the pilots and crew. That made the stories told by the veteran fighter pilots—men who had been awarded Silver Stars and Distinguished Flying Crosses— much more real.

Military life is very social, and much of what I learned about World War II came about in conversations at barbecues, picnics, parties, get-togethers at our house, or visiting my father's office. When these veteran flyers talked "shop," history came alive for me. Too timid to approach such larger-than-life heroes, I simply listened, gleaning much merely from the decorations they wore on their uniforms. Those colored ribbons wrote a kind of hieroglyphic history, telling what skills they had mastered, where they had fought, and how brave they had been.

"Gee, Dad," I would say after my parents' guests went home, "Colonel So-and-So has two Silver Stars."

"Yes, son," my father would say, "he shot down eleven Messerschmitts over Germany."

After the Korean War, when I attended elementary school, my father was public affairs officer at Alexandria Air Force Base in Louisiana (later called England AFB) and produced a radio show for a local station. His commander and golfing buddy, Col. Bill Daniel, had been a hot fighter pilot in World War II. During that period, I also met the amazing Joseph McConnell—a "triple ace" who flew F-86s in Korea. (An ace is a pilot who has shot down at least five enemy planes.) Producers shot portions of a movie about McConnell starring Alan Ladd at Alexandria. Prior to the filming, McConnell appeared on my father's radio show. Meeting him, I felt pure unadulterated awe, as other boys might feel if they had met Babe Ruth.

Years later, I felt that childhood veneration return when shaking hands with Frank "Gabby" Gabreski, who had the distinction of being an ace in two wars. Flying P-47 Thunderbolts, Gabreski shot down twenty-eight German planes during World War II. In Korea, he was credited with six and a half MiG kills. Stunned to see the elderly Gabreski in 1994 at an air show in Dallas, I became that nine-year-old kid again for a few moments, thrilled to get the autograph of a double-war ace.

When I was graduated from high school in 1962, the Vietnam conflict was little more than a blip on the radar screen for most people. Avoiding the draft had no influence on the decision I made after high school to attend Vanderbilt University.

Not an Appealing Career

The military held no appeal to me as a career—my interests lay in economics and business administration—but I planned after earning a bachelor's degree to enlist. I believed that America's freedoms could not be protected without a strong military. And like many who came of age in the era of the Peace Corps and the civil rights movement, I accepted John F. Kennedy's credo—"Ask not what your country can do for you, but what you can do for your country."

Another reason for joining the armed forces was pragmatic. The military provided excellent training for leadership, and the GI bill could help pay for graduate school. My father took my decision in stride. He would have been disappointed if I had chosen not to serve my country at all, but Dad never pressured me to make the military my life.

The majority of my friends at Vanderbilt did not come from military families, and they planned to go on to law school, medical school, or Wall Street. But in 1965, the war started heating up. America sent combat troops to Vietnam, and the draft began pulling more young men into military service. Suddenly some of my friends were making decisions about their lives based on avoiding the draft, as if the sword of Damocles hung over their heads.

After graduating from Vanderbilt in 1966, I discussed Vietnam with my father. Only months away from retirement, Dad revealed that senior officers—concerned that decisions regarding Vietnam were being made for political, not military, reasons—were beginning to express dissatisfaction about the war. They felt that the Johnson administration was implementing combat operations piecemeal, that we were tiptoeing into an Asian war without any clear strategic objective. Many good officers in the upper ranks began to consider retirement.

Secretly elated by the war, an emotion spawned by both the adventurous nature and the outright stupidity of a young man, I wasn't deterred by my father's report. For the professional warriors of my father's generation, World War II had been the highlight of their lives. If the American military was involved in a war, I wanted to know what it was like, but I also wanted to get out as quickly as possible.

The Christmas before graduation, I visited all the recruiters in Little Rock to determine which branch of the service had the shortest commitment. The logical choice was the Air Force, but slightly high blood pressure and an inner-ear problem meant I couldn't pass the pilot physical. The shortest commitment—three years—was the Army. Later, I often wondered how the son of an Air Force career officer ended up in the Army, let alone in an infantry unit.

The Taste of Mud

I flew to Fort Jackson in Columbia, South Carolina, and entered hell, otherwise known as basic training. During the Vietnam era, almost nine million young men would go through the same rite of passage. After a barber shaved my head in less than fifteen seconds, I peeled off my civilian clothes and pulled on a green uniform identical to the one worn by the other 199 hairless recruits in C Company. Thus began the process of methodically stripping us of any personal identity.

The Army's intent was to subdue our individuality and mold us into a unit that took orders and protected the unit above all else. The sheer physical agony of basic training shocked me. Though reared on military bases, as the son of a colonel I had always been granted a certain amount of privilege and deference. A week before, I had been playing golf with my father's friends—colonels and generals—on a beautiful, manicured golf course. Now, a private, I was the bottommost slime on the face of the earth, taking abuse from lowly corporals.

My platoon was made up of half college graduates who had enlisted to go to Officer Candidate School; the rest were high school graduates or dropouts who had enlisted or had been drafted. No matter. Whether you possessed a master's degree and were destined for OCS or were a draftee with a tenth-grade education, you were treated the same—like an earthworm. "You have no mama, you have no papa," screamed the drill sergeant. "You just got me and the United States Army." And it was true. You had nothing and were nothing.

In September 1966, I completed basic training and was assigned to advanced infantry training at Fort McClellan, outside Anniston, Alabama. The military was gearing up for ground combat in Vietnam, and as the first infantry troops to go through McClellan in more than twenty years, we essentially had to rebuild the facilities, which were overrun with ragged trees, grass, and weeds.

Unlike basic training, most of my peers now were college graduates; several had law degrees. Like me, most had fathers who had served in World War II and felt an obligation to serve. The men training us were pre-dominantly hard-nosed noncommissioned officers, determined to make the college boys as miserable as possible. And they did.

Advanced infantry training required practical application of what we had learned in theory. For eight weeks, we mastered the use of weapons, dug foxholes, dressed "wounds," and practiced escape and evasion, night patrols, and ambushes. We learned how to pull a bayonet out of a man's chest without getting the blade stuck in his breastbone, how to throw live grenades without killing ourselves or our buddies in the process. Fledgling soldiers looked at each other and realized that statistically it was impossible for all of us to come back in one piece. We were on a conveyer belt, going to one destination, a war—with two goals, to kill the enemy and to survive.

As the end of training neared, I contemplated the possibility that in a few weeks, I could be leading a platoon of fifty men into combat. Throughout basic and advanced training, I mentally examined what I had been taught about killing by my church, by my parents, by an expensive education, and by society. Many men worried whether they had the courage to stand and kill. Taking an enemy soldier's life in combat caused me no qualms, but the possibility that I could make a flawed decision that could cause men under my command to be killed profoundly disturbed me.

Something else bothered me as well. All of us had signed up for the infantry. Soon we would be slogging through swamps and crawling in the muck. Some loved that blood-and-guts life in the dirt; I dreaded it. But before we graduated from AIT, the Army opened up the Ordnance Officer Candidate School at Aberdeen Proving Ground in Maryland and began accepting volunteers. Aberdeen was where my father had received his commission in 1943, and not only was training at Aberdeen a family tradition, ordnance duty got me out of the muck and mud of the infantry. In late November, Sgt. B. G. Burkett reported to Aberdeen for the six-month OCS course.

In the Army, the Quartermaster Corps supplies all the soft goods, like food, toilet paper, cots, and uniforms. Army Ordnance handles all things metal or explosive: guns, ammunition, explosives, and trucks. As an ordnance officer, I could be put in charge of an ammo dump, a maintenance facility for vehicles or guns, or assigned to a pizzazz job, like "EOD": explosive ordnance disposal, the "bomb squad" of the Army.

More Pressure in OCS

In OCS, the psychological pressure doubled. Rigid protocol controlled everything from chewing our food to making our beds. Drill instructors screamed constantly in our ears. The idea: to make us oblivious to the things that do not matter and able to react decisively to the things that do.

The Army wanted me to surrender totally to its system. I hung by a thread, refusing to give 100 percent of myself. Golf was my method of defiance. I kept my clubs and a change of clothes in the trunk of my car. Whenever I had thirty minutes of freedom after dinner, I raced to my car, slipped on a golf shirt, and drove the half-mile to the post driving range. After hitting a bucket of balls like a machine gun, I jumped back in my car and raced back to the ordnance school in time for study hall. The frantic routine seemed absurd, but it was my attempt to remember who I really was—and what I hoped to return to.

In May 1967, I graduated from OCS. Of course, all of those who started didn't make it to graduation. A couple went AWOL (Absent Without Leave), several flunked out, and a handful quit. For the graduation ceremony, my dad sent me his old second lieutenant's bars, and after being commissioned "an officer and a gentleman" I pinned them on my uniform. Before, I had always been part of the system. Now, as the second generation of my family to serve as an officer in the U.S. military, I was inside.

Before the end of the course, officers from the Pentagon came to the base and put us through two weeks of "charm" classes, teaching us the protocol of being officers in the U.S. Army. One day near the end of the course, while we were putting down our preferences for our first assignment, a major strode to the front of the room. "Gentlemen," he announced, "I need ten of you to volunteer for Vietnam immediately."

Stunned silence. We sat frozen, unwilling to attract attention. We looked sidelong at each other like, "What? Now? You're kidding." Ten days from graduation and we hadn't even had a beer at the officers' club.

I refused to volunteer to go to war as an inexperienced second lieutenant. Even the NCOs look down on "butter bars." I preferred to go as a first lieutenant, with at least a year's experience in a division. Typically, that's what the Army did. But the military was in the middle of a massive troop buildup for Vietnam. They needed Army officers ASAP.

"Gentlemen, you either volunteer or I'm going to pick ten of you anyway," the major said. He pointed out that any volunteers would receive thirty days of leave. "Hell," he bellowed, "you're all going to Vietnam anyway!" As we looked at each other, a few hands slowly went up. My arms clamped firmly at my sides, I held my breath and tried not to move. He picked ten other men, and I sighed in relief. My time would come.

It never occurred to me that I might not make it to Vietnam at all.

Arrival

Assigned to the 1st Armored Division, I was stationed at Fort Hood, near Waco, Texas. With fifty thousand troops, the base had the heaviest concentration of tanks in the free world. Technically, my MOS (military occupational specialty) was "4815" or mechanical engineer, but because I had taken some computer classes at Vanderbilt, I was assigned to a computer project.

In the mid-sixties, the Army began computerizing the enormous job of tracking logistics, supplies, and personnel for an armored division. I was thrust into a computerization project that called for a full colonel, a lieutenant colonel, and eleven captains. Because the demand for field grade officers in Vietnam and Germany was so high, we had only one major and twelve second lieutenants. Ours was a diverse group: whites, one Hispanic, and one or two blacks, with educations ranging from high school to the Ivy League.

Though none of us had any real experience in the traditional paper requisition and inventory system of moving men, armor, and supplies, we quickly were given substantial responsibility. We were trying to superimpose a computer system on top of the old way of doing things, a clear case of the stone-blind leading the hopelessly nearsighted.

After nine months on the computer project, I had only fifteen months left to serve. Since a tour of duty was twelve months, if I was going to Vietnam, I had to do it quickly. Several hundred lieutenants out of Fort Hood each month were being sent to the war. But when I made a formal request of the battalion commander to be assigned to duty in Vietnam, I hit a snag. The commander said my status was frozen.

Technically, any job in the military is interchangeable with any job with a similar MOS. The military could plug me in for any mechanical engineer in an armored division. However, because the computer project was unique, my MOS was meaningless. I could not be transferred until the completion of the project; then I had to train my replacement. My time in the Army would run out before I made it to the war.

Here's where familiarity with the military helped. I contacted the Army assignments officer at the Pentagon, who controls all appointments for a particular specialty every month. The officer agreed that every Monday morning, he would give me a list of openings in Vietnam.

An old Army adage says: If you don't want to do something, volunteer for it, and they won't let you do it. Every Monday morning I called, volunteered, and was turned down. This became the routine. I wrote several letters to congressmen seeking an assignment to Vietnam and received only form letters in reply.

My persistence became a unit joke. Several NCOs who had already been to Vietnam worked in my office. One had been wounded three times and assumed I was a lunatic. A barrage of friendly banter greeted me every morning. The NCOs made sure to put the weekly casualty reports on my desk. In April 1968, when my campaign succeeded and orders for Vietnam came through, my emotions fluctuated wildly, from "Oh, boy, I'm finally going to get in the game," to "Oh, shit, what have I done?"

Don't Volunteer for Anything

Before shipping out, I returned home on leave. I didn't tell my parents I had volunteered for Vietnam; I knew my mother wouldn't understand. My dad, who had retired and was teaching ROTC at a high school in Columbus, Mississippi, sat me down one night and gave me the standard father-son speech: Don't volunteer for anything you don't understand, don't do anything stupid, and come back in one piece.

With my few days of leave running out, I began to feel a rising sense of anxiety. I had always hated good-byes, and this one would be especially tough. At the airport in Columbus, there was the typical handshaking and hugging, but I had an intense desire to get it over as quickly as possible. I had a sinking feeling that I would choke up if it lasted too long. As I walked away from the huddled group, my sister Barbara followed for a few steps. With my typical morbid sense of humor during uncomfortable events, I left her with an impossible task. "If they send me home in a box, have me cremated and scatter my ashes at Augusta, after the last putt drops at the Masters. That will at least get me fifteen seconds of immortality each spring." As Barbara grimaced, trying vainly not to cry, I turned and walked to the plane.

After I was seated, I peered out the window to get one last look at the only people on earth who loved me unconditionally and who were loved unconditionally by me. Fighting back tears, trying not to think of the pain my death would cause them, I felt a strange sensation of completely detaching myself from my family; I refused to think about never seeing my parents and two sisters again.

At Fort Lewis, I reported for overseas processing and shipment, and filled out endless forms, including a grim slip that asked in the event of my being wounded, whether to contact my parents (and in the event of my demise, where to ship my body). I rejoiced to learn of my promotion to first lieutenant. At least I would not arrive in Vietnam as the lowest of the low.

But first there came three tedious days of sitting around the flight line at McChord Air Force Base outside Tacoma, Washington, twiddling my thumbs until they had a seat on a plane for a first lieutenant. Only 10 percent of the seats were reserved for officers, and every colonel, major, and captain in the U.S. military seemed to be headed to Vietnam that week. I was last on the list.

Sitting in the waiting area, I met an NCO also going to Vietnam.

"Goddamn, lieutenant," he said, pointing to something sticking three inches out of my duffel bag. "What the hell is that?"

"Sergeant," I said, "that's my golf club." I had stuck a wedge and three golf balls in the bag.

"Lieutenant, you're going to a war, not a goddamn golf tournament," he said with an incredulous look.

I made a lame joke about taking out some of the enemy with my wedge, but in truth that club was my attachment to my family. I could grip that golf stick and smell the green grass of home. Wherever I went—that iron was going.

On June 11, 1968, I finally boarded a plane to Anchorage, the first leg of the flight to Vietnam. On board sat two hundred troops, all aware that this was the real thing. We were going to war.

Each of us sat silently as if in suspended animation, every man lost in his own thoughts. At home on leave I had slipped two photos into my wallet, placing them among my other family pictures. One was of my mother, Helen Reidy, taken shortly after she married my father, and the other was of my father in uniform not long after he had been commissioned a second lieutenant. Gazing at those photos had a hypnotic effect: Would I marry? Have children? Teach a daughter to ride a bicycle? Or a son to hit a baseball? Would I lose a leg, an arm, or my sight? Would I see my family again? Did I have any future at all besides death?

This time tears rolled slowly down my cheeks. Fortunately I had a window seat and was able to gaze out at the bright billowing clouds until I could compose myself.

Looking around the plane, I saw those of my generation who had made a choice, taken a stand—a stand with a price. With a rush of resolve, I knew I was right where I belonged, right where I wanted to be.

From Anchorage, the trip to Yokota took ten hours. Planes carrying troops to Vietnam flew into Yokota at night in order not to offend the sensibilities of the Japanese. Pretty stewardesses bustled about the cabin, serving meals and Cokes, but none of the men pestered them. The only sound was the muffled roar of the engines.

Wearily disembarking from the plane in Japan, we lined up and walked across the dark tarmac past a line of Vietnam veterans trudging the other way—onto the plane we had just left, now making ready to fly back to the United States. The contrast was striking, as if they came from a different generation. They carried themselves like combat-hardened soldiers, faces worn by what they had seen and done. Seeing them brought home the reality that not everyone on our plane would return to the states whole and healthy—or even alive.

"In-Country"

After twenty-two hours on airplanes, pink fingers of sunrise began to creep into the black sky. Through the plane window appeared an enormous white sand bar jutting out into the impossibly blue South China Sea: Cam Ranh Bay, where the U.S. military had a huge installation. I was about to become one of the 2.7 million Americans who would ultimately serve "in-country."

As I walked off the plane, an oven blast of air hit me, sucking my breath away. The temperature had to be over one hundred degrees with almost 100 percent humidity. After an hour on the ground, death by heat prostration seemed imminent.

Assigned to Qui Nhon before leaving the states, I had written the unit and received a reply, but that assignment was virtually meaningless. The military sent new troops to units based on its immediate needs. Several infantry lieutenants and I dumped our things in the wooden-floored tents where newcomers were billeted. After chow, we asked where the beach was. A tired GI in a sweaty T-shirt pointed. We walked three hundred yards and there it was, a fine, white, sandy beach—clear aquamarine water, green mountains in the distance. Nurses in bikinis strolled in breaking surf. Was I at a war or a college spring break?

To figure out our assignments, we checked the posted roster every hour. On the second day, the roster revealed I had been assigned to the 199th Light Infantry Brigade. The next day, I reported to the airstrip at Cam Ranh and boarded an American C-123, a two-engine cargo plane. The three-man crew was American, but all the other passengers were soldiers of the Army of the Republic of Vietnam (ARVN)—our allies—in full combat gear. They spoke no English, and I spoke no Vietnamese. In my new khakis, I felt as if I had been plopped down among Martians.

We strapped ourselves into the nylon web seats lining the sides of the plane, and the aircraft took off, heading south to Bien Hoa, an air base near Saigon.[1] The plane quickly passed over the coastal plain, and we caught a glimpse of the mountains, densely covered with lush vegetation. *My God*, I thought, *You could lose New York City in that jungle.*

As the plane made its landing approach, the pilot's voice crackled over the intercom: Due to sporadic fire on one side of the air base, he was going to make a steep descent. "It would be better if everybody gets on the floor," he said. Quickly, I clambered out of the web seat and hunkered on the deck. Though the Vietnamese troops had not understood a word the pilot said, they took one look at me and en masse, as the plane abruptly dived, hit the floor.

At Bien Hoa, I asked a group of Air Force personnel where I reported to the 199th Light Infantry. Nobody seemed to know. A debate ensued. "Oh, they're not even in this part of Vietnam," one guy said. Somebody else grabbed the phone to find out where I was supposed to go and came back with instructions. "Catch this bus and wait. They'll come to you."

An Army bus with metal mesh instead of windows arrived. The driver calmly informed me the screens kept out enemy grenades. At the 90th Replacement Battalion, I waited around some more until a sergeant from the 199th appeared. He threw my duffel bag in a Jeep, shook my hand, and called me "Sir." Instantly I felt like I belonged. As we drove, the sergeant regaled me with war stories.

The 199th was based at a camp a few miles northeast of Bien Hoa. Easily deployed, able to move quickly, its motto was "Light, Swift, and Accurate." The brigade had four infantry battalions, one artillery battalion, and one combat support battalion. Assigned to combat support, I entered the command shack and heard the crackling sound of urgent radio traffic; apparently I had arrived in the middle of a major operation. I handed my records to a buck sergeant. "Sir, we'll process this right away," he said. "Go to the mess hall. You'll probably be shipped out to the field right away. We're short several rifle platoon leaders."

"Oh shit, oh shit, oh shit," I thought. Terrified at the prospect of being assigned in the field without preparation on the first day, barely able to think, I made my way to the mess hall and sat there, drinking a cup of coffee and thinking about Harry Horton.

From Texas City, Texas, Horton had been one of my three roommates at Fort Hood. After dropping out of the University of Texas, he had gone through OCS, and he was the first of the four to go to Vietnam. "I'm dead," he told us when his orders came through. Throughout training, Harry had often said he was convinced he would be killed in Vietnam. One quiet night I asked him why—if he believed he was doomed to die in combat— he had not taken one of the ways out many others had taken, heading for the Canadian border or faking a medical condition? "Because America needs me," he said jokingly, trying to cover his embarrassment. But he meant every word.

The night before he left in early November 1967, Harry divided up all his possessions among us. He gave me a hunting knife, which I later slipped back in his bag. Horton was acting crazy with this death stuff. He would want the knife when he arrived in Vietnam.

"Deceased"

A month later we sent him a Christmas card, but the mail came back marked "Deceased." Later, we discovered that after he had been assigned to his unit in the 25th Infantry Division in Vietnam, Harry had been sent into the field as a rifle platoon leader.

In the intervening years, I have often thought of Harry. I think there may be no greater courage than to confront the thing you fear the most. When his platoon was ambushed and pinned down, Harry single-handedly charged an enemy machine gun bunker only to be cut down. His posthumously awarded Silver Star citation read, "Lieutenant Horton's personal courage and outstanding leadership are in keeping with the highest traditions of the military service and reflect great credit upon himself, his unit, the 25th Infantry Division, and the United States Army." Horton never hesitated. He did his duty to America without flinching.[2]

Harry wasn't an intellectual, nor was he particularly athletic or even very handsome. He was simply the heart, soul, and backbone of America. In times of crisis, it isn't the politicians or generals who save us. It's the Harry Hortons. Had he lived, Harry would have a wife, two kids, and a house in the suburbs. He would teach his children honesty, integrity, patriotism—and probably how to put frogs in the teacher's desk and play hooky. He'd make sure they all went together to church on Sunday. America didn't even notice the passing of Harry Horton, but she is substantially poorer in his absence.

As I sat in the mess hall trying not to panic, a major walked up to me. "I know you," he said, apparently recognizing me from the computer project at Fort Hood. "Have we got a job for you!" he said. "Don't go away."

The major returned twenty minutes later and took me to meet the executive officer of the 199th. The XO brusquely said he needed a "materiel readiness expediter," the official name the Army had given to a quasi-official position in every army of all ages. The job description: You will get what we need when we need it. If you steal it, we don't want to know about it. If you get caught, it's your problem. (The Navy has another name for it: "dog robber.")

The XO thought somebody with computer knowledge could be a good "materiel readiness expediter." Knee-weakening relief rolled over me. Convinced an hour before that I would be dropped into a jungle firefight that afternoon, instead I had been assigned a Jeep and a driver and given a formal "letter of authority." This letter gave me an aura of officialdom, a kind of paper chutzpah. If I needed to bluff a transport plane out of the Air Force, I simply showed them the letter. Often it actually worked.

To me, the letter said that B.G. Burkett was not going to find himself crawling through the bush in a firefight. (The clerk had been playing the typical enlisted man's trick on a green lieutenant. Despite Horton's tragedy, almost no one was sent into the field his first few days with his unit.) Elated, exhausted, and excited, I grabbed the letter and my duffel bag, then made my way to the barracks that would be home for the next eleven months.

Home Sweet Home

The official name of the base was Camp Frenzell-Jones, named after the first two men from the 199th to be killed in Vietnam. But we called the camp the "BMB" (Brigade Main Base), built by GIs in a bare orange mud field outside the small town of Hoi Nai—by Vietnamese standards a populated urban area. The two-story, wood-frame barracks had a corrugated tin roof and housed forty officers. For the next year, I lived in a stuffy plywood cubicle eight by nine feet square.[3]

All the officers started with a bare bunk, a blanket, and a footlocker, and then created a bit of home, tacking up posters, scrounging chairs, adding a rug or a lamp scavenged from military supply or bought at the PX. There also were gifts from family, and things left over when other men left Vietnam. My predecessor had left a lamp, and I found a little folding beach chair in a corner somewhere. I had a radio and later bought a tape recorder to listen to music, all the current hits from America.

Like a small city, the base even had a weekly newspaper, the *Redcatcher!* (exclamation point included). While the paper's reporters described enemy activity, operations, combat awards, and GI humor, they also chronicled the everyday affairs of any small town: sports, comings and goings, hobbies, and upcoming parties.[4]

I arrived shortly after the historic Tet Offensive, during a period known later as "mini-Tet." Significant enemy activity still occurred in the area. The absolute height of the war in terms of troop strength was April 1969, near the end of my tour, with 543,400 American servicemen in-country. But the image that most people have of the war—that most of those troops were slogging through the jungle, shooting at the enemy twenty-four hours a day for their entire tour—was far from reality. The structure of the U.S. military in Vietnam was like a giant pyramid, with 80 percent of the troops at the bottom providing various services so that the other 20 percent could fight. Most servicemen were like me, performing support work at a rear base.

An Army of a half-million men must be supplied with necessities, and the U.S. military had to ship everything needed from the States: generators, gas to run the generators, and trucks to move the gas. Not only ammunition, guns, tanks, medical supplies, and food, but also toilet paper, talcum, toothpaste, and typewriters. The base PX stocked all kinds of electronic gadgets: small appliances, little refrigerators, televisions, and lawn chairs. The biggest arrival of every month was the ship carrying that all-important staple—beer. Our beer consumption was astronomical. Budweiser should always be so lucky.

But the infrastructure of Vietnam wasn't equipped to handle distribution of all this stuff. Everything—roads, docks, airstrips, warehouses, hospitals, wells, mess halls, barracks, latrines—had to be built. American troops spent far more man-hours building warehouses, constructing roads, and drilling water wells than in combat. We brought in millions of pounds of concrete. Those men not building were cooking, repairing trucks, typing up paperwork, running the PX, handling security, and performing endless other jobs.

I became the official "dog robber" for the 199th, serving with B Company of the 7th Combat Support Battalion. Each officer was assigned extra duties as well as his main job. One of mine was fire marshal. I had to make sure that all fire extinguishers were operating in my area. The water system was nonexistent; rain and sand barrels were available to fight any fire started by incoming rockets. But my main extra job was leader of a rifle platoon, a "ready reaction force."

Every camp was responsible for its own defense from enemy attacks. This was a semitransient camp, where one or two battalions would come for rest, training, and medical treatment after being in the field. With battalions going in and out, you could never depend on who was going to be there to defend the camp in case of an attack. Though directly in a combat zone, the camp was rocketed or mortared only about once a month.

Because I had been in the infantry as an enlisted man, I was given command of one of the three reinforced rifle platoons formed to defend the main camp. Each platoon leader had fifty to sixty troops, two gun-Jeeps, three separate machine gun crews, and often an armored personnel carrier, with one .50 caliber machine gun and two M-60 machine guns mounted on that. Half of the men were service personnel, such as cooks and clerks. The other half typically were combat veterans back in camp for a variety of reasons—perhaps minor wounds or a touch of malaria.

In the first three months of my tour, I drove every single day into Saigon to prowl the military docks. The city was fifteen or twenty miles south, on a direct asphalt road built by Americans. (Jeeps were outfitted with tall metal arms in front in order to trigger trip wires sometimes strung across the roads by the Communists.) Our brigade was nicknamed "The Palace Guard," as the last defense for Saigon on its northern perimeter.

Like any job, the war became a routine: a lot of hard work, discomfort, and monotony interrupted by periodic bursts of terror. True, there were Green Berets out eating snakes in the highlands. Navy SEALs went into the jungle to snatch Viet Cong prisoners or to blow up radio sites. Infantry soldiers went out on search-and-destroy missions in free-fire zones. But most of us lived in self-contained communities where we ate, watched movies, went on R&R. Even now, I can read the letters I wrote to my sister Barbara and remember keenly the details of my year in Vietnam.

Thursday, 19 Sept. 1968

Dear Barbara,
Things have been quiet, except for the ammo dump the VC blew up about an hour ago. A guy could have a nervous condition before he gets out of here....

Love, Jug

The two things I remember most vividly about Vietnam are the weather and the smells. On the coast, Vietnam had two seasons. In the "monsoon season," from September to early February, the temperature hovered around ninety-three degrees. Every day about 5 P.M., rain poured in torrents. The high humidity sapped willpower. In the "dry season," the mercury registered ninety-five degrees, but there was no rain. Three inches of red, powdery dust coated everything.

The intense heat heightened the smells. The local cuisine depended on spicy ingredients, and their pungent odors permeated the small houses. But other aromas were less appealing: the sour mildew, the rotten-egg swamps, the rancid rice paddies, the oily diesel engine fumes, and the stench of the barrels where we burned the crap from the latrines. You couldn't avoid the stink, the dust, and the bugs, especially the sticky flies that flew in your nose, your mouth, and your eyes.

Each morning we woke up at 0500, when the water trucks rumbled by to fill the tanks. Anyone who wanted a shower before the water was gone had to take it as soon he rolled out of bed. I hated that early morning shower. Though the day would be scorching hot by noon, the well water ran ice cold. After I woke up, I plugged in my hot plate to start heating water, ran to the shower, stood under the freezing drizzle, then raced back to my room. After shaving in the blessedly warm water, I threw the rest out the door, put on my uniform, then headed for the mess hall—the only building that had air-conditioning—and ate a cheese omelet. Hit the office at seven to catch up on the endless paperwork. Midmorning, I took the

Jeep and driver and began tracking down emergency items the brigade needed. Maybe someone had to replace a 105 howitzer gun barrel, but there were none to be found. I scrounged around on the docks or found another artillery battery that had an extra gun barrel and offered to trade for something they needed.

The U.S. government was spending millions of dollars to get goods to Vietnam, but ships were backed up, sitting idle in the South China Sea for up to six weeks, waiting their turn to be unloaded at the docks. Food was rotting in the holds. The backlog became a political problem. Gen. William Westmoreland finally put out an order: Unload the damn ships. In a matter of days, thousands of huge crates and boxes were unceremoniously dumped on the docks, with no organization or system in place to retrieve them. Finding any given item was a nightmare.

Everything was shipped in plywood crates marked with an eleven-digit code. Because of the computer project, most of the essential codes were familiar. I told my drivers to write down the numbers on the crates they saw every chance they had, then used those to create my own inventory system.

When we needed a howitzer part, I looked on my inventory list to find boxes stamped with the right code. Knowing the supply personnel would automatically say, "We don't have that," I first requisitioned the item legitimately. Turned down, I'd ask for authority to look for the item, grab the box already located, then trade the excess to another division, the Koreans, or the South Vietnamese.

Sometimes I found weird things, like an Air Force fighter pilot's helmet, very specialized headgear, quite different from an Army helicopter pilot's helmet, lost for some reason in the Army's supply system. Knowing no one in the 199th would ever need it, I made a note of the location, just in case.

Sure enough, my battalion commander eventually called me in and asked me to find a fighter pilot's helmet. He wanted to paint a special logo on the headgear and present it to Gen. Frederic Davison, the commanding general of the 199th. I showed up with that helmet an hour later, flabbergasting the hell out of my commander. He probably thought a contingent of Air Police would arrive any minute claiming I stole it.

Sunday, 20, Oct. 1968

Dear Barbara,

Things have started to hop. I woke up Sat. morning and we had firefights going on three sides of us. Then last night we had a typhoon, which blew off a few tin roofs, and dumped a lot of water, not much else. The VC were busy too. They mortared the depot and blew up the BOQ. [Bachelor Officers Quarters.] All the officers just happened to be at a party. Rockets flew over and really gave me a scare, but they hit in Bien Hoa and didn't do much damage. What was I saying about being bored? Like this morning, it was still raining. In the latrine you sit on a soggy seat, use soggy toilet paper, and sit there while the rain blows over you. This afternoon I plopped on my bed and was immediately asleep.

Love, Jug

Saigon hummed with life, making it easy to forget that a war raged in other parts of the country. People ate lunch at bustling sidewalk cafes. They went to the bank, they shopped, they sat and talked on benches under resplendent red-flowered trees. I was always amazed on my trips into Saigon to see billboards advertising Kodak film or Coca-Cola. There was even a Buick dealership in the center of town. But the beautiful city also held hidden dangers.

For instance, one day, while a Jeep from our base crossed a bridge in Saigon, a VC with a knife leaped on the hood. The driver slammed on the brakes and threw him off before anyone could fire a shot. The man melted into the crowd. The Viet Cong had been known to walk up to Jeeps driving slowly on the jammed streets of Saigon, lay a live grenade on the canvas top, then disappear well before the grenade exploded. Authorities recommended that when we went into Saigon, we remove the canvas. No shade meant roasting in the ruthless South Vietnamese sun; I kept the top on my Jeep. To be safe, while in Saigon, I constantly scoured the crowds for anything suspicious.

The "white mice," local police who wore white hats and shirts, directed traffic in Saigon at many of the intersections and traffic circles. Their efforts at orchestrating the anarchy seemed to have little effect. Few streets had marked lanes; pedestrians and pushcarts scurried across roads swarming with various vehicles—military vehicles, motor scooters, bicycles, pedal rickshaws called "cyclos"—a chaotic situation that inspired paranoia. One day, my driver and I were waiting at a stoplight when an old man on a sputtering little Lambretta scooter came up beside me. The man reached up and grabbed the canvas of the Jeep above my head as if to steady himself. Convinced he had placed a grenade there, I grabbed the cocked .45 caliber pistol lying in my lap and jammed the barrel between his eyes. He reared back, lost his grip on the Jeep, and fell over just as the light changed and the vehicle began to move forward. I punched the canvas over my head. No grenade. Behind us, the man had fallen to the ground and was untangling himself from his moped, probably thinking, *crazy damn American.*

In many ways, Vietnam was the great leveler. The war taught you not to evaluate situations and people the way you had before. You couldn't say,

"They can't draft me, I'm a doctor." Or, "They can't kill me, I'm the mayor's son." Education, wealth, parents—all that had no meaning. Everything in your previous life had been stripped away. Going to Vietnam was almost like taking a religious vow of poverty. All you had was your character, your internal abilities, and your physical and mental strength.

I can remember the first time I came under fire, and thinking, *Those silly bastards are actually trying to kill me! What the hell did I do to them?* It was an overwhelming feeling to suddenly realize twenty million Asians woke up every morning intent on killing B.G. Burkett. You quickly took it personally.

When you first arrived in-country, you asked yourself this question: What is the worst the enemy could do to me? The answer: Kill me. Nobody wanted to be with someone who had not come to terms with that reality.

It wasn't denial. It was acceptance. Once you made peace with that, it no longer had any power over you or had the ability to interfere with what you had to do. Like that old saying, "That which does not kill you makes you stronger."

This reality was acted out in strange, unexpected ways. For example, our base had a tall, good-looking first lieutenant who had been a college basketball star—a hero, right?—yes, back in the states. One night, the base under heavy mortar attack, he cracked, crumpling to the ground, crying, asking for his mother. From then on, the star basketball player was regarded as a coward.

Then there was Jeff, a short, dumpy enlisted man with thick glasses, who talked constantly about nothing, irritating others trying to read or write letters home. One evening, Jeff was riding shotgun in the lead truck for a convoy to supply camps toward Tay Ninh when it was hit by a Viet Cong RPG (Rocket Propelled Grenade). The driver was decapitated, leaving the lead truck stalled in the road, the convoy unable to move forward and vulnerable.

The attack blew Jeff's thick glasses into shards, rendering him nearly blind. But he jumped on the dead driver's torso, slammed the accelerator to the floor, and while firing his M-16 out the window, drove the truck down the road so the convoy could escape the ambush.

Who did you want around when something bad happened? The short dumpy guy who drove you crazy. Jeff later received a Purple Heart and a Bronze Star Medal for valor.

No Medal for Me

One night I nearly earned my own Purple Heart. The camp was on red alert status so I went to sleep wearing my boxer shorts, T-shirt, and socks, cuddling an M-16 in case of an enemy attack. In the middle of the night, mortar rounds exploded into the camp, jarring me from an uneasy sleep. Barely awake, I jumped into my boots, grabbed my pants, shirt, helmet, and weapon, and ran out the door. With mortar rounds impacting in the area, I sprinted to my unit's assembly point on a nearby hilltop. But I didn't know a carpenter had started to build wooden steps up the steep slope. Just as a flare brilliantly lit the whole scene, in full sight of my platoon, I tripped over the jumble of planks and went crashing down the hill, ripping a chunk of flesh out of my knee. Clutching my pants, I half hobbled, half crawled to the top of the hill.

A medic came over as I struggled into my clothes and tried to assess the attack. Blood ran into my boot. "Looks like you can get a Purple Heart for this one, sir," the medic said as he wrapped my knee with a field dressing. Embarrassed, I thought at first he was kidding. But he was dead serious.

The medic technically spoke the truth. I had suffered a "wound under fire" that required medical attention. We all knew men who received Purple Hearts for very minor wounds. Stories went around the camp about one soldier who was attending an open-air movie in Saigon when a terrorist grenade went off in the street. He jumped up and cut his finger on the seat. Bingo! Purple Heart.

I looked down at my gouged knee. How could I tell my grandkids that I had been "wounded in action" by tripping down a rocky hill in my underwear? I was supposed to be a competent leader, and my platoon had seen me sprawled on a hill in my boxer shorts. My only hope of salvaging any dignity was that the entire platoon would have mass amnesia the next day.

Dogs Saved Thousands

Early on, I met the leader of Dog Platoon, also based at the 199th BMB. A patrol going on a mission might be assigned a German shepherd and a handler. The dogs' ability to sense motion and smell people in the jungle was credited with saving thousands of American lives in Vietnam. (The U.S. military has had dogs as far back as the Civil War.)

One Sunday, the only day we had free time, the Dog Platoon's leader asked me if I wanted to go swimming. I had visions of bobbing in some nasty river along with parasites and floating crap and begged off. "No, no, it's a swimming pool," he promised.

We drove to a charming French villa near Bien Hoa that had been commandeered by the American military. We walked through some wrought iron gates, and I gulped in amazement: There, lounging around a gorgeous pool with clear blue water, were nurses and stewardesses in bathing suits. (Civilian stewardesses knew to bring their bikinis for those six-hour layovers.)

On occasional trips to Cam Ranh Bay, I swam and snorkeled at a picturesque beach reserved for officers. We fired up a barbecue pit, grilled steaks, and broke out the beer. Booze, barbecue, and babes: Cam Ranh beach was an exotic version of Fort Lauderdale.

Typically, in the evenings after chow we had little to do. Alcohol was very cheap—a dime for a can of Black Label beer and twenty cents for a shot of Scotch—so many men just sat and drank. Most nights, on a sheet strung up near the barracks, we showed current movies. During "intermission," we played cartoons or short porno flicks while someone ran the reel to another group and brought the next reel back. We'd throw a Jiffy Pop on a hot plate, grab a beer, and be back in time for the next film segment.

Religious services on Sunday were always packed. Going to war inevitably prompts thoughts of the eternal. I attended mass each week. Even men who didn't have a formal religion made peace with their God in some way. Our brigade priest, Capt. Charles (Angelo J.) Liteky, epitomized the combat chaplain. Athletic, deeply tanned, tough as leather, he often accompanied platoons on combat missions. On December 6, 1967, the Viet Cong had ambushed a patrol while Father Liteky was with them. The fierce fighting killed twenty-one men and wounded seventy-four. Though injured in the neck and foot by shrapnel, Liteky refused to leave the battle. The priest walked among the dying, administering last rites. He personally rescued more than twenty wounded men pinned down by fire from automatic weapons and Claymore mines. Liteky became one of three Catholic priests who received the Medal of Honor in Vietnam. The other two were awarded posthumously.[5]

You know the unit's tough when the brigade priest is a war hero.

On Sunday, our unit helped out at the local Catholic orphanage, but mostly we read, played guitars, and watched TV. Some tank units carried small television sets with them in the field. At night, they put out security guards, set up their lawn chairs, plopped the TV on the tank and watched *Perry Mason*.

I bought a small black-and-white set for five dollars from a guy who was going home. My favorite show, *Shell's Wonderful World of Golf*, aired every Sunday.

Friday [no date] 1968

Dear Barbara,

Everything is getting pretty boring, no firefights or air strikes or artillery. I guess that's good, but it sure makes time drag. This TV I've gotten helps at night and I've been doing a lot of reading. As a matter of fact, I'm probably doing more reading now than I did in college. We're watching the Dom DeLuise show. At home you'd change channels, but here you've only got one! Of course, if you understand Vietnamese, you can watch their channel.

Love, Jug

And, of course, I played golf—sort of. After scrounging an old scrub brush from the mess hall, I buried it in the clay so the stiff bristles barely stuck out of the ground. Using the brush as my tee, I slammed golf balls into the tarp slung between two poles for an hour at a time. As a three-year letterman on the golf team at Vanderbilt, I had played some of the finest courses in the South. Fantasy golf transported me out of Vietnam and brought back thoughts of home and my childhood.[6]

As a kid tagging along with my dad as his caddie, we were able to spend a lot of time together at the golf course. Golf is life. It was where my father taught me about honesty, tradition, integrity, self-reliance, and responsibility. In golf, as in life, you either make things happen or let things happen to you.[7]

In midsummer, I visited Col. Ben Shields, the base commander at Tan Son Nhut. Back home, I often had played golf with him and my dad. We talked about his (very good-looking) daughters, and he invited me to golf with him at an old French course near the base. I made excuses—I had no clubs, no golf shoes. The colonel said he had plenty of equipment, and he would send a chopper for me. Though greatly tempted, I begged off. I had real misgivings about telling my commanding officer I was taking off Sunday afternoon to play golf with Colonel Shields and that a helicopter was being commandeered to fly me to the course. He didn't know my father was career military, and he might see the whole thing as pretty damned uppity. Saying no was one of my biggest regrets of my eleven months in Vietnam. Later while on R&R in Australia, I played golf at a breathtaking public course on a cliff overlooking the Pacific Ocean near Sydney. But most of my golf was limited to watching television every Sunday.

We tried not to think about what was going on in the states politically. To all the GIs in my acquaintance, the antiwar protests were like people doing a rain dance to stop a hurricane. We looked at their activity as treason, actively encouraging the enemy to kill us. The soldiers who suffered most were soldiers in the bush with line companies.

In Vietnam, actress Jane Fonda was the most visible symbol of the antiwar movement. Fonda was involved in an organization called F.T.A., which we all knew stood for Fuck The Army.[8] She epitomized everything we hated about the antiwar movement: She had wealthy parents and knew nothing of the reality of the war. To me, protesting government policy was legitimate; traveling to North Vietnam and making broadcasts saying you supported the people trying to kill American troops and destroy a democratic nation was nothing short of collaborating with the enemy.

My mother wrote to me twice a week. Those letters were the history of my family for a year. But after I had been there a few months, the military began advising us to read our mail and then burn the letters from home. Why? The Jane Fondas of America.

The Fonda Effect

Military authorities told us that mail found on the bodies of dead Americans had been passed by the North Vietnamese to antiwar protesters back in the states. Parents of the dead men had gotten harassing letters and calls from people using information they had gleaned from personal mail. So we began burning letters from home. When my mother died, I felt the loss of those letters acutely. To this day, I believe Jane Fonda personally stole a piece of my family history. For many Vietnam veterans, the feelings are even more severe; to them, it is as if Fonda murdered a member of their family and then beat the rap.

In October, I hit six months in-country. That made me eligible for R&R, a week of rest in the country of my choosing, selected with brochures courtesy of the Military Tourist Bureau. Counting the days until I flew to Bangkok, I dreamed not of pretty women and beautiful scenery but of flush toilets and a hot shower. My plan was to sleep in every single day.

Saturday 2 Nov. 1968

Dear Barbara,
Needless to say, Bangkok was great! What amazed me was that it's a completely modern city, clean, neat, beautiful buildings, etc. . . .
Johnson has really upset us over here with his bombing halt. First he restricts the targets so we can't hit any important targets, and then he ends that without getting a single thing from Hanoi. If the military had been allowed to fight the war, it would have been over with half the casualties, but no, they have to play politics. Just watch, Hanoi will demand more before they even agree to really talk. They haven't even admitted they have troops in the South!

Love, Jug

Shortly after I arrived in Vietnam, the enemy blasted another nearby base camp with mortars four or five nights in a row. The attacks illuminated the ink-black sky like Fourth of July fireworks. Red-orange fireballs erupted wherever mortars impacted, and enemy green tracers crossed paths with friendly red tracers. Occasionally "Puff the Magic Dragon" appeared to work its wicked sorcery. The Air Force had converted the venerable C-47 cargo plane into a hellacious weapons platform. Sporting several miniguns aimed out one side of the plane, the pilot flew in a circle around a target, putting thousands of rounds into enemy positions. Puff sounded like the whine of a mammoth buzz saw, and the streak of tracers made it look as if the "dragon" was belching flames. When the firing ended, an orange streak of death emerged from the plane and plunged into the target, and then there would be darkness. I could only be thankful the enemy had no similar "dragons."

Up on a small hill, our base looked down on the embattled camp. When the mortar rounds started exploding next door, we dragged our lawn chairs and beer coolers into position and watched the show. Seeing the colorful pyrotechnics, it was easy to forget how deadly the attacks could be. The American tracers poured out in defense, and the enemy tracers converged inward like a million fireflies at war. Fireworks on the Fourth of July have made me slightly uneasy ever since.

While snapping photos of a particularly spectacular daytime air strike, I heard a high-pitched mechanical shriek. A chunk of shrapnel whistled past my cheek and smashed a fist-sized hole into a Jeep behind me. Heart pounding, feeling asinine, I put the camera away.

Typically, when a large enemy unit moved into the area, intelligence from electronic sensors, patrols, and the South Vietnamese put us on alert. That meant I had to be more careful about checking passwords at night. If mortars hit at 2 A.M., my job was to pull my platoon together and find out our assignment. Not allowed to keep personal firearms in our barracks, we raced to the weapons area, grabbed our rifles, then piled into the bunker line or took cover if mortars and rockets were coming in.

Once during an attack, the duty sergeant claimed he needed the commanding officer's direct order to unlock the weapons bunker. To me, the objective of shooting the enemy coming through the fence seemed more important at the time than observing command protocol. (And I didn't even have an MBA yet.) Instantly I had one of my men chop the door down with a fire ax. I suspect the duty sergeant found a job after the war as a bureaucrat at a rules-bound agency. No one in authority ever mentioned the incident.

When alerts were over, we checked all the weapons back in, like cowboys disarming at the saloon door in the Wild West. Early on, I learned the wisdom of this. One night, when an alert ended, I walked to the mess hall while my men checked in their guns. But another platoon leader headed to his barracks; instead of turning in his sidearm, he took it with him. The lieutenant, who had been in Vietnam eleven months and had only one month to go, stretched out on his bunk, put the gun to his temple, and blew his brains out. His roommate theorized that the officer, a deeply religious man, was depressed because he had gone to Thailand on R&R and shacked up with a prostitute for the whole week. He had a fiancée back home and felt ashamed.

If I died in Vietnam, it would not have been at my own hand. There were plenty of other ways to die. One day, I hitched a ride with a helicopter crew flying to Vung Tau, the old French resort city on the coast where Australian troops were based. Always scrounging and snooping, I had heard through the grapevine the supply depot at Vung Tau contained some interesting goods. En route, we overheard frantic radio traffic from an Australian unit engaged in a furious firefight against an entrenched enemy tree line. The Aussie was pleading desperately for whatever help any unit in the sector could provide. Below, I could see little more than deep green, flat coastal plains punctuated by canals feeding into a delta of the muddy Saigon River. Instantly, the American pilot banked and swept his chopper over the area. I was just supply hunting, and suddenly we were in the middle of a raging battle.

The skin of a helicopter provides as much protection from gunshots as a beer can; an enemy .51-caliber round pierces the thin metal membrane as easily as a child's BB gun blows holes in a paper target. Still, I immediately squatted on the floor next to one of the two doorgunners, hooked one of the seat belts to the back of my fatigue pants, and said a quick prayer.

With my new camera, a Canon bought in the PX for a hundred dollars, I snapped pictures as the pilot made a gut-churning dive low over the tree line. The doorgunners let rip with a stream of ear-splitting M-60 machine gun rounds, trying to provide cover for medics on the ground frantically working on a few wounded Australians. Over the pounding roar of the rotor blades and the machine guns, a gunner screamed into his microphone that we were taking fire. As the helicopter bucked and lurched, I kept clicking the shutter. I knew we were all going to die, but my combat photographs were going to be in *Life* magazine.

Miraculously, American fighter planes materialized in the sky above. The helicopter pilot peeled off, and we resumed our trip to Vung Tau. From their casual attitudes, I could see that my worst nightmare had been just another day at the office for the pilot and doorgunners. When we finally landed at Vung Tau, grateful to be alive, I herded the helicopter crew into a pose in front of the chopper for a picture only to discover that in my panic, I had stripped the film. No award-winning photos.

But, other than attacks on our base camp at night, I saw very little combat. That was also true of many troops in the field. A soldier with Dog Platoon told me he had gone out on twenty-two patrols in four months; in all that time neither he nor anybody in his platoon had fired a shot, nor had they seen the enemy. Others weren't so lucky.

One morning on base, I saw a rifle company coming back from several days in the field. Slogging through the mud, they had not bathed in days. The only food they had eaten was C-rations. They looked like whipped dogs.

They were taking off their gear and putting things away, when I heard one baby-faced soldier whistling as he rolled his poncho and put his rucksack in order.

"Trooper, what the hell are you so happy about?" I asked him.

"Sir?" he said, jerked out of some private reverie.

"What the hell are you so happy about?" I repeated.

"Sir," he said with a wide smile, "I'm only nineteen years old, and I've already seen the worst day of my life."

Whenever I'm a little depressed, I think of the best and purest optimist I ever met. I hope he made it.

Saturday, 9 Nov. 1968

Dear Barbara,

Things have really been busy. I pulled off a great legal triumph today. I was defense counselor in a marijuana drug trial and I got a verdict of "not guilty." Even I found it hard to believe....The trial counselor thought he had it sewed up, so he didn't really prepare, and he had little experience. I just made my point and then let him stumble over himself. Had I been trial counselor, I know I could have gotten a conviction in twenty minutes....

Love, Jug

Any drug you wanted to buy in Vietnam—marijuana, heroin, opium—was cheap and available. Kids sold joints on the side of the road for fifty cents apiece. But there was no place to hide illicit goods. Although officers had their own rooms, there was precious little privacy for enlisted men who were subjected to frequent searches.

Typically, we junior officers staged a surprise inspection once a month. We didn't look exclusively for drugs, but any kind of dangerous contraband, such as live ammunition or weapons, souvenirs pilfered off the dead, even enemy documents that might be valuable intelligence. Virtually every shakedown revealed something illicit. One inspection turned up a stolen, loaded M-60 machine gun a soldier had stashed in his bunk. During a search of three hundred men, authorities usually found one or two men with half a joint. He would be slapped with an Article 15, the equivalent of a misdemeanor, which mostly affected privileges and promotions.

Nearer the combat zones, there was less oversight, fewer inspections, and more ability to hide drugs. But there was great peer pressure not to let others down. Few men wanted to go out on patrol with somebody stoned. Though it increased later, the rate of drug usage during the period when I was in Vietnam would have been the envy of any high school principal in America. I did not use drugs in Vietnam and did not have friends who did. No one in my immediate command ever got caught using drugs. But I served as either defense or prosecution counsel on a half-dozen courts-martial for men accused of drug offenses while in Vietnam.

Alcohol presented a bigger problem. Each of us had a ration card for one or two cases of beer a month, plus we could go to the clubs and drink if we wanted. The heaviest drinkers tended to be senior NCOs who had been around a while. A scary incident kept me on the side of sobriety.

One night, after a friend's unexpected promotion, we threw a spontaneous party near a creek bank. We were grilling steaks, drinking beer, and listening to music. The party expanded, with people bringing more food and booze. I kept eating and drinking—and drinking and drinking and drinking.

The next morning—with 81 mm mortars pounding in my head and the feeling that a large water buffalo had sat on my stomach—I woke up on the bank of the creek as the local Vietnamese workers were coming in for the day. Around me, twenty young American officers were strewn out across the ground. If the VC had paid us an impromptu visit that night, all we could have done was puke on them. Even though I had gone to sleep and not passed out, the idea of being incapacitated terrified me. I don't think I had more than two beers at a time after that.

Despite the ever-present awareness of the war, Vietnam had its compensations. Troops in Vietnam were better equipped, had more ammunition, better mail service, and often ate better than troops did in World War II and Korea. Though troops in the field had to eat C-rations, the food in our mess hall was gourmet cuisine, considering the fact that Army cooks were dishing it out. We frequently had steak and baked potatoes. Thanksgiving meant even better food than usual. Our menu read like one you'd find in a nice stateside restaurant: turkey, dressing, cranberry sauce, mashed potatoes, sweet potatoes, green beans, rolls, pumpkin pie, coffee. That 1968 Thanksgiving in Vietnam, I pushed myself away from the table as gorged as I had ever gotten at my mother's dinner table.

And despite the occasional heavy labor and the boring nights, we had numerous Vietnamese employees to make the load easier. There were waitresses in the mess hall and elderly men doing manual labor like filling sandbags and pulling weeds. All the laundry was done by housegirls, who charged by the piece. In our barracks were three housegirls, sisters in their mid-twenties or early thirties: Hat, Van, and Phan. The officers each paid them ten or fifteen dollars a month to do laundry. I enjoyed talking with them, using a hodgepodge of words I had acquired in French and Vietnamese aided by a large dose of pantomime. As unofficial negotiation officer, I explained the women's fees to new officers and set up their work arrangements.

"Buddhist or Catholic"

The housegirls and I joked and bantered every day. They were Catholic and so am I; that really made a connection with them. Only two religions existed in their world. When a new officer arrived, the first thing they asked me in their pidgin English was: "Buddhist or Catholic?" I couldn't make them understand that one new man, a Presbyterian, was a Christian. To Hat, Van, and Phan, anyone who didn't belong to the Catholic Church was a Buddhist.

One sister had been married to a soldier in the South Vietnamese army who had abandoned her and their children. The two other women were single. Everything I wanted for my family and future children, the housegirls wanted for their children. Freedom was at the top of the list.

Even though I knew the sisters hated the Communists, one day I teased one of the women about favoring the North Vietnamese. Furious, not understanding that I was jesting, she stormed out. The other women told me later that two Viet Cong soldiers had come into their village, taken their brother outside the house, and shot him dead because he was a member of the militia. The sister I had inadvertently infuriated had grabbed their brother's weapon and killed the two VC. Shortly after that, fearing deadly retribution, the sisters left their village to go work for the Americans. I got the message.

The women also despised the Japanese because of what they had done to the Vietnamese during World War II. When a Japanese-American lieutenant was assigned to our battalion, the sisters saw him come into the area and became very agitated. "Japanese! Japanese!" they began wailing and backing away. They could not comprehend that he was an American. It took me four days of cajoling before they finally agreed to do the new officer's domestic chores.

Sunday, 15 Dec. 1968

Dear Barbara,

We've had no more rockets but there have been a few snipers out each night. Seeing those helicopters go after them is something. Sleeping is difficult because the artillery and B-52s go all night long. There's no doubt the NVA is out there, beaucoup of them....

We sleep with our weapons, in our clothes. A lot of guys are even sleeping in the bunkers.

One of my men went off his nut. Threatened to kill the NVA and any GI or officer, including me, who got in his way. They're sending him to the hospital . . . Have a Merry Christmas and a Happy New Year.

Love, Jug

Christmas meant goodie boxes from home and a tree decorated with beer cans. For the Christmas of 1968, the state of Mississippi sent the 199th Brigade several thousand dollars; we used the money to import entertainers—meaning singers and strippers—from the Philippines.

During the Vietnam War, except during the Tet Offensive and a few other periods, South Vietnam remained open to tourists. Pan Am flew visitors, typically from Europe, Australia, and New Zealand, into Saigon, where residents went about their business. And there were hundreds of eighteen-to twenty-one-year-old Australians who toured South Vietnam, singing at base camps. They traveled from camp to camp, making a hundred dollars a night, sleeping in their Volkswagen vans. A hell of a summer job. As far as I know, none were killed or injured.

Other "visitors" on tourist visas included young journalists, often with obscure publications. Usually male, they wanted experience as "war correspondents" they could put on their resumes—or maybe they just craved adventure. Most lived the good life in Saigon, though to listen to their reports, they were always out in the field in the thick of combat.

Assume a day in Vietnam has one thousand parts. Then assume that one hundred of those parts—10 percent—were actually involved in attempting to engage the enemy, a fairly accurate percentage even at the height of the war when I was there. Maybe three of those one hundred parts actually involved some actual combat. The rest of us would be drinking beer, popping popcorn, watching TV. But that intense slice of combat was the news that people in America saw on their televisions at 6 o'clock that night. The next day, the same thing happened. Telescoped in time and perspective, the sporadic combat made it appear that all troops in Vietnam were facing constant, unrelenting battle.

That was misleading even at the peak of the fighting, when an average of four hundred troops (out of a half-million in-country) were killed each week. And about one-sixth of those deaths were caused not by the enemy but by other causes. Almost half the helicopter crashes in Vietnam occurred in noncombat conditions, but often when a helicopter went down, the media portrayed the crash as a combat-related loss.[9]

I saw this media distortion firsthand. During an NVA attack of a nearby village, several South Vietnamese civilians suffered burns when the enemy torched their homes. The injured civilians were brought into our dispensary for medical treatment. Two reporters appeared at the main gate to do a story on how the Americans "accidentally napalmed" the village. The village had not been napalmed. There had been no air strike. But the reporters had decided in advance what the story was. They wrote that the village had been napalmed.

In the middle of my tour, we went on alert when a unit of about four hundred NVA crossed a river north of us and were boxed in by American tanks and South Vietnamese infantry. A ferocious firefight erupted. The NVA refused to surrender; a dozen troops battled their way into the small village of Hoi Nai. The residents took refuge in the Catholic church, much more substantial than their tiny houses, which were made mostly of cinder blocks with tin roofs.

The American advisor to the South Vietnamese troops wanted our allies to take one or two platoons to rout the NVA stragglers, who had holed up in the abandoned houses. The South Vietnamese commander adamantly refused. That would put his troops at risk. He demanded that the Americans call in an air strike so he would not lose any men. The commander and the American advisor began arguing. Knowing that if anything in the hamlet was destroyed, we would rebuild it, the village chief weighed in, insisting on an air strike as well.

Meanwhile, a network television news correspondent and his cameraman roared up in a Jeep. Based on the demands of the South Vietnamese, the American advisor called in an air strike. The scene was now incredibly dramatic: Fighters screaming in, dropping bombs, lots of noise and fires.

Network "News"

A few nights later, I saw the event on network television: the noise, the bombs, the dust rising, buildings burning. One of the cameras focused on an old Vietnamese lady, clearly terrified, huddling with a group on the front steps of the packed church, gripping a little girl, probably her granddaughter. The reporter's commentary was that Americans had destroyed a pro-American village, and he ended by speculating, "Who knows how many civilians were killed or wounded by American soldiers today?"

While virtually annihilating the NVA, these attacks caused no civilian loss of life. In the next few days, our engineer unit cleared up the debris and rebuilt the houses that had been destroyed. An officer set up a process by which the residents were compensated for the loss of their possessions: So much for a bicycle, so much for a pig. All Catholics, the villagers were extremely pro-American before and after this incident. In a bizarre way, they felt a great sense of satisfaction; they had resisted the Communists.

What the reporter had shown on camera was all real. The woman was real, the child was real, the bombing was real, the destruction was real. What the reporter said was in the form of rhetorical questions. "Who knows how many villagers have been killed?" But the impression left with the American public was that their troops had destroyed a village and maybe killed hundreds of civilians. The pictures apparently coincided with the words the reporter was saying. But they had nothing to do with what really happened.[10]

One vivid image often shown on American TV news was a downed cargo plane at Khe Sanh being licked by fire. In reality, the plane had crashed months before, and the flames came from the burning of the latrine waste in trenches behind the plane. The TV people simply used the scene as a vivid backdrop whenever they needed to show a burning aircraft.

On January 23, 1969, with only a few months to go in Vietnam, I turned twenty-five. "It's a hell of a thing to have a birthday in Vietnam, sir," one of my enlisted men said to me. "What are you going to do on your next birthday?" It struck me as a preposterous question. Thoughts of tomorrow could get you killed. In Vietnam, you had no future, only today. The military typically pulled men out of combat within thirty days of their DEROS (Date Eligible to Return from Overseas). Men started fantasizing about hopping on the Freedom Bird. They often got sloppy and ended up dead.

But contemplating the future was unavoidable. I began planning an R&R to Australia and in order to apply to various universities for graduate school, arranged to take the Graduate Record Exam in Vietnam. Twenty other prospective graduate students and I sat for the difficult test in a wood frame building on the edge of an airstrip at II Field Force Headquarters near Bien Hoa and Long Binh. An artillery battery began firing rounds into the countryside directly over the building. Each boom made us jump, then black residue from the guns trickled down, dribbling like rain on the tin roof. Occasionally, a helicopter landed on the nearby helipad, generating gusts of wind that made the metal roof panels flap.

Scorchingly hot, like the inside of a barbecue pit, the room's only breeze came from a single fan, which blew a stream of air in our direction. Soon drenched in sweat, we had to lean over our papers at an angle so the droplets landed on the floor and not on our papers. I took off my shirt. Several men stripped to their underwear. We joked about how many extra points we deserved for taking the test in such ridiculous conditions. I could only pray that my score would be high enough to get me into graduate school somewhere, anywhere.

Sunday, March 1969

Dear Barbara,
I got my graduate score. 524. Not good, but not bad. It should get me in.
We'll see.

The XO called me in to try to get me to take captain and stay in at least one more year. Supposedly I'm rated among the top 5 percent of lieutenants.

Impressed? He told me, being a service brat, I probably wouldn't be able to adjust to civilian life! Watch me!

  Love, Jug

I felt conflicting emotions about leaving Vietnam—elated but also guilty, as if I was abandoning friends. Saying good-bye to my platoon would be like going to the locker room in the middle of the fourth quarter of a hotly contested football game. My DEROS was May 5, 1969, but graduate school did not start until September. Despite what I told my sister, I did consider extending my tour. But one night that spring, rockets and mortars bombarded our camp, hitting several men. I remember thinking, *If I come home without my legs because I volunteered to stay a few extra months, what will I tell my mother?* That made my decision easy. I was out of there.

My driver was leaving at the same time, so for a week before we left, he and I took sightseeing trips to Saigon and several pagodas en route, snapping photos and playing tourist. I intended to spend a few weeks touring the Orient after I left, but I couldn't find anyone to go along. Homesickness set in. I was ready to get the hell out of Southeast Asia.

In early April, I began turning in my equipment. I made flight arrangements and underwent final medical exams. Once a month, we had a going-away dinner for those leaving, with presentations of plaques, citations, and awards. Now it was my turn.

My last night in camp, I handed my platoon over to another first lieutenant. Nostalgia and loneliness flooded over me. I had built a rapport and mutual respect with the men. Now I had to turn them over to someone who was inexperienced. And I felt sad leaving Hat, Van, and Phan. I wondered if the three vivacious sisters would survive the war.

On May 5, 1969, I hitched a ride the few miles from BMB to the 90th Replacement Depot, where I had arrived eleven months earlier, green and filled with barely contained dread. And again, I waited for my name to appear on a manifest for the next plane out.

Senior officers bumped me off the first few flights. Late on the second night, someone came into the barracks. "Lieutenant Burkett!" he shouted. "Pack it up. You're out of here." I hustled into my clothes, grabbed my duffel bag, and raced to the bus. "Lieutenant Jesse Burkett?" called out a sergeant. Wrong Lt. Burkett. Deflated, I trudged back to bed. Later the next day, I finally caught the Freedom Bird. As the aircraft lifted off the ground, I thought I would feel a great sense of relief, but there was nothing, just numbness.

After the plane took off, the pilot announced: "Gentlemen, we're passing over the coast of South Vietnam." A brief cheer rose, then silence. Each of us was aware that many of our companions on the arriving flight had already gone home either in hospital planes or in silver metal coffins, stacked one on top of another in the cargo hold of an Air Force transport.

Role Reversal

In Yokota, I was now in the line of veterans trudging past the newcomers. There really was a difference in the two lines of men. In our line, there was a certain resolve. We had passed through the fire and become steel. They were apprehensive, but we had no anxiety. We had survived. I felt old.

My God, I thought, looking at the men coming off the plane in the other line, *they're sending children.*

From Yokota, we flew to Anchorage. Like the flight over, there was no chitchat. You'd think two hundred sex-deprived men would flirt with the civilian stewardesses, but there was little conversation. Immersed in thought, we were more interested in eating a hot meal than hitting on women who were undoubtedly inured to the attentions of the most persuasive GIs.

In Anchorage, stiff as hell, I located a restroom, shaved and washed up at the sink. Back in the lobby, I ran into three teenagers, all Air Force service brats like I had once been, probably heading to college. I tried to strike up a conversation with them. But their world revolved around the college campus, where the war was an abomination, and I was clearly a soldier. Only a few years older than they, I could not connect with them.

Another weird sensation. Vulnerability. I did not have a gun. Looking around, I realized nobody else had weapons. "How do they protect themselves?" I wondered, feeling literally naked.

But being on the air base in Anchorage comforted me. More than any other place, I felt at ease on an Air Force base. Planes on the ramp, people in uniforms bustling about—in Anchorage there was a feeling that I was home, even if it was one of home's farthest-flung outposts.

From Anchorage, we flew to McGuire Air Force Base adjacent to Fort Dix, New Jersey, where we were to be processed out of the Army. We arrived about 9 P.M. Not only was there no welcome, there was no food. The mess hall was closed. We asked a duty sergeant where we were supposed to stay. He had no idea. Another lieutenant and I found an empty barracks. There were no mattresses on the beds, so we slept on the bare springs with our duffel bags as pillows.

The next morning, aching from the long flight and the steel springs, we located the mess hall. "Chow line's closed, sir," the sergeant told us. The last man had been fed and they were already cleaning up.

"Well, we got in from Vietnam late last night, and we haven't had anything to eat in twenty-four hours," I said. A specialist four stepped up. "Sir, I'll make you some bacon and eggs, sir," he said.

Later we walked to the processing area, where several hundred men were going through the exit process, an irritating, interminable procedure that takes hours. At lunchtime, again, there was no place for us to eat.

This time, we took matters into our own hands. We hitched a ride to the officers club and each wolfed down a huge T-bone steak. When we emerged from the club, the sky had turned black and was pouring rain. Just then, a major general drove up in his chauffeur-driven staff car. We saluted as the general walked in. His driver was wearing Vietnam service ribbons. "Sergeant, if you can get us back to the processing area, in about an hour we're going to be civilians," I said. "The general is eating lunch. He won't miss you."

He glimpsed our Vietnam decorations, grinned ear-to-ear and said, "Gotcha sir. Get in." The staff car, its red flag with two silver stars flapping in the wind, drove up to the processing area. Everyone in uniform snapped to attention. The driver opened the door and saluted sharply, playing it to the hilt. Then two first lieutenants climbed out. "Carry on, gentlemen," I said, saluting the astonished onlookers. Two hours later, I was no longer a member of the U.S. Army.

Still in uniform, we boarded a shuttle to the Philadelphia airport. At the terminal, I shook hands with my companion and sat down for the two-hour wait for a flight to Nashville to visit relatives, and from there, my parents' house in Little Rock. Feeling weary, disconnected, I thumbed through the exit packet from Gen. Creighton Abrams given to servicemen on leaving Vietnam ("A grateful nation thanks you for your service,") and a pamphlet titled, "Your Year in Vietnam," with pictures of the country.

At Fort Dix, there had been no formal leave-taking, no acknowledgment of what we had done. The Army's attitude was, "Don't let the door hit you in the butt as you leave. We're finished with you. Next!"

2

Welcome Home, Baby Killer

THE PROFESSOR stood at the front of the class, a look of contempt on his face. "I want one thing to be perfectly clear," he announced. "I do not want Vietnam or the U.S. military mentioned in this class." If we ever discussed our experience in the military or referred to our experiences in the service for case studies, he promised to give our project papers lower grades.

That marked the beginning of my second quarter in graduate school in January 1970, at the University of Tennessee. In an evening class on industrial management, we had just gone around the room and introduced ourselves. Of a dozen students, five were business executives from a local manufacturing firm. Like me, two other students had returned to civilian life after tours of duty in Vietnam; another Vietnam vet student was an active duty officer.

The professor's syllabus demanded that students use case studies from their previous work experience to illustrate management problems and solutions. The executives could draw on their careers. The veterans had only college or their experiences in the military. I had managed large groups of men and organized a complex system of ordnance inventory under very difficult and changing conditions, but in the eyes of this arrogant professor, that counted for nothing. I would have to draw on my experiences in the Boy Scouts and selling lemonade in order to pass this business course.

The professor's ban on our discussion of military matters didn't extend to him, however. Over the course of the semester, he spouted antiwar and antimilitary opinions, repeatedly making negative references to the U.S. armed forces. Whenever he referred to the military, his purpose always was to illustrate a breakdown in the ethics and morality of workers.

I could understand being opposed to the Vietnam War. But the entire

U.S. military? The same military that fought for the professor's right to stand in front of a classroom and speak his mind freely?

Although rankled, I didn't vent my anger. I had come home. It was time to make my way in the world, to earn my first million. But how? After serving as both defense and prosecution counsel in court-martials in Vietnam, I considered going to law school. Earning a law degree took at least three years; obtaining an MBA would be faster, and maybe I could start my own company. The sky was the limit.

After World War II, the government paid for veterans' tuition, room, and board at the college of their choice. If a veteran had the brainpower to be accepted at Harvard, the government paid his tuition. But the GI Bill for Vietnam veterans provided only a small stipend for college, about $175 a month, which hardly paid for a decent apartment. I had saved most of my money in Vietnam and had a little over five thousand dollars by the time I arrived at the University of Tennessee. Still, after tuition, books, and living expenses, my savings wouldn't go far.

I decided to take a double load and complete the two-year MBA program in twelve months, an ambitious plan that left little room for a social life. The people who had attended undergraduate school at Vanderbilt with me had been out in the business world for three years, making their fortunes. I had to catch up.

When I enrolled at UT, which had a student body of thirty-five thousand, the veterans' coordinator told me that more than one thousand students also were veterans. Based on the percentage of members of the service who went to Vietnam, I guessed at least a third had fought in the war. Still, I didn't seek them out. Typically, I didn't know another student was a Vietnam vet until he introduced himself in class. We had no social group where we swapped war stories. That was yesterday.

Serious Business

What we all had in common was our age, three or four years older than the typical graduate student. We didn't party; we buckled down to business.

Despite that management professor, the university was no hotbed of antiwar protest. Although a small nucleus of activists occasionally demonstrated, the campus was relatively conservative. Still, Vietnam dominated our lives like an invisible presence. The world was debating Vietnam. At parties, confrontations about the war erupted during casual conversations. Someone might make a ridiculous statement like, "I think it's awful we're killing all those babies." I could not let a comment like that go without challenge.

Invariably, the people forcing confrontations didn't know what they were talking about. Few people knew why we were there. "We had a treaty with South Vietnam?" one college history teacher asked me. He didn't know that North and South Vietnam had never been one country, that the conflict was not legally a civil war. Most of their information came from television or at a teach-in, and bore little relation to the reality of the war. That didn't stop them from arguing. They believed they knew more from watching Walter Cronkite than someone who had been in Vietnam. And since they were "antiwar," if you disagreed with them, then you were "pro-war." They couldn't understand that you could be against war but in favor of defending your country's treaties and commitments to other countries. The complexities of reality were ignored. The "atrocity" label got slapped on a GI who accidentally shot a civilian in Vietnam but not on an antiwar protester who blew up a police officer and a bystander. Conversations about the war were so frustrating that eventually, when somebody brought it up, I would fade into another part of the room.

At first, I took great interest in the news concerning Vietnam, reading newspapers and watching television news in particular for information on the 199th. Over and over, I saw reports I suspected were outright lies. One story about a certain battle discussed how the Americans "made no effort to avoid civilian casualties." When I was there, troops made an enormous effort to avoid civilian casualties at whatever cost. I knew that did not change when Burkett left the war.

Another story that appeared shortly after my return home discussed "antiwar sentiment among the GIs in Vietnam." I couldn't imagine where they had gotten their information. I had roamed over much of South Vietnam, and there was no antiwar sentiment among the troops when I was there. Certainly many soldiers felt dissatisfaction with the way the politicians were running the war, but none I knew aligned himself with the Jane Fonda faction.

For a few months, I communicated with men in my unit, but one by one they left to come home. The three Vietnamese housegirls sent me pictures and a dress they made for my sister. But then I lost track of them and often have wondered about their fate.

As school began to take over all my time, my interest in war news began to wane. In the spring of 1970, after the Cambodian invasion, a national movement tried to shut down college campuses in protest. When veterans at the business school were casually asked how many would attend class on the designated walkout day, we told the professors: "We paid our tuition. We'll be here; you damn well better be here." The picket line avoided the business school. Most of the students taking graduate business courses went to class as if it was just another day.

After graduating from Tennessee with a good academic record in September 1970, I began interviewing with firms in Nashville and Atlanta.

At twenty-seven, older than the typical entry-level employee, I tried to stress my maturity, my life experience. But offers were few.

During one meeting with an executive at an Atlanta bank, the man looked at my resume then abruptly stopped reading.

"I'm not hiring any Vietnam vets," he said as he ripped up my resume. "Get the hell out of here. I'm going to get a cup of coffee, and I don't want you here when I get back." He walked out of his office, leaving me sitting there feeling as if he had spat in my face.

I thought back to other interviews. Were the offers not coming because of stiff competition? Or were the offers few because of Vietnam? Most Vietnam veterans learned to put down on their resumes something like "Military requirements satisfied," or "Military obligations: none." That meant you were not going to be drafted. Proud of my military service, I refused to do that. At the same time, I realized my insistence on including Vietnam on my resume set me up for nasty reactions.[11]

Meanwhile, I went "home" to Dallas, where my father's company had transferred him. In addition to my parents and two sisters, some fraternity brothers from Vanderbilt were living in Dallas. The city, in the center of both the Sun Belt and the Bible Belt, was booming. Dallas had family, friends, opportunity, and good weather for golf. That was enough for me.

Vet Friendly Skies

Several companies, such as Southwest Airlines and Federal Express, had reputations for being friendly to Vietnam vets. (When you boarded a Southwest Airlines plane in the seventies, the pilot likely had been making bombing runs on North Vietnam two years before.) And there was Ross Perot's Electronic Data Systems. Perot, a graduate of the U.S. Naval Academy, ran EDS like the military. The grapevine buzzed that EDS was aggressively pursuing Vietnam vets. I applied for a job at EDS and interviewed with an executive who was a former Marine.

"You have only one tour in Vietnam," he said, glancing at my resume.

"Yes, sir," I replied.

"Most of us have more," he said, continuing to read.

He glanced up. "You only have one year of command duty," he said.

"Yes, sir," I said, wondering what the point was.

"Most of us have more," he replied. Great, I thought, now I'm *not enough* of a Vietnam vet.

EDS asked me back for more interviews. But I had lived in a regimented environment all my life and wasn't anxious to return to it. In the fall of 1970, I accepted an offer selling computers at Burroughs. Because of my interest in the stock market, Burroughs assigned me area brokerages as potential clients. After a year, I was hired to work in the Dallas office of

Underwood, Neuhaus Inc., a prestigious old-line, family-owned securities firm based in Houston. Quickly, I became successful as a stockbroker, typically calling on small institutions and trust departments, following oil industry stocks and stocks based in the Southwest. I started building up my own portfolio, with each year better than the one before.

Promoted to junior partner and after years of saving money and focusing on my career, I was ready to settle down and have a family. For a year, I dated a woman who worked as a legislative aide in Austin, the state capital about two hundred miles south of Dallas. In 1977, after a commuter romance, we decided to marry. Almost instantly, both of us realized the marriage was a disaster. The long-distance romance simply could not survive the realities of wedded life. As a Catholic, the divorce and religious annulment were very traumatic for me, far worse than Vietnam had ever been.

As my career as an investment broker evolved over the next fourteen years, I rarely thought about Vietnam. When I socialized with friends who were veterans, we felt a rapport, but we rarely talked about our experiences in Southeast Asia.

The Memorial

One day in July 1986, a friend from the Vietnam years called.

"Hey Burkett, I'm going to this meeting," said the unmistakable Georgia drawl of Paul Russell. "They're trying to build a Texas Vietnam veterans' memorial. Let's go hear what they have to say."

A Vanderbilt grad, Russell had received a Vietnamese Cross of Gallantry as an advisor to the South Vietnamese during two tours in Vietnam. After the war, Russell had worked his way up to president of a major construction firm in the Southwest. We frequently ran into each other at Vanderbilt alumni functions. But until that day, we rarely talked about the war.

Russell had been contacted by Art Ruff, president of one of the largest real estate development companies in the country. During the war, Ruff had been an artillery officer serving primarily as a forward observer—the guy who called in artillery strikes, a dangerous combat position. Hit twice by shrapnel, Ruff had received two Purple Hearts and a Bronze Star Medal. After Vietnam, he had returned to Dallas and worked in the development business, ultimately building his company into a multimillion-dollar corporation.

Because of his great connections in the Dallas financial community, Ruff had been approached to help raise money for a memorial to all Texans killed in Vietnam. Although Ruff didn't know Russell personally, he had heard through the grapevine that he had some financial savvy. Russell, in turn, was asking me, thinking I might know something about marketing and raising money.

Texas had lost 3,427 men in the war—3,271 killed and 156 missing in action. Certainly these men deserved recognition by their home state. I had not seen the National Vietnam Memorial, but I felt that the mothers and fathers, sons and daughters of those Texas servicemen should not have to go to Washington, D.C., to honor their dead. Texas should pay homage to their sacrifice, just as it had recognized the sacrifice of men in World War II. Feeling a psychological and moral obligation to help, I agreed to attend the meeting.

The first effort to build a Texas Vietnam Veterans Memorial had actually started in 1974, only two years after the last combat troops left Vietnam. The endeavor had fizzled. In the late seventies, another group tried again only to end up deeply in debt. A new group of Vietnam veterans incorporated a nonprofit corporation in 1981. Torn apart by internal politics and turmoil, the effort whimpered to a halt. Two years later, some of the remnants of that board resurrected the effort, feeling that if they just tried harder, the enterprise would succeed. Their goal was ambitious—raise $2.5 million. They proposed to build the memorial in Fair Park, a facility owned by the city of Dallas. The veterans thought Texans would respond with a flow of cash like oil from Spindletop. But by mid-1986, the effort was one hundred thousand dollars in debt and foundering badly.

Ruff, Russell, and I believed passionately that the Texas KIAs deserved recognition; they had paid the highest price for their country. We agreed to help.

The National Vietnam Veterans Memorial had been completed in 1982 amid controversy and criticism about the "black gash of shame and sorrow." That did not seem to have much bearing on what we were trying to do; this memorial was more traditional. We felt that if we could line up Texas veterans—all veterans, not just those from Vietnam—behind the memorial effort, raising money should be easy. After more than a decade of others failing, we believed we could convince Texas to stand up, sing the Star-Spangled Banner, and open its wallet. There was no question of interrupting my career. I planned to sell stock when the market was open, then handle my end of the project on the off-hours and weekends. I never dreamed that the memorial would become the dominating focus of my life.

Fund-raising

Early on, Ruff had approached John Stemmons, a Dallas patriarch who had made his fortune in real estate development. Ruff asked only for a pledge, to be paid when we built the memorial, but Stemmons said no way—cash on the barrelhead or nothing. Stemmons knew Dallas executives would not ante up unless they knew others had put money on the table. "I will put in fifty when I see your fifty," Stemmons told Ruff. They both wrote checks for fifty thousand dollars. That meant we were starting from zero.

One of Ruff's early successes was a $250,000 grant from the Meadows Foundation. The catch was that we had to raise a matching $250,000. I became the bean-counter and chief day-to-day fund-raiser. Before I began soliciting, Jay Dee Allen, another Vietnam veteran and real estate developer, warned that my task was not going to be an easy one. He had gone to one of the wealthiest men in Dallas and asked for a donation for the memorial, thinking the request was a slam-dunk. "Why the hell should I give any money to those bums?" the entrepreneur asked him.

I just brushed off his comments, thinking that the man had simply had a bad experience with someone who had served in Vietnam. That fall I began telling longtime clients about the memorial before hitting them up for donations.

"Why the hell are you involved in something like that?" one man asked me.

"What do you mean?" I said.

"Why would you be involved with people like Vietnam veterans?" he said.

"Well, I'm a Vietnam veteran," I told him.

"You're kidding me," he said, looking at me as if I had just confessed I had syphilis.

Another said, "Hell, I've dealt with you for years, and I never figured you were a Vietnam veteran." I was confused. How was it supposed to show?

In office after office, the scene repeated itself. The public's perception of Vietnam veterans became abundantly clear. They were losers, bums, drug addicts, drunks, derelicts—societal offal who had come back from the war plagued by nightmares and flashbacks that left them with the potential to go berserk at any moment.

Astonished, I thought of all the Vietnam veterans I knew. Not one had come back from Vietnam so messed up he couldn't function. Some had been POWs, some terribly wounded, others had endured terrible combat conditions. But if anything, as a group they seemed more socially confident, more self-directed than those who hadn't gone. A few had become alcoholics, but I also knew nonveterans who had become alcoholics. Some had divorced, but that seemed to be epidemic in the culture, not a manifestation of trauma induced by Vietnam.

When I suggested this, pointing to a successful Vietnam veteran—say, Richard Knight, then city manager of Dallas—they shrugged. "Well, yeah, but he is different," they insisted. What about Hugh D. Robinson, retired general and president of Cityplace Development Corporation? U.S. Congressman Sam Johnson, former POW?

The answer invariably was, "Those are the exceptions."

Stymied, I tried another fund-raising direction, asking a simple question: Who are Vietnam veterans?

Answer: Many airline pilots are Vietnam vets. Almost 70 percent of the six hundred members of the Southwest Airlines Pilot Association were once members of the armed forces. Several Texas pilot associations agreed to start campaigns among their members. Southwest Airline's pilots alone raised sixteen thousand dollars. Once the pilots were on board, I tried to persuade the executives at Delta, American, and Southwest airlines to match their contributions and then extend the campaign to the rest of the airlines' employees.

Thinking that Texas-based defense contractors who had made millions off the war would be particularly receptive, I targeted companies such as Bell Helicopter, General Dynamics, Texas Instruments, Brown & Root. After all, they had a stake in the memorial; soldiers are their constituency.

I couldn't have been more wrong. Brown & Root, which had sold billions of dollars' worth of goods to the U.S. military and was a primary contractor for the port at Cam Ranh Bay, turned me down cold. Rockwell International and Varo Corp., which manufactured night vision equipment and missile launcher systems, also declined.

Fort Worth-based Bell Helicopter manufactured 70 to 75 percent of all helicopters used in Vietnam. They built the AH-1G (Cobra), the OH-58 (Kiowa), and the UH-1 (Huey) helicopter, which became the most enduring symbol of the Vietnam War. While we had modest success with the unions at Bell—raising twelve hundred dollars through a notice in the employee bulletin—the company donated nothing. An employee campaign at Texas Instruments, along with a corporate matching grant, raised twenty thousand dollars. But of all the companies that profited from the war, the only corporation that was really forthcoming was General Dynamics, which made a gift of fifty thousand dollars.

Frustrated, I identified the top five hundred private and top five hundred public corporations in Texas and mailed out hundreds of solicitation packets. At the slightest bit of interest, I moved in, asking to address the company's philanthropic committee personally. Over and over, the answer came back. *No, no,* and *hell no.* I had a public relations nightmare on my hands, an obstacle to my goal far greater than the logistics of mailings and tracking fund-raising efforts.

This negative perception was so pervasive, I began looking at the history and the rhetoric of the Vietnam veteran and how that intersected with what people thought about the war.

Absurdities on Film

One of the hottest movies out in 1986 was *Platoon*, Oliver Stone's cynical version of life as an enlisted man with a combat unit in Vietnam. He depicted average soldiers doing drugs while on patrol, another shooting a Vietnamese woman in the head and threatening to kill a little girl, and a soldier killing his sergeant. A ferociously intense movie, *Platoon* drew raves as a realistic, uncompromising look at war. But the film was also absurd, about as authentic a depiction of the average soldier in Vietnam as John Wayne's *McClintock* was of ranchers in the West. Stone had served as an enlisted man in Vietnam and had to know better.

In fact, almost all films that featured a Vietnam veteran usually showed him as a misfit, a loser, or a nut. In the 1976 film *Taxi Driver*, Robert De Niro played a crazed, pill-popping Vietnam Marine vet obsessed with a teenage prostitute. In 1978, *The Deer Hunter* showed Vietnam vets as alienated or suicidal. And there was 1983's *First Blood*, with Sylvester Stallone as pumped-up, traumatized Green Beret John Rambo, whose last name became synonymous with a guy on the rampage.

It wasn't just Hollywood. In the press, stories about successful men who are Vietnam veterans rarely made reference to that status. But when a street person dressed in camouflage garb shot wildly at pedestrians, the story became "Vietnam Veteran Goes Berserk." For certain types of crimes, especially murder and rape, if there were any Vietnam connection, *that* became the touchstone for the story and usually was referred to in the headline.

Baffled, I began to buy books about Vietnam veterans and to clip stories from the newspaper. And I began to see *them*:

At a red traffic light, a squalid man, clearly homeless, holding a sign: "Vietnam Vet. Will Work for Food."

At Memorial Day events or Fourth of July parades, men in ratty fatigues or the tattered remnants of a Vietnam-era uniform.

On the streets of downtown Dallas: men in ponytails, needing a shave, wearing jungle boots with blue jeans and jackets bedecked with military decorations and patches. Men wearing green berets drinking from bottles tucked into paper bags, bragging loudly about their exploits in the war or bitterly discussing Agent Orange or their nightmares.

With a shock, I realized I had seen them all along but not the way the public did, the way those executives did. I began to understand that to the typical American, the homeless fellow in the sloppy fatigues was the real Vietnam veteran, not me in my suit or Congressman Sam Johnson or senator and soon-to-be Vice President Al Gore.

My mandate became clear. If I was going to raise the money, I had to counter the image. I had to equate the men who died with the winners, not the bums, to show that they were men worthy of recognition. But, until much later, I didn't ask the big questions: How real was the image? And who the hell are those people?

The Money Pit

Revamping the existing direct mail campaign was a major fund-raising nightmare. The group was spending about five hundred dollars to send out mailings of a thousand envelopes at a time to the general public. On average, only 2.3 envelopes were returned with a check. The typical donation was twenty-three dollars, a negative return. Something had to change. I called the legendary B.T. Collins, a former Green Beret who lost an arm and a leg in Vietnam. After the war, Collins had served as chief of staff to Gov. Jerry Brown and as director of the California Conservation Corps. In the mid-1980s, Collins began raising money for a Vietnam veterans memorial in California. He gave me several good ideas; the best was a folding, self-addressed, postage-paid envelope. If we could distribute the envelopes in mass quantities, we had to pay postage only on envelopes sent back to us with donations.

The state chapters of the American Legion and the VFW each had about 110,000 members. I asked the boards of both organizations to send out our envelope in an issue of their monthly newsletter. The idea seemed like a no-brainer. Veterans are supportive of other veterans, right? I did not realize that many veterans of World War II and Korea had little respect for Vietnam veterans. Those same perceptions were at work, with the additional negative attitude that we had "lost" *our* war.

Although membership in the VFW is open to Vietnam veterans, the organization leans heavily toward World War II vets. Our request triggered battles on both boards. Ultimately, the two organizations reluctantly agreed to send out the envelopes in newsletters that carried a story about me and the memorial effort. The first week after the VFW newsletter went out, our mailbox was stuffed with hundreds of envelopes, more than we had generated on any other campaign.

But the big return was a cruel prank. Few of the envelopes contained any money. Apparently people at various VFW posts had collected the envelopes, sealed them and mailed them back empty so we had to pay the postage.[12] The rest were filled with Christian pamphlets and hate letters, calling me names like "baby killer" and "pot-smoker."

"Fucking scum, crybabies, World War II vets are real men, you are drug-using wimps," someone had scribbled on one envelope. "Why don't you bums go to work and quit playing GI Joe?" wrote another. "I would be glad to contribute if you will include the names of the boys who died from Agent Orange and suicide because of the war," wrote a woman.

Appeals through the American Legion newsletter, as well as several other military alumni associations, didn't work any better. Vietnam veterans were an incredibly hard sell, even to other Vietnam-era veterans. They saw the newspapers and the movies. They read the books. They saw the bums. They didn't believe the stereotypes about themselves or their friends, but the perceptions were so pervasive, they must be true about…those other guys.

The memorial effort began to take over my life. At any given time, I had as many as a dozen fund-raising campaigns going. As my commissions plummeted, my bosses became increasingly unhappy with the amount of time I was devoting to this weird effort.

So was Stephanie, my new wife. I had remarried in November 1987, and she was aware that I had taken on the responsibility of the memorial. But by that summer, Russell, Ruff, and I realized our original estimate of six to nine months had been a spectacular miscalculation. We still needed to raise more than $1 million. Then in October 1987, the stock market crashed, wiping out much of my personal portfolio. Stephanie began to express concern about how much time I was spending on this memorial thing.

Every now and then there was a bright spot. Popular Dallas disc jockey Terry Dorsey, a Vietnam veteran, put on an eighteen-hour Veterans' Day marathon in 1988 for the memorial fund, bringing in more than $150,000 in pledges and a lot of positive goodwill. But every time we took a step forward, a story appeared in the newspaper like "Homeless Vietnam Veteran Shoots Cop," sending us three steps back.

When that happened, the next week would be filled with heckling. "Hey, Mr. Burkett, I see one of your boys was active again," one prospect told me after a negative story about a Vietnam veteran appeared in the morning paper. There was nothing I could say.

The image factor seemed insurmountable. To counter the negatives, I needed hard statistics about Vietnam veterans—who went, who died, who came back, and what happened to them after the war. Was the popular image of the Vietnam Veteran, so deeply imbedded in the psyche of Americans, real?

In any given population, some people will suffer from alcoholism, drug addiction, homelessness, mental illness, and suicide. Of the 3.3 million men and women who served in-country and in surrounding waters, a certain percentage would commit suicide, rob banks, or murder strangers. What I wanted to know: *Were they, because of their experience in the war, more likely than their peers who didn't go to Vietnam to suffer problems or commit crimes?*

The answer surprised even me.

3

Will the Real Vietnam Vet Stand Up?

AMERICA WON World War II. Vietnam was "the only war America ever lost."

In World War II, everybody pulled together. Vietnam was the class war, the war in which wet-behind-the-ears, poor, uneducated, minority men were chopped to pieces while college boys thumbed their noses in campus antiwar protests. Brave American soldiers in World War II bested the evil armies of Hitler and Hirohito. In Vietnam, confused, drug-addicted soldiers killed women and children.

World War II's veterans came home to stirring parades, ready to sire the Baby Boom and forge a supernation. Vietnam veterans trickled back in dishonor, fighting drug habits and inner demons. Or so say the stereotypes.

Let's take just one: The war in Vietnam was fought by teenagers barely old enough to shave, while World War II was fought by men. A much-repeated statistic claims that the average age of the Vietnam soldier was nineteen, while the average age of the World War II soldier was twenty-six.

But more fifty-two-year-olds (twenty-two) died in Vietnam than youths of seventeen (twelve). The oldest American serviceman killed was sixty-two. Almost 11 percent of those who died were thirty years of age or older.

The average age of men killed in Vietnam was 22.8 years, or almost twenty-three years old. This probably understates the average age of those in Vietnam by several months, because those who faced the enemy in combat roles typically were the younger, healthy veterans, not the older career soldiers. While the *average* age of those killed was 22.8, more twenty-year-olds were killed than any other age, followed by twenty-one-year-olds, then nineteen-year-olds.[13]

Despite the image that only enlisted "grunts" fought and died, officers accounted for 13.5 percent of those killed, although they represented only 12.5 percent of the troop strength in Vietnam. Twelve generals died in Vietnam. The Army lost a higher ratio of its officer corps in Vietnam than in World War II; twice as many company commanders (captains) died than did second lieutenant platoon leaders. (The Army didn't send inexperienced second lieutenants directly into combat after commissioning if it could be avoided.)[14]

Volunteers accounted for 77 percent of the combat deaths in Vietnam. That percentage goes up for younger men. Almost 86 percent of the nineteen-year-olds and 97 percent of eighteen-year-olds killed were volunteers. Even among draftees, the number-one age to die was twenty, then twenty-one, twenty-two, and twenty-three. (Age eighteen wasn't even in the top eight.)

When people are asked how many eighteen-year-old draftees died in Vietnam, they invariably answer with a number such as "seven thousand" or "ten thousand." The correct answer: 101, fewer than 1 percent of those who died in the war. (Because the image is that the war took the heaviest toll on young minorities, people are further astonished to learn that only *seven* eighteen-year-old black draftees died in Vietnam.)

It's actually easy to see that the impression of unwilling youngsters dying in the war is illogical. All males had to register for the draft at eighteen but could not be drafted until they were eighteen and a half. Local draft boards were given a monthly quota. During the sixties, as in the forties, draft board policy was to draft from the top down. If a local board had a quota of twenty men in a month, it was most likely to pick the older ones first, before they grew too old to be eligible. With the months of training required, few men arrived in Vietnam as eighteen-year-old draftees.

Men could be drafted up through age thirty-five during World War II, but numerous exemptions kept most older men out of the service. Most men older than their mid-twenties were not drafted until later in the war. The World War II figure of twenty-six apparently was generated by surveying discharged veterans at war's end and did not pinpoint when they were in combat.

Other statistics comparing the two eras are difficult to find, but by extrapolating from Vietnam KIAs and comparing them to World War II, it becomes clear that the average age of the fighting soldiers was similar. "A notable feature of the Second World War is the youth of most who fought it," wrote Paul Fussell in his book *Wartime*.[15]

But age is only one of the many misconceptions about the Vietnam War. Let's start at the beginning. The Gulf of Tonkin Resolution—the quasi-official start of the Vietnam War—was opposed by only two U.S. senators. A poll taken subsequently revealed that 85 percent of the public supported America's involvement in Vietnam. And despite the impression that Americans supported all our military interventions until the "evil war," a 1937 poll showed 64 percent of Americans regarded our entry into World War I as a blunder. Even World War II, "the good war," was not universally popular. Two years after the fighting ended, an October 1947 poll indicated that 25 percent of Americans regarded the United States' participation in World War II as a mistake.

One of the worst things that happened to my generation of Vietnam veterans, however, was taking the torch from the generation who fought World War II. In many cases they were our fathers, our uncles, our mentors. We did everything we could to make them proud, but somehow the torch was stolen from us. The press portrayed us as victims, marched off to war, maimed, poisoned, drug-ridden from our trauma, then dumped back on society. Many veterans of the World War II era became our worst critics, labeling Vietnam vets crybabies, whiners, losers.

We didn't drop the torch. The men who fought in Vietnam performed well and courageously. "The United States military did not lose the war in Vietnam, period," Gen. Norman Schwarzkopf has said. "In the two years I was in Vietnam, I was in many battles. I was never in a defeat—came pretty close a couple of times, but we were never defeated. The outcome of the Vietnam War was a political defeat, but it was not a military defeat."[16]

But in the fighting and the aftermath of *both* wars, distortion and misinformation shaped popular opinion to such an outrageous extent that every assumption must be tested against the facts.

Franklin D. Roosevelt's propaganda machine cranked up before the first American soldier ever set foot in Europe, painting a stirring patriotic image of the war and why we were fighting there. The negative realities of World War II were glossed over, misrepresented, or unreported by a patriotic press dependent on the cooperation of the U.S. military for access to the war zone. In Vietnam, the press seized on the horrific realities of war and spotlighted them. Every facet of the war was filtered through a negative media lens that ultimately projected itself onto the Vietnam vet, portraying him as a victim, a loser, a sucker who was too stupid to stay out of the war.

The reality is far different.

The Draft

Active for only thirty-eight years throughout America's history, the military draft has always proved unpopular with the age group facing conscription. For my generation, the draft was this huge rock in the path of life: You could not go over, around, or under it. You had to deal with it. Every decision a young man made had to factor in the draft. But was that so different from the reaction to Selective Service in other eras?

The United States has employed the draft as a way to raise military manpower since the Civil War, when military squads were sent house to house to round up eligible males. Those thus "drafted" could pay cash instead of serving or hire someone to take their place—hardly an egalitarian system. Grover Cleveland, who later became president, paid a man to take his place when he was drafted during the Civil War—a practice that was legal. The draft proved so unpopular that during 1863, protest riots killed one thousand people in New York City.

A less abusive, presumably fairer draft system was set up in 1917 in response to World War I (also an unpopular war at home). But still there was widespread grumbling, and many refused to serve.

A fundamental assumption about World War II is that patriotic Americans lined up by the thousands outside recruiting offices on Monday, December 8, 1941, the day after the Japanese attack on Pearl Harbor.

That's not what happened. In 1941, the U.S. military was the thirty-eighth largest in the world. When Congress declared war on Japan, little infrastructure and few large training facilities existed. Time was needed to build bases to house and train men to fight. Although the draft was revived again in 1940 (approved by a one-vote margin in the House of Representatives), the procedure did not become fully operational until 1943.

President Roosevelt understood he had to enlist the American people's hearts and minds to win the war. He "drafted" director Frank Capra to make eight films depicting the necessity and glory of fighting for America. Still, a large minority of Americans opposed our entry into a war in Europe. Many prominent citizens such as Charles Lindbergh vocally protested the war. Actor Lew Ayres, who starred in the original Dr. Kildare movies and the Oscar-winning film *All Quiet on the Western Front*, created a furor when he became a conscientious objector. Although there was considerable resistance to American involvement in what many regarded as Europe's fight, the press rarely reported that opposition. That was considered unpatriotic.

Another significant difference: In 1941, the Depression was still lingering in some pockets of the country. To many, any job was better than no job. Contrast that with the Vietnam generation. The economy was booming—jobs were everywhere. Suddenly Uncle Sam was saying, "No, you're not going to law school or Wall Street. You're going to be a private earning ninety bucks a month."

Still, despite the need for jobs, many American men in the forties were not any more thrilled with the idea of going to war than their sons would be twenty-five years later. The image of millions of men thronging induction centers came from Hollywood; the majority who served during World

War II waited to be drafted rather than join voluntarily. Ultimately, during the 1940s, some fifteen million men were inducted into the armed forces. Of those, only 33 percent enlisted; 67 percent were drafted.[17] Initially set up to bring in men twenty-one to thirty-four, the draft age had to be lowered to eighteen because there were not enough volunteers.[18]

Draft-dodging during World War II wasn't elevated to the high art it became during the 1960s, but many men scrambled to obtain sought-after draft deferments that came with the build-up of the war industry. They also faked illness, bribed draft boards, and refused to register. As the rumor circulated that married men would not be taken, America had one of the biggest increases in marriages in modern times. When scuttlebutt spread that men with children would not be drafted, a bulge in the birthrate followed nine months later.

After World War II, Selective Service did not end. Men were conscripted to fight in Korea. (That war cost the lives of fifty-four thousand Americans, almost as many as were killed in Vietnam, but in only three years.)

American involvement in the Vietnam War began gradually and did not have a shocking event like the attack on Pearl Harbor to galvanize popular support. Instead, our commitment grew out of the country's political and military desire to contain the spread of communism.

French Indochina had been split into various countries—Cambodia, Laos, South and North Vietnam—prior to the withdrawal of the French. Before French colonialism, these territories had been controlled by feudal lords and were not concise political entities. In 1954, the South Vietnamese attempted to set up a democratic government, ultimately joining the South East Asia Treaty Organization. The United States provided the fledgling administration economic and military aid, sending in military advisors to show them how to defend themselves against internal and external enemies of democracy. Most of the advisors were Army counterinsurgency experts, although the Navy and Air Force also had advisors. In the early sixties, as China and Russia started giving more military aid to North Vietnam, we increased our assistance to include ground troops. One of the first major Army units in South Vietnam was the 173rd Airborne, an all-volunteer unit, as were Marine units sent in early on.

As American involvement in Vietnam escalated, the draft became a bigger issue. The draft pool during the Vietnam era was the largest in the history of the United States. During the entire Vietnam era—from 1964 to 1972—twenty-seven million men came of draft age.

Of the 8.7 million men who served in the Vietnam era, 2.7 million were actually stationed in Vietnam. (An additional six hundred thousand received the Vietnam Service Ribbon by serving in the fleet offshore or Air Force units based in Guam or Thailand while conducting combat operations.) About one-third of Vietnam-era veterans entered the military through the draft, far lower than the 67 percent drafted in World War II. And once drafted and inducted, many men volunteered for the Airborne, Special Forces, or other duty likely to send them to Vietnam.

In addition, at least 10 percent of draftees, like Jan Scruggs, the founder of the Vietnam Veterans Memorial in Washington, actually *volunteered* to be drafted. Most Vietnam veterans know someone who did this. Why? If you were drafted, you owed Uncle Sam only two years instead of the three or four years required of those who enlisted. You'd go to your draft board and say, "Look, I'm coming out of college in May of 1966, ending my student deferment. Don't take me then. I want to be drafted in September." You spent the summer working, playing golf, traveling, or whatever, then reported for induction. The draft board was only too happy to agree. They had a quota for September as well as May. So they made their quota for that month. You planned when you went in, and you had to serve only two years.

The downside: You risked an unpleasant assignment. Those who enlisted for four years had a wider choice of jobs, such as Signal Corps. (The draft affected only the Army. The Air Force, Marines, and Navy were all volunteer, although at the height of the war, the U.S. Marine Corps did take some draftees.) The Army invested a great deal of time and training in the most desirable assignments, and they wanted someone who agreed to serve longer than two years. Draftees were far more likely to end up in the infantry, where there were greater manpower needs, and the training was not as intensive or expensive.

Still, someone with a few years in college had a good shot, if he had high test scores or valuable skills, to end up in a decent job far from the combat zone, like my computer job. Two-thirds of the people who went into the service did not go to Vietnam anyway. And while many outside didn't know this, men could avoid going to Vietnam once they were in the military. In most units if a soldier stated a firm preference not to go to Vietnam, most commands did not force him. Leaders didn't want a dissident in the group causing trouble. Although there was strong peer pressure—few men wanted to be seen as a coward—many of us knew people in the service who opted out of going to Vietnam.

Nonetheless, most of the men I knew in Vietnam felt an obligation to be there. Of course, there were a handful of servicemen who thought they were too important to have to serve their country. A doctor in my unit had been drafted, which he considered a most outrageous injustice because he was far too valuable to be stuck in the war. The doctor thought because he had the money and intelligence to go to medical school, he shouldn't be subject to the rules that applied to everyone else.

Although there were more than half a million of various kinds of "draft dodgers" during the Vietnam era, only 8,750 were pursued and convicted of draft evasion.[19] But compare that to World War II, when there were more than 350,000 cases of draft evasion and thousands were sent to federal prison. And few people know that while about ten thousand Americans fled to Canada to avoid the draft, up to thirty thousand Canadians entered the U.S. military, and about ten thousand served in Vietnam.[20]

A major difference between Vietnam and World War II was the way draft dodgers were perceived. In the 1940s, avoiding the draft was a shameful thing, not bragged or even talked about. I was astonished when I came back from Vietnam to discover that dodging the draft had somehow become an ethical, moral thing to do—a badge of courage—while those who enlisted were somehow considered morally inferior. Stupid. Suckers.

During the Vietnam era, the antiwar movement accomplished an astonishing feat. "They had not only been smart enough to duck the threat of death in combat—they had also managed to shift the onus onto those who fought," the journalist and novelist Tom Wolfe has written. "Never mind Ho Chi Minh and socialism and napalmed babies and the rest of it. The unspeakable and inconfessible goal of the New Left on the campuses had been to transform the shame of the fearful into the guilt of the courageous."[21]

But draft dodgers during Vietnam were just like those who avoided service during World War II. They were not morally opposed to all wars. After Vietnam, few American antiwar activists protested the Soviets' invasion of Afghanistan. And in April 1975, when North Vietnam violated its agreement with the United States that had ended America's participation in the war by invading the South, the antiwar movement didn't make a peep. They were opposed only to the war they might have to fight.

William Smith, dean of the draft lawyers during the Vietnam era, helped about three thousand men avoid the draft. "Most of them—regardless of what they said—were primarily motivated by not having their lives interrupted," Smith said in a 1988 Los Angeles Times story about draft dodgers. "It became very obvious to me that it was mostly a personal, selfish thing. We could just about guarantee we could get anybody out, and we did—but somebody always went in their place."[22]

Many of those who avoided the draft have now expressed second thoughts. Lobbyist Steve Gorelick escaped the war when the draft ended just before the expiration of his student deferment. "I can't look back and say my not going to Vietnam and my getting a college deferment was an act of political conscience," said Gorelick. "I wish I could look back and see more political courage in my behavior, but all I can see is that I was out to save my behind."

Novelist Mark Helprin, officially designated a 4-F, although he had a perfect physical rating except for corrective lenses, has gone even farther. "I am absolutely certain that in not serving, I was wrong," Helprin said in an address he delivered at West Point in 1992. He felt justified in staying out because Vietnam "was the wrong place to fight," and he disagreed with the conduct of the war. But he later decided he'd made a serious mistake, calling his decision to avoid Vietnam a regret he would carry to his grave.

"Neither a man nor his country can always pick the ideal quarrel, and not every war can be fought with moral surety or immediacy of effect," Helprin said. "It would be nice if that were so, but it isn't." To make amends, Helprin left America for the Middle East, where he served in the Israeli army and air force.

"And although I did, it can never make up for what I did not do," Helprin said. "For the truth is that each and every one of the Vietnam memorials in that cemetery and in every other . . . belongs to a man who may have died in my place. And that is something I can never put behind me."[23]

I have great respect for two types of war protesters: The ones who went to prison as a result of their beliefs and the conscientious objectors who agreed to serve but refused to carry weapons. During my tour, all three of my platoon's combat medics were conscientious objectors. They agreed to go to Vietnam but refused to bear arms.[24]

Education

"The best and brightest" started the Vietnam War, "but they did not send their sons," wrote Myra MacPherson in her Vietnam book *Long Time Passing*. She quoted a draft dodger with the pseudonym "George," who faked mental instability to avoid the draft: "In the main, the average IQ of those who went to Canada or became COs or found a way out were higher than those who went to war."[25]

Since the war in Vietnam, this idea has become the conventional wisdom among academia and the media: *Only the poor, the minorities, the not very bright who had few options in life served.* The best and the brightest didn't go. If you were smart, you found some way out of Vietnam, leaving America's disadvantaged to fight and die.

The controversial Project 100,000 is often used to "prove" this point. Proposed by Defense Secretary Robert McNamara, the program was created as a way not only to provide manpower for the military but also to right social ills by taking underprivileged and low-aptitude men into the services between 1966 and 1971. The project brought in thousands of draftees and volunteers who scored well below average on standard military tests, recruits unofficially labeled "McNamara's morons." Most were assigned to jobs not requiring technical knowledge, especially the infantry.

A study later determined that Project 100,000 was "less than successful in its stated goal of providing low-aptitude and disadvantaged youth an avenue for upgrading their skills and potential through military service. The military doesn't appear to be the panacea for struggling youth."[26]

Few people know this was not the first experiment of that nature. During World War II, one hundred thousand felons were released from prison and inducted into the military with the promise that if they honorably completed their term of service, they would be pardoned—assuming they survived the war. A disproportionate number of these men found themselves in combat units.

While men who have money and connections always have found ways to avoid going to war, in reality the force that fought in Vietnam was America's best-educated and most egalitarian in the country's history—and with the advent of the all-volunteer Army, it is likely to remain so.

Look at the facts. In World War II, only 45 percent of the troops had high school diplomas. Many were virtually illiterate. At one point, the numbers of inductees who were unable to pass both the draft physical and the mental ability test created a crisis.[27] During the Vietnam War, almost 80 percent of those who served had high school diplomas, even though, at the time, only 65 percent of military age youths in the U.S. had a high school degree.

Throughout the Vietnam era, the median education level of the enlisted man was about thirteen years. Proportionately, three times as many college graduates served in Vietnam as in World War II.[28]

In most wars, the better-educated typically find themselves in support roles, while the less-educated end up in combat units on the front lines. But that wasn't as true of Vietnam as in World War II. Draftees in Vietnam typically had more years of education and scored higher on aptitude tests than nondraftees. Since many college-educated men tended to take their chances with the draft rather than volunteering, they often ended up in infantry units. "Since most draftees ended up in combat," said George Q. Flynn in The Draft, "it meant that the U.S. Army was, in an unprecedented fashion, using brainpower on the front."[29]

Flynn quoted Col. Dan S. McMillin, commander of a training regiment at Fort Knox. The draftees during the Vietnam build-up were "head and shoulders above the last generation of soldiers in education, desire, and sense of responsibility," McMillan said. Reports from the battlefield confirmed that draftees made good fighting men. "Draftees were less guilty than volunteers of violating military rules and regulations and had fewer problems with drugs," Flynn wrote. "The draftees' higher level of education and intelligence, middle-class background, and maturity contributed to their superior performance as soldiers."[30]

A vast majority of the officer corps in Vietnam, which made up 12.5 percent of the force in-country, had bachelor's degrees. Only the Army took some noncollege graduates into OCS; all ROTC officers of all branches were college graduates. During my tour in Vietnam, I briefly had a Jeep driver with a master's degree. A specialist fourth class, he had been drafted while working on his Ph.D. He had completed all but his dissertation for his doctorate. Everybody called him "Doctor."

The Class War

Author Myra MacPherson and others contend that the Vietnam War was fought mostly by poor minorities who saw the military as their ticket out of the ghetto, while the smart, well-educated sons of bankers and lawyers and doctors dodged the draft or were dragged kicking and screaming into serving their country when their deferments ran out.

The assumption that the suffering of the Vietnam War fell disproportionately on the poor and working class has been promulgated equally by the left and the right, by everyone from Dr. Martin Luther King, Jr. to Ronald Reagan. Over and over, authors, politicians, and activists have claimed that working-class minorities made the ultimate sacrifices while the white, well-to-do boys sat in their college dorms. In 1975, defense analyst James Fallows wrote a story for the *Washington Monthly* called "What Did You Do in the Class War, Daddy?" drawing on his experiences avoiding the draft at Harvard. Another draft dodger assuaged his conscience in a 1990 confessional piece in *Life* magazine by dismissing the Vietnam era military as "a fighting force made up largely of minorities and the poor...."

In the 1993 book *Working Class War*, author Christian G. Appy maintained that Vietnam, a predominantly infantry war, took its heaviest toll on young, noncareer enlisted men in the Army and Marines. He contended that the war was fought "primarily by the nineteen-year-old children of waitresses, factory workers, truck drivers, secretaries, firefighters, carpenters, custodians, police officers, salespeople, clerks, mechanics, miners and farmworkers." Appy used interviews with unnamed veterans he met in a "rap group" to build a case that these men were brutalized by vicious training and sent to Vietnam without knowing why they were fighting, tragic symbols of the American military's supposed "doctrine of atrocity," doomed to return home damaged and broken.[31] (The term *rap group* changed dramatically from the 1970s to the 1990s; he's talking about group therapy, not musicians.)

Supported primarily by anecdotal evidence, the class-war concept seems logical. Whites faced with the draft had a higher propensity to go to college than Hispanics or blacks. And they had access to doctors and lawyers who could keep them out of the military. The argument that the military, therefore, had to turn to blacks and Hispanics at a disproportionate rate seems hardly worth arguing about.

But this assumption ignores the fact that blacks and Hispanics both had lower rates of high school graduation and, therefore, were less likely to meet the military's basic educational requirements. (In addition, higher rates of felony convictions kept more blacks and Hispanics out of the military.) In reality, the main factor which discriminated between who fought and died was not geography or economics but educational goals, according to Dr. John F. Guilmartin Jr., Lt. Col. USAF (Ret.). A Vietnam veteran and professor in the Ohio State University Department of History, Guilmartin examined Appy's book in the influential journal *Reviews in American History*.[32]

"Young men who reached age eighteen without college plans did not get student draft deferments," Guilmartin wrote. "While the more affluent were no doubt more likely to attend college, whatever economic bias they may have introduced into gross casualty rates by community was almost entirely offset by deaths among college-educated graduates of ROTC, OTS (Officer Training School), and service academies"—all officers, as Guilmartin pointed out.

Although the Vietnam computerized war casualty list doesn't include socioeconomic status, it does record race. About 5 percent of those who died were Hispanic and 12.5 percent were black—making both minorities slightly under-represented in relation to their proportion of draft-age males in the national population. (This will be discussed further in a later chapter.)

The only large population group not represented among the combat deaths in proportion to their U.S. demographics were those who designated themselves Jewish. Based on an American Jewish population of 2.5 percent, you would expect to find more than one thousand war-related deaths of Jewish men. But only 269 of the men who died in Vietnam identified themselves as Jewish, or 0.46 percent of the total KIAs.[33]

Why? Jewish youth probably were more likely to go to college and stayed in college longer. But it's also true that many of the leaders of the antiwar movement were Jewish, and perhaps there was less family or community support for young Jewish men to enlist in the military.

That doesn't mean Jews didn't serve well and heroically. Two rabbis died in Vietnam. Two Jewish servicemen, John L. Levitow and Jack H. Jacobs, received the Medal of Honor. But David Epstein, a retired Jewish Army colonel, has said he was ostracized in the Jewish community for fighting in Vietnam. "Few of us have failed to experience the embarrassed silence and looks of pity and contempt or, conversely, vicious verbal attacks when in Jewish groups it became known that we served in Vietnam," Epstein wrote in a 1989 article protesting two prominent Jewish organizations honoring Jane Fonda for work on behalf of Soviet Jews. "Couple this with the memory of a plethora of Jewish names among the luminaries of the antiwar movement, and you may begin to understand our sense of isolation."[34]

Years after the war, a study approached the question of socioeconomics in a scientific way. Arnold Barnett, professor of operations research at the Massachusetts Institute of Technology, heard conservative pundit William F. Buckley Jr. on public television saying that all you needed to do to avoid military service in Vietnam was to be well-born and/or affluent.[35] Realizing that a "class war" was an issue fraught with public policy questions, Barnett teamed up with Capt. Timothy Stanley of the Department of Social Services at West Point to test the idea.

"If untrue, the belief that affluent citizens were conspicuously missing from the Vietnam War dead is harmful to all Americans," they wrote. "It demeans the sacrifices of the wealthy by implying that such sacrifices were nonexistent. It demeans the sacrifices of the nonwealthy by suggesting that, manipulated and misled, they shed their blood in a conflict in which the privileged and influential were unwilling to shed theirs."[36]

Their 1992 study compared the socioeconomic status of the fifty-eight thousand Americans killed in Vietnam to fifty-eight thousand randomly chosen contemporaries by rating their home-of-record according to per-capita income. They discovered that 30 percent of the KIAs came from the lowest third of the income range; but 26 percent of the combat deaths came from families earning in the highest third. This result was startling—and far from the expectation that wealthier Americans were sheltered from the war.

The research also looked at what death rates could be expected if proportionately distributed throughout American communities and found that per capita death rates were only slightly lower in affluent American communities than in others. Neighborhoods where the median family income was in the lowest 10 percent nationally had twenty-eight deaths per one hundred thousand residents—not much different than neighborhoods with median family incomes in the top 10 percent nationally, which had twenty-three deaths per one hundred thousand. In fact, there was scant association between death rates and family income.

In his narrative, Fallows had cited four affluent communities: Beverly Hills, California; Belmont, Massachusetts; Chevy Chase, Maryland; and Great Neck, New York. He suggested that if parents in such influential communities—instead of families in rural and inner-city neighborhoods—had been receiving the gold stars, the war might have taken a far different course.

But the MIT study indicated that three of these cities—Belmont, Chevy

Chase, and Great Neck—actually had a per capita death rate *higher* than that of the country as a whole. Even Beverly Hills sent young men to the war. Actor Gregory Peck's son served in Vietnam. Academy Award-winner Jimmy Stewart lost a stepson in Vietnam—U.S. Marine 1st Lt. Ronald Walsh McLean, who died only days before his twenty-first birthday. A member of a six-man reconnaissance team attacked by the enemy while patrolling in Quang Tri Province, McLean received a posthumous Silver Star. Men like McLean from wealthy communities actually were about 10 percent more likely to die in Vietnam than other soldiers—probably because of the disproportionate presence of the affluent in hazardous roles such as pilots or infantry officers.[37]

For the MIT researchers, the question arose: Are the KIAs who cited Belmont and Chevy Chase as their hometown the sons of the maids and the gardeners, their residence belying their true socioeconomic status? To test this hypothesis, the researchers located the next of kin for eighteen hundred KIAs to determine the family's true demographics. The answer was no, they were not the sons of the servants. They were the "best and the brightest," men who could have used their family position or money to avoid the military, but who believed in serving their country.

Perhaps, as the war dragged on, discontent among the affluent would have resulted in fewer of their sons going to Vietnam. Maybe, but the data suggested that the deaths of soldiers from the richest 10 percent of the nation had the same distribution over time as the deaths of other servicemen.

Although thousands of men used college deferments to avoid the war, others earned their degrees and then enlisted. Texas A&M University lost 111 students, officers ranging from Maj. Gen. Bruno A. Hochmuth, class of 1935, to CWO Phillip R. Pannell, class of 1972. Twelve men from Texas A&M are missing in action; four were POWs. Checks of other universities reveal a similar trend. Yale University lost thirty-five graduates to the war, four from the class of 1968 alone, serving and dying at a rate consistent with the national average.

"One could plausibly assert that middle and upper-class Americans had greater access than less affluent youths to student and occupational draft deferments, and to doctors who could identify and attest to disqualifying physical ailments," the authors concluded. "But to reconcile that observation with the findings in this paper, one would have to infer that the affluent did not proceed en masse to exploit their special advantages. Less vulnerable than other youths to unrelenting pressure to serve in Vietnam, they nonetheless appear to have gone there in sizable numbers. That possibility has scarcely been mentioned in discussions about Vietnam casualties, but it deserves a place in any balanced assessment of what happened."

Drugs

Another common negative image of the soldier in Vietnam is that he smoked pot and shot up with heroin to dull the horrors of combat. Drugs certainly were widely available in Vietnam, as they were in America. In 1966, the U.S. Military Assistance Command surveyed the accessibility of illegal drugs, primarily marijuana and opium, in Saigon, Cholon, and Tan Son Nhut. They not only found twenty-nine fixed outlets, they discovered drugs were easy to buy from anybody just about anywhere.

And they were cheap. In 1967, marijuana joints cost from twenty cents in Saigon to a dollar in Da Nang. Opium could be obtained for a dollar per dose. Morphine cost five dollars a vial. Heroin had not yet appeared on the market. But drugs were not a major problem for most of the war. In 1967, the Army in Vietnam had 1,391 drug-related investigations, involving 1,688 individuals, for use of marijuana. That year, the drug use rate of twenty-five per one thousand troops in Vietnam was *lower* than the Army-wide rate of thirty per one thousand troops. There were only twenty-nine cases prosecuted involving use or possession of opium or morphine.[38]

The drug problem grew worse as the war wound down: In 1970, when American troops began to withdraw, drug court-martials rose to 11,058—or eighteen times the 1966 rate. (About 90 percent of the cases involved marijuana.) The problem wasn't the horror of combat. It was the boredom.[39]

What gets lost in the rhetoric is that these soldiers were drawn from a culture where drug use was becoming increasingly prevalent. During the withdrawal years, one estimate indicated that 18 percent of U.S. troops used marijuana; however, about half of these men started smoking pot before they entered the armed forces. A profound cultural shift was at work.

Soldiers during World War II used their own version of dope—alcohol— to cope with wartime stress. "The soldier, especially the conscript, suffers so deeply from contempt and damage to his selfhood, from absurdity and boredom and chickenshit, that some anodyne is necessary," wrote Paul Fussell in the book *Wartime*. "In Vietnam, drugs served the purpose. In the Second World War the recourse was to drunkenness." Fussell pointed out that "although not widely publicized, very heavy drinking of hard liquor had been a notable custom in the peacetime American Army. Army public relations labored to conceal the facts about military drinking from the public." That problem was magnified in wartime.[40]

The British were legendary for their capacity for alcohol, according to Fussell, but even they were horrified by the American excesses in World War II. "One British officer, commenting on the American and British troops being kept apart after the American defeat at Kasserine Pass: 'Although we are not angels,' he says, 'an Army which is drunk all day is no good to be associated with.'"

The problem grew so acute near the end of the war that from October 1944 through June 1945, more troops died in the European theater due to alcohol poisoning than from the rampant communicable diseases. In the Pacific, after the battle for Manila, the U.S. military put up billboards to warn the troops away from Filipino moonshine: "Deaths from Poison Liquor to date: 48."

Except for the last couple of years of the war, drug usage among American troops in Vietnam was lower than for American troops stationed anywhere else in the world, including the United States.[41] Even when drug use started to rise in 1971 and 1972, almost 90 percent of the men who had ever served in Vietnam had already come and gone. America had virtually thrown in the towel. Idleness and declining troop morale led to escalating drug use that reached crisis proportions.

Despite the fears that Vietnam veterans, hooked on cheap, easily available heroin, returned home addicts, a study in the early seventies at Washington University showed that most who tried the powerful drug in Vietnam quickly stopped when they returned home. The study examined a sample of men on active duty and another who tested positive for heroin on leaving Vietnam. The men were reexamined a year later, then followed up again two years after that.

Only 5 percent of the men who became addicted in Vietnam relapsed within ten months of their return; only 12 percent returned to the drug even briefly within the next three years. The study found that soldiers in Vietnam were not especially vulnerable to narcotic use, nor did Vietnam service increase the risk of long-term heroin addiction. They used heroin because the drug was inexpensive, pure, easily available, and those family members and friends who might disapprove were far away.

The research also showed that those who became addicted began using opiates almost as soon as they arrived in Vietnam, before they went into combat. The users rarely reported that they took heroin to overcome the fear or stress of battle, but because the drug was "enjoyable" and "passed the time."

Other studies have confirmed that combat did not compel soldiers to turn to heroin. "Veterans who saw combat were more likely than others to use heroin, but this association existed only because both combat experience and heroin use were correlated with a high level of preservice antisocial behavior," wrote Lee N. Robins, Ph.D., university professor of social science and professor of social science in psychiatry at Washington University, in the December 1994 Harvard Mental Health Letter, published by the Harvard Medical School.[42]

In other words, before they went into the military they had major problems and were prone to use drugs. "Many of these men were in combat because they had never acquired the skills that kept others behind the lines," Robins said. "The stress of war and the easy availability of opiates did not break the link between early antisocial behavior and later opiate use that is commonly seen in the United States."

The drug problem in Vietnam was the mirror image of the drug problem in American society. "Preservice fighting, truancy, drunkenness, arrests, and dropping out or being expelled from school were associated with heroin use in Vietnam just as strongly as in the United States," Robins wrote. (Robins pointed out that when the study was reported in the press, skeptical journalists charged that the results of the research were distorted to vindicate the Department of Defense.)

Despite the image that Vietnam veterans are more likely than others to use drugs, a study after the war by the VA showed drug usage of veterans and nonveterans of the Vietnam age group was about the same. Another study, the "Vietnam-Era Research Project," concluded that drug use was more common among *nonveterans* than Vietnam-era veterans.

Unfortunately, the illegal drug business—amounting to a $150 billion a year industry—now is a virtual fact of life in America. In the late eighties, an estimated twenty million Americans smoked marijuana, nearly six million regularly used cocaine, and a half million were addicted to heroin.[43] Many years after Vietnam, military authorities—just like civilian authorities—are still fighting the problem of substance abuse. In 1980, 27 percent, almost one-third, of all uniformed military personnel reported they had used some illegal drugs in the previous month.[44] In 1982, a survey showed that 48 percent of sailors eighteen to-twenty-four years old were using illegal drugs, a statistic so alarming the Navy initiated random drug testing.[45]

And there was no war to blame it on.

Desertion

Despite the sentiments of many World War II soldiers that Vietnam GIs were less committed than they were, during the Vietnam War not a single American platoon ever surrendered to the enemy as a unit. Indeed, incidents abound where entire platoons in Vietnam chose near certain death over surrender.

In the early 1990s, Lt. Gen. Harold G. Moore, of Ia Drang Valley fame and coauthor of *We Were Soldiers Once, and Young*, met the officers who led the Vietnamese regiment he fought two decades earlier. These NVA leaders repeatedly emphasized to Moore that they had truly been astounded by the "fanaticism" displayed by the American soldier. The average GI in Vietnam consistently insisted on fighting despite the odds, forcing the North Vietnamese to account for that tenacity in their battle plans.

The antiwar movement paraded Vietnam soldiers who had deserted their units as "proof" that it was an immoral war. But in World War II, the Army's overall desertion rate was 55 percent *higher* than during Vietnam; several thousand American GIs even went over to the Germans and fought with the German army. One American pilot defected with his P-38 to the Germans and ultimately commanded a German SS unit.[46] After refusing to take an oath of allegiance to America, several hundred Japanese-Americans were deported and fought with the Japanese army.

Literature on World War II portrays the Battle of the Bulge heroically. But the day the attack started, more than twenty thousand American GIs were AWOL in Paris alone. Before D-Day, the American military had to resort to using British jails because all the military prisons were filled to capacity with people who refused to fight. Many units threw down their arms and surrendered without firing a shot at the Battle of the Bulge. (The 101st Airborne Division became trapped in Bastogne because many on their flank quit fighting.)

In World War II, twenty thousand troops were convicted of desertion in the war zone. Desertion was such a massive problem that General Eisenhower made one soldier a vivid example for his troops. After twice deserting his unit, which was in combat in France, Pvt. Eddie Slovik was court-martialed and condemned to die. He was shot by a firing squad January 31, 1945. Although forty-nine deserters were sentenced to death, Slovik was the only one executed.[47]

Of the five thousand who deserted for various causes during the Vietnam War period, only 5 percent did so while attached to units in Vietnam. Only twenty-four deserters attributed their action to the desire to "avoid hazardous duty." Of AWOLs, only 10 percent were related to opposition to the war.[48]

An abundance of material contradicts many of the other negative images that surround Vietnam vets.

- The GI in Vietnam was in the combat zone an average of three months longer than the GI in World War II. (Many battles in World War II were very intense but short.) In addition, soldiers in Vietnam served an average of three months longer in the military than soldiers in World War II.
- Over a ten-year period, 230 soldiers in Vietnam were victims of non-combat homicides. Compare that to Houston, a city of 3.1 million, in which there were 701 murders in one year (1981) alone.
- Ninety-seven percent of Vietnam veterans received honorable discharges, exactly the same rate for the military in the ten years prior to the war. Vietnam veterans received dishonorable discharges at less

than half the rate of Vietnam-era vets who did not serve in the war
zone.

- The death rate in Vietnam was lower than in the two previous wars.
  In Vietnam, the mortality rate was twenty-two per one thousand
  troops, compared to forty-three per one thousand in Korea, and fifty-
  two per one thousand in World War II.[49] A soldier wounded in
  Vietnam was two times more likely to survive than the wounded soldier in World War II. While some of the difference can be attributed
  to improved antibiotics and medical techniques, the helicopter was
  the main reason. The average time from injury to hospitalization was
  2.8 hours in Vietnam; in World War II, it took 10.5 hours.[50] That's also
  one reason Vietnam had a higher rate of those permanently disabled;
  ten thousand men lost a limb, more than World War II and Korea
  combined. Many of those who were severely disabled in Vietnam
  would have died in previous wars.[51]

It's a Crime

Fear of returning combat veterans is as old as war itself. After the
Revolutionary War, an American judge blamed a wave of violent crime on
former soldiers who had grown accustomed to killing and looting their
English enemies. After the Civil War, organized gangs of ex-soldiers roved
the country, plundering and threatening civilians. (The best known were
Frank and Jesse James, veterans of Quantrill's Raiders.)

After World War I, attorney Clarence Darrow proclaimed that veterans
"inoculated with the universal madness" of the war were preying on citizens. World War II brought the same fears. A cartoon in *Back Home*, artist
Bill Mauldin's classic 1947 book about World War II, featured a woman
reading the paper to her husband just home from the war. On the front
page of *The Daily Dirt* was the headline "Veteran Kicks Aunt." The wife
reads: "There's a small item on page seventeen about a triple ax murder. No
veterans involved."[52]

Mauldin pointed out that in the immediate years after the war, every
time an ex-soldier was accused of some crime, his veteran status was
pointed out in the headline. "The sad fact was that such headlines gave
added impetus to the rumor that always appears in every country after a
war—that the returning soldiers are trained in killing and assault and are
potential menaces to society," Mauldin wrote. "Police records show that
World War II veterans committed no more and no fewer crimes in proportion to their numbers than the rest of the citizenry, and after a while most
reputable newspapers stopped headlining veterans every time they got into
trouble."[53]

But World War II veterans said, "We're not going to take it anymore."

The powerful lobby formed by the VFW, the American Legion, and the VA screamed bloody murder when World War II veterans were maligned.

However, when the same negative image was heaped on Vietnam veterans, no one rose to their defense or made any effort to negate the criticism. Although the prison population actually went down as soldiers returned from the war, Vietnam veterans were connected to an increasing crime rate and every possible deviant conduct identified in society.[54]

Nowhere was that image more prevalent than on television. In 1974-1975, a survey of programming over an eleven-month period found more than twenty episodes involving Vietnam veterans. Invariably, the veteran was portrayed as a "dangerous, drug-abusing psychopathic criminal," subject to flashbacks and "uncontrollable lapses in which he would act and think as if he were in combat."[55]

What happened? The antiwar movement had painted Vietnam veterans as criminals. And the aftermath of the Vietnam War coincided with the "victims' movement," which sought to shift the blame for personal problems from individuals to society. Most Vietnam veterans, stung by the criticism they received from the public when they returned home, faded away, leaving a vacuum that was filled by activists with a "victim" agenda. They took up the chant: "Yeah, we're bums, we're screwed up because of the war."

The Veterans Administration and Vietnam veterans' groups such as VietNow and Vietnam Veterans of America (VVA) became some of the main purveyors of the gospel that Vietnam veterans were broken, damaged men. A 1981 VA study concluded that 25 percent of those in combat during the war had ended up in prison.[56] In the mid-1980s VietNow, one of the first Vietnam veterans' organizations to receive a VA grant for delayed stress counseling, put out a pamphlet claiming:

- More veterans have committed suicide than were killed in Vietnam.
- One-third are functionally impaired, and seven hundred thousand suffer delayed stress syndrome: depression, marital problems, insomnia, and irrational rage.
- Vietnam veterans have much higher rates of alcoholism, drug abuse, and crime: Seventy thousand are behind bars, while more than two hundred thousand are on probation, parole, or out on bail.
- Forty percent are unemployed and 25 percent earn less than seven thousand dollars per year.[57]

The more mainstream VVA has claimed that 5 to 12 percent of the prison population at any given time are Vietnam vets, with up to three hundred thousand in the criminal justice system. (A porn magazine called *High Society* reported in 1995 the "fact" that one-quarter of all those imprisoned in America were Vietnam vets![58])

All this information is based on self-reporting by prisoners. But in every major study of Vietnam veterans *where the military records were pulled from the National Personnel Records Center in St. Louis and the veterans then located for interviews*, an insignificant number have been found in prisons.

Besides, logically, it makes little sense that high numbers of Vietnam veterans have served in prison. Do some extrapolations. Currently, there are slightly more than one million men in state and federal prison. Of those, only fifty-seven thousand are between the ages of forty-five and fifty-five, the group that encompasses the vast majority of Vietnam veterans.

Of those in prison, approximately 80 percent are not high school graduates. But currently, about 90 percent of Vietnam veterans have their high school diplomas. That whittles that fifty-seven thousand down even farther. Add to that the effect of race. Of those in prison, 55 percent are black. But only 10.5 percent of Vietnam veterans are black.

In addition, a vast majority of those incarcerated come from broken homes. During the Vietnam era, however, most youths lived in families with a mother and a father, another factor that is overlooked. Finally, a large percentage of those incarcerated in this age bracket received their first felony conviction as a youth offender. You cannot serve in the U.S. military with a felony on your record.

My personal guess is that only about thirty-five hundred Vietnam veterans currently are held in state and federal prisons—less than .001 percent of the total 3.3 million who served.

In any large population group, some people will commit crimes. The question becomes: Did Vietnam put them there?

"There are Vietnam vets in prison whose problems have nothing to do with the war," Dr. John P. Wilson, a professor of psychology at Cleveland State University, told the *VVA Veteran* magazine. Wilson studies PTSD. "You'll find folks in there who are just plain nasty, they just happen to be veterans."[59]

Unemployment

A corollary to the prison myth is the belief that substantial numbers of Vietnam veterans are unemployed. To see what kinds of employment studies had been done on vets, I contacted the Labor Department and the Department of Veterans' Affairs and combed through journals at the library. Although few studies were limited to Vietnam veterans, one done by economist Sharon Cohany made references to subgroups, like "draft-age males" or "Vietnam-era males." Cohany became interested in my research and subsequently did studies specifically about Vietnam veterans.

Cohany's research revealed that Vietnam veterans were no more likely to be unemployed than men who did not serve in Vietnam and, in fact, had a lower unemployment rate than those who didn't serve. Figures from 1994 showed that the unemployment rate for U.S. males eighteen and over was 6 percent. The unemployment rate for all male veterans was 4.9 percent. Among Vietnam-era veterans who served outside the Vietnam theater, it was 5 percent.

For Vietnam veterans, the rate went down to 3.9 percent. (These figures do not include those Vietnam veterans currently serving in the military—and of course are fully employed.) Cohany's research also indicated that more black ex-GIs work in white-collar, public-sector jobs than do black males who never served.[60]

When We Came Home

In the winter of 1991, Americans sat entranced at their television sets, watching in amazement and pride as U.S. troops decimated the Iraqi army and liberated Kuwait. An exultant nation welcomed the troops with jubilant ticker-tape parades. Columnists and TV pundits declared our victory in Desert Storm an exorcism of the demons of Vietnam, the clear-eyed and professional all-volunteer military a vast improvement over the pot-smoking, disaffected soldiers who fought in that unpopular war in Asia.

What went virtually unnoticed is the fact that Vietnam veterans—and the troops they commanded—won the Gulf War.

After Vietnam, tens of thousands of those who fought stayed in the military. Moving up the ranks, these officers resurrected the armed forces from the low morale and internal dissension that followed the pullout of American troops from Indochina. By the time America defeated Iraq, most of the Army senior officers from the brigade level on up were Vietnam veterans, including Barry McCaffrey, Norman Schwarzkopf, and Colin Powell. Despite the hostility many in America displayed toward the armed forces throughout the 1970s, these vets made the military their career, working hard to rebuild the esprit de corps that had existed before our nation's citizens repudiated its warriors.

These three now-famous generals of Vietnam were up-and-coming young junior officers who saw the worst of the war. When Iraq invaded its neighbor, they remembered well the lessons of Vietnam. They focused on attacking Iraq instead of Kuwait, in contrast to Vietnam, when the focus was defending the South.

And these senior officers understood that before American troops went to war, they needed the total support of the American people and their political leaders. Once they obtained that support, they deployed their troops and weapons systems to wreak maximum destruction on the enemy's army as quickly as possible. They gave Iraq no time to recruit, rearm, or resupply as we had done in Vietnam. They just crushed them.

Operation Desert Storm made "Stormin' Norman" Schwarzkopf a household name and Powell a potential presidential candidate. In 1996, McCaffrey retired from the military and was named drug czar by President Bill Clinton. Like the vast majority of Vietnam veterans, they refused to be victims and instead became heroes.

Powell, Schwarzkopf, and McCaffrey are not aberrations. Throughout America, Vietnam veterans have ascended to the upper levels of leadership in business, the legal system, law enforcement, the media, and politics.

They did it quietly. A good example is the experience of James W. Hall-Sheehy. An infantryman and Army journalist in Vietnam, Hall-Sheehy returned home in the early 1970s and applied for a job at a small manufacturing company. His interview with the plant manager was going well until the manager noticed on his resume that Hall-Sheehy had spent a year in Vietnam. "I just don't think I can take a chance on you," the manager told him. "There have been so many stories about that place and what it did to people. It's nothing personal. It's just business. If I were you, I'd forget I had ever been there."

Dumbfounded, Hall-Sheehy took his advice. For his next job interview, he listed only his dates of military service. "Any service in Vietnam?" asked the interviewer.

"No," he lied.

"Good," she said. Hall-Sheehy had learned his lesson. For years after that, Hall-Sheehy kept his Vietnam service a secret. He did his job, drawing quietly on the lessons he had learned in Vietnam, and moved up the ranks into management.

Years later, as assistant vice president for personnel at American General Fire and Casualty Company, Hall-Sheehy surveyed men identified by their employers as effective managers. Of 390 people mentioned, he found that 139 were Vietnam veterans. As in his case, most did not reveal their Vietnam service on their resumes.

Hall-Sheehy's research on the effect that Vietnam service had on men who ended up in the business world was reported in the *Harvard Business Review* in 1986.[61] His findings led him to conclude that Vietnam was "an important management training ground for a generation of men and women"—teaching them not only leadership skills but also discipline, tenacity, perseverance, empathy, and sensitivity. On the response form, one veteran wrote: "As far as I'm concerned, Vietnam was the ultimate graduate school for handling stress. Nothing on my job compares with what I experienced then."

The same could be said for people like Frederick W. Smith. After graduating from Yale, Smith served a tour in Vietnam as a Marine pilot. After the war, Smith went on to success as the founder of Federal Express, connecting a network of twenty-five cities using a hub-and-spoke technique like the logistics air net connecting bases in Vietnam. Like Southwest Airlines and EDS, Federal Express hired large numbers of Vietnam vets. The three companies now rank in the Fortune 500.

Other Vietnam pilots, whether they flew fighter planes, bombers, helicopters, or transport aircraft, found their expertise in demand after the war. Dozens of pilots who had flown in the war became astronauts.

With their weapons training and military discipline, many Vietnam veterans found a niche in law enforcement—as police officers, state troopers, and federal agents. The list of Vietnam veterans who became doctors and paramedics could be endless.

A Super Bowl Winner, Twice

"Vietnam Veteran Wins Super Bowl." Of course, you didn't see that headline. But one did. Twice. Graduate of the United States Naval Academy, Roger Staubach served in Vietnam as a supply officer. After the war, the Heisman Trophy winner quarterbacked the Dallas Cowboys to Super Bowl victories in 1971 and 1972. Staubach now runs a commercial real estate company in Dallas.

Some Vietnam veterans turned to acting and the arts. Patrick Duffy of *Dallas* fame served in Vietnam, as did another actor in the show, Steve Kanaly, who played Ray Krebs. A newscaster in Chicago before he was drafted, Pat Sajak spun records as a military disc jockey in Saigon; now he spins television's *Wheel of Fortune*. Dennis Franz, who won an Emmy in 1995 and would later add two more for playing detective Andy Sipowicz on *NYPD Blue*, spent eleven months as a scout observer and rifleman in Vietnam.

The CEOs and heads of businesses who served in Vietnam are too numerous to list. Many veterans found places at TV stations, newspapers, magazines, and publishing houses. Donald Graham, publisher of the *Washington Post*, one of the country's most prestigious newspapers, served in Vietnam. So did *Post* editor Lou Marano and foreign correspondent Herb Denton, and Walter Anderson, editor of *Parade* magazine. Vietnam veterans Roger Parkinson and Dick Schlosberg have been publishers of major newspapers. Gerald Byrne, publisher of the widely read bible of the entertainment industry *Variety*, was a Marine in Vietnam. Steve Kroft served in the war as a sergeant in the 25th Infantry Division; he's now an award-winning editor and correspondent for *60 Minutes*.

"In Vietnam I learned how to fish with hand grenades, slay rats with a mongoose, [and] win hearts and minds with Tina Turner," wrote Vietnam veteran Guy Gugliotta, now a staff writer at the *Washington Post*. "My mother sent Nixon a protest note," he said. "I wrote back that it wasn't so bad."

The commanding officer of a small patrol boat, Gugliotta called Vietnam not only the most important event in his life but also a powerful, positive experience that shaped whom he later became.

Vietnam gave Gugliotta confidence, strength, and the ability "to cut out the nonessentials." He paid a price, certainly. In eleven months, Vietnam "leeched away my youth and high spirits." But he came away with much more that was positive.

"My gains were personal, but that's the way it is in an expeditionary force in an unpopular war," Gugliotta said. "Winning or losing isn't your problem. Finishing as a whole person with your self-respect intact is what it's all about."[62]

Journalist Terry Anderson, who spent 2,455 days in captivity in Lebanon, is a Vietnam veteran. Anderson's book *Den of Lions*, about his years as a prisoner of the Shiite Moslem extremists known as the Islamic Jihad, was released to critical acclaim in 1993. Anderson credited his six years as a Marine and service in Vietnam with getting him through the ordeal.

The list of Vietnam veterans who have received acclaim for their fiction writing is long, and includes Winston Groom, author of *Forrest Gump*, Phil Caputo, John Del Vecchio, Tobias Wolff, and Tim O'Brien, who won the National Book Award for his 1978 Vietnam novel *Going After Cacciato*. For three consecutive years, Vietnam veterans won Pulitzer Prizes for writing: Lew Puller in 1992 for his autobiography *Fortunate Son*, Robert Olen Butler in 1993 for his book of short stories called *A Good Scent from a Strange Mountain*, and Yusef Komunyakaa in 1994 for his book of poetry called *Neon Vernacular: New and Selected Poems*. Photographer and Vietnam vet Robin Hood won the Pulitzer Prize for photography in 1977.

And Vietnam veterans have made an impact in Hollywood. William Broyles, founding editor of *Texas Monthly* and author of a book called *Brothers in Arms*, co-created the TV show *China Beach*, about nurses in Vietnam, and received an Oscar nomination for the screenplay of the 1995 film *Apollo 13*.

Vietnam veteran John Poindexter became National Security Advisor. Commander in Chief of U.S. Naval Forces in Europe, four-star Admiral James B. Busey IV, was named head of the Federal Aviation Administration in 1989. Other government officials who served in Vietnam include Vice President Al Gore and former Secretary of State Alexander Haig. Former Secretary of the Navy James Webb, author of the gripping Vietnam novel *Fields of Fire*, was a rifle platoon leader in Vietnam. Vietnam veterans who have been elected governors of their states include Mike Hayden of Kansas, Tom Ridge of Pennsylvania, Robert Kerrey of Nebraska (now a senator), and Charles Robb of Virginia, now a senator. In 1997, the Senate had six members who served in Vietnam, and the House of Representatives had nineteen veterans of the war.

Of all those Americans who served in Vietnam, none endured more than the POWs. Bombarded by anti-American propaganda, malnourished, and isolated, many POWs suffered psychological terrors as well as physical injuries. After living in inhuman conditions, brutally treated for months and sometimes years, many of the POWs from Vietnam returned home to situations often drastically changed from when they left for war. Many marriages collapsed, and three POWs committed suicide after their return. Many POWs continued to have severe health problems. Among the disabilities considered by the VA to be linked to incarceration by the enemy are beriberi and pellagra, chronic dysentery, nutritional ailments, posttraumatic osteoarthritis, anxiety, depressive neurosis, irritable bowel syndrome, and peptic ulcer disease.

Still, despite the horrors they endured and the great adjustments they faced at home, many excelled in later life. Some even remained in the military and fought again. Three former POWs of North Vietnam—Col. Dave "Bull" Baker, Lt. Col. Rick McDow, and Bill Byrns—flew planes in Desert Storm. Capt. Bob Naughton, a POW for six years, stayed in the military and became commanding officer of the Dallas Naval Air Station.

POWs Wes Schierman, Gordy Paige, Guy Gruters, and Bob Jeffrey became pilots with major airlines. Pilot and POW Denny Moore went to work flying a 727 for an Arabian prince. Former POW Fred Flom flies for American Airlines.

Navy Lt. Everett Alvarez Jr. became the *first* American airman to be captured in the war on August 5, 1964, when his Skyhawk fighter-bomber was shot down over the Gulf of Tonkin. Alvarez spent eight and a half years as a POW in the infamous Hoa Lo prison Americans nicknamed the "Hanoi Hilton." After the war, Alvarez earned a law degree from George Washington University and served as deputy director of the Peace Corps, then became deputy administrator of the VA.

A POW for Six Years

Sam Johnson endured six years and ten months in captivity, much of the time spent in a concrete cellblock that he and his fellow captors dubbed "Alcatraz," reserved for troublemaking POWs. They suffered malnutrition, terrible beatings, and severe deprivation for refusing to denounce their government. Of the ten men who survived "Alcatraz," four entered public service. After his release, Johnson served seven more years in the military. He is now a U.S. representative from Texas. Other former POWs elected to the U.S. Congress include Rep. Pete Peterson (D-Florida), Sen. Jeremiah Denton (R-Alabama), and Sen. John McCain (R-Arizona).

Vice Admiral James Bond Stockdale, a Navy pilot shot down after two hundred combat missions, was held prisoner in the Hanoi Hilton for more than seven years. After the war, Stockdale was appointed president of the

Naval War College in Newport, Rhode Island, and served for a time as president of The Citadel. While a senior fellow at the Hoover Institution, he came to national attention when Ross Perot chose him for his vice-presidential running mate in the 1992 presidential election.

"We brought no psychotics home from Hanoi," Stockdale said. "That may have been our greatest achievement."

The Pollsters

In every category for which I could find statistics, Vietnam veterans were as successful or more successful than men their age who did not go to Vietnam. Louis Harris and Associates Inc. released a study in 1980 called *Myths and Realities: A Study of Attitudes Toward Vietnam Era Veterans.* Commissioned by the VA, the Harris study showed Vietnam veterans were less likely to be high school dropouts and more likely to have post-high school education, were much more likely to have incomes above thirty thousand dollars and less likely to have incomes under twenty thousand dollars than non-Vietnam vets, and more likely to own their own homes.[63]

A *Washington Post*/ABC News survey released in April 1985, on the tenth anniversary of the fall of Saigon, reinforced the findings of the earlier Harris study. The *Post*/ABC survey randomly polled 811 veterans who served in Vietnam and Southeast Asia and 438 Vietnam-era veterans who served elsewhere. "Ten years after the fall of Saigon and after the trauma of their return home, most Vietnam veterans have successfully entered the mainstream of American life," wrote *Post* staff writers Barry Sussman and Kenneth E. John.[64]

The poll revealed that only 9 percent of Vietnam veterans had not graduated from high school compared to 23 percent of their peers. A Vietnam veteran was more likely to have gone to college than a man of his age not in the service. Nearly 30 percent of Vietnam vets had some college education, versus 24 percent of the U.S. population.

That educational edge translated to employment rates similar to nonveterans of the war. In 1985, three of every four said their annual household incomes exceeded twenty thousand dollars. Almost half made thirty thousand dollars or more per year. Seventy-eight percent were homeowners, paying mortgages on traditional, single-family homes—and more likely to own a home than their peers who did not go to Vietnam. Eight of every ten surveyed were married, and 90 percent had children.

In many ways, there was little difference between those who went to Vietnam and those who didn't. About the same percentage in each group was registered to vote, and political party affiliation was similar. More Vietnam veterans than nonveterans classified themselves as independents, however.

Strikingly, the *Washington Post* survey indicated that, despite the negative attitudes of the public, Vietnam veterans had positive feelings about their experience.

- Seventy-four percent said they "enjoyed their time in service."
- Eighty percent disagreed with the statement "the United States took unfair advantage of me."
- Fifty-six percent of Vietnam veterans said they benefited in the long run by going to Vietnam. Only 29 percent said they were set back.
- Ninety-one percent of those who served in Vietnam were "glad they served their country."[65]

The 1988 Vietnam Experience Study was an even larger examination of how Vietnam vets had fared after the war. Researchers at the U.S. Centers for Disease Control studied fifteen thousand randomly selected veterans who joined the Army between 1965 and 1971. Half had served in Vietnam, half in other posts. There were no important differences in background characteristics between Vietnam and non-Vietnam veterans in regards to race, age, aptitude test scores. All of those studied had a pay grade at discharge no higher than E-5 (sergeant).[66]

The study showed that more than 90 percent of both groups were employed. In both groups, more than 60 percent of those who married were still married to their first wives. More than 90 percent of Vietnam and non-Vietnam veterans felt satisfied with their current personal relationships. At the time of the study, few men in either group were in jail, institutionalized, or mentally or physically incapacitated.

"We're not trying to minimize the importance or the severity of psychological problems," said CDC epidemiologist Scott Wetterhall in 1988. "But in the vast majority of cases, the facts do not support the stereotypes."[67]

With this ammunition, I was ready to fight the image battle. But I had forgotten about "Them."

4

The Ragtag Brigade

ARMED WITH my statistics, I began to make real headway with individual donors. When people could see solid evidence that the stereotypes were wrong, they opened their wallets.

When we first came on board, Art Ruff and I had met with the management of Channel 5, the Dallas/Fort Worth NBC affiliate, where a Vietnam veteran named L.B. Lyon was the news director. The station probably donated in excess of $1 million in free advertising to the memorial effort. On certain "hook" days, such as Memorial Day, the station needed stories on veterans. I began to give them ideas for segments, like a mother who had lost two sons in Vietnam or a former POW flying for a local airline. The reporter aired the human-interest angle then put in a plug for the memorial.

Since it worked with Channel 5, I began offering story ideas and my demographic information to newspapers and other TV stations. The editorial boards and management departments of the newspapers were usually receptive to my requests. The *Dallas Times Herald* gave us several "donations in kind"—printing a big poster we could put in store windows, for example. The Belo Foundation, the charitable arm of the company that owns the *Dallas Morning News*, also made a donation to the memorial effort. But trying to break through most writers' and assignment editors' knee-jerk reactions to Vietnam was like trying to empty the Tonkin Gulf with a teaspoon. Convincing top management to donate to a worthy cause was one thing; persuading presumably "objective" journalists to see another side of the story was another.

At the *Dallas Morning News*, I first called the lifestyles department, explaining to a young female editor that I wanted to interest the paper in a story on the many successful Vietnam veterans in Dallas, mentioning the various studies I had found.

"Now, Mr. Burkett, I will concede that there are a few of the men who served who managed to put their lives back together," she said. "But you and I both know that most of the people who served in Vietnam are pretty screwed up. I don't quite see what the story is here. But I understand what you're trying to do. I have your number, and if we decide to do a story, I'll call you." She didn't call.

Stuart Wilk, then assistant city editor for the paper, was almost as unreceptive. "I don't know what the news is in that," Wilk said dismissively when I suggested a piece about successful veterans. But he assigned a reporter, who wrote a small story. And Wilk hooked me up with Larry Powell, who made a brief mention of successful Vietnam veterans in one of his columns. At the *Morning News*, only Jim Wright, an editorial writer who had served in Korea in the Marine Corps, wrote anything of significance sympathetic to Vietnam vets.

The *Dallas Times Herald* proved more open-minded. Reporter Dean Takahashi did a package of stories on successful Vietnam vets, featuring some of Dallas's up-and-coming professionals. But his editors deleted most of the positive statistical data I had gathered.

A Problem of Identification

Then on August 20, 1986, a man named Patrick Henry Sherrill went berserk in a post office in Edmond, Oklahoma, killing fourteen employees before turning a gun on himself. The press descended on the story. "It has been reported that Henry Patrick Sherrill was a Vietnam veteran," announced Bud Gillet, reporter for Channel 4, live from the scene on the 5 o'clock news.

Earlier that day, the tragedy had been reported by radio, quoting a Navy spokesman who released a statement that Sherrill was *not* a Vietnam veteran. Sherrill had served in the Marine Corps in the mid-1960s but had not left the United States. The *Dallas Morning News* had called me and asked for a statement, which they ran in their late edition.

Irritated that Channel 4 was repeating false information, I called the station and asked for the newsroom. I told them about the Navy's statement that Sherrill was not a Vietnam veteran. But at 6:00 P.M., Gillet, still live at the scene, repeated his earlier description of Sherrill as a Vietnam vet.

I phoned the station again. The producer hemmed and hawed, claiming they could not verify that Sherrill wasn't a Vietnam vet. "Just call the damn Pentagon," I said. At 10:00 P.M. the final newscast came on, with the same reporter live at the scene. "The suspect is Patrick Henry Sherrill, who *may or may not have been* a Vietnam veteran." (Emphasis added.) The next day, I fired off angry letters to the station's news director, the station manager, and the chairman of the board of CBS. I received no reply.

For several weeks afterward, the media carried stories about the victims, seven men and seven women. All were consistently described in extremely positive terms: PTA members, Boy Scout leaders, and so on. A terrible irony was never acknowledged by 99 percent of the journalists who covered the story. Two of the seven men murdered were Vietnam veterans. One of them—Paul Michael Rockne, the grandson of famous Notre Dame coach Knute Rockne—was a decorated war hero, recipient of a Bronze Star Medal.

The thing most people remembered about this incident would be those early frantic reports. "Vietnam Veteran Kills 14."

"Vietnam Vet Goes Berserk"

By 1988, the paid office staff of the Texas Vietnam memorial effort was down to one woman, an Army veteran who did secretarial work. We instituted a policy of spending absolutely nothing on benefit events. With that policy in place, we could raise the money. We just had to live long enough.

Then another story exploded in Dallas that repeated the "'Nam Vet Goes Berserk" pattern. While writing a traffic ticket on a downtown Dallas street on January 25, 1988, a police officer named John Glenn Chase scuffled with a mentally ill street person, who tried to intervene. Somehow, the demented man snatched the officer's gun. Some people waiting for the bus began chanting, "Kill him, kill him!" The vagrant shot Chase in the face, then began calmly walking down the street as the officer lay dying. Two off-duty policemen heard the gunfire and after cornering the suspect in a parking lot, shot him to death.

Dallas Times Herald reporter Lori Montgomery identified the dead suspect as Carl Dudley Williams. "County records show he was a Vietnam veteran," her story said.[68] Dick Hitt, a columnist for the *Times Herald*, wrote about the incident several days later, describing his conversation with a man who had gone to Williams' funeral: "I'm thirty-eight and he was four years younger, but he used to be one of my heroes," the funeral-goer told the columnist. "Hell of a thing," Hitt replied. "Do you think Vietnam did that to him?"[69]

Was Williams even a Vietnam veteran? I decided to find out. A contact at the National Archives told me that parts of an individual's military record are public, available through the federal Freedom of Information Act. I sent off an FOIA request and quickly received a summary of Carl D. Williams' military service: Williams had entered the Navy August 30, 1974— seventeen full months *after* all combat troops had left Vietnam. Released five months later for mental problems, Williams had not set foot in

Vietnam.[70] The information was available to any reporter who was interested enough to check.

I wrote to *Times Herald* publisher Arthur E. Wible, pointing out the reporter's error.[71] He sent back a condescending letter. "We have editorialized, we have reported, and we have done some sensitive pieces about the *special problems* that many veterans faced and continue to face years later," Wible wrote (emphasis added).[72] The paper didn't correct the story.

Eventually, after months of pestering reporters with story ideas, some of them began to call me on their own when they needed a source for a veteran story. A female reporter from the *Dallas Morning News* called saying she wanted to do a piece on nurses in Vietnam. *Wow!* I thought. *This is great. It's finally working.* From my research, I had numerous positive stories about nurses, several who ultimately became generals.

"No, no, no," she interrupted me. "We want people who are having problems, like depression, drug abuse, posttraumatic stress, nightmares. You know, general psychological problems because of the war." It was a reverse women's rights ploy: "Why should men get all the space for their problems and not the women?" But when I tried to explain I knew no nurses who were having recurring problems because of the war, I could hear her clicking off mentally. She really wasn't interested in anything I had to say, just in finding sources to fit a preconceived idea, which is exactly the kind of story they later ran.

Using FOIA

For months, I had a quiet, ongoing fight with some local veterans' groups and their ragtag contingents. Some members were sincerely trying to help the memorial, but I often wished they would stay away. They had a tendency to appear at veterans' events in shabby military regalia, reinforcing that "Vietnam vet as bum" image.

One of them was Jesse Duckworth, who donned combat fatigues and a green beret on holidays such as Memorial Day. He wore his beret at a jaunty angle, often signing autographs for awestruck kids. He frequently bragged that not only had he been awarded the Silver Star for combat heroism, he also had even been nominated for a Distinguished Service Cross. A younger man named Rocky Manrique, who also dressed in military garb and wore a green beret, went with him everywhere. They had served together in Vietnam, and Rocky confirmed Duckworth's many war stories.

But Duckworth did not look like any Green Beret I ever knew. Slovenly, he always needed a shave and stank of alcohol. In my experience, those who'd earned the right to wear the beret of the Special Forces had too much pride to be seen like that in public. Of course, photographers gravitated to Duckworth at parades and wreath-laying ceremonies. Journalists asked him for quotes on Agent Orange and VA programs. On Veterans' Day, November 11, 1986, an Associated Press photographer shot a picture of Duckworth at the Vietnam Veterans Memorial on the Washington Mall, saluting a pair of jungle boots. The photo appeared in hundreds of newspapers around the country.[73]

"Damn, Jug," Russell asked me after we encountered Duckworth and his cronies at a veterans' event. "Did you ever know people like that in Vietnam?" Impulsively, I sent an FOIA request for Duckworth's record. When the documents came back, my suspicions were confirmed. Duckworth had never been a Green Beret. He was awarded no medals for heroism, and he had not served in Vietnam.

J.W. Duckworth had been a private first class in the Army; his only overseas duty was in Germany. Court-martialed while at Fort Hood on two charges of AWOL, Duckworth had been given forty days hard labor and reduced to private E-1 before being discharged.[74]

His friend and defender, Roque "Rocky" Manrique, had served in Vietnam as a telephone operator in the Signal Corps, the equivalent of a clerk. He had never been a Green Beret.[75]

Why had Duckworth lied? For attention? To make himself feel better about his poor military record? To provide a ready excuse for a failed life? I had no idea. But his charade made me furious. Duckworth was pretending to be something he was not, stealing the honor and recognition of men who had rightfully earned those medals and the green beret, tainting the image of true Vietnam vets. I slipped the records to a TV reporter. After a story appeared revealing his fraud, Duckworth disappeared from the local veterans' scene.[76]

In the fall of 1988, not long after I requested Duckworth's record, I spoke at a symposium on the Vietnam War at a community college in Dallas. Also on the panel was Joe Testa, president of the Dallas Vietnam Veterans of America (VVA) chapter. Testa had a dry, personable wit and actually had been one of my better volunteers. Although he often wore fatigues decked with sergeant's stripes, they were clean and neat, not slovenly. According to his resume, Testa had been drafted in 1967 and served eighteen months with an infantry division headquartered west of Saigon. Twenty years later, when Oliver Stone's movie *Born on the Fourth of July* was being filmed in Dallas, Testa appeared at calls for extras, wearing a Silver Star and walking with the help of a cane, as if suffering from an old war wound. During filming, he became friends with author Ron Kovic.

But Testa constantly reinforced the idea of Vietnam veterans as victims. Because he was the president of the Dallas VVA Chapter, reporters turned to Testa when they wanted to write about veterans and Agent Orange, posttraumatic stress disorder, drug abuse, or homelessness.

At the symposium, Testa said something about the war that struck me as odd, a minor technical point. Prior to being able to obtain military records, I would have ignored it. Now, curiosity piqued, I sent an FOIA request for the military records of Joseph Testa Jr.

Testa, too, was a phony. He had enlisted in the Army and started basic training at Fort Polk, Louisiana, on September 13, 1967. After going AWOL twice, he received court-martial sentences totaling nine months of hard labor. Testa did not serve in Vietnam, received no valorous decorations, and was discharged under conditions "other than honorable." He had even lied about graduating from high school; records indicated he had dropped out in the tenth grade.[77] Other records showed that since 1977, Testa had been convicted four times of credit card abuse and theft by check in Dallas County.

I gave Testa's record to several local reporters, who did stories unmasking him as a fraud.[78] The front-page exposé rocked the VVA. Testa was removed as chapter president and, like Duckworth, vanished from the Dallas area.

Heroes and Phonies

My fund-raising for the memorial was causing tension at home. I was working late into the night, seven days a week. My wife was patient, but she couldn't help asking, "God, when is this thing going to be over?" I had no answer.

By August 1988, we had raised donations and pledges of about $1 million. The board realized that we needed two more years to raise the remaining $1.5 million. Art Ruff pushed us to pare back the memorial design, bringing the construction costs down to about $1.16 million, plus an endowment fund for maintenance costs. We still needed to raise about five hundred thousand dollars, but the end was in sight.

Even though we didn't have all the money, Russell urged the board to buy and engrave the granite tablets, then put them up in a temporary display at Fair Park. "It'll give the project more credibility," he argued. "People will be able to see and feel the names." Maybe the tablets would push donations up over our goal. And besides, Russell pointed out, "if we can't get the rest of the money, the city will be stuck with them and have to do something."

The board agreed and gave the go-ahead to quarry the massive tablets. The most expensive part of the memorial, the four granite slabs with the names of those killed in action are ten feet long, eight feet high, and eight inches thick. The fifth tablet, for the names of those missing in action, measures six feet high and five feet wide at the base. The tablets were quarried near Marble Falls, Texas, and shipped to Memphis, Tennessee, where they were engraved with a special photographic process by Binswanger Glass Company, which had engraved the national Vietnam Veterans Memorial.

As I was proofreading the final tally of names for the Texas monument, I came across the name of Timothy Honsinger, Army private first class. His date of death was September 11, 1966, but his date of birth was blank. The Department of Defense list also omitted his birth date. I couldn't leave a blank on the memorial, so I made an FOIA request for his record.

The documents revealed that after enlisting at age eighteen in 1965, Honsinger had been manning a machine gun on an armored personnel carrier during a search-and-destroy mission in Vietnam's Boi Loi forest. When his platoon came under heavy enemy fire, an antitank rocket tore off his right forearm.

His arm pumping blood like a hose, Honsinger jammed something in his armpit to stop the bleeding and kept shooting. He helped evacuate eight wounded men before passing out himself. Medevacked out by a dustoff helicopter, he apparently had died en route to the field hospital. For his heroism, Honsinger was awarded a Silver Star. Strangely, it was not designated "posthumous."[79]

Trying to locate his next of kin, I called a clerk at the VA benefits office. She found Honsinger's file. "But there's a problem here," the clerk said. "This file has disability checks signed in 1971." She couldn't tell me much more. I contacted the regional veterans' center in Waco and found out that someone named Honsinger still was receiving military disability compensation. Outraged, convinced that someone had assumed his identity and was collecting money as Honsinger, I asked buddies in law enforcement and the media to help me track down the impostor. They discovered someone with that name working for a law enforcement agency and living in a small town near Dallas.

One weekend, I went to the house, but no one was home. The next weekend, when I returned, a woman answered the door. After I explained that I was doing research on the Texas Vietnam Veterans Memorial, she called to someone inside. A tall, bearded man wearing only gym shorts came to the door. His right arm was missing to the elbow. Behind him, a citation for the Silver Star was hanging on the wall.

Honsinger didn't die in Vietnam, I thought with a chill. *He's standing right in front of me.*

The man provided military records proving he was Timothy Honsinger. After sustaining his terrible injuries, Honsinger had been medevacked out by a helicopter. Separated from his unit, he had been shipped back to the

United States without his company ever knowing his fate. He had returned to Texas, gone through rehabilitation, and found a job as a radio dispatcher. Needless to say, he was *very* shocked to hear that his name was on the national memorial as killed in action. "I can verify that he's very much alive," his girlfriend said with a smile.

I called some reporters who ran stories about Honsinger.[80] I felt oddly elated, like the man who found the "lost sheep." Finding Honsinger triggered my thinking about Duckworth and Testa, people who inflated their military experience, awarding themselves medals they did not deserve, claiming to speak for Vietnam vets although they had not served in the war. Honsinger, a genuine hero, had not boasted or sought acclaim. He went on to become a police lieutenant. The pretenders had stolen something Honsinger and others had earned with their valor, pain, and wounds, devaluing what they had done for their country.

So I became a detective of sorts. Whenever I saw someone in the media described as a Vietnam veteran, I sent off for his or her military record. Most often I checked those I call the "image makers," the veterans used by reporters to illustrate stories on homelessness, PTSD, Agent Orange illnesses, criminality, drug abuse, alcoholism, and war crimes.

The key was having an accurate and complete name. (For common names, it is virtually impossible to get records without a service number or information like hometown or date of birth.)

Often, the records revealed that the veteran I investigated was bogus—had never been there. Or if he had, he wasn't the hero he claimed to be. Those claiming to be involved in covert operations or members of elite military groups like the Navy SEALs or Green Berets, were even more likely to be impostors.

Some of the phonies had built elaborate frauds, going to incredible lengths to forge and steal documents and photographs, then altering them to support their pretensions to heroism. They bought medals at flea markets and through catalogs. They cried on camera when talking about their dead buddies, about witnessing atrocities. Some had fooled their wives, congressmen, psychiatrists, even military commanders who had also been in Vietnam.

I contacted military buffs all over the country for help in verifying records; they in turn called me when they ran across something interesting. Unintentionally, I became a sort of clearinghouse with a network of sources that stretched from Alaska to Florida. I gathered records on veterans from actor Brian Dennehy to writer Ron Kovic, author of *Born on the Fourth of July*. By 1989, I was pumping out an average of one FOIA request per day. (In 1991, I was named along with Dean Allard, the director of the U.S. Navy's historical center, and other academics to participate in a study of the system by an agency associated with the National Archives.[81] When I asked why, an Archive official kidded me that I was probably the Archives' number one individual FOIA user.)

Whenever I found documentation that veterans cited in the press had lied or outrageously inflated their wartime service, I contacted the journalists who wrote the stories and offered to give them a copy of the vet's military record. The reporters often reacted as if I had offered to mail them a live cobra. Most didn't even know that they could request military records. Whether they were with *The New York Times* or the *Podunk Press*, journalists rarely attempted to verify the stories they wrote on veterans' personal histories. Few wanted to acknowledge that they had been fooled.

Construction Begins

After almost three years, we had raised most of the money for the memorial; now we had to obtain final permission to install the monument at the Fair Park site. The site had been a frustration all along. Owned by the city of Dallas, the land is managed by the city's Parks and Recreation Board. In late 1988, we had to go before the park board to ask for site approval.

The board was headed by a black woman. "I'd like to say something right here," she announced when our turn on the agenda came up. "This is a worthy project. Everybody knows that the majority of those killed were poor black kids." The room went quiet. *Damn*, I thought. *I hope nobody asks me the percentage.* From the demographic studies, we knew that was a myth. But nobody questioned it. After our one-minute spiel, the panel unanimously voted to approve our request, and we fled the meeting in a hurry. That was the only time common misconceptions about the war worked in our favor.

In April 1989, we received final permission from the Dallas City Council to build the project, to be completed by Veterans' Day, November 11, 1989. Honorary chairman George Bush had been elected president. We were thrilled to learn that Bush had agreed to appear at our ceremony, which would make ours the only Vietnam memorial to be dedicated by a president. (President Ronald Reagan, wary of the controversy surrounding the national Vietnam Veterans Memorial, had declined to attend that ceremony.) The tablets had arrived, and the president was coming. The end finally was in sight.

We still had to raise about two hundred thousand dollars. On top of what he had already given, Art Ruff had loaned the memorial sixty thousand dollars in order to finish construction, with my pledge not to quit until I had raised the money to repay him, plus another $126,000 to endow a maintenance fund.

Then, on the Fourth of July, two veterans opened the Vietnam War

Museum at the Alamo Plaza in San Antonio, the only museum of its kind in the country. To the pulse of rock 'n roll from the sixties and seventies blaring from hidden speakers, thousands of visitors toured rooms filled with everything from scale models of fire bases to artifacts taken from captured Viet Cong prisoners, including the tanned pelt of a booby-trapped Vietnamese tiger. Dozens of veterans provided videotapes of their memoirs of the war. One room recreated a soldier's life in a "hooch" littered with automatic weapons and equipment.[82]

Put together by Gaylord O. Stevens and Kenneth M. Bonner, two men who called themselves highly decorated Vietnam veterans, the "museum" looked more like a cross between a surplus store and a hobby shop. Stevens, the director, was gaunt and bearded, seemingly hardened by his service as an elite Navy SEAL in Vietnam during 1968–1969. His assistant, Bonner, claimed to have served in the U.S. Army Special Forces (Green Berets) in 1971–1972.

The museum's goal was to present a "truthful" picture of Vietnam, Stevens told a newspaper reporter. "We *know* war is horrible," Bonner added. Both gave the reporter their discharge papers to authenticate their war service.

The two men organized volunteers to solicit money on the street—wearing ragged military garb, of course—to start and maintain the museum. The volunteers' aggressive fund-raising tactics prompted the alarmed San Antonio City Council to pass a law limiting solicitation of money on city streets.

After reading about the museum in the *Dallas Times Herald*, I had a sixth sense that something was strange. Maybe my antenna went up because getting a Navy SEAL and a Green Beret together at that time was like a duck mating with a chicken. And neither appeared to be the kind of man who had been a member of such elite units. "I can't really explain why, but I think those guys are fakes," I told John MacCormack, the reporter.

For the first time, I encountered a journalist who took great umbrage at the idea of being deceived. MacCormack agreed that if I could prove they were not who they said they were, he would run another story. There was one problem. The men had shown him their military records but had only given him their first names. MacCormack went back to them, obtained their full names, and I requested the records.

Sure enough, both were impostors. Stevens had not been a SEAL; he had served in the Coast Guard from 1969 to 1972 and had not left the United States. Stevens also had a lengthy criminal record for theft and fraud.[83] Bonner did not enter the Army until 1978, three years after the war ended. He was not a Green Beret and had added seven years to his age in order to appear old enough to have served in Vietnam.[84]

Confronted by MacCormack, the men admitted they had lied. Ironically, neither man knew the other was bogus. They followed the unwritten rule of veterans: Unless he volunteers, don't question someone else's military service.[85]

MacCormack's story of the two pretenders made national headlines when *New York Times* reporter Roberto Suro picked it up. Both veterans insisted their hearts were in the right place, that they were merely trying to tell the Vietnam story through the eyes of those who were there. Although the men offered to resign, the board of directors of the museum asked them to stay on, contending that they had started something valuable.[86] (The museum later shut down, but Stevens still resurfaces periodically trying to resurrect it.)

In many ways, uncovering the fakes at the San Antonio museum was a watershed event for me. I realized that there were some reporters who cared about the truth. And I realized that these phonies were not just a few "bad apples" but a national phenomenon, a weird ripple in the American psyche.

The Memorial Dedication

In early November, workers scrambled to finish the construction. On Veterans' Day 1989, my wife and I drove to Fair Park for the dedication of the Texas Vietnam Veterans Memorial. I felt like I had gone fifteen rounds with Muhammad Ali and was still on my feet. The big moment had come. The president and his wife would be there. CNN was scheduled to show the dedication live. I had never spoken in front of more than one hundred people before, and now I was going to make a speech in front of the president on international TV. I feared that when I opened my mouth, nothing but a squeak would come out.

A security fence surrounded the memorial area, courtesy of the Secret Service. I was pleased to see that the ragtag "'Nam vets" crowd had been kept behind the fence. As Art and I and our wives passed through metal detectors and entered the designated gate, we were stopped by an officious man in a suit.

"Hold it right there," he said. "Where are you going?"

"We're cochairs of the memorial effort," I said. "We're going down to the podium."

"Oh no, you're not," he said.

"Who the hell are you?" I asked him.

"I'm the guy with the gun," he said.

Art Ruff started laughing, but the guy did not crack a smile. He was a Secret Service agent. The confusion took fifteen minutes to straighten out.

By that time, President Bush and his entourage had arrived at the reception tent and had shaken hands with everybody but us.

We finally climbed onto the dais. Although it was November, the afternoon was extremely hot and growing hotter by the minute. The platform had reinforced metal plates beneath the red, white, and blue bunting to provide protection for the president, and it reflected heat like an oven. By the time I started my speech, I felt as if I had been basted and baked.

I thanked President and Mrs. Bush, and all those who'd been involved in the memorial effort. "Every man who ever served in wartime remembers the names of fallen comrades," I said. "Just as our president remembers the names Ted White, Jack Delaney, Jim Wykes, and Tom Waters, my generation of veterans remembers the names engraved here." The president turned, obviously surprised, and looked at me; I had named a handful of men close to Bush who had fought and died in World War II. I thought about Harry Horton, my roommate at Fort Hood.

"We remember names like Gregg Hartness and Charles Bryan and Russell Steindam. Some of the names represent individuals decorated with Navy Crosses or Medals of Honor, but death makes no such distinction. Each one of these 3,427 young men was an American doing his duty. Each was someone's father, someone's brother, someone's husband, or someone's son.

"Remember them, ladies and gentlemen, remember them all," I said in closing, "and especially remember the pain and suffering of their families, for it is because of their sacrifice and the sacrifice of past generations of veterans that this great nation remains free." Somehow, I finished my speech without squeaking or choking up. I introduced Texas Governor Bill Clements and sat down, exhausted.

After all the speeches, we paused and looked up. Against impossibly blue autumn skies, four Navy jets screamed overhead, one peeling off in the "missing man" formation, followed by four Marine jets. An Air Force B-52, followed by a KC-135, both flying only a few hundred feet off the ground, came rumbling over. Then came the pounding, throbbing sound everyone who was there associates with Vietnam, as four Army National Guard Huey helicopters swooped in low over Fair Park.

The tune of taps began, a bugler on the ground echoed by another on the roof of the baroque Dallas Music Hall, in a sound so lonely, so lovely I was near tears. The ceremony ended with the president and the first lady shaking hands all around, cameras flashing.

We had been told we had to be out of Fair Park by 3 P.M. The Rolling Stones were playing in the Cotton Bowl. Mick Jagger was expected to draw more than sixty thousand people, six times as many people as we had drawn, and we had to clear out. As we headed to our cars, I realized we had raised more than $2 million against incredible odds. But I felt no great sense of satisfaction. I was just desperately tired. We had built this stone edifice but had changed nothing. A true memorial is what we feel in our hearts, and America in her heart still did not believe those who fell in Vietnam were worthy. At best, we had given a handful of families a massive tombstone.

That night, I watched news coverage of the event. All three local network affiliates couldn't resist going to the ragtag crowd. We had kept them on the periphery, but in the end, the image—Vietnam vets as bums, derelicts, losers —won out. They had learned how to be vets from the media, then in turn reinforced the image. A giant circle, with no beginning and no ending.

One reporter ended his story about the memorial dedication by inter-viewing "Joe," a tall, scraggly "Vietnam veteran" wearing a boonie hat adorned with unit patches.

"Joe, how do you feel about today?" the reporter asked. "Do you feel good?"

"This is long overdue," Joe said. "I've had posttraumatic stress for seven years and nobody gave a damn."

I wanted to scream.

When the dedication was all over, what kept coming back to me wasn't the ceremony, but all the research—the statistics, the stories, the official military records. To me, the memorial mattered less than the files, which had the power to prove that the dishonorable stereotypes and clichés stand on little more than myth and distortion.

In the three years we took to raise the money, an image kept recurring. The mental picture that characterized Vietnam vets for the American public, by far, was that of men like "Joe," haunted by memories of the war, struggling with flashbacks and nightmares, likely to go berserk at any moment.

Among those most responsible for perpetuating that image in the media were Dan Rather and producers at CBS News. In "The Wall Within," an hour-long 1988 television show, Rather and his producers, Paul and Holly Fine, had tackled the issue of posttraumatic stress disorder, ascribing its symptoms to hundreds of thousands of Vietnam vets.

"Bull!" was my initial reaction when I watched "The Wall Within" in 1988. If soldiers were suffering PTSD, why hadn't Rather? He'd covered the war. And what about other war correspondents like Ted Koppel, David Halberstam, Stanley Karnow? And the combat officers such as Colin Powell, John Shalikashvili, David Hackworth?

Was Rather's contribution to the image of the Vietnam vet a documen-tary or an outrageous fiction? With FOIA, I knew how to find out.

5

CBS Hits "The Wall Within"

THE FAMILIAR, urgent voice of Dan Rather spoke as the camera panned across a dark forest, reminiscent of Southeast Asia. "Twenty years ago, the United States military trained young Americans for combat operations in Vietnam," Rather said. "Since then, a number of these men, haunted by their deeds, became seriously ill." The troubled face of a middle-aged man with salt-and-pepper hair and a bushy mustache appeared on the screen. "He asked us to call him only Steve," Rather said.

Rather told how Steve fought for almost two years "behind enemy lines." Steve looked off into the trees. "I think I was one of the highest trained, underpaid, eighteen-cent-an-hour assassins ever put together by a team of people who knew exactly what they were looking for, and who [was] used to the maximum and then dumped it back on society to take care of," said Steve somberly.

The opening minutes of "The Wall Within" made for arresting television, daring the viewer to turn away. For weeks, CBS aired ads promoting the hour-long special, hailing it as the "rebirth of the TV documentary."[87] Jay Sharbutt of the *Los Angeles Times* said the special was not the typical "quick-hit, hot-topic" TV show.[88] Fourteen months in the making, the documentary was an attempt to keep flying the tattered banner of the crown jewel of CBS—its once-distinguished news division.[89]

"The Wall Within" precisely fit what Americans have grown to believe about the Vietnam War and its veterans: They routinely committed war crimes. They came home from an immoral war traumatized, vilified, then pitied. Jobless, homeless, addicted, suicidal, they remain afflicted by inner conflicts, stranded on the fringes of society.

In a review, *Washington Post* writer Tom Shales described the program as "extraordinarily powerful," the story of Vietnam vets who "wrestle with demons they cannot drive out."[90] Another critic described his first reaction as sympathy for the traumatized vets. His second: a sense of fear that so many of these unhinged veterans were loose on the streets.

Rather and his producers, Paul and Holly Fine, focused on veterans in Washington state, men who drifted to the Northwest so they could live hidden in isolation. All suffered from posttraumatic stress disorder, which Rather described as afflicting perhaps a million Vietnam vets. Possibly as many as one hundred thousand vets had been driven to suicide over the war, Rather announced. The program profiled six veterans, "outcasts, broken spirits," who had come out of hiding to appear. All apparently had received treatment at Department of Veterans Affairs (VA) Vet Centers in the Northwest.

"At age sixteen, Steve was a Navy SEAL, trained to assassinate," Rather gravely intoned. "For almost two years, he operated behind enemy lines, then he broke. He came home in a straitjacket, addicted to alcohol and drugs."

On camera, Steve described how, crippled by PTSD, he almost strangled his own mother, mistaking her for a Viet Cong. Unable to hold a job or function in society, his marriage falling apart, Steve fled to the forest, where he lived in hollow logs and stumps. He tried to drown his anger in alcohol and drugs, "punishing himself with twenty-three car accidents," Rather said, which left him permanently crippled. But the hate continued, his character permanently distorted by military trainers who programmed him to kill with vicious, mind-altering techniques.

What had so deranged him? Rather coaxed Steve to reveal he had been forced by his superiors to massacre Vietnamese civilians, leaving Chinese and North Vietnamese literature tacked to the mutilated corpses to disguise the war crime as the work of the Communists—all part of the CIA's sinister "Phoenix Program," the elimination of the enemy support base. When the generals landed with the press, the covert operatives melted into the jungles.

"You're telling me that you went into the village, killed people, burned part of the village, then made it appear that the other side had done this?" Rather asked.

"Yeah."

"For propaganda purposes at home."

"That's correct."

"This is not something you made up. This is not a hallucination?" Rather said, looking searchingly at Steve, as if to probe his heart.

"Oh, no," Steve shook his head.

But something happened. One day, Steve could not kill anymore. "The day he came out of action, Steve knew he was sick," said Rather. "He knew combat had made him different. He asked for help; that's unusual, many vets don't. They hold back until they explode."

Here again Vietnam vets were being portrayed as deranged, perpetrators of war crimes, baby killers. However, it was absurdly easy to see that Steve had lied. Rather had covered the Vietnam War as a correspondent in 1965 and 1966. He had to know there were no sixteen-year-old Navy SEALs in Vietnam or anywhere else. The minimum enlistment age is seventeen; in modern times, it is extremely difficult to enlist in the military without a valid birth certificate. Even if Steve had lied about his age to enlist, after entering the Navy it requires an average of two years training to join a combat SEAL team. In Vietnam, the youngest SEALs were in their twenties.

Rather's next PTSD victim was identified as George Grule, who described the terror of working on the flight deck of the aircraft carrier the USS *Ticonderoga* during intense night operations off the coast of Vietnam. When a close friend moved toward the spinning propeller of a plane, Grule leaped forward to save him, but his move came too late. "He walked into the prop right next to me," Grule said. The blades chopped his friend to pieces, spattering Grule with his blood.

The sight of such a gruesome death and guilt at not being able to save his friend traumatized Grule, leaving him a hyper-vigilant "outcast." Although he served three tours, Grule returned home feeling his contribution to the war effort was a waste. Now unable to function in civilian society, he slept only two hours a night, he told Rather. To escape his memories, he drove aimlessly for hours through the Washington hills while his family slept. "I got to cool the feeling that—not to explode and do something that I'll just be guilty for again," Grule said, "I just may say to hell with it and end it."

Grule's story ended with Rather's grave pronouncement: "Had George not served, George would not be ill."

All six men described how their nightmares, flashbacks, hallucinations, abusive behavior, and addictions ruined not only their lives but also the lives of their wives and children as well. Their anguished faces made their pain all too real. Of the six vets profiled, the most grisly story was told by Terry Bradley. Clearly disturbed, the former "fighting sergeant" was driven to madness by the atrocities he had been forced to commit in Vietnam and misdiagnosed as a paranoid schizophrenic by a medical profession ignorant of PTSD.

In a shocking scene, Bradley claimed to have skinned alive up to fifty Vietnamese men, women, even babies, in an hour, stacking their mangled bodies in heaps, holding butchered hearts in his hands. "Could you do this for one hour of your life, you stack up every way a body could be mangled, up into a body, an arm, a tit, an eyeball, a soldier that, turned over, that don't have no face, guts, maggots, because they been there more than a day, whatever, and the stink and the smell and stuff like this. Imagine us over there for a *year* and doing it intensely," Bradley said. "That is sick."

"You've got to be angry about it," Rather soothed. "I'm suicidal about it," Bradley said.

Devastated by his PTSD, Bradley could not work. Each month, he received a Social Security check of $931 and a $400 check for VA compensation for PTSD. The VA's reaction to Bradley's trauma? To throw drugs at him. Spilling out a cardboard box of antipsychotic medication, Bradley offered Rather a sample. The newsman declined. "Massive drug therapy medication has left him with organic brain damage," Rather said. "He's legally incompetent." Like the other vets, Bradley sought sanctuary in the woods. The camera followed Bradley at night in a dark forest, showing him howling at the sky like a wounded animal.

Using statistics without naming their source, Rather claimed that more Vietnam vets had died by their own hand than the fifty-eight thousand dead listed on the National Memorial, that one in three Vietnam veterans was suffering from PTSD, that one out of three homeless men was a Vietnam veteran. A subsequent segment on *60 Minutes* that week called "P.T.S.D." blasted the VA for not doing enough to help traumatized vets.

"These are American sons and daughters who went into a green jungle hell and came out with nightmares that won't go away," Rather told the *Chicago Tribune.* "I won't kid anyone. This is not happy-time viewing. This hour is not a movie. This is real. But if you want to know how it was and how it is, watch this program."[91]

If that was "how it was and how it is," why hadn't CBS instigated an investigation into the atrocities described by "Steve" and Terry Bradley? There is no statute of limitations on war crimes. If the two men had done what they claimed, they and others deserved to be held accountable.

The documentary was so acclaimed it became part of the CBS video history series on the Vietnam War. Dignified with a formal introduction by Walter Cronkite, once the nation's premier war correspondent, the series sold for $150. Designated as official "history," marketed to schools and other institutions, the video now forever perpetuates the image of the Vietnam vet as a walking time bomb.[92]

That single issue—that Vietnam veterans carry a deadly seed of trauma in our brains that could explode at any moment, regardless of how outwardly calm and rational we seem—had distorted the image of those who served more than anything. All the other issues—suicide, homelessness, criminality, alcoholism, drug abuse, wife beating—are offshoots of PTSD. *If he hadn't gone to war, he would not have* (fill in the blank).

Where had Rather and his crew found their shocking statistics? How had they chosen the veterans profiled? Were their stories true? The show raised even larger questions. How had PTSD become the defining hallmark of Vietnam vets? How many veterans really suffered from the problem, and was combat trauma worse for Vietnam than for soldiers in World War II or Korea?

With my new skill at filing FOIA requests, the first step was getting the military records of all six vets featured. And just for good measure, I sent off for Rather's military record, too.

The Records

Most of the men featured had received counseling at Tacoma and Spokane-area Vet Centers. I opened a road atlas and drew circles around the two cities. I called every county courthouse and motor-vehicle office in the circles, searching for records pertaining to Terry Bradley, George Grule, Guy Iredale, John Michaelson, and Michael Rice, the names listed on the CBS transcript. (CBS gave no last name for "Steve.")

To find addresses and phone numbers for each man, I worked my way through the various departments: property, lawsuits, divorces, birth records, arrests. I checked area high schools to see if anybody with those names had been graduated. I often called at lunchtime, whenever the regular staff people were out and neophytes were operating the phones. Whenever I hit on the right name, I attempted to bluff somebody into giving me a Social Security number, which I could use to obtain a service record for common names.

At one courthouse, I asked about Michael Rice. "Mike Rice?" asked one clerk. "I went to high school with him." She explained I was looking for the wrong spelling; his name was "Mikal."

After obtaining correct names for Rice, Iredale, and Michaelson, I sent in FOIA requests for their military records to the NPRC in St. Louis. The records revealed that all three had served in Vietnam, but two had less hazardous duties than they had claimed on the program. Only Elvis "Guy" Iredale could be described as a true combat "grunt." The recipient of a Purple Heart and a Combat Action Ribbon (a Marine award denoting thirty days under enemy fire), Iredale was the only one who had experienced the kind of intense combat so-called experts say causes PTSD.[93]

Rather said John A. Michaelson's symptoms were "alienation, hostility, and distrust." He had transferred PTSD to his wife and children. His twelve-year-old son Elijah lived in an institution because of his own violent tendencies, and his teenage daughter repeatedly had been in trouble with the juvenile justice system. But contrary to Michaelson's self-description as a grunt "walking point," he actually had served as a guard with the USMC MAG-36, a Marine helicopter unit stationed at Ky Ha Airfield at the Chu Lai Base, a relatively secure location in I Corps as was mine near Bien Hoa. Michaelson's military record listed no valorous combat decorations or Combat Action Ribbon.[94]

On camera, Mikal C. Rice described horrific flashbacks, triggered by thunder or cars backfiring, which brought back the memory of trying to help "Sergeant Call" during a grenade attack at Cam Ranh Bay. Rice broke down, sobbing as he described discovering Call's body had been blown in half. "He died in my arms," Rice told Rather.

Military records revealed that Mikal C. Rice had been a guard with the 981st MP Company at Cam Ranh Bay from 1969 to 1970.[95] According to casualty records, only one Army "Sergeant Call"—Richard Joseph Call—died in Vietnam. Sgt. Call burned to death on April 4, 1968, when his armored vehicle was struck by enemy rocket fire during an engagement seventy miles northwest of Saigon. Call was killed several hundred miles from Cam Ranh Bay, months before Rice arrived in-country, and thus could not have expired in Rice's arms.[96]

In a moving finale, Michaelson, Rice, and Bradley visited the Vietnam Veterans Memorial in Washington with Rather to find the names of the dead who haunted them. Michaelson said he had cradled Lance Cpl. Ralph Knutsen as he died on Christmas Eve. Knutsen's name was not on the wall.

"I guess we missed one, huh?" Michaelson said to Rather. "He was killed from friendly fire, you know? I mean, one of our own guys got him. And maybe they didn't put them down, huh?"

If Knutsen had been killed by friendly fire, his name would be on The Wall and in the casualty records. The engraved names include victims of car accidents, homicide, suicide, heart attacks, and disease, not just enemy action. The only criterion is that they died in Vietnam as a member of the armed services. But casualty records show nobody by the name of Ralph Knutsen died in Vietnam of any cause.

And Bradley's dead friend, Bentline, "torn to pieces" in front of him? I could find no evidence that anyone named Bentline had served in the military in Vietnam.

A Sixteen-Year-Old Navy Seal?

The military records that proved hardest to obtain were those of "Steve," Terry Bradley, and George Grule.

CBS cloaked Steve in anonymity. Then Accuracy in Media, a conservative media watchdog organization that had condemned CBS for using a few individuals' tragedies to smear all Vietnam vets, reported that Steve's last name was Barbe, and he lived in Jefferson County, Washington.[97] His story had appeared in the *Bremerton Sun* a few days after the documentary aired. "There are those of us who were on the front line who no longer wish to be in a state of denial," Steve told reporter Julie McCormick when asked how he responded to those skeptical about the seriousness of PTSD.[98]

After contacting the courthouse in Jefferson County, I located a divorce record for Steve Barbe. The documents provided his ex-wife's full name and address; her number was in a Puget Sound-area phone book. Janice Jaman acknowledged that her ex-husband Steve had appeared in the CBS segment, but that wasn't the first time Barbe had told his story. He had also been featured in an earlier BBC film called "Haunted Heroes."

Jaman felt that Steve's PTSD had been triggered by his combat experiences as a Navy SEAL. She had gone to the Vet Center with her husband, listened to his stories, and sat in on rap sessions in an attempt to understand what had happened to him during the war. But PTSD made him impossible to live with. In Jaman's mind, Vietnam had ruined her marriage.[99]

Jaman explained that her husband had served during the war under a different name. He took Barbe, his mother's maiden name, after the service. His real name was Steve Southards. His ex-wife mailed me his DD-214, which showed Southards indeed had served in Vietnam. Now, having his service number, I filed an FOIA request for the official military record of Steven Ernest Southards, which confirmed that he had not been in the Navy at age sixteen. Southards reported for active duty on August 24, 1965, two days after his seventeenth birthday, and served until April 2, 1969. Southards did spend some time in Vietnam, assigned to the U.S. Naval Support Activity Detachment in Qui Nhon from August 1966 until August 1967.

But Southards was not a SEAL, nor had he taken any SEAL training. There had been no military trainers creating an "eighteen-cent-an-hour assassin," no participation in secret programs to murder Vietnamese civilians.[100]

In reality, Southards was an "internal communications repairman," assigned to rear area bases, and had no combat decorations. His only special training was a "motion picture operation course (16mm)," at Subic Bay in the Philippines. Southards did receive a Navy Unit Commendation Medal, as did all members of his unit for meritorious service in providing "logistic support" to U.S. Navy, U.S. Coast Guard, and free world naval forces. After his transfer to the Philippines, Southards spent several months in the brig for going AWOL six times. Little that Southards had told Rather was true except that he had been in the Navy, and that his first name was Steve.

In June 1991, shortly after obtaining Southards' record, I received a letter from Andrew Weir, a reporter for BBC Television Features in England. The BBC was preparing a documentary series on aspects of the Cold War and wanted to delve into issues of the intelligence side of the war in Vietnam. After seeing "The Wall Within," they were trying to track down "Steve" in order to interview him as a former "Special Forces" officer. When Weir contacted his ex-wife, Jaman had given him my phone number and address.

"She told me that you were investigating people who had appeared as ostensible witnesses to atrocities, but who had faked their credentials and whose testimony was thus dubious at best," Weir wrote. "We are concerned that we are not exploited by any such people in our researches, and I would appreciate hearing from you about any cases of deception in this area which you may have been able to expose." I talked with Weir and gave him a rundown on Southards' record. This BBC producer decided not to interview Southards.[101]

The irony was inescapable. I, a rank amateur, had been able to verify with several phone calls and an FOIA request that the description Steve had given of his military service and his tales of atrocities were fraudulent. Before interviewing Southards, another producer had tried to verify his background and found his ex-wife, as I had. Apparently CBS, while meticulously preparing its trumpeted "return to the documentary" for over a year, had made no effort to obtain Steve's record independently.

The "Fighting Sergeant"

Terry L. Bradley had claimed to have slaughtered fifty Vietnamese civilians in an hour, flaying and stacking them in heaps as part of his combat role. But the area of operations of the 25th Infantry Division was too close to Saigon for such atrocities to have gone undetected, and no record exists of large numbers of Vietnamese civilians murdered in this area during Bradley's tour of duty, according to *Red Thunder, Tropic Lightning*, an oral history of the 25th Infantry Division in Vietnam.[102]

Bradley's own military record shows that although he had served in Vietnam, he was not a "fighting sergeant," as described by Rather, but an ammo handler in the 25th Infantry Division. And he was not a "success" in Vietnam, as Rather claimed. In three-and-a-half years of service, Bradley spent three hundred days either AWOL or in the stockade. [103]

Spokane *Spokesman-Review* columnist Doug Clark interviewed Bradley after the CBS broadcast. He discovered that Bradley's emotional problems began long before the war. "His father and mother drank," Clark wrote. "He dropped out of his freshman year and joined the Army, he says, to get away from 'too much stress.' " After he returned to the states, Bradley was diagnosed as paranoid schizophrenic but refused to take his medication.[104]

Schizophrenia is an organic brain disorder that is not triggered by combat or any other trauma. Bradley had not been unhinged by his duties as a cold-blooded assassin but was betrayed by his own brain, something that would have been easily apparent to the CBS producers had they chosen to check the facts. Instead, Rather praised Bradley as a "truth-teller."

Death on the Flight Deck

The story told by George Grule presented an interesting challenge.

He had described witnessing a harrowing propeller accident aboard the aircraft carrier USS *Ticonderoga*. The *Ticonderoga* log verified that a man had been killed in a propeller accident in 1967 while the ship was off the coast of Vietnam. But the accident report for that incident did not list Grule as one of the twelve witnesses, nor was he a member of the ship's crew at that time.[105]

In fact, I could locate no military record for George Grule. It was not until 1994, when *Reader's Digest* began preparing a story about my work, that I learned that CBS had misspelled his name in the program transcript. Military records show that George Lee Greul, a high school dropout, had served in the Navy from February 2, 1969 to December 28, 1972, assigned to the *Ticonderoga*. He had received a Vietnam Service Medal; for a portion of 1969, the ship sailed in the Tonkin Gulf off the coast of Vietnam. But no propeller accident had occurred during the period that Greul was aboard ship in the Tonkin Gulf.[106]

Malcolm McConnell, writer and roving editor for *Reader's Digest*, called Vet Center counselor Bruce Webster, trying to verify the facts of Greul's case. After hearing from Webster, Greul called McConnell. The writer explained that he had the record of an accident in 1967, but Greul was not listed as a crewman. "Oh, that was a different accident," said Greul, who now lives in Port Angeles, Washington.[107]

Greul told McConnell the death of his friend occurred between July and October 1971, when the ship was off the coast of Vietnam on "secret presidential orders" to mine Haiphong Harbor. Greul verified that he had been declared 100 percent disabled by the psychological trauma the accident caused; he receives $1,952 a month in service-connected compensation payments from the VA. (The Vietnam Veterans' Readjustment Act provides for Vietnam veterans to receive disability compensation payments for service-connected PTSD. Terry Bradley was also receiving compensation.[108])

McConnell and *Digest* researcher David Levy obtained the declassified ship's log for July through October of 1971, and found another aircraft-propeller accident that resulted in the death of twenty-four-year-old Seaman Ronald J. Becker. The log showed that the *Ticonderoga* had been converted to an antisubmarine warfare carrier in 1970, during Greul's service. After

that, the ship operated in the Pacific on routine patrols, not combat operations. In the summer of 1971, the time of Becker's death, it was not in
waters off the Vietnam coast on a "secret mission," as Greul had claimed to
Rather. The *Ticonderoga* was then deployed on a training mission a few
miles off the coast of San Diego, California.[109]

The military record of Ronald Joseph Becker indicated that he had been
killed during the same period that Greul was aboard ship. I obtained the
investigative report on the accident from the Office of the Judge Advocate
General, Department of the Navy.[110]

According to the JAG report, the gruesome accident occurred in the
early morning on August 19, 1971. Plane captain Becker came on duty the
night before about 7:00, with his partner and bunkmate, Kenton F.
Gleason. Both were on deck at 12:30 A.M. when an S-2E aircraft landed. On
deck, the plane's propellers continued to spin; by customary practice, the
engines are kept idling until the initial tie-down is installed. Both men
walked toward the aircraft, each carrying two tie-down chains. Becker
installed one tie-down on the nose gear, then walked slowly upright on the
starboard side of the plane.

Gleason completed his second tie-down on the other side of the aircraft.
Kneeling, he glanced under the plane to see how Becker was doing at precisely the moment his partner walked into the starboard propeller. Doctors
could do nothing. Becker's injuries were so extensive he died either immediately or soon after being transferred to the sick bay operating room.

Investigators interviewed all those who had been on the flight deck or
called to the deck when the accident occurred. Of the twelve people on the
flight deck, only Gleason had seen the accident. It was a very dark night;
the investigative report said that the state of the seas could not be observed
due to darkness. The pilot and co-pilot heard a resounding chunk against
the aircraft and felt it shudder. Out the windows, they could see a man
lying on the flight deck, but neither saw the accident happen.

But listen to Greul talking to Dan Rather on camera.

"Did you lose any friends in Vietnam?" Rather asked.

"Yes," Greul said, with a catch in his throat. "On the flight deck, night
operations, recovered aircraft, prop job. He was directing it, or waiting for
it to be directed, I can't recall exactly."

"Then what happened?" Rather said.

"He just simply walked into the prop, right next to me," Greul said. "My
attempt [to save him] was too late. My attempt wasn't executed like I had
done before and after. I made the mistake of thinking what he thought, and
that's what caused it."

But Greul was not listed as one of those on the tightly controlled flight
deck. It's extremely unlikely that Greul, a repairman, had been on deck

after midnight. If for some reason he had been on deck, it's highly unlikely he was close enough to the aircraft to see it happen and certainly not close enough to reach out to Becker. Yet each month, Greul receives a government check for PTSD disability—for an accident he heard about. When asked by *Reader's Digest* about the death of Becker, Greul became belligerent and threatened to sue anyone who printed anything that could end his disability compensation.[111]

However, if anyone had been traumatized by the accident and deserved compensation, it was Kent Gleason. He and Becker shared a room aboard ship for a year, making them close friends. Gleason's record, obtained through FOIA, confirms his version of his military service.[112]

Gleason now lives in Washington state. He remembers Becker's death vividly. "I went underneath the plane and tied up one wheel," Gleason says. "I threw the other chain under the aircraft. I turned to look at him, and I saw him look at me." In that instant, Gleason saw his buddy walk into the propeller. "The blood came back on me. I saw his arm go off. I could see he was hit in the head, and I could see his brains. I knew he was dead. I don't know what he was thinking of because he was a smart man. He'd been to college. I think he got distracted."[113]

Gleason turned to run for help and stepped on something. He looked down and saw Becker's severed arm. He raced to the tower and grabbed a medic. "I had a hard time talking," Gleason says. "I was going into shock. The next thing I knew I was in the sick bay." Given a tranquilizer shot, he woke up three days later.

He was ordered to report to the ship's commanding officer, who had a chaplain waiting to help Gleason. "I was shaken, very shaken," Gleason says. He told his C.O. how the accident happened. "I asked if he [Becker] was still alive. He said no. I was told they'd called for blood, but he was already dead."

The commanding officer told Gleason he had two choices: He could go back to the base on a helicopter, or he could stay and continue his job. Gleason chose to remain on board and work.

"Okay," the C.O. said. "What if I put you back on nights again?"

Gleason told his commander that the only way he could get through the situation was to confront his fear. "So he put me back on nights," Gleason says.

A few days later, the commanding officer asked Gleason if he would be the military escort for Becker's body. Gleason agreed; he accompanied the casket by helicopter to Anaheim, California, where he met Becker's bereaved family, including his fiancée. He attended Becker's full military funeral.

When the ship redeployed, Gleason went back to work. "I was scared as hell every time I went underneath an aircraft," Gleason says. "I knew it could have been me. He just made a mistake." But he confronted his fear and went on.

After Gleason left the service and moved home to Washington state, he had vivid memories of the accident and continued to mourn the loss of his friend. He attended community college on the GI Bill for a year and studied forestry. In school, he met a veteran from one of his squadrons. "We got together and talked," Gleason says. "That really helped."

Gleason's first wife told him he used to wake up screaming, but he did not remember having nightmares. He had no survivor's guilt; hearing about the war or about Navy fighter planes didn't upset him. The memory of Becker's death never disappeared, but Gleason did not use drugs or turn to alcohol to cope. After school, he found a good job doing road maintenance that he's held ever since. His second marriage has endured.

When Gleason heard about Greul's claims, he was astonished. It had never occurred to him to seek compensation for PTSD. The idea that someone was cashing in on Becker's death—and talking about it on national TV—disgusted him.

Rather's Statistics

The statistics used by Rather in "The Wall Within" were no more reliable than the stories by Greul and the others. "There have been between twenty-six thousand and one hundred thousand suicides, depending on which reputable source you believe in," Rather claimed.

After the segment aired, Thomas K. Turnage, then administrator of the VA, condemned CBS for its many distortions. "I would have applauded any honest attempt to portray the largely successful readjustment of the vast majority of Vietnam veterans and of the many effective efforts to help those who have had difficulty," Turnage wrote to Howard Stringer, president of CBS. "However, by your unfounded exaggeration and by presenting several of the most unfortunate individuals you could find, CBS left no doubt you intended to have the public believe, 'These are your veterans of Vietnam.' There is absolutely no justification for CBS to leave such an impression on the American public."

Turnage challenged their statistics. "Yes, our Vet Centers have seen over five hundred thousand *Vietnam Era* (emphasis added) veterans, with about one-third of them meeting the accepted diagnostic criteria of PTSD . . . [but] your anecdotal reports can hardly be the basis for concluding that hundreds of thousands more Vietnam veterans manifest the disease or its symptoms and have further avoided contact with our outreach program."

He also disputed the CBS assertion that between twenty-six thousand and one hundred thousand Vietnam vets committed suicide after the war.

"Nothing we are aware of that is reasonably 'reputable'—including a mortality study we ourselves did—would confirm exaggerated numbers of Vietnam veteran suicides. CBS obviously didn't take the time to examine the normal rates of suicide in the general population since 1964, when the Vietnam Era began. It is clear that if there had been double to quadruple the number of expected suicides among Vietnam veterans, the total U.S. rates would have been drastically affected. That simply did not happen."[114] (See Chapter 13 for more on Vietnam vets' suicide rate.)

With the contention that "one out of three homeless men is a Vietnam vet," CBS again was playing fast and loose with the statistics. "Estimates of the homeless population vary widely," Turnage wrote, "but the VA does not dispute the general belief that one-third of homeless men are veterans —veterans of *all* wars. This is reasonable given the fact that about 45 percent of adult males in the general population are veterans. However, there are no indications Vietnam veterans are over-represented among the homeless." (See Chapter 14 for more on homelessness.)

Stringer wrote back, defending their statistics and their criticism of the VA for not providing enough help to PTSD victims. "Your criticisms were not shared by a vast majority of our viewers," Stringer contended. "CBS News and its affiliates received acclaim from most quarters." He cited reports that VA offices and counseling programs were deluged with requests for therapy by veterans. "In sum, this was a broadcast of which we at CBS News and I personally am proud," Stringer concluded. "There are no apologies to make."[115]

Except for the fact that little of it was true.

Marvin, the Trip-Wire Vet

The image of the Vietnam veteran as a hapless victim of an unjust, illegal war in which monstrous atrocities were commonplace lies so deeply ingrained in these members of the media that they were willing to accept the patently ludicrous story of a sixteen-year-old SEAL assassin and grotesque details of massive, previously unreported war crimes.

Stung by Accuracy in Media's criticism of the documentary, producer Fine told *Electronic Media* that "thousands" of veterans suffering from PTSD had been interviewed before the six were selected.[116] CBS President Stringer wrote to Accuracy in Media saying that "hundreds" of afflicted veterans had been interviewed and that "six were chosen as representative." The Fines and Rather had talked to numerous vets who had been successfully treated for PTSD at Washington Vet Centers but had rejected their stories in favor of the outrageous, the sensational, the bogus. They wanted to believe the crazies.

The bizarre genesis of the "The Wall Within" can actually be traced to

1983, when the *Tacoma News-Tribune* ran a sensational series on "trip-wire" Vietnam vets supposedly driven into the wilderness by PTSD.

The stories were written by Marlowe Churchill, then the military affairs reporter for the *News-Tribune*, circulation 120,000. In the fall of 1983, a contact at the Washington VA approached the young writer about a novel program being launched to reach Vietnam veterans with PTSD who were living in remote areas—some so antisocial they lived in makeshift homes in the forests. One of the counselors called them "trip-wire" vets, referring to Vietnam booby traps and the wires used to trigger them. But the term had a double meaning; the second was a warning that these Vietnam veterans could explode at any moment.

Drafted in 1966, Churchill could not serve because of degenerative eye disease. But he had great empathy with those men who had seen combat. The idea that some soldiers had been mentally crippled by their war experiences intrigued him. Posttraumatic stress disorder, first codified in 1980 in the *Diagnostic and Statistical Manual* (*DSM-III*), the psychiatric profession's diagnostic "bible," was still little understood. Clearly Washington state was leading the way, providing innovative programs for the forgotten vets of Vietnam. To Churchill, the story sounded very interesting and worthwhile —not to mention an old-fashioned scoop, every reporter's passion.[117]

Churchill and photographer Russ Carmac spent a weekend attending rap sessions in Port Angeles on the rural Olympic Peninsula. He met about twenty Vietnam veterans and listened as they bared their souls, telling war stories so grim and gruesome Churchill was shocked. All of them had had trouble adjusting to society since the war; most were coping with guilt, unemployment, and marital problems. Some seemed so disturbed, Churchill wondered if they didn't belong in a psychiatric hospital instead of a counseling session.

Thirty-three-year-old Marvin, a skinny, somewhat spooky character, told the most unsettling stories. A Special Forces "commando" who had tracked Viet Cong through the jungles of Vietnam for four years, Marvin acted as a sniper and assassin in Vietnam before being wounded in 1971. His murderous duties even included shooting American deserters. Finally, the killing became too much, and Marvin's mind had snapped.

Marvin came back to the United States confused and full of self-loathing. He began living in the mountains, trapping animals, wearing animal skins, and living in caves and hollow tree stumps. But he was not alone. Marvin knew of many other vets driven from society by shame, anger, and guilt who were living in the woods.

At first, Churchill was skeptical of Marvin. Photographer Carmac, a Navy veteran who had been based on an aircraft carrier in the Pacific during the war, was even more suspicious. But the counselors told them that the Vietnam vets knew a "bullshitter" when they heard one. And Marvin was no bullshitter. The vets in group therapy comforted Marvin, wrapping their brotherly arms around him, praising him for opening up. One man who said he had served with the 82nd Airborne Division in Vietnam in 1970 swore to Churchill that Marvin's experiences were just the sort of thing he saw during the war. (Churchill did not know that the 82nd Airborne had left Vietnam in December 1969; the unit was not there in 1970.) Even a man who said he had been a Navy SEAL vouched for Marvin.

Churchill and Carmac returned to Tacoma and met with the paper's editors. "We realized, shit, this is pretty hot stuff," Churchill says.

But could Marvin's stories be true? Churchill asked the psychologist who introduced him to the men to tell him if Marvin was legitimate. The psychologist said he could not divulge any patient confidences, but he felt Marvin was telling the truth. Churchill tried sources at the CIA and the Department of Defense. They could only venture that although unlikely, Marvin's story was possible. "Nobody could or would say this is outrageous," Churchill says. His editor at the paper thought the story credible as well.

Churchill did verify Marvin had been in the Marine Corps. Port Angeles psychologist Bruce Webster had diagnosed him as suffering from PTSD, and Marvin had been admitted to the veterans' counseling program. "You work on faith that somebody had checked them out or screened them," Churchill says. And the other vets were so sincere, their stories so poignant, so terrifying. They had been through so much. The government should do something about these pitiable men. There clearly was a need for counseling. Churchill rationalized away his misgivings. "The War Inside," Churchill's three-part series on "trip-wire vets," appeared in late December 1983.

Descriptions of Marvin's desolate life in the wild—hunting and living off the land—ran as the first story called "Lost in the Woods," accompanied by Carmac's vivid pictures. It told how as a seventeen-year-old recruit from the backwoods of Colorado, Marvin served as a "Special Forces scout" hand-picked for an elite assassination team after the Marines discovered "he could hit the bull's-eye ninety-eight times out of one hundred from three hundred yards and could track—even smell and sense—animals from afar." The Marines sent Marvin alone into the jungle to track and kill VC. He often entered Viet Cong camps undetected to steal food and medical supplies, eating raw monkey meat when nothing else was available.

His commanders sometimes ordered Marvin to kill South Vietnamese collaborators and U.S. soldiers who had deserted. "There's a lot the public don't know and probably never will know about what happened in 'Nam," Marvin said. "After the first eighteen months, I got tired of killing and only killed when I absolutely had to. I lost my bloodthirstiness."[118]

Marvin claimed that if he had not been severely wounded, his superiors would have ordered him killed after all the atrocities he had committed. Back in the United States, Marvin drifted to the only place he felt comfortable—the forest. "The only job skills I have are those that might be useful to a hitman for the Mafia," Marvin complained. He had a "pet" mountain lion that he had taught to come close enough to touch. A photo depicted Marvin, barefoot and shirtless, tracking a mountain lion on a forest trail.

Mike McWatters, a private consultant and "acknowledged expert on veterans' problems," and himself a Vietnam vet who suffered from PTSD, claimed there were as many as a thousand such men living in the wilderness of Washington state—on the Olympic Peninsula and in isolated areas north of Spokane in conditions as primitive as those of mountain men in the eighteen hundreds. McWatters had developed the outreach program implemented by five Washington Vet Centers in order to provide counseling for these men. As many as eighty-five "trip-wire" vets who had been living in the forests were reentering society with the help of therapy, according to McWatters. A picture that ran with the third story in the series showed Marvin surrendering a knife to therapist Webster in an "act of psychological liberation."[119]

The series caused an instant sensation. Veterans' groups around the country announced that the problem dramatically illustrated the government's insensitivity to veterans' issues. The Associated Press picked up the articles, with Marvin as the lead story, sending the report international. Other reporters inundated Churchill with calls, asking him to put them in touch with Marvin. (Churchill had kept Marvin's last name confidential.) A reporter from *People* magazine appeared. The story was printed by *The New York Times*, which headlined the piece "U.S. Wilds Hide Scars of Vietnam."[120]

TV reporters and documentary filmmakers descended on Washington in search of trip-wire vets. A French news team arrived, and the BBC sent a film crew. HBO wanted to base a series on Marvin. A female film producer wined and dined Churchill, trying to seduce him into giving her Marvin's last name. The reporter refused and later heard that she was more successful with someone else who knew Marvin. Everybody wanted a piece of Marvin and the wild men in the woods.

But a few Vietnam veterans called Churchill, expressing anger about the story. "This is bullshit," one told him. "I was there, and I never saw anything like that." Churchill wrote off the naysayers. After all, there had been almost three million men in Vietnam, and the critics couldn't know everything that happened.

A couple of weeks after the first series appeared, Churchill wrote a follow-up story about anonymous threats Marvin claimed he had received.

Sinister voices on the phone told him to "shut up or you die." Marvin, saying he was under orders not to discuss secret missions until thirty years after the war, insisted the threats came from within clandestine U.S. military units.[121]

The furor died down to a dull roar. A few months after the series ran, a freelance writer interested in doing a story on the Phoenix Program and assassination teams in Vietnam came to Washington state. Churchill took him to see Marvin.

"The writer and I both saw Marvin's story unraveling like a bad sweater," Churchill says. "Frankly, I thought Marvin by then was just plain crazy. He began calling me about CIA types who were staking him out. I tried to calm him down, even taking a day off driving 150 miles to allay his obvious paranoia. I thought the media hype just freaked him out."

The wildly successful series boosted Churchill's career. He won a national journalism award and accepted a job at a bigger newspaper, *The Press-Enterprise* in Riverside, California, where he moved in 1985. Work soon commenced on *Distant Thunder*, a film starring John Lithgow as a crazed trip-wire vet hiding in the forests of Washington state, a character based on Marvin.

But a year later, Churchill received shocking news. His original source on the trip-wire story, a VA employee, called him out of the blue. The administrator had discovered Marvin's whole tale was a hoax. Marvin had not been an assassin. Marvin did not really live in the woods. Marvin was not even a Vietnam veteran. He had washed out of Marine boot camp in California after only a few months. Churchill had been scammed by a loser who had faked his PTSD. The VA, the Vet Center psychologist, other veterans, and the press had been completely hoodwinked. Nobody had ever checked Marvin's record to verify his wild stories.

The revelation made Churchill feel sick to his stomach. "I began doubting my abilities," the reporter says. "I did some serious drinking over Marvin." He could not bear to look at his journalism award.

Churchill's source was even more devastated. He told Churchill that he had served in Vietnam as a member of Special Forces and had seen heavy combat. After the war, he had adjusted to civilian life with few problems, although being around the PTSD vets had stressed him out. The administrator agonized about writing a story or a book exposing the ruse. Churchill agreed to help. But ultimately neither the original source nor Churchill ever published anything explaining how Marvin had fooled them.

"I just didn't want to touch it," Churchill says. "To be burned so badly, and in front of the world. There's a lot of guilt over it, the realization that I could have done a better job." The experience taught him a valuable lesson.

Churchill quotes Pulitzer Prize-winning reporter Bob Greene: "If your mother says she loves you, check it out."

The Origin of "The Wall Within"

In 1987, when TV producers Paul and Holly Fine decided they wanted to do a story for CBS on "trip-wire" vets, they began calling veterans' therapists in Washington state. Lloyd Humphrey, a counselor for the Vet Center in the Colville/Kettle Falls area of Washington, told them about a Vietnam veteran who called himself "Cajun James."

His real name was James Eugene Howard. In 1981, Howard had quit his job as an electrical contractor, changed his name to "Cajun," bought some horses and moved his family into the wild foothills to live in a teepee. In 1986, Howard moved back to town to run for the office of county auditor, listing himself as Cajun James and a general store as his residence. Cajun James wrote to Paul Fine, telling him there were hundreds of Vietnam vets living in armed camps in the rugged wilderness of the Northwest woods. If Fine came to Washington, Cajun James promised to lead the producer to them.

"I guess there's a bonding that happens between two people sometimes that just clicks." Fine wrote back to Cajun James. "If you can gain permission for us to meet these vets, I must film them in July because this special will be broadcast in September. Please call me collect anytime, day or night."[122]

The Fines, Rather, and their crew came to the Colville/Kettle Falls area to shoot footage of the "wilderness vets" for a documentary to be called "Missing in America." Cajun James was hoping his connection with Fine and CBS would help him stage a benefit concert for veterans' programs featuring major stars. In return for his help, Fine gave him the names of some of the stars' agents. But Cajun James could not lead CBS to large numbers of vets living in the wilderness. Why? There weren't any. Even Cajun James was living in town.

To find veterans for his "trip-wire" documentary, Fine turned to the local Veterans Center, where counselors assured him that they had one of the largest populations of veterans with PTSD in the country. The counselors put out the word that CBS wanted to talk to Vietnam veterans suffering from PTSD, and dozens agreed. (Marvin's legacy was felt in the CBS presentation. "I used trip-wires," Southards told Rather. "I lived in logs. I lived in stumps.")

Even before the documentary aired, many local people believed that the *60 Minutes* crew picked out the most sensational stories. "We felt all along that CBS committed tremendous exploitation of some very sick individuals while they were here," said Colville resident Sarah Lee Pilley, who runs a restaurant where the CBS crew dined. She talked to writer Doug Clark, who wrote about the New Yorkers' descent on Washington before the piece aired. "I got the distinct feeling that CBS had a story they had decided on before they left New York. Then they came out here and filled the bill for what they wanted by talking to those people who would fit in best with their script."[123]

Mrs. Pilley told Clark that CBS initially expressed interest in interviewing her husband, a retired Marine lieutenant colonel who had seen heavy combat in Vietnam. But they lost interest when they realized how successful he had become after the war. The crew interviewed eighty-seven Vietnam veterans before choosing the "four or five saddest cases to put on film," Mrs. Pilley said. "The factual part of it didn't seem to matter as long as they captured the high drama and emotion that these few individuals offered."

After the documentary was broadcast, Sarah Pilley condemned it as "emotional exploitation of the mentally ill." She was not the only one who felt CBS exploited the veterans. After Cajun James' promise to lead CBS to an armed encampment fell through, Lloyd Humphrey, leader of a rap group at the Stevens County Counseling Center in Colville, had helped the Fines locate other vets to interview. The producers had filmed individuals who had worked through their trauma and were making a success of their lives, Humphrey said. But the CBS producers did not use any of that footage. They wanted the crazy ones.

"There are 'Nam vets with strong delusional tendencies," said James Funke of the Vietnam Veterans' Outreach Center in Spokane. "But that's the minority; that's not the type we see. There have been a couple of crazy guys who have come through here, but there have been thousands of others."[124]

In any sample of a large enough population—World War II vets, Vietnam vets, employees of the Cincinnati Transit System, even journalists—you're going to find people with emotional and mental problems. CBS apparently did little to check the veterans' stories beyond to verify that they were clients at a Vet Center and had spent some time in Vietnam.

"It would seem reasonable to expect better journalism from the network of Murrow and Cronkite," wrote Clark.

After "The Wall Within" aired in 1988, the concept of trip-wire vets continued to make the rounds, migrating to other locations where it was picked up by other journalists. In 1992, ABC's *20/20* aired a story on "bush vets" living in the jungles of Hawaii. Anchor Tom Jarriel repeated the usual false statistics: More than one-half of all Vietnam vets have suffered from emotional disorders, marital abuse, and inability to hold a job. One in ten is homeless. Nearly half a million Vietnam-era vets now suffer from PTSD.[125]

I did the same thing I did with "The Wall Within"—sent off for the transcript and started making calls. The story originated much the same way the CBS "documentary" began. I tracked the story back to a Honolulu TV station's news department, which had picked up the idea from a local newspaper. From there it went national, with "Hawaii bush vets" appearing in a piece called "Lost in America" in *Time* magazine.[126] From there it went to *20/20*.

For the most part, the handful of veterans in the various stories were the same. Unlike those on CBS, the vets picked by *20/20* didn't manufacture elaborate war histories to include assassinations, civilian murders, and the deaths of buddies who did not exist. Methodically, I tracked down their records, but because their names were common, I was able to locate only four or five. Of the Hawaii vets I was able to locate records for, some had exaggerated, but none had created stories out of whole cloth.[127]

When confronted by Malcolm McConnell for *Reader's Digest* and Glenna Whitley for *Texas Monthly* with the evidence that "The Wall Within" was a fraud, Rather and producers Holly and Paul Fine refused to comment. "The producers stand behind their story," said Kim Akhtar, a spokeswoman for CBS. "They had enough proof of who they were."[128]

Rather holds himself to be virtually alone in the world of serious TV journalism, often making the point in public pronouncements. On September 30, 1993, in an address to the Radio and Television News Directors Association, Rather chastised other television reporters for producing entertainment, not serious, hard-hitting pieces like "The Wall Within."

"It's the ratings, stupid, don't you know?" Rather said. "They've got us putting more fuzz and wuzz" on the air so news can compete with entertainment programs for "dead bodies, mayhem, and lurid tales." Invoking the memory of newsman Edward R. Murrow, he invited mass repentance. "We should all be ashamed of what we have and have not done, measured against what we could do."[129]

Rather lashed out at his own network, although not by name, for airing an entertainment show in the spring of 1993 about the purported discovery of Noah's Ark, which turned out to be a hoax. That time would be better spent on making a documentary, Rather said. He warned that other news organizations, including CBS, couldn't rejoice over the *Dateline NBC* disaster, when NBC producers were caught using tiny rockets to fake a truck crash test. "It could happen to us," Rather said.[130]

My point exactly.

Why won't Rather and CBS admit their "documentary" was a fraud, that it perpetrated an unwarranted, false picture of men who fought in Vietnam?

Rather certainly has experience with the military. During the Korean War, when men could be drafted out of college, Dan Irvin Rather joined the Army Reserves while attending Sam Houston University in Huntsville, Texas, thus avoiding the possibility of being drafted. On graduating in 1954, well after the Korean War was over and the killing had ended, Rather quit the reserves and enlisted in the Marine Corps. (This is the same national broadcaster who, night after night during the 1988 presidential campaign, hammered Republican vice presidential candidate Dan Quayle for avoiding Vietnam by joining the National Guard.) Although the press often refers to Rather as an "ex-Marine," he did not finish Marine recruit training. He joined the Marines on January 22, 1954, but was discharged less than four months later, on May 11, for being medically unfit. (As a boy, Rather had suffered from rheumatic fever.)[131]

Perhaps Rather and the Fines—obviously very important journalists—don't believe they can be fooled by ordinary people telling extraordinary stories.

Marvin's Legacy

From "trip-wire vets" to "The Wall Within" to "bush vets," the image of the Vietnam veteran barely holding on to sanity now was firmly entrenched. In April 1995, ABC aired a made-for-television movie called "Redwood Curtain," starring John Lithgow and Jeff Daniels. A young Amerasian girl adopted by Lithgow's character searches for her real parents; all she knows is that her father was a soldier in Vietnam and her mother a Vietnamese woman who owned a flower shop.

Both Lithgow and Daniels portray Vietnam veterans with PTSD. Lithgow's character has become enormously successful, his adoptive daughter a concert pianist. But he drinks heavily, still tormented by the war despite his apparent readjustment. When he dies, the teenager moves to live with his sister in the Pacific Northwest. There, she meets Marvin's direct descendant—Jeff Daniels playing a twitching, grunting, barely functioning Vietnam vet living in a makeshift forest sanctuary.

The image of the "dysfunctional Vietnam veteran" now has spread beyond Hollywood and the media and become institutionalized within the counseling apparatus of the VA system, through the Vet Centers and lobbying efforts of veterans' groups.

But PTSD and its association with Vietnam vets actually has roots in the nexus of the antiwar movement and the official creation of the diagnosis of posttraumatic stress disorder. These negative images of the Vietnam veteran possess extraordinary credibility and durability because antiwar activists and journalists with agendas formed and reinforced them over time.

They painted American soldiers as killers and sadists, every bit as vicious and amoral as Nazi storm troopers. "Last week, somewhere in the Midwest, he took his girl for a walk and bought her a soda at the local emporium," wrote author and antiwar activist Mark Lane in 1970. "In six months, he may be murdering unarmed women and children in Vietnam."[132]

The government was evil because it drafted misfits and minorities to serve as cannon fodder in a war that by definition was immoral. After the end of the war, these former soldiers underwent a metamorphosis, criminals still, but also victims—of the military-industrial complex, of American imperialism, of their own inner demons. Psyches shattered by the horrific atrocities they had committed, they could no longer fit into the lives they left behind when they went to Southeast Asia. Tormented by flashbacks and nightmares, prone to uncontrollable bursts of anger and violence, once-reviled Vietnam veterans offered final proof that the war was not only a disaster for the Vietnamese, but for America.

With the reality of posttraumatic stress disorder, revulsion against the soldiers gave way to pity; they were transformed into "the haunted generation," a national tragedy—men who suffered not only in war, but came home to experience high rates of unemployment, alcoholism, drug addiction, criminality, homelessness, and finally, suicide.

To heal the Vietnam veteran, to heal the country, became a national agenda. But it's an agenda based on a myth.

PART II

The Trauma of War

6

Atrocities: The Good War Versus the Bad War

A MAJOR TACTIC of the antiwar movement was to portray the men fighting in Vietnam as sadistic killers who had little regard for civilians — and to claim that wanton butchery not only was common but also was the policy of the American armed forces.

"The war in Vietnam is one of the most barbarous wars in history," said one antiwar pamphlet, quoting United Nations Secretary General U Thant.[133] The media led the American public to believe that the level of atrocities committed by American troops was not only substantially higher than in any other war but also totally unprecedented. The 1968 massacre at My Lai became the example of what was ostensibly common throughout the war.

With the assumption that this level of brutal killing was widespread, inferences were made about the men who came home from the war: Veterans were unable to adjust or, if they had any conscience at all, were completely broken in spirit over the terrible deeds they had done. "We have nothing against the soldiers, but the war is just so immoral it is turning them into animals," was a common protester's plaint.

Many of the assumptions were not only far-fetched, they also were deliberate lies spread by political foes of the war, calculated to turn American public opinion against our intervention. As early as 1965, families of soldiers killed in Vietnam were subjected to organized telephone harassment campaigns accusing the men of committing evil in Vietnam. "Your husband got what he deserved," one caller told the widow of Capt. Christopher O'Sullivan. "I am glad. It serves him right."[134]

111

For twenty years, Ho Chi Minh's followers had used unspeakable brutalities to terrify and subdue the people of South Vietnam. One early victim of the Viet Cong was Swiss freelance cameraman Pieter Van Thirl, who was stabbed, tortured, and had his eyes cut from their sockets after his capture in May 1965. Jack Wheeler, chairman of the Vietnam Veterans Memorial Fund, has said that seeing pictures of a pregnant South Vietnamese woman disemboweled by Communist soldiers to terrify villagers into submission was one of the things that convinced him the Vietnam War was worth fighting.[135]

But that reality was drowned out by the antiwar left in this country. Captured directives from North Vietnam in the Indochina Archive of the University of California show that two of the most powerful factions of the American antiwar movement, the People's Committee for Peace and Justice and the National Peace Action Committee, were working hand-in-hand with the North Vietnamese.[136] The propaganda campaign by the Communists—which started well before My Lai—encouraged their allies to portray the conflict as a "civil war," an indigenous rebellion independent of the government in Hanoi. And the corollary to this was that the U.S. "imperialists and their puppets," were "cruel, weak, cowardly, vicious, immoral, and corrupt," while the North Vietnamese and their adherents were "kindly, strong, brave, heroic, moral, and scrupulously honest."[137]

American antiwar activists complied. Writer Todd L. Newmark, who served in the Army Signal Corps from 1969 through 1970, has pointed out how the left portrayed the war in Vietnam as just the most recent manifestation of America's decadence. "Certain themes and slogans came into currency," wrote Newmark. "On the domestic front, America was a 'police state,' while in foreign policy we were 'policeman of the world.' We were committing 'atrocities' in Vietnam and acting like 'fascists' both here and abroad. We were a 'violent' people, a 'violent' society, except for idealistic youth. The administration 'lied,' 'deceived,' and continually 'escalated,' while the New Left quested only for truth and justice."[138]

However, Ho Chi Minh was painted as a "man of the people," a "nationalist," Newmark said. "It followed from this that he must be humane, peace-loving, and certainly not 'aggressive,' as we were. He was a 'patriot,' and a pretty decent, self-effacing fellow when you got right down to it. He wanted only to 'liberate' the South, free it from the 'neoimperialists,' and he hadn't the slightest interest in places like Cambodia or Laos. So why were we beating up on a little old man in sandals?"

America's allies, the South Vietnamese, were depicted as corrupt and evil, far worse than the Communist alternative. Antiwar authors such as Frances Fitzgerald, Susan Sontag, and Mary McCarthy praised the North

Vietnamese government, the same inhuman and oppressive regime that now rules with an iron fist. (Which brings up another important question: If the Vietnamese people were so mistreated by American soldiers, why was the United States the number-one destination of the thousands who fled when the Communists took over South Vietnam?)[139]

A classic example of twisting reality on its head was the so-called 1970 Winter Soldier Investigation, touted as "an inquiry into American war crimes."[140] The reporting of such trumped-up tribunals by the press indicated little willingness to examine very closely the stories and those who told them. War crimes by the North Vietnamese were virtually never discussed. When the Communists took over North Vietnam in 1954, they murdered fifty thousand, and hundreds of thousands died in forced labor camps.

In his 1982 book *Why We Were in Vietnam*, Norman Podhoretz, the editor of *Commentary Magazine*, defended America's involvement in Vietnam from those who labeled it an immoral war.

"The intervention was a product of the Wilsonian side of the American character—the side that went to war in 1917 to 'make the world safe for democracy' and that found its contemporary incarnation in the liberal internationalism of the 1940s and the liberal anticommunism of the 1950s," Podhoretz said. "One can characterize this impulse as naïve; one can describe it in terms that gave it a subtly self-interested flavor. But there is no rationally defensible way in which it can be called immoral."[141]

The efforts to portray American troops in Vietnam as war criminals also displayed an incredible ignorance of the realities of war. The soldiers who fought in Vietnam were contrasted with those who fought in World War II; alleged "baby killers" versus benevolent GIs handing out candy bars to children. In "the good war," American troops were tough but righteous warriors, killing Nazis and fascists in combat. In Vietnam, American troops were confused, dispirited drug addicts lashing out at anything that moved, usually killing civilians in the process.

One antiwar pamphlet distributed in 1967 portrayed an American soldier with a gun standing next to a South Vietnamese woman, her hands clasped as if asking for mercy. "At a cost of 59.9 percent of our total national budget, the U.S. fighting man is the best equipped soldier of all time. For what? For this? To make war on women and children?"[142]

Of course that's not what the picture shows. It depicts a soldier standing next to a woman. But that single image—men forced to kill women and children—has become attached to Vietnam veterans in such a tenacious way that even today, the assumption that all American combat soldiers in Vietnam were variations of William Calley and his men at My Lai permeates the way they are treated in the press, in movies, in books, and even the VA health care system. In the movie *Born on the Fourth of July*, paralyzed Vietnam veteran-turned-antiwar activist Ron Kovic and a fellow paralyzed veteran argue about killing babies.

Far more representative of Vietnam soldiers were men like Lt. Thomas Gray Jr. A platoon leader and operations supply officer of the 1st Infantry Division's Supply and Transport Battalion, Gray set up an orphanage during his off-duty hours. He persuaded folks in his home state of Maine to put together a support network to assist the effort. But Gray wanted to earn a Combat Infantryman Badge before he left the war and persuaded his division commander to transfer him to an infantry battalion. Gray died in a Viet Cong mortar barrage shortly after arriving at his new assignment. There were many more like him. The Green Berets alone during their decade in Vietnam dug 6,436 wells, repaired 1,210 miles of road, and built 508 hospitals and dispensaries.[143]

This is not to say that atrocities committed by Americans did not happen. However, the unfortunate reality is that what happened at My Lai *was not* unprecedented in the annals of American warfare. But a tightly controlled U.S. government propaganda machine and the willingness of the American press to censor itself created an image in World War I and World War II that such things never happened. Author Paul Fussell has written about the legendary cynicism and verbal subversion of soldiers in World War II, which led to the creation of such terms as SNAFU (Situation Normal, All Fucked Up).

"It was not just the danger and fear, the boredom and uncertainty, and the loneliness and deprivation," Fussell said. "It was the conviction that optimistic publicity and euphemism had rendered their experience so falsely that it would never be readily communicable. They knew that in its representation to the laity, what was happening to them was systematically sanitized and Norman Rockwellized, not to mention Disneyfied."[144]

Those same "tricks of publicity and advertising" might have succeeded in changing the American public's view of the war in Vietnam, Fussell suggested, if not for television and the presence of an uncensored press—and the absence of an easily identifiable enemy. "Because the Second World War was fought against palpable evil, and thus was a sort of moral triumph, we have been reluctant to probe very deeply into its murderous requirements," Fussell said.

Even antiwar activist Daniel Ellsberg, who served in the war zone, has written that Vietnam was "no more brutal than other wars in the past." But the idea that brutality characterized most Vietnam troops created a corollary—that their savagery inevitably armed internal timebombs that continued to tick for years afterward.

The Tragedy of My Lai

On March 16, 1968, 1st Lt. William Calley and his platoon—1st Platoon, C Company, 1st Battalion, 20th Infantry, Americal Division—were on a search-and-destroy operation in the Quang Ngai province when they ventured into My Lai, a hamlet of Son My Village. Some said later that they began to take sniper fire, but that is open to question. When it was over, hundreds of unarmed civilians—old men, women, and children—had been herded into a ditch and gunned down, murdered by Calley and members of his platoon.

How could something so egregious, so hideous have happened? Theories that the platoon had snapped under the pressure of heavy combat were refuted. Charlie Company had been in Vietnam only three months. Although the company had experienced little direct contact with the enemy, it had suffered casualties from mines and booby traps, which tended to enhance anxiety and frustration.

Since then, millions of words have been written about what happened at My Lai. But when the North Vietnamese captured the city of Hue six weeks earlier during the Tet Offensive and held the area for five weeks, they cold-bloodedly executed thirty-five hundred to five thousand South Vietnamese—schoolteachers, civic leaders, doctors, and other "enemies of the people." That was merely a story in passing in the American press, not the feeding frenzy that was triggered by My Lai. Although fewer people died at My Lai, the difference was that the enemy perpetrated the crimes in Hue.

The military hierarchy of the Americal Division hushed up what occurred at My Lai. The carnage became an object of investigation only when a soldier heard about it through the grapevine. He found out that not only was it true but also that a substantial number of photos of the slaughter had been taken that day. He pushed a congressman into taking action. The resulting U.S. Army investigation became the Peers Report. The story hit the national consciousness on December 5, 1969, when *Life* magazine published a story and photographs about the slaughter at My Lai.[145]

Many people who had served in Vietnam were not surprised to hear that a company in the Americal Division was involved in the atrocity. Among all the major units in Vietnam, it had the reputation of being the most disorganized, with some companies populated by less-than-sterling soldiers. Charlie Company was not the typical cross-section of "All-American youths," as later portrayed. It was a catastrophe waiting to happen.

The Creation of Charlie Company

Formed originally on the battlefield during World War II, the Americal Division fought gallantly in the Pacific, primarily in the Philippines, and was deactivated in 1946. In keeping with Army practice, when the U.S. military needed another new division in Vietnam, they resurrected the name and tradition of a previously deactivated division.

What the military has never publicly conceded is how such a unit typically is created during the expediency of a war. Each of the major components of the Americal Division—the 196th, the 198th, and the 11th Infantry Brigades—was formed at different locations, but by the same method. Cadre were assigned, then existing units were ordered to provide a certain number of men to the new unit to fill the ranks. This method has several virtues: A commander who has worked hard to train his unit and create a superb fighting machine is not penalized for his hard work by losing his top men. But what occurs in reality is a great purging of misfits.

There are always ne'er-do-wells in the military. Some are actually sent there by judges, who give young criminals and juvenile delinquents a choice—jail or the military.[146] And when inducted, American soldiers bring their culture with them. The military—just like society—has its share of antisocial behavior, drug users, alcoholics, and racists. A man's entrance into the military doesn't suddenly cleanse him of his faults. Recruit training can shape an individual into a functioning member of the military but rarely purifies his soul.

The command structure believes that these "purged" men are given a new start. The new unit is sent into intensive training, the kind the military steadfastly believes can smooth the roughness off anyone and mold disparate men into a cohesive combat force.

Calley was one of those men who should never have been thrust into a position of leadership. Although he had flunked out of junior college and had a poor academic record, he was selected for Officer Candidate School and graduated without learning to read a map properly, according to William Wilson, the Army colonel assigned to investigate My Lai.[147]

Lack of proper training was pinpointed by the Peers Report as the ultimate antecedent of the My Lai incident. But nowhere does the report mention that the selection process itself may have been flawed. To do so would create culpability at the highest policy-making levels. But anyone who has witnessed one of these selection operations knows that it can create the potential for disaster.[148]

Even once the unit arrived in Vietnam, it suffered another command-induced disruption known as "infusion." Every man in the unit was scheduled to go home 365 days later, all on the same day. In order to stagger the return dates, so that all the experienced troops didn't leave at the same time, large groups were swapped with units already in Vietnam. For example, the Americal would send one hundred men to the 1st Infantry Division; the 1st Division in turn would send back one hundred men with staggered dates to return home. Once again, commanders got to purge troublemakers and send them to the Americal. But even more devastating to the unit morale, the cohesion and bonding created during training was shattered.

Although later portrayed as the kids next door, many in the Americal Division were not the equivalent of men in other units in Vietnam, and the Army knew it. (The last witness at the Calley trial, Col. Oran Henderson, testified that the brigade commander asked for a sixty-day extension to train his troops before they shipped out to Vietnam. He believed they were not ready for combat. The request was denied.)

In a 1971 court-martial, Calley was convicted of killing twenty-two unarmed civilians and a variety of other offenses; he was sentenced to hard labor for life. His sentence was later reduced to ten years, making him immediately eligible for parole. After serving only three years under house arrest, Calley was released in 1974 and now works in a jewelry shop in Georgia. (Twenty-eight officers, including two generals, were accused of serious offenses related to My Lai—from giving false testimony to failure to report war crimes. None was convicted.)

I don't know any Vietnam veteran who condoned or excused what Calley and his platoon did. They sullied the reputation of every single one of us. Calley should have been tried for murder, found guilty, and executed, with disciplinary action proceeding up the chain of command to every officer and man who had a part. Calley was not a scapegoat, a victim of U.S. military policy. He was a criminal.

"None of us had any tolerance for what Calley did," says Marine Col. Hays Parks, an infantry officer and military prosecutor who tried Marines for murder while in Vietnam and now works with the Pentagon's International Law Branch. Calley "did not deserve to be in the military, let alone command men. Had there been any strength of leadership—either at the company, battalion, or brigade level—My Lai wouldn't have happened."[149] Parks concurs with the Peers Report that My Lai was the result of a command breakdown.

The reality is that thousands of soldiers in Vietnam experienced heavy combat and conditions far worse than Charlie Company faced and did not commit atrocities. David Halberstam, the Pulitzer Prize-winning journalist who covered the war for *The New York Times*, has said that, "For every Calley, there were [large numbers of] young American officers who were brave and selfless and treated their men and the enemy with respect."[150]

Even war correspondent Peter Arnett has said that in all the units he accompanied, he never saw anyone kill a civilian or assault a child. "They didn't even think of it," Arnett has said. "Every unit I was with, [the GIs] went out of their way to be kind and decent with the people."[151]

Although a fierce critic of the war, CBS News correspondent Morley

Safer, in his book *Flashbacks*, praised the average American GI: "My mind drifts to a dozen acts of supreme courage that I had witnessed in Vietnam, of tenderness shown by fearsome-looking men to village children whose older brothers had planted mines and booby traps. I remember one black sergeant, an enormous man, who had himself been raised in the most appalling conditions in Chicago, dancing across a dike during a mortar attack and pulling two children to safety."[152]

One person often left out of the My Lai discussion is Hugh Thompson Jr. On March 16, 1968, Thompson, a twenty-five-year-old recon helicopter pilot, flew his chopper over My Lai as Charlie Company rampaged through the village. When Thompson grasped what was happening he landed, and with his crew chief and doorgunner, rescued eleven Vietnamese civilians, including a tiny baby—showing incredible moral courage by putting himself between his fellow soldiers and their targets.[153]

Thompson also rejected the theory that atrocities were a daily occurrence. "People say [My Lai-type incidents] happened all the time in Vietnam," Thompson said. "I don't believe it." And then there was Ron Ridenhour, who reported the massacre after hearing about My Lai from one of his buddies—hardly the act of a man who routinely had witnessed atrocities.[154]

It was a travesty of justice that no one paid a heavy price for what occurred at My Lai. On the other hand, what army in the history of the world, in the middle of a war, has publicly examined the actions of one of its officers, generating massive propaganda material for its enemies? After the war, the North Vietnamese Communists told their American counterparts that they were amazed—and impressed—with the fact that the United States tried Calley while the war was still going on. However, once the My Lai episode became known, the antiwar movement seized on the massacre as the universal experience of Vietnam soldiers. The press picked up the theme.

Wilson, the Army's investigator, was deeply disturbed by the horrific events at My Lai. He rarely talked to anyone about his work on the case. "I do remember being startled when the public seemed to make a hero out of Rusty Calley, or at the least a victim," Wilson has written. "It sure didn't look that way from up close."

Pictures Worth a Thousand Words

Much of what people think they know about the Vietnam War can be summed up in a few photographs.

A famous photo of a naked little South Vietnamese girl named Kim Phuc fleeing down Highway One in terror after her clothes had been burned from her body in a napalm attack became the perfect illustration of

America's "indiscriminate" napalming of civilians. It was used by media around the world as an example of an American atrocity. Walter Cronkite used the photo, by Nick Ut of the Associated Press, as a dominant image in the introduction to his video history series on the Vietnam War.

A picture may be worth a thousand words, but it also can distort reality. There were no American planes involved, and there were no American ground troops at the scene. It happened in June 1972, when Communist troops broke through Route 1 and occupied the marketplace in Trang Bang, and a South Vietnamese Skyraider dropped napalm on orders of a South Vietnamese officer. (This happened when almost all American combat units had been withdrawn.)

After the fall of South Vietnam, the Communists tried to use Kim Phuc and her injuries as propaganda against the Americans. But she rebelled, fleeing to the West. She now lives in Toronto.

Another famous image that became an example of Americans supporting a brutal, corrupt regime—also used in the Cronkite series—was the point-blank execution of a man in civilian clothes by the Saigon police chief, Brig. Gen. Nguyen Ngoc Loan. Photographer Eddie Adams of the Associated Press won a Pulitzer Prize for the photograph, which captured the man's hideous grimace at the instant the bullet pierced his brain.

The shooting occurred during the 1968 Tet Offensive. Thousands of Viet Cong cadre in civilian clothes had infiltrated the city of Saigon and the surrounding area. A Viet Cong lieutenant had executed a South Vietnamese police major and his entire family. When he was captured by Loan's military troops, who policed Saigon, Loan used the VC's own gun to kill him. The shocking image drew condemnation of Loan and America from around the world. *Look what the leaders of the American allies in South Vietnam do for fun.*

Adams later expressed regret that his photograph had been used to discredit both General Loan and America's participation in the Vietnam War. The city was under martial law. Loan, as the head of the Saigon police, was within his authority to order the execution of an enemy soldier in civilian clothes who had murdered a family.[155] But Americans were not used to seeing the realities of war. In World War II, the press had a policy of usually not showing a dead body, let alone someone in the act of killing another human being. And certainly not an execution.

But similar executions have occurred in other American wars. During the Battle of the Bulge, a special hand-picked unit of English-speaking German soldiers was outfitted in American uniforms and inserted into the midst of American units still reeling from the ferocity of the German attack. The German mission was to sow confusion and disorganization, changing road signs and giving improper instructions to American columns of vehicles. They partially achieved their objective; the Americans did not know whom to trust. Ultimately almost all of the German saboteurs were captured or killed. General Eisenhower almost immediately issued orders to have the dozen or so prisoners executed without the benefit of a trial. On Christmas Eve, the Germans were blindfolded, trussed up to poles, and shot by firing squads.

General Eisenhower was completely within his authority to order the executions. So was General Loan. The difference in the two situations was the treatment by the press and the fact that Loan did not order someone else to perform the execution.

Sound Bites

Distortions built an image that dripped on the American psyche daily. In his book *Hazardous Duty*, Maj. Gen. John Singlaub described one such "drip" created by an American reporter in Saigon. The reporter's news magazine ran a story on ARVN officers more concerned with procuring prostitutes for GIs than in fighting the Communists—a charge that had come directly from Viet Cong propaganda leaflets. "That evening, Bill [Donnett, Singlaub's senior embassy advisor], encountered the reporter who wrote the article on the terrace of the Caravel Hotel," Singlaub wrote. "Bill lit into him over the piece. The reporter, an honest old-school newspaperman, was chagrined. 'I filed my story citing that as VC propaganda,' he complained. 'But my editors rewrote it the way they wanted.'"[156]

Most of the journalists lived in Saigon. Some, like Peter Arnett, even had families there. Arnett made a reputation as a war correspondent in Vietnam. But two of his reports have become part of the war's most enduring myths. He reported that the U.S. Embassy had been taken by the enemy during the Tet Offensive, a story that was picked up by others and continued to circulate for days despite official Army denial. In reality, none of the attackers made it into the embassy building.[157]

And another famous phrase came from a story Arnett did on the Battle of Ben Tre during the Tet Offensive. He quoted an unidentified American major as saying, "We had to destroy the town to save it." The implication was that the Americans had battered Ben Tre indiscriminately, killing civilians in the process of killing the enemy. The phrase caused an uproar. The antiwar movement seized on the quote, saying it proved what they had been contending all along, that Americans were systematically destroying the land and people of Vietnam with little regard for human life. Here the horror was being attested to by a military participant in that destruction.[158]

Ben Tre was a provincial capital in the Mekong Delta with a population of about fifty thousand people, not a village. Only a handful of American advisors lived in a small compound in the city at the time of the Tet

Offensive. Curious about the accuracy of the story, I tracked down the senior officer who commanded the group of advisors, Army Maj. Phil Cannella, who now lives in Illinois.

Cannella remembered being interviewed by Arnett, who he thought was a good reporter, after the attack. But he confirmed that Arnett misrepresented what happened at Ben Tre. Arnett attributed the destruction to the Americans; however Cannella said most of the devastation was created by the enemy trying to dislodge the small band of Americans.[159]

Cannella and his men had only small arms to defend themselves. When the Viet Cong overran outlying South Vietnamese units around Ben Tre, they captured large quantities of arms and ammunition, including many 105 howitzers. The VC promptly used the howitzers to lay siege to Cannella's small compound from across the river, systematically blasting away with flat trajectories toward Cannella's position—demolishing buildings and killing civilians in the areas near the compound. For fifty hours, Cannella and his men held out, unable to get any supporting American artillery or air strikes to counter the enemy's attack. Artillery and aircraft resources during Tet were stretched to the breaking point, and Cannella's small unit was low on the priority list.

Eventually, the Navy sent gunboats down the river to attack the enemy troops firing at Cannella and his men. Finally, tanks and troops of the 9th Infantry managed to break through to Ben Tre. After the airstrip was secured, Arnett flew into Ben Tre on military transport and interviewed Cannella and Air Force Maj. Chester L. Brown about what had taken place. Cannella remembers telling Arnett that in defending the town it was a shame that some of it was destroyed, but the quote was later attributed to Maj. Chester L. Brown.

Although Cannella made clear that the destruction was almost completely wreaked by the Viet Cong, not the Americans, Arnett's story gave the opposite impression, stating that in the first few hours of the battle, American artillery and bombs rained down on Ben Tre. Arnett has steadfastly defended the secrecy of his source by claiming that Military Assistance Command Vietnam (MACV) started an investigation to identify the loose-lipped major, as if there was some type of military witchhunt to shut down dissenters. Cannella assured me there was no such investigation; in fact, he had never been asked about the news story by anybody except me. As senior officer, if any investigation had occurred, Cannella would have been the first one questioned.

But the phrase, "We had to destroy the village to save it" took on a life of its own. As late as 1995, antiwar activist and "professional" Vietnam veteran Bobby Muller told *People* magazine, "Destroying a village to save it from communism doesn't make much sense."[160]

The way the two wars were reported still affects how the American public views the men who fought in Vietnam.

Here's a quote: "What kind of war do civilians suppose we fought anyway? We shot prisoners in cold blood, wiped out hospitals, strafed lifeboats, killed or mistreated enemy civilians, finished off enemy wounded, tossed the dying into a hole with the dead, and boiled the flesh off enemy skulls to make table ornaments for sweethearts or carved their bones into letter openers." The paragraph sounds like something written about Vietnam. But these words were published in the February 1946 edition of the *Atlantic*, written by war correspondent Edward L. Jones about World War II.

War Crimes

The only American ever convicted specifically of the charge of "war crimes" was Cpt. Henry Wirz, a Confederate soldier and medical doctor in charge of Andersonville Prison in Georgia during the Civil War. Conditions were so bad, 12,912 men died there.[161] Although widely considered a scapegoat, Wirz was convicted of conspiracy to kill in violation of the laws and customs of war, and murder in violation of the laws and customs of the war. His trial set a legal precedent invoked eighty years later for the Nuremberg Trials after World War II, when Germans were tried for war crimes.[162] (The Nuremberg tribunal was given jurisdiction over the crimes of the vanquished but not the victors.)

"War crimes" and "atrocities" can include looting; taking grisly souvenirs, such as body parts of dead soldiers; the torture and killing of POWs; and wanton rape and murder of noncombatants. All are against the rules of war laid down by the Geneva conventions. But who gets charged with which war crimes usually depends on who wins and who loses.

For years after returning from Europe, World War II veterans freely admitted they stole nearly everything that was not nailed down, and even fifty years later, pieces of stolen art are still surfacing at a remarkable rate. In the late eighties, a valuable collection of manuscripts, crucifixes, and ancient coins called The Quedlinburg Treasury surfaced in Texas. Hidden in a mine shaft south of Berlin, these priceless artifacts had been stolen by Army Lt. Joe T. Meador, who brought them to his home in Whitewright. After Meador died in 1980, the Lutheran Church of Quedlinburg had to sue his heirs for the return of their precious religious relics.[163]

Even before My Lai, the murder and brutalization of noncombatants was a charge often raised in Vietnam. The NVA and VC shielded their forces by placing them in civilian villages. They fired on American soldiers from pagodas and populated areas, knowing that any return fire alienated the villagers and provided propaganda against the Americans. The antiwar movement not only condemned the troops for the deaths of civilians caught in the cross fire but also claimed that the murder of noncombatants was the official policy of the American military.

Hanson W. Baldwin, retired military writer for *The New York Times*, took antiwar activists to task in May 1971 for their inflation of civilian combat deaths in Vietnam. Sen. Edward M. Kennedy's Senate Subcommittee on Refugees had issued an estimate that up to 1.1 million South Vietnamese civilians had been killed or wounded in the war between 1965 and 1971. Baldwin pointed out that these were extrapolations based on extrapolations; actual statistics of civilian deaths in Vietnam were far lower. From October 1967, when reasonably valid information was first available, through 1970, about twenty thousand had been killed and another forty-eight thousand to fifty thousand wounded. And most of those deaths were attributable to the Viet Cong and North Vietnamese.[164]

Although the antiwar movement insisted that the country's population had been decimated by the war, in truth, by 1971 the population of South Vietnam had increased by about two million over 1965. The population of North Vietnam had also grown by hundreds of thousands. "The extreme critics of the government have lost their cool to such a degree that the Big Lie has become a part of our daily fare," Baldwin wrote. "The attempts to denigrate, to tear down, have one universal quality—to 'poor-mouth' the United States, to attribute to our government, our military command, and our fighting men a rapacity, cruelness, and ruthlessness that is a gross caricature of their true image."

Although critics contended that U.S. policy condoned killing of non-combatants, the American armed forces never had authorization to harm civilians. To prevent the indiscriminate use of force, MACV issued directives establishing rules of engagement. Capt. Eugene M. Kotouc, the task force intelligence officer, told the jury hearing the My Lai case that he ordered his officers to respect the lives of South Vietnamese civilians.

Clearly, telling Calley and his crew was not enough to prevent a tragedy. But as Guenter Lewy in *America in Vietnam* and others have pointed out, no evidence substantiates the charge that My Lai was typical. "Nor is it likely, given the number of antiwar journalists reporting on Vietnam, that if other such atrocities had occurred, they could have been kept secret," said Norman Podhoretz. The proportion of civilians among overall casualties in Vietnam was about 45 percent, about the same as it was in World War II and much lower than it was during the Korean conflict, when it was estimated at 70 percent.[165]

In *Vietnam*, a history magazine about the war, writer A. Francis Hatch examined the portrayal of American soldiers as "bloodthirsty barbarians." He quoted Nuremberg prosecutor Telford Taylor: "It has been said that the 'massacre at Son My [My Lai] was not unique,' but I am unaware of any evidence of other incidents of comparable magnitude, and the reported reaction of some of the soldiers at Son My strongly suggests that they regarded it as out of the ordinary."[166]

Antiwar protester Daniel Ellsberg agreed. "My Lai was beyond the bounds of permissible behavior, and that is recognized by virtually every soldier in Vietnam. The men who were at My Lai knew there were aspects out of the ordinary." Otherwise, why try to hide what happened?[167]

The response of soldiers to an event that occurred in the Central Highlands in 1966, which later was reported in the book *Casualties of War*, by Daniel Lang, illustrates that most American soldiers did not tolerate the criminals who took advantage of the war to commit egregious offenses.[168] (The book was the basis for the 1989 Brian De Palma movie of the same name.)

A sergeant named Meserve announced to his buddies that they were going to kidnap a South Vietnamese woman to take along for a little "R&R" on a five-man reconnaissance patrol. Only one other man expressed interest in this crime, but the woman was abducted. Meserve and three other members of the patrol raped her. But despite taunts and threats of death from the other men, one soldier named Sven Eriksson refused to assault the woman. Meserve and the other men later killed her.

If raping and murdering unarmed peasants were daily occurrences in Vietnam, then Eriksson would have looked the other way. But he reported the crime. Eventually all four men were court-martialed and convicted of rape and/or premeditated murder.[169]

De Palma's movie changed the story to indicate that the incident was precipitated after a fellow soldier died as a result of a deadly trap set by a South Vietnamese villager previously thought friendly to Americans. Supposedly this makes what happened later easier to understand. But that's dishonest. What Meserve and his cronies did was premeditated rape and murder, not a metaphor for the Vietnam War, despite De Palma's attempt to portray it that way.

While not trying to excuse crimes against civilians in Vietnam, they must be compared to what has happened in other wars. The movie *Breaker Morant* was based on the true story of an Australian soldier executed for murdering civilians in the Boer War in South Africa.

Stephen Ambrose, a World War II historian and biographer of Presidents Eisenhower and Nixon, has said that incidents such as My Lai are "a universal" in war. "I don't think that [My Lai] was an exception or an aberration," Ambrose said at a scholarly conference held in New Orleans on the twenty-fifth anniversary of My Lai. But that said, Ambrose added, "hundreds and hundreds of other platoon leaders in Vietnam were just as provoked, and they never lost control."[170]

American War Crimes and World War II

It's a common misconception that Pvt. Eddie Slovik was the only American soldier executed during World War II. But according to documents in the National Archives, in the European theater alone, the U.S. Army condemned 443 of its own soldiers to death for war zone capital offenses, mostly rape and murder of civilians. Of those soldiers condemned, at least ninety-six were executed from December 7, 1941, to June 1946. Most are buried outside the wall of a U.S. military cemetery in France. Military authorities refused to give these criminals the privilege of being buried with those killed in combat.[171]

That number does not include Army Air Corps troops, the Navy, or any troops in the Pacific. The total number of American servicemen executed in all theaters was approximately three hundred.

Most death penalty cases involved the rape or murder of women—mostly German, but also women in Allied countries. Two typical cases, chosen at random from National Archive files on executions of American GIs in the European theater, involve the rape of noncombatant civilians. (In Vietnam, the equivalent would have been the rape of a South Vietnamese woman.)

Four soldiers, members of a unit that made one of the initial landings in the American invasion of Sicily on July, 9, 1943, wandered into the small village of Marretta, near Gela, Sicily, one afternoon about a week after the invasion. The four men gang-raped an Italian woman. Later apprehended by MPs and identified, their punishment was swift and sure. All four American GIs—David White, Armstead White, Harvey L. Stroud, and Willie A. Pitman—were tried and convicted of rape within days of the attack. A little more than a month later, the four privates were executed by hanging.[172]

A few months after the invasion of Normandy and the fall of the German-occupied French port of Cherbourg to the Americans, Pvt. William P. Pennyfeather and two companions, assigned to the 3868th Quartermaster Truck Company, went looking for a whorehouse on the afternoon of August 1, 1944. None of the Cherbourg sporting establishments was open for business.

Pennyfeather had a shave and a haircut, then spent most of the early evening drinking cognac, going from cafe to cafe with his companions until the establishments all had shut their doors for the night. Shortly after midnight, they heard sounds of laughter coming from a rooming house at 1 Rue

Emmanuel Liais and muscled their way in, claiming they were looking for "Boche" (Germans). Pennyfeather sexually assaulted a French woman. Tried and convicted of rape on September 2, 1944, Pennyfeather was hanged at Fort Du Roule, France on November 18, 1944, along with another soldier who had been convicted of an assault on a French woman in Octeville.[173]

Bombs Away

The goal of the so-called International War Crimes Tribunal, convened by Bertrand Russell in 1968, was to "expose barbarous crimes reported daily out of Vietnam." America was committing "genocide" of the Vietnamese people, Russell claimed, particularly through air operations that dropped more bombs on North Vietnam than all those dropped by the United States during World War II.[174]

That was true in terms of tonnage, but according to the *Vietnam War Almanac*, most bombs used in Vietnam were dropped on uninhabited areas along the Ho Chi Minh Trail in an attempt to block enemy infiltration. The North Vietnamese later admitted that nonmilitary targets were never specifically targeted.

In 1971, Sen. George McGovern called American bombings in Vietnam unprecedented "since Hitler's Germany." A year later, antiwar activists condemned what they called the "Christmas bombing" of Hanoi in December 1972. McGovern, who had himself been a World War II bomber pilot, again weighed in, calling it "the most murderous aerial bombardment in the history of the world." Sen. Harold Hughes compared the raid to the bombing of Hiroshima and Nagasaki.[175]

But the bombing was none of those things. Called Operation Linebacker II by the military, it did not happen on Christmas, and Hanoi's figures showed that the official death toll was 1,318 even though U.S. antiwar activists urged them to claim ten thousand killed. (The North Vietnamese had killed more civilians days earlier in an artillery barrage of the town of An Loc.) In addition, some of those killed in Hanoi may well have been victims of friendly-fire; the North Vietnamese threw millions of rounds of ammunition and missiles into the air, all of which had to come crashing back to earth.[176]

During World War II, the Allies deliberately targeted dams, intending to deny the enemy their electrical power and water supplies. The British RAF Bomber Command formed a squadron of specially modified Lancaster bombers for the purpose of destroying dams in Germany. On May 16, 1943, the nineteen RAF aircraft took off from Scampton, England, for their goal —three dams near the Ruhr industrial areas. Flying at night, at a precise speed and at an extremely low level, the aircraft dropped bombs designed to sink to the most effective depth before exploding. Wing Cmdr. Guy

Gibson, who led the raid, was awarded the Victoria Cross for his role in the effort. The operation later inspired a film called *The Dam Busters*.[177] Compare that to Vietnam, when crews of Phantom bombers were sent to bomb a hydroelectric plant in North Vietnam. They were ordered not to hit a nearby dam. Flying straight and level allowed them to drop their bombs more accurately, but that strategy also made them an easier target for antiaircraft weapons.

Worse, in World War II, the Allies targeted cities that had absolutely no military importance. On one night alone—February 13, 1945—two thousand night bombers hit the German city of Dresden, congested with some six hundred thousand refugees. Up to 135,000—mostly women and children —were wiped out in the bombing or burned to death in the subsequent fires. Not a single Allied plane was lost; the city had no antiaircraft guns.[178]

In early 1945, the U.S. military began a systematic bombing campaign of Japan against primarily civilian targets in an effort to end the war. "They'd run sixteen thousand pounds of napalm per plane," retired Air Force Maj. Gen. Chuck Sweeney said in 1995. "Hundreds of planes a night, for months on end."[179]

On the night of March 9, 1945, American aircraft bombarded Tokyo with napalm for three hours. The resulting firestorm was so intense water in the rivers reached the boiling point. The attack killed about eighty-four thousand civilians and injured another forty-one thousand. About sixteen square miles of the city were reduced to ashes. Christopher Lew, writing in *World War II* magazine, called the barrage the greatest urban disaster, man-made or natural, in all history. That was not the end of it. The Americans continued to attack Japanese cities, and in the next ten days destroyed thirty-two square miles of urban landscape. Ultimately, bomb runs reduced Tokyo, Osaka, and Nagoya to rubble and killed tens of thousands of civilians.[180]

And, of course, there were the atomic bombs dropped on Hiroshima and Nagasaki, which killed outright more than one hundred thousand civilians, with thousands more dying of radiation sickness in the years after the war ended. The crews of the bombers were not proclaimed war criminals. After Col. Paul Tibbets landed the *Enola Gay*, Gen. Carl "Tooey" Spatz, commander of all Air Forces in the Pacific, pinned the Distinguished Service Cross on the chest of Tibbets' flight suit.[181]

Grisly Souvenirs

In Vietnam, there was talk of grunts lopping the ears off the bodies of dead Viet Cong to keep track of "kills"—vivid proof of American soldiers' barbarity, and to listen to the antiwar activists, unique to Vietnam. On October 13, 1967, General Westmoreland issued a directive expressly prohibiting the practice of cutting ears off enemy soldiers. In August 1971, Army CID announced its policy to seize any severed body parts that troops attempted to bring home.

But that was not the first time the American military had to address the issue. That occurred twenty-five years earlier in September 1942, when a directive from the commander-in-chief of the U.S. fleet in the Pacific prohibited the taking of body parts as war souvenirs. Customs agents during World War II routinely asked if travelers entering the U.S. were bringing in items such as bones. In April 1943, the *Baltimore Sun* ran a story about a woman who asked American officials to allow her son, a soldier in the Pacific, to send her an ear he had severed from the head of a Japanese soldier.[182]

One World War II American sniper company, raising "souvenir-taking" to psychological warfare, was known for scalping their German victims.[183] Such things weren't limited to the European theater. In a memoir called *With the Old Breed*, World War II veteran E.B. Sledge describes two bitter Pacific campaigns, that of Peleliu and Okinawa. He told of a Marine using his Kabar knife to wrench the gold teeth from a helplessly wounded Japanese. "Because the Japanese was kicking his feet and thrashing about, the knifepoint glanced off the tooth and sank into the victim's mouth," Sledge wrote. "The Marine cursed and cut his cheeks open from ear to ear."[184] Such an atrocity would have gotten you crucified in Vietnam.

A number of books about Vietnam tell of mistreatment of prisoners by American troops as if this was routine behavior. Mistreatment of POWs happened in Vietnam, as it certainly does in all wars. The brutality of war makes it difficult for combatants to turn off their anger and aggression even though enemy soldiers have been stripped of their weapons.

In a World War II novel called *Winds of War*, author Herman Wouk told the story of an American submarine commander who sinks a Japanese ship, then has the survivors machine-gunned. Most Americans took this as a piece of fiction in which Wouk was taking literary license. We all know Americans didn't do such things.[185]

But several such incidents actually happened. After a Japanese convoy was sunk in the Bismarck Sea in 1943, American and Australian aircraft strafed the survivors in lifeboats or clinging to wreckage.[186]

Lt. Cmdr. "Mush" Morton, one of the icons of the Submarine Corps, was an old, experienced hand by the time of Pearl Harbor. In January 1943, Morton was the commander of the USS *Wahoo* when the vessel single-handedly sank a four-ship Japanese convoy. One of the first two ships that went down was a troop transport; the others were supply ships. Such vessels often carried civilian laborers and captured prisoners. When the ships went down, troops and passengers ended up in the water, frantically swimming in search of life rafts and anything else that would float. "There must be ten thousand of them," one of Morton's officers said.

Morton gave orders, and crewmen with small arms and the deck guns of the *Wahoo* proceeded for over an hour to shoot at the life rafts and people struggling in the water. Under the circumstances, sailors could not distinguish a soldier from a civilian, a woman or child from a soldier, or even a Japanese from a Korean slave laborer. Hundreds of people died indiscriminately in the hail of gunfire from the *Wahoo*.[187]

For this infamous action, instead of facing a war crime tribunal, Morton won wild acclaim from military authorities. The *Wahoo* incident merits only oblique mention in most books about Morton. Had Morton been German, I have no doubt that at the end of the war the Navy commander would have been tried as a war criminal. If the commander of a Navy ship had done the same thing during the Vietnam War, he would have been charged with genocide, and director Oliver Stone would have made a movie called *The Wahoo Incident*. But the battlecry in the Pacific was, "Kill Japs!" and Morton was duly awarded the Navy Cross as well as the Army's Distinguished Service Cross.

An investigation ordered by Eisenhower into mistreatment of POWs in the European Theater indicated a number of violations of the Geneva Convention by American troops. Problems with strong-arming POWs during interrogation and pilfering their personal property were so prevalent in the 9th Infantry Division that orders prohibiting such behavior were issued on four separate occasions.[188]

What came to be known as the Webling incident occurred on April 29, 1945. A platoon of Americans with the 222nd Infantry Regiment, 42nd Infantry Division, entered a small farm hamlet inside Germany a few miles north of the concentration camp of Dachau. The American soldiers took forty-three German troopers prisoner and shot them to death.[189]

After the liberation of Dachau, 122 German soldiers surrendered to the Americans. A few members of an American squad delegated to guard duty began cursing at the German POWs until all the Americans were chanting, "Kill 'em, kill 'em!" Enraged, a GI named "Smitty" grabbed his machine gun and let off a long burst at the German prisoners who were standing unarmed with their hands over their heads. As bodies fell, Smitty continued to shoot.

"Stop that crazy bastard!" shouted Col. Robert Wiley, who charged into the scene. As Smitty let go with a final burst, Wiley kicked him in the head to push him away from the machine-gun. But Wiley was too late. All 122 POWs were dead. The incident was hushed up. Charges filed by the division commander against Smitty and the platoon were dropped. Nazi war criminals were being tried for crimes against humanity, and nobody wanted to mention American breaches of the rules of war.[190]

A final example to show that brutalization of enemy prisoners occurs in all armies: In Israel, the military enjoys a lofty status as "morally superior" to other armies. It lives by the slogan "purity of arms"—meaning they do not murder, rape, or plunder. To suggest that Israeli soldiers might be other than heroic borders on blasphemy. But in 1995, Israel's foreign ministry launched an investigation after a retired Israeli general claimed that during the 1956 Sinai campaign, he and other Israeli soldiers killed forty-nine Egyptian prisoners.

That revelation was followed by allegations that during the 1967 Middle East War, the Israeli army's elite Shaked infantry unit took three hundred Egyptian prisoners at El Arish in the Sinai and shot them. "In effect, in a matter of hours, the whole Egyptian force was liquidated," Israeli historian Arieh Titzhaki said on national radio. The unit was under the command of Lt. Col. Binyamin Ben Eliezer, who later became housing minister.[191]

The stories of Israeli atrocities provoked a national debate. Military historians contended that military censors covered up the atrocities, abetted by a willing public that venerated the military and its "purity of arms" tradition, stated succinctly by David Ben Gurion, an Israeli pioneer. The Jews, he said, were a "virtuous people" who needed a "virtuous army," and a virtuous army "preserves purity of arms."[192] Unfortunately, that tradition, even for the Israelis, is a myth.

The Tribunals

"As perfectly ignorant of Vietnam as the men who sent them there, [soldiers] found themselves monkey in the middle of a people's war so savage that babies were routinely used as trip plates for bombs and disemboweled cadavers swung from village signposts," wrote Paul Solotaroff in *Rolling Stone* magazine in a 1993 story about homeless Vietnam veterans.[193]

His piece later evolved into a 1995 book called *The House of Purple Hearts*. Solotaroff's inverted reasoning illustrates common attitudes of the left.

"One register of the savagery in which Vietnam vets were steeped is the degree of fear and loathing they inspired back home. At the airport in Oakland, California, people spat upon them and jeered, hurling rocks and plastic bags of chicken blood. That scrim of opprobrium seemed to lift somewhat ten years ago when the Vietnam Memorial was unveiled. America was reminded that these men were its sons and began seeing them as victims as well as demons."[194]

First criminals and demons, now victims. Solotaroff repeated this recurring theme, which has remained remarkably consistent since the early seventies. As its dominant tactic in their battle against the war, the antiwar movement successfully demonized Vietnam veterans by calling a series of "tribunals" or hearings into war crimes. But like Solotaroff's book, they were packed with pretenders and liars.

On January 31, 1971, an organization called Vietnam Veterans Against the War (VVAW) convened what came to be known as the Winter Soldier Investigation. Some of the major organizers included Jane Fonda, Dick Gregory, Phil Ochs, Graham Nash, David Crosby, and actor Donald Sutherland. For four days in a hotel in Detroit, "veteran" after veteran told grisly tales of horror—of using prisoners for target practice and throwing them out of helicopters, of cutting off the ears of dead VC, of burning villages and gang-raping women.

Lawyer and activist Mark Lane was one of the organizers of Winter Soldier. In 1970, Lane had published a book called *Conversations With Americans*, in which Vietnam veterans told their stories of committing atrocities and witnessing endless war crimes committed by their fellow soldiers.[195] Many of these tales were obviously absurd. As James Reston Jr. pointed out in a review of the book, Lane quoted one man's contention that a female Communist sympathizer was interrogated, tortured, and then raped by every soldier in his battalion. "Lane does not explain that in Vietnam an American battalion runs anywhere from one thousand to twelve hundred men," Reston said.[196]

Lane's book was blasted by writer and war correspondent Neil Sheehan in *The New York Times Book Review* as a hack job. Sheehan repeatedly showed that many of Lane's so-called "eye witnesses" to war crimes had never served in Vietnam or had not served in the capacity they claimed.[197]

Veteran Chuck Onan, for example, claimed he had attended parachute, frogman, and jungle survival schools and had received special training in torture techniques, such as stripping women prisoners, spreading their legs, and driving pointed sticks into their vaginas. "They told us we could rape the girls all we wanted," he said. Onan became a member of an LRRP (Long Range Recon Patrol) unit but deserted before he was sent to Vietnam, fleeing to Sweden so he did not have to kill. "They just went too far," Onan said.[198]

But Sheehan pointed out that, contrary to his fanciful claims, Onan's military record said he had attended Aviation Mechanical Fundamental school in Memphis, not frogman, parachute, and jungle survival school. Onan had not belonged to an Army LRRP unit; he worked as a stock room clerk at a Marine base in Beaufort, S.C. The torture school was also a product of his vivid imagination. The Marines did not give courses in tormenting prisoners. Onan deserted after receiving orders to go to Vietnam, where his lackluster record indicates that, even if he had gone, he would have been assigned to work as a mechanic or to a mundane administrative job.[199]

Another "Winter Soldier" named Michael Schneider testified that he had shot three peasants in cold blood, had been told by a sadistic lieutenant to attach wires from a field telephone to a man's testicles, and was ordered by his battalion commander to kill prisoners. After a year and a half as an infantry squad leader, then platoon leader with the 101st Airborne Division and the 196th Light Infantry Brigade, Schneider couldn't take the trauma of war any longer. Although he had been awarded the Bronze Star Medal, the Purple Heart, and the Silver Star, Schneider deserted and fled to Europe.

Schneider also told Lane a fascinating story about his family, claiming that his father replaced George Patton as the commander of the 11th Armored Cavalry Regiment in Vietnam. "He was a captain in World War II," Schneider said. "In the Nazi army."

Lane took this at face value. "Your father is a colonel in Vietnam?" he asked.

"Full colonel. Commanding officer in 11th Cavalry Regiment now," Schneider said, contending that his father changed his name after the war from Dieter von Kronenberger and switched loyalties to the American military.[200]

Lane's point was clear: *Nazis are running large American units in Vietnam. Vietnam soldiers are just like the Nazis.* But Sheehan pointed out that at the time there was no Colonel Schneider or Von Kronenberger in the U.S. Army, and no one by that name ever commanded the 11th Armored Cavalry Regiment. Schneider's stories about his father were bogus, as were those about his own service: Schneider deserted from Europe, not Vietnam. After surrendering to Army authorities in New York, he deserted again and was arrested on an Oklahoma murder charge. His last recorded residence: The maximum security ward of Eastern State Mental Hospital in Vinita, Oklahoma. Hardly a credible witness.[201]

Sheehan also shed some light on a story told in Lane's book by Terry Whitmore, a black Marine who had deserted to Sweden. Whitmore claimed that he took part in a planned atrocity—the extermination of an entire village of several hundred people, much like the My Lai massacre.[202]

Whitmore had been in Vietnam during the time that he claimed the war crimes took place. But his battalion was operating in an unpopulated area near the DMZ. And both his former battalion commander, still on active duty, and a former platoon leader in his company, who had left the military to work as a teaching assistant at a university, said that no such massacre took place. These two men told Sheehan of an earlier incident involving Whitmore's company. The company commander, a captain, and an enlisted man had been involved in an action in which four Vietnamese—

two women, a man, and a child—had been shot to death. The action happened at night in a hostile area. The two American soldiers were court-martialed on murder charges but acquitted. The company had been fired on; it had been impossible in the dark to distinguish friendlies from the enemy. Sheehan speculated that Whitmore had taken that story and inflated the numbers. Although a terrible incident, it was far from the planned massacre of hundreds of civilians.[203]

According to Sheehan, another man in Lane's book, Garry Gianninoto, who claimed that as a Navy medical corpsman he had witnessed numerous atrocities, had actually been assigned to an aid station at a battalion head-quarters, well out of the combat zone. He had been court-martialed for refusing orders to work in areas where he might have been shot. In the brig, he signed a statement admitting that he "had committed a homosexual act and had taken morphine," prompting the Navy to boot him out of Vietnam to a hospital for evaluation. (Otherwise, he would have had to finish his thirteen months in Vietnam when he was released from the brig.) He went AWOL in New York and was given an undesirable discharge.

When asked by Sheehan about the many lies and misrepresentations in his book, Lane admitted he did not check military records. "It's not relevant," Lane said.

"This kind of reasoning," Sheehan wrote, "amounts to a new McCarthyism, this time from the left. Any accusation, any innuendo, any rumor, is repeated and published as truth." An editor at Simon & Schuster, asked by Sheehan whether they compared the soldiers' tales to their military records, "equated the idea of searching the military records with taking a radical medical theory to the American Medical Association. 'They'd just say it was wrong,' he said." The editor admitted to Sheehan that the book was published as an antiwar protest.[204]

That same disrespect for the truth was in operation during the Winter Soldier hearings. After all the atrocities were dutifully taken down, the transcript was inserted into the *Congressional Record* by Sen. Mark O. Hatfield, who asked the commandant of the Marine Corps to investigate the many crimes, particularly those perpetrated by Marines.

"The results of this investigation, carried out by the Naval Investigative Service are interesting and revealing," said historian Guenter Lewy in his book *America in Vietnam*.[205] His history of the war was one of the first to rely on previously classified documents in the National Archives. "Many of the veterans, although assured that they would not be questioned about atrocities they might have committed personally, refused to be interviewed. One of the active members of the VVAW told investigators that the leadership had directed the entire membership not to cooperate with military authorities."

One black Marine who testified at Winter Soldier did agree to talk with the investigators. Although he had claimed during the hearings that Vietnam was "one huge atrocity" and a "racist plot," he could provide no details of any actual crimes. Lewy said the question of atrocities had not occurred to the Marine until he left Vietnam. His testimony had been substantially "assisted" by a member of the Nation of Islam.

"But the most damaging finding consisted of the sworn statements of several veterans, corroborated by witnesses, that they had in fact not attended the hearing in Detroit," Lewy wrote. "One of them had never been to Detroit in his life." Fake "witnesses" had appropriated the names of real Vietnam veterans.

Lewy pointed out that incidents similar to those described at the Winter Soldier hearings did occur. "Yet these incidents either (as in the destruction of hamlets) did not violate the law of war or took place in breach of existing regulations," Lewy wrote. Those responsible were tried and punished.

"In either case, they were not, as alleged, part of a 'criminal policy,'" Lewy said. Despite the antiwar movement's contention that military policies protecting civilians in Vietnam were routinely ignored, Lewy said the rules of engagement were implemented and taken very seriously, although at times the rules were not communicated properly and the training was inadequate. That's what made the failures so notable.

"The VVAW's use of fake witnesses and the failure to cooperate with military authorities and to provide crucial details of the incidents further cast serious doubt on the professed desire to serve the causes of justice and humanity," Lewy wrote. "It is more likely that this inquiry, like others earlier and later, had primarily political motives and goals."[206] (Although it has been thoroughly discredited, the Winter Soldier "investigation" is still being cited today as "proof" of American servicemen's barbarity. Writer Susan Brownmiller referenced it in *Newsweek* in a 1993 story on gang rape by soldiers.[207])

In April 1971, the VVAW staged a demonstration it called Dewey Canyon III, a "limited incursion into the country of Congress." The protest was named after an operation in 1969 that sent elements of the 3rd Marine Division into Laos. About this same time, an ad appeared in *The New York Times* signed by forty-nine American servicemen from the 1st Air Cavalry Division urging support for antiwar demonstrations. But as United Press International later reported, the men, members of a Mekong Delta-based helicopter unit, had neither read nor paid for the ad.[208]

Dewey Canyon III featured Vietnam veterans marching on Washington in a very dramatic, emotional way. Long-haired, scruffy, dressed in camouflage and the remnants of military garb, and draped in medals, they presented the image of men who had obviously been tested in battle and had seen the horrors of war, like bedraggled Southerners returning home from the battle of Gettysburg.

After being blocked from holding a ceremony honoring the war dead at Arlington National Cemetery, the veterans marched to the Capitol to present sixteen demands to Congress. At the end of the day, they held a candlelight march around the White House. After a man who said his son died in Vietnam blew taps, the soldiers began flinging their war medals over a high wire fence in front of the Capitol: Purple Hearts, Bronze Star Medals, Silver Stars—bits of ribbon and metal hurled in the face of the government that had so betrayed them. Some, after throwing away what had cost them so dearly, broke down and cried.

One of them was John Kerry, Vietnam Navy veteran and aspiring politician who had been among those who organized the protest. Kerry flung a handful of medals—he had received the Silver Star, a Bronze Star Medal, and three Purple Hearts—over the fence. Kerry spoke later that week before the Senate Foreign Relations Committee, putting a face on the antiwar movement far different from the one seen before—the scruffy hippie or wild-eyed activist. Kerry represented the All-American boy, mentally twisted by being asked to do terrible things, then abandoned by his government.

From start to finish, the public took Dewey Canyon III at face value, not understanding that they were watching brilliant political theater. Kerry, a Kennedy protégé with white-hot political aspirations, ascended center stage as both a war hero and as an antiwar hero throwing away his combat decorations. His speech, apparently off the cuff, was eloquent, impassioned.

But years later, after his election to the Senate, Kerry's medals turned up on the wall of his Capitol Hill office. When a reporter noticed them, Kerry admitted that the medals he had thrown that day were not his.[209] And Kerry's emotional, from-the-heart speech had been carefully crafted by a speechwriter for Robert Kennedy named Adam Walinsky, who also tutored him on how to present it. TV reporters totally ignored another Vietnam veteran, Melville L. Stephens, a former aide to Adm. Elmo Zumwalt, chief of Naval Operations, who that same day urged the Senate not to abandon America's allies in South Vietnam. "Peace for us must not come at the cost of their lives," Stephens said in a speech he wrote himself.

Kerry did not return from Vietnam a radical antiwar activist. Friends said that when Kerry first began talking about running for office, he was not visibly agitated about the Vietnam War. "I thought of him as a rather normal vet," a friend said to a reporter, "glad to be out but not terribly uptight about the war." Another acquaintance who talked to Kerry about his political ambitions called him "a very charismatic fellow looking for a good issue."[210]

How many of the other participants in Dewey Canyon threw away "props"? How many were really Vietnam veterans?

Well, let's take one example: Al Hubbard, the VVAW's executive secretary and one of the organizers of Winter Soldier. He wrote a poem that appeared at the beginning of *The Winter Soldier Investigation*, a book of testimonies from the hearings:

"This book is dedicated to you,

> America
> *Now,*
> *Before the napalm-scorched earth*
> *consumes the blood of would-be-fathers*
> *and*
> *have-been-sons*
> *of*
> *daughters spread-eagled*
> *and*
> *mothers on the run.*
> *Reflect.*
> *See what you've become,*
> *Amerika."* [211]

A scathing commentary by one of those who could no longer stomach the fight, right? Wrong. Hubbard first claimed he was a decorated Air Force captain who had caught shrapnel in his spine flying a transport plane into Da Nang in 1966. But after NBC received a tip that Hubbard was lying about his rank, a reporter confronted him. He confessed on the evening news and the *Today Show* that he actually served as a sergeant, not a pilot or captain, in Vietnam.

John Kerry defended Hubbard, citing the confession as proof of Hubbard's integrity. "Al owned up to the rank question," Kerry said. "He thought it was time to tell the truth, and he did it because he thought it would be best for the organization."[212]

William Overend, a CBS reporter sympathetic to the antiwar movement, later pointed out that Hubbard only confessed when he was confronted. Then the Defense Department issued a news release. "Alfred H. Hubbard entered the Air Force in October 1952, reenlisted twice and was honorably discharged in October 1966, when his enlistment expired," the statement said. "At the time of his discharge he was an instructor flight engineer on C-123 aircraft with the 7th Air Transport Squadron, McChord

Air Force Base, Tacoma, Washington. There is *no record of any service in Vietnam* [emphasis in the original], but since he was an air crew member he could have been in Vietnam for brief periods during cargo loading, unloading operations, or for crew rest purposes. His highest grade held was staff sergeant E-5."

The announcement that Hubbard had no record of service in Vietnam jolted Overend, who had been impressed by Hubbard's leadership qualities. He began looking into Hubbard's background independently. Hubbard claimed he had been severely wounded. Overend called the VA, which confirmed that Hubbard had a sizable medical record and had a service-connected disability rating of 60 percent. At the time, he was receiving disability compensation of $163 a month. But the VA refused to say how, where, or when Hubbard was injured. Overend checked Hubbard's medals and decorations: Hubbard had no Purple Heart or Vietnam Service Ribbon, which can rightfully be claimed by any member of an air crew serving in Vietnam, no matter how briefly.

Hubbard refused to discuss his record. Overend finally discovered that Hubbard had suffered a rib injury during a basketball game in 1956, and a back injury in 1961 during a soccer game. Hubbard had not been wounded, nor had he ever served, in Vietnam. But the story was too long for television, and when Overend tried to sell the piece to a liberal publication, no one would touch it. The truth might hurt the antiwar effort. Overend finally published the story in July 1971 in the *National Review*.

Other major VVAW leaders, like Michael Harbert, also had problems with their credibility. Harbert claimed he was an ex-sergeant who had flown forty-seven missions over Vietnam during 1967 and 1968. "I had fantasies that they were going to take me prisoner because I was in the Air Force and flew in bombing missions over the North," he said after returning to Hanoi in the 1980s. "Suddenly I was back on my last combat mission after the Long Binh Bridge, over the Red River. I closed my eyes, and I was right back in the AWACS, directing an air strike...and the MiGs are in the air, and the surface-to-air missiles are after us." Hearing the explosions brought that fear back.

But Harbert's record showed that he was a member of the 964th Airborne Early Warning and Control Squadron, based at McClellan Air Force Base in California throughout the Vietnam War. The 964th flew EC-121D aircraft on what were known as "College Eye" missions—well out of danger zones, usually along the coast of Siberia or China and not in range of MiG attacks and surface-to-air missiles. Harbert's awards and decorations include the Air Medal with one oak leaf cluster but no Vietnam Service Medal. His only overseas service was in Taiwan from November 28, 1967, to April 9, 1968.[213]

Victims and Executioners

Despite abundant evidence that what happened at My Lai was an aberration, those with political motives manipulated the media images brilliantly, and in the process, they draped disgrace over every Vietnam veteran. A handful of antiwar activists built careers on it.

"My Lai epitomizes the Vietnam War not only because *every* returning soldier can tell of a similar incident, if on a somewhat smaller scale," said psychiatrist Robert Jay Lifton, who was instrumental in the Winter Soldier hearings, "but also because it is an expression of the psychological state characteristic for Americans fighting that war. The Vietnamese people are, of course, the victims, with the American GIs caught in the middle and rendered both victims and executioners."[214]

That belief crystallized in Lifton's contribution to the creation of "post-traumatic stress syndrome" diagnosis. The most recent edition of Lifton's book *Home from the War* said that at least nine hundred thousand Vietnam veterans have had full-blown PTSD and an additional 350,000 currently suffer from the disorder in a milder form. Those with PTSD, Lifton maintained, are five times more likely to be unemployed than those without it and up to six times more likely to abuse drugs and alcohol.[215]

More than any other single person, Lifton perpetrated the "villain-victim" image of Vietnam veterans. But how did Lifton's assumptions spread and become solidified as national policy? The answer lies in the peculiar nexus of the antiwar movement, the burgeoning psychiatric industry, and the guilt of a nation.

7

The Creation of Posttraumatic Stress Disorder

EMOTIONAL and mental reactions to combat have been obvious since antiquity; the condition cuts across cultures and generations. An Egyptian warrior named Hori wrote about the fear of going into battle some three thousand years ago: "You determine to go forward. Shuddering seizes you, the hair on your head stands on end, your soul lies in your hand."[216]

In the Civil War, it was called "soldier's heart." Military records of that terrible conflict indicate about twenty soldiers per thousand suffered from "paralysis" and about six per thousand from "insanity."

"Shell shock" was the term used in World War I to describe the disorienting effects of combat. "Sixty thousand nerve-wracked soldiers back from the trenches by spring, if war continues!" said *Forbes* magazine on October 13, 1917. "That is the estimate of a neurologist who points out that now is the time for American women to take training which will enable them to help in the reconstruction of the soldier. Many of our soldiers may never fully recover from paralysis and mental disorder resulting from shell shock and trench hardships, but for thousands of them, 'occupational therapy' will offer a road to recovery."[217]

Shell shock was thought to be physiological in nature, caused by damage done to the brain by exploding shells. The military was skeptical, suspecting that those afflicted were malingerers or cowards. But late in the

Great War, the U.S. military introduced "the Salmon plan," named for its senior psychiatric consultant, Dr. Thomas Salmon. He recommended identifying and treating stress reaction as close to the front as possible, returning men to combat quickly. The plan seemed to bear fruit; after treatment, 65 percent of psychological casualties returned to the fight.[218]

After the war, Sigmund Freud described the condition as an internal conflict of a different nature, a battle between a soldier's "peace ego" and "war ego." But when America entered World War II, the Freudian theory lost out to the coward theory in military circles. To cut down on psychiatric casualties, the military instituted psychological screening to sort out the "marginally adjusted." Draft boards waived more than a million men from service during World War II as mentally unfit.

But war neurosis did not disappear. During one period in 1942, the Army discharged more soldiers from duty on psychiatric grounds than the service took in. Psychological trauma took a heavy toll on the 1st Army in Europe, which suffered an estimated 102 psychiatric casualties per 1,000 troops. Doctors began calling the condition "combat fatigue," because it afflicted men who had been screened for preexisting psychiatric conditions and sometimes struck soldiers who had fought bravely in earlier battles. The military in 1944 reactivated the Salmon plan, giving each division a psychiatrist who attempted to treat combat fatigue and return soldiers to the front lines quickly.

A study after World War II examined the nature of psychiatric casualties in combat. A special commission described several factors as playing a part in psychological stress reaction: lack of effective leadership, death of comrades, killing of the enemy, poor morale, and miserable living conditions. The experts deemed combat psychiatric casualties different from other recognized psychiatric syndromes—a "situational psychosis," perhaps. Early in the Korean conflict, psychiatric casualties accounted for almost one-quarter of all evacuations from the battlefield, or about fifty out of one thousand troops. Again, a renewed Salmon plan reduced that to about thirty casualties per one thousand.[219]

In 1952, the American Psychiatric Association (APA) published its first edition of the *Diagnostic and Statistical Manual (DSM-I)*, a reference book for physicians to classify patients' diagnoses, manage records, and to process insurance forms. Portions drew on the work of psychiatrists who served in the military in World War II and included diagnosis for "gross stress reaction," which could occur among soldiers in combat even though they had no history of mental health problems. Although some studies indicated that the reaction might occur long after the battlefield experience and persist for years, the *DSM-I* described it as a temporary condition caused by extreme environmental stress, which should disappear after the patient was removed from the anxiety-producing situation.

By the time combat troops were being sent to Vietnam, the U.S. military had learned its lesson and put the Salmon plan into place early on. Each major unit had medical personnel to treat psychiatric disorders close to combat zones. The expectation was that soldiers would be treated and returned quickly to the fighting. The psychiatric casualty figure dropped to five troops per one thousand in 1965-67. One study pointed to the positive morale, individualized one-year tours, brief and sporadic combat, relative lack of indirect fire from the enemy, and high-caliber medical and psychiatric care as the reasons for the low rate of mental disorders among Vietnam troops.[220] Another factor surely had an effect: In the mid-1960s, the American people overwhelmingly supported the war and its soldiers.

In 1968, the year of the Tet Offensive, the APA published the *DSM-II*. This version did not include any mention of combat-related disorders, lumping such things under headings like "inability to adjust to adult life." Emotional trauma or distress during or after battle came under the standard diagnosis of depression, schizophrenia, and other mental illness.

Wilbur J. Scott, a former platoon leader in Vietnam and a sociology professor, described the changing description of the terror wreaked by combat over four wars in his 1993 book *The Politics of Readjustment*.

Scott pointed out that those writing the *DSM-II* had no experience in treating war neurosis in World War II or the Korean War. Initial indications from respected psychiatrists in Vietnam were that the standard nomenclature covered the range of disorders they encountered there," Scott wrote. Not everyone agreed. But the *DSM-II* was not just a "scientific" reference work in which medical and psychiatric experts dispassionately described the maladies afflicting mankind; politics played a large role in the compilation of the *DSM-II*, a role that became glaringly obvious in the creation of posttraumatic stress disorder.

In the late 1960s, the antiwar movement began to gain stature within the psychiatric community. Prominent members of the APA held antiwar sessions at the organization's conferences. Some delivered papers on the responsibilities of therapists to be antiwar advocates.

One of the prime movers and shakers among the antiwar psychiatrists was Robert Jay Lifton, a former Yale psychiatry professor and former Air Force psychiatrist in Korea. Lifton had studied victims of the Holocaust and Korean POWs, and equated the bombing of Hiroshima, intended to bring the war with Japan to a speedy end and save millions of American and Japanese lives, with a war crime. (His 1995 book, *Hiroshima in America*, contended that the bombing caused the "psychic numbing" of America.)

By November 1969, Lifton, already a zealous opponent of the Vietnam War, had read an account of My Lai and vowed to intensify his protests. In articles denouncing the military and the Vietnam War, Lifton urged his fellow psychiatrists and therapists to take up the cause. Vietnam was even worse than wars that had gone before, Lifton asserted. He was one of the first to suggest that soldiers would suffer severe psychological effects specific to the Vietnam War. He called the military psychiatrists in Vietnam "technicist" professionals who had collaborated with an "absurd and evil organization"—the U.S. military—by treating soldiers only to send them back to combat.

At the 1970 APA convention, the board of trustees began developing an official antiwar resolution. "As psychiatrists, we have specialized deep concern about its [the war's] grave effects on morale and on the rise of alienation, dehumanization, and divisiveness among the American people," read a portion of the trustees' statement, published a year later. "Therefore: The board hereby expresses its conviction that the prompt halt to the hostilities in Southeast Asia and the prompt withdrawal of American forces will render it possible to reorder our national priorities to build a mentally healthier nation."[221]

In March 1971, a poll of APA members found that 67 percent wanted the government to terminate all military activity in Vietnam. A year later, the APA and seven other mental health organizations released a public statement: "We find it morally repugnant for any government to exact such heavy costs in human suffering for the sake of abstract conceptions of national pride or honor."[222]

No word on what these concerned psychiatrists intended to do about the mental health of all the South Vietnamese we eventually abandoned to execution, concentration camps, and overcrowded escape boats. Prozac had not yet been invented, so we couldn't simply drop pills on our forsaken allies and urge them all to take one and lie down until the Communists went away.

"Of special note is the assumption that a mentally healthy nation (and thus each individual within the nation) is by definition opposed to the war, and that the war itself is a pathology, one that alienates, dehumanizes, and divides," wrote Phoebe Spinrad, an associate professor of English at Ohio State University, in a 1994 paper called "Patriotism as Pathology," in the *Journal of the Vietnam Veterans Institute*. Spinrad served as an administrative Air Force officer who participated in the evacuations from South Vietnam at the end of the war. Like I did, she became interested in why Vietnam vets were seen as a class of damaged people and began looking at the language used in PTSD literature. If the Vietnam War was a pathology, she says, then its warriors could not be discussed using terms like "shell shock" and "combat fatigue," those phrases from previous conflicts.

"All these earlier terms placed the veteran in the context of physically painful (rather than morally objectionable) activities, and assumed as part of the treatment that the veteran must extract some sense of purpose from the pain," Spinrad said. "Such definitions and treatments obviously could not be used for participants in a pathology rather than an activity."[223]

In the popular media and in professional journals, Robert Lifton tirelessly spread the word that Vietnam veterans would prove to be a national nightmare. He suggested that the Vietnam War would produce a "very large pool of young, embittered veterans" who had more mental problems than veterans of other wars. "The inability to find significance or meaning in their extreme experience leaves many Vietnam veterans with a terrible burden of survivor guilt," Lifton told the *Washington Post* in 1970.[224]

"Some are likely to seek continuing outlets for a pattern of violence to which they have become habituated, whether by indulging in antisocial or criminal behavior—almost in the fashion of mercenaries—offering their services to the highest bidder," Lifton said. "Sometimes disturbances may not be evident for five or eight or ten years." In other words, the vets may look normal, but they could go berserk at any moment.

But if sheer savagery of battle is what triggers PTSD, veterans of some World War I and World War II battles would be more likely to suffer from the condition than most Vietnam veterans. During World War I, in the Battle of the Somme, sixty thousand men died in four hours. Of the five thousand Marines who landed on the beaches of Tarawa the first day of the assault in November 1943, fifteen hundred had become casualties by nightfall. According to writer Paul Fussell, a coxswain at the helm of a landing vessel went insane during the battle of Tarawa, "perhaps at the shock of steering through all the severed heads and limbs near the shore."[225]

In six weeks of fighting in Normandy, Fussell said, casualty rates were so high the 90th Infantry Division had to replace 150 percent of its officers and more than 100 percent of its men. "If a division was engaged for more than three months, the probability was that every one of its second lieutenants, all 132 of them, would be killed or wounded," Fussell said. After the Normandy campaign, the commanding officer of a British army company found an average of five original men remaining of about two hundred in each rifle company.

One study of fear in American soldiers in World War II revealed that more than 25 percent of the GIs in one division admitted they had been so scared in battle that they vomited; another quarter said they had been so frightened at certain moments that they had lost control of their bowels.[226]

Many soldiers in World War II were so afraid of combat that they went to extreme measures to avoid fighting. In France following the Normandy invasion, General Eisenhower was shocked to discover that in one hospital alone there were more than one thousand cases of self-inflicted wounds, "men who had shot themselves through the foot or some other nonvital part of their bodies to get out of the firing line."[227]

Combat was not all soldiers in the Second World War had to face. American and British troops suffered so severely from dysentery in Burma that they cut holes in the seats of their trousers "to simplify things," Fussell said. "But worse was the mental attrition suffered by combat troops, who learned from experience the inevitability of their ultimate mental breakdown, ranging from the milder forms of treatable psychoneurosis to outright violent insanity."[228]

Most people who suffered horrors in combat went on with their lives. In 1995, during the fiftieth anniversary of World War II, Hiroshima bombardier Tom Ferebee addressed the rumors that PTSD—insanity, nightmares, nervous breakdowns, and suicides—plagued the crew of the plane that dropped the atom bomb. "If I've been nuts all these years," Ferebee said, summing up the crew's feeling, "I'm glad no one told me."[229]

However, the image of the disturbed veteran did not stick as tenaciously to veterans of other wars as it did to Vietnam veterans—thanks to Robert Lifton. "[My Lai] illustrates the murderous progression of deception and self-deception—from political policy to military tactics to psychological aberrations," Lifton told the Congressional Conference on War and National Responsibility convened in Washington in 1970.

Lifton was one of the organizers, along with leaders of the tiny but vocal Vietnam Veterans Against the War, of the Winter Soldier "investigation" held in Detroit in January 1971. For days, veterans told grisly stories of war crimes they had seen and committed. But like Mark Lane's book *Conversations with Americans*, the so-called "investigation" was packed with phonies.

Lifton himself testified, describing the horrors patients had told him in "rap groups" he led with members of the New York Chapter of the VVAW. These men suffered from psychic numbing, from dehumanization, from guilt over being part of the "filth" of the war. How could they not? The war itself was immoral.

Not long after Winter Soldier, Lifton was quoted in the *New York Daily News* saying the responsibilities of psychiatrists within the military were to the soldiers—not to the goal of returning them to fight—a responsibility that is true in all wars but "excruciatingly true" of the Vietnam War.

"If the combat veteran suffers anxiety, guilt, or confusion over his role, the psychotherapist should, ideally, help the GI examine his actions and emotions more closely and feel them more acutely," reported the *Daily News*. " 'But if the psychiatrist were to do so,' Lifton says, 'most GIs in Vietnam whom he treated would refuse to continue fighting.' " [230] Of course Lifton had no scientific evidence of this, just his own opinion.

Lifton would later admit that his information did not come from a random sample of Vietnam vets. "Almost all of them belong[ed] to the minority of Vietnam veterans who emerge with an articulate antiwar position," he wrote. "I made no attempt to gather data from a 'representative' group of veterans." [231] Lifton wanted the ones with an antiwar position, men who could be public advocates by horrifying the American public, who would then urge the politicians to end the war.

"Antiwar veterans generate a special kind of force, no less spiritual than political, as they publicly proclaim the endless series of criminal acts they have witnessed or participated in," Lifton said. "The groups differed from street-corner psychiatry in their second function, important from the beginning, of probing the destructive personal experiences of the Vietnam War for eventual dissemination to the American public. For a number of them, and at varying intervals, political activities become inseparable from psychological need." [232]

Were they even Vietnam vets? Call me cynical, but I suspect Lifton did not look too closely at military records.

It appears that even before most Vietnam veterans had returned home, Lifton had decided that they would be plagued by mental afflictions. A *Washington Post* reporter quoted Lifton on May 3, 1969, as saying that the unpopularity of the war was making it difficult for returning servicemen to justify their participation with a "minimum of inner guilt." [233]

Soldiers from World War II didn't suffer from inner guilt. Why did Vietnam vets? Because the war was immoral. Lifton went on to lay the groundwork for what would become the dominant image of Vietnam vets.

"This may intensify the violence in his [the Vietnam veteran] collective behavior," Lifton told the *Post*. "It creates a jingoistic attitude. It's not an organized jingoism they respond to but a hatred of all Vietnamese because of particular things that may have happened to them in Vietnam. It creates an unsteady equilibrium that could express itself in any direction."

"Unsteady equilibrium." "Violence." "Inner guilt." As Lifton and his fellow antiwar therapists developed rap group programs to treat veterans, those who objected to Lifton's radical politicization of psychiatric treatment were invited to leave. "Those of us who held a more radical view of the groups tended to outlast the others in the general program," Lifton admitted later.

Spinrad pointed out that those patients who couldn't admit "sufficient guilt" were bullied until they left the group. "One former infantryman, although bitterly opposed to the war and increasingly committed to the rap groups, repeatedly insisted, 'I just can't *feel* any guilt.' Members of the group bombarded him verbally until he burst into tears and acknowledged feeling guilt," Spinrad said. "His 'crimes' had been killing some North Vietnamese troops and having sent his men out on patrol, where they subsequently died."

Such events are always traumatic experiences in any war, but they were not atrocities or war crimes. "Nor did the infantryman give any indication that he sent out the patrol in error or with insufficient equipment or support," Spinrad pointed out. His offense? Simply doing his job as a soldier.[234]

For another view, Spinrad quoted novelist and Vietnam veteran John Del Vecchio: "Killing should hurt the killer—that, thank God, it does indeed cause lasting emotional scars—even if that killing is considered justified." And sometimes killing another human being is necessary.

"In the past several years I have spoken to thousands of veterans," Del Vecchio wrote in 1985. "Almost all have expressed a feeling that we were not there to kill but were there to save lives. If I killed someone in Vietnam, I believe that action saved the lives of other Americans and, more importantly, saved the lives of many South Vietnamese citizens."[235]

Certainly not all Americans agreed we should be fighting the war (just as not all thought we should fight World War II), but soldiers who serve at their country's behest, killing enemy soldiers in combat, are not lawbreakers. In Lifton's view, every deed committed in the war was the same as an illegal act, therefore, soldiers must bear the same guilt as criminals. The soldier in Lifton's rap group who was finally coerced to admit his guilt received congratulations, but shortly thereafter he disappeared from the group. Apparently, he had had enough "therapy."

Another case Spinrad cited from Lifton's book involved four or five veterans who angrily condemned a former rap group member for "still being a first sergeant" and not "going along with the program" of the rest of the group.

"The target of rage was a man from among them who held tenaciously to an identity element they had pointedly rejected," Lifton wrote, "causing them to doubt their own capacity to rid themselves of that element and undergo change." In other words, for being proud of his military service, he was driven from the group.

"The important point in this case, however, is the ominous note struck by Lifton's phrase, 'causing them to doubt their own' new identities," Spinrad said. "The unrepentant veteran has become a personal danger to the others, and must be destroyed or driven away."

After two years of working with such rap groups, Lifton's book was published in 1973 to great acclaim in the media. The "patients"—all those who had fought in Vietnam—had been properly diagnosed by a psychiatrist. All had committed "atrocities," all were suffering "psychic numbing" from their deep internal guilt, and the only way to cleanse themselves was to admit they were war criminals and force the world to acknowledge that reality as well. Logically, only those Vietnam veterans who acknowledged these awful "truths" were able to help others heal.

A year earlier, Lifton had sponsored the First National Conference on the Emotional Needs of Vietnam-Era Veterans in St. Louis, Missouri. Ten VA employees attended and met the antiwar therapists who later would influence the design of the VA counseling system. By the late 1970s, hundreds of rap groups, modeled on those developed by Lifton and his inner circle, had spread across the country. Those who led the groups came out of therapy under the aegis of Lifton and his cohorts. They had passed the test: Admit guilt, be cleansed, obtain healing, help others do the same.

One of the most important groups was the Flower of the Dragon, a veterans' counseling program in Sonoma, California, which became one of the models for Vet Centers set up by the VA. The assumptions of the therapy provided there were Lifton's: the military as dehumanizing agent, the war as a producer of atrocities, and "psychic numbing" and paranoia as the distinguishing traits of Vietnam vets.

Charles R. Figley, who later became one of the most influential voices in the PTSD literature, was one of the leaders of the Vietnam veterans' therapy movement. Figley had participated in the Dewey Canyon III demonstration with Lifton's group of antiwar veterans. Another leader was Arthur Egendorf Jr., a veteran and author. "From the time I entered the military," Egendorf said in 1972, "it became increasingly obvious that the heroes of this war were those who fought it in the streets of American cities or in the courts or in the jails or by leaving the country rather than lend their support. Whatever the personal cost, all of them—exiles, deserters, and resisters of every stripe—answered the call to fight in a senseless war with the most appropriate response—an outright refusal."[236]

This perfectly illustrated the attitude of those who dominated the dialogue, Spinrad said: Only those who opposed the war had something to be proud of. "Thus, a proud veteran is demoted to the status of a coward or loser," she said.

Against the Tide

Lifton's was not the only voice. During the war, studies showed no link between combat-engendered psychiatric difficulties in Vietnam that were treated in the war zone and later psychiatric problems in readjustment to civilian life. Military psychiatrist H. S. Bloch said that in his experience, those soldiers who struggled over the morality of combat were most often driven by psychological conflicts that existed before they arrived in Vietnam.[237] And soon after the end of the war, opinions of psychiatrists outside the antiwar movement debunked the idea that Vietnam veterans suffered "adjustment woes."

Dr. Jonathan F. Borus, of Massachusetts General Hospital and Harvard Medical School, reported a study in April 1974 that showed Vietnam combat veterans had no more adjustment problems than had servicemen who were not in Vietnam.

Borus studied troops at an East Coast Army garrison post while with the Walter Reed Army Institute of Research in Washington, D.C. He examined the military records of 577 Vietnam veterans and 172 servicemen who served elsewhere. The study indicated that 23 percent of Vietnam veterans had adjustment problems in their first seven months back in the United States. But 26.2 percent of veterans who *didn't go* to Vietnam, but served in other areas, had adjustment problems as well. Was the cause the war or something else?

His findings challenged the "assumptions that the Vietnam experience or the reentry transition itself are debilitating stresses for the majority of returning veterans," Borus said. He admonished mental health professionals "who have added politically colored reports to both the public and professional literatures."[238]

But in the media, anecdotal evidence by Lifton and his acolytes pushed out a more scientific approach. "Viet Veterans Called 'Time Bombs'" headlined a story in the *Baltimore Sun* on January 15, 1975. The article quoted Dr. Leonard Neff, a psychiatrist working at the VA hospital in the Brentwood section of Los Angeles. Neff claimed many Vietnam veterans were "walking time bombs" whose "frustration, disillusionment, and anger could erupt violently, anywhere, anytime."

Neff called the condition "post-Vietnam syndrome," and referred to an incident in which a supposed Vietnam vet held two rangers and a hiker hostage at rifle point. He cited no controlled studies and no evidence that he was really treating Vietnam vets, not just people who said they were. But Neff echoed Lifton: If organized, these men were quite capable of mounting an armed assault against society—attacking a government building perhaps. Certainly the mental state of Vietnam vets should be a concern not only to the veterans but also to the whole nation.[239]

Influential columnist Tom Wicker took up the issue in *The New York Times* on May 27, 1975, telling the story of a former Army Ranger who slept with a gun under his pillow. During one of his frequent nightmares about combat, his wife tried to wake him. He shot and killed her. "That was only one example of the serious but largely unnoticed problems of 'post-Vietnam syndrome,' or PVS, the label by which the extraordinary psychological difficulties of *hundreds of thousands* of Vietnam veterans have come to be identified," Wicker said. (Emphasis added.)

How did Wicker know that hundreds of thousands of Vietnam veterans have such difficulties? Because people like Lifton said so.

Wicker cited a series of articles in *Penthouse* magazine as the source for these shocking statistics:

- Of those who were married before they went to Vietnam, 38 percent were separated or getting divorced six months after their return.
- About five hundred thousand have attempted suicide since discharge. (Remember, this is in 1975!)
- As many as 175,000 "probably" have used heroin since getting out of the service.[240]

Frightening statistics often cited by activists—but with absolutely no basis in fact. They were guesses and estimates and suppositions, not based on studies of Vietnam veterans as identified through military records.

About six months later, on November 11, 1975, the *Los Angeles Times* printed a story called "Viet Veterans Melting Into Society." The piece quoted Lifton: "Unlike World War II, where the symbol of the vet was GI Joe, the lovable, typical young American, the veteran who came home from Vietnam was perceived as something sinister, disturbing, frightening," Lifton said. (The story did not say he was one of those primarily responsible for that image.)

But *Times* reporter David Lamb looked beyond Lifton's rhetoric. "There is ample evidence to suggest that the vast majority of Vietnam veterans has melted back into society as successfully as any soldier from any war," Lamb wrote. "Little has happened to challenge the theory of historian Dixon Wecter who wrote in 1944: 'War colors the mainstream of a citizen-soldier's life, but seldom changes its direction.'"

Lamb pointed out that both the American Legion and the VFW had enjoyed their greatest growth in recent years. Of their 4.5 million members, 22 percent were Vietnam vets. And Vietnam veterans were using the GI Bill for education in numbers higher than those from other wars. Only 2 percent of Vietnam veterans used narcotics in civilian life, a figure similar to nonveteran drug usage. Indeed the transition from war to peace was marked by a "strong tendency to discontinue narcotics even by men familiar with them before Vietnam," according to a psychiatrist in charge of a government-sponsored study on drug usage among veterans.[241]

In fact, "the American soldier in Vietnam was psychologically healthier than his counterpart in previous wars. His rate of hospitalization for mental reasons was half that of the World War II soldier."

The rates of psychiatric problems in Vietnam increased as the unpopularity of the war grew. In 1967, there were ten psychiatric casualties per one thousand troops in the war zone. In June 1970, that had risen to thirty-eight per thousand. Since there was no particular change in the way the war was being fought, the increase probably had more to do with the way vets felt they were perceived by those back home and by the fact that soldiers were unwilling to risk anything in a war the U.S. had already unofficially declared over. Who wants to die for a lost cause?

In conclusion, Lamb quoted a VA psychiatrist: "Our society was scared by the image of the Vietnam veteran coming home and shooting up the community, of being a junkie," said Dr. Charles A. Stenger. "It was a distorted image that the veteran is still paying for. There is no evidence that Vietnam has produced a disproportionate share of people who are maladjusted to society and no evidence that the primary contributor to that maladjustment was military service."

But the "time bomb" image, perpetrated by therapists with a vested interest and those who found Vietnam a convenient scapegoat for their problems, refused to go away. "Thousands of young men who fought for their country have returned to their hometowns to find no way to reorder their lives," said the *Detroit Free Press* on April 25, 1976. The reporter interviewed a handful of men who *said* they were Vietnam veterans and described their devastated lives, including one who said he saw a Viet Cong coming through his door at work. "I grabbed him and assaulted him, but he was just a paperboy," the man claimed. Again, anecdotal evidence was the proof that large numbers of Vietnam veterans were suffering mental problems.

In the seventies, vet counseling groups around the country began to publish small studies on Vietnam veterans and PTSD, based on those showing up for counseling. Inevitably these produced high rates of the disorder, leading activists to proclaim that up to two million veterans were suffering readjustment problems. A study in New York, the basis for a $2 million jobs program, said that Vietnam vets who experienced heavy combat, about one-fourth of the total, had three times the unemployment rate of those who saw only light combat. And 45 percent of the heavy combat vets continued to have PTSD symptoms. Did the study check military records to verify either Vietnam status or combat status, or did the research rely on self-description by vets? Reports didn't say.

As Spinrad has pointed out, literature on PTSD projected the image of damaged, broken man onto *every* Vietnam vet. A handbook for clerics published by the Disabled American Veterans (DAV) called *A Pastoral Response to the Troubled Vietnam Veteran* drops the adjective "troubled" on the second page. "The Vietnam veteran describes guilt and shame. Like a heavy yoke carried on his shoulders, guilt burdens the veteran and diminishes creativity and vitality," read one passage written by Chaplain Melvin R. Jacob. "The reality of Vietnam ate away at the spirit of many of its soldiers. The constant inconsistencies and incongruities, the gut-wrenching absurdities, and the endless emptiness left their indelible marks on the hearts of American warriors."[242]

Author Judith Lewis Herman published *Trauma and Recovery* in 1992. Herman echoed Lifton: "The study of war trauma becomes legitimate only in a context that challenges the sacrifice of young men in war. The moral legitimacy of the antiwar movement and the national experience of defeat in a discredited war had made it possible to recognize psychological trauma as a lasting and inevitable legacy of war."[243]

Blatant antimilitary attitudes permeate much of the PTSD literature. In his essay, Chaplain Jacob called even stateside and peacetime military service "brutalizing" and "dehumanizing."[244] In her book, Herman advocated that trauma sufferers repudiate the source of the harm—not the enemy soldier but the American military.

"Significantly, the latest villain in much of the current literature is John Wayne," said Spinrad, "whom one writer rejects scornfully as having 'indoctrinated' young men with such outmoded notions as the 'values of honor, courage, sacrifice over survival and the resiliency of the human spirit.' What terrible values to be 'indoctrinated' with: honor, courage, and sacrifice. Heaven forbid that any of our young men accept such things. And yet, this repudiation of ideals is the final step in the process that began in the 1960s and is being carried on in the VA today."[245]

Despite earlier studies showing Vietnam vets had no significant readjustment problems, media reports about disturbed veterans and Hollywood's portrayals of Vietnam began to take hold, particularly among those who influenced the VA system. A 1980 Harris Poll found that 52 percent of the general public saw Vietnam veterans' problems as more serious than those of World War II or Korean War vets. But when the same question was asked of those who identified themselves as antiwar activists, 75 percent said that Vietnam veterans' problems were worse. (Most of those therapists treating former soldiers defined themselves as "antiwar.") But the perception was growing even among Vietnam veterans themselves, with 56 percent feeling that their problems were worse—maybe not for them but the other guys.[246]

The Creation of the VA Vet Centers

Following the official end of the war in Vietnam in 1975, veterans' activists, often the same ones who had been involved in Vietnam Veterans Against the War, began to demand more services for what they perceived as the unique needs of Vietnam veterans. Not only had Vietnam vets come back to an indifferent, even hostile nation, they also were forced to go for help to a system set up to treat the older veterans of World War II and Korea.

In response, the VA brought in younger physicians more sympathetic to the attitudes of Vietnam veterans and added activities geared toward the younger patients, not the geriatric World War II vets. When Vietnam veterans began pushing for more outpatient services so they would not have to go to the VA hospital for treatment of substance abuse and other kinds of counseling, the VA reacted.

In 1971, therapist Floyd "Shad" Meshad was hired at the Brentwood VA Hospital in Los Angeles to write a report about Vietnam veteran patients. Meshad knew about the problems of Vietnam veterans firsthand—even the horror of being wounded. In *Long Time Passing*, author Myra MacPherson said Meshad was shot down in a helicopter. "I split my head," Meshad said. "I was scalped. I could feel my whole face slipping. Like an old basset hound, my face just kinda fell down. I tied a bandanna around it to hold it up." After his return home from Vietnam, Meshad said, he had a difficult time coming to terms with the war. His wounds required several painful operations.[247]

Because of those experiences, Meshad identified strongly with Vietnam veterans and felt the government's services were deeply inadequate. He wrote a scathing report, saying the "veterans were hostile, the staff was afraid, and the traditional VA services useless." His report was backed up by others on the staff. The Brentwood director appointed Meshad to do something about the rancorous atmosphere. Meshad and others formed the Vietnam Veteran Resocialization Unit, with the goal of creating a setting where veterans could talk about and make sense of their experiences in war. That led to the unusual situation of a social worker calling the shots in a hospital, where physicians typically reign supreme. Because of Meshad's philosophy, everything—individual therapy and so-called "rap sessions"—was geared toward dealing specifically with problems resulting from combat. Psychiatrists and clinical psychologists who disagreed with Meshad's radical approach were kicked off the ward, with the backing of the VA authorities. Meshad's approach coincided with that of Lifton, who was doing the same sort of rap sessions in New York.[248]

But just as Lifton's philosophy of treatment grew out of his opposition to the war, so did Meshad's. A commissioned officer assigned as a "mental hygiene consultant" in Vietnam, Meshad had boasted that he conducted antiwar activities while still working with troops in the combat zone. He claimed he decided to make himself a martyr of the war by taunting military authorities and refusing to clip his mustache, eliciting the expected court-martial. (Although he told MacPherson and others that he was severely wounded, Meshad's military record shows no wounds, no Purple Heart, and no hospital stay.[249])

Like Lifton, Meshad profoundly affected the VA system. Feeling that most Vietnam veterans who needed help would not approach a VA hospital, where rules and regulations were paramount, Meshad set up a network of storefront clinics throughout Los Angeles where he held rap groups so veterans could talk about their war experiences. Veterans did not have to prove eligibility. Don't have your DD-214, your official discharge form? No problem. There the motto was "when in doubt, err on the side of the vet."

The work of reclaiming these broken, wounded men was his passion, his obsession. "I was a madman, a maverick," Meshad later said. "Had long hair, a beard, wore a field jacket. But they referred vets from all over the country to me."[250]

In 1977, as pressure built to provide more services to suffering Vietnam veterans, the VA hired Meshad as a consultant for the development of a national outpatient system because of his experience with storefront veterans' counseling centers.

Two years later, Congress passed Public Law 96-22, directing the VA to establish Vietnam Veterans' Readjustment Counseling Centers apart from the existing VA medical center system. Called "Vet Centers," these storefronts and community clinics were staffed primarily with former antiwar protesters turned therapists, such as Meshad, and others who had gained experience as counselors in programs like Flower of the Dragon and Swords into Plowshares. The intention was that this would be a short-term program to deal with a special but temporary idiosyncrasy in veterans' needs. MacPherson pointed out in her book that almost every Vet Center worker she talked to was antiwar—especially those who said they were veterans themselves. Like the storefronts, the Vet Centers' position was to believe the vet.

But a final piece of the puzzle was needed: The inclusion of posttraumatic stress disorder in the new *Diagnostic and Statistical Manual-III*.

To counter the belief by some psychiatrists that no separate classification was necessary to diagnose the problems of veterans, a group of Lifton's colleagues called the Vietnam Veterans Working Group joined forces. They collected case histories of troubled Vietnam veterans until they had data on more than seven hundred, chosen apparently in the same way Lifton selected those for his book. One of the members was an antiwar psychoanalyst from New York named Chaim Shatan, who was one of the first to begin using the term "post-Vietnam syndrome" to describe the vets he was seeing in the self-help groups. "The so-called Post-Vietnam Syndrome confronts us with the unconsummated grief of soldiers—

impacted grief, in which an encapsulated, never-ending past deprives the present of meaning," Shatan said.[251]

Another was Sarah A. Haley, a social worker fresh out of graduate school who began working for the Boston VA Hospital in September 1969. Haley told author Wilbur J. Scott she had heard stories about war and atrocities from her father, who had served in North Africa during World War II as a special agent for the "Overseas Secret Service"[sic]. (Perhaps she meant the World War II Office of Strategic Services.)[252]

On her first morning of work at the VA, evaluating Vietnam veterans for psychotherapy at an outpatient clinic, Haley had her first contact with a Vietnam vet, a new patient who was anxious and agitated. A few days before coming in for treatment, he had broken down, becoming easily startled and experiencing insomnia and terrifying nightmares. His company in Vietnam had killed women and children at a village called My Lai, he told Haley, although he had not joined in the carnage. He kept saying one of his buddies wanted to kill him, but there was no evidence to prove that beyond his obvious agitation.[253]

What an incredible coincidence. On Haley's *first day* at work, she gets a witness to what becomes the defining atrocity of the Vietnam War. Haley does not identify her patient. Like the sinner in the confessional who has purged his soul and become clean, he is protected by that therapist/patient confidentiality.

Had the patient really been at My Lai, or had he—like mental patients have been known to do—latched on to the story and made the trauma his own? Although Haley has said she had not yet heard anything about the breaking case, the Calley inquiry had begun months earlier. Ron Ridenhour had written a lengthy letter to the president, sending copies to twenty-three members of Congress, the Secretaries of State and Defense, the Secretary of the Army, and the Chairman of the Joint Chiefs of Staff, on March 29, 1969. For months, investigators had been interviewing members and former members of Calley's platoon. Stories had already appeared in the press about the massacre, and the grapevine was working overtime. On September 5, 1969, Calley had been arrested and charged with multiple cases of murdering "Oriental human beings."

Haley accepted the man's story at face value, but the other VA staff members thought he was delusional; he had been previously diagnosed as paranoid schizophrenic. Haley pooh-poohed this diagnosis. Her father had been a secret agent. He knew all about war atrocities, and here was proof in the living flesh.

Later, when Haley and Lifton met through the New York City and Boston chapters of the VVAW, she introduced the man to Lifton, who later wrote about him. Lifton's book identifies him only as "the My Lai survivor," although everyone in Charlie Company had been named by this point.[254] (Why call this guy a "survivor" of My Lai? No one was shooting at him. Vietnamese civilians died, not Americans. Lifton's phrase smacks of that ritualized cleansing offered by the anointed psychiatrist.)

That encounter not only escalated Lifton's antiwar protests, it also shaped Haley's career. She began examining the issue of troubled Vietnam veterans who claimed they committed war crimes. "When the Patient Reports Atrocities," Haley's study of 40 of 130 men she had evaluated or treated over a period of three years, appeared in the *Archives of General Psychiatry* in February 1974 and caused an enormous reaction.[255]

Her report began with a poem to show how a real Vietnam vet would feel:

> *Sacrificing a portion of your*
> *consciousness so you won't have*
> *to deal with*
> *Being there*
> *and*
> *building mental blocks*
> *so you won't have to deal with*
> *having been there.*[256]

The poet? Al Hubbard, who had already been exposed for lying about his service in Vietnam.

Haley did not claim that the forty veterans were representative of all Vietnam soldiers. "Because many veterans shun the VA or other 'establishment' health care facilities, we have attempted, where possible, to contact veterans' groups on campuses or other 'antiestablishment' veterans' groups." In other words, Haley and her cohorts sought the most radical, alienated vets among the returning soldiers. Nothing in the methodology of the study indicated that Haley checked military records to find out if her patients were Vietnam veterans.

Her report said that the psychiatric literature on Vietnam presented an often "misleading" finding of a lower incidence of psychiatric casualties from Vietnam than Korea or World War II. "The twelve-months' duty assignment in Vietnam exposed men to a time-limited stress, and many veterans did not react immediately to this stress and only became 'psychiatric casualties' months and even years after their return to the United States." And those early combat stress studies did not examine "acknowledged combat atrocities." Acknowledged how? By people in the self-help groups like Lifton's.

"As therapists we most often work with patients who have neurotic guilt over unconscious wishes or impulses, experience psychic distress at the breakthrough of such wishes or with patients who 'act out,' usually symbol-ically, their internal distress," Haley wrote. "The 'crimes' of these patients are usually in the form of fantasies or nonlife-threatening behavior."[257]

But not these patients. "How can the therapist respond to the issue of actual participation in atrocities and the varying subjective states associated with those acts?" Haley asked. "These reports may be accompanied by varying degrees of guilt, casualness, or even pride and bravado. The thera-pist's ability to acknowledge and tolerate both the veteran's objective responsibility and his varying views of himself is of crucial importance in the therapist's sense of 'being with' the veteran as they work toward under-standing and resolution of conflict." In other words, what these patients were reporting was not unconscious wishes or impulses, but reality.

Three case studies followed. "John," a drug abuser failing college, had joined the military and volunteered for Vietnam after his older brother was killed in combat. He told one atrocity story after another: killing prisoners after entreating them to surrender and murdering civilians without provo-cation. But after guarding a high-ranking group of Viet Cong prisoners for a week, John grew to know them as people. When his commanding officer ordered him to "blow them away," he refused, standing frozen as his com-mander and other soldiers executed them. Back home, his guilt led to drug use and repeated suicide attempts.

Haley, who had no military experience, accepted this story at face value. (She passed right over the tip-off that "John" was a drug user and a college dropout *before* he went to Vietnam.) Like John, she said, "other veterans who reported guilt were able to do so only after a trusting relationship had been established." Or possibly after the veterans realized Haley believed anything they said, and, in fact, pricked up her ears when they reported "atrocities."

Her next veteran was "Bob," a twenty-three-year-old ex-Marine referred by the VA after he threatened to kill his wife. A squad leader in Vietnam, he was brutal to POWs and civilians alike, staying thirteen months "in the bush" and refusing R&R because he was "too into killing." Bob reported the murder of a superior officer who ordered his squad up a hill defended by the Viet Cong, although he left ambiguous who did the actual killing. When his squad camped outside a supposedly pacified village, they awoke the next morning to find themselves encircled by booby traps. (No expla-nation for why Bob's squad violated a fundamental rule of infantry tactics by having 100 percent of its members asleep at the same time in a combat environment.) After getting safely away, Bob and his squad returned to the village and "blew them motherfuckers away."

On return from Vietnam, Bob felt angry and sad all the time and was unable to hold a steady job. While other symptoms subsided, he continued to feel a "murderous rage" toward his mother, wife, and "peace nuts."

Haley attributed all this to Vietnam, where an invisible enemy ruled the night. Curiously, Haley doesn't seem interested in exploring Bob's hostile feelings toward his mother and wife except as an extension of his Vietnam experience.

Her last case study was "Bill," a twenty-one-year-old former Marine who served as a radioman in Vietnam. Bill described Marines who routinely killed prisoners and took ears from enemy bodies as "trophies." He refused to commit atrocities but admitted that he came close. Bill also refused R&R out of loyalty to his squad. After eleven months in the bush, Bill had lost forty pounds. Sent to a field hospital and diagnosed as having tuberculosis, Bill said that instead of being evacuated he was returned to combat with a month's medication, "if I lived that long."

With a week left to serve, his unit was overrun in the night. Shot, he tried to pick up his already dead lieutenant, who "fell apart" in his hands. With multiple wounds to his chest, Bill watched helplessly as an enemy soldier, later shown to be twelve years old, prepared to finish him off. But the young boy was shot by a Marine, and his body fell across Bill, who was pinned under the dead Vietnamese boy for an hour. Bill was referred to the psychiatry unit of the VA because he felt continually guilty and depressed. (Bill's claim to have been diagnosed with tuberculosis and sent back to combat might have raised a red flag for anyone who had been in the military, as would the claim that he had been pinned down for an hour by the body of a twelve-year-old.)

"Each of these men had held positions of strategic importance to their combat units," Haley reported. "Each was in receipt of one or more Purple Hearts, and each had been decorated for bravery. They each sought help at a point of crisis after a period of time spent trying to 'forget.' This pattern of 'delayed reaction' is typical of the Vietnam combat veterans I have seen who have been involved in atrocities."

Or at least typical of the psychiatric patients who confessed war crimes. Haley made clear that the therapist's role is to believe. "The therapist should not deny the reality of the patient's perception of his Vietnam experience, because if he does the patient may correctly assume he is being 'cleaned up' or 'whitewashed' in order for the therapist to tolerate and treat him. The veteran needs the strength of the therapeutic alliance in order to tolerate 'remembering,' working through, and eventual repression." Although she admitted that combat veterans might play down or embellish their war stories, "the only report that should not be accepted at face value, although one might choose not to challenge it initially, is the patient's report that combat in Vietnam had no effect on him."[258]

Remarkably, Haley pointed out that this group of patients was usually "chronically anxious, angry, or frankly paranoid. Self-defeating or self-destructive behaviors predominate; they lose jobs, alienate friends/family, provoke arrest/imprisonment, and are in frequent automobile accidents." But she attributed that to their experiences in Vietnam, not mental disorders that had nothing to do with their military service. Haley saw what she wanted to see.

Haley's study was one of the first in a long string of ostensibly scientific examinations of Vietnam veterans with psychological problems. But there was little effort to truly measure what these therapists were seeing in a scientific way. Were the patients really Vietnam veterans? Had they actually seen combat? Did their military records confirm any of their stories? What psychological problems existed before their military service? The only self-reporting not accepted at face value was that Vietnam caused patients no psychological distress—whether they were cooks or combat snipers.

Even ordinary life experiences—indeed, nothing more than the climate—could trigger the reaction. "Hot humid weather like that of Vietnam can bring on nightmares, flashbacks, depressions," wrote Tom Wicker in *The New York Times* in 1975, quoting Chaim Shatan. "One mental specialist, Sarah Haley of the Veterans Administration in Boston, has found that even ordinary child-rearing can bring on symptoms of PVS (Post-Vietnam Syndrome). When young children enter an aggressive stage, fathers who are veterans sometimes find a forgotten aggressive instinct triggered in themselves."[259]

Despite a lack of solid empirical evidence, the diagnosis of PTSD as defined by people like Haley, Lifton, and Shatan—that stress reactions to combat can occur years after the events that triggered them, with dramatic consequences—was included in the *DSM-III* published in 1980. "PTSD is in *DSM-III* because a core of psychiatrists and veterans worked consciously and deliberately for years to put it there," wrote Scott. "They ultimately succeeded because they were better organized, more politically active, and enjoyed more lucky breaks than their opposition."[260] The diagnosis of PTSD shifted the disorder's cause from the patient (and his individual psyche) to the cause (the war), and in so doing became the textbook definition of "Vietnam veteran."

The Definition of PTSD

The *DSM-III* definition of PTSD takes up a page. Although the primary impetus of PTSD's inclusion in the manual was Vietnam veterans, psychiatrists were careful not to limit the disorder to combat soldiers, extending the definition to include victims of rape or assault, natural disasters, or any traumatic incident:

> "The person has experienced an event that is outside the range of usual human experience, and that would be markedly distressing to almost anyone, e.g., serious threat to one's life or physical integrity;

serious threat or harm to one's children, spouse, or other close relatives and friends; sudden destruction of one's home or community; or seeing another person who has recently been, or is being, seriously injured or killed as the result of an accident or physical violence."

The traumatic event is "persistently reexperienced" in dreams, nightmares, or flashbacks and may be triggered by symbolic events such as the anniversary of a battle. Or the patient might experience detachment, avoiding thoughts of the event. Also present should be at least two symptoms (not present before the trauma) such as insomnia, irritability, difficulty concentrating, hypervigilance, and exaggerated startle response.[261] In order to diagnose PTSD, patients must manifest a certain number of the symptoms. Sounds straightforward.

But in practice, therapists began telling Vietnam vets that they might not know they had PTSD, and they broadened the list of "common" symptoms of the disorder to include psychic numbing, feelings of helplessness, depression, aggressiveness, fear of crowds, anxiety and panic attacks, anxiety-related headaches or backaches, and intrusive thoughts.

Those who exhibit any of the symptoms are urged to seek counseling immediately. But the symptoms are so generic, so widespread. Who hasn't felt depressed, hopeless, aggressive, or had a backache at some point? As for guilt, even those who *did not* go can claim that. In the September 1983 issue of *Esquire*, writer Christopher Buckley wrote a story called "Viet Guilt" — he felt bad that he had avoided the Vietnam draft by pleading asthma.

Buckley raised the astonishing possibility that perhaps the experience in Vietnam was positive for some people. "I have friends who served in Vietnam," he wrote. "One was with Special Forces, another was in Army intelligence, another with the CIA. They all saw death up close every day and many days dealt it themselves. They're married, happy, secure, good at what they do. They don't have nightmares, and they don't shoot up gas stations with M-16s. Each has a gentleness I find rare in most others, and beneath it a spiritual sinew that I ascribe to their experience in the war."[262]

But those people were not in Lifton's rap group.

The assumption that Vietnam veterans were traumatized by their experiences in an "immoral war" were the roots of the tree. From the roots grew a sapling, with the proliferation of the storefront counseling centers manned by antiwar activists turned psychological counselors, whose aim was to "heal" those damaged by their war service.

The *DSM-III* designation of PTSD as a definable psychiatric disorder nourished the sapling and "proved" the need for the counselors. By 1980, the storefronts gave way to the incorporation of the treatment into the official, government-funded VA system, with Vet Centers providing outpatient treatment and the hospitals providing inpatient care for PTSD. Limbs began to spring from the tree as counselors and "professional veterans" created a cottage industry—writing books, putting on seminars and workshops, leading group therapy sessions. Therapists could bill for treating the "forgotten casualties of the Vietnam War," all those hundreds of thousands of wandering time bombs waiting to go off if not given the treatment they desperately needed. Of course, in addition to that altruistic motive, the more patients therapists could find, the more money they could make.

That same year, another important event gave the tree planted by Lifton a shot of fertilizer. In October 1980 the VA recognized PTSD as a service-connected disorder. Now psychiatrists could designate veterans as disabled due to service-related PTSD, making them eligible for monthly compensation payments by the VA. Monetary incentives were now firmly in place on both the supply and the demand side, with the diagnosis of 100 pecent service-connected PTSD disability the pot of gold at the end of the rainbow. The sapling has become a sequoia.

In 1981, *Newsweek*, in a story called "The Troubled Vietnam Vet," reported the results of a five-volume study by the Center for Policy Research in New York, which indicated that a third of those in heavy combat suffered from PTSD.[263]

The story quoted Dr. John Caknipe, chief counselor at Detroit's Flight of the Phoenix Vet Center, who told of an anguished vet he had treated. The veteran described a "hand-to-hand night battle" that wiped out his entire unit. When the sun arose, the soldier found himself surrounded by the "grotesquely mutilated bodies" of his men and thirty-six wounded Vietnamese. Realizing there was no hope of medical aid, he shot and killed all of those still alive. His superiors forbade him to tell of what had happened. "When he finally broke," Caknipe said, "he cried for three hours. Then he stood up and said, 'I feel light. I feel light.' And he left."

The magazine described a handful of other veterans who were struggling. One, Dan Spranger, returned home from Vietnam only to meet such hostility that he refused to talk about Vietnam, telling friends he served his hitch as a cook. "At least no one could ask me if I had killed any kids or women," Spranger said.

Spranger suffered from nightmares, dreaming often that he was back with his buddies at Tiger Lair, a 9th Infantry Division firebase in the Mekong Delta. In his nightmare, the men laugh as they load mortars, firing and loading again while the mortar rounds fall and explode on a nearby hamlet. People run screaming, but they are not Viet Cong, they are American women and children. In the rubble huddle his wife and daughter. The trauma of his Vietnam experience haunted Spranger to such an extent that he lost his job, and his wife divorced him. His daughter was born with birth defects that Spranger attributed to battlefield exposure to Agent Orange.

Newsweek also mentioned Steven Cytryszewski, plagued by flashbacks, nightmares, and panic attacks after his experience in Vietnam. "I smell the sulfur from the ammunition, and I feel the heat of the sun," he said. "Sometimes I wake up screaming 'Incoming rounds!' When I drive along a road with trees on both sides, I don't look at the road, I look at the trees. I'm looking for snipers." Cytryszewski was enthusiastic about the Vet Centers, where the therapists took his stories seriously.

But the Center for Policy Research study, which did not check military records, was about as valid as the veterans' stories told in *Newsweek*. Spranger's military record revealed he *was* a cook in Vietnam; he has no record of combat.[264] And Cytryszewski? According to his military record, Cytryszewski was a supply clerk in Vietnam with the 9th Infantry.[265]

Although the veteran in the story told by Caknipe was not identified, he told a tale similar to others told by fakers: After a terrible battle in which war crimes are perpetrated, he is forced to kill fellow Americans. The only survivor, burdened by horror and guilt, he is forbidden to tell of the atrocities by his evil superiors. But his story was absurd on its face—no American unit was completely wiped out in Vietnam. So-called "lone survivors" peddling grandiose tales should raise immediate suspicion.

In 1981, the American hostages were released from Iran, inevitably evoking images of the 1973 prisoner exchange with North Vietnam. The country welcomed them home with an outpouring of warmth and adulation, which stood in stark contrast to the response given Vietnam veterans and further reinforced the need for the Vet Centers.

Although trickles of men like Caknipe's patient began coming into the Vet Centers, it took an occurrence outside the realm of clinics and psychiatrists to firmly etch in public perception the image of the broken, wounded Vietnam veteran, an event that eventually would send hundreds of thousands of those who fought in Vietnam—or at least said they did—into the VA hospitals and Vet Centers howling that they were traumatized.

That event was Rambo.

8

Rambo: An American Hero

SCRUFFY John Rambo, carrying a bedroll and wearing a field jacket emblazoned with an American flag, stares down at a quaint country house by the side of a sparkling lake, with snow-capped mountains in the distance. A black woman hangs freshly laundered clothes on a line.

The first scene in the 1982 movie *First Blood* appears idyllic. But tension lurks beneath the surface. Rambo tells the woman he's looking for a friend; they served on the same team in Vietnam. She looks at the picture he gives her with bitterness. "Delmar's dead," she says with quiet pain. "Cancer. Brought it back from 'Nam. All that orange stuff they spread around."

Stunned, bewildered, resigned, Rambo heads for the highway and walks toward the small town of Hope. He's just looking for something to eat when he's accosted by Sheriff Will Teasle. Burly, blustering, Teasle literally runs the unshaven, long-haired veteran out of town. But Rambo refuses to be bullied. Deliberately, he walks back toward Hope (get it?), only to have the hard-assed sheriff toss his butt in jail.

As a deputy takes Rambo's fingerprints, the falsely accused vet catches a glimpse of a window crisscrossed with bars. Flashback to Vietnam— Rambo in a bamboo cage, being abused by his North Vietnamese captors. Following Teasle's orders to clean up Rambo, a deputy orders him to strip, gaping as Rambo removes his shirt to reveal a sculpted back and chest viciously scarred by a whip, a legacy of his days as a POW. Pounded by water from a fire hose, unnerved by the flashbacks, pushed to his limit by the sadistic sheriff, Rambo goes berserk, attacking the deputies, fighting his way to freedom.

But the war has just begun. Rambo, using nothing more than his wits and a hunting knife, takes on the sheriff's posse. He survives a leap from a cliff, evades a pack of hunting hounds, kills a helicopter sniper using only a rock, rigs booby traps in the forest to incapacitate (but not kill) the sheriff and his deputies, and escapes from an abandoned mine, collapsed by a bunch of weekend warriors with a rocket launcher.

Through the wilderness of the Pacific Northwest, clearly a metaphor for the jungles of Vietnam, Sheriff Teasle and his deputies pursue their resourceful quarry, but they become the hunted.

Exciting, suspenseful, with spectacular stunts, *First Blood* is a stunning film, an adolescent male's fantasy of the super war hero, misunderstood by the society that turned him into a killer and then abandoned him—first by refusing to let him win the war they sent him to fight, then by rejecting him when he returned to the nation he loves.

Rambo can see no life for himself in the real world. "You just can't turn it off!" Rambo howls. "Back there I flew helicopters. I could drive a tank. I was in charge of million dollar equipment. Here, I can't get a job!" Flashing back to the horror when a friend was blown up at his side, Rambo—the Green Beret, the hardened combat hero—dissolves into an incoherent mess.

First Blood was a turning point. Before 1982, other movies about Vietnam featured the victimized, suicidal Vietnam veteran, traumatized by his memories. He was often portrayed as a vagrant, dirty, drifting through life. The other option: He was crazy as a loon. Prior to Rambo, the two most successful Vietnam movies were not likely to encourage anyone to identify with the soldiers in them. *The Deer Hunter*, winner of five Oscars, was not a hero's story. And *Apocalypse Now* was a surrealist exercise in absurdist excess.

But *First Blood* perfectly captured The Hero as Victim—of society, of war, of his own inner demons. It was *because* he is the perfect fighting machine that the Vietnam veteran can't cope with the world, *because* he is a real man. Rambo's ire was directed toward the government, always a safe target. *The government is evil. The government betrayed us.* Hollywood finally caught up with the image of the dysfunctional vet created first by the antiwar movement and veterans' advocates and added its own mythic twist: Vietnam vet as dysfunctional superman.

There are several ironies about the movie and its two sequels, *Rambo: First Blood Part II*, and *Rambo III*. They introduced a new word in the American lexicon: "He's a Rambo." Now Vietnam veterans are forever identified with macho-gone-berserk.

And both actors who starred in the original film are, to be charitable, pretenders. Sylvester Stallone, who played steroidal fighting machine John Rambo, now the epitome of the Vietnam veteran, managed to avoid military service and spent 1965 to 1967 as girls' athletic coach at the American

College of Switzerland in Leysin.[266] (Ironically, in one of his earliest movies, the 1969 *Rebel*, Stallone portrayed Jerry Savage, a college student and "modern-day, urban rebel" who drops out of school to protest the Vietnam War.)

And the sadistic sheriff is portrayed by character actor Brian Dennehy, who appeared in dozens of movies, such as *Presumed Innocent, Cocoon, Semi-Tough, Foul Play, Gorky Park, Silverado, F/X, Legal Eagles, Best Seller,* and *Street Legal,* as well as numerous TV movies and the series *Birdland.*

The actor publicly maintained for years that he was a Vietnam veteran. Dennehy told a *New York Times* reporter in 1989 that he had suffered a concussion and shrapnel wounds during combat.[267] In a *Playboy* interview in 1993, Dennehy was described as serving a "five-year" tour as a Marine in Vietnam, where he suffered minor wounds in combat.

"Ever kill anyone?" asked *Playboy. "Is there a Vietnam movie that nails the experience?"*

As for killing someone, anyone in combat would agree that it's pretty much accidental," Dennehy said. "It's not what you're thinking about. You spend a considerable amount of time just trying not to be in a combat situation. You're trying to avoid coming face-to-face with anything. So when something bad happens, it's usually accidental. But the implication in war movies is that war has this rational beginning, middle, and end. And of course none of it does. It's absolutely fucking chaos. *Apocalypse Now* is the movie. Even more interesting is that it was made so soon after the war was over. It was about the war and a parable about the war. It was and is the most sophisticated overview of the experience."[268]

Dennehy seems like a nice guy, and he is a terrific actor. At six foot three, with the build and the craggy face of an Irish boxer, Dennehy looks the part of the combat-hardened Marine. (He played the tough Marine gunny sergeant in *A Rumor of War.*) But he's not a Vietnam veteran. A scholar-athlete while attending Columbia University, Brian Manion Dennehy was on active duty from September 15, 1959, to June 4, 1963. His military record contains no Vietnam Service Medal, no Armed Forces Expeditionary Medal, no Combat Action Ribbon, no Purple Heart, and no transit orders showing him going to Vietnam. His records show no indication Dennehy was ever wounded, unless he suffered a sprained knee from his duty on his only overseas assignment—as a Marine football player in Okinawa during 1962.[269]

After obtaining the record, I contacted Dennehy's agent and told him there were discrepancies. At his suggestion, I wrote Dennehy a letter; there was no response. I suspect that Dennehy's exaggeration of his military experience started as a way for the actor to gain credibility as a tough guy for the movies.

Rambos 'R' Us

First Blood became a touchstone for pretenders, a pattern to follow consciously and unconsciously. Released one year after the completion of the national Vietnam Veterans Memorial, the movie marked a change in our nation's perception of Vietnam veterans.

During the decade after the war, few real Vietnam veterans wanted to identify themselves as such. The divisiveness, the anger, the confusion made it safer, wiser to file that part of ourselves away. As a Vietnam veteran, society rejected me. But as long as I did not identify myself as a Vietnam veteran, I was accepted. So I assumed my other identities: Vanderbilt graduate, golfer, stockbroker, husband, father.

But Rambo made it okay, even heroic, to be a Vietnam vet. Politicians began to claim Vietnam service while campaigning for office. Sen. John Kerry, who had made a dramatic public splash with his antiwar stand, now wrapped himself in his Vietnam veteran status.

After the release of the second Rambo movie in 1985, counselors in Vet Centers across the country saw an influx of Vietnam veterans seeking help to vanquish their inner demons. Even to counselors who had never been in the military, some were clearly impostors, like the man who went into a Pittsburgh Vet Center in 1988 wearing a Marine Corps shirt and claiming he had served in Da Nang. He was not a day over thirty, making him a preteen during the war.[270] Others wove their stories so well genuine combat veterans were fooled.

Many of these pretenders became "professional" Vietnam vets. Today, they fool psychiatrists, reporters, editors, even the military hierarchy. They learn how from Hollywood and from journalists and authors who swallow their tales and print them for others to study.

The Bogus Vet Phenomenon

Phony war heroes are nothing new. They sprout after every war, claiming heroism they never displayed and wearing medals they never earned.

Since the dawn of civilization it has been the lot of men to be warriors: We go out to the hunt, to protect our women, to fight our enemies. In Greek mythology, the Spartans were regarded as the most ferocious fighters in the ancient world. Spartan mothers were said to give their young sons this grim admonishment as they went off to war: "Come back with your shield or upon it." The saying meant fight well and return to me, or fight well and die honorably. But don't dare be a coward.

Some men fight and return; some stay home and say they went. Military writer and Vietnam vet Dan Cragg has written that phonies claiming combat may have something to do with the feeling of failing an important test of manhood. He pointed to a stanza spoken by King Henry V, on the eve of the Battle of Agincourt, in Shakespeare's famous play:

> And gentlemen in England now a-bed
> Shall think themselves accurs'd they were not here,
> And hold their manhoods cheap whiles any speaks
> That fought with us upon Saint Crispin's day.

Cragg served two tours in Vietnam without ever being shot at or firing a shot. "I can relate to those 'gentlemen in England now a-bed,'"

Cragg said, "When the battles at the Ia Drang were raging I was back in Saigon on General Westmoreland's staff. I didn't know then how lucky I was!" Cragg actually served in the military in Vietnam and felt left out because he wasn't in the thick of combat. Others who were never anywhere near a battlefield may feel that regret even more intensely and make up stories to compensate.

In February 1991, author William Marvel wrote a story for *Blue & Gray*, a history magazine about the Civil War, describing his efforts to determine whether Walter Williams of Houston was indeed America's last surviving veteran of the Civil War. Williams had been granted that status on March 16, 1959, when John Salling, the only other remaining Civil War veteran, died. Despite some cynics who wondered if Williams really was old enough to have fought in the Civil War, the State of Texas and the federal government both confirmed Williams' claim and granted him pensions. When Williams died, his funeral procession became a virtual parade through the center of Houston. Schoolchildren were released from classes, and nearly one hundred thousand people lined the city streets to watch a part of American history laid to rest.

But Marvel's research of census information revealed that Williams was a fraud. Williams had been five years old in 1860, and only ten when the war ended. Not until 1932, when Williams applied for a Confederate pension, did he begin identifying himself as a Civil War veteran.

That was not the end of the tale. Marvel also revealed that "Civil War veteran" Salling also was a pretender; he had been born in 1858, two years before the war began. "Every one of the last dozen recognized Confederates was bogus," Marvel wrote, including all three attendees at the last United Confederate Veterans' reunion. While some faked their status for notoriety, Marvel attributed the motives of most to money. They had falsified their ages during the Depression years to qualify for state pensions.[271]

Marvel identified the last real veteran of the Civil War as Yankee Albert Woolson of Minnesota. A drummer boy during the war, Woolson died in 1956 at the age of 108. But Williams probably will forever be referred to as the last surviving veteran of the Civil War, at least until *Blue & Gray* goes on-line for reporters to access.

Actors like Dennehy have long used military careers to enhance their stature. After the Spanish-American War, actor Tom Mix, one of the highest-paid stars of the silent screen, appeared in more than four hundred movies. He buffed up his masculine image by claiming he had charged up San Juan Hill with Teddy Roosevelt and the Rough Riders.

Mix had been in the Army at the time of Roosevelt's famous charge, but he never left the country or saw combat. Far from being the brave hero, Mix had gone AWOL and was eventually listed as a deserter in military records. (Mix also claimed he had been wounded in desperate gunfights while trying to capture outlaws during his days as a United States marshal. But Mix, who died in 1940, apparently was shot only once—by his wife Victoria, who grabbed one of his collection of small caliber handguns during a domestic altercation.)[272]

William Rich, a World War II fighter pilot with twenty-one combat missions over Europe to his credit, heard about the March 1995 funeral of James Harris Reed, one of America's last World War I veterans. Reports said that Reed had been a flying ace who shot down thirteen German planes on the Western Front, an astonishing feat in the early days of fighter planes. That record made Reed the U.S. Navy's greatest flying ace of World War I.

Reed regaled friends at his nursing home with tales of battling the Red Baron and of his friendship with the great American flyer Eddie Rickenbacker. He talked of being captured by the Germans three times and his two daring escapes. When Rich heard about Reed's exploits, he visited the funeral home and wondered why no official representative of the U.S. government was there. Rich asked the family to donate Reed's medals and pilot's log to the Millville Army Air Field Museum. They complied, but when he received the items, Rich could tell something was wrong. Nothing in the log book looked right. The cover seemed to have been erased, then written over.

Rich discovered the truth when an archivist pointed out that Lt. (j.g.) David Ingalls, with five kills, was the Navy's only ace during World War I. According to military records, Reed had served in the Navy, but as a seaman second class, not a pilot—and not during World War I. Reed was born on July 22, 1907, making him eleven years old when World War I ended.[273]

Johnny Comes Marching Home

The fakers from World War II began even before the war was over. As early as 1943, people recounted stories about buying drinks for soldiers home from the front on leave only to discover their uniformed guests had never left the country. But the nature of the war stories of World War II were dramatically different from those of Vietnam. World War II phonies emphasized the myths of that war—they were all heroes, there was no friendly fire, no fragging, no war crimes, just the boys next door saving America from the Nazis and the Japanese.

Sen. Joe McCarthy told people he was wounded in action as a tailgunner in World War II. In reality, he spent the war behind a desk as an intelligence officer interviewing fliers who had returned from missions and was "wounded" when he got drunk at a party, fell down a ladder, and broke his leg.

A radio announcer named Douglas R. Stringfellow ascended to Congress as a congressman from the First District of Utah based on his tales of courageous clandestine heroics during World War II. After the war, Stringfellow gave hundreds of speeches throughout the state about a dangerous OSS mission that took him and other men behind German lines. Stringfellow maintained that as a private in the Army Air Corps, he had been chosen to participate in a "star" unit of highly qualified men, then surreptitiously was commissioned as an officer to lead the group.

These remarkable American covert operatives parachuted into a wood just south of the great Nuremberg stadium where only days before Hitler had reviewed his elite guard, the SS storm troopers. Once on the ground, they took over the strategic center that was "paramount in all the German Army," and for eleven hours sent and received false messages that completely disrupted the German's war effort, creating weaknesses in the Siegfried Line and upsetting Hitler's timetable for conquering the world. These "cloak-and-dagger boys" later captured one of the key atomic physicists of Germany. Whenever he told the tale, Stringfellow's implication was that he and his group literally had won the war for the allies.

Sadly most of the men were killed. (Note the "dead men can't talk" theme.) Stringfellow and four others were captured by the Germans and ended up at Bergen-Belsen concentration camp where they were beaten and tortured. But with Stringfellow's leadership, they heroically escaped to Allied territory in France. There Stringfellow suffered his most serious injury of the war. While checking out a "jet propulsion factory" the Germans had secretly set up on French soil, Stringfellow was paralyzed by a "bouncing Betty" mine and confined to a wheelchair. Although he had made a remarkable recovery, whenever he appeared in public Stringfellow leaned on a cane. For his heroism, he received a Silver Star.[274]

This absurd story was pockmarked with gaping holes, but the cane and Stringfellow's stirring message of prayer, hope, and righteousness mixed with stories of spies and deeds of daring won over credulous voters.

Skeptics were reluctant to attack his unbelievable stories because Stringfellow clearly was crippled. In 1952, Utah voters elected the thirty-year-old Stringfellow to Congress.

Stringfellow's remarkable heroics were featured on the TV show *This Is Your Life*. But in 1954, when Stringfellow came up for reelection, his political opponents began circulating information that called Stringfellow's clandestine heroics into question. A tear-stained Stringfellow admitted during a televised program called *They Stand Accused* that his dramatic tale was a hoax and withdrew from the election. In reality, Stringfellow had risen no higher than private, had not been involved in clandestine activities, and had never been captured. He saw no combat and received no valorous decorations. Stringfellow's wounds were real, but they occurred when he stepped on a land mine while on a routine training assignment in France on November 19, 1944.

The most amazing thing about Stringfellow's story was the reluctance of some of those around him—who privately had expressed their suspicions—to reveal his lies for what they were. Even after he was exposed on camera, the messages of support that poured in to the TV station indicated that Stringfellow might still have been reelected had he stayed in the campaign!

More than fifty years after the end of World War II, veterans of that war continue to peddle sham tales of heroism to the public. Veteran David Rubitsky of Milton, Wisconsin, claimed that he had "single-handedly" killed six hundred Japanese soldiers in World War II but had been denied the Medal of Honor because he was Jewish. He spent more than sixteen thousand dollars in two years to press his claim with the Army. Rubitsky's heroism was supported by a yellowing photograph of a group of Japanese soldiers. Behind them a message in Japanese says, "Six hundred fine soldiers died because of a solitary American soldier."

But Army spokesmen said there was "incontestable evidence" that Rubitsky had not performed the heroic deeds he had claimed. The evidence included information from Japanese military experts and an investigation of the photograph, which confirmed that the handwriting and words could not have been written by a native speaker of Japanese.[275]

Another World War II veteran took his claims even further. More than twenty-five years after the war ended, Charles Gordon Vick sued the United States government. Vick claimed that, as an enlisted private during the Marine Corps attack on Peleliu in 1944, he penetrated Japanese lines and obtained Japanese maps and plans for the defense of the Japanese homeland. Vick's heroism prompted a battlefield promotion; his commanding general told him that President Roosevelt had appointed him colonel, but he had to keep the promotion secret for twenty-five years. In addition, Vick claimed, he was promised a future promotion: to commandant of the Marine Corps, with the rank of general. When he sued, Vick said he would pass on the position as commandant and would be satisfied with the pay and other emoluments of a full colonel—retroactive to 1944—plus the Medal of Honor and Purple Heart.

Vick had been arrested years earlier for falsely impersonating an officer but was acquitted on the ground that he was insane at the time. During the 1970s, Vick had pressed his claim for retroactive pay and honors through administrative channels; his claimed rank escalated over time. Finally, in 1982, Vick took his claim to the United States Court of Veterans Appeals. It was denied.[276]

For years, a mysterious man known as "General Dennis," claiming to be a highly decorated World War II vet, hung out at conventions of the Orders and Medals Society of America. At one convention, General Dennis dressed as the French equivalent of a major general. His regalia increased over the years until he was wearing the insignia of Marshal of France, the highest possible rank. He boasted numerous foreign medals in combinations that were virtually impossible, all earned on "secret" missions for the French Republic. Not until he appeared wearing most of the American valorous decorations did someone confront him, warning him that wearing unauthorized American medals was illegal.[277]

In 1993, the *San Bernardino Sun* in Southern California ran a story about an area resident who was the nation's "most decorated war hero." William "Bill" Gehris, an Army sergeant during World War II, told the paper he had received fifty-four decorations for his military exploits both in the Army and the Marines. Gehris had been among the first wave of soldiers to hit Utah Beach and had fought with Patton at the Battle of the Bulge. The crusty old sergeant had become well-known for his advocacy on behalf of veterans and had been appointed to California Congressman George Brown's Veterans Affairs Committee. Gehris also served on Congressman Bob Dornan's veterans advisory committee. Selected by the National Veterans of Foreign Wars as national aide-de-camp, Gehris often spoke at veterans' events and participated in parades. In a place of honor at the Redondo Beach VFW post hung an oil painting of Gehris in an Army uniform adorned with his many medals, including the Distinguished Service Cross, the Distinguished Service Medal, six Silver Stars, four Bronze Star Medals, a Legion of Merit, a Soldier's Medal, given for heroic action in saving a soldier's life, and numerous campaign medals from both World War II and the Korean War.[278]

Oddly, Gehris didn't have a Purple Heart. How could anyone receive the DSC and six Silver Stars, given only for heroism in combat, and not be wounded at least once? And Gehris said he received the DSM for charging a German pillbox with a flame-thrower in June 1944. But that medal is rarely given to enlisted personnel, only high-ranking officers for "meritorious service in a position of great responsibility."

While portions of Gehris' file had been destroyed in a fire at the National Personnel Records Center in St. Louis in 1973, many of the documents had been reconstructed. (While many phonies mention this fire as the reason they have no records, very few Vietnam-era records were damaged. Those with the heaviest damage were Army records from 1912 to 1959. Some 1947 to 1963 Air Force records in surnames I through Z were less seriously affected. Many of these records are duplicated at other locations such as the VA and the military finance office and, therefore, can be reconstructed.[279])

His record revealed that Gehris served in the Army from 1941 to 1945, and from 1951 to 1954, when he was discharged as a sergeant. Gehris' Army record showed no decorations for valor. His one Bronze Star Medal had been awarded to all Army infantrymen for meritorious service; the others were service awards given to the typical soldier in the thick of the European campaign. Further, the Marine Corps checked its records and could find no evidence that he had served with them.[280]

The *San Bernardino Sun* features editor reacted with hostility to my suggestion that Gehris' claim to be the most decorated veteran in the nation was false. Gehris had provided documentation for his medals, the editor insisted, and she was satisfied he was real.

Marlowe Churchill, the reporter who had been fooled by "Marvin the trip-wire vet," was working at the Riverside *Press-Enterprise* in Southern California not far from San Bernardino. He wrote a story exposing Gehris, but Gehris refused to back down from his lies. "There are people who don't believe six million Jews were killed, either," Gehris told Churchill.[281]

A few years later, another audacious fraud was exposed in the same region. In 1995, a group of top enlisted men recommended that the Air Force's prestigious 1st Sergeant of the Year Award be named for retired Chief Master Sgt. Spencer B. Dukes, who had an office in the retiree affairs section at March Air Force Base near Riverside. For years after World War II, Dukes frequently stood before groups of airmen, telling the inspiring tale of how he had survived not only the ghastly Bataan Death March in the Philippines (in which hundreds of Allied captives died) but also forty-two months in a Japanese prison camp and the atomic bomb attack on Hiroshima. His many decorations included the Silver Star, the Purple Heart, and the Army's Combat Infantryman Badge.

The first Dukes Award was given that October only to be quietly recalled two months later after retired Chief MSgt. Robert Brown, who did survive the Bataan Death March, raised questions about Dukes's claims. Brown saw a story about Dukes called "A Hero to Look Up to," in the Air

Force Sergeants Association's magazine. He became suspicious of Dukes's claims that he had served with the Philippine Scouts and that he had lived in a prison camp along the Mongolian-Russian border. Brown knew that no U.S. enlisted men worked with the Philippine Scouts. And Brown had been imprisoned in that same camp; he did not remember Dukes, nor was he on the roster of prisoners. In addition, Dukes was not a member of any of the major Bataan survivor's organizations. But Brown's efforts to get someone in authority to check Dukes's service record were rebuffed by Chief MSgt. David Campanale, who declined to look into the matter and even suggested that Brown owed Dukes an apology.

Finally, a notice Brown posted in a veterans' newsletter prompted an investigation by the inspector general. A check of his military records revealed Dukes was not a Bataan survivor. Nor was he a Japanese prisoner of war. He did not even serve during World War II.[282]

Even the "forgotten war," the label now attached to the Korean conflict, produced pretenders. At the dedication of the Korean War Veterans Memorial in Washington, D.C., in July 1995, Oregon Congressman Wes Cooley told reporters that the United States should have accepted nothing less than an unconditional surrender. He also described his service in Korea, saying he had trained with a five-hundred-man Special Forces group as a "demolition expert," with instruction in special tactics, mountain climbing, and escape methods. He added that he could not reveal details of secret missions, and although he left the Army in 1954, he was never officially discharged. Cooley contended he had continued to perform volunteer intelligence work for the United States in his travels in later life.[283]

Cooley's official biography listed him as a Special Forces veteran of the U.S. Army in Korea from 1952-1954. And throughout his campaigns for the House of Representatives, Cooley repeatedly referred to his Korean War service. But a reporter for the Ottaway News Service grew suspicious. He called me and I helped him obtain Cooley's military record.[284]

Cooley's record indicated no Korean service and no combat. When pressed for more details by reporters, Cooley claimed that he had been "in and out of Korea" on sensitive clandestine operations for which records would be limited. Journalists for the Washington Bureau of the Ottaway News Service finally turned to an authoritative source to settle the dispute. An examination of morning reports and duty rosters—the daily records of military units, in which company clerks record the comings and goings of the troops—revealed Cooley had not left the United States during his military service. He did not even finish training until after the war ended.[285]

Cooley's prevarications weren't limited to his military service. It turned out Cooley lied about being Phi Beta Kappa in college, lied about living in the district he represented in Congress, and lied about being a farmer so that he could get a tax break on his land. Cooley and his wife faced a federal criminal investigation when it was discovered she had collected widow's benefits totaling $141,169 after the death of her Marine husband in 1965—benefits she was not entitled to if she were married, as the Cooleys represented themselves to be. Cooley was convicted of campaign fraud by the state of Oregon.[286]

The Victim Hero

Although the phony war hero phenomenon has always existed, after Vietnam it took root and flourished in a way not seen after other wars. For many men (and a few women), the need to explain failed or disappointing lives is perfectly fulfilled by describing themselves as traumatized Vietnam veterans. After all, how could anyone not be affected by all the terrible things one had seen and done in that immoral war? The pretender could be a hero and a victim at the same time.

The dedication of the Vietnam Veterans Memorial in 1982 indicated to the nation that the soldiers who died were worthy of being remembered, and the first Rambo movie, released in 1983, proved to America that despite his victimhood, the Vietnam vet was one tough, patriotic guy.

The shift was most obvious in the political arena. In 1984, Connecticut Rep. Robert Sorensen assured everyone that—although he was opposed to a proposal to open each session of the legislature with the Pledge of Allegiance—he was patriotic. Sorensen's proof? "My patriotism should not be questioned by anyone because when it was necessary, and when my country called me into service, I fought in Vietnam," the thirty-two-year-old Sorensen said on the floor of the state house.

Under pressure from his opponent in his reelection campaign, the politician admitted in an emotional statement to fellow legislators that he had not served in Vietnam.[287] Even as he 'fessed up to his deception, Sorensen tried to dance around it. "For the first time ever, the American public had before them a war in their living rooms," he said. "Every single person in this United States fought in that war in Vietnam. We were all a part of that war in Vietnam because of what was coming to us, what we were feeling, what we were seeing. We all felt the pain. We all felt the anguish that those people felt. So in a sense a part of us was there with every single person that fought there. So in a sense I was there."

That's like a proud father-to-be saying that in a sense, he's just as pregnant as his wife. Sorry, she's the one with the swollen ankles and the labor pains. Still, Sorensen's deceit signaled to the national media that the tide had shifted. "His trespass against legitimate veterans was unfair, but it does certify one constructive change of climate," said an editorial in *The New York Times*. "True or false, service in Vietnam is finally worth boasting about."

By the late eighties, when I began raising money for the Texas memorial, the Rambo image had taken on a life of its own, like a runaway locomotive roaring through a one-horse town. More and more people saw the advantage of getting on board, and they assumed the expected role, repeating the stereotypes they saw in movies and the media.

The presentation of pretended posttraumatic stress can actually take many forms. In 1985, psychologist Loren Pankratz presented a paper at the American Psychiatric Association meeting in Dallas in which he described how patients wove false stories of PTSD into their personal pathology. Although many are malingerers or persons with personality disorders, some have somatoform disorders (focused on physical symptoms), schizophrenia, or other psychiatric disorders.

Many of these phonies have repeated their "memories" of combat so often, they have come to believe them, like those who recover "false memories" as adults. An extreme version of this condition is *pseudologia fantastica*, in which the faker creates a web of reality mixed with unreality, dressing as a Green Beret or SEAL, surrounding himself with the medals and memorabilia to buttress his fantasies and impress others.

Most who make up tales of Vietnam heroism/victimization probably are people with low self-esteem, who feel alienated and rejected by society. When the Rambo image hit Hollywood, they identified with him much more quickly than did the Vietnam veterans who had high self-esteem, who went into the military with a large amount of pride and patriotism, did their jobs, and returned home. Inevitably, when pretenders are exposed, their close friends and family refuse to believe that they have been so completely fooled.

After researching the bogus Vietnam vet phenomenon for almost a decade, I realized that although they overlap, most fakers fit into a handful of loose categories. The list could be endless, but the cases in the next chapter illustrate common elements.

9

Would I Lie to You?

STALLONE'S RAMBO embodied a twisted logic: He failed in life precisely *because* of his combat competence. (One of Marvin's friends in the trip-wire vet series howled that none of them could hold a job because they were trained only to kill, a refrain repeated by Steve in "The Wall Within.")

This reasoning collapses when you look at all the soldiers, Marines, and sailors who rise to prominence in civilian life. Usually those who excel in the military do well outside the armed services. But symbols are more powerful than logic. Everyone "knows" that a Vietnam veteran is a broken individual who has a difficult time functioning in society. For the homeless, undereducated, or jobless, claiming Vietnam vet status can mean restoring self-respect. The war persuasively explains their inability to function in society.

Why the deceivers lie probably emerges from deep feelings of inadequacy, the need to be seen as a man's man, bigger than life. For some, belonging to a group defined as "warriors" is irresistible. Darrow (Duke) Tully, publisher of the *Arizona Republic* and *Phoenix Gazette*, often bragged to friends and reporters that he was a decorated Air Force pilot who had flown 105 missions over Korea and Vietnam. He often wore full dress uniform to formal events. Tully was forced to resign as publisher in 1985 after the Maricopa County attorney revealed that he had never served in the Air Force or *any* branch of the military.[288]

The media helps many pretenders portray themselves as heroes. At times, journalists' gullibility reaches ludicrous levels, as in the tale of Kevin Holt, a former Howard University groundskeeper. In January 1996, reporter Dana Priest of the *Washington Post* wrote about Holt after the

175

Defense Department ordered him detained in Bosnia for questioning about terrorist activities. Holt had appeared at an earlier interview with another *Post* reporter carrying an M-16 assault rifle, dressed in Army camouflage fatigues, and draped with Vietnam War paraphernalia. In the story, Holt was described by Priest as a Vietnam veteran in his "mid-thirties"—making him about twelve when the war ended. Priest even mentioned that Holt had been arrested previously for posing as an American serviceman, but the story didn't question his claim that he had served in Vietnam.[289]

Patterns emerge when comparing pretenders and why they lie about Vietnam service. While some use it to excuse their failures, others use it to polish their professional image, to hide criminal behavior, to get attention, to extort money from sympathetic people, even to get elected.

The Failed Life

- In the summer of 1979, a pregnant twenty-eight-year-old house-keeper was found dead in a hotel room in Newport News, Virginia. The young woman had been handcuffed and shot three times in the abdomen with a high-powered rifle. In a duffel bag left in the room the previous week, police found photographs of twenty-five-year-old Reginald Kilpatrick in full Marine Corps uniform, along with three diaries of his service in Vietnam. Kilpatrick had written about slaying some of the enemy, having a "license to kill," and about "killing some civilians when he got back in the United States." He also wrote about undergoing "reeducation" in Okinawa so he wouldn't kill when he returned to the United States.[290]

  A shipfitter, Kilpatrick looked every inch the Marine. He kept to himself, although others in the hotel could hear him playing a recording of the Battle Hymn of the Republic and the National Anthem before he went to work. A friend described Kilpatrick as "different," always thinking someone was after him. "I think he was a little messed up in the head," a clerk told a reporter. "He told us he had been wounded in the Marines."[291]

  After the murder of the housekeeper, a police bloodhound tracked him to a wooded area near the inn. After a ten-hour standoff, a nine-man SWAT team captured the heavily armed, camouflage-garbed Kilpatrick when he jumped from his hiding place, screamed, and pointed a high-powered carbine at police. Although he was wearing a flak jacket, Kilpatrick was seriously injured when he was shot in the buttocks and torso with buckshot. In his pocket was a Marine identi-fication card with an April 1977 expiration date. Before he died of his wounds, Kilpatrick told investigators that he had shot a vending machine repairman and gone into hiding in the woods. He had returned to the hotel for his duffel bag when the housekeeper confronted him. Kilpatrick confessed to her murder.

Investigators later learned that Kilpatrick had been stationed with the Marine Corps at Camp Lejeune but was discharged in 1977 after being convicted of making obscene phone calls to a member of a local school board. He had not served in Vietnam. His "diaries" were elaborate fabrications.

- Mechanic Richard Dale Moore made a habit of fixing neighbors' cars and helping them do repairs on their mobile homes in Grand Prairie, Texas. If he had a violent temper when he was drunk, which was frequently, and if he routinely carried a knife, and if he was often arrested for driving while intoxicated, well, that was understandable. He told everyone of the horrors he had seen as a Marine in Vietnam.

  One night in October 1993, people attending a party near his home called police, complaining that Moore was intoxicated and "out of control." Officers Gene Evans and Lisa Thomas escorted Moore home. But a few minutes after the officers left, Moore, furious at those who had called the police, tried to return to the party with a shotgun. Someone saw him and again alerted police. Moore scurried home and tried to hide the shotgun, followed by the two police officers. Although his wife attempted to calm him down, Moore threatened to release a dog on them. When the officers tried to subdue him with pepper spray, Moore pulled his ever-present lockblade knife and came at the police. Officer Evans shot and killed the mechanic.

  The tragic story was reported in the *Dallas Morning News*, which pointed out that Moore was a former Marine and Vietnam veteran— yet another man whose life was ruined by 'Nam.[292] But according to military records, although Moore had served in the Marine Corps from 1971 to 1977, he never had left the United States during his enlistment. A tenth-grade dropout, Moore spent most of his service as a motor vehicle operator in North Carolina.[293]

- In 1988, when former teacher Michael Spradling ran for a local school board in North Texas, he told reporters he had been a federal drug agent and a hospital administrator and was working on a doctorate degree. Spradling also liked to tell people he was a Vietnam veteran, a war hero. Spradling frequently grabbed a loaded gun and threatened people who ventured onto his property. His ex-wife described him as a "walking time bomb."

  Four years later, after Spradling sent sexually explicit letters to female students, he was charged with felony distribution and display of harmful material. A state district judge voided Spradling's teaching certificate and fined him one thousand dollars. His mental condition deteriorated. Spradling built a house with no windows because he did not want people to look in. He started fires outside and threatened to kill his family. A psychiatrist prescribed lithium, a common treatment for manic-depression. But Spradling refused to take the medication.

The "time bomb" exploded one Sunday in 1992 when Spradling became increasingly agitated because his children were not getting dressed fast enough, and they were going to be late for church. Spradling's fourteen-year-old son Kris, pushed to the limit by his dad's emotional and verbal abuse, grabbed a .38-caliber pistol and shot his father five times. After the shooting, which Spradling survived, his ex-wife told reporters that although Spradling loved to play the war hero, he had not served in Vietnam. Spradling had been discharged from the Marines after suffering heat stroke in boot camp.[294]

Meaningful Ribbons, Medals

In the military, rank sets the tone of every conversation. Every person knows his or her position in the hierarchy. But beyond rank, what most distinguishes status among peers are ribbons and medals on uniforms. They show campaigns served, wounds suffered, valorous feats performed.

A highly decorated military man or woman is automatically thought to be a leader, someone destined for higher rank. Often in the competitive world of military promotions, the individual who prevails is the one most decorated. Because the mission of the military is to fight and win wars, combat experience is highly valued.

Adding medals and decorations to your "fruit salad" is not unlike resume inflation in the civilian world, with one big difference: Wearing unearned military awards is illegal, punishable by prison and a fine. When committed on active duty, such fraud can result in a dishonorable discharge and loss of retirement benefits.

- His peers in the 1st Special Forces Group at Fort Lewis, near Tacoma, Washington, regarded chaplain Maj. Gary Probst as one of their most decorated and highly regarded soldiers. A Green Beret and Ranger in Vietnam, Probst was a master paratrooper, an expert field medic, and an explosives expert.

  After returning to the states, Probst, a minister, became an Army chaplain. He wore the Bronze Star Medal, the Ranger Tab, the Special Forces Badge, the Vietnam Campaign Ribbon, the Marine Corps Expeditionary Medal, and other decorations. But Probst did not graduate from the elite Ranger or Green Beret schools and was not a master paratrooper, explosives expert, or field medic, and he never served in Vietnam.

When Probst's lies were exposed in 1990, he hinted that he wore the decorations and badges showing expert training to gain the trust of soldiers, as all good chaplains must. "If anything, those things can be helpful at times," Probst told a reporter.

A Special Forces soldier in his unit didn't see it that way. "He tried to make himself look like some kind of war hero when he wasn't," the soldier told a reporter. "For a Green Beret—or a Ranger—that's just about the worst thing you can do."[295]

• As a judge advocate in the U.S. Marine Corps, Capt. Jeffrey Zander was a rising star. Unlike most military lawyers, whose combat experience is limited to battling rivals with their tongues, Zander wore numerous impressive combat decorations. Zander had been involved in Operation "Frequent Wind," the evacuation of Saigon in April 1975. After seeing a bus full of refugees hit by mortar fire, Zander rushed from his position of safety, pushed the badly injured driver aside, and steered the bus to shelter, saving many lives. For that heroism, Zander became the first American Marine to be awarded the prestigious Croix de Guerre by the French government since 1917. He also received the Bronze Star Medal for valor and a Purple Heart for shrapnel wounds inflicted during the attack.

When he became a military lawyer, that wartime experience paid off in many ways. Zander's prior enlistment and Vietnam service "adds an 'indefinable' character to his presence," said one superior reviewing the attorney's performance, according to Lincoln Caplan, a lawyer who wrote a cover story about Zander in the March 1995 issue of the *ABA Journal*.[296]

In 1988, Zander ranked number one among the three hundred graduates of his judge advocate training class. The next year as a prosecutor in Okinawa, Japan, he obtained convictions in all but one of his sixty-four cases. Several years later he was picked for a master's program for American military lawyers. The only problem was that Zander had not passed the bar exam. He had doctored papers to gain entrance to the Judge Advocate General Corps. And his claims of combat heroism and service in Vietnam were lies. Zander had not enlisted until 1976.

Runaway ego and burning ambition apparently prompted the wholesale fraud. Upon leaving active duty and joining the Marine reserves, Zander had used the GI Bill to attend law school at Brigham Young University. But his prospects of getting into the Judge

Advocate General Corps were slim; few new lawyers were being brought in. Pressed by financial problems, too stressed to prepare himself for the bar exam, Zander doctored a certificate granting membership to the California bar to another lawyer named James Henry Zander, then forged a document showing he changed his name from James Henry to Jeffrey.

Then Zander created a counterfeit DD-214 (discharge paper) showing he had joined in 1974 and served in Vietnam. Not content to claim mere service, Zander began awarding himself medals—not only the Croix de Guerre, Bronze Star Medal, and Purple Heart, but also the Combat Action Ribbon, National Defense Service Medal, Armed Forces Expeditionary Medal, Humanitarian Service Medal, Navy-Marine Corps Parachutist Wings, and (bizarrely) the Antarctica Service Medal.

The ruse unraveled in 1993 when Zander was charged with incompetence and found himself on trial. Convicted of felony violations of the Uniform Code of Military Justice, he was expelled in disgrace from the Marine Corps and sentenced to 120 days in the brig at Quantico, Virginia. The Marine Corps was forced by the military court of appeals to overturn the convictions of more than fifty servicemen Zander had represented.

Zander's fraud prompted a change in the Marine code of honor. Judge advocates now are required to submit proof of their good standing in a bar. It's called the "Zander Rule."

Impress the Boss

- Shouting "lock and load!"—the supposed battle cry of 'Nam—was the way Wall Street whiz Jeff Beck pumped himself before big meetings at Drexel Burnham Lambert during the merger mania and financial shenanigans of the 1980s. Beck built a reputation as a "rainmaker," participating in some of the largest corporate takeovers in history. Friends affectionately called him "Mad Dog," his nickname from two tours of duty in Vietnam.

  The high-stakes high-roller told awed business colleagues gruesome stories of combat, telling how as a Green Beret he slit enemy soldiers' throats and performed covert ops for the CIA. During a fancy dinner party, Beck might roll up the left sleeve of his shirt and point to a scar on his wrist etched there by an AK-47 round ripping through his flesh during a battle in the Ia Drang Valley. Only a tough Seiko watch had saved his hand, Beck told awed listeners. Before returning to the United States, his heroics had earned him a Silver Star, two Bronze Star Medals, and four Purple Hearts.

To some, the war seemed to have left Beck mentally disturbed. He had a reputation for doing wild and outlandish stunts, like gobbling down a box of dog biscuits while talking to the chairman of RJR Nabisco, making barnyard noises in the halls of his firm's offices, and concealing fake vomit in his tuxedo jacket at fancy dinners for use as a practical joke after the soup course.

Beck snared a bit part in the movie *Wall Street* when director Oliver Stone hired him as a consultant. At a dinner for the cast, Stone and Beck swapped war stories. Stone thought he was talking to a fellow veteran, one still disturbed by Vietnam. Actor Michael Douglas, star of *Wall Street*, proposed making a movie called *Mad Dog* based on Beck's Vietnam experiences.

But Beck's tough-guy, Vietnam hero image was a sham. "Mad Dog" Beck had enlisted in the Army reserves to avoid the draft. His record indicated that he did not serve in Vietnam, nor did he ever serve on active duty other than for training. In early 1990, when a reporter for the *Wall Street Journal* exposed Beck's fraud, a woman who knew him between his three marriages described how combat-trauma nightmares left him trembling. "The guy lied in his sleep!" the outraged woman told the reporter. Beck's explanation of the difference between his stories and his records: He had been an intelligence agent, and thus his records were "classified," an alibi that has become a lame cliché.[297]

- Another of Wall Street's most ambitious executives was James Darr, who from 1979 to 1988 headed the limited partnership unit of Bache and Company, a major investment house. Darr's unit proved so profitable that higher-ups left him alone to build his empire.

  The son of a shoe salesman, Darr assiduously cultivated a macho war hero image. He bragged to some that he flew an F-4 Phantom jet fighter on undercover operations for the CIA during his tour in Vietnam. To other acquaintances, Darr boasted that as a helicopter pilot, he and his cronies liked to fly at treetop level over rivers in Vietnam, trying to drop low enough to make the aircraft's wheels spin by touching the water. Some friends were told by Darr that he served in Special Forces, others that he was a civilian who worked for the CIA. Later Darr chucked those stories for a new one: He had not been in Vietnam at all, but because he spoke fluent Farsi, he spent the war years on assignment for the CIA in Iran to support the Shah.

  In reality, Darr spent his years of active duty in the Air Force as a logistics officer at Hill Air Force Base in Utah, which provided parts and maintenance for F-4 jet fighters and other weapons. He never served in Vietnam. Darr's empire crumbled in 1991, when the value of the limited partnership unit tumbled, and he came under scrutiny for conflicts of interest. Under investigation, the lies about his service exposed, Darr quietly resigned.[298]

Elect a Hero

Throughout two centuries of American history, a superlative military record was considered an absolute prerequisite for attaining high political office. Very few U.S. presidents—Bill Clinton aside—have had no military service. Briefly during the 1970s, Vietnam service was more likely to cost candidates elections rather than help them, but that changed in the 1980s. In 1986, Royall H. Switzler, a Republican state representative, ran for governor of Massachusetts touting his status as a Green Beret in Vietnam to take advantage of the newly emerging respect for veterans of the war. But Switzler had not been a member of the elite Special Forces in Vietnam, as he claimed; he had served a peacetime hitch in Korea. When the charade was exposed, he first attributed the "embellishment" to his campaign staff. Switzler finally went on television and admitted that he had lied.

"I pretended to be someone I wasn't," Switzler said, adding that he felt his real hitch in the Army hadn't been quite heroic enough. "My pretense took on a life of its own and almost became real."[299]

He then explained his mendacity as a form of flattery. "I owe an apology to those who served in Vietnam," Switzler said. "It was out of the high esteem that I hold for you that I took your honor as my own and in doing so did you a grave injustice."[300]

During a 1992 bid for the presidency, Sen. Tom Harkin of Iowa claimed that he had served as a pilot in Vietnam. His claim had surfaced eight years before, during a 1984 bid for reelection to the Senate, when Harkin boasted that he had served one year in Vietnam flying F-4s and F-8s on combat air patrols and photo-reconnaissance support missions. Challenged by Sen. Barry Goldwater, Harkin did a quick shuffle, claiming that he had actually flown combat sorties over *Cuba* during the sixties. Harkin finally admitted he had not seen combat but had served as a ferry pilot stationed in Atsugi, Japan, flying aircraft to be repaired from Atsugi to the Philippines. When pressed by reporters to explain how much time he really spent in Vietnam, Harkin estimated that over a year, he flew in and out of Vietnam a dozen or so times. But Harkin's military record showed no Vietnam service decorations. He finally conceded he had not flown combat air patrols in Vietnam and began describing himself as a Vietnam *era* vet.[301]

Candidates for president and governor receive intense press scrutiny, but the claims of many of those running for lesser elective offices who wave their Vietnam service as proof of their patriotism may undergo little serious analysis—except by their opponents.

- In 1990, former Ku Klux Klan Grand Wizard David Duke ran for the U.S. Senate in Louisiana. He bragged about his exploits in covert operations in Vietnam, where he instructed anti-Communist officers and volunteered to go on rice drops behind enemy lines on Air America, the airline run by the CIA.

  "I went over to Southeast Asia to fight communism," Duke boasted in one campaign appearance, claiming he worked for nine months in Laos for the U.S. State Department. He flashed pictures of himself on an airplane in Laos, contending that he had flown twenty "rice runs" out of the Laotian capital Vientiane. On one flight, Duke claimed, the plane caught enemy fire and "a piece of mortar lodged in my belt." At a rally in Chalmette, Duke told a crowd that he often volunteered to go behind enemy lines. "A couple of times I almost didn't come back," Duke said.

  Vietnam veterans protested Duke's statements, pointing out that the airport used for rice runs out of Laos was Watty Air Base, not Vientiane. In reality, Duke had gone to great lengths to avoid military service. His only contact with the military had been a brief stint in the ROTC while he was enrolled at Louisiana State University. Duke was forced to leave the school because of his Nazi leanings.

  Duke inflated a visit to Laos into a tour of duty behind enemy lines. His only contact with Southeast Asia came in 1971 when Duke stopped briefly in Laos during a stopover while on a worldwide vacation. His father, who worked in Laos, found him one of those jobs routinely arranged for visiting children of Americans—teaching English to a handful of Laotian military officers. He was fired after about two months when he drew a Molotov cocktail on the blackboard.[302]

- Retired Lt. Col. Michael Donley was well known among his peers as a black Vietnam War hero who was still struggling to put the horrors of combat behind him. The first vice president of the Dallas-area NAACP, an elective office, Donley claimed he used religion and the teachings of Martin Luther King and Malcolm X to overcome the trauma the war caused in his life.

  Drafted while a student at Howard University in 1972, Donley joined the Air Force. At age nineteen, he began attending Officer Training School, but didn't actually have to report to his unit until much later, allowing him time to finish his bachelor's degree. Donley then volunteered for a year of survival training, which took him to Alaska, Panama, and Spain.

Somehow, he accomplished all that school work and military training in time to ship out for Vietnam in 1973. His first day in-country, Donley was ordered to lead the rescue of a downed Huey transport helicopter in the Delta region. "By the time we'd gotten there, VC had overrun the position, and our job really became retrieving the bodies," he told a reporter. Donley said his squad had to walk out on foot because ground fire made landing air transport impossible.

A few months later he was again aboard a Huey, this time on a classified mission. "We lost our rotor," Donley said. "All we could do was spin down." When Donley was shot in the leg, his sergeant threw him over his shoulder and carried him two hundred yards to cover. Treated in Japan, Donley was sent back into combat. Five months later, Donley was shot in the same leg. Finally, two Purple Hearts to his credit, he was sent home where he retired from the military as a lieutenant colonel.

But his ordeal had just begun. Donley struggled with his war memories, waking in the night with the memories of the stench of burning bodies, the sounds of screaming. The internal pressures cost him two marriages. Not until he met a fellow veteran running an out-reach center and accepted Jesus "as my Lord and Savior" did Donley's nightmares of combat end.

"We all did what we had to do," Donley said. "It's long past time to put it behind us. A lot of veterans are angry they were never wel-comed home. The only time I was told 'welcome home' was two years ago."[303]

That may be because Donley did not actually serve in Vietnam. Military records show Donley was stationed at Webb Air Force Base, Texas, during his tour of duty—as an enlisted inventory management specialist. A supply clerk. Not an officer nor a retired lieutenant colonel. No combat. No Purple Hearts. Only an active imagination.[304]

- During his campaign for city council in Addison, a suburb of Dallas, William Archie "Bud" Akin boasted that he had served as a lieutenant in Vietnam and piloted A-4 Skyhawks for five years in the U.S. Navy. After his stint in the service, Akin worked for twenty-five years as a corporate pilot, an important skill in a town that prided itself on its small but busy corporate airport.

His other qualifications were also impressive. Student for two years at the University of Alabama. Former city council member in

Perrine, Florida. Developer and manager of a $12 million real estate project. Likable, apparently talented, Akin was duly elected. But his tenure was marked by turmoil. Accused of "meddling" in an important lawsuit against the city, hiring friends for contracts, and wasting city funds, Akin became the target of a recall campaign.

That's when voters discovered that Akin was one of the biggest impostors to ever gain public office in Texas. Few of the accomplishments Akin had claimed were true. The town of Perrine did not have a city council after 1949, so he could not have served as a councilman. Akin did not attend the University of Alabama; he did not even have a high school diploma.

After obtaining a GED, Akin joined the Navy at age seventeen in 1960. But Akin's rank at discharge after three years of active duty was E-3, not lieutenant, as he claimed. Akin did not serve in Vietnam. He was assigned to the USS *Bon Homme Richard*, an aircraft carrier. Although the ship sometimes cruised the waters off Southeast Asia, records revealed that the only award Akin earned was the Good Conduct Medal, an indication the ship did not sail in Vietnam's coastal waters when he was aboard.[305] And the closest Akin came to flying Skyhawk jets was in 1988, when he took out a student pilot's license. He allowed it to lapse before qualifying for his pilot's license.

After the Addison *Register* printed the results of its investigation of Akin, the city councilman abruptly disappeared from town.[306]

- In the late seventies, Bill Church of Chattanooga had a problem. He wanted to start a splinter group of the Ku Klux Klan known as the Justice Knights. But there was hot competition in his region for new KKK recruits. Desperate for attention and publicity, the six-foot-three, three-hundred-pound Church let the world know that not only was he a martial arts expert, he also was a combat-hardened Vietnam vet with experience in Green Beret and Ranger units.

"I'm one of these 'Nam vets who believes in violence," Church said. "If someone gets in my way, he's liable to get blown away himself."[307]

Church planned to offer combat and survival-type training—for a small fee, of course. He liked to carry weapons and made sure his motley band of recruits displayed plenty of firepower at their meetings. In April 1980, Church and members of his small group of followers were charged with four counts of assault with intent to commit murder after a cross-burning turned bloody, leaving four elderly and middle-aged black women wounded. Church was acquitted when another Klansman confessed to firing the shotgun blasts that injured the women.

Church's pathetic group was short-lived. Still, his boasts left the impression that a PTSD-crazed veteran turned KKK leader after his horrendous experiences in Vietnam. But Church was not a Vietnam veteran. Born in October 1956, he didn't turn seventeen until six months after American troops withdrew from Vietnam in 1973. He entered the Army in 1976, and his MOS was "metal body repairman." Church spent only a year and eighteen days on active duty.

• When private investigator James Joseph Young Jr. went into business in Dallas, he made much of his experiences as a Special Forces colonel who saw combat in three wars—World War II, Korea, and Vietnam. He used the title "Retired Colonel" and scattered military memorabilia throughout his office. Young proudly talked about his experiences in covert operations and his many decorations, which included the Distinguished Service Cross, two Purple Hearts, and more than fifty commendations from the Army. Young spoke regularly at local high schools, helping to recruit young men and women for the Army. In November 1986, he was given the prestigious task of serving as presiding officer of a Special Forces Association ceremony at the JFK memorial in downtown Dallas, asked to say a few words in memory of the fallen president.

But Young had served in only World War II and had been discharged as a private first class when the war ended. No heroics, no covert ops, no Korea, or Vietnam. Young's elaborate fantasies were exposed in a bizarre way by a true hero.

In 1987, Young was hired by a Dallas developer to kill his estranged wife. Young turned to an acquaintance to help him find a hitman. The friend was the late Fred William Zabitosky. As a Green Beret in Vietnam, Zabitosky was assistant team leader of a nine-man Special Forces recon team. The group was operating deep within enemy territory on February 19, 1968, when a larger NVA force attacked. Although seriously wounded himself, Zabitosky rescued the injured pilot from a burning helicopter while under heavy enemy fire. He received the Medal of Honor for his heroism.[308]

After being approached by Young, Zabitosky immediately contacted the FBI. He cooperated with federal agents by setting up a sting, telling Young he wasn't interested but that he could find someone who was. Taped by Zabitosky talking about the hit, Young ultimately pleaded guilty to his involvement in the proposed murder-for-hire and went to prison.[309]

• In twenty years as a private eye in Houston, Ed Pankau wowed clients and reporters alike. As head of Intertect Inc., a burgeoning investigation firm with offices in eight states, Pankau's colorful back-ground provided spice for stories about him in *Business Week*, *The New York Times*, and other publications. He frequently appeared on local and national television programs as a fraud and security expert. Pankau's 1992 book, *Check It Out!* garnered attention in everything from women's magazines to *Playboy*.[310] The self-proclaimed son of a bootlegger, Pankau handed out a resume that painted the image of a clever, resourceful sleuth who had been toughened in battle and trained by law enforcement and other government agencies to sniff out criminals and put them away. Pankau told reporters he had been a Green Beret in Vietnam and that he had been wounded in battle. After the war, Pankau said he had worked as a special agent for the IRS and as a police officer in Florida. Like a character in a pulp detec-tive novel, Pankau was always pulling off some outrageous case. Pankau claimed that he helped bust the infamous "Murph the Surf" gang of jewel thieves and brought down a presidential candidate by videotaping Sen. Gary Hart in the illicit company of Donna Rice. Even as parachutes of American troops blossomed above his head, Pankau, on assignment in Panama for another case, rushed into a blazing building and grabbed a computer printout documenting where Panamanian leader Manual Noreiga had stashed $800 million in assets. After a story about him called "A New Breed of Sam Spade" appeared in *The New York Times*, publishers came calling. Pankau made a deal with Macmillan Inc. for his autobiography.[311]

Pankau had already written a partial manuscript called *Easy Money* about his extraordinary life. "Based on the true life experiences of Ed Pankau, president of Intertect, Inc., *Easy Money* is the story of the fraud, greed, and corruption causing the breakdown of society throughout the United States," the summary said.

The manuscript described how Pankau, during a tour of duty in Vietnam as a "Sneaky Pete" Special Forces sergeant, was forced to assassinate a guard. Pankau and his squad had been sent to Vietnam "to bring a cannibal tribe into the modern world of personal warfare. We taught a tribe of Muong (sic) cannibals how to kill much more effectively with machine guns, mines, and Claymores than the machetes, spears, and blowguns that they had used for thousands of years.

"That first patrol was where I put months of specialized training to use where they had me crawl through the muck of a rice patty (sic) up to and behind a sentry guarding the entrance to a VC supply base. I remembered the feel of pulling the sentry's back into my col-larbone and driving six inches of cold, hard steel into the front of his throat and the smell of his lifes (sic) blood as it ran down my arm."[312]

His writing was amateurish, but one agent was excited because the manuscript promised juicy details about top government officials consorting with crime figures and people Pankau called "unknown Keatings," white collar criminals who had stolen millions in the savings and loan debacles of the 1980s. If true, Pankau's tidbits about celebrities and major political figures could create a sensation when the book was published. But after working on a proposal, one potential collaborator backed out of the project. While doing normal background research, the experienced writer realized the details Pankau had provided about his military background and specialized training were not completely accurate.

Another author, Robert Pack, spent six months researching Pankau's life. He also abandoned the project. "I do not believe it is possible to produce a true, libel-free, original book about your life and career," Pack wrote Pankau in April 1993. The letter became public after Pankau filed a defamation suit against Pack seeking more than $5 million in damages, and a story about the lawsuit appeared in the *Wall Street Journal*.[313]

According to military records, Edmund Pankau served in the Army from June 10, 1963 to July 23, 1964, but not as a Green Beret killing people behind enemy lines and training mountain cannibals in methods of modern warfare. Pankau's highest active-duty rank was private first class during a period in which he earned no Special Forces qualification, no Combat Infantryman Badge, no Vietnam Service Ribbon. Pankau served as a parachute rigger. The closest he came to the war was during an eighteen-day stint attached to the 1st Special Forces Group packing chutes in Okinawa, more than a thousand miles from Vietnam.[314]

Pankau had also distorted his other credentials. The Tallahassee Police Department searched its records and found no record that Edmund Pankau or "Edmund Von Pankau" had been employed by them as a police officer, as he had claimed. His eyewitness account of seeing American troops airdrop while he was in a downtown Panama City building was ludicrous; the drop zone was sixteen miles away. And Pankau had not been a special agent for the IRS; he was a trainee who failed the background check and stayed less than a year.

The Association of Certified Fraud Examiners revoked Pankau's certificate and expelled him from the organization after a three-member board of review conducted its own investigation and concluded that the flamboyant private detective had "made numerous conflicting public statements about his alleged role, if any, in several different investigations."[315]

Wall Street Journal reporter Laura Johannes pointed out that Pankau may have let slip one of the secrets to his success in his book *Check It Out!* regarding uncovering the truth about people. "The true secret of the supersleuths is often a glib-tongued, smooth-talking little pretext, a white lie that often falls into the gray area, but not illegal, realm of the law," Pankau wrote.[316]

The Mysterious Hero

Although he may work as an accountant, mechanic, or not work at all, this type of pretender loves to talk about serving with elite units like Green Berets and SEALs, going on secret missions with classified orders, or running covert "ops" with the CIA.

The mysterious hero typically is a great actor and storyteller, instinctively understanding something all good con men know: An aura of mystery allows other people's imaginations to run wild. He gives his listeners just enough details and allows their minds to manufacture the rest. The kicker is that the stories can't be proved or disproved. When a records search shows he was never in the military or that he was a clerk, the clandestine warrior just says, "Of course, there are no records. The types of missions I was on were highly classified."

Don't believe that excuse. People who are chosen for those types of missions must have extensive training, and that *does* show up on military records. And don't trust someone who insists the citations for his heroic medals are "classified." Citations for covert operations are just like citations for other combat missions. The only difference is that they are purposely vague about locations and other details.

- During a 1990 Desert Shield panel discussion, "veteran" Dennis J. Tierney talked about his ongoing battle with the symptoms of post-traumatic stress disorder, and sported a Vietnam POW-MIA hat. As chief executive officer and general manager of The Highground, a veterans' memorial in Wisconsin, Tierney often told people that he served with the U.S. Army Special Forces during the Vietnam War from 1967 to 1972, when he was wounded.

  To those he knew well, Tierney provided more juicy details. In Vietnam, Tierney claimed, his orders came from the CIA. "I did stuff you guys normally didn't do," he told a Highground board member. When pressed for details, Tierney hedged: "I'm not in a position or at liberty to discuss that with you." But he continued to sow hints that he was a covert operative, signing one letter to supporters this way:

"Dennis Tierney; Grandma's Helper; U.S. Army 5th Special Forces; S.O.G. 'Up Country' 67-72; Zulu P-5-L." Because Tierney "talked the talk and walked the walk," there was no reason for his fellow Vietnam vets to doubt him. But finally someone grew suspicious and began looking into his military record.[317]

During the period he said he was in Southeast Asia, Tierney was actually working at a Chicago-area pickle factory. And divorce court records showed he had a job in Detroit for at least part of 1968 and 1969. Tierney received a ticket for speeding in the Chicago area in January 1970, and he applied for an Illinois driver's license in March 1971, both periods when he was supposed to be in Vietnam. No records could be found to indicate Tierney ever served in the military.[318]

- One night in 1988, a psychiatric social worker named Keith Roberts told a pretty young woman whom he had treated for depression at a Dallas-area psychiatric hospital to meet him at a local hotel and to bring a dog leash and a change of clothes. At the hotel, Roberts tied her up, slipped a black leather hood over her head and a red dog collar around her neck and attached a leash to it. While having sex with her, Roberts told her he had been part of an assassination team in Vietnam, highly trained men who infiltrated villages at night and slit civilians' throats. The grisly story terrified the young woman. Roberts' message was clear: Tell and you're dead.

  Roberts used the story not just in bizarre seduction ploys. He told others around the hospital the same wild stories of assassinating civilians in Vietnam. But the truth came out when the young woman filed a personal injury lawsuit against Roberts and the hospital where he worked: The psychiatric social worker had not served in Vietnam. The young patient was awarded $1.1 million.[319]

- For twenty years, Dennis Chapman kept his silence about the many secret missions he had performed as a SEAL in Vietnam. But in 1987, after moving to the small town of Bend, Oregon, he decided to come clean. Chapman regaled his new friends with awesome tales of bravery, describing how he rescued a pilot shot down behind enemy lines with a thousand NVA troops in hot pursuit. Before Chapman's military career was ended by combat wounds, he had been awarded the Silver Star, two Bronze Star Medals, the Purple Heart, and two Presidential Unit Citations.

  He joined a number of Oregon veterans' groups, able to devote time and effort to their projects by virtue of monthly checks Chapman received from the VA as a result of being declared 100 percent disabled. Although Vietnam was in the past, Chapman told his buddies of another tragedy, more recent and still raw: The untimely death of his mother from a heart attack.

Chapman's many secrets might have remained concealed except for one thing. In 1990, he applied for a permit to carry a concealed weapon. The routine background investigation was alarming. Chapman's mother had been murdered execution-style in Arizona not long after her son had sold her a $1 million life insurance policy. Indicted and jailed for the murder, Chapman was released on a technicality.

After that disturbing news, an Oregon veterans' group began looking into Chapman's past. He had not been a SEAL, had not seen combat, did not earn awards for heroism, had not been wounded, and hadn't served in Vietnam. Chapman had been discharged from the military as unsuitable.[320]

- Fewer than 1 percent of all VFW post commanders are granted the distinction of being named "All American" by the Veterans of Foreign Wars. But Joe Bennett, former post commander in Middlesex County, New Jersey, was one of those men. Bennett was distinguished in another way. He had served in Southeast Asia for thirty months. After training in underwater demolition and "sniper and survival school," Bennett was assigned to a Marine recon unit. His clandestine operations took him to Laos, Cambodia, Thailand, and Vietnam. From early 1960 to the end of 1962, Bennett said, he spent most of his time in the jungles of South Vietnam, training indigenous tribesmen to fight the North Vietnamese. One of the ways they convinced the tribesmen to fight the Communists was to ship them to the Philippines and send them on free shopping trips at the Subic Bay PX.[321]

Bennett's official VFW bio said that after thirty months in Southeast Asia, he was reassigned to Camp LeJeune and—"as fate would have it"—his tour was extended six months by "presidential orders" because of the Cuban Missile Crisis. He served with a recon team with "U.D.T." [Underwater Demolition Team] and was honorably discharged December 20, 1962.

Hard to imagine how Bennett fit it all in. But the experience took a toll. During a rocket attack in Southeast Asia, he "got blown out of a barracks" and broke both legs. And of course, there were the memories. "He'd wake up suddenly in the middle of the night and put his hands around my neck," Melba Bennett said. "Now, he's still a little jumpy."

In reality, Bennett's military record showed that he served on active duty in the Marine Corps from October 30, 1957, to December 18, 1962. His MOS was 3516 (automotive mechanic). Sent to the U.S. Naval Base, Subic Bay, Philippines, in January 1960, Bennett served there as a guard, a dispatcher, and a mechanic. He had no Special Forces training and did not serve in South Vietnam, Cambodia, Thailand, or Laos. Bennett's record showed no wounds or a Purple Heart or any combat decorations.

When someone within Bennett's VFW post challenged his wild stories, the VFW hierarchy handled the situation by verifying that, by virtue of his overseas service as a mechanic in the Philippines, Bennett was eligible for membership.

• The editorial in the December 31, 1984, issue of *The New York Times* probably moved many readers to tears. After hearing reports that a secret helicopter unit of the 101st Airborne Division made raids into Central America to assist pro-American forces, and that families of casualties were told their loved ones died in accidents elsewhere, Tom Dammann felt a pang of recognition. Dammann, a journalist who wrote foreign dispatches for a newspaper syndicate in the sixties and who was an occasional contributor to the *Times*, published an op-ed piece titled "Military Accidents?"[322]

"Shortly after Christmas last year, I learned that my son, Thomas L. Dammann Jr., had made five covert parachute jumps into North Vietnam in 1959 and 1960, when Dwight D. Eisenhower and John F. Kennedy were presidents. Tommy's leg was shattered in the aftermath of his fifth drop. He was twenty years old."

Officials at Fort Benning, Georgia, told the family that Tommy suffered the injury in an auto accident near the base only one day before his discharge was due. For twenty-four years, his father wrote, Tommy clung to his secret, limping through life on a leg left two inches shorter than the other because of the accident. After his discharge, Tommy went to college, married, and worked for the *San Francisco Chronicle*. But by the mid-1960s, his life was crumbling. Embittered, angry, Tommy lost his wife and his job. Tommy demonstrated against the Vietnam War and once ended up in jail. He went to Europe, then returned home and lived with his parents. Tommy tried to write but, afraid of rejection, refused to submit his work to editors. Tommy moved to a remote area of Michigan where he lived in isolation. He fell victim to alcoholism and was hospitalized several times.

No one in the family knew Tommy had been in Vietnam until his wife Marilyn called his parents to explain he was in the VA hospital in Tomah, Wisconsin, being treated for PTSD. He had become enraged while watching the nightly news and started screaming about the similarities between the war in Vietnam and the situation in Central America, prompting his frightened wife to take him to a VA hospital.

"It was only then," Dammann wrote, "that Tommy finally revealed that the auto accident was a cover-up." Tommy reluctantly told his father of his covert operations. "I was dropped into North Vietnam five times, Dad; four times from Libya and the last time from Fort Benning." Dammann said that later he learned more from Marilyn and the Vietnam veterans in the rap group Tommy had joined.

"They say that after completing their first four missions, Tommy and his buddies came out of North Vietnam two by two, but that on the last foray their commanding officer ordered them to rendezvous someplace where they were, in Tommy's words, 'blown up.' Heavy fighting resulted. People were killed. Of twenty-five men, Tommy was one of three survivors. One died on the plane en route from Southeast Asia to Fort Benning.

"My son's traumatic experiences, and his tortured life, don't prove anything about the Reagan Administration's tactics in Central America," Dammann said. "Moreover, we may never know the whole truth about our government's covert activities, either in Central America today or in Southeast Asia more than twenty years ago. I am certain of one thing, though—Tommy will never again reveal his secret. He died last June, apparently in a fall on his stairs at home." Georgia officials could offer Dammann no information on the supposed twenty-four-year-old accident, apparently confirming Tommy's story. Was Dammann suggesting his son was killed so that he couldn't reveal information about covert activities?

The military records of Thomas L. Dammann Jr. reveal far more than the heartfelt story by a bereaved father that ran in *The New York Times*.

Tommy Dammann Jr. enlisted in the U.S. Army in October 1957, attended basic training at Fort Ord, California, and advanced training at Fort Belvoir, Virginia. In May 1958, Dammann was sent to Wheelus Air Base in Libya, where he spent about fifteen months. Dammann's duties at Wheelus likely involved performing topographical surveys, not covert ops into North Vietnam. After Libya, Dammann finished most of his military service at Fort Benning, until his discharge August 24, 1961, from Letterman Hospital, after a car accident caused a broken leg and internal injuries. His rank at discharge was private first class. But Dammann had no Airborne training, nor was he Special Forces qualified, absolute prerequisites for any of the "secret" operations he claimed.[323]

The Storytellers

- For years, Bill Kane, honors graduate of Princeton University and Yale Law School and former Fulbright scholar, made a good living in law, real estate, and banking. After graduating from law school in 1970, he worked for banks in Tokyo and London and began setting up real estate syndications in California, amassing a fortune worth up to $4 million. But friends eventually realized that Kane had a secret life. During his sophomore year at Princeton, he had taken some time off. He later revealed he had been skirmishing in jet fighters above the jungles of Southeast Asia and had been awarded a Medal of Honor for his exploits.

  Writer David Margolik told the "strange but true" story of Bill Kane in *The New York Times* on April 29, 1994. Kane's military career didn't end with the Vietnam War. Kane told friends he had continued working for the government, at times with the Defense Intelligence Agency, the CIA, or various other intelligence groups of the armed forces. He helped catch Gen. Manuel Antonio Noriega in the Panama operation and claimed he was paid $1 million by a wealthy Jew to locate a Nazi war criminal in South America.

  Kane bragged that, as a "dollar a year" consultant to the Pentagon, he helped mastermind the strategy of the Persian Gulf War from his home in Malibu, using his home computer and a telephone linked to the White House, the Pentagon, and the military's Cheyenne Mountain strategic complex in Colorado. His secretaries overheard him shouting on the phone, giving directions to underlings on where to look for Scud missiles. At the twenty-fifth reunion of his Princeton class in 1991, he regaled former classmates with accounts of his part in Operation Desert Storm.

  In October 1991, Kane wrote a last letter to his children, mentioning his role in the bombing of Iraqi soldiers as they fled Kuwait and saying he was concerned that he might be disciplined for war excesses or become a target of Iraqis seeking revenge. Kane then checked into the penthouse suite of the Mirage Hotel in Las Vegas, took a handful of sleeping pills, and pulled a plastic bag over his head. His death was ruled a suicide.

  Kane's obituary in the Princeton Alumni Weekly mentioned his "intense involvement" in the Gulf War. But when his girlfriend, Deborah Hecht, tried to have Kane buried with military honors, complete with a fly-over by jets, she discovered that the armed services could find no record he had ever served. His first wife, married to him during the early 1970s, told Margolik that Kane was a draft dodger during the Vietnam War. During his last years, as his financial empire collapsed, he suffered from depression and abuse of alcohol and cocaine.

"Total bull," his son said of Kane's tales of military derring-do. "But he had this incredible ability to weave together stories, and you really had to work to find the inconsistencies."[324]

- The word came in Vietnam that seventeen-year-old Steve Boyle was needed in the United States: President John F. Kennedy had been assassinated. The nation was in mourning. Boyle, who had played second trumpet in the Air Force Band before being shipped to the combat zone to perform daring helicopter rescues, was taken aside by a lieutenant colonel who said he was being shipped back to the states to play taps at JFK's funeral. One slip-up, the officer warned him, and Boyle would be court-martialed.

  During the state funeral at Arlington Cemetery, the eyes of the world upon him, a scared Boyle lifted his trumpet to cold lips. Six notes into his rendition of taps, overwhelmed by emotion, he cracked a note. Terrified, Boyle trembled, knowing that after the funeral he was going to be chewed up and spit out by the lieutenant colonel. Instead, after the ceremony Boyle was pulled into a long black limousine near the gravesite. An ancient general told him that his bobble reflected the mood of the nation, and he didn't need to worry about retribution. The man reassuring him was Omar Bradley, the famous World War II commander.

  Thirty hours later, Boyle found himself back in Saigon. "It was almost like a dream or a nightmare, I don't know which," he said. "It was a very high honor to have been able to say for the world 'goodbye.' I will always carry that memory." Boyle spent another seven years in Vietnam, including two as a prisoner of war, and he still suffered from the horrific memories.

  Later Boyle became a volunteer fireman in Homer, Alaska. He told his amazing story in November 1993 on the air at KBBI, the area National Public Radio station. It broadcast the story in recognition of the thirtieth anniversary of Kennedy's death. The remarkable tale was picked up and printed by the *Homer News*. Boyle declined the paper's request for an interview, but his wife and three grown children affirmed that Steve had repeated the anecdote to them and friends many times.

  It was a sweet, sad, moving story. The response to the radio station was tremendous. "People called to say they were in tears," said David Webster, the radio reporter who had coaxed Boyle to tell his account on the air.[325]

But none of Boyle's poignant tale was true. The bugler who played taps at the president's funeral did bobble a note, but that musician was a sergeant named Keith Clark, solo bugler for the U.S. Army Band. Boyle had not been a prisoner of war. He had not even served in Vietnam. The hoax was revealed after a listener called KBBI saying the details did not square with a piece that also ran on NPR mentioning Clark.[326]

What was most remarkable about this story was the response of the *Homer News*. Editor Mark Turner admitted that they had been fooled and apologized in an editorial headlined, "Taps Hoax Shows Lack of Attention to Newsgathering Basics."[327] (In my years of researching this issue, most reporters have resisted the idea that they had been fooled, often hanging up on me or refusing to print a correction. When I saw Turner's editorial, I felt like I'd discovered one of the last honest reporters in America, and he'd been exiled to Homer, Alaska.) And Boyle was one of the few fakers I have ever heard about who apologized. His explanation for the lie was pitiful.

"I fabricated the whole thing out of a lifetime of being a nobody," said Boyle. He had been telling a version of the story for twenty-five years. "I tried to be somebody. It was an incredibly stupid mistake. I've created a monster, and now I guess I have to deal with it."

• As a member of the local VVA speaker's bureau, John G. Osterhout often entertained audiences around Newburgh, New York, with tales of eating monkey meat while working in the jungles of Vietnam training Montagnard hill people to fight the Viet Cong. A former Green Beret, promoted on the battlefield to major during one of his two tours in Vietnam, Osterhout's DD-214 (discharge paper) indicated that he had received the DSC, the Silver Star, the Bronze Star Medal, and four Purple Hearts. Other members of the local VVA chapter were awed by Osterhout. They invited him to be the grand marshal of the 1994 New Windsor Memorial Day parade. That day Osterhout, smoking a big cigar, rode next to a Gold Star mother, his chest emblazoned with all his medals.[328]

Osterhout did serve in the Army Security Agency, a semiclandestine electronic intelligence gathering group. However, his highest rank was not major. It was specialist fourth class. Any monkey meat he ate would have had to be imported from the jungle to Hokkaido, Japan, where Osterhout, a Morse code operator, sat in a listening post from 1960 to 1961. Osterhout served only one tour in Japan and none in Vietnam. During the time Osterhout claimed he was serving a second tour in Vietnam, from 1961 to 1966, he was actually living with his first wife, Pat, in Montgomery, Alabama.[329]

His ruse was uncovered when Osterhout ran into a Marine who really did serve with the Montagnards. "The Marine said Osterhout didn't know the language and wasn't familiar with the customs," a local VVA official told the Newburgh *Sunday Record* in November 1994. Osterhout had fooled the local VVA group very easily by whiting out portions of his real DD-214 that said he was a Morse code specialist, and typing in his new heroic identity. Run through a copier, the paper gave legitimacy to his boast that he had received the Distinguished Service Cross. In reality, the highest award Osterhout had earned was a Marksman Badge.

- When Bruce Jackson met "Jim Bennett," he had already abandoned an earlier idea of doing a book of oral history about the Vietnam War. But Bennett's enthusiasm, and his amazing stories of combat in Vietnam, persuaded Jackson to resurrect the project. In a 1996 issue of the *Journal of American Folklore*, Jackson, filmmaker and professor at State University of New York at Buffalo, told how Bennett, a former Green Beret, convinced him to make a documentary film on men who had served in Vietnam.

  Jackson and his partner prepared applications for grants to do the project, putting Bennett down as the director because he could supply the access to the vets and expertise in understanding their stories. (Bennett was a pseudonym that Jackson used for the story.) Bennett's own story would be the documentary's centerpiece. Bennett claimed that most of his work was with the Phoenix Project, attached to the CIA, and that he was ordered to assassinate not only village officials but also their "wives and children and goats and chickens."

  Trained in the whole array of infantry weapons, Bennett's specialty was the crossbow. He was also an expert on the use of nitroglycerin. He had once been on an assassination mission with his crossbow. After a successful kill, he was wounded in enemy territory. Bennett hid in the jungle, treating his wound with maggots from a dead animal, a technique he learned from a Buddhist monk.

  The secret nature of his work, and the havoc it wreaked with his records, impeded Bennett's ability to obtain treatment at the VA for a lung disorder he believed was caused by Agent Orange. And he had lost all his medals in a move, rendering him unable to prove he had been in 'Nam at all.

  Bennett's stories were amazing, but Jackson had no reason to question his veracity. Another friend, a newspaper reporter, finally opened Jackson's eyes. The reporter quoted writer Dashiell Hammett on checking the facts, especially the ones that are so good they are almost too good to be true. With that in mind, Jackson told a friend one of Bennett's stories about the time his Special Forces camp at Lang Vei was overrun by tanks and drenched with napalm, killing nearly everyone before the survivors could return safely to the Marine base at Khe Sanh. A friend recognized the story of this famous battle as straight out of Michael Herr's *Dispatches*. A Special Forces vet verified that Bennett was not one of a dozen or so men who survived that battle. The Special Forces Association had no listing for Bennett at any rank.

Another veteran, present when Bennett brought up using nitro in Vietnam, finally called his bluff. "You're full of shit," he told Bennett. Nitroglycerin is unstable at temperatures over eighty-five degrees. In Vietnam, the thermometer soared above eighty-five degrees every day.

Eventually Jackson learned that Bennett had never been in Vietnam at all. Bennett had served overseas in Germany and left the military under less than honorable conditions. One former Green Beret confided to Jackson that he knew the guy was a liar all along, but he did not blow the whistle on him. Why? Because Bennett told such great stories. "I loved listening to him tell those goddamned stories," the friend said. "I mean, I was *there* and I couldn't tell stories like that guy."[330]

Vietnam Vet Phonies or Phony Vietnam Vets

Perhaps the most aggravating pretenders I investigate are those who are real Vietnam vets, but they feel the need to buff their image. These men should know better. Instead of being proud that they were good clerks, truck drivers, or mechanics, they claim Special Forces or heroic combat deeds. Some even use their status as "heroic veterans" to plead for money from other vets or to run scams.

- When a publisher in Kentucky decided to do a yearbook about the Vietnam history of the 173rd Airborne, individuals were allowed to send in their names and a brief biographical sketch. One bio accompanied a photograph of the helmeted Lowell W. ("Squeeker") Olds in mid-parachute jump.

  "Participated in battles in Dak To, Tet Offensive, and Tuy Hoa. Discharged as an E-4. Most memorable experiences include the 'Hell of Dak To, Christmas at Tuy Hoa, and Martha Raye's U.S.O. show.'"

His decorations supposedly included the Bronze Star Medal, Purple Heart, and the Distinguished Service Cross.[331]

Maybe the part about Martha Raye was true. Olds served in Vietnam but not as part of the 173rd Airborne. According to his military record, Olds was a radio telephone operator whose duties in-country included driving a truck and operating a forklift. Olds was not Airborne qualified, had not been promoted above private first class, and he had no valorous decorations.[332]

- Jerry Wayne Graham's lifeless body was found on the streets of Salt Lake City on September 9, 1989, his battle with the bottle finally over. The former Green Beret was a victim of alcohol poisoning and the Vietnam War, his sister told the press.

  "One thing he talked about when he got out was the killings," his sister Leslie Oyler of Stockton, California, told a reporter for the *Deseret News*. "It affected him very badly. Like someone on drugs, there were flashbacks."[333]

  Members of the local VFW banded together to give Graham, who died penniless, a funeral suitable for a decorated soldier. A local mortuary donated its services and paid for the casket and opening and closing of the grave. Others who wished to remain anonymous donated the rest of the costs. The government provided a white military headstone. Veterans, most of whom had not met Graham, paid tribute to the former soldier. A fellow Vietnam veteran pinned his own Combat Infantryman Badge to Graham's chest before the casket was closed. Taps was played and a twenty-one-gun salute ended the solemn proceedings. *Bravo*, a veterans' magazine, headlined its story about the death of Graham "Another Vietnam Unknown KIA—Killed in America."

  "A bottle of vodka had done for the Communist Vietnamese what they could not do with their AK-47s during his tour as a Green Beret in Vietnam," the story read.[334]

  Graham's military record showed that while Graham was attached to Company A, 5th Special Forces in Vietnam for nine months in 1970, he was service personnel, not a Green Beret. Graham was a clerk-typist.[335]

- At six foot eight and more than 250 pounds, itinerant preacher Robin Wright appeared every inch what he claimed to be before he turned to serving God: A highly decorated Navy SEAL. Wright told his amazing tale in the July 1987 issue of *Guideposts*, an inspirational magazine.

  During his third tour of duty in Vietnam, Wright's C-1A aircraft came under fire while operating off the aircraft carrier USS *Enterprise*. The crew was on a resupply mission when snipers in the jungle between the beach and the Da Nang airfield shot down the plane. Wright, the only survivor of the crash, tried to stay afloat while Viet Cong shot at him from the beach. He was saved when a helicopter swept in and dropped a paramedic into the waves. As he and his rescuer were being hauled in by a helicopter hoist, Wright was hit in the back by two bullets.

For his wartime heroics, Wright said he received the Navy Cross, "two or three" Silver Stars, the Distinguished Service Medal, and at least one Purple Heart. He was saved, but at a terrible cost. His crushed sciatic nerve caused paralysis from the waist down. In the hospital, he met a Marine who had lost all his limbs when he threw himself on a grenade. (Never mind the physics of that!) This Marine led Wright through an intense spiritual experience. Suddenly and miraculously, Wright was completely healed and walked out of the hospital.

Larry Bailey, a retired Navy SEAL captain and freelance writer, dissected Wright's story—described both in *Guideposts* and in Wright's own cassette tapes—for *Soldier of Fortune* magazine in November 1994.[336]

Bailey pointed out there was no strip of jungle between the Da Nang airport and the beach where enemy soldiers could hide. No qualified SEAL ever served as a "combat aircrewman," as Wright had claimed. And there are no military records showing Wright had ever trained as a SEAL.

When Bailey pointed out the numerous errors in Wright's story to the editor of *Guideposts*, he declined to correct or retract the story. "To do so might cast doubt over the veracity of the other stories in the magazine," the editor told Bailey. But Wright's wild claims popped up again in the *News-Herald* of Panama City, Florida. That newspaper, contacted by a former SEAL who was suspicious of Wright's story, also declined to question Wright's credentials any further.

Not until Wright left his wife and moved in with a woman from his congregation was the preacher exposed. His wife's divorce attorney requested Wright's military records, which showed that he had earned only a National Defense Service Medal, the Vietnam Service Medal, and the Republic of Vietnam Campaign Medal. He had not attended SEAL school, had not been in a military plane crash, and had not been shot twice while being rescued. In fact, Wright had not been ordained a minister and was wanted on a variety of state and federal charges, including theft, nonpayment of child support, and interference with the custody of his new wife's son.[337]

• In October 1984, disabled "Special Forces veteran" Bill Callahan ran 120 miles to Tampa to visit a scaled-down model of the Vietnam Veterans Memorial to honor his fallen comrades. His efforts made the newspapers, prompting various veterans' groups to give him donations along the way. Callahan's determination was inspiring, especially because the former Green Beret had suffered serious spine and leg injuries from shrapnel during a rocket attack near Phu Bai at the end of his third tour of duty in Vietnam.[338]

After his successful run, Callahan was honored by Florida Gov. Bob Graham. The next March, Callahan walked 1,250 miles from Florida to New York City to publicize the plight of American servicemen missing in action in Southeast Asia and that of Vietnam veterans back home who still suffer psychological scars. Callahan's arrival in Manhattan was met by front-page headlines in the *New York Post* and *New York Daily News*. An instant celebrity, Callahan while in New York led a national homecoming parade for Vietnam vets.[339] Two months later, Callahan received a standing ovation from a crowd of more than fifty thousand at Yankee Stadium.

But he was physically unable to finish the return leg of his announced trip. His noble mission incomplete, Callahan called a press conference in June 1985. Dressed in spit-shined boots, camouflage pants, and olive drab muscle shirt, he announced that he planned to walk 1,250 miles in two months from Crystal River, Florida, to San Antonio, Texas.[340] Callahan's determined face appeared in newspapers all along the route. To reporters along the way, he told more details of his story.

Before the attack that disabled him, Callahan had survived firefights in Laos and Cambodia. "I dove into a culvert, and the next thing I knew, there was an explosion," Callahan told reporter Jim Tunstall for the *Tribune* in Tampa. "When I finally got my bells back together, one of my buddies was laying on top of me and another was across my leg." Fourteen friends died in that attack, he said. Callahan was one of only two men who survived. He not only lost part of one leg, his spine was shattered. He received the Bronze Star Medal and Purple Heart, but his ordeal was just beginning. For several years, Callahan was forced to undergo back surgery to repair the damage war had done to him.

But the psychological damage of returning home "a man without a country" was harder to repair. After years of anger and confusion, he joined a veterans' group that held rap sessions and lobbied for veterans' issues. Despite his injuries and a heart attack, Callahan set out on his runs listening to Marine drill tapes and wearing a jacket that said "'Nam-Vets. Run For Life. POW-MIA." Then he began his cross-country runs for the POW-MIA cause.[341]

The truth about Callahan was far less dramatic, as was revealed shortly after he finished his San Antonio trek in October 1985. A local veteran, retired U.S. Army 1st Sgt. Tom Thomas, had initiated an investigation of the "walking vet" and alerted the newspaper that Callahan was not what he claimed.

According to his military record, Callahan served in Germany and Alaska during most of his seven years in the military. He spent only nine months in Vietnam, not three tours, with the 589th and 84th Engineer Battalions, and the 159th Aviation Battalion. He was not a Green Beret and had not trained with the Airborne Rangers, as he claimed. His record showed no awards reflecting combat, no Purple Heart or Bronze Star Medal. Callahan worked primarily as a carpenter.[342]

The *Tampa Tribune* ran a story comparing Callahan's claims to his service record. A spokesman for the Department of the Army confirmed that Callahan had suffered an injury while working as a military policeman in Fort Leavenworth, Kansas. Callahan suffered a concussion when he tackled a man attempting to gain access to a restricted area.[343]

- After watching the jubilant homecomings of soldiers on television after Operation Desert Storm, freshmen at Williams High School in Plano, Texas, were appalled to hear of the less sympathetic reception janitor Reggie Gutierrez had received when he returned home from Vietnam two decades earlier.

  They heard his stories when Gutierrez, at the request of the school's history teacher, spoke to fifteen different classes about his experiences in the war. One of the history teachers even performed Gutierrez's custodial work while he spoke.

  Gutierrez told the students that after undergoing jungle training, he served as an M-60 machine gunner in an Army unit that delivered ammunition and supplies to the troops. When his Jeep hit a mine during the 1968 Tet Offensive, the explosion took out all his top teeth; his right leg was crushed when the Jeep landed on top of him. Gutierrez considered himself lucky. Another passenger died.[344]

  After the war, Gutierrez suffered from PTSD. Spooked every time there was a loud noise, he couldn't find work. He reenlisted in 1971, going through basic training with a brace on his leg. He stayed in the military until 1979. By then, his body had started reacting to exposure to Agent Orange, breaking out in blisters and rashes. Gutierrez still needed to wear leg braces, and his teeth had never been properly fixed. Gutierrez told the students it was his dream to visit the Vietnam Veterans Memorial, to pay homage to his fallen comrades. But with fifteen children and eighteen grandchildren, he could not afford the trip.

The students, most of whom knew little about Vietnam, were very touched. Thus began "Operation: The Wall." Through bake sales and donations, 380 students raised $464.97 to pay Gutierrez' plane fare and hotel expenses to Washington, D.C., to visit the memorial. After a TV news report about the students' surprise presentation of the trip, a local chiropractor matched their donation so that his wife could accompany him. Gutierrez' bowling team pitched in ninety-six dollars, and a few other families donated fifty dollars. In all, he received about $1,900 for the trip.[345]

I obtained Gutierrez' military record, which revealed that he arrived in Vietnam on April 27, 1968, two months after the Tet Offensive ended. He received no personal combat decorations or Purple Hearts. Gutierrez served as a truck driver for a support company.[346]

• Albert "Bud" Porter, a burly man who said he served in Vietnam as a Navy SEAL, was a common sight as he led Memorial and Veterans Day ceremonies in the Port Townsend, Washington, area. At various times commander of the local VFW, AMVETS, and American Legion chapters, Porter wore the dark beret with the gold emblem of the SEAL commandos as well as the Navy Cross, two Silver Stars, two Bronze Star Medals, and rows of other Vietnam combat decorations. He frequently visited the local high school to talk to students about his wartime exploits as a frogman on an Underwater Demolition Team in the 1950s, then as a SEAL in Vietnam in the sixties. He boasted that he had served in secret operations in Vietnam.

The commander of American Legion Post 26 in Port Townsend and member of numerous other veterans organizations, Porter was regarded as the unofficial leader of the close-knit community of veterans on the northern Olympic Peninsula. Fellow vets backed up his claims. A local Marine said he met Porter in Vietnam in 1966, when the SEAL "swam into my post." When a reporter questioned Porter's story that he'd been shot eleven times and received numerous Purple Hearts, another vet defended him, explaining that Porter had undergone an operation in 1994 during which a "half pound of shrapnel and bullets," as well as large lesions, were removed from his body.

But American Legion officials in Washington, tipped off by veterans suspicious of Porter's claims to be a SEAL, contacted me for help in investigating his background. Porter's record showed he had served honorably in the Navy from 1950 until 1970, when he retired as a chief boatswain's mate. And Porter did receive a Purple Heart for a minor wound while serving in 1966. But Bud Porter wasn't a SEAL. He had not attended any of the special training schools required of either UDT or SEALs, nor had he received any valorous combat decorations.[347]

Porter refused to answer questions about his record except to point out that he was involved in "classified" operations. Porter resigned as commander of the American Legion Post 26 but continued to participate as a member, prompting a lawsuit against the post by several veterans, including a Marine who had lost an eye in Vietnam.

In late 1995, the Post 26 membership committee voted not to ask former commander Porter to document his military service record, allowing him to retain his membership. "We don't judge whether our members tell war stories or not," said one legionnaire. "These guys served. That's all we care about." But both the national VFW and the state AMVETS organization officially expelled Porter over his public claims and appearances wearing valorous combat decorations that he had not earned.[348]

• When retired Staff Sgt. Gerard Patrick Miserandino ran for junior vice commander of the Washington, D.C., Department of the National VFW in 1987, many of his colleagues agreed that the charismatic disabled Vietnam veteran was an excellent choice.

Only those veterans who have served overseas in a war are eligible for full membership in the VFW. The Vietnam generation has been reluctant to join groups top-heavy with vets from previous wars. But the World War II generation is dying off, and the VFW needed someone who could attract Vietnam vets and pump up their membership in an effort to restore the group to its glory days on Capitol Hill.

That was why Miserandino, a captivating public speaker, could be such an asset. Many had served in Vietnam, but few who survived had given as much as the highly decorated Miserandino, who lost both his hands during a "secret mission" in Vietnam.

During the election campaign, Miserandino circulated a flyer showing a miniaturized version of his DD-214 (discharge paper) and listing his various decorations: Silver Star, two Bronze Star Medals, three Purple Hearts, two Presidential Unit Citations, Combat

Infantryman Badge, RVN Gallantry Cross, the European Occupation Medal, and many other awards denoting special training, such as the Parachute Badge, Ranger Tab, "Jungle Expert," Expert Badge with Rifle, and Pistol and Machine Gun Bars.

The flyer described how Miserandino returned home from the war in 1967 and was the first Vietnam veteran to become a VFW post commander in 1969. Employed by the VFW as an appeals consultant at the National Veterans Service, Miserandino had been elected chairman of the New York State Veterans' Legislative Coalition, composed of twenty-nine veterans' organizations.

But during the campaign for junior commander, suspicions arose. Presidential Unit Citations were rarely given out; how had one man received the decoration twice in one short tour? Miserandino assured his supporters that he had received all the medals he claimed, including the Silver Star, given only for heroism in combat. But when a supporter asked him to come to the post and answer questions about his decorations, Miserandino refused. As evidence mounted that Miserandino's record was not what he claimed, the VFW convened a court-martial, charging him with "conduct unbecoming a soldier and gentleman" and submitting false military service documents. In the middle of the proceedings, Miserandino stalked out.[349]

The evidence proved that Miserandino had served six weeks in Vietnam with Company C, 4th Battalion, 12th Infantry, 199th Infantry Brigade from October 28 to December 27, 1966. According to an affidavit by retired Maj. Gen. James Boatner, former commander, the 4th Battalion did not conduct combat operations during this period and never conducted secret operations during his command, as Miserandino claimed. Boatner said it was not bravery during a covert operation that cost Miserandino his hands but a sad, unfortunate accident. On the morning of December 27, during training for night ambushes, Miserandino had attempted to remove a hand grenade that had been set out as an American booby trap. As he reached around a tree trunk to replace the pin in the grenade, the device exploded. The explosion blew off his hands; the tree trunk saved his life by protecting his head and body from the blast. Miserandino was medevacked to a hospital and later sent back to the states.[350]

At the evacuation hospital where he was a patient, Miserandino did receive one Purple Heart, but not three as he claimed. His battalion had not been awarded the Presidential Unit Citation, and Miserandino had no decorations for heroism. Miserandino, working his way up the hierarchy of the VFW, had fabricated the stories of heroism to further his ambitions. When his lies were revealed, the panel convened for the VFW court-martial voted that Miserandino be dishonorably discharged from the organization.

The irony is that Miserandino, although in Vietnam for only six weeks, was genuinely eligible for membership in the VFW. With his personality and communication skills, he did not need to lie about his war service to go far in the organization. But he, like many others, felt obliged to add "hero" to his resume.

- A group in Washington state known as "Operation We Remember" provides all-expenses-paid trips to the Vietnam Veterans Memorial for disabled Vietnam veterans. In 1990, a Tumwater resident named Edward Allen Harrelson presented himself as a possible participant. A tall, beefy man whose red beard was beginning to turn gray, Harrelson wore about eighteen medals, including the Navy Cross, Silver Star, Bronze Star, Diver's Helmet, and three Purple Hearts, making him one of the most highly decorated Vietnam veterans in the region. Purple Heart license plates adorned Harrelson's car, exempting him from paying motor vehicle taxes.

Harrelson told friends he spent a decade, from 1965 to 1975, as a Navy SEAL. He confided that most of his work in Vietnam was done behind enemy lines on highly secret missions, the records of which were still classified. He showed them a citation supposedly awarding him a Navy Cross, which described how, while on "Bright Light classified directive," ABH1 Harrelson and "members of his Special Operations Force" encountered heavy enemy resistance. During the ensuing firefight, Harrelson was wounded while extracting a known North Vietnamese government official in a "secured, sedated, breach-carrying position, descending a mountainous cliff region." Automatic weapon fire penetrated the official's body, wounding Harrelson in the base of his spine.

Harrelson tumbled fifty feet to a sandy riverbed below, his fall cushioned by the enemy official secured to his back. Unable to walk, under intense enemy ground fire, Harrelson began crawling, returning fire and retrieving weapons, supplies, and a radio while pulling a wounded team member to safety. (Presumably Harrelson unstrapped the guy from his back.)

After radioing for a "hot rescue," Harrelson laid down a "rim of fire," and directed the pilot to extract all other team members. He wiped out the remaining enemy, permitting his own rescue. "Post firefight and rescue intelligence reports indicated that ABH1 Harrelson had repelled the advance of three (3) North Vietnam Army Regular platoons, and one (1) mortar squad," the citation said.

The attack left Harrelson, who worked as a veteran's benefits counselor at Western Washington State Hospital, disabled because of "war wounds" in his back. Harrelson had difficulty walking; his wife had to do all the heavy-duty chores around the house. Based on his DD-214 (discharge paper) and the sponsorship of a local VVA chapter, Harrelson was approved by Operation We Remember for financial assistance to visit The Wall.[351]

A producer named Marc C. Waszkiewicz filmed Harrelson talking about his service in Vietnam and his trip to The Wall as part of a documentary called "Vietnam: An Inner-View," to be accompanied by a companion book.[352] After the trip, Harrelson's story was picked up by local and national TV programs. Harrelson testified in front of committees at the state legislature on veterans' issues. Harrelson claimed his involvement in secret ops had not ended in Vietnam. He boasted that billionaire H. Ross Perot had contacted him to participate in the rescue of American POWs in Vietnam and bragged that he had been in the war room at the Pentagon to discuss top secret missions.

The citations and the Purple Heart license plate seemed authentic. Still those around him began to wonder about Harrelson. He always parked in spaces reserved for the handicapped, but if he was disabled, why did he pick up and move a log in the woods? When Harrelson borrowed about two thousand dollars from Operation We Remember to repair his truck in order to drive to Washington, D.C., he did not repay the money. But mostly they picked up on a bunch of little things, facts that didn't mesh, tales that did not ring true. Harrelson frequently complained of flashbacks and nightmares, but these problems seemed to be little more than excuses for being in a bad mood.

Several veterans began to talk to each other about their doubts. After staying up all night making notes of the discrepancies, one suspicious acquaintance who worked for the state government called the Washington Department of Corrections. Within ten minutes, the word came back. Ed Harrelson was a registered sex offender. He had been sent to prison for raping his stepdaughter.

That was just the beginning. His DD-214 was a forgery. Harrelson had been in the military, but he was not a Navy SEAL. His real military record showed that he had been an enlisted sailor aboard the USS *Lexington* and the USS *America* from 1965 to 1969. Because the ships spent some time in waters off the coast of Vietnam, Harrelson received the Vietnam Campaign Medal and Vietnam Service Medal. But his highest rank was E-3, and his service was marred by several periods of AWOL. Records show Harrelson was declared a deserter from a naval air station in Georgia in September 1969.[353]

Harrelson had been charged with armed robbery, auto theft, passing hot checks, and forgery committed during the period he was AWOL.[354] From 1971 through 1977, a period Harrelson claimed he was a SEAL in Vietnam, he was actually in prison in North Carolina.

After getting out of the penitentiary, Harrelson moved to the West Coast, where he was married. Convicted of incest in the first degree in Thurston County, Washington, in 1988, Harrelson was sentenced to fourteen months in prison.[355] The veterans who investigated him turned over their information to the governor's office, which ordered an inquiry into how a registered sex offender obtained a job as a veterans' benefits counselor at a state hospital. Placed on suspension pending the outcome of the investigation, Harrelson resigned and left the state.

• A cover story called "Terror on an Eight-Hour Shift" in *The New York Times Magazine* in November 1995, focused on the brutal, terrifying job of being a prison guard at the maximum-security prison in Lucasville, Ohio. In 1993, inmates at Lucasville had rioted, holding eight prison guards hostage and killing six inmates. Some of the scariest inmates were held in the Special Psychiatric Unit, the "nut block." One was Lee Seiber, a forty-seven-year-old inmate with "cadaverous cheeks and eyes that look as if they could burn through sheet steel." Seiber, known as "Crazy Horse," had been on death row for murder until 1995, when his death sentence was commuted. Seiber promptly sued for the right to die rather than live out his life in prison.[356]

Writer Bruce Porter described Seiber as a two-tour Vietnam veteran who served with the 4th Infantry Division. He told how "Crazy Horse" and a prison guard enthusiastically reminisced about the inmate's favorite weapon in Vietnam, the M-79 grenade launcher. "He says he got two hundred to three hundred Viet Cong with it, before his discharge for being a little too enthusiastic for Army work," wrote Porter. "It probably had something to do with the dozens of heads he says he cut off and staked around his compound." Despite the military's rejection of his work ethic, Seiber still received ninety dollars a month in veterans benefits from the government.

Seiber told Porter various stories about what led to his imprisonment. He shot a man in a bar in Columbus who was threatening him with a beer bottle. Or maybe it was two men, or two men and a woman. No matter. "Here's the big thing," Seiber said. "This is 1995, and you're still paying me for all the people I killed for you in '66 and '67, and here I kill one guy for myself, and I'm locked up for the rest of my life. There's something wrong with that, isn't there?"

That was the same tune Seiber sang at the sentencing phase of his trial. According to the prosecutor, Seiber went into a bar in Columbus one night in the early eighties and started harassing a waitress, insisting that she examine the tattoo on his penis. When another bar patron told him to back off, Seiber pulled out a gun and shot the man to death. After his conviction, while the jury was trying to determine punishment, Seiber muttered out loud in court, "What's the big damn deal? I killed all those people in Vietnam for you. Why can't I shoot one for myself?"[357]

Regardless of the mathematics of that sentiment, Seiber's military record showed that his description of his service in Vietnam was highly exaggerated. Lee Edward Seiber served in Vietnam from December 17, 1966, to December 16, 1967, but not as a rifleman with the 4th Infantry, as he claimed. Records show Seiber was a specialist fourth class radio operator assigned to the 167th Signal Company, 54th Signal Battalion.[358] Seiber worked in a radio station that was part of the all-important military communications grid. These stations were so vital to the war effort that they were placed in areas that were not vulnerable to enemy attack. Seiber served not in the field—where he claimed he killed hundreds of Viet Cong and staked their heads around his compound—but inside an air-conditioned building in one of the safest places in Vietnam.

• During Desert Storm, a Seattle "Vietnam veteran turned peace activist" named Michael Gayler demanded the right to speak in public schools in response to military recruiters being allowed access.

Gayler told reporters and talk show hosts that he was a Vietnam veteran who had been wounded by grenade fragments in battle and decorated for bravery. But after coming to the conclusion that the war was morally wrong, Gayler said, he asked his commander to move him to a noncombat role. The request was rejected. As a political protest against the war, Gayler said he deserted and lived with a South Vietnamese family in Saigon for nine months until he was arrested by MPs.[359]

In her column for King Features Syndicate, writer Linda Ellerbee took up Gayler's cause. "It's nice to know that even now, when the war is over, in at least one of our cities, Gayler and others like him will be out there counseling peace," Ellerbee said. Gayler's demand for equal time was granted, and he began going into schools, telling of the atrocities and evils he had seen in Vietnam.[360]

But writer Doug Clark with the Spokane *Spokesman-Review* became suspicious of Gayler and called me. I helped Clark obtain Gayler's military record, which showed that before he ever set foot in

Vietnam, Gayler repeatedly had gone AWOL. In reality, during his three-year stint in the military, Gayler was court-martialed, busted in rank three times, and racked up 247 days of bad time. Probably the only reason he received an honorable discharge was because he had earned the Army Commendation Medal and a Purple Heart—that and the fact that he was only two months away from the end of his second tour in Vietnam when he was last picked up for AWOL.[361]

Confronted by Clark, Gayler admitted that his AWOL incidents had nothing to do with political protest, just getting drunk with his buddies. One time, Gayler laughed, they all traveled to Montreal to see the World's Fair. His "political convictions" were purely motivated by personal convenience and comfort. "Gayler didn't walk to the nearest U.S. Embassy [in Saigon], drape himself in an American flag, and then wait for a CBS camera crew to show up and film his protest for the 6 o'clock news," Clark wrote. "Gayler left his fellow soldiers in the field and then hid like a common criminal."[362]

A year after he was exposed, Gayler was arrested and cited for malicious mischief after he splashed a blood-colored substance on retired Gen. Norman Schwarzkopf during a promotion for his book, *It Doesn't Take a Hero*, in a Seattle suburb. Local publications again described Gayler as a "decorated" Vietnam veteran who served two tours as an Army Ranger.[363]

- When I read a story in the Phoenix *New Times* in August 1994 about Robert George Abbott, fifty-year-old ex-Marine, I immediately fired off an FOIA request. The Marine Corps' recruiting slogan is "A Few Good Men." And Abbott was no longer a man.

  Shown roller-blading around Phoenix, wearing curly black, shoulder-length hair, penciled-in eyebrows, and pink short-shorts, Robert had legally changed his name to Donna Marie Abbott. Hormone shots had given the new Donna respectable-sized breasts, but her feminine look was a little at odds with the tattoo on her left arm: a dramatic winged horse emblazoned with the words "Viet Nam 65–67."

  Abbott claimed that in his life as a man, he served as a Marine in Vietnam. When he and two other members of his company were captured by the enemy during a covert mission, they refused to reveal military secrets. The NVA castrated them.

  "Basically, we were sniping and we got caught in the wrong place," Abbott told *New Times*. "I'm kind of old-fashioned—I believe in God, Mom, apple pie, and my country, so I didn't talk." Abbott returned home after Vietnam and became a transvestite.

Reclassified as a "disabled female," Abbott began receiving hormone treatments at the VA Hospital.[364]

When the FOIA came back, I got a shock. Donna Marie Abbott, also known as Robert G. Abbott, had indeed been a rifleman in Vietnam. But Abbott had not been a POW, nor had he been castrated by the enemy during clandestine operations. His record indicated Abbott suffered a "frag wound" in the left thigh and received a Purple Heart for injuries suffered in combat.[365] (Abbott said he was captured in 1966, which meant that he was still in Vietnam one year after he claimed the enemy castrated him. Not likely.)

But, for the record, the New Times story does say that Abbott liked to dress up in women's clothes even before he became a Marine. In their campaign to recruit a "few good men," they got at least one good transvestite.

Pretenders Across Enemy Lines

Vietnam War phonies aren't limited to Americans. James R. Reckner, director of the Center for the Study of the Vietnam Conflict at Texas Tech University, told me about a conference on the war he attended in Denver in the spring of 1995. A group of Americans met with a delegation from Hanoi. The delegation included two active duty PAVN (People's Army of Vietnam) officers, a colonel, and a lieutenant colonel. Eight of the fifteen men in the Hanoi delegation were described as PAVN veterans of the war, including one who looked much younger than the others. Later in the week, one older PAVN veteran told Reckner that the younger man was lying; he was not old enough to have fought in the war. Even the North Vietnamese have problems with fakers![366]

That story causes a chuckle, but an even better one came to my attention several years ago. During one of the American Legion's periodic campaigns to attract members, an Asian-American in Washington state submitted an application showing that he held an honorable discharge and was a veteran of the Vietnam War. The American Legion readily accepted him; he became a valued member of the local chapter. Eventually, he won office as the chapter commander.

But questions arose about the American Legion chapter commander's eligibility. An investigation of his records revealed that he was indeed a Vietnam veteran with an honorable discharge—from the North Vietnamese army. For years, his fellow vets had assumed he was from South Vietnam and had fought in an American unit against the North. When questioned, the man was forthright about his true service; nobody had ever bothered to ask him before. He had fled Vietnam after the war and made his way to America. Despite his popularity in the chapter, his service as an enemy soldier disqualified him from membership in the American Legion.

The pretend war hero has always existed. But in the traditional sense of our country's conflicts, the Vietnam War had no heroes, only villains. In the seventies, the growing psychiatric industry, well-represented by antiwar activists such as Jay Lifton, trumpeted the prediction that U.S. soldiers in Vietnam—now pariahs of society—were forever mentally scarred by the war. The evolution had begun; PTSD proved these men were no longer villains, they were victims. With the help of Hollywood, Rambo combined the victim/hero into one persona. If the Vietnam vet was not socially acceptable, at least he was someone worthy of help.

With the heat of antiwar rhetoric fading, a nation beginning to feel ambivalent about the way it had treated Vietnam's veterans now saw a way to make amends. An act of Congress salved the guilt of a nation and institutionalized the idea that Vietnam veterans not only were worthy of redemption but also of being financially compensated for the rest of their lives.

As my economics professor at Vanderbilt preached, if you want a social activity to diminish, tax it. If you want that activity to increase, pay a cash stipend. We have now a congressionally mandated epidemic to prove that economic wisdom.

The VA and the PTSD "Epidemic"

ON OCTOBER 24, 1979, in the town of Bend, Oregon, an enraged Vietnam veteran named Michael C. Pard armed himself with a rifle and a handgun and grimly set off in search of his ex-wife and her husband. He found and confronted the newly married couple, who jumped in their car to get away from him. Pard leaped in his own vehicle and began firing shots at them as the two vehicles raced wildly through the town. Terrified, his ex-wife and her husband found safety by driving into police headquarters. Pursued by a state trooper, Pard ended up in a shootout and was wounded in the leg, hand, and head before being captured.[367]

Originally charged with three counts of attempted murder, Pard entered a plea of not guilty by reason of insanity. At the veteran's February 1980 trial, psychologist Kevin McGovern took the witness stand to testify that Pard suffered from posttraumatic stress disorder and, therefore, was incapable of conforming his conduct to the requirements of the law.

The jury returned a verdict of not guilty on two counts of attempted manslaughter and one count of attempted murder. The judge placed Pard under the jurisdiction of the Oregon Psychiatry Security Review Board, which committed him to the Oregon State Hospital for thirty years. But after only eight months, the staff concluded he suffered not from PTSD but from a personality disorder and did not need hospitalization. Pard was released under state supervision with the provision that he seek outpatient treatment.

But that was not the end of the case. After his release from the hospital, Pard promptly applied for VA disability compensation. Based on his descriptions of traumatic experiences in Vietnam and subsequent symptoms, two VA psychiatrists declared him a victim of PTSD. They granted

Pard a temporary 100 percent service-connected disability rating—a designation indicating he was completely disabled because of his military service in Vietnam—and therefore entitled to monthly payments from the
government.

Although Michael Pard was one of the first Vietnam veterans to successfully use PTSD as a defense in a court of law in the United States, the
diagnosis was becoming increasingly more common in the late 1970s, as the
condition was refined by the psychiatric profession. I could see it in my own
circle. In the late 1980s, when I began working to build the Texas Memorial
and constantly needed volunteers for events that occurred during the business day, certain Vietnam veterans were always available. Although they
had no outward sign of disability, they did not work. They didn't have to.
The veterans received a livable income from the federal government
because they had been diagnosed as suffering from PTSD. In fact, these
men wore PTSD as a badge of honor.

Like them and thousands of other Vietnam veterans, Michael Pard had
been examined by VA psychiatrists who determined the psychological
wounds of war had damaged him to such an extent that he could no longer
work. The diagnosis allowed them to claim heroism, to boast they had
been certified by the government as traumatized by the horrors of war
and, therefore a grateful nation—and its taxpayers—would compensate
them for the rest of their lives.

But when Pard's disability rating was reviewed, his permanent rating
was reduced to 30 percent. So in 1984, Pard and his new wife Kerry sued the
U.S. government and the VA for $8.5 million in damages, claiming negli-
gence because therapists had not diagnosed his PTSD in a timely manner.
Because of the VA's failure, Pard claimed, his mental condition steadily had
deteriorated, resulting in his attempt to kill his ex-wife.

Four experts testified in federal court that Pard suffered from PTSD
resulting from his war experiences. During the trial, Pard stated under oath
that during his four and a half months as a doorgunner in Vietnam his helicopter gunship registered "more than four hundred" confirmed kills. Pard
said he witnessed the death of four fellow crewmen during that short
period and narrowly escaped death several times himself. During one particularly harrowing mission, his helicopter was shot down, and he was
forced to shoot three Vietnamese children in self-defense. On another
extraordinary occasion, his helicopter crew rescued a general. Pard testified
that he received the Distinguished Flying Cross for his part in that daring
effort as well as a Bronze Star Medal for valor for his other wartime service.
But what stuck most in his mind was the death and dying he saw.

"You saw your buddies dying around, you know, all over the place," Pard
said when he appeared on NBC Magazine with David Brinkley on December

5, 1980, to talk about his case. "I lost my pilots, I lost doorgunners. I was wounded over there, got shot down twice, and just never knew if I was going to make it to the next day." Newsman Brinkley stressed that Vietnam veterans received little recognition when they returned to the states. "Although Michael was awarded the Distinguished Flying Cross, Bronze Star Medal, and a Purple Heart," Brinkley said, "he didn't come home a hero—there were no parades, only protest marches, and he was bitter."[368]

At trial, the assistant U.S. attorney offered three witnesses who served in Vietnam with Michael Pard: his commanding officer, a pilot, and a fellow crewchief. The testimony of the three men revealed that Pard's helicopter was not a gunship used in combat but a utility helicopter that transported supplies and ferried the commanding officer and his staff from place to place. Pard's ship and the unit's two other helicopters were not sent on combat assault missions and registered no confirmed kills; members of the unit saw little or no action against the enemy.

Pard's commanding officer told the court that none of the unit's helicopters was ever shot down during the time Pard was in Vietnam. They didn't save a general. No Vietnamese—children or adults—were ever shot by the unit's men. Pard had not received the Distinguished Flying Cross or the Bronze Star Medal. Pard had been injured but not by enemy fire. In early 1968, Pard's machine gun malfunctioned, and a piece of the gun lodged in his arm, resulting in his return to the United States after only four months in Vietnam.

On June 20, 1984, U.S. District Judge Gus J. Solomon issued a twenty-page ruling that Pard did not suffer from PTSD and that the violence he committed against his ex-wife had nothing to do with his experiences in Vietnam.[369]

Portland psychiatrist Dr. Edward Colbach testified for the government that Pard's attempt to blame his violent actions in 1979 on a fabricated story about Vietnam amounted to a "con of such brazenness and magnitude, to end up in federal court like this, that it can only be pulled off by an antisocial personality."

If Pard hadn't suffered trauma in Vietnam, why had the psychiatrists at the VA testified that he had? Why was Pard certified disabled due to PTSD—and given monthly payments—if he had experienced no combat in Vietnam whatsoever?

The answer lies in the politics of an epidemic. The epidemic is real, but the disorder is often feigned.

PTSD: The Presumption, Not the Exception

Moving quietly, Marine Sgt. Byron "Rusty" Norman, crept forward with his platoon, probing for booby traps just across the border of Vietnam into

Laos. Hearing gunfire nearby, he stood motionless and listened for a few moments, every nerve straining to detect any sound of the enemy. When Norman stepped again, his foot came down on a punji stick—a sharpened bamboo stake the Viet Cong had dipped in excrement. The pain was excruciating, the foot broken and infected by the time he was evacuated to a hospital ship.

Norman's story was told in a 1991 story by *Dallas Morning News* columnist Bob St. John. Since the war, Norman had to wear a brace on his badly scarred foot. VA doctors refused to acknowledge his injury was service-connected because the wound was not listed on his military record. But there was a logical explanation for that, Norman said: The government did not want to admit the U.S. military was operating in Laos at the time.

After Vietnam, Norman had earned a college degree and married. But in the 1980s his life began to fall apart. He couldn't keep a job, then his marriage crumbled—all because of posttraumatic stress disorder. Finally, with the help of counseling at the VA, he was able to pull his life together. Still, the nightmares and physical pain lingered.[370]

Reading Norman's story of secret missions and PTSD prompted me to send an FOIA request for Norman's military record. It showed that the Marine veteran had served one short tour in Vietnam from June through December of 1969, then returned for a few days as a member of a landing party in 1970. But he was not in Vietnam in March 1969, when the only Marine cross-border raid into Laos occurred (Operation Dewey Canyon). His record indicated no decorations related to combat, no wounds, and no hospital stay.[371]

I didn't know what happened to Norman in Vietnam; but according to his military record, it's unlikely any injuries or trauma occurred the way Norman described. Had he suffered psychological problems before he went into the service, or did something else happen to him in 'Nam?

Being in a war zone changes all soldiers. The experience certainly changed me, although I never fired a shot at the enemy. In Vietnam, my mind was always two steps ahead, thinking about the consequences of my actions. At home, I have a tendency to see things sooner than I might have before. I'm more cautious and aware of potential dangers. But merely being in Vietnam didn't cause my life to fall apart.

Norman's military record in hand, I visited Bob St. John, who expressed concern that Norman had misrepresented his wartime service. The writer said he had gotten the story through a friend, a mental health professional at the Vet Center where Norman had gone for PTSD counseling. St. John approached his editors about making a correction. But the paper's bottom line: The guy was a Vietnam vet and that was good enough for them.

Not long after that, I met with C.W. Gaffney, the regional director of the

VA Vet Center in Dallas. A Vietnam veteran, Gaffney had served in 1969 with the 1st Cavalry. He told me that he supervised about one hundred counselors; about sixty-four were Southeast Asian theater vets, although Gaffney admitted employees' military records were not checked beyond a DD-214, which they provided to the VA. But that really wasn't an issue, Gaffney insisted. If someone was a fake, he and the other vets would spot him.[372]

I told Gaffney about the guy in St. John's column and my irritation with those who tell bogus Vietnam stories to explain their present problems. "Now, Mr. Burkett, you don't know what traumatized this individual," Gaffney said. "Why are you doing this?"

"I have a major problem with people claiming combat had ruined their lives when they weren't actually in combat," I said.

But Gaffney turned the conversation into an opportunity to psychoanalyze me. "Is this compulsion related to Vietnam?" he kept asking. "Do you think this will make you feel good? What do you hope to be remembered for?" Gaffney began talking about how the whole country suffered from PTSD over Vietnam. He was really into counseling not as a solution *but as a process.* Gaffney said he could not wait for the Gulf vets to begin hitting the Vet Centers.

I persisted, but Gaffney finally had enough. He looked me in the eye. "You don't understand that you are suffering from posttraumatic stress."

Taken aback, I started chuckling. "What makes you think that?"

"Mr. Burkett, you are obviously in denial," Gaffney said.

"In denial?" I asked.

"Yes, you are denying the trauma and the experience of Vietnam," Gaffney said. "That's why you are obsessed with tracking these individuals down. You're delusionary in thinking that you weren't traumatized and they weren't traumatized, when in fact, this is a symptom that shows that you did suffer."

By this time I was laughing. I couldn't believe it. I pointed out to him that the pretender phenomenon wasn't my delusion. I told him about the so-called "trip-wire vets" and "The Wall Within." I added that *Time* magazine had just updated the trend with a story on "bush vets" in Hawaii.

An uncomfortable expression came over Gaffney's face. He told me that while a regional director of a Vet Center in San Francisco, he had initiated the creation of the Vet Centers in Hawaii, hiring a counselor with combat experience who moved to Kona and began setting them up. But the counselor had lied not only about his academic credentials but also about his experience in Vietnam as well. The faker was fired when the VA discovered he had fabricated much of his combat record and academic credentials.

Gaffney was candid about the incident. He even admitted that he did not know you could obtain military records from St. Louis. Gaffney had only once checked a veteran's record through the VA computer system and then only for a client's dates of service. But Gaffney saw Norman's fabrication as an isolated case, not a systemic problem. I left that day frustrated but curious about how PTSD had become such a widespread assumption about Vietnam vets that I could not convince this sincere therapist that *I didn't* have it.

Vietnam Made Me Do It

Military training doesn't suddenly make everyone a law-abiding citizen. In any group of 2.7 million men, a certain number are going to commit criminal acts. But the creation of the PTSD diagnosis was a boon to defense attorneys who now had another weapon in their arsenal to defend criminals. Now, those who preyed on society had an excuse for their crimes: *Judge, it's all because of Vietnam.* (A book called *Defending the Vietnam Combat Veteran*, published in 1989 by the Vietnam Veterans' Legal Assistance Project, reminded attorneys to look not only at PTSD symptoms but also at exposure to Agent Orange when defending their clients.[373])

That connection between Vietnam and crime gave rise to the idea that as many as a quarter of all Vietnam vets were incarcerated, driven to offenses against civilians by their depraved behavior in war.

When convicts are asked if they are Vietnam vets, I'm sure many raise their hands. But in 1988, a federal Centers for Disease Control (CDC) study of Vietnam veterans, which meticulously checked military records, found the incidence of incarceration extremely low—about the same as nontheater veterans.[374]

Strangely, when criminals seize on PTSD as a way to explain their misdeeds, VA officials are happy to accommodate them. In Silverton, Oregon, a Vietnam veteran named Duane Samples was charged in December 1975 with murder after he disemboweled a woman named Fran Steffens. Another woman, Diane Ross, who was staying with Steffens, survived an assault that same night and identified Samples as her attacker. The cause? Vietnam, Samples claimed.

Samples was a smart man, in the top 5 percent on intelligence tests and a graduate of Stanford University. He told prosecutors he had gone into the Army after receiving his degree in psychology and served in Vietnam in 1966–67 as a forward observer, calling in artillery strikes against enemy positions. But after Vietnam, his idealism destroyed, Samples drifted from job to job, drinking and smoking dope to endure long stretches of unemployment. He finally found a position counseling people with addictions near Salem, Oregon. When Samples pleaded guilty to Steffens' murder in exchange for the dismissal of the attempted murder charges and received a sentence of fifteen years to life, those who knew him concluded that the attacks were an aberration, possibly induced by drugs.

Former FBI Special Agent Robert K. Ressler told the story of Samples in his 1992 book, *Whoever Fights Monsters*. Ressler, one of the founders of the FBI's Criminal Personality Research Project, asked Samples in 1980 to participate in the program, which studies serial killers. From the brutality and gruesome nature of the crimes, as well as substantial evidence of Samples' obsession with sexual mutilation, Ressler believed that he shared many similarities with serial killers like Ted Bundy and was a classic sadistic sexual psychopath. Samples declined, saying he didn't see himself as the same sort of person as the mass murderers Ressler had been interviewing. Samples told Ressler that after his release from prison, he wanted to earn a doctorate in psychology. He asked the agent if he could go to work with the FBI's Behavioral Sciences Unit. Taken aback, Ressler explained that the FBI probably would not hire someone with a prison record and left, thinking he would have no more involvement with Samples.[375]

But in 1981, Ressler was informed by the prosecutors that Oregon Gov. Victor Atiyeh had commuted Samples' sentence, and he was going to be released from prison. Samples claimed he had been rehabilitated and that in 1975, psychiatry had just begun to recognize his disease—PTSD. "His experiences in Vietnam, Samples claimed, had left him shattered, and, after years of torment, it had tragically surfaced in his murder of Fran Steffens," Ressler wrote. "With counseling in prison, Samples now felt he had conquered this disorder that had once pushed him to snuff out a life."[376]

Two psychologists supported Samples' efforts. One, an academic, had extensively examined Vietnam veterans suffering from PTSD. The other was a psychologist in private practice who was receiving VA funds to counsel Samples in prison on a regular basis. Samples had convinced the VA to send him a private therapist and had won a monthly PTSD disability compensation check based on his trauma during the war.

Samples claimed that while in Vietnam, he had seen two fellow officers, Hugh Hanna and Randy Ingrahm, die horribly of disemboweling wounds. The academician's report described how Samples watched his close friend Ingrahm "literally being shredded by a Claymore land mine." Forced to pick up the pieces of his friend, Samples recalled placing the "bleeding parts of his body into a basket for Medevac and seeing the blood run out of the basket as it was lifted up into the helicopter." Although he had been decorated for bravery in Vietnam with the Bronze Star Medal, in his nightmares Samples saw his medals as being "the color of dried blood."

Prosecutors, alarmed that the governor had commuted Samples' sentence and concerned that he was still dangerous, asked Ressler for help. A reserve officer in the Army's Criminal Investigation Division, Ressler knew how to obtain and evaluate military records. He discovered that Samples' military records showed no Bronze Star Medal for valor, as Samples had claimed, nor any other awards for combat or bravery.[377]

Ressler learned that while men with the names Hanna and Ingrahm had been wounded during the time Samples was in Vietnam, neither had died. Randy Ingrahm, an enlisted man, not an officer, did not remember Samples. Hugh "Bud" Hanna, promoted to major, had stayed in the military. Ressler located him at a U.S. military base in Belgium; Hanna remembered Samples well. Samples had arrived in Vietnam as Hanna's replacement as forward observer. But as a newly minted psychology graduate, Samples was counseling enlisted men against the war, so Hanna's superiors sent him back to his post until they figured out whether Samples was going to work out. After returning to the war zone, Hanna had been severely wounded, shot in the mouth, tongue, and palate. When the time came for Hanna to testify against Samples for his antiwar activities, he could not speak, so the issue was dropped.

Col. Courtney Prisk, Samples' commanding officer in Vietnam, told a newspaper that Samples "was a guy I thought needed frequent counseling to keep his spirits up. He was strange—not peculiar—but strange." Prisk said that there had been only one casualty in his unit from a Claymore mine, and that had occurred three hundred yards away from Samples. "I believe Samples has taken two or three things he saw or heard about and fabricated them into something," Prisk said.[378]

The evidence uncovered by Ressler and others was presented to the governor at a commutation hearing. Samples reacted with fury, saying that the man who died was not Ingrahm (his previous claim), but "Ingraham." In 1983, Mike Wallace, correspondent for *60 Minutes*, did a sympathetic story on Samples and post-Vietnam stress syndrome, claiming that the attempt to refute Samples' tale had failed. On the air, Samples came across as an intelligent, polite, believable man who had suffered much. Wallace said that he had located the lieutenant colonel who had served with the "real" Ingraham in Vietnam, who confirmed that he was killed. But Wallace did not name the lieutenant colonel or put him on camera, so there was no way to check that information.[379]

Gov. Atiyeh, finally listening to the experts who showed that Samples had a long history of pathological fantasy that had nothing to do with Vietnam, reversed his commutation decision. But Samples almost succeeded in worming his way out of his sentence by clever manipulation of both the prison system and the VA. Ressler pointed out that Dr. John Cochran, a forensic psychologist with the Oregon State Hospital, believed that Samples, a clerk in the prison's psychological section, had doctored his own prison records to buttress his claim that he had been rehabilitated; later, some of Samples' records disappeared. Despite Cochran's contention that Samples was a classic sexual sadist, and thus not capable of rehabilitation, the "powers that be" did not listen to him. The VA not only provided Samples with a private therapist at government expense, they also gave him monetary compensation—all without ever checking to see if what he said about his service in Vietnam was true. Ultimately Samples was paroled and currently lives in California.

Another killer who tried to use Vietnam PTSD as a defense was Arthur J. Shawcross. Arrested in 1969, Shawcross was convicted of raping and strangling an eight-year-old girl. He also admitted killing a young boy. After serving fourteen years in prison, Shawcross was released on parole, then went back to his murderous ways. Arrested again in 1990 in Rochester, New York, he was charged with the brutal murder and mutilation of eleven women, most of them prostitutes. Shawcross pleaded not guilty by reason of insanity.

His lawyers floated a three-pronged defense: sexual, psychological, and physical abuse as a child; a mental condition of "altered states" similar to multiple personality disorder; and posttraumatic stress disorder from his experiences in Vietnam.

Shawcross told the press that his lust for violence blossomed during the war. Sent to Vietnam in 1968, he was a twenty-two-year-old loner with a troubled history that included torturing animals. Assigned to a supply depot at a military base "near the front lines," Shawcross said he soon became a "one-man army," heading into the jungle on unauthorized patrols, his M-16 fitted with "baby-bottle nipples" so he could quietly pick off enemy snipers. "I was a ghost in the jungle," he bragged.[380]

He described witnessing numerous atrocities, such as his fellow soldiers cutting open a prostitute with a machete or forcing an old woman to drink battery acid. Shawcross told a reporter he also committed war crimes, raping and cannibalizing two young Vietnamese women he came across in the jungle. "I was becoming a monster of sorts," Shawcross claimed. "Vietnam taught me how to kill." His mother described his letters home from 'Nam as "descriptions of hell," reeking of "blood and horror." In handwritten accounts and psychiatric interviews, Shawcross described numerous grotesque murders of Vietnamese women in loving detail.

A VA psychiatrist for the defense echoed his assertions. "He became a serial killer, trolling the jungle for victims," said Dr. Joel Norris. Shawcross applied for VA benefits and obtained disability compensation of seventy-three dollars a month for combat wounds to his arm.[381] (He also applied for Agent Orange benefits, claiming the defoliant caused health problems.)

But Shawcross could provide little information about his activities in

Vietnam—no names or nicknames of buddies or officers, and only vague place names like "north of Kontum." And his anecdotes varied with each telling. Still, Shawcross seemed so believable, describing his horrific exploits with a sure, matter-of-fact manner.

FBI agent Ressler obtained Shawcross' military records, which indicated he had seen no combat and that his tales of seeing atrocities on patrol were lies. Sp4 Arthur Shawcross earned no combat decorations, no Purple Heart, and no medals for bravery, as he had claimed.[382]

Shawcross actually served two six-month tours as a supply and parts specialist at Camp Enari, headquarters of the 4th Infantry Division, a military complex at Pleiku complete with first-run movies, air-conditioning, service clubs, a chapel, and swimming pool—far removed from the heavy action. The Army confirmed that Shawcross never accompanied jungle patrols. Ressler located a colleague who had served in the same area at the same time. He confirmed that they had seen little enemy action.

Two reporters, Steve Mills and J. Leslie Sopko with the Rochester *Democrat and Chronicle*, located members of Shawcross' unit; none of the veterans remembered Shawcross either by name or description. "Two dozen soldiers who served in his unit said that it is unlikely he would have seen much fighting," they wrote. Toward the end of his tour in Vietnam, Shawcross was disciplined repeatedly and finally sent to Fort Sill, where he was assigned to weapons repair.[383]

Pretrial motions by the prosecution debunking his claims of PTSD were so strong and unequivocal, Shawcross's attorneys didn't even mention the subject at the five-week trial. Shawcross was convicted on ten counts of murder in the second degree and one count of homicide and was sentenced to 250 years to life in the penitentiary.

Ressler, who has studied hundreds of serial killers, took the psychiatric profession to task for relying on self-reports of patient-offenders. In his book, the former FBI agent told the story of Monte Rissell, a young man who saw a psychiatrist on a regular basis and was described as making good progress—and all along he was raping and murdering young women. While using Rissell as an example of the manipulative genius common to some serial killers in a presentation, Ressler encountered Rissell's psychiatrist. Mortified at having been gulled by his patient, the psychiatrist felt that if he had been more astute about the case, the lives of several women might have been spared.

"In my view, the problem stemmed from the historic reliance of traditional psychiatry on self-report," Ressler said. "That is, that the patient will truthfully tell the doctor everything that has happened and will willingly participate in the healing process. Forensic psychiatry has learned not to rely solely on self-reports, to use outside reports, court records, and the like, and to continually question the accuracy of what a patient-offender discloses about his life and actions."[384]

But VA psychiatrists rarely do this. The numbers of Vietnam veterans who make use of PTSD as a criminal defense are minuscule compared to those who demand compensation, saying war trauma has screwed up their lives. And they do so with the complicity of VA psychiatrists, psychologists, and social workers who need patients in a system serving a steadily declining number of veterans.

The Numbers Are Staggering

Since the war's end, veterans' activists have claimed that anywhere from 250,000 to 2 million of the approximately 3.3 million men who served in the Vietnam theater of operations "currently" suffer from PTSD. Those are astonishingly high figures, especially since fewer than 15 percent of those who served in Vietnam were in direct line combat units, a figure that stayed consistent throughout the war. Personnel in support units might conceivably suffer PTSD from terrorist or rocket attacks on their bases; however, with the exception of the Viet Cong terrorist campaign of 1965 and the Tet Offensive in 1968, most rear areas were relatively free from these attacks.

But as the conviction that massive numbers of Vietnam vets were emotionally disturbed grew more pervasive and in response to lobbying by veterans' advocates, the government realized the need to measure just how big the problem of Vietnam veterans with PTSD really was. In 1983, Congress passed Public Law 98-160, which mandated the Research Triangle Institute in North Carolina to undertake such a study.

The investigation took more than four years and cost $9 million to complete. When the National Vietnam Veteran Readjustment Study (NVVRS) was released in 1988, Sen. Alan Cranston, then chairman of the Senate Veterans' Affairs Committee, called its findings "nothing short of shocking."

According to the NVVRS, 15.2 percent of male Vietnam theater veterans, or about 479,000, suffered from PTSD. Among white veterans, the incidence of PTSD was 13.7 percent. The rate was even higher for black veterans (20.6 percent), and highest for Hispanic veterans (27.9 percent).

An additional 11 percent of veterans were currently suffering "partial" PTSD. That brought the number who suffered from "partial" or full PTSD at the time of the study to 830,000, or about 26 percent of all Vietnam vets.

But even more amazing was the study's estimation of the "lifetime" prevalence of PTSD—that 30.9 percent of males and 26.9 percent of females had PTSD sometime in their lives. The report added those figures to the "lifetime partial" PTSD among male veterans of 22.5 percent and female veterans of 21.2 percent and came to a staggering conclusion.

"These findings mean that over the course of their lives, more than half [53.4 percent] of male theater veterans and nearly half [48.1 percent] of female veterans have experienced clinically significant stress-reaction symptoms," the study concludes. "This represents about 1.7 million veterans of the Vietnam War." Not only that, but "about one-half of the men and one-third of the women who have ever had PTSD still have it today," the report said.[385]

The study tied the disorder to high levels of combat exposure: "The prevalence of PTSD and other postwar psychological problems is significantly, and often dramatically, higher among those with high levels of exposure to combat and other war-zone stressors in Vietnam, by comparison either with their Vietnam era veteran and civilian peers or with other veterans who served in the Vietnam theater and were exposed to low or moderate levels of war zone stress. This suggests a prominent role for exposure to war stress in the development of subsequent psychological problems and confirms that those who were most heavily involved in the war are those for whom readjustment was, and continues to be, most difficult."[386]

In-country vets suffered many other readjustment problems. Forty percent had been divorced at least once. Violent and hostile acts were reported by 46.8 percent. Ten percent said they had been homeless or vagrant at some point. However, the study downplayed the fact that in each category, Vietnam veterans' problems were not significantly different from those of Vietnam-*era* vets who did not serve in the war.

But, strangely, another survey released the same year conducted by the Centers for Disease Control as part of the Vietnam Experience Study, found much different results. The CDC study concluded that about 15 percent of Vietnam veterans experienced *some* symptoms of combat-related PTSD at *some time during or after* military service. That meant a soldier could have had a flashback a week after a firefight—or he could have suffered depression a decade after the war. That study found that only 2.2 percent had the disorder during the month before the examination.[387]

Even more significantly, the CDC study found few differences in psychological adjustment between Vietnam veterans and nontheater veterans. About 14 percent of Vietnam veterans reported problems with alcohol dependence compared to 9 percent of non-Vietnam veterans. Anxiety was reported by 5 percent of the Vietnam veterans compared to 3 percent of nontheater vets. Five percent of Vietnam vets suffered depression, compared to 2 percent of non-Vietnam veterans. And fewer than 1 percent in either group met the criteria for current drug abuse. At the time of the study, few men in either group were in jail, institutionalized, or mentally or physically incapacitated.

The research indicated that "current poor psychological status was more prevalent in veterans who were not white, who had been young (younger than nineteen years) at enlistment, or who had lower general technical scores at enlistment," regardless of whether a veteran had served in Vietnam. Other characteristics, including military occupational specialty, "*were not* associated with current poor psychological status." (Emphasis added.) Tellingly, poor psychological status among those who were in Vietnam was 13 percent for those with tactical military occupational specialties—those more likely to serve in combat—and 12 percent for those with a nontactical MOS. Was it the war or something else that caused their difficulties?[388]

"Military service in Vietnam was, undoubtedly, an emotionally and psychologically difficult experience for many U.S. servicemen," concluded the CDC study. "Fifteen to twenty years later, more Vietnam veterans have psychological and emotional problems compared with veterans who did not serve in Vietnam. These psychological problems, however, are not of a magnitude that has resulted in Vietnam veterans having, as a group, lower social and economic attainment."

Why the vast difference in the findings of the two studies?

The NVVRS examined only sixteen hundred Vietnam veterans and 750 non-Vietnam vets. The CDC study was much larger, comparing 9,324 Vietnam veterans to 8,989 non-Vietnam veterans. But the real answer lies in the artful way the NVVRS was constructed.

Seek and Ye Shall Find

The creators of the National Vietnam Veterans' Readjustment Study did begin with the military records of Vietnam veterans, obtained from the National Personnel Records Center and the Defense Manpower Data Center. According to *Trauma and the Vietnam War Generation*, the final NVVRS report, the records were pulled at random to fit a prescribed formula so that the study's sample "universe" included a certain number of veterans from each service, a certain number of officers, so many enlisted men, and so many women—a universe that theoretically matched those who served in Vietnam.[389]

But the predominant data extracted from the military record was the veteran's address or other locator information. Because each service person was to be interviewed in person, *the substance and circumstances of the veteran's military service was not extracted from the military record*. For that, the researchers relied on the veteran's personal testimony without examining his military record. If the veteran said he was a squad leader with two tours of heavy combat, they accepted his description at face value.

Then the study's designers created a control group of 225 Vietnam veterans who had already been diagnosed as PTSD patients. Most were undergoing psychiatric treatment; their chart diagnosis and their diagnosis by "an expert clinician" agreed on the presence of PTSD. Their conditions were matched against the larger sample group to identify those veterans with PTSD. The researchers did not obtain the military records of those already diagnosed patients to verify they were in Vietnam. They assumed that the patients actually were Vietnam vets; after all, the VA system had already identified these men as Vietnam veterans with PTSD. So the PTSD "validation" instruments the study created were compromised before the study even began.

Another major problem for the researchers occurred immediately, when they realized that among the control group many of those diagnosed with PTSD *did not in fact meet the criteria* established in the *DSM-III*. At least 40 percent of those diagnosed as suffering from PTSD did not report enough symptoms to qualify for the diagnosis. Although this was an astonishing admission, in order to compensate, the researchers simply adjusted the definition of PTSD. Ironically, this new definition eventually became the criteria for PTSD in *DSM-IV*, after its supposed "validation" by the NVVRS. (The CDC study required that those diagnosed as PTSD meet the full criteria.)

With those inherent flaws built into the study, the research was further skewed by the creation of the sample universe, which was composed of 20 percent Air Force and 20 percent Navy, far over-representing these two branches of the service in Vietnam, where the brunt of combat was borne by the Marines and the Army. Except for pilots and combat-zone aircrews, and men patrolling on river boats, the Navy and Air Force collectively should have suffered the least amount of stress. The study also excluded all those Vietnam veterans still on active duty in the mid-eighties, although men who made the military a career are more likely to have served in combat, many for more than one tour of duty.

Although the Officer Corps in Vietnam constituted approximately 12.5 percent of personnel, the sample included only 7 percent officers. Officers typically are older, have a higher education level, and are known to be less susceptible to combat stress than younger, less-educated enlisted men. The sample also included several hundred women, the great majority of whom were nurses. Interestingly, six of these women claimed their stress was caused by being a POW of the enemy. Apparently no one involved in analyzing the survey realized that not a single American military woman was *ever* a prisoner in this war.

The study also divided the participants into categories of low/moderate and high exposure to combat. Each veteran was asked questions to describe his combat experiences and then assigned to a category. But no attempt was made to verify that the claimed combat experiences actually happened.

The combat rating scale included questions such as: Were you on a ship or aircraft that passed through hostile waters or air space? Did you ever see a body? Did you ever see the enemy? Was your camp ever shelled by artillery or rocket fire? Were you ever shot at by small arms fire? By the study's standards, I served in heavy combat. But I certainly would never describe my experience in Vietnam that way. To me, combat is actively out looking for the enemy, shooting at him, and being shot at.

Because low was lumped with moderate, virtually everyone in the study was assigned to "low/moderate" or "heavy" combat exposure. Where were all the cooks, the lifeguards, the troops running the ice cream factories and water purification plants, the tens of thousands of clerks who served in Vietnam? (In theory, the oversampling of Air Force and Navy personnel would result in lower exposure to combat.) After choosing fifteen hundred Vietnam theater vets, the study sample was then "augmented" with one hundred theater veterans with service-connected disabilities. The report doesn't say how these veterans were chosen or whether they were representative of the number of veterans with such disabilities.

Among male respondents, more than 25 percent claimed to have received "combat" medals; 6 percent of female respondents said they received combat medals. But there's no definition given for these decorations. A Combat Infantryman Badge, given to infantrymen for thirty days under hostile fire? A Silver Star or Bronze Star Medal for valor? Because the term "combat" medals is not defined, it's impossible to tell what that means.

And about 19 percent of the males surveyed said they were wounded or injured in combat in Vietnam; 13 percent said they received a Purple Heart. Approximately 220,000 Purple Hearts actually were issued during the entire Vietnam War—which works out to about 7 percent of those who served. Of the 220,000 that were issued, about 47,000 went to men who were killed in combat; in addition, my guess is that approximately 10 percent of the Purple Hearts were multiple awards to the same individual. I know men who received as many as five. That brings the percentage down even farther to about 4.7 percent of those who survived the war. The study sample contained three times that number of recipients of the Purple Heart.[390]

Either the study's creators placed a heavy emphasis on choosing those who were wounded and the most likely to be traumatized, or they had a high ratio of liars. I would guess the latter.

The NVVRS began with a faulty design—relying on self-reporting, not verifying the information through military records, skewing the sample. But the methodology of obtaining the facts from the subjects further distorted the results. Interviewers were hired and given a ten-day training course on how to conduct the examinations. Their goal was to obtain answers to all items on the questionnaire. In addition, each interviewer carried a large card listing the symptoms of PTSD. Early in the conversation, the interviewer asked the subject—symptom by symptom—which he had experienced. At the end of each phase of the questionnaire, the interviewer repeated each of the questions about PTSD symptoms again.

The interviewers were trained in getting answers to potentially sensitive questions by a team of "recognized expert clinicians experienced in diagnosing and treating stress disorders, particularly among combat veterans." These apparently were VA therapists in various PTSD programs who, as we've seen, have a spectacular inability to discern fakes from the real thing.

If, throughout the interview, the veteran persisted in giving negative replies to the questions about symptoms, the intrepid examiner was to try a different approach. Rather than ask if the veteran had insomnia, the interviewer inquired if he suffered from any "sleepless nights." Once the man admitted sleepless nights, that was written on the card next to insomnia, showing the man did in fact suffer a symptom of PTSD. "The interview was purposely designed to allow respondents *multiple opportunities* to tell the interviewer about traumatic events," the report said. (Emphasis in the original.)

Each veteran was interviewed for three to five hours; with these instructions, it's a safe bet that some of the veterans probably felt that their interviewer would not leave until they gave the "right" answers. In The Family Interview Component, the spouses or live-in partners of 450 veterans were interviewed, called upon primarily to confirm the veteran's testimony about his symptoms. Finally, researchers telephoned the veteran to verify the answers.

"In addition to determining the scope of issues connected with PTSD for the family, our survey [of the spouse] had another purpose: verification," the report said. "There are those who believe that some or all Vietnam veterans are 'faking it' when they describe PTSD symptoms, that they only want sympathy or to obtain veterans' benefits. There are some who question the very existence of PTSD. Yet our study found a strong correlation between PTSD symptoms reported by the veterans themselves and reports of the veterans' symptoms from their spouses. Furthermore, there was no incentive in our survey to motivate respondents to claim to experience symptoms they did not experience. We believe that these factors provide strong indications that Vietnam veterans are not 'making up' symptoms—a reality of which many husbands, wives, and children are already aware."391

Because a wife confirms that her husband acts like a jerk, can't hold a job, and blames it on the war, he must be telling the truth about his service in Vietnam? And although it was subtle, the message was there: If the results of this study come out well, you may be eligible for government money.

The results were predetermined. Of course the study found high rates of PTSD; the researchers changed the definition, then persisted until the veterans finally admitted some symptoms. Also, because of the interviews with the wives and children, the researchers laid the groundwork for a second assault on the taxpayers' money by claiming the family and children might well have to be treated, too. (Among those on the editorial board to the publisher of the report: antiwar activists Sarah Haley, Robert Lifton, and Chaim Shatan.)

One example of how bizarre these results are: The study said that 23.7 percent of Marine enlisted men in *nontactical* jobs suffered PTSD, almost the same rate as the 26.3 percent of Marines in *tactical* assignments. Did Marine cooks, truck drivers, and clerk-typists really experience the same trauma as Marine riflemen heavily engaging the best the North Vietnamese had to throw at them?

Interestingly, the study indicated that, by far, those most likely to report trauma were veterans who were high school dropouts, the unemployed, and those making less than twenty thousand dollars a year. The lowest rate of PTSD was among those who served on active duty for twenty or more years—although those career military servicemen were more likely than others to have seen heavy combat. The prevalence of current PTSD also was higher among male theater veterans who were members of veterans' organizations—maybe because the word had gone out in those groups about veterans' disability benefits. And the level of PTSD among those who had some contact with the VA since leaving the service was twice the rate of those who had not contacted the VA.

But perhaps one of the most significant findings was that male theater veterans who said they experienced "high war-zone stress" had higher rates of nine psychiatric disorders—including anxiety disorders and depression—than did era veterans and civilians. Of those Vietnam veterans with PTSD, 42 percent had a lifetime diagnosis or recent symptoms of antisocial personality disorder. (Remember Michael Pard?)

"Men exposed to high levels of war stress reported lower levels of life satisfaction and happiness, were more socially isolated, had more often been homeless or vagrant, expressed higher levels of hostility, had committed more violent acts, and more often had been arrested or jailed and convicted of a felony than those exposed to lower levels of stress in Vietnam," the study said.

To the researchers, this "proved" the trauma of war. The logic of relying on people with high rates of antisocial personality disorder and other psychiatric illnesses to accurately describe their war experiences *without verifying their reports with military records* eludes me.

The NVVRS book *Trauma and the Vietnam War Generation* includes a war trauma poem from that ubiquitous sham "Vietnam veteran" Al Hubbard and a familiar quote from antiwar therapist Sarah Haley: "The only report that should not be accepted at face value is the patient's report that combat in Vietnam had no effect on him."

However, the researchers did not accept one finding at face value, because the results disagreed with what they expected to find. Among those veterans who said they experienced high war-zone stress, the rate of drug abuse was only 8.4 percent. Overall, the rate of drug use for Vietnam vets was similar to civilian rates. "This appeared to indicate an underreporting of drug use among veterans as well, based on the presumption of high levels of drug use in Vietnam," the report stated in a transparent bit of political correctness.

The study also found so few Vietnam veterans—fewer than 1 percent—in jail or prison that they could not assess the relationship between postwar psychological problems and incarceration. Researchers explained this anomaly by suggesting that percentage clearly was not accurate, that the veterans they were unable to locate were probably incarcerated. But people in state or federal prisons are easier to find than just about anybody. And the study did not explore another interesting finding—that there was no correlation between immediate combat-generated psychiatric problems in Vietnam and psychiatric problems in readjustment to life after the war. In other words, those who were psychiatric casualties had no increase in postwar problems.

The Gold Standard

In 1993, Dr. Arthur Blank, at one time the VA's chief of psychiatric services, defended the NVVRS findings, insisting that they were highly accurate. The CDC study "missed three out of four cases of PTSD," according to Blank.

Blank contended that the level of PTSD was higher among Vietnam veterans than those of World War II or Korea because veterans returned abruptly to a hostile social environment. In World War II, ground troops returned intact and often had many months of "decompression" with their comrades to work through their stress and grief. In World War II and Korea, Blank said, soldiers had more thorough psychiatric services, and the Army intervened more directly to treat combat stress.[392]

But he's wrong. Psychiatric casualties were actually *lower* in Vietnam, because the military followed the Salmon plan early on. (Granted, the social atmosphere on returning home was more positive for both World War II and Korean War vets.)

Then Blank argued that the problem of fabricators is an "irrelevant sideshow" to the clinical treatment of vets with PTSD. While liars could be a problem for researchers, he said, that was not a problem at the clinical level because "skilled clinicians and counselors can weed out the fakes." The real story, Blank insisted, is that PTSD is readily treatable in the VA system and has a high recovery success rate. Neither of those statements is true. And for that matter, "skilled clinicians" probably do *not* weed out fakers.

And Blank, as national director of the War Veteran Counseling Service, had a vested interest in the study finding high numbers of veterans with PTSD. The NVVRS was conducted at the demand of Congress as a condition of continuing to fund the Vet Centers. The VA has a stake in building the largest PTSD patient base possible.

The study was typical government pork: Ask a panel of artists to determine whether a subsidy should be paid to artists, or a panel of accountants to determine if the tax laws should be made more complex. The VA and those who feed off its enormous bureaucracy—therapists, psychiatrists, social workers—must have patients who need treatment, so they created a study that justified their existence. "It is important to note that only a mental health professional can accurately determine if you have PTSD," the report cautioned.

Sacred Cow

The VA, which has a budget of more than $15 billion, has been under fire for the last fifteen years for being a bloated, inefficient agency in which too many dollars chase too few needs. In 1990, the Inspector general found that twenty-one of the 131 surgeons at six VA hospitals "spent no time in the operating room at all during the year." An audit of three other hospitals in 1994 revealed the situation had not improved. Thirteen of the seventy-nine surgeons on staff—paid an average salary of $135,000—did no operations during the year. Although the rest of the federal work force shrank 8 percent, under the Clinton administration, the VA work force grew 1.4 percent, to 264,000, and the Veterans' Affairs budget has steadily climbed.[393]

New York Times columnist William Safire created a firestorm in January 1995, when he called the VA a "sacred cow" and charged that its services could be better provided through health care paid for by private health insurance. He pointed to a study showing that the VA had more than three hundred administrators making more than one hundred thousand dollars a year and that its cost-per-patient was twice that of the private sector.[394]

However, while costs have risen, the number of veterans has actually dropped, from 30.1 million in 1980 to 26 million in 1995. Because of eligibility requirements and private insurance, the VA system cares for only about one-tenth of all veterans. In 1996, the VA budget was in line to receive $16.6 billion, about twice as much as the Department of Defense spends on the eight million active duty service personnel and their families. A quarter of the beds in the VA's 173 hospitals stand empty as surviving soldiers of World War II move into their geriatric years. The VA has shut only two hospitals since the 1960s, both because of earthquakes. But when Edward J. Derwinski, the secretary for veterans' affairs for President George Bush, suggested admitting nonveterans to underused VA hospitals, the outcry from the veterans' groups was so loud he was forced to resign. And the VA's 1996 budget proposed by Clinton's Secretary for Veterans' Affairs Jesse Brown did not close any hospitals but advocated that the agency spend $343 million to build two more![395]

These trends have been going on for more than a decade. So it was in the interest of everyone connected to the study and the VA to show there was a serious need. Like the inclusion of PTSD in the *DSM-III*, the continuing push to show that Vietnam veterans are severely afflicted by PTSD—which advocates say can manifest itself twenty years after the triggering incidents —is political, not scientific.

When the results of the NVVRS were announced, the VA and veterans' advocates exuberantly waved them like a banner, claiming the research "proved" the need for more Vet Centers, more funding, more jobs. The VA called the study the "gold standard" in PTSD research.

During yearly hearings of the House and Senate Committees on Veterans' Affairs, the research invariably is raised as justification for expansion of PTSD programs. The CDC study, which involved eight times as many veterans and stuck to the definition of PTSD, is dismissed as irrelevant. But all the NVVRS really proved was that if "scientists" ask the questions in a biased way, they get the answers they are seeking.[396]

Since the creation of the Vet Centers, the funding for diagnosis and treatment of PTSD has mushroomed. By the end of 1991, the VA system had established the National Center for PTSD Research at West Haven, Connecticut. Currently there are twenty Specialized Inpatient PTSD Units; nine Evaluation and Brief Treatment Inpatient Units; eight Residential Rehabilitation Units; fifty-seven PTSD Clinical Teams; nine outpatient-based Substance Abuse Disorder/PTSD Teams; four inpatient-based PTSD Teams Substance Use Disorder demonstration projects; and a study authorized and funded by Congress of PTSD in Native Americans and Asian Pacific Islanders who served in the Vietnam War.

In 1994, the cost of administering PTSD programs through the VA medical facilities had grown to more than $47 million a year. Add that to the Vet Center program, which has 201 centers and now costs $58 million a year. (That does not include millions in disability compensation.) The PTSD programs are not shrinking; they are growing as they find more "victims." The National Center for PTSD established a women's division, targeting not only female veterans but also spouses of veterans.

The validator of PTSD, the National Vietnam Veterans' Readjustment Study, was a welfare bill for mental health professionals. Continually referenced in congressional hearings and publications, this study has taken on a life of its own. A press release from the VA put it succinctly: "Future size of the Readjustment Counseling Service will be determined by need and utilization."[397]

During the war, the goal of the left was to show that the Vietnam conflict was so immoral it permanently damaged the psyches of those who fought it. The bottom line now is money. If truly damaged Vietnam veterans were being helped, that would be one thing. But VA hospitals and PTSD programs are havens for malingerers who manipulate the system for their own psychological and financial ends and will ultimately cost taxpayers billions.

The Vietnam Veterans' Guide to Tax-Free Living

RESIDENTS in the working class neighborhood of Stratford, Connecticut, watched anxiously from behind blockades as SWAT police trained their weapons on a basement apartment. A Vietnam veteran had barricaded himself in a building and threatened to shoot any officer who came near. All morning, police officers and a VA psychiatrist negotiated with the man by phone.

"He said he wanted some respect," a police captain said later.

The April 14, 1995, standoff started after "Dr. Darnell," a psychiatrist with the Veterans' Medical Center of West Haven, notified police about 11:20 that morning. His patient, Kenley Barker, had phoned to tell the doctor he had a gun and was holed up in his apartment. Apparently intoxicated, forty-eight-year-old Barker insisted that if police came through his door "there would be a big mess."[398]

That morning, Barker had told his landlord's mother, Phyllis Valentino, that he was depressed over killing one hundred men as a Marine during the Vietnam War. While the woman tenderly held his hand, Barker moaned that he suffered from Agent Orange syndrome and worried about its effects on his son, who had cerebral palsy. Barker had been recently released from the VA hospital where he was undergoing treatment for a drinking problem and PTSD. He told Valentino he did not want to go back to the VA hospital because they might send him to a treatment center in Massachusetts.

It was not the first time Barker had created a standoff situation. He was awaiting a court appearance from an earlier incident that occurred on Christmas Day, 1994, when Dr. Darnell called police and told them he was worried about two of his patients. Officers were dispatched to a North Haven apartment where Barker was holed up with another Vietnam veteran, Joe Coyle, both apparently inebriated. Barker was threatening to commit suicide.

"I don't want you here when they show," Barker had yelled at Coyle, apparently talking about the police. "I'm going to take them out. I don't care what happens to me." As police officers tried to coax them from the apartment, Barker had continued to shout at Coyle. "I'll end everything and anybody who gets in my way. I don't want you to see this, so leave." After ten minutes, Coyle left the room, but Barker had refused to follow him. "If you want me, come and get me, and it will be over," Barker had yelled. Police finally succeeded in getting Barker's rifle and a knife.[399] After that incident, both Barker and Coyle had been taken into custody and were committed to the VA Medical Center. But for some reason, they had been released.

The second standoff in April finally ended after three anxious hours when police negotiators persuaded Barker to give up. A waiting ambulance whisked Barker to the VA hospital for observation.

The impression left by the story in the *New Haven Register* of Barker's breakdown was that yet another Vietnam veteran, tormented by the faces of those he killed, had gone berserk. Perhaps the psychiatrist believed that as well. According to sources at the West Haven VA, Barker and Coyle were long-term patients in their PTSD program. The psychiatrists at the center believed that the two men were deeply troubled Vietnam veterans.

But according to military records, Kenley Barker of Easton, Connecticut, had joined the Navy—not the Marines—on September 30, 1965, and had been discharged on April 22, 1966. Barker served on active duty for less than a year. During that six-month period, Barker had been stationed at the U.S. Naval Training Center in Great Lakes, Illinois, the U.S. Naval Base in Charleston, South Carolina, and the U.S. Naval Air Station in Pensacola, Florida. For part of that time, he apparently was treated at the U.S. Naval Hospital.[400]

Barker had not served in Vietnam and thus could not have "killed one hundred men as a Marine." Barker certainly has mental problems, but they are completely unrelated to the Vietnam War. (Coyle is not a Vietnam veteran either. He served in the Army as an electrical repairman from February 26, 1962, to February 25, 1965, all in the United States.[401]) So how was it possible that both men had been treated for Vietnam-related PTSD for all those years?

While VA psychiatrists and social workers feed off the PTSD phenomenon, the biggest beneficiaries are the thousands of Vietnam-era men and women who qualify for medical treatment and a service-connected PTSD disability rating of 100 percent. That diagnosis can net veterans more than three thousand dollars a month tax-free—even if they never saw combat, even if they never set foot in Vietnam.

Not All Veterans Welcome

The Department of Veterans' Affairs manages the largest health care system in the United States. Throughout the fifty states, Puerto Rico, and the Philippines, the system includes 171 hospitals, 128 nursing homes, 37 residential care facilities, and 191 community clinics, and employs about 268,000 people. Annually, about 2.6 million veterans—approximately 10 percent of the total number of veterans—receive care from the VA. That works out annually to about 10 patients per employee.

In 1992, 542,894 veterans accounted for a total of 922,524 admissions to VA hospitals. More than 97 percent of those patients were men. The bulk, about 40 percent, were veterans of World War II; another 26 percent were Vietnam veterans. Even more are seen by the Vet Centers, clinics run by the VA Readjustment Counseling Service. In 1995 alone, the Vet Centers saw 138,407 veterans; 84,253 were new veteran clients.

But the pool of veterans is shrinking. World War II ended more than a half-century ago; the Vietnam War ended more than twenty years ago. There were twenty-seven million veterans in 1994, but by the end of the century, that will have dropped to twenty-four million. With the all-volunteer armed services and no draft, the country's supply of veterans is getting smaller and smaller, but the VA's budget just keeps growing.

Most people assume that the VA medical system treats all veterans, but not every veteran is eligible, whether or not he served in combat. To determine eligibility, veterans must take what is called a MEANS test. Any veteran with a total household income of less than nineteen thousand dollars a year is eligible for free VA treatment even if his problem is not service-related. (The threshold is twelve thousand dollars a year for outpatient care.) All former POWs are also eligible for free treatment. And veterans who are disabled by injury or illness incurred or aggravated while on active duty—"service-connected" disorders—can qualify for free treatment for that disorder at VA hospitals as well as disability compensation payments from the Veterans' Benefits Administration. About half of those treated have service-connected disabilities.

A veteran with a higher salary and nonservice-connected problems may receive treatment if the VA facility has room, but he or his insurance company has to pay. The result of the MEANS test can be ironic: VA facilities will treat poor veterans for nonservice-connected problems but may turn away more prosperous veterans who have problems that resulted from their military service. (Each VA facility has its own guidelines and standard operating procedures, resulting in confusing and inconsistent policies from hospital to hospital. To add further confusion, an individual hospital may change its policy back and forth.)

Veterans with service-connected disabilities ratings of 50 percent or above qualify for free treatment of that problem regardless of their income. The rating is determined by one of the VA's Regional Office Rating Boards. This board assesses the degree of disability, measured in percentages ranging from zero to 100 percent in increments of ten. (A 100 percent rating means 100 percent disabled. By adding up ratings for various problems, the rating can actually go above 100 percent.) The board looks at time missed from work and loss of work efficiency to determine the rating.

Psychiatric disability is rated at six levels, from zero to 100 percent. In mid-1993, disability compensation payments ranged from $85 to $1,730 a month, tax-free. Veterans with ratings of 30 percent or higher can qualify for additional money for dependents—a spouse, a minor child, a dependent child over eighteen attending school, or a dependent parent. Those with ratings of 50 percent or higher qualify for free medical care, whether the problem is service-connected or not, regardless of their income. Each year, compensation payments are adjusted for inflation.

Most veterans who qualify for 100 percent PTSD payments also qualify for Social Security and other benefits, such as payments for dependents. Although disability compensation payments can reduce Social Security supplemental income, it is exempt from federal and state income taxes.[402]

Those who lost limbs or eyesight in Vietnam also qualify for disability payments. While the amputation of a leg is obvious, PTSD is subjective, its symptoms surprisingly easy to fake.

Fraudulent claims of PTSD not only denigrate Vietnam vets who truly suffer from trauma, they cost the taxpayers millions of dollars—in treatment dollars, hospital costs, and disability compensation. According to Dr. Douglas Mossman, a former VA psychiatrist, a single veteran designated 100 percent disabled by PTSD in 1994 received the same after-tax income as a Cincinnati, Ohio, resident who works full-time to earn $30,040 a year. In addition to VA compensation, the veteran can qualify for Social Security payments, spousal benefits, tuition for children, and other benefits that may be available to the disabled. (In Texas, disabled veterans are exempted from certain taxes.) Where's the incentive to get well and return to work?

The potential cost is staggering. In 1991, the VA system paid out almost $10 billion in disability compensation to more than two million veterans. Each year veterans file more than six hundred thousand claims for service-connected disability benefits. Some are new claims; some are requests for increases in disability ratings. About half are granted. The VA estimates that about three hundred thousand veterans suffer from psychiatric disabilities severe enough to receive compensation. A 1995 analysis of VA benefits said that 153,486 veterans received compensation payments of 70 percent or more for a psychiatric disorder. (The VA could not provide data on how many were disabled due to PTSD versus other mental disorders.)[403]

Periodically, these veterans must go back to the system and prove that they are still disabled by undergoing treatment for PTSD. If a veteran maintains his rating for twelve years, he receives a "total and permanent" letter, meaning PTSD has rendered him totally and permanently disabled. After that, it doesn't matter what he does. He never has to go to treatment again. His disability rating cannot be changed.

Many other veterans are given ratings of something less than 100 percent and receive smaller payments. Most of these vets are constantly attempting to maintain their ratings or have them upgraded, a process that can require inpatient evaluation care for up to three months, treatment by doctors and therapists, and ongoing paperwork.

In addition, veterans with lower ratings who are hospitalized receive full disability payments after twenty-one days for the rest of their hospitalization. It's called a "twenty-one-day certificate." For example, assume a patient with a 30 percent rating for PTSD, who is receiving five hundred dollars a month, is admitted to the hospital and stays twenty-one days. After that three weeks, his disability payments are raised to 100 percent, or more than eighteen hundred dollars a month for the time he is hospitalized, a "raise" of thirteen hundred dollars. After another month in the hospital, at discharge he receives a compensation check for thirty-six hundred dollars. All the while, his "three hots and a cot" are provided. A nine-month hospitalization for a malingering PTSD veteran can net more than fifteen thousand dollars, tax-free. The VA system provides a monetary incentive for being sick—not for getting well.

Thousands hear about the money train and apply for the benefits every year. From 1984 to 1988, the number of Vietnam veteran inpatient PTSD cases jumped five thousand to nearly eleven thousand, with outpatient visits increasing even faster. (This has occurred despite the fact that the war —and its memories—are growing ever more distant.) Vet Centers report that up to 80 percent of the veterans seeking help say they suffer from combat-related psychological problems.

In a 1993 book called *Cutting Ties*, VA psychologist Tutsie Silapalikitporn argued that the costs of determining ratings and upgrade requests for emotionally disabled veterans *alone* cost taxpayers about $1.3 billion per year. Silapalikitporn said that the government could save millions of dollars by giving all veterans who claim they are traumatized by war a 100 percent disability rating.[404]

Dr. Laurent S. Lehmann, the Department of Veterans' Affairs associate director of psychiatry, has downplayed the number of those faking the disorder. "Yes, it's possible that someone might have sufficiently low self-esteem that he could claim to be suffering from PTSD when he isn't," Lehmann said. "Or he could be suffering from something else and think it's PTSD. But these are a very small percentage. The bigger problem may be the guy who has it but, for whatever reason, doesn't want to admit it."[405]

But with such powerful monetary incentives in place, it's naïve to think that all, or even most, of those veterans who claim they suffer from PTSD —like Kenley Barker—ever served in Vietnam.

A second, more difficult question to answer can be whether those PTSD patients who did serve in some capacity in-country truly were traumatized —or just say they were.

"Nobody Had a Typewriter"

On December 17, 1988, a pickup truck driven by David Franklin Hollingsworth III collided with an eighteen-wheel tractor-trailer in Thibodaux, Louisiana. Hollingsworth sued the owner of the truck, alleging that the accident not only resulted in physical injuries but also exacerbated his PTSD from Vietnam and prevented him from working. The litigation began a series of depositions in which Hollingsworth described his war experiences.

Hollingsworth enlisted in the Army in 1964. He testified that he had been assigned to the 101st Airborne, the Screaming Eagles, where he received instruction in the Russian language. After six months, Hollingsworth was transferred to the 173rd Airborne in Okinawa, where he took "jungle survival training." In May 1965, Hollingsworth claimed, he arrived in Vietnam as part of the 173rd Airborne Brigade and 5th Group Special Forces and was assigned to Bien Hoa.

Although his primary MOS was turret artillery, and he was permanently attached to a maintenance outfit, Hollingsworth said, the unit had nothing for him to do. So on a daily basis, Hollingsworth was assigned TDY—temporary duty assignment. "They put up a roster, and I could go do what I wanted to do, pretty much," Hollingsworth said. They put him in with Special Forces, and he became a Green Beret. "My C.O. had trust in me. I was a doorgunner for a while, went and worked Montagnard camps for a while. I did a little bit of everything, demolitions, blew up tunnels. My whole tour was TDY, just about."[406]

In Vietnam for fourteen months, Hollingsworth testified, he was wounded twice, in his right arm and in the back, and he received two Purple Hearts. Oh, and he also had been hit in the eye with a hot piece of shrapnel. Since he and his unit were being chased by the enemy at the time, Hollingsworth just pulled out the shard of metal; the only medical treatment he received was an eye patch, which he wore for about three weeks.[407] (In a subsequent deposition, he added a fourth wound to his testimony.[408]) Hollingsworth claimed he earned a Vietnamese Cross of Gallantry, two Bronze Star Medals for valor, Combat Infantryman Badge, and two Purple Hearts.

One Bronze Star Medal was awarded, Hollingsworth said, when he was serving as a doorgunner with a helicopter company and assisted in the evacuation of Army personnel from an intense fire zone. "As I was helping [another soldier], something hit him and exploded his head right in front of me," Hollingsworth told the attorneys. "Parts of him went all over me, in my open mouth, and I almost lost it totally. The guys in the helicopter had to pull me back in and literally sit on me until we got back to a base camp." But he never actually received a citation for that Bronze Star Medal. "Nobody had a typewriter," Hollingsworth said.[409]

Later, Hollingsworth was shifted from the helicopter unit to three different Green Beret A-Teams. But he refused to talk about that. "It was classified when I was there, and I don't know if it's been desensitized," Hollingsworth said. "If you'll notice in my records, there's a warning to me not to give any information out."[410]

Hollingsworth claimed his psychological troubles began in Vietnam. "I'm a classic case," Hollingsworth said. "I had severe problems in Vietnam. I can tell you horrible things. I was involved in more ungodly horror than you can imagine. I had to burn people to death and pull them out of holes. I had little children this big, bodies that I had to take and pick up. I can sit here and tell you horror stories that you won't sleep for weeks."[411]

After he left Vietnam in 1967, Hollingsworth had difficulty keeping a job and difficulty controlling his anger. In the seventies, Hollingsworth often provoked confrontations. "[I'd] see the biggest guy in the bar and walk up and smack him and hope that he would fight. I was immensely violent. I had this huge inner anger inside of me."[412]

Frequently arrested for disorderly conduct, fighting, and destruction of property, he was indicted in 1980 on charges in Orleans Parish that he murdered his ex-girlfriend and his best friend. Hollingsworth pleaded guilty to manslaughter. Sentenced to four years in prison, he was released in 1982.[413]

Hollingsworth testified that he did not know he had PTSD until after the accident with the eighteen-wheeler. He began to have sleeplessness, nightmares, and flashbacks of Vietnam. After he contacted a local veterans' outreach program, a VA psychologist named Jim Russell took one look at a test Hollingsworth took and said, "My God, you've got to have PTSD. I think the best thing you can do is come to my group." Russell, Dr. Madeline Uddo, and Dr. Arthur Burden of the VA all made the assessment that Hollingsworth had PTSD.[414]

Hollingsworth attended Russell's group for about a year, then was made co-counselor of the group; he was given a 50 percent disability rating for PTSD. Even with medication, Hollingsworth contended, his PTSD was so severe he could not work. In addition to his VA compensation, he received Social Security and Workmen's Compensation benefits, for a total of twenty-one hundred dollars per month. He also obtained a handicap license plate for his truck, courtesy of the Disabled American Veterans (DAV).[415]

Hollingsworth seemed the epitome of the traumatized Vietnam vet: overweight, long hair, and a graying beard, unable to cope with life because of the terror he had experienced in Vietnam as a tough, heroic Special Forces commando.

Before they went to trial, the attorneys representing the truck company's insurer obtained Hollingsworth's military records. Hollingsworth had served in Vietnam from July 25, 1965, to July 8, 1966, with Company D, 173rd Support Battalion, 173rd Airborne Brigade near Bien Hoa. The battalion's job was building a base camp. Hollingsworth served as an artillery repairman, then as a cook's helper. Hollingsworth was not a Green Beret war hero. Despite his boasting, Hollingsworth received no valorous decorations and no Purple Hearts.[416]

A constant disciplinary problem, Hollingsworth went AWOL for six days in Saigon and was busted from E-5 to E-3. But his troubles with authority had begun long before Vietnam. His school records show a history of truancy before he dropped out of school in the tenth grade. When Hollingsworth was sixteen, he had been arrested for breaking and entering and larceny.[417] When confronted with the disparities in his testimony and his military record, Hollingsworth insisted that his records were inaccurate because his activities in Vietnam were still "classified."

At trial, Col. S. Malave-Garcia, Hollingsworth's commanding officer in Vietnam, testified that not a single soldier in the company was involved in combat during Hollingsworth's time in Vietnam. He signed no TDY orders for Hollingsworth to serve as a doorgunner or to participate in any Special Forces activities. The only time Hollingsworth came to Malave-Garcia's attention was when he was given an Article 15 and reduced in rank for AWOL.

But defense attorneys were prevented from telling the jury that the psychiatrist who examined him on their behalf diagnosed Hollingsworth as suffering from antisocial personality disorder—and so had the VA psychiatrist, Dr. Arthur Burden, although he contended it overlapped his PTSD. (The VA apparently was determined to make Hollingsworth a PTSD patient from the beginning. The intake assessment when Hollingsworth presented himself at a VA facility in March 1989, said he was interested in Agent Orange information. "[He] was advised to be screened for PTSD even though he is not bothered anymore by the war," the report said.)[418]

The judge also excluded from evidence Hollingsworth's conviction for double-manslaughter and any information on his disability benefits. Hollingsworth had made it clear to a vocational rehabilitation specialist that he was expecting a large settlement in the near future and had no interest in returning to work.

At trial, a jury found Hollingsworth 50 percent liable for the accident and granted him only a token payment. Hollingsworth appealed and won the right to a new hearing on compensation for damages. (The case is still pending.) He gets yet another bite at the apple—and, meanwhile, continues to draw VA disability compensation for PTSD.

The Doorgunner's Guide to Tax-Free Living

*1st Co., 2nd Bn., 505th Inf., 82nd Airborne [name deleted] needs witnesses to verify that while stationed in Vietnam in 1969 he pulled two buddies who couldn't swim out of a river. After rescuing his platoon sergeant, he dove into the river again and pulled out another member of his platoon. But the platoon sergeant fell back in and drowned. [Name] now suffers from PTSD. Contact—*from a personal notice in *The American Legion Magazine*, April 1995.

Notices like these appear in numerous veterans' magazines, usually placed by people building cases to persuade VA psychiatrists that they have been permanently disabled by PTSD.

Another ad from *Vietnam* magazine: "Combat Veterans: You can receive monthly VA money and benefits for combat stress (PTSD) by submitting one letter. Expert, guaranteed personal help. If you feel war has changed your life, get the benefits you deserve! Send $10 to—" A similar advertisement has run in *Survivalist* magazine: "Let us help you get PTSD disability." Ironically, this magazine advertises itself as promoting "self-reliance."

A Vietnam veteran in Aurora, Indiana, named Dennis C. Latham publishes *The S-2 Report*, a bimonthly newsletter that deals with the VA and PTSD. He served in the 1st Battalion, 3rd Marines in Vietnam during 1967 and 1968. One of his first jobs was stripping wounded and dead bodies while serving on a landing team based on a helicopter carrier. Out in the field, Latham served on an intelligence field interrogation team, during which he saw prisoners tortured. Then his best friend was killed in an ambush on the Fourth of July, 1968. When Latham returned home, he couldn't cope and was "forcibly retired" from a job at the post office. He discovered he had PTSD in 1981 after his wife at the time complained that he called her a "gook" in his sleep and tried to strangle her.[419]

After obtaining a 50 percent service-connected disability himself, Latham wrote a booklet called "How to Receive Disability for PTSD," which was approved by the VA as an informational handout. "Filing a PTSD claim is a one-time shot which can be worth thousands of dollars in benefits and money if done right the first time," says his ten-dollar booklet, which is advertised in *Vietnam* magazine.[420]

Latham also assists veterans in obtaining PTSD disability compensation, usually by editing stressor letters for forty-five dollars to sixty dollars, which he learned on the job at a Vet Center. "Every combat vet who has followed my instructions has been service-connected," says Latham. Now he aids other vets. "One veteran did show up at my house just to see if I existed," Latham said. "I helped him with his letter, and he got 30 percent going in after years of unsuccessful attempts."[421]

Another book, published in 1993 by the Vietnam Doorgunners Association, showed veterans exactly what to do. Called *Posttraumatic Stress Disorder: How to Apply for 100 Percent Total Disability Rating*, by Roxanne Hill, president of the organization, the twenty-dollar book gives all the ins and outs of dealing with the VA bureaucracy, finding and filling out the right forms, filing a claim, gathering witness letters, and undergoing oral interviews with psychiatrists. Hill's book provides an eye-opening glimpse into the VA system for determining PTSD compensation, showing just how subjective and easy to manipulate the process is.[422]

The date you file your claim is important, according to Hill's book. The sooner the better, because if you succeed in getting a disability rating, the VA will then give you "back pay" to the date you first filed. If it takes eighteen months to obtain that golden 100 percent rating, for example, you might receive up to thirty-five thousand dollars (tax-free!)—or whatever lump sum accrued during those eighteen months—then start receiving those delightful monthly payments.

"One helpful note," Hill wrote. "Most veterans don't think they have PTSD, and even after they are diagnosed with PTSD they don't think they are disabled." But that shouldn't stand in your way!

You must insist on being admitted into a PTSD Clinical Team (PCT) unit for an evaluation. "Don't take NO for an answer," said Hill. "You will need to be involved in treatment to get 100 percent disability for PTSD, but you will not have to remain in treatment once you receive your award."[423] Why enter a hospital if you don't need inpatient care? Because you will need letters of support from the staff of the PCT Unit.

The book described step-by-step what to do and say, accompanied by actual documents of a successful candidate for 100 percent PTSD disability with the name redacted.

"Tell them all about the symptoms you have that you read about from paragraphs 1) through 6). Tell them about your marriage(s). Tell them about your anger and rage. Tell them how you don't trust people. 'ESPECIALLY THE GOVERNMENT'! Tell them how you think the VA is screwed to the max and this PCT program is probably just as screwed up. Let the tears start to come if you are able. Tell them how screwed up life has been since you got back from 'Nam. And, tell them for some reason, things seem to be getting worse for you, harder to handle. The older you get the harder it is for you to hold back the anger and the sadness inside. Tell them sometimes you just don't think you can take much more of this life."[424]

Hill tells potential claimants they should never talk about their childhoods during intake assessments at the VA. "Beginning with the first doctor at the mental health clinic or during the PCT interview, if anyone asks you about childhood, tell them as far as you know that time of your life was normal. Don't volunteer any information about childhood. You had a normal childhood. Even if you didn't, for the purpose of the interviews, you did." No abuse, no parental alcoholism, no unhappiness whatsoever.

Why? Because childhood trauma can affect whether you qualify for a 10 percent, 30 percent, 70 percent, or 100 percent rating. You want no doubt in the doctor's mind: Vietnam screwed you up, not child abuse or an alcoholic father.

"You need to always keep the appearance of your lifestyle before Vietnam as average and normal. This will keep the VA from trying to say your problems are due to your lifestyle before you entered the armed forces."[425]

Have trouble with alcohol? Tell the doctor. Like to fight or carry guns? Been arrested? *For sure* tell the doc.

And please, don't mask those PTSD symptoms. "If you act like nothing is wrong, you will be considered cured and sent away from the program improperly diagnosed (not having PTSD sever [sic] and chronic)."

Let's brush up on our symptomology. "Patients with PTSD are quick to be angered and display that anger. They rarely trust anyone, especially authority figures. They are usually depressed and have a difficulty with the ability to relate their feelings to others (doctors and psychologists), because they are not in touch with themselves."

Got that?

But hey, it's not all bad. While you're going around being depressed and sad for ninety days (the typical inpatient PCT stay), after twenty-one days, you will automatically receive temporary compensation at the same rate as someone 100 percent disabled!

Pay attention to your psychiatrist. You may see this doctor only a few times, but he or she is the one who counts at the rating board, not the consulting clinical psychologists, who do most of the counseling. Ask the psychiatrist to write a letter for you to the rating board. If he agrees, pull out the letter you have already drafted, which will save the doc considerable research time!

Don't forget your own "stressor" letter, a description of a tragic incident that happened to you in Vietnam. "If you have a specific event which took place, but you did not receive any award or Purple Heart during the event, then perhaps you can get in touch with some other Veterans who also witnessed the event." Ask them to write a short letter. Collect letters from your wife, your pastor, your father, all testifying that you're a basket case.

But you do not have to have been awarded any medals or Purple Hearts to have PTSD or receive compensation for PTSD. "Just being in Vietnam under a long-term, sustained life threat can cause PTSD."

To qualify for a 100 percent disability rating from the rating board, the patient wants a ruling like this: "The attitudes of all contacts except the most intimate are so adversely affected as to result in virtual isolation in the community. Totally incapacitating psychoneurotic symptoms bordering on gross repudiation of reality with disturbed thought or behavioral processes associated with almost all daily activities such as fantasy, confusion, panic, and explosions of aggressive energy resulting in profound retreat from mature behavior. Demonstrably unable to obtain or retain employment."[426]

The determined veteran seeking the golden diagnosis can read between the lines: Say this, do that, or kiss that lifetime paycheck good-bye.

Unbelievably, the process is virtually risk free. The VA will even reimburse applicants for travel expenses. If the VA psychiatrist finds you don't have PTSD, the VA will send you to a second psychiatrist outside the VA for another diagnosis. If that civilian doctor says you have the condition, you may be sent to yet another doctor for another session—all paid for by the VA. Organizations like the DAV, VVA, VFW, American Legion, and AMVETS often help veterans obtain benefits at no cost. The DAV's primary purpose is helping veterans obtain disability benefits. "Opening a claim can just be a phone call away," says Latham's booklet.

And it's all tax-free. "When you receive an award for 100 percent total disability," says Hill's book, "you no longer have to pay or file taxes. You also are ready to apply for Social Security Benefits and the Agent Orange Veteran Payment Program (AOVPP)."[427]

Even before I read the "Doorgunners' Guide to Tax-Free Living," I realized the VA process of determining PTSD compensation held vast potential for fraud. After my conversation with Gaffney, the director of the Dallas Vet Center, I began talking to VA therapists around the country trying to figure out what safeguards were in place. Phonies fooled their families, the police, vets groups, even the military. How many had also fooled the VA system?

After reading a column written by a VA psychiatrist affiliated with the West Haven VA Medical Center about a deranged Vietnam veteran in the news, I called the psychiatrist to point out that the guy was a pretender. (I had already researched his record after his case appeared on TV.)

The West Haven VA became one of the national centers for the study of PTSD under a large VA grant. Using a database of hundreds of men in ongoing treatment for the disorder, many who are receiving 100 percent compensation for PTSD, West Haven's doctors and researchers have published at least eight studies on the subject.

The psychiatrist, a very down-to-earth person who did nothing but treat PTSD inpatients at a VA hospital, was taken aback by my claim that the veteran was bogus. I asked if the doctor had ever gotten a patient's military record to verify a DD-214 or to compare against a patient's claims.

"Oh, hell, we never check a military record," the psychiatrist said. "Why would we check a record?"

The psychiatrist assumed that every patient in the VA system has been screened by the admissions office and certified as a veteran. However, that isn't necessarily true.

Military Records and the VA

On the first day a member of the armed service reports to recruit training, his or her name and Social Security number are sent to the VA system. On the day he or she leaves active duty service, the military notifies the VA. When a patient comes into a VA hospital facility, a clerk enters the name into the computer system and verifies that the patient is eligible. A veteran needs only to have one day of honorable service to qualify for medical benefits (but as much as 180 days to qualify for educational and other benefits). Veterans who receive dishonorable discharges are not legally eligible for VA medical benefits.

However, if a veteran has an eligible discharge prior to receiving a dishonorable discharge—as someone might who reenlisted—he is fully eligible for VA benefits. Take the example of a veteran who is honorably discharged. He reenlists, then kills the base commander's wife. Convicted, given a dishonorable discharge, and sent to prison, he can continue to collect VA benefits. The VA either can't or won't identify those with dishonorable discharges receiving veterans' benefits even while in prison. The number could be in the thousands.

Once inside the hospital, the veteran can inform the clerks and doctors that he was a POW. That goes in the record. He can tell them he was a Green Beret. That goes in the record. He can tell them he committed atrocities in Vietnam and is haunted by memories of killing children. That goes in the record. But clerks usually do not request the patient's military record from the National Personnel Records Center in St. Louis to allow physicians to verify those claims.

Not one of the VA employees or doctors I have ever interviewed—with one notable exception—said they knew they could obtain a military record to verify someone's background. They, like many of their patients, are under the impression that military records are strictly private.

People who are not even veterans can get around the VA system by going directly to the Vet Centers. There, the prevailing philosophy is "No Hassles." As proof of their clients' MOS and war experiences, Vet Centers typically accept DD-214 forms. But those are easily doctored with whiteout and a copy machine. Dozens of printing mills churning out counterfeit DD-214s have sprung up around the country to help self-made veterans illegally obtain VA benefits and services, civil service points, admission to veterans' organizations, and credibility from the media.

At the Vet Center, each client receives a "C-Card," a purple plastic card with a magnetic stripe that designates him an official member of the VA family. Nobody checks further. They don't know if he's eligible. They don't care. They need warm bodies to maintain their funding and their jobs.

From there, it's not terribly hard to gain admittance to a VA hospital. Perhaps a client at a Vet Center complains that arthritis in his knee has aggravated an old war wound. The counselor may refer him to a VA hospital for treatment. Once there, the admitting clerk may not bother to check the patient's record. The patient has circumvented even the VA's limited validation process.

Some pretenders use the Vet Centers to authenticate their forged documents, getting a clerk to stamp "POW" on a fake DD-214 or asking for letters that buttress their tales of combat. They then take those papers to the VA. While clerks are trying to sort out the mess, the veterans are admitted into the system. Others have actually appropriated real veterans' names and Social Security numbers.

"Things are beginning to make sense," the West Haven psychiatrist explained after hearing for the first time about the validation process. The doctor admitted having frequent doubts about patients' histories, particularly during group therapy sessions where patients were always trying to one-up each other with war stories. And "delayed" trauma, in which a veteran's PTSD appeared many years after the stressor, was particularly hard for the psychiatrist to understand based on what was known about PTSD. Research has shown that the biochemistry of trauma is such, the psychiatrist said, that a crippling disability manifests itself within the first five years or not at all.

The psychiatrist was shocked to discover vets—even those with no service-connected disability—received 100 percent disability payments after they had been in the hospital twenty-one days. That monetary incentive made the doctor realize why many patients are very resistant to leaving hospital treatment; they often use the fear of "anniversary reactions"— stress triggered by anniversaries of battles in Vietnam—to stay in the hospital long enough to qualify for those disability payments. Then suddenly, miraculously, they are well and able to go home.

Like most VA psychiatrists, this doctor had not been in the military and could not challenge a veteran's claim that on a given date, say, the 101st Airborne was in the Mekong Delta and came under fire. And mistakes like mispronunciation of place names (Bien Hoa as "Ho-ah" instead of "Wa," for example), details that another veteran might perceive, went right by the psychiatrist. If a patient says what doctors expect him to say, he is believed.

The psychiatrist told me that many of the patients in the PTSD program were "very lost people" with weak personalities and antisocial traits, "lost souls" who might have been maladjusted even if they had never served in the military. In many cases, these patients were habitual losers who found in PTSD the perfect crutch to explain their problems.

But the psychiatrist would not challenge them. It is politically incorrect to doubt patients who have come in for help. Indeed, a real disincentive exists for everyone involved to doubt patients' authenticity.

A common sense test of how many Vietnam vets are truly victims of PTSD is to look at the profile of the PTSD patient showing up for treatment at VA Vet Centers. The vast majority are one-term enlisted men. If exposure to combat is the principal cause of PTSD, why aren't more career NCOs among the victims? Most served multiple tours in Vietnam and saw more combat.

The problem of sham combat veterans permeates the VA system. Pittsburgh counselor David McPeak told the *Baltimore Sun* about one of his experiences in group therapy at a Vet Center. The handful of Vietnam veterans shared many difficult and troubling feelings. At his turn, a recent arrival told the group how he had suffered seven rifle wounds to the leg, evoking a reaction of sympathy from the other vets.

One veteran, assuming the poor man's leg had been incapacitated by such extensive wounds, asked gently what the man did for a living. He was a mailman. Outraged, McPeak stood up and escorted the phony from the room.[428]

Over and over, I have heard directly from therapists or in media accounts that they can tell a phony from a genuinely traumatized vet. But the truth is this: Most can't and they don't. Therapists don't want to admit it, but I'm convinced that many of those claiming PTSD were clerks who say they were Green Berets, truck drivers who never left the States, and washouts who latched onto Vietnam as a way to explain failed lives. I firmly believe that in some VA facilities, most of those being treated for PTSD have less than honorable discharges.

Inside Group Therapy

When I first told a writer friend who works for a national publication that he could obtain PTSD compensation even if he was not a Vietnam veteran, he didn't believe me. I made him a bet: He could walk into a Vet Center and be certified 100 percent disabled. He didn't even have to have a good story. He could tell them PTSD caused amnesia.

"You're on," the writer said.

My friend—let's call him Jack—did not serve in Vietnam. He was an Army reservist in the 1950s. During the war, Jack was a Foreign Service officer in Africa and later spent three months in Vietnam as a civilian. But he knows the lingo, and he knows the history of the war. His experiment revealed not only that it is possible to fake PTSD in the Vet Centers, the counselors will actually teach you how.

First, to find out if he could enter therapy even though he was not a veteran, Jack's wife telephoned VA Vet Centers in New York, Miami, Chicago, Denver, Seattle, and Houston. Using a ruse, she explained her brother was a troubled Vietnam veteran who needed help for stress and alcohol abuse. But he did not have his discharge papers or anything else to prove his military service. At each Vet Center she contacted, a spokesman or counselor explained that her brother could be treated as an inpatient while the VA obtained his correct records from the NPRC in St. Louis.

That process could take up to six weeks, longer in cases where names and service or Social Security numbers don't match the records. If someone uses a common name, the VA database can show several individuals with that name as authentic Vietnam vets, extending the process indefinitely. Meanwhile, the patient can get free psychiatric counseling and even inpatient care, if the situation is a crisis.

Then Jack visited an East Coast VA Vet Center in August 1993. That morning, he called the counselor and said he was a Vietnam veteran suffering from "stress problems." The man told Jack to come into the center for an assessment.

The center is a storefront facility in the inner city. The writer arrived about 3:30 that afternoon and was greeted by the counselor, "Peter," a pleasant man in his forties. He asked if Jack wanted to discuss stress problems. When Jack said yes, the counselor asked for his name, date of birth, address, and Social Security number. My friend gave the counselor his correct name but said he had served on active duty in the Army from March 1964 to April 1967, giving the rank of specialist five.

In a semi-private alcove, Jack explained to the attentive counselor that he had been a MACV advisor to the 37th ARVN Ranger Battalion. The writer told a story he had hatched about a December 16, 1965, battle in which "Specialist Whitmoyer" and "Captain Celeste" had been killed. Since Whitmoyer's daughter contacted him a few months before, Jack said, he had been having recurrent nightmares of the battle and had started binge drinking.

Incredibly, the counselor didn't ask his new patient to describe the other symptoms he was suffering. Instead, he gave Jack a photocopied Vet Center handout which listed the symptoms of PTSD and asked if he had any of them. The writer read down the list and picked out "anxiety reactions," "self-esteem problems," "sleep disorders," "nightmares," and "substance abuse."

At that point, another counselor, whom I will call "Bill," joined the discussion. The two therapists agreed that Jack had the "classic symptoms of PTSD," undoubtedly triggered by his contact with the fictional Whitmoyer's daughter.

Group therapy was the best way to heal PTSD, Bill said, but added that the Vet Center could possibly arrange a "private contractor" counselor nearer his home. He invited Jack to join his therapy group that night. Bill said that his group was very close and supported each other. He handed his new recruit a color picture of the group visiting the Vietnam Veterans' Memorial in Washington. Most of them were wearing camouflage BDU fatigues with medals and assorted military regalia. The clear impression was that they were all hardened combat veterans. Bill cautioned Jack: "Never try to visit The Wall alone." His implication was that veterans were too emotionally fragile and needed professional guidance or group support to face the trauma of The Wall.

Gruffly paternalistic, Bill openly expressed antiestablishment attitudes, as if patriotism or satisfaction in military service were absurd. Although the VA maintains that its counselors are supposed to be neutral about the war, most therapists don't follow those guidelines. These counselors echoed most of the professional literature on PTSD, which assumes that at best, the Vietnam War was a senseless bloodbath, and at worst, an outright evil, tainting all those who participated. When Jack noted with pride that the 37th ARVN Ranger Battalion had received U.S. Presidential Unit citations, Bill scornfully said: "Try taking *that* to McDonald's."

Bill warned that the VA was pressuring Vet Centers to reduce their budgets and speculated that one day soon there would be no funded programs. Then, he said, "vets will only have other vets." He gave Jack a brochure to read before coming to the group therapy that night: *Readjustment Problems Among Vietnam Veterans, the Etiology of Combat-Related Posttraumatic Stress Disorders*, by Jim Goodwin, Psy.D. In effect, Bill was giving Jack a primer on how to act if you have PTSD.

That night, the writer returned to the Vet Center at 6:00 P.M. and joined Bill and seven members of his group in a conference room. The group leader was a man named Roger, who said he had been a medic in an Evac hospital in Qui Nhon. The other members of the group were Robert, who said he had served with the U.S. Marine Corps "west of Da Nang;" Aaron, a middle-aged man who had been a supply clerk at MACV headquarters at Tan Son Nhut in Saigon; Bob, who was apparently with the 9th Division; Paul, who had been a military policeman in I Corps; and two other men, an Army squad leader for six months in Vietnam and a combat engineer along the coast with II Corps.

Counselor Bill asked the group to explain to Jack why they had come for PTSD counseling. Roger explained that he had substance abuse problems and had been maladjusted ever since returning from duty in Vietnam. Robert, the Marine, said he drank too much and had problems with uncontrollable rage. Aaron suffered from recurrent stress from the danger of being on supply convoys between Tan Son Nhut and Bien Hoa. (The writer knew that with the exception of the Tet Offensive in 1968, this was the safest area in Vietnam until the withdrawal of U.S. forces in 1973.)

Bob, the man in the 9th Division, had a strange story. He had severe alcohol problems and had been repeatedly incarcerated and institutionalized. Bob had "memory blackouts" of his Vietnam service, and the VA had no record of his military service and "had screwed up my DD-214." The counselor explained that the VA was trying to "fuck Bob over," but that the Vet Center was supporting him and giving him books to read so that he could recall details of his service in the 9th Division in the Mekong Delta.

Paul, the ex-MP, was the most obviously maladjusted of the group. He said he had alcohol and drug-related brain damage and had been institutionalized and homeless on a number of occasions. Paul had recently attempted suicide by drinking three quarts of medical alcohol. On Bill's urging, Paul described how his MP battalion had taken part in the "Chicago riots" (although when was not clear) and had been immediately shipped overseas, first to Germany, then Vietnam.

A recent PBS program, said Paul, showed documentary film footage of him being taken from a burning building in Hue, bleeding from the ears. This had triggered the suicide attempt. He also said he had seen heavy combat at the "Rockpile, near the Cambodian border."

At this point, Jack was convinced that Bob and Paul were probably pseudo-PTSD victims and possibly not even veterans. Jack knew the "Rockpile" was nowhere near the Cambodian border. And Bob had said that the court had ordered him to attend these counseling sessions as a condition of his parole. He may have pleaded for mercy as a traumatized Vietnam vet, then was forced to adopt a false history to explain the lack of military records to support his tale.

Then Jack told the group his concocted story. They listened carefully, nodding when he talked about his insomnia, his alcohol problem, the fact that he belonged to the American Legion where he could drink cheaply. Bill performed a spot diagnosis, stating unequivocally that *the* reason he abused alcohol was PTSD. The counselor agreed that he needed to join his group and urged him not to consider other vet groups.

Roger also encouraged him to stick with the group, saying that not only Vietnam combat vets but all "Vietnam-era vets" needed counseling because of America's rejection of them. Both Bill and Roger contended that *all* World War II and Korean combat vets had PTSD but were repressing the symptoms through alcohol abuse. Jack was not convinced. Their categorical assertion that all Vietnam combat vets were crippled by PTSD was illogical. That would mean officers such as Colin Powell, Norman Schwarzkopf, and all the senior service officers, as well as most of the senior pilots on all of America's airlines, were also "crippled" by PTSD.

A few days later, Jack walked into another East Coast VA Vet Center and was greeted by a team leader for the Readjustment Counseling Service. We'll call him Tony. Jack gave Tony a forged DD-214, which he had altered through the use of correction fluid and a photocopy of a correctly completed form found in a U.S. Army administrative manual. He assumed the identity of Melvin A. Brown, born March 3, 1944.

Jack told this counselor the same tale he had used earlier about being an advisor to 37th ARVN Ranger Battalion, and added that he had been jailed twice for drunk and disorderly since meeting with Whitmoyer's daughter and sister in the spring. He said he had lost all his ID papers in a homeless shelter theft and had only his DD-214, or discharge paper.

Tony, a Marine combat vet and an amputee with experience in I Corps, recommended ongoing counseling at his center and inpatient treatment at the local VA medical center. He started a file for Jack and said that the information on the DD-214 would stay at the Vet Center. Tony gave the writer a medical consultation sheet to take to the VA medical center. Under "reason for request," the counselor wrote: "This forty-nine-year-old white male employed and separated from wife (three years) and desires to get treatment inpatient. Veteran also complains of nightmares of Vietnam, sleep disorders, illusion of dead people outside door."

The counselor was compassionate and very accommodating. He was also thoroughly convinced that Jack was a traumatized Vietnam veteran.

Jack told the counselor he would visit the hospital for a consultation, then return to the Vet Center for another therapy session. But my friend cut short his charade, not willing to actually commit fraud for the sake of journalism. The exercise dramatized vividly not only that a patient could get treatment at the VA without proper identification, but once in, the counselors and group therapy would lead him to properly manifest the symptoms of PTSD. Had he stayed in the program, Jack had no doubt he could have qualified for a disability rating and monetary compensation.

12

PTSD Made Easy

IN EARLY 1993, a frustrated nurse at the VA Medical Center in Gainesville, Florida, came to counselor Richard Burns and asked for help. She told him that a Vietnam veteran, diagnosed as 100 percent disabled by PTSD, had been drawing disability payments for ten years. After a bout with binge drinking, the veteran had been hospitalized in the inpatient substance abuse unit. But the extreme symptoms of PTSD were interfering with his treatment. The man refused to talk to anyone, insisting they would not understand his problems because they had not been with Special Forces in Vietnam.

Burns worked in the outpatient substance abuse clinic, where he screened patients to decide whether they belonged in an inpatient program and did individual and group therapy. He is also a combat veteran of Vietnam who later completed a career serving with the 5th and 10th Special Forces groups. Although Burns now sports a beard, he still has the proud bearing and muscular build of a professional soldier as well as a genuine concern for fellow veterans.

After agreeing to help, Burns arranged to "accidentally" run into the beefy patient, who was wearing a T-shirt adorned with the distinctive flash and crest of Special Forces pulled over his considerable gut as he walked in a hospital hallway. "Hey, hi, how ya doing?" Burns asked the vet, making a point to be warm and engaging.

"Man, I served in 'Nam with Special Forces," the veteran said with a hang-dog look.

"Yeah, I hear you're having trouble relating to anybody 'cause you were in Special Forces," Burns said. "Let's sit down and talk."

In Burns' experience working at the hospital since 1989, if a veteran had indeed served in Special Forces, when he met Burns two things would happen: first, the patient would interrogate Burns to find out who he was and what he had done in the military. Second, satisfied that Burns had indeed served in Special Forces, the veteran would latch onto him like a fly on honey. The unique camaraderie of Special Forces always created an instant bond.

This veteran just looked at him. Burns wondered if the man was taking Thorazine, a common medication for some psychiatric patients. He decided to give the patient the benefit of the doubt. "What special project or A-Team were you on?" Burns asked, expecting an answer like Sigma, Project Delta, or ODA 132.

The man hesitated. "You don't know what Special Forces team you were on?" Burns asked. "What the hell did you do in Special Forces?"

"Well, I was attached," the patient said. "That's why Special Forces is not on my records."

"Attached? What do you mean?" Burns asked, by now very suspicious.

"I was a doorgunner," the patient said. "I was assigned to 82nd Airborne Division, and they attached me to Special Forces to fly doorgunner."

Burns had been in Vietnam during February 1968, when the 82nd Airborne arrived in Vietnam. As a Pathfinder—a scout who went before combat troops to mark out landing zones—he spent two or three weeks with the 82nd at Bastogne Fire Support Base.

"Oh, really?" Burns asked. "What year were you there?"

"I was there in '66 and '67," the vet said.

That's when Burns hit him with the hard stare. "That doesn't make sense to me," he said, sounding perplexed. "The 82nd arrived in-country in 1968."

"Well, those of us that flew doorgunner in aviation went over there early," the patient said. "Most people don't know that."

Burns told the veteran he didn't think that was true. "I'll look at the *Vietnam Order of Battle* tonight," Burns said, referring to the book that outlines when and where troops served in the war.

The patient began to mumble, backing away from Burns. "I can't talk right now," he said, walking away. "I don't want to be hassled."

Burns went to the nurse who had asked him to talk to her patient. "Carla, the guy's a phony," he told her. "Another one?" she asked. They both laughed. But the laughter was mixed with frustration and irritation. Both knew the patient's 100 percent disability was based on his traumatic experiences with Special Forces in Vietnam. But his Special Forces experience did not exist. Since Burns had started working in the VA system, the same thing had happened to him at least fifty times.

Burns is in a unique position. A Special Forces veteran who served two tours in Vietnam, Burns experienced combat first as a Pathfinder with the 101st Airborne Division. On his second tour, he went over as a Pathfinder with the 1st Air Cavalry Division and as an advisor to the Vietnamese Airborne Division. Burns retired after twenty years in the military and then earned a bachelor's degree in psychology and a master's degree in public administration.[429]

When Burns first began doing counseling for substance abuse, he was taken aback by the number of those in supposedly elite units who talked about "losing control" or "going berserk" when faced with problems at home. Then Burns noticed that the ones who talked like that were usually obvious fakers, not the real combat vets. "It takes a hell of a lot of self-control to do those things you need to do in combat," Burns says. "And *now* he's out of control? That doesn't make sense." The only real combat veteran Burns has ever dealt with who had trouble controlling his anger had experienced sexual abuse as a child.

That doesn't mean that intense combat doesn't affect people. Burns himself has experienced some symptoms of PTSD. After Vietnam, he had problems with intimacy. After seeing men he cared about die, Burns was reluctant to allow himself to grow close to his wife. He doesn't want to feel that sense of profound loss again. And Burns had anger after returning from Vietnam—not from combat, but from the way his peers and his country reacted to him. But serving in Vietnam also gave him strength. His war experiences built confidence and taught him self-discipline. Burns believes he is less likely to lose control than someone who did not experience battle.

"Combat builds character," Burns says. "I know if I can make it through combat I can make it through anything."

Even the most horrifying experiences had some positive results. When he was only eighteen years old, he saw men killed—but years later, that gave him the ability to give CPR without panicking to a woman badly injured in a car accident. Although the woman died, Burns was able to say that he had done his best and go on. "Am I desensitized or do I simply accept death as part of life?" Burns asks. "Traumatic emotional events change your perception, your values, the way you react. But so do other things. And it doesn't mean it debilitates me for the rest of my life."

The common problems Burns sees with true combat veterans from Korea and Vietnam are "survivor's shame" (they did not die and others did); leadership guilt (that their actions or decisions may have caused others to die); lack of closure because neither Korea nor Vietnam was "won;" and stress caused by coming home to a country that rejected their service.

But all those problems are easily treatable, he says, especially if the counselor understands the nature of combat. Burns treated one Korean vet with true PTSD who had been misdiagnosed for forty years. The veteran felt guilty for pushing his unit up a hill too fast; a friendly artillery round exploded, killing six of his men. Years later, a civilian psychiatrist, treating him for a ten-year period, gave the veteran antidepressants and told him he had done nothing wrong, that he should just forget about it. But the veteran could not erase the memory of his men's deaths. He drank heavily and several times attempted suicide.

Burns confronted the real issues.

"You did screw up," Burns told the veteran. "You should have known better than to keep them bunched up like that." The veteran looked at him in amazement and gave a sigh of relief. "You're the first person in forty years who's agreed with me," he said.

Then Burns asked the man if he wanted to forget about Korea, about his troops. "No," the vet said. Burns agreed that there was no way he could forget his combat experiences—nor should he want to forget his buddies, especially those who died.

"Well, then, let's take the guilt and put it in its proper place," Burns told him. He pointed out that the veteran had been only eighteen or nineteen years old when given a tough combat leadership position—a heavy burden for someone so young. Getting the veteran to forgive that eighteen-year-old was the first step toward being healed.

Sheep-Dipped

During the years Burns worked at the Gainesville Veteran's Administration Medical Center (VAMC)—1989 to mid-1996—when a veteran came into the hospital, he was screened at the front desk to determine his eligibility for treatment. If the veteran said he was in Vietnam and was having emotional or mental problems, he was seen by a PTSD clinical team made up of a psychiatrist, psychologist, and social worker. If the vet was using alcohol or drugs, he was sent to Burns. Since virtually everyone treated for PTSD abuses something, Burns saw most of the PTSD patients.

Once the diagnosis of PTSD was made, the veteran was put into group and/or individual therapy. "If he's a Vietnam vet, the therapists are going to treat him for PTSD even if they don't believe him," Burns says. "If the guy starts telling wild stories, the counselors can't say the patient's full of shit. They have to treat him."

Unlike most therapists, Burns can quickly tell when patients are lying to him about their military experiences. They misuse acronyms, mispronounce geographical names of places in Vietnam, have no knowledge of the real structure of various units, and describe combat actions that could not have happened. They boast of "fifty confirmed kills" in combat, something Burns knows was impossible to verify. Most claim they were involved in secret missions in Cambodia, Laos, or North Vietnam. (Conveniently, all their buddies are dead and of course can't talk.) Often, their exploits are based on World War II movies.

According to Burns, the main reason the fakers claim covert operations is to avoid the problem of the alleged combat not being on their DD-214s. "I can't tell you what I did; it's classified," they say. Or they claim the reason they have no documents proving they were in Vietnam is that the government has tried to disavow their clandestine activities by wiping out ("sheep-dipping") all their records.

Burns has a complete history of Special Forces operations. He knows that when a soldier goes on a classified mission, the military record might not say *specifically* where he was, but the serviceman is still eligible for the awards and decorations for that mission with perhaps the location changed. And a vet's record indicates the specialized schools necessary to become a Green Beret, a Lurp (Long Range Reconnaisance Patrol—LRRP), or a SEAL.

Some patients use altered records; they may doctor documents or use false records created for them unwittingly by the VA. One of Burns's colleagues had a client who had been receiving 100 percent disability compensation for combat-related PTSD for a decade. The patient's medical record said he served with Military Assistance Command Vietnam, Studies and Observations Group (MACV-SOG), 5th Special Forces Group and had been a POW. But something about his stories didn't ring true. The colleague, who had no military experience, asked for Burns's help.

The man's medical record included a two-page summary written by a VA psychiatrist. The summary explained that the patient had been hand-picked to serve on an eight-man squad on a secret mission deep inside Laos. (The team was captured, and everyone but the patient was killed and dismembered.) During his escape, the patient was wounded several times. The entire experience traumatized him to such an extent he was declared 100 percent disabled because of PTSD and given disability compensation.

But Burns obtained the patient's true military record, which showed he had been a private in Vietnam, a personnel specialist who did not have jump wings or any of the other training required of someone chosen for such a mission. He had no Purple Heart or any other awards or decorations to substantiate his story. The veteran's name was not on the POW list. And the unit that he claimed was attached to MACV-SOG was actually an infantry battalion in the 173rd Airborne. The supposed commander of his unit never served in Special Forces or MACV-SOG and did not claim he had. (The officer had written a Vietnam book; perhaps that's where the patient found his name.)

The patient's entire story was false; the psychiatrist had been completely hoodwinked. Because the physician didn't cross-check his interview against the man's military record, the medical summary in the file assured that the man received the special status of POW and that his story about a secret mission in Laos from then on would be accepted at face value by others within the VA system. But when Burns told them the patient was a pretender, neither the counselor nor the psychiatrist blew the whistle. The fabricator is still receiving at least thirty-six hundred dollars a month tax-free in VA disability compensation and Social Security, plus three hundred dollars a month for Agent Orange exposure. The POW sticker is still on his VA file.

This story is hardly an aberration. Burns has encountered only two psychiatrists within the VA system who have a military background; both served in World War II. But even if the psychiatrist had cross-checked the interview against the record, he may not have realized he was being fooled if the veteran had a good line of bull to explain away the inconsistencies. Burns, who knows which units did classified operations, can blow fraudulent accounts apart in minutes.

It's not a minor problem. Charlatans can cause significant disruption of therapy groups. Burns was leading a substance abuse therapy group when one of the veterans began talking about how he became sexually aroused while killing people in combat. From his own experiences, Burns knew that sex is the farthest thing from a combat soldier's mind when faced with staying alive. He had to cut the man off whenever he began to talk in group. But Burns never challenges frauds in front of others, especially their family members, who probably believe the tales.

Burns learned quickly that when he told VA doctors and psychologists that a patient was lying, they usually did nothing. Few VA officials want to take on the challenge of getting rid of the pretenders. Although there are provisions for prosecution under Title Eighteen of the U.S. Code for defrauding the veterans benefits system, the VA usually elects to ignore the problem.

A handful of people within the VA do care about the truth. One VA social worker in Gainesville came to Burns in 1992 and asked for help with a group of eight Vietnam veterans who had been in his group therapy for a year. All claimed they had been in elite units—Lurps, Green Berets, SEALs. But the social worker was concerned because no matter what he did, the men refused to take responsibility for their lives—to behave like decent human beings. When the social worker tried to encourage them to shape up, they flung back that he did not understand, he had not been in 'Nam.

"I really wonder about these guys, Richie," the social worker said. "I think some of them are bullshitters." He asked Burns to come to his group to show them that a Vietnam veteran with combat experience could earn a master's degree and build a career.

"I can't get through to them," he said. "You'd be a good role model."

Burns took to the therapy session a copy of his DD-214 and documentation of his Silver Star, Bronze Star Medals, and Purple Hearts to show them he was really a combat veteran with Special Forces experience and could understand their problems. He faced a ring of eight tense, scowling men, most with arms folded in front of their bodies. All were slovenly dressed. Some had on berets or hats with MACV logos or patches with the skull and crossbones symbol of a SOG forward operating base. Four or five were wearing camouflage fatigues. Burns felt a cringe of irritation on seeing the cammies. (The only people who wore such uniforms in Vietnam were members of a few units, such as Rangers, Pathfinders, Special Forces, SEALs, snipers, and Marine Force Reconnaissance.)

All the men in the group were being treated with psychotropic drugs and antidepressants for PTSD. To break the ice, Burns told them a little about himself. How after graduating from high school at seventeen, he went into basic training, jump school, and Pathfinder school, then joined a Pathfinder unit that was sent to Vietnam. He described being wounded three times, his combat decorations, and what it was like to experience MACV Recondo training, something only three thousand men went through during the entire decade of the war.

Burns could see as he spoke that most of the men didn't know what the hell he was talking about. As soon as he ended his narrative, they started attacking.

"How do we know you're for real?" one man said. Burns showed them the folder with his documents. One challenged him on MACV Recondo training, but his questions did not make sense. Another asked him if he knew about another operation, using an acronym that was not legitimate.

"No, because that wasn't a real operation," Burns flung back.

"It was classified," the vet responded.

Burns tried to encourage them to talk about their experience, but they refused to open up.

"Man, you don't know nothing," another said. "We've been through a lot more than you."

Burns realized with a shock that *not one* of the eight vets had done what they were claiming to have done in Vietnam. All eight were phonies. As he left, the social worker apologized to Burns. But no action was taken against the pretenders; they continued to stay in group therapy, spinning their yarns and leeching off the VA system.

That experience was typical of what happens when fakers run into real combat vets who know the difference between true trauma and bogus war stories. That's one reason Burns filled his office with military memorabilia —his retirement photo in Green Beret regalia, jump wings, certificates for

Jungle Expert, MACV Recondo School, Special Warfare Center and School, as well as citations for the Silver Star, Bronze Star Medal, and Purple Hearts —to put veterans on notice that he knows what he's talking about. But they still try to sell him the same stories of sham trauma they've been telling others for years, even with direct evidence that they are lying.

One veteran who was receiving PTSD disability compensation told Burns, who was interviewing the man to determine if he was eligible for substance-abuse treatment, that he had served in Vietnam with the 101st Pathfinders, 101st Airborne Division in 1968. Burns informed the patient that was impossible. The Pathfinder Detachment was a fourteen-man unit, and during 1968, Burns was a member of it. Burns knew every man personally, and the patient was not one of them.

This information did not faze the patient. Burns clearly was mistaken, the patient declared firmly, continuing to insist he had served with that unit. Although Burns gave him every opportunity to change his story, the patient refused to budge. He believed he had served with the Pathfinders. His friends and family believed it. It had become his identity.

When Burns began writing a column called "Burns Ointment" for *Behind the Lines*, a magazine about Special Operations, he used the term "wannabes" to refer to phonies who have been telling their lies so long the stories have become real to them. Burns estimates that out of the fifty or so patients he saw a month who claimed they were Vietnam veterans with disabling PTSD, about five—*only 10 percent*—truly suffered from the symptoms. So far in his career, Burns said he's seen only a handful of real combat vets who actually were disabled by PTSD. "I doubt if five of the hundreds I've seen deserved 100 percent compensation," Burns says.

That means that fully 90 percent of the vets he sees are "wannabes" seeking to wangle something out of the VA. Many are good at manipulating people, excellent story-tellers who have the gift of gab. They are often living with their parents or with women who completely accept their tales.

"Most of them are just damn lazy," Burns says. "They're doing drugs, drinking alcohol, they don't want to get jobs. A lot of them are not capable of working because they're drinking and drugging too much." He believes many have discharges other than honorable—indicating a lifetime of adjustment problems. Most are angling for that coveted diagnosis of "100 percent service-connected disability" so they can travel, buy a little ranch, or use drugs without the pesky problem of having to work. "Wouldn't you rather be diagnosed a hero suffering from war trauma and given three thousand dollars a month than diagnosed as somebody who's got an antisocial disorder?" Burns says.

The fraud is so pervasive that even those who have no mental disorders jump on the money train. Burns knows two real combat veterans who obtained 100 percent PTSD disability pensions although they admitted to him that they had no psychological problems from the war. One spent a decade filing requests for PTSD disability compensation and even quit his job to show he was completely disabled. The other qualified for the compensation as well as Social Security disability and now clears three thousand dollars a month. Benefits include college tuition for his children and free VA medical treatment. Essentially retired, all he must do is visit a civilian psychiatrist once a week. He throws his medications down a toilet.

The veterans' rationale for their scam is simple. They risked their lives for their country. The liars are getting the dough, why shouldn't they?

Hitting the Jackpot

According to Burns, the procedure to qualify for PTSD disability compensation varies widely. One veteran may see a psychiatrist once and walk out with a 100 percent recommendation. For others, qualifying may take months of going to group therapy and repeated hospitalizations. "There's no rhyme or reason to it," Burns says. "It's very subjective." Burns contends that if a veteran is determined and persistent, if he makes it his *job* to qualify for a PTSD disability, then eventually he will be successful.

Veterans teach each other about the process of getting disability compensation. Burns describes how the game often works: A veteran comes to the VA hospital for the first time for substance abuse problems. During inpatient treatment, he'll talk to another veteran also in the hospital.

"I'm in here for a tune-up," the old-timer tells the newcomer. "I've got PTSD." The experienced veteran has been diagnosed as having some level of PTSD disability. To maintain his rating or be granted an increase, the vet has to show problems significant enough for hospitalization. Thus the "tune-up." He arrives at the VA psych ward threatening suicide, knowing that he won't be turned away. That puts on record his "suicidal behavior."

The old-timer shows the new guy how to work the system. Before you go in for treatment or evaluation, don't shave for three or four days. Wear old fatigues, some unit patches, an old beret. Study the symptoms of PTSD. Some men come in for therapy using the medical language they read on the brochures. When a guy with an eighth-grade education tells Burns, "Doc, I've got intrusive thoughts," words the man would not say just talking to his friends, Burns knows the veteran has been reading PTSD literature. Another clue: men who are able-bodied with marketable skills refusing to work. "You've got to be disheveled, have family problems, unable to work to qualify for a PTSD disability," Burns says.

The veteran insists his problems are so bad he must be admitted to an inpatient PTSD program. If that is accomplished, he's well on his way to getting an "award letter" from the VA regional office notifying him that he has been given a disability rating for PTSD. If he gets a 30 percent rating, the quest begins for the 50 percent, then 70 percent.

A year later, the vet takes the treatment discharge summary and the progress reports to the hospital and tells the doctors that his PTSD is getting worse, not better. He asks for an increase in his disability rating and often gets it. Sometimes the men make arrangements with their buddies to check into the hospital for "tune-ups" together, giving them somebody to talk to and play cards with while they are going through the motions of therapy.

Every two years, those with disability ratings face a Compensation and Pension hearing or a "C&P." This hearing can mean their disability will be increased or decreased.

"These guys are terrified they are going to get cut," Burns says. "Before the C&P, everyone's anxious. They throw on some cammies, take off their gold jewelry, don't shave or bathe for days." When they go in for the hearing, they know to act depressed and withdrawn or anxious and violent. They cry, they shout about what "fucking 'Nam" did to them. "The better the acting, the more they get," Burns says.

The ultimate goal is the "total and permanent" disability letter. "That's what they're all striving for," Burns says. "That's their Medal of Honor." A pecking order prevails among the PTSD vets, with those who can boast a 100 percent "total and permanent" disability at the top of the heap.

Some are frank about their motives. One VA therapist treated a Marine veteran who said he had suffered trauma in Vietnam, particularly "helping with the wounded at Quang Tri in the fall of 1968." He kept saying that he served in "the bush" but could or would not name anyone who served with him. Emotionally abusive to his family, the unemployed veteran's PTSD symptoms—reports of flashbacks and anxiety—were very convincing.

The Marine managed to obtain a diagnosis of "PTSD, chronic, severe," with the stressor described as "Vietnam combat." He was also diagnosed as suffering chloracne from Agent Orange. Then the veteran hired a lawyer who specialized in helping people obtain Social Security benefits; together, the former Marine's VA compensation and Social Security benefits could total up to $3,400 a month, or $40,800 a year. With a 100 percent PTSD rating from the VA, the man's lawyer knew he most likely would succeed in getting Social Security payments for his client—and a legal fee of at least four thousand dollars for himself when the veteran received back pay.

The Marine and his wife were very open with the counselor about their purpose in coming to the VA. The wife didn't believe his Vietnam stories, but she wanted him to qualify for the disability so she could quit work. "I've been with him for twenty-five years," she insisted. "I deserve something. And after we get it, I'm never going to work again." (More often, veterans refuse to allow Burns to talk to their wives. Under VA rules, he cannot unless the veteran signs a release.)

The man's therapist, who knew Burns and had been alerted to the problem of pretenders, checked his record. The Marine had no Combat Action Ribbon. He had served only one month in-country before being kicked out of the Marine Corps for emotional problems relating to child-hood. But he's still in the system, still pursuing his 100 percent disability. The therapist felt he couldn't confront the lying Marine without risking his own job.

"The VA is very afraid of challenging these guys," Burns says. "If we say they're not real or we take them off their meds, they'll act out, they'll call their congressmen. The doctors don't want patients making waves. They don't want some congressman calling and saying why aren't you treating this fine Vietnam vet?" Every therapist in the VA system fears these "con-gressionals" who write politicians complaining that, by God, they served their country and the big, bad VA is beating up on them. Most counselors have seen the heat come down from an elected official who wants to curry favor with veterans' groups—regardless of whether the "congressional" is a liar.

Occasionally, the system does challenge pretenders. One Marine veteran tried to climb onto the PTSD gravy train at the Miami VA Medical Center only to be turned away by an alert psychologist who noticed that the man's DD-214 listed no Combat Action Ribbon and information about "bad time" had been whited out. The veteran then took his act to the Augusta VA Medical Center. He gained admittance to the inpatient unit there and obtained a diagnosis of service-connected hearing loss and PTSD triggered by Vietnam combat.

"He may have been in combat, but he doesn't have PTSD," says Burns. "Now he's trying for Social Security. He says he'll get it. I think he did drugs in Vietnam and gave his sergeant shit all the time. He has an antisocial per-sonality."

Burns knows that if the veteran was unsuccessful in getting into Augusta, he would try another hospital. "You could try every inpatient pro-gram in America if you have enough money to get there," Burns says. Even if a counselor managed to expose a veteran as a phony, the VA employee has no way to flag the patient's chart in the computer system, preventing the man from fooling someone else.

Cases like these take time, energy, and financial resources away from treating true combat veterans with PTSD. And real combat vets who truly need help end up in group therapy with phonies, get disgusted, and quit treatment.

Burns once sent a real Marine combat veteran of Vietnam to PTSD group therapy. During one session, another participant claimed to have served in the true combat vet's unit during the same time period and told outlandish stories about men in the unit killing babies, urinating, and defecating on the dead. The Marine, outraged because the men he served with were honorable, became so frustrated, he stood up and angrily confronted the liar. But who was kicked out of group therapy? The real combat vet.

"When wannabes receive treatment, disability compensation, or other services from the Veterans Administration as a reward for their fantasies, it only succeeds in supporting their delusions and compounding their lies," Burns says. They need treatment—for the "wannabe syndrome," not PTSD. "It's a sickness, a mental disorder," Burns contends.

When treating schizophrenics, who often have delusions of grandeur, mental health professionals usually try to confront them with facts, pointing out that their belief systems are untrue. "You put reality in place so you can work with them," Burns says.

But VA psychiatrists and psychologists usually refuse to confront these patients with their lies. "I had a psychiatrist say to me, 'I only believe what [PTSD vets] tell me. I take them at face value,'" Burns says. "I asked him, 'You wouldn't do that to a schizophrenic, would you?' He didn't answer."

The elaborate tales and sham trauma are the basis of the wannabe's delusions, and when mental health professionals don't challenge those stories, Burns contends, they validate those self-delusions. The payoff for the man claiming false combat experience isn't only monetary compensation but is the ability to use his "medical condition" to justify often abusive and bizarre behavior.

But challenging malingerers is not in VA therapists' best interests. "We are judged by the number of people we see, not by the quality of our treatment," Burns says. "It's a numbers game. You keep your jobs, your funding, by the numbers."

Wandering Impostors

As an inpatient in the nursing home of the Castle Point VA Medical Center in New York, Vietnam veteran Michael Lormand had serious problems. He checked into the facility in January 1990 for treatment of multiple sclerosis, PTSD, Agent Orange, and other war-related disorders. A difficult patient who demanded special treatment from doctors and nurses, Lormand claimed he had been a POW in Vietnam. His status as a POW is what allowed him admission to the nursing home unit, which had a long waiting list. But when Richard Darcy, chief of Medical Administration Service, tried to verify Lormand's status as a POW, he discovered that another veteran with the same name, Social Security number, and date of birth was simultaneously receiving treatment in the Topeka, Kansas, VA Medical Center.

An investigation by Bruce Sackman of the Office of the Inspector General revealed that the Michael Lormand at the Castle Point VA was actually an impostor named Philip J. Tulotta, a man who had been discharged for homosexual activity after spending only eighty-one days in the U.S. Coast Guard.[430]

According to Sackman's "management implications report," Tulotta had appropriated Lormand's identity to obtain treatment at fourteen different VA Medical Centers, receiving care worth an estimated $107,000. But that was not the extent of Tulotta's deception. Under his own name, Tulotta had been treated since 1975 in twenty-one different VA Medical Centers, at a cost estimated at more than five hundred thousand dollars— for disorders he did not have and for services to which he was not entitled. Several times Tulotta conned his way into lengthy PTSD programs.

His story becomes even more outrageous. Sackman discovered that on January 12, 1981, Tulotta had been admitted to the Brooklyn VA Medical Center, claiming that he suffered night terror, seizures, and flashbacks from Vietnam. When Tulotta told doctors he had terrible pain in his legs from war trauma, the physicians performed a venogram. After the needless procedure resulted in complications, Tulotta filed a civil malpractice suit against the Brooklyn VAMC. Although they proved he had lied about his service, Tulotta received ten thousand dollars.

At the conclusion of the litigation, the VA District Counsel told Tulotta he should never return to a VA Medical Center. That's when Tulotta assumed the identity of Michael Lormand, a man Tulotta knew was a real Vietnam veteran. "Tulotta was clearly a predator upon the VA Health Care System," the IG report concluded. The impostor not only cost the system hundreds of thousands of dollars, but by conning his way into programs, he deprived other deserving veterans of treatment. And he placed the real Michael Lormand at risk by creating an inaccurate medical chart.

IG authorities wanted to know if Tulotta's case was an isolated incident or if it revealed defects in the VA health care system nationwide. The investigation of Tulotta led them to Dr. Loren Pankratz, a clinical psychologist at the Portland, Oregon, VA Medical Center and an internationally recognized expert on malingerers, factitious (fake) disorders, and Munchausen Syndrome, in which people feign the symptoms of an acute illness to gain medical care. Once inside a hospital, these patients often create an uproar, demanding services, special medications, and even unnecessary surgery.

The psychiatric syndrome is named after German Baron Von Munchhausen, who lived during the eighteenth century. After his service in the Russian Army, Von Munchhausen returned home to regale friends with humorous tales of his life as a soldier and sportsman. He became legendary after the publication of a storybook called *The Adventures of Baron Munchhausen* by Rudolf Eric Raspe, who turned the baron's comic stories into outrageous tall tales. Eventually, the name became synonymous with liar or fantasizer.[431]

In 1951, the term "Munchausen Syndrome" (with only one "h") was first used to describe patients who travel to seek medical care and tell dramatic falsehoods, conning doctors while playing the role of the sickly patient. They often study the diseases they imitate or keep other diseases active by neglecting serious disorders.

In a paper called "The Ten Least Wanted Patients," Pankratz and psychiatrist Dr. Greg McCarthy described a Korean-era veteran, nicknamed "Major Munchausen" in the psychiatric literature.[432] The major, who always wore clothes of understated elegance, crisscrossed the country after his discharge from the Army in 1958, gaining admittance to VA clinics and hospitals, where he variously impersonated a fighter pilot and war hero, an oceanographer with Jacques Cousteau, a minister of the Church of Scotland, a professor of psychology from Nicaragua, a Boeing corporate executive, a nuclear physicist with NATO, a Strategic Air Command (SAC) bomber pilot, a personal representative of famous senators, and more. The major claimed his numerous abdominal scars were the result of war wounds or operations while he was a POW, but his military record revealed he had never seen combat. He feigned various illnesses, including heart attacks and kidney failure, and said he had undergone forty-eight major operations. Surgeons at one hospital performed emergency surgery on the major's failing kidney only to discover the kidney had already been removed.

When the major walked into the emergency room of the Portland VAMC in 1980, Pankratz recognized him from various descriptions in medical literature. Pankratz collected what he could of the major's medical chart, which he discovered included more than three hundred admissions. Pankratz later realized the real number was probably more than five hundred if civilian hospitals were included. In his wanderings, the major accumulated costs estimated to be more than $7 million. The major died in 1983 at a Tennessee hospital, probably of infections related to drug abuse.

When contacted by the IG investigator, Pankratz had known Tulotta as a Munchausen patient from previous years. Pankratz had actually invited Tulotta to a conference on patient deception that he had sponsored for VA doctors in the region. There, Tulotta told the group how he had fooled everyone with his stories.

After obtaining a search warrant for Tulotta's personal effects, IG investigator Sackman found a collection of books and articles on PTSD and Agent Orange. He also discovered Tulotta had been charged with fraud and forgery in a local state court. On March 9, 1990, Tulotta pleaded guilty in the Southern District of New York to two counts of fraud related to his impersonation of Lormand and signed an "injunction on consent" barring him from ever entering a VA medical facility using any name or Social Security number other than his own.

From his career at the Portland VAMC, which started during the Vietnam War, Pankratz knew that Tulotta's case was far from unique and, in fact, represented a startling and outrageous reality about the entire VA medical system. Far from being an "irrelevant sideshow," as Art Blank contends, liars like Tulotta and the major cost the VA and the American taxpayer millions of dollars a year.

And the VA does virtually nothing about it. Indeed, Tulotta is still using the VA periodically.

Liars, Frauds, and Wannabes

Loren Pankratz went to work in the VA hospital in Portland, Oregon, in 1969. As a psychology graduate student, he had been somewhat oblivious to the war because he had remained one step ahead of the draft. He remembers when Vietnam vets began to dribble into the system.

"The young vets didn't treat the doctors with respect, and the doctors didn't respect them," Pankratz says. An emotional and psychological gulf existed between the doctors and the impatient, aggressive, bright young Vietnam veterans. "Don't trust anybody over thirty," was the cry of the age.

Early on, in 1971, Pankratz surveyed all Vietnam veterans admitted to medical and surgical services at the Portland VAMC. The image of the alienated vet had already begun. Pankratz was curious, so he asked patients about their drug use, their combat experiences, and what they expected next in life. Pankratz was young and had long hair; the vets opened up to him. What he found surprised him.

"Most of those who used drugs in Vietnam weren't using any more," he says. "It was situational. These guys were all in their twenties, and they were now trying to get integrated back into the mainstream—to get jobs, buy a pickup, get married."

That early casual survey impressed him with how ordinary these Vietnam vets were. Later, when the PTSD diagnosis became part of the diagnostic manual, Pankratz was skeptical about the massive numbers claimed. Also, he knew the concept of delayed onset violated basic psychological principles of mental stress: Symptoms of trauma should decrease, not intensify, with the passage of time.

Pankratz looked forward to asking about this when a PTSD researcher from the Midwest was scheduled to speak at the Portland VAMC soon after the diagnosis of postwar trauma appeared in the *DMS-III*. "This expert was to spend an extra hour with the handful of psychologists at the hospital," Pankratz says. "But he arrived at our meeting with two veterans wearing combat fatigues, and one sat on each side of him. Scientific questions about his methodology seemed inappropriate. This man came to tell us what to believe. It was like a religion."

The Portland VA set up satellite clinics, manned with Vietnam veterans turned counselors, to treat PTSD. VA counseling teams began to discover the disorder everywhere. At one clinic, a particular psychologist seemed to be a magnet for PTSD patients with dramatic symptoms. The therapist claimed there were Vietnam veterans living in the woods or in bunkers, stockpiling guns. He worked sixteen-hour days and seemed always to be trying to solve the problems of some crazed veteran. The clinic was in constant turmoil. But as soon as that psychologist left, the problems disappeared.

After a few years on the psychiatry inpatient ward, Pankratz became the consulting psychologist for the medical and surgical services. He continued to sleuth out malingerers, Munchausen Syndrome patients, drug seekers, and pretenders. He enjoyed working with difficult and noncompliant patients, illustrated by his article on what he calls "geezers," or cranky old men, published in the *Journal of the American Medical Association* in 1988.[433] In 1989, he was promoted to full professor at the Oregon Health Sciences University in the Departments of Psychiatry and Medical Psychology. In his desire to understand clinical error, Pankratz became an amateur magician and a collector of antiquarian books on fraud.

One day, a physician asked him to examine a Vietnam veteran who was giving the nurses trouble. The doctors were trying to create some structure for the patient, but the unruly vet repeatedly caused turmoil. He had an injury to the groin that had become reinfected, and he was fighting their attempt to treat it. When Pankratz talked to him, the patient claimed he had been captured in Vietnam and tortured by the enemy. He went into a tirade, describing how the enemy had jabbed him with bamboo sticks dipped in feces, and now the staff was torturing him, too.

The patient's wild railings prompted Pankratz to doubt his story. The psychologist had learned that deceptions are often covered by exaggerated claims and overly dramatic expression of feelings. Pankratz immediately checked POW records and discovered the patient had not been held captive in Vietnam. Not only that, the patient had never served in Vietnam—*he wasn't even a veteran*. The man had finagled admittance to a VA hospital even though he had never been in the military.

Pankratz discovered that was easy to do. "You walk in the door and say you're a veteran," says Pankratz. "They have to assume you are. That's the law." Theoretically, the hospital or clinic eligibility clerk checks a master database within forty-eight hours to see if the veteran is indeed eligible for VA treatment. But Pankratz found that clerks might take up to two weeks to run the records—and sometimes failed to do it at all. "A lot of times I'm the one who finds these patients are not veterans," Pankratz says. "I go down to admitting to double check the veteran's status, and they have not even run the name yet."

Patients who claim PTSD trauma can spin any tale they want to tell; neither the clerks nor the doctors obtain their military records to verify the stories. "It was always amazing to me that they never checked to see if the people were really there in Vietnam," Pankratz says. "I want to be confident that we are treating the correct problem, not something the patient made up."

But the VA system makes it hard for physicians to check military records. After becoming interested in deceptive patients, Pankratz befriended clerks at the regional office, three miles away from the hospital, where patients' "C-files" are kept. Each veteran's C-file includes his claims for benefits, such as educational training, medical treatment, or service-connected disability compensation. An administrative file, not a military record, the C-file nonetheless often contains a copy of the veteran's DD-214, as well as information about previous marriages and children, defaults on student loans, multiple attempts to obtain service-connected status, and angry letters to congressmen.

Soon, whenever Pankratz encountered a patient with a story that sounded strange, he began checking the patient's C-file, especially alert to patterns of lying and dishonest or self-serving behavior. After he began researching deceptive patients, Pankratz believes he became the number-one user of C-files in a clinical setting within the entire VA system. What he found was often astonishing.

Physicians frequently asked Pankratz, as consultation psychologist, to evaluate patients with unusual symptoms or pain complaints. Even before seeing the patient, Pankratz would check the C-file. "It was not unusual to discover that an individual had recently requested an increase in benefits for his service-connected disability," Pankratz says. "Discovering this piece of the assessment puzzle often allowed the physician to replace a million-dollar work-up with careful monitoring. The medical team is at a terrible disadvantage without this important information."

Pankratz had been prepared for such surprises ever since the publication of the first of his many articles on deceptive VA patients. In 1978, Pankratz and psychiatrist Dr. John Lipkin published a paper entitled "The Transient

Patient in a Psychiatric Ward: Summering in Oregon" in the *Journal of Operational Psychiatry*.[434] They described fourteen transient patients who migrated to Oregon, usually in the summer, to gain admittance to the VA. These patients took up valuable bed space, wreaked havoc on the psychiatric ward, but benefited little from their treatment. These rootless patients usually gained admittance on the weekends or at night, often by saying they were suicidal. One started a fire and another went to a medical ward and threatened people as a way to force doctors to commit him to the psychiatric ward.

With the exception of one man, all abused drugs or alcohol. Several seemed to view the VA as a Holiday Inn. One man flew in from Hawaii. Brought to the hospital by airport police, he presented himself as "totally confused and desperately suicidal." Once admitted, the veteran strolled into the dayroom and asked, "Is the Notre Dame-USC game on TV tomorrow?" Another patient who received 100 percent service-connected compensation for schizophrenia used his money to travel the country, staying in the finest hotels and VA hospitals. Once admitted, his psychotic symptoms quickly vanished. He was clean, considerate, and helpful, which resulted in longer-than-average stays in the hospital.

Another patient was a Florida resident who heard about Oregon from another patient while in a Florida VA hospital. He and the other patient drove across the country, arriving in Portland without money or medication to live in cooler climes during the summer. The Florida man tried for two days to gain admittance to the hospital and finally succeeded during a night shift. Several days after the man was admitted, Pankratz tried to interview him for his study but couldn't find him. The patient was on a hospital ward fishing trip off the coast.

Although the average stay for regular patients was twenty-two days, a handful of the transient patients stayed more than five weeks. These rootless patients had characteristics of Munchausen's Syndrome: truculent, evasive, and hostile, taking up staff time, and disrupting the ward. Pankratz' study showed that these manipulative patients easily gained access to the system simply by demanding care. Once inside the hospital, they avoided identifying problems and took no responsibility for personal change.

While investigating such patients in the 1970s, Pankratz began to see an increasing number of veterans who came in complaining of symptoms similar to PTSD. Many of them were similar to the transient patients and seemed to be using VA facilities for their own purposes. In 1983, Pankratz and psychiatrist Landy Sparr published the first study to ever document "factitious" or counterfeit posttraumatic stress disorder. The paper described five men treated at the Portland VA medical center. All claimed to be Vietnam veterans suffering PTSD; three said they were former POWs.

"Taken at face value, and using *DSM-III* criteria, the cases reported here are fairly convincing examples of posttraumatic stress disorder," the authors wrote in the *American Journal of Psychiatry*.[435] Each person complained of sleep disturbances, difficulty in concentrating, and reexperiencing old traumas. Emotionally constricted and disinterested in others, they claimed their difficulties began after they left Vietnam, and the symptoms had persisted for more than six months. All likely would be diagnosed as suffering from PTSD.

But they were all phonies. None of the five patients had been a prisoner of war, four had never been in Vietnam, and although admitted to a VA facility, two had never even been in the military.

One twenty-nine-year-old man came in to the emergency room with his wife, who told doctors that her husband had suffered a shoulder injury while a medic in Vietnam. Unemployed, he had told his wife that he was having nightmares and other difficulties, including extreme irritability, memory impairment, and feelings of remorse over events in Vietnam. Married only six months, they had moved up their wedding date because he told her he was terminally ill with heart disease. He also told doctors he had suffered a heart attack at twenty-seven and was an insulin-dependent diabetic.

But physicians found no evidence of diabetes or a heart attack. His shoulder injury had been caused by a motor vehicle accident in Germany while he was in the service. And he had been in the military not for five years, as he claimed, but for eighteen months. He had never served in Vietnam.

Another patient, an unemployed thirty-year-old photographer, came to the emergency room saying he was having "intrusive" thoughts of combat in Vietnam, particularly of the time when he was held as a prisoner of war. He said he had been exposed to Agent Orange in the war and thought that might have done something to his nerves.

This patient had been adopted at age three after his natural mother set fire to her home with her children inside. He enlisted in the Marines to go to Vietnam because he thought the war would be like an adventure movie. In therapy, he later confessed that he was never a POW and had told the story to impress others.

A thirty-four-year-old man, who also said he was a former prisoner of war, came into the emergency room complaining of pain in his thigh and knee due to an "old shrapnel wound suffered in combat." He described all the classic PTSD symptoms: preoccupation with violence, intrusive thoughts of combat experiences, nightmares, and detachment from other people since leaving Vietnam. He had a long history of drug and alcohol abuse, and claimed to have a service-connected disability for a "nervous condition."

Announcing that he was on the verge of "going crazy" because of all he had experienced in Vietnam, the veteran demanded to be admitted to the hospital, or else he might go "out of control and hurt someone." He hinted that he had acted on those wild impulses in the past, "wasting" some people in the Philippines and Panama with a submachine gun.

The veteran was admitted to a detoxification unit. Meanwhile, the authors discovered that the man had served time in prison as an accessory to a burglary. While incarcerated, he became acquainted with a Navy veteran who was familiar with the VA system; he told him all about veteran entitlements. Doctors finally discovered that not only had the patient not been a prisoner of war, he also had never served in Vietnam and, in fact, had never served in the military! Named after his father, he was using one of the World War II-era veteran's military cards.

Another veteran, a thirty-year-old student, came to the emergency room with his wife, who had discovered that for the previous seven months her husband had been pretending to attend classes in a physician's assistant training program.

"His wife felt that much of his trouble was due to adverse incidents in Vietnam. [He] had told his wife and in-laws that he had difficulty coping because of atrocities he witnessed. He described buddies being killed and maimed, sudden ambushes, and suffocating heat and humidity. He spoke of his gradual disenchantment with the war and his cynicism upon returning home. This all sounded authentic because his stories were principally derived from the book *A Rumor of War* by Philip Caputo." The student claimed to be receiving GI benefits; in reality, he had secretly pawned some of their belongings to get money. The veteran had been in the military from 1975 to 1978, but he had never served in Vietnam. He confessed to doctors that he told the stories to gain sympathy.

These case histories illustrate one of the main problems of diagnosing PTSD. "Simulating is easy, since the symptoms described by *DSM-III* mostly reflect private phenomenology and since by definition the symptoms are caused by events now past," the authors said. "Patients may manufacture or exaggerate symptoms and misidentify their origin. It is not always easy to determine if distortions are outright lies or subtle misperceptions. These difficulties are a diagnostic snare, especially when it is known that compensation may be available to those with a positive diagnosis."[436]

In 1990, Pankratz reminded the medical community that problems of factitious PTSD were still occurring. Again writing in the *American Journal of Psychiatry*, he described three cases that he had seen within one month at the Portland VAMC.[437] One was the first woman he had seen who claimed to have Vietnam PTSD. A second was Pankratz' first Grenada PTSD patient. Although the veteran claimed he could no longer read after being shot in the head during the Grenada invasion, there was no evidence of a penetrating head wound. Pankratz discovered the veteran had never been in Grenada; his injury had resulted when the patient tumbled down the steps in a mess hall.

The third patient was a Navy veteran who had been hospitalized in two VA PTSD treatment programs. He claimed his trauma had occurred aboard ship during the Korean conflict and, when challenged, blamed a nonexistent head injury for confusion or memory loss. An outpatient psychiatrist became suspicious of the veteran's vivid tales because he had served on a companion ship. The psychiatrist obtained the log of the patient's ship, which revealed that the stories were fabrications.

Pankratz says that the hallmark characteristics of these pretenders is outward boldness and seeming sincerity. He believes most malingerers know their stories aren't true, although stories can create a life of their own if acted out over long periods of time.

In 1985, Dr. J. DeVance Hamilton, affiliated with the Houston VA Medical Center, also reported case studies of what he called "pseudo-post-traumatic stress disorder."[438] He described three "Vietnam veterans" who complained of flashbacks, nightmares, insomnia, irritability, substance abuse, and other symptoms of PTSD. One was a thirty-four-year-old man who said he served eight years as a Navy underwater demolition expert and frequently had been exposed to "life-threatening enemy fire."

During his hospitalization, doctors discovered the "frogman" had served only seventeen months in the Navy. None of the three men had been in Vietnam. "It is clear that graphic stories of trauma are not conclusive proof of PTSD," Hamilton wrote. "The accounts presented by pseudo-PTSD patients can be just as vivid and detailed as those in the genuine disorder." One man presented his symptoms whenever he needed bed and board in a VA hospital, an example of "malingering" or using illness to seek secondary gain.

"As is often the case with malingered symptoms, an antisocial personality disorder was also present," Hamilton wrote. "Although occasional reports of malingered traumatic neurosis go back at least as far as World War I, the experience on our service has been that true malingering as a cause of pseudo-PTSD is quite rare." (Or perhaps, as a cynic might remark, quite rarely detected.)

Other impostors may claim they have flashbacks or similar psychiatric complaints to "get out of legal entanglements" or as a way to avoid criminal charges. "Some of these folks live very marginal lives," Hamilton told one reporter. Saying they are Vietnam veterans can make them feel "important, even heroic."[439]

In his report, Hamilton brought up another group of very interesting patients. "These patients served in Vietnam, often in combat, and were confused and embittered by the response of American society and government when they got home," Hamilton said. "They remain preoccupied with how to integrate their war experiences into their lives, but they do not suffer from the very specific symptoms of PTSD. Nonetheless, because of well-publicized but loosely applied terminology, they may present with the sincere belief that they suffer from 'post-Vietnam syndrome' or 'delayed stress.'" These patients have a different explanation for their problems: An ungrateful nation—not Vietnam—screwed them up.

After years of treating veterans, Pankratz agrees with Burns that there are many cheats demanding VA treatment and that a relatively large number of eligible veterans fraudulently seek PTSD compensation. If they don't succeed at one VA facility, they go to another one.

But the professional skepticism of Pankratz, Burns, and Hamilton about PTSD claimants has been consistently ignored in favor of the politically correct and self-serving naïveté of people like VA psychologist Art Blank and psychiatrist-activist Jay Lifton. That shows no signs of changing—although Pankratz has made a major effort to force the VA to recognize the enormous problem.

In the early 1990s, Pankratz discovered a way of using the computer on his desk to search the administrative files of the VA Data Processing Center in Austin, Texas. This center receives administrative information on every veteran who appears at any one of the 159 different VA medical centers. The information was of great benefit for understanding an individual patient's clinical history. However, Pankratz recognized the larger issues revealed in this data.

Working with James Jackson, an assistant to the director of the Portland hospital, Pankratz decided to identify patients who had been admitted to four or more *different* hospitals in the VA system within one fiscal year. These admissions might not be unnecessary or fraudulent, but such high rates of admission can be difficult to justify in one hospital, let alone different hospitals. Their findings were published in the December 1994 issue of the *New England Journal of Medicine*.[440]

For the year 1991, Pankratz found 810 patients who accumulated 6,266 admissions at four or more different hospitals. Each of these veterans averaged more than one hundred days of inpatient care that year. Pankratz also identified thirty-five individuals who continually wandered over the five years of the study. These "habitually wandering" patients averaged about thirteen admissions a year, running up a total estimated bill of $6.5 million for medical care during five years.

The most active wanderer managed fifty-four admissions during a single year—more than one a week, plus an additional 143 outpatient visits during the same period of time. Hospitals seemed helpless against these patients, and doctors were obviously confused by their stories. One patient received eleven different psychiatric diagnoses in ten different states during a two-and-a-half year period.

Homelessness did not appear to be the explanation for their transient lifestyle. They often checked out of residential care facilities and nursing homes against medical advice before their treatment was completed. But physicians did not want to believe the problem existed. "I had great difficulty," Pankratz says, "convincing physicians they were being fooled so much."

Pankratz points out that deceptive patients use all sorts of strategies and personal styles—charming, abusive, suicidal—to get what they want. Sometimes the goal is drug seeking; for others, the objective is not apparent. But overall, most of these patients are men with personality disorders whose lives are chaotic, characterized by poor social skills, poor work records, and substance abuse.

It's impossible to tell how many wanderers and deceptive patients are claiming PTSD. But obviously those determined to obtain PTSD compensation who are turned down at one facility will make attempts at multiple places. Different areas of the country have higher rates of acceptance of PTSD disability claims. Patients can exploit weak points along the application process.

The award of service-connected status is supposedly the work of a team. However, the team may not communicate much with the psychiatrist who is hired to complete the assessment. This psychiatrist has perhaps only two hours to complete the whole process, which is certainly not adequate to evaluate what the patient might have concocted in months of preparation. For example, the psychiatrist usually will not even know if the patient has presented his story at a hearing in another state or if his current story is consistent with the previous presentation.

Each VA medical center has a computer system for its own hospital, but these computers are not centrally connected or networked. Thus, a clinician who makes the effort to search for past records will discover only those within that hospital. If a patient does not divulge his total VA history, records at other hospitals will not be known. This is ideal for the traveling Munchausen patient, the patient who wants drugs, or the individual unhappy with a past VA decision.

"We are very poor at finding deception," Pankratz says. "It would help if the VA stopped behaving like 159 separate units and became a unified health-care system."

After discovering Tulotta's fraud, investigator Bruce Sackman of the New York Inspector General's office wrote a strong report supporting Pankratz and his recommendations for changing the system, especially better data-base coordination. But officials at VA headquarters in Washington, D.C., sat on Sackman's report. Apparently someone in the IG office wanted to solve the problem administratively, bypassing the clinical issues.

In 1995, Pankratz took early retirement from the VA and started an independent practice, mostly consulting on health fraud. He continues to insist that most psychiatrists, psychologists, and social workers do not understand the extent of the problem of patient deception and are not sufficiently aware of their vulnerability to impostors. "I know all the scams and all the common presentations," he says. "Yet I am often captured by the charm of the charlatan. That's why I gather the records and review them so scrupulously. Many clinicians don't have the time or the expertise to investigate thoroughly. They don't have the courage to label deceptions or the hope that it will make a difference if they do." He agrees that the presence of such widespread fraud tarnishes much of the research in the system.

Since his 1983 paper on factitious PTSD, Pankratz has been a reviewer for the prestigious *American Journal of Psychiatry*. He has consistently criticized articles that fail to check records and that do not provide safeguards against confirming the authors' biases. "The scientific enterprise," Pankratz emphasizes, "is an attempt to search honestly by guarding against one's own expectations. Sissies need not apply."

Many presumably "scientific" studies fail to provide meaningful information because the subjects understand exactly what the researcher wants to know and expects to find, says Pankratz. Common sense tells us that combat will leave a lasting impression on an individual. So will poverty, chronic illness, and bad luck. Identifying the cause of symptoms often proves elusive. Honest patients easily misattribute the source of their distress, and a correlation between combat and distress does not mean that one caused the other.

How many so-called Vietnam vets claiming they have PTSD are fakes? That question should plague many mental health professionals who have years invested in studying veterans and PTSD.

Publish or Perish

Since 1990, doctors at the National Center for PTSD at West Haven, VA, Medical Center have published numerous papers on the disorder, including some benchmark studies that were published in the two leading psychiatric journals: *Archives of General Psychiatry* and *American Journal of Psychiatry*. The subjects of the studies are drawn from a pool of PTSD patients who have undergone treatment at the center. Each study is based on very small samples of PTSD victims: from thirteen to fifty-three veterans. They are variously described as "twenty male patients with PTSD," "Vietnam combat veterans who sought treatment for PTSD," or "subjects with PTSD [who] were Vietnam veterans."

The bulk of their research indicates that large numbers of Vietnam veterans suffer from PTSD, although they are able to function reasonably well in society, according to Dr. Dennis Charney, chief of psychiatry at West Haven. But the studies all show a clear association with combat in Vietnam and severe symptoms of PTSD.

Charney says that all the veterans involved in the West Haven studies were in prolonged, ongoing PTSD treatment within the West Haven medical center, not taken from Vet Center counseling groups. While it "might have been possible" for some pseudo-PTSD fabricators to have come into the program, it was highly unlikely, Charney says, stressing that the psychophysiological studies were especially rigorous.[441]

However, a psychiatrist involved with the studies at the center, who talked to me on condition of anonymity, admitted researchers made no serious effort to validate patients' Vietnam combat service other than the veterans' own statements, or in some cases their DD-214s, which are easily forged or which might show their presence in Vietnam but no combat duty.

Given the prevalence of deceitful claimants in the VA system, this failure to rigorously verify the subjects' claims of Vietnam combat by obtaining military records from the NPRC calls into question the data obtained in the West Haven research. Other studies of PTSD published in prestigious medical journals suffer the same fatal flaws, rendering almost all the "scientific" data of PTSD and Vietnam veterans thoroughly useless.

The failure at West Haven, this psychiatrist maintained, was not intentional misrepresentation. Researchers were naïve and believed that anyone coming forward and presenting himself as a traumatized Vietnam veteran was de facto genuine because it was such a stigma. Besides, the veterans wore the fatigues and the medals. They "looked the look and talked the talk," the psychiatrist said.

But badly flawed studies like those done at West Haven further stigmatize the Vietnam veteran. Internally, the researchers recognize the problem. In 1994, a group of psychiatrists with the West Haven center who are aware of my work proposed a study to look at three hundred Vietnam vets with 100 percent disability compensation to determine the quality of their treatment. None of the patients was still undergoing therapy; their files were inactive.

The goal was to determine whether veterans had been appropriately treated. The protocol called for the hospital to obtain each man's military record then examine it against the veteran's interviews to see if what he said happened to him matched his military history. Because the doctors had no experience reading military documents, which use abbreviations and terminology not familiar to civilians, they proposed that I examine the records and compare them to unit histories. With money from a private grant, I was to be hired as a private consultant to examine each record—with all names and identifying numbers removed to maintain patient confidentiality.

Although designed to determine whether their treatment had been appropriate, the study also would have determined how many of the patients designated as 100 percent disabled due to PTSD were genuine Vietnam vets. But after months of discussion, the proposal was shelved. The stated reason was that examining military records was an unnecessary invasion of patients' privacy. But I suspect the real reason is because the VA does not want to acknowledge that as many as *three-fourths* of those receiving PTSD compensation are pretenders.

To admit so many are malingerers could affect the medical center's funding as well as sully the researchers' reputations and harm their careers. So they ignore the glaring phony vet issue and hope the whole problem will go away. They still do not verify what research subjects say about their service by independently obtaining their true military records from the National Personnel Records Center in St. Louis. As word of the pot of gold —PTSD compensation—continues to spread, the problem will only become worse.

One study performed jointly by Yale and West Haven may shed some light on the true nature of these patients. Researchers gave thirty-four "Vietnam combat vets" diagnosed with PTSD a personality disorder examination. The results were intriguing. The study found a high rate of character pathology in both inpatient and outpatient groups. The most frequent disorders for which criteria were met were borderline personality, obsessive-compulsive, avoidant, and paranoid personality disorders. The authors concluded that "war-related PTSD in treatment-seeking Vietnam veterans is often accompanied by diffuse, debilitating, and enduring impairments in character."[442]

But my humble conclusion is that pretenders who lie about their combat history and have managed to weasel their way into the West Haven PTSD program are people with psychiatric problems or long-standing personality disorders. One common-sense question might weed out numerous impostors: Do PTSD claimants continue with therapy and Vet Center counseling after they successfully obtain PTSD disability compensation? Valid sufferers would persevere, seeking alleviation of their suffering; malingerers would not.

The VA doesn't cure PTSD; it teaches PTSD. Giving a veteran disability compensation for PTSD is tacitly admitting the treatment has failed. The therapy has to fail for the malingerer to gain what he wants—money.

Dr. Sally Satel, then a psychiatrist at the West Haven VAMC, raised the issue of the "entitlement/disability culture" of the VA in a paper that appeared in *The Psychiatric Times.* "[Some patients] have found themselves seduced into an institutional dependence that stunts rehabilitation," she wrote.[443] Satel pointed to Vietnam veterans with chronic PTSD as an example of the unintended consequences of the current system.

"In the VA, a person is not just a patient, but a veteran. Long lengths of stay in relative isolation from nonveterans help consolidate that identity. Housed on their own unit and steeped in elicited war memories, many of our veterans sought to recreate the platoon. Dog tags appeared around necks. A few men even returned from weekend passes sporting new tattoos of wartime images and symbols. What happened to *readjustment?*" Many within the VA regard these veterans as virtually untreatable. Labeled as suffering "malignant PTSD," their problems extend beyond the standard symptom checklist in the current *DSM-IV* to include serious problems with aggression, addictions, unemployment, and homelessness—social pathology that Satel said most likely reflects a complex interaction between war trauma and the personal, prewar devastation many of them suffered.

But when does peer support and sharing experiences give way to "insularity, group regression, and the indignation of victimhood?" Satel asked. "One warning sign may be the wish to be officially designated 'disabled.' Sadly, so many of our patients wanted this. Committed to obtaining VA disability payments, they ignored the old adage, 'Don't get money, get better.' And once they obtained the benefit, they froze, further incapacitated by the fear of losing it."

Some patients even boast about how much they "earn" as career patients in the VA, Satel said. "Preserving this guaranteed income took on a life of its own, closing off veterans from the therapy of work and, ultimately, reentry into the community," Satel said. "In the VA, it can literally pay to be ill. Thus, pronouncing these veterans untreatable seems unfair since elements of the treatment system itself may have impeded, however unwittingly, functional improvement."

The bottom line is that many PTSD—real or fake—patients get worse with VA treatment.

Researchers at the Augusta VA Medical Center studied treatment outcomes for veterans with PTSD. Fifty consecutively admitted patients at the Specialized PTSD Unit for Vietnam veterans were put through a five-week treatment program. The results suggested that "veterans with chronic PTSD are resistant to short-term treatment or that the type of intensive crisis treatment typically provided these patients [focusing on reliving Vietnam experiences] does not produce positive outcomes."[444]

The bottom line seems to be that, despite all the dollars thrown at it, there is no effective treatment for PTSD. In 1996, researchers at the Center for Traumatic Stress at Hadassah University Hospital in Israel analyzed the results of eighty-one studies of PTSD treatment since 1981. While some of the studies looked at survivors of car accidents and various trauma, most involved war veterans. Their conclusion: "No study claimed to have achieved durable remission in chronic PTSD, thereby reflecting many clinicians' belief that the disorder is rather unresponsive to any form of treatment." In other words, while treatment can help, it cannot cure—locking those treated by the VA for PTSD into the system for life.[445]

The report of one study from the Augusta VAMC was unintentionally hilarious. In examining the well-known problem of the high number of Vietnam veterans in treatment for PTSD who exaggerate their symptoms, the researchers said: "One reason might be that Vietnam combat veterans are just now 'learning' to respond to years of dormant thoughts and feelings about their condition. During this dissonance reduction process they are 'seduced' into exaggeration, overreports, and even factitious reports when confronted with their pathology. In a sense they must make an effort to 'really' be a Vietnam veteran again and must sell themselves and their helpers. Given that many other veterans are also involved in this process, this can become a 'cathartic or contagion process,' where facts and fiction are interchangeable."[446]

The researchers concluded by suggesting that exaggeration should be considered a symptom of PTSD!

Rich Burns said that the VA's approach to treating PTSD not only fails to confront liars; it also completely ignores accountability. "These guys can do anything—tell the psychologists to go fuck themselves, beat their wives, lay around the house—because they've been traumatized," Burns says. "They have no job except to show up for their appointment."

A handful of VA clinicians are starting to admit this. An article titled "At the VA, It Pays to Be Sick," by former VA psychiatrist Dr. Douglas Mossman, appeared in a periodical called *The Public Interest* in the winter of 1994.[447]

"Sadly, a program with good intentions has yielded a series of perverse incentives that reward illness, encourage patients to view themselves as incapacitated, and poison the relationships between patients and their care-givers," Mossman wrote. "The result of the VA's cost-free hospital treat-ment and its disability compensation is that veterans are provided with financial incentives to use inpatient psychiatric services frequently and for lengthy periods. Veterans are, in effect, encouraged to be (or appear) ill and unable to work or function socially. Unsurprisingly, one commonly finds that the overwhelming majority of Vietnam combat veterans undergoing psychiatric treatment at VA hospitals have applied for disability compensa-tion."

Mossman pointed out that because of eligibility rules, most of those treated at the VA have limited financial prospects. "The typical psychiatric inpatient, even if he had a strong desire to work, would have very little hope of obtaining employment that would give him an income as high as 100 percent SC (service-connected) status," Mossman wrote.

But aside from the cost, Mossman said the current system represents the "antithesis" of good psychiatric treatment. "A disability-benefit system that makes it financially attractive to be too ill to work is contrary to psychi-atry's therapeutic goals," Mossman said. "The VA system 'rewards' a person for existing psychopathology. As one Vietnam veteran put it: 'The object is to convince people you are hopeless. When this occurs they both believe you and then help you with compensation.'"

Mossman suggested several changes in the VA system: Eliminate the financial reward for remaining hospitalized more than twenty days; once a veteran has accepted a disability payment, findings of psychological injury and disability level should be permanent; compensation should be tied to a realistic estimate of lost earning potential; and patients should pay a modest portion of their treatment costs.

I disagree that the disability rating should be permanent; that locks in the phonies forever. Burns has an even simpler solution to the problem of fakes within the VA: Require everyone seeking treatment or compensation to sign a VA Form 180, allowing the VA to obtain their full military record. Hire a veteran who knows how to read records and has a head for military history. Pay him or her a GS-11 salary, about forty thousand dollars a year, to screen the C-file and military record of every vet claiming combat-related PTSD. Burns is convinced many pretenders would take their cha-rades elsewhere.

Under the current system, however, that won't happen. In 1995, I talked to Kenneth R. Atkins, special agent in charge for the Dallas Office of Inspector General, Department of Veterans' Affairs. He had seen an article about me in a San Antonio newspaper and asked if I was aware of anyone committing fraud at the VA. "Absolutely yes," I said.

But Atkins wanted to know if I knew of any counselors or psychiatrists "selling" false diagnoses of PTSD or "facilitators" who sold counterfeit documents. When I told him the bigger problem was the massive numbers of people lying about their combat experience to qualify for compensation, Atkins shrugged. "We're not concerned with those," Atkins told me. "Vietnam veterans kind of got a bad rap." He implied that the compensation was justified if they were legitimate veterans and eligible for any VA benefits.[448]

Neither the VA, which needs warm bodies, nor the powerful veterans' lobbies, which need issues, will admit that deceptive patients are costing taxpayers tens of millions of dollars a year. It will take a president and a Congress not frightened of the veterans' groups to demand accountability.

Despite the 1988 CDC study showing that only 2.2 percent of Vietnam vets suffer from PTSD, the myth has charged on, fueled by TV programs like "The Wall Within," poorly designed VA studies, and self-serving therapists.

In 1991, the *St. Petersburg Times* used the Gulf War as an opportunity to haul out all the old myths and add some new ones. The reporter claimed that nearly a half million Vietnam veterans—a sixth of those who served—suffer from some form of posttraumatic stress disorder; that Vietnam veterans are nearly twice as likely to have been divorced as nonveterans; and (a new one to me) that some are compulsive blood donors because of guilt feelings.[449]

The PTSD myth reached the level of high farce with the 1994 publication of *Achilles in Vietnam: Combat Trauma and the Undoing of Character*, by psychiatrist Jonathan Shay, who for many years has treated Vietnam veterans for the Boston Department of Veterans' Affairs Outpatient Clinic. On the faculty of Tufts Medical School, he trained staff for the New England Shelter for Homeless Veterans. Shay's book received acclaim in publications ranging from the *Wall Street Journal* to *Time* magazine.

Shay used a cross-disciplinary approach to examine the effect of war on fictitious persons from classic literature, such as Achilles, who goes berserk at the end of Homer's epic poem *The Iliad*. War, Shay contended, not only causes lifelong disabling psychiatric symptoms, but also can ruin good character. "The painful paradox is that fighting for one's country can render one unfit to be a citizen," he wrote. And nowhere, he said, was that more obvious than in Vietnam.

English scholar and Air Force veteran Phoebe Spinrad has taken Shay to task on his selective use of characters from Homer and Shakespeare. Shay doesn't point out that despite equal provocation, the other warriors in *The Iliad*, including the Trojans, whose families and homes are attacked, do not go berserk like Achilles. Wouldn't they be suffering PTSD, too?[450]

Shay's attempts to show the links between literature and psychiatry are murky at best. He overgeneralizes from his tiny batch of veterans claiming PTSD to "all combat veterans" and inflates statistics to an absurd extent. But what's most ridiculous about the book are the improbable stories the Vietnam veterans—all anonymous, of course—told in therapy.

A member of a LRRP team described to Shay the reaction of his unit on night patrol on the coast of South Vietnam when they saw a group of junks in the water. Assuming they were Viet Cong soldiers, the team ambushed the entire fleet. When dawn arrived, they realized in horror that they had massacred hundreds of Vietnamese fishermen and their families. Shay repeatedly returned to this story as an example of the terrible events veterans suffered. (It's interesting to note that the massacre of innocent people in sampans is straight out of the movie *Apocalypse Now*.)

But this ludicrous action violates virtually every practice of the Lurps. Teams of four to six men, Lurps are the "eyes and ears" of larger units. Their mission is observation and stealth, and they often move at night. The weapons they carry are individual infantry weapons used only in self-defense. Lurps are never given the responsibility of ambushing larger units or engaging in spontaneous firefights. In fact, they are to avoid getting engaged because they face a difficult extraction process. In effect, they are on their own.

If a LRRP team spotted junks in the water, the men would report the sighting; by attacking, they risk complete annihilation themselves. Perhaps helicopter gunships with searchlights would have been dispatched to the scene or the Lurps would fire artillery flares over the enemy fleet; artillery barrages could have been rained down on the boats without exposing the team to discovery. If this man really was a patient of Dr. Shay's, he should have been treated for his fantasies, not PTSD. The other stories in the book are just as nebulous and absurd. But Shay's book was taken very seriously by book reviewers, hailed as a literary look at how combat invariably erodes character.

Before the book's publication, Shay heard about Richard Burns through Professor Barry Lowe at West Point, the commander of the Lurps in peacetime. (Burns' daughter graduated from West Point and his son is a Ranger.) Shay asked Burns—who, remember, is a former Recondo, Pathfinder, and Green Beret who has written about PTSD—to review his manuscript.

"I got through the introduction of the book, and I knew something was wrong," Burns said. "The guys he did the studies on were phonies. It was all crap. To me it was a slap in the face to real Lurps." Burns felt that veterans the psychiatrist had interviewed had fed the doctor false and far-fetched tales, painting the picture of Vietnam combat troops as ill-trained, out of control, and undisciplined, like the soldiers often seen in Vietnam movies. From experience, Burns knows that men in those elite units are highly trained, disciplined, and skilled professionals. They have to be or they don't live through their difficult tasks. Of course, the psychiatrist had used pseudonyms, so none of the wild war stories could be verified.

Burns pointed out to Shay the numerous inconsistencies in the stories. "I understand you're trying to help veterans," Burns told Shay. "But I don't believe any of these guys." Shay immediately became defensive, but he admitted he had not verified any of the men's records. Nor did he have a military expert working with him to evaluate the veterans' stories. Instead of dealing with the falsehoods riddling his book, Shay started to personally attack Burns, saying that since he was a "lifer," his observations about the military in Vietnam were not valid.

"But I wasn't a lifer on my first tour of duty," Burns pointed out. "I was eighteen years old." Shay's response was that his Vietnam experiences marred his perception. He insinuated that Burns' attitude toward combat service and patriotism were mental disorders.

"Because I'm a Vietnam veteran, therefore my perception is marred," Burns says. "But I'm the one who's the expert, not a psychiatrist who has never been in the military." Burns says Shay called him at work four or five times, each time to defend himself and attack Burns' expertise. After several conversations, with Burns repeatedly stressing that the veterans' stories were not true, Shay said he was going to publish the book anyway.

"Then his book came out, and of course the VA thinks it's great," Burns says, shaking his head in disgust. "Most of the mental health professionals hold that opinion, and that's one of our problems with treatment."

I contacted Shay, who confirmed he didn't obtain military records to document the veterans' stories. "Until someone gives me a strong reason to disbelieve, I won't check," he said.[451] Shay thinks he's championing America's abused and damaged combat soldiers, righting the wrongs that have been done to them. I'm sure any suggestion that he is perpetrating a libel on Vietnam veterans would shock him.

Shay also assured me he has taken to heart the legions of America's "disavowed veterans." That was a phrase I had not heard before. I asked him to explain. Shay said that disavowed veterans are combat soldiers who have been repudiated by the federal government. They were involved in secret, sometimes illegal operations in Southeast Asia for which the government wanted to hide all their tracks. So the government completely purged all their records, wiping away any trace of their service. Because of this, these men are denied benefits and proper treatment for all that ails them.

In other words, the government is the liar. Shay is fully convinced that he is righting a massive wrong perpetrated by an evil system. I do not question Shay's sincerity. But of all the mental health professionals I have ever talked to, he is by far the most naïve. Frauds frequently use that "government-wiped-out-my-records" complaint.

Again, *every* armed service veteran has an official, permanent record of his or her service. If an Army or Marine recon specialist, for example, was assigned to a MACV-SOG or CIA operation (in Laos, perhaps), his chronological record of assignments might state: "Classified assignment," with the applicable dates. When a man or woman serves in the military, every day of his or her service must be accounted for—transit times, hospitalizations, leave, and, of course, time spent in the stockade or brig.

In addition to "disavowed vets," Shay has taken on another dubious cause. In a July 1995 editorial in *The New York Times*, Shay and Congresswoman Maxine Waters (D-CA) pleaded for the restoration of veterans' benefits to Vietnam-era veterans who received less-than-honorable discharges, so called "bad-paper" vets.

"A great number were in combat," they wrote. "Many bad-paper veterans are among the 250,000 ex-combat soldiers who suffer from posttraumatic stress disorder. They have a higher incidence of unemployment, violent behavior, alcohol and drug abuse, family problems, and homelessness than other veterans. Most soldiers discharged less than honorably committed their offenses after their combat duty; many did so because of psychological injuries suffered in battle."[452]

Shay's support of bad-paper veterans ignores the fact that most of those who received dishonorable discharges were not combat soldiers. In the military, a dishonorable discharge is the equivalent of a felony conviction in civilian life. Shay's proposal rewards those who were the criminals of the military system. Since a general or honorable discharge automatically qualifies a veteran for a wide variety of VA benefits, that's as ludicrous as pardoning civilians who are convicted of felonies and giving them monetary benefits and college scholarships.

But with the encouragement of Shay and Waters, legislation prepared in consultation with veterans' groups proposed a solution: Establish a procedure to automatically upgrade bad-paper discharges. A side benefit would be to allow more dysfunctional vets into the system to be counseled by gullible psychiatrists like Shay, who could help them in their quest to feed at the taxpayer trough.

Vets like Dave Goff.

The CIA Assassin

David Goff stood stiffly at attention, his mustache drooping over the sides of his mouth and thinning hair combed across the top of his head. The audience watched as U.S. Congressman James T. Walsh (R-NY) carefully pinned a colorful collection of medals and ribbons to the chest of Goff's dark civilian suit.

"This is my greatest privilege since I took office," Walsh said. A small group of fellow veterans stood nearby, also receiving from Walsh belated medals due them from the war in Vietnam. But none received valorous decorations as prestigious as those awarded to Goff twenty years after he left Vietnam.

Goff received both a Distinguished Service Cross and the Distinguished Service Medal, the two highest decorations given by the Army except for the Medal of Honor. In addition, Goff acquired the Silver Star with one oak leaf cluster, Bronze Star Medal for valor, Soldiers Medal, Purple Heart, Army Commendation Medal, Meritorious Service Medal, Air Medal, National Defense Medal, Vietnam Service Medal, Vietnam Cross of Gallantry with Palm, Good Conduct Medal, and the Vietnam Campaign Medal. The medals pinned on by the congressman that 1989 spring day made Goff one of the most highly decorated Vietnam veterans in the state of New York.

Unknown to those in the audience, no citations accompanied the medals Goff received that day. Goff told the congressman's aides the operations in Vietnam were so secret the citations still were classified. One of the aides scribbled down Goff's accounts of the combat actions so that the congressman had a description of his heroism to read as he made the presentations. Many of those in the Syracuse area, especially those who knew Goff through the Vet Center, thought the recognition he received that day was long overdue.

It seemed as if there were two Dave Goffs. There was the Goff employed as superintendent of the Department of Public Works in Morrisville—married, the father of two kids. And there was the Goff, the Vietnam veteran who worked with local veterans, crying and counseling with them through many long nights. Goff cofounded Chapter 293 of the Vietnam Veterans of America (VVA) and as president of the chapter worked to bring vet outreach programs to the rural county where he lived. For four years, Goff had hosted the annual VVA Memorial Day "watch fire" on his father's farm to commemorate those who died or are still missing in Vietnam. Goff had even helped set up a VVA chapter at the Auburn Correctional Facility.

A 1989 news story in the Syracuse *Post-Standard* by Marie Villari after the presentation by Walsh described the horrific road Goff had traveled, how he had gone from a desperate man needing help to one reaching out to others.[453] Several years later, reporter Melanie Hirsch of the *Post-Standard* followed that piece with an article entitled "Exorcising a Demon Called Trauma," describing Goff's triumph over PTSD.[454]

From those accounts, here's Goff's story:

One drizzly day as Goff drove to work, he looked through the windshield of his car and saw—clear as day—four NVA soldiers pointing AK-47s at him. In a six-mile drive, Goff had three frightening flashbacks. He was diagnosed as suffering from PTSD. "It's an SOB going through it [therapy]," Goff said. "Because you've locked it up so long. But you've got to go back."

He and his wife Brenda had married in July 1969, just before he left for duty in Okinawa. After his discharge in 1970, Goff came home to the small-town life in New York state. For more than a decade, he had not spoken about his experiences in the war. As far as his wife knew, he had never left Okinawa. But in reality, Goff told reporters, he had been involved in brutal clandestine operations in Vietnam.

"I hid it," Goff told Villari, who interviewed him at his Peterboro home where his den was filled with Vietnam War memorabilia. "The analogy that I use in the rap group is, I stuffed it in the closet and locked the door. Every so often one of those boxes falls off the shelf, and I have to pick it up and throw it back in there."[455]

But eventually Goff could no longer keep the terrors of war tamped down. He slept with a .357 Magnum under his pillow. Depressed, Goff began drinking up to a quart of Scotch per day. He experienced recurrent flashbacks and nightmares. Many nights he lay awake and contemplated killing himself. In 1984, he and his wife separated. "I got to the point where suicide seemed the only way out," Goff said.

Finally, after seeing enemy soldiers aiming guns at him in the middle of the road, Goff received help from the VA. Accepted into the therapy program for PTSD, Goff's truth began to come out. "I have seen enough death and destruction in Vietnam to last me a lifetime," he wrote during therapy. His counselor advised him to tell his family about the past. Goff's wife was dumbfounded to hear what had really happened to her husband during his time in the military.

What Goff told his family was indeed shocking. After enlisting in 1968, he was assigned to the 101st Airborne Division, attached to MACV— Military Assistance Command Vietnam—with the "Special Operations Group." As part of the Phoenix Program, Goff said he took orders from the CIA. His team performed thirteen top-secret missions in Vietnam, Laos, and Cambodia, carrying cyanide pills to commit suicide in case they were taken prisoner. "Our biggest thing was assassinating—political officials, military in the North Vietnamese Army—creating chaos with the government," Goff said. "It was working."[456]

But the missions succeeded at a great personal cost to Goff. Running on pure adrenaline, Goff couldn't handle the chaos being wreaked on his psyche. During one patrol, a fellow soldier, hit by gunfire three or four times in the chest, pleaded with him, "Hold me." Goff turned away, too callused by the death and destruction he had seen and dealt to help the dying man. Then one night, when Goff fell asleep on guard duty, VC soldiers slipped in and slit a buddy's throat. After eight or ten missions, Goff said, he had inured himself to human feelings. Goff had a nervous breakdown and was shipped to Okinawa.

The Army's reaction to Goff's trauma? A chaplain who offered soothing words and two water-size glasses of warm Scotch. Assigned for the last six months of his tour to the mail room, Goff said, he was debriefed by superiors using electric shock treatments. These unnamed "superiors" warned him never to talk about his covert missions, threatening to yank Goff back into active duty if he violated the secrecy rules.

No wonder he was so screwed up! After months of therapy, relieved that his true story was finally out, Goff began working closely with the Vet Center in Syracuse, coordinating four rap groups for Vietnam vets, and another for vets and their wives. Goff often heard knocks on the door late at night from Vietnam vets struggling with their own memories. Goff told these Vietnam vets that they could get past their PTSD like he did. "People ask me, 'How does it feel to be a hero?'" Goff told Villari. "I was caught in the wrong situation at the wrong time."

I first read about Goff in the *Dallas Times Herald*, when Villari's 1990 story was picked up by a wire service and circulated around the country. His tale later popped up in a veterans' magazine and Laura Palmer's "Home From the War" column headlined "Vietnam Vet Finds Peace in Truth."[457]

Assassination squads, electric shock debriefing, the Distinguished Service Cross, *and* the Distinguished Service Medal—to me, Goff's story sounded as fishy as discount cat food. For one thing, SOG does not stand for "Special Operations Group," but Studies and Observations Group. And the Distinguished Service Medal, which recognizes merit, not valor, is only awarded to senior commanders in positions of great authority. Goff clearly did not fit that description.

What infuriated me most about Goff was that he was a walking billboard for all the negative stereotypes of Vietnam vets—assassin, suicidal, alcoholic, PTSD sufferer. And on top of all that, he was claiming to be a hero. But would a congressman agree to present the medals to Goff if they were not valid?

After a series of phone calls, I identified Goff's full name and filed an FOIA request for the military record of David Jerome Goff Jr. In a few months, my suspicions were confirmed. Goff had never been assigned to MACV-SOG. No Special Forces duty. No covert CIA operations. The banal truth about Goff: He had been a clerk in Okinawa, his highest rank E-4.[458]

I talked to an editor at the Syracuse *Post-Standard*, who was skeptical but assigned a reporter to call me back. I explained to the dubious reporter that Goff's record showed that he had not served in Vietnam. Goff, the reporter insisted, was one of the most upstanding citizens in the Syracuse area. How could I—fifteen hundred miles away—know something about him that the Vet Center, Congressman Walsh, other Vietnam vets, and the original reporter did not know? But when I explained how he could obtain Goff's record himself, the reporter agreed to file an FOIA request.

When he received Goff's record, the journalist and I talked. "That's proof positive that he lied," I said. "No, it's not, Mr. Burkett," the reporter said patiently, as if talking to a small child. "Mr. Goff has explained that. The government has doctored these files because they are trying to cover up the activity he participated in. Everybody knows that the CIA doctors records."

If the CIA had truly done all that has been attributed to it in Vietnam, there would have been no reason for the rest of us to be there. I tried to explain that Goff's stories of assassination squads and electric shock debriefing were ludicrous, but the journalist brushed me off.

"Mr. Burkett, we've spent a lot of time on this," the reporter said with a hint of exasperation. "We're satisfied that David Goff is genuine. We'd like you not to call us anymore about this. If you do, we're not going to accept the phone calls."

Frustrated with the newspaper's disinterest in the truth, I did not return to the Goff case until 1993, when Malcolm McConnell, the author of a number of military books (and the coauthor of a biography of Maj. Gen. John K. "Jack" Singlaub, one of the first commanders of MACV-SOG), decided to write a story about my work for *Reader's Digest*. Particularly interested in David Goff, he filed his own FOIA request for Goff's record.

The record said that Goff had been assigned to the 30th Antiaircraft Artillery Brigade, "USARV" (Republic of Vietnam). But the 30th Artillery did not serve in Vietnam; the unit was based in Okinawa. Any TDY to Vietnam—even if the assignment was classified—would be reflected in Goff's chronological record of assignment. Records had no indication of temporary duty in Vietnam. In a further check, the Records Center in St. Louis examined pay records, confirming that Goff signed for his money at his unit in Okinawa each payday.

McConnell called Goff, who repeated the basic details of the stories he had told various reporters: He had been a member of an assassination team based in Okinawa, taking training in jungle warfare and other specialized schools on the island. When McConnell pointed out that Goff's military record indicated only that he served as both a clerk and a mail clerk, Goff insisted that was not his true record. He adamantly stuck to his story about thirteen secret missions to Vietnam, TDY from Okinawa, assigned to MACV-SOG under control of the CIA.[459]

But when McConnell asked Goff exactly which unit to see if he knew the MACV-SOG operational structure (i.e., Op 34, Op 33, and so on) he just said, "CIA." Asked where he staged from, Goff seemed confused at the question. Goff claimed his team was briefed at a "safehouse" in Saigon, but he was unfamiliar with the layout of the city. He said he had never met the MACV-SOG commander during his thirteen missions. (McConnell knew that was highly improbable; anyone on sensitive cross-border operations was generally briefed in the presence of the MACV-SOG commander.)

Goff supposedly received the Distinguished Service Cross for rescuing two wounded members of a five-man assassination team, but Goff could not remember the place or date of that action. "I've been in a lot of therapy and have tried to forget most of this stuff," he said.

Goff claimed he had obtained his full, "updated" service record several years before, which included all his classified assignments, but that several days after receiving the file, some unnamed person called him and told him to return the file and make no copies. Goff could not remember to whom he returned the file but claimed that the material had to remain classified until the year 2000. "The U.S. government does not want to reveal its assassination campaign to Southeast Asian governments," Goff said.

His many medals and decorations, Goff said, had been sent a few at a time over a period of many years. Goff had received a form DA-1577, which listed all the awards and decorations to which he was entitled. He showed that paper to Terry Bersina, a veteran service representative of New York State, and a VA official named Gary Williams. They helped Goff obtain the decorations he had not yet received, which in turn were presented to him by Walsh. (The VA's Gary Williams also received medals that day.)

Goff mailed McConnell the DA-1577, showing he was entitled to all the medals Walsh presented. Goff also sent a copy of what purported to be a MACV-SOG identification card with his picture, identifying David J. Goff Jr. as a member of Special Forces acting under the direct orders of the president of the United States. "Do not detain or question him!" the card reads. "He is authorized to wear civilian clothing, carry unusual personal weapons, transport and possess prohibited items, including U.S. currency, pass into restricted areas, and requisition equipment of all types, including weapons and vehicles."

McConnell was not impressed. He knew the card was a commercial gimmick that anyone could obtain through an ad in *Soldier of Fortune* magazine.

Finally, Goff's contention that his decorations were "classified" were not true. There are *no* classified general orders or classified special orders for

Army valorous decorations, according to Maj. Michael Wawrzyniak, U.S. Army Military Awards Office. If a decoration is awarded for a classified "black operation," the order and citation is generically worded or the after-action report of the operation is declassified. By 1993, all decorations regarding covert operations of the Vietnam War had been declassified. Wawrzyniak verified that the Distinguished Service Medal is *never* awarded to junior enlisted men. And, although in rare cases, the DSM has been awarded to full colonels (O-6) and senior NCOs, this important decoration is usually reserved for general officers.[460]

McConnell called Congressman Walsh's office and told him what he had learned about Goff. The revelation stunned Walsh and his staff. "We couldn't believe it," said John McGuire, Walsh's district director and himself a Vietnam vet. "We were dumbfounded."[461]

Walsh's office asked Goff to sign a Privacy Act Release so that they could obtain his records for themselves. Goff refused. So Walsh filed his own FOIA request. The records Walsh received verified McConnell's assessment and showed fraudulent documents in Goff's file attesting to the decorations. Walsh's office then forwarded the records to the U.S. attorney's office. "I now believe a fraud was committed by one of the veterans awarded medals, a Mr. David Goff, and attach evidence herein and request your office take appropriate action under law," Congressman Walsh wrote.[462]

That letter triggered a call to the FBI, which began looking into the allegations against Goff. Federal agents verified that Goff was ineligible to receive virtually all of the medals bestowed by Walsh. The only awards Goff had really earned during his service were the Good Conduct Medal, a Sharpshooter badge with rifle bar, and the National Defense Service Medal, given to anyone who completes basic training during wartime.

In March 1994, two weeks before the five-year statute of limitations ran out, David Goff was charged in federal court in Syracuse with violating the rarely invoked federal law prohibiting unlawfully wearing medals and decorations. If convicted, Goff faced six months imprisonment and a fine of five thousand dollars. The U.S. Justice Department found only two other instances of the medals fraud rule being enforced since October 1990.

"I still believe in David Goff," said Ben Barrett, secretary of the local VVA chapter, after the indictment. (Goff was then vice president of the chapter.) "For them to say he's not a Vietnam vet, they'll have to prove it to me."[463]

But Goff proved it himself.

"I admit at this time that I fraudulently made military documents, to include DA Form 1577 dated February 17, 1989, and DD Form 214, reflecting my processing out of the military on December 24, 1970," read Goff's signed confession. "I personally typed in the DD-214 the section in box 24 where it makes reference to my being commended for the National Defense Service Medal, the Vietnam Service Medal, and the Vietnam Campaign Medal."[464]

Five years to the day after Walsh pinned on the medals, Goff waived his right to trial. Surrounded by a dozen supporters, Goff admitted in court that he had lied about his service record and that he had never served in Vietnam. He pleaded guilty to the charge that he "knowingly wore medals he was not entitled to wear." Goff later was sentenced to two hundred hours of community service and fined $2,170. The judge ordered Goff to undergo counseling. He was not required to return the medals. (It's not illegal to possess military medals, only to display or wear them as if entitled to them.)[465]

About a month after Goff pleaded guilty, McConnell's story, "The True Face of the Vietnam Vet," ran in the May 1994 issue of *Reader's Digest,* revealing that I was responsible for exposing Goff as a fraud. I was inundated with letters, some congratulating me, some asking for help in exposing a prevaricator. But others were from Goff's supporters, blasting me and defending their friend.

What prompted Goff to make up such wild tales? Goff's confession to the press blamed drinking and depression, saying that his good works with veterans' groups outweighed any negative impact of his fraud. I disagree. Looking for attention, pumping himself up by spinning outrageous lies, Goff denigrated the U.S. military and the Vietnam vets he claimed he wanted to help. Much of the public perception of Vietnam vets—that they are perpetrators of war crimes, alcoholics, suicidal, sufferers of PTSD—has been spun by the Dave Goffs of the world. That ugly image solidifies every time a wannabe like Goff grabs center stage.

Diagnosed with PTSD, adorned with medals, Goff was eligible for PTSD disability compensation, Social Security payments, and disability retirement from the state of New York, where his war record helped him establish seniority as a civil servant. Fortunately the FBI investigation intervened before he qualified for compensation.

But Goff did not give up. Two years later, I heard from a Syracuse contact that Goff was trying to hire an attorney to pursue his claim of PTSD compensation with the VA.

I have no doubt that if he persists he will get it. In late 1996, the Department of Veterans Affairs published new regulations changing the way the VA rates mental disorders. The change makes it easier for veterans to win claims for service connection for PTSD because it requires the VA to use the criteria currently used by the American Psychiatric Association, as codified in the *Diagnostic and Statistical Manual of Mental Disorders, 4th*

Edition (DSM-IV). That definition now includes "learning about the sudden, unexpected death of a family member or close friend." In other words, just being part of the human race now qualifies you for PTSD compensation.

Honey, the War Shrank My Hippocampus

Psychiatrists and psychologists at VA Medical Centers around the country have churned out papers on PTSD and Vietnam veterans for the last twenty years. They always report a strong link between combat and serious mental illness, between PTSD and Vietnam.

The papers just keep coming.

In 1995, the Dallas VA Medical Center reported that 51 percent of its seriously mentally ill veterans—diagnosed with manic-depressive disorders, schizophrenia, and other psychoses—served in war zones, and 43 percent of those were in combat. Finding so many veterans with mental problems surprised the researchers. "It has been a common assumption that the majority of severely mentally ill veterans were marginally adjusted when they entered the service and washed out during basic training," said Dr. Robert Fowler, chief of psychiatry at the Dallas VAMC. "Our findings indicate this assumption is incorrect." Or does it? There's no indication the researchers verified the men's stories by checking military records.[466]

That same year, the West Haven VAMC published another in a long series of studies on PTSD. This research used MRI (magnetic resonance imaging) brain scans to show that veterans with PTSD had up to 8 percent shrinkage in the hippocampus region of their brains compared to non-PTSD veterans. The hippocampus controls short-term verbal memory. The study suggested that the shrinkage could account for a common symptom of PTSD—memory loss. But the researchers could not answer the obvious questions. Which came first, the smaller hippocampus, leaving veterans more vulnerable to PTSD? Or did the trauma cause the hippocampus to shrink? Do they really know what they are measuring at all? Perhaps liars and wannabes have smaller hippocampuses.[467]

Researchers at the West Haven VAMC focused on veterans of a different war for a study grappling with the relationship of PTSD to traumatic combat. The startling results were reported in the *American Journal of Psychiatry* in February 1997. They examined fifty-nine National Guard reservists from two separate units who participated in the Gulf War. The reservists answered nineteen questions about the nature of their war experience one month after the war ended and again two years later. The veterans were asked specific questions about significant events—such as seeing others killed or wounded, being involved in firefights, observing the bizarre disfigurement of bodies—as well as more subjective questions, such as whether they faced "extreme threat to personal safety."

An astonishing 88 percent reported changes in memory for traumatic events during Operation Desert Storm; 70 percent recalled events at the two-year evaluation that they had not reported at one month. After checking "no" at one month, eleven of the fifty-nine veterans recalled "extreme threat to personal safety," fifteen reported seeing bizarre disfigurement of bodies, nine said they had seen others killed or wounded, five reported seeing a close friend killed, and five reported being involved in a firefight. One veteran even remembered being wounded, something he hadn't mentioned just one month after the war. Those who remembered trauma that they had not reported earlier had more symptoms of PTSD.

Did the veterans simply forget? Was the trauma repressed or denied? The researchers have no way of knowing. They didn't check military records to see what kind of trauma these veterans really faced. But the implications of this study are far-reaching.

"Numerous investigations, including two earlier studies on this same population of Gulf War veterans, repeatedly have shown that level of combat exposure is significantly correlated with level of PTSD," the researchers said. "However, if memories of trauma are inconsistent, then statistical analyses such as correlations involving retrospective accounts of trauma are highly suspect.

"This study suggests that the relationship between the development of PTSD and level of combat exposure is not as clear as previously believed. Factors other than combat, such as childhood trauma and preexisting personality may also play an important part in symptom development."[468]

Although the study suggested strongly that the definition and diagnosis of PTSD is deeply flawed, an editorial in the same issue of the *American Journal of Psychiatry* made it clear that mental health professionals will not run out of patients. "Military and Veterans Affairs psychiatrists need to develop collaborative clinical and research programs that target early recognition and intervention. It is hoped that these efforts will curtail the development of chronic PTSD and the associated social and occupational impairment that have proved so devastating to treat in *Vietnam veterans*." (Emphasis added.)[469]

Regardless of the facts, PTSD has become the defining hallmark of the Vietnam veteran, a reality "proved" by therapists and advocates by the "fact" that large numbers of Vietnam vets commit suicide or end up on the streets as homeless people.

Or do they?

13

"Vietnam Killed Him"

Suicide

NAVY AIRMAN Robert Fife often wept as he told his wife Nancy of the squalor and torture he endured after his plane was shot down and he was captured by the Viet Cong in early 1966. Able to escape after fifteen days in captivity, he was one of the lucky ones.

Nancy Fife had not known her husband until a few months after he returned from the war. They married and had two children. Although he rarely said much about Vietnam, the brutal ordeal for the Navy navigator never really ended. During the twenty-three years of their marriage, Fife struggled with memories of the terror he had experienced at the hands of the enemy. One night he went berserk merely at the sight of his wife's sneakers. He later explained his frightening outburst. When his captors came to his bamboo cage to beat him and urinate on him, they wore sneakers. And the enemy soldier whom Robert had strangled during his daring escape also had worn canvas shoes.

The intensity of her husband's reaction was all the proof Nancy needed that his anguish was real. As his life disintegrated, Robert sought counseling. Nancy went with him to his first session with a therapist in 1986. Fife's therapist diagnosed him as suffering from posttraumatic stress disorder, caused by his horrific experiences in Vietnam as a navigator for a USS *Ranger*-based F-4 fighter and his subsequent ordeal as a POW.

Finally, Fife's struggle ended. In June 1989, at the age of forty-six, the former airman took his own life with carbon monoxide. A tombstone provided by the VA said: "Robert J. Fife, U.S. Navy, Vietnam."

After his suicide, Nancy found among her husband's effects a citation for heroism and a 449-page manuscript, Fife's vivid and frightening autobiography of his time in Vietnam.

In her grief, Nancy Fife realized that while her husband had physically survived the war in Vietnam, it ultimately killed him just as surely as if he had taken a bullet to the brain. She petitioned the Utah Vietnam War Memorial committee to include his name on the wall of that monument. In support of her effort, his therapist wrote a letter calling Fife a casualty of the Vietnam War.

"He was clearly depressed, guilt-ridden, angry, alienated from people, and viewed the world in a very negative manner as a result of his military service experiences, particularly as a prisoner of war," wrote Dr. Corydon Hammond to the committee.

Fife's sad death was a perfect example of one widespread belief about Vietnam veterans. In the CBS documentary "The Wall Within," Dan Rather said that "possibly as many as one hundred thousand Vietnam vets have been driven to suicide after the war." If true, that means that suicide, the final act of the tragedy that is PTSD, has killed more members of the armed forces than died in the war.

With Fife's suicide, Vietnam had claimed yet another warrior. Nancy Fife's campaign to honor her husband on the memorial made local headlines. After much debate, the committee agreed to add Fife's name to that of the other 389 men from Utah who would be listed on the memorial.

An Associated Press reporter decided to write a story about Fife, the man who had bravely flown 130 combat missions and survived a prison camp only to die by his own hand more than two decades later. In an attempt to find someone who had served with him, the reporter obtained Fife's military records. As an artisan was preparing to engrave Fife's name on the monument, the reporter discovered the bizarre truth.

Robert Fife had not flown 130 combat missions, as he had claimed. He had not been captured by the Viet Cong. Fife had never set foot in Vietnam or the Southeast Asia theater of operations. Fife had enlisted in the Navy in September 1965. Fife wanted to be a hero, but he had been given a medical discharge from the Navy after eight months of stateside service because bones in his right foot had not mended properly after a childhood accident.

Described as unreliable, angry, a dreamer, Fife was also a pornography addict and a gambler. Apparently illegitimate, according to a relative, he had never known his father and blamed his mother for making him "a bastard." Fife had created an inner world of heroics, writing a manuscript describing amazing military exploits. The tales of bravery and competence in war allowed him to forget his shortcomings.

After discovering the truth, his wife told a reporter: "I feel like I've been raped."[470]

Fife told his stories so convincingly that neither his wife nor his therapist had a clue to his deceit. To back up his tales, he had acquired a certificate that appeared to be from the USS *Ranger* Committee. The paper said that Lt. (jg) Robert J. Fife, after 130 missions over enemy territory, was "one of only four naval aviators to escape from enemy prison camps." Signed by Admiral Thomas H. Moorer, retired Chief of Naval Operations, the certificate listed all the medals Fife was entitled to, medals Fife told relatives he had burned. The list included the Navy Cross, the service's highest award for valor. In reality, Fife's only award was the National Defense Service Medal.

Fife had appropriated the heroism of a man named Dieter Dengler, who served on the USS *Ranger* and was one of only a handful of POWs to ever escape the enemy during the Vietnam War. After the war, Dengler spoke on the lecture circuit for a few years. Perhaps Fife heard him speak. Fife's effects included newspaper stories about Dengler and copies of his Navy Cross award and citation.

Since the early 1980s, the supposition that suicide is a leading cause of death among Vietnam veterans is periodically boosted by the publication of papers or studies that purport to prove the correlation statistically. The daily press reports the studies, often packaged with stories about men like Fife, men so undone by combat experiences that they end their lives.

"If we put the names of all that have died since we came home on the Wall, tragically, we could walk through a canyon down there," Steve Bentley told syndicated columnist Laura Palmer. Bentley was then director of the Veterans' Employment and Training Services program in Portland, Maine, and a leader in the Vietnam Veterans of America. "In the last year here, we've had at least a dozen (suicides). I know what killed them was unfinished business from Vietnam they never got away from, but the death certificate won't say that."[471]

Hollywood reinforces the theme of "suicidal vet" with movies such as *Coming Home*. In that film, a Marine officer and Vietnam veteran played by Bruce Dern, whose wife (Jane Fonda) falls in love with a disabled Vietnam vet (Jon Voight), walks into the ocean and—you guessed it—drowns himself. Suicidal Vietnam veterans are stock characters in all the subgenres of Vietnam films, said author Michael Lee Lanning in his 1994 book *Vietnam at the Movies*. "While the success and method of self-termination vary, the reason behind the death wish is always the same: The vet is unable to deal with what he saw and did in Vietnam and cannot adjust to a "normal" life when he arrives home," Lanning wrote. "The message of the Vietnam-veteran suicide film seems to be that the veteran is better off dead by his own hand than alive and attempting to survive with the guilt of the war on his shoulders."[472]

Other films that include suicidal vets are *Flatliners*, *Full Metal Jacket*, *Lethal Weapon*, *The Big Chill*, *Distant Thunder*, and *The Prince of Tides*. In *The*

Deer Hunter, a soldier played by Christopher Walken stays in Vietnam after troops are withdrawn in order to make money taking part in a Russian roulette contest. Eventually, of course, he blows his brains out.

Even when Vietnam vets are good, they're bad. Randy Quaid stars as a nutty, alcoholic Vietnam vet in the 1996 special effects extravaganza *Independence Day*. A crop duster who guzzles booze while he flies, Quaid's character suffers from war trauma and the unsettling experience of being abducted and probed by aliens. The only way he can redeem himself in the eyes of his teenage son is in a final, fiery act of heroic suicide.

The Tunnel Rat

Self-proclaimed experts like Bentley say that the suicides of many Vietnam veterans are more subtle—a car driven into a tree, an "accidental" overdose. An example: In 1989, Vietnam veteran John Kolosowski just walked into a vacant field in Houston, lay down and died. In his pocket was a dog-eared card of the Brotherhood of Vietnam Veterans, which ran a shelter for the homeless in Houston. The poor man had nothing else to his name.

Kolosowski's sad end became a cause celebre in the Houston media. *Houston Chronicle* reporter Evan Moore ran a handful of stories on the veteran's death and his pauper's funeral attended by only a few. One said the VA refused to pay the costs of his burial because he didn't die in a government hospital. Kolosowski's tale was picked up by the Associated Press, syndicated columnists, and veterans' newsletters as an example of how Vietnam veterans—abandoned by their government, afflicted by their demons—ultimately self-destruct.

Moore found veterans who said they served with Kolosowski. They described the diminutive Marine as a "tunnel rat," a man with a tight, wiry frame who could wiggle his way into the hidden maze of tunnels dug by the Viet Cong. They described how he had been lowered into the holes with a flashlight in his mouth. For years, they said, Kolosowski had dreamed about the things he saw—rats, sharpened spikes, grenades suspended inside the tunnels on fish hooks, poisonous snakes, hidden enemy soldiers waiting to kill. As a result, the former Marine battled alcoholism for years after the war, drinking to numb the war memories, drifting from place to place.

"We called him 'Ski' back then," said another Vietnam veteran named Johnny Bacot, who identified himself as a former Marine sniper. "Every company had what they called a 'house mouse,' who was usually the smallest guy in the bunch, and Ski was ours."[473]

One story dubbed him "the forgotten vet." After hearing of his circumstances, ten veterans' groups banded together to give Kolosowski a full memorial service with flowers, a bugler playing taps, a color guard, and a twenty-one-gun salute, all presided over by a former Air Force chaplain.

"It took him sixteen years with the open end of a whiskey bottle, but he killed himself just as sure as if it had been a gun he'd stuck in his mouth," Gary Thomas of the Brotherhood of Vietnam Veterans told a reporter. "I don't know how many of these funerals I've been to. Nobody there, nobody cares. Just a couple of guys and a coffin and somebody who started dying a long time ago in Vietnam." The government promised Kolosowski many benefits in return for his service in Vietnam, Thomas said bitterly, but in the end, refused even to pay three hundred dollars to have his body embalmed.[474]

A sad story about an undoubtedly difficult life. His military record shows that Kolosowski, an orphan from Brooklyn, left high school after one year. In October 1970, at age seventeen, he joined the Marine Corps. Despite the stories his "fellow veterans" told reporters, Kolosowski was not a "tunnel rat."

And he did not serve in Vietnam.

Kolosowski was discharged only two months after he enlisted because of "mental inaptitude" and "defective attitude."[475] (Oddly, Kolosowski's friend Johnny Bacot, who described himself as a "Marine sniper," and reminisced about Ski's tunnel exploits, is the real thing. Records show Bacot served six years in the military and earned a Combat Action Ribbon, as well as a Vietnam Service Medal and a Vietnam Campaign Medal. But he could not have served with Kolosowski in Vietnam.[476])

In *Long Time Passing*, author Myra MacPherson recounted the stories of several veterans driven to suicide by the war despite all the help they received from their local Vet Center.

MacPherson described the government's resistance to providing counseling for Vietnam veterans until it could no longer ignore "the frightening statistics." She cited a study done for Ralph Nader's Center for the Study of Responsive Law: "Suicide appears to be one of the leading causes of death among Vietnam veterans in general and disabled veterans in particular."[477] Her explanation: Vietnam veterans returned so traumatized by their depraved experiences in the war—evil they've committed and evil done to them—that they are driven to self-destruction.

One of MacPherson's suicides was Gerald W. Highman, who had been undergoing counseling at the Vet Center in Columbus, Ohio. "The twice-wounded former Marine was 'pretty-mixed up' when he came home," MacPherson wrote, quoting his father Merrill Highman. "After years of depression and combat flashbacks, Highman seemed to be doing better." Finally, Highman pulled himself together. He married his childhood sweetheart and found a job. Gerald started going to the Vet Center for counseling, and he often seemed to be his "happy old self."

But one terrible morning Gerald called his father. The son asked if his father had slept well, then calmly announced: "I just killed Joann." Next, Gerald told his father, he was going to commit suicide. Merrill Highman pleaded with his son not to kill himself, then called police and hurried to his son's home. He was too late. Joann, Gerald's wife of only six months, lay dead in a pool of blood; Gerald died after being rushed to the hospital.[478]

Did Vietnam cause Highman's actions? Military records show that Gerald Wayne Highman, hometown Gahanna, Ohio, served in the Marines in Vietnam from July 1969 to October 1971. But he received no Combat Action Ribbon, the Marine Corps decoration given to those who engage in combat, and no Purple Heart. His record showed no wounds or hospital stay. Highman was actually an "office machine repairman," who fixed typewriters and mimeograph machines at a large permanent base camp.[479]

Another Vietnam vet in MacPherson's book who took his life is Eddy Erikson. (The story of Erikson's death was also included in a *Newsday* story about haunted Vietnam veterans in 1979.[480]) MacPherson described him as an "eighteen-year-old doorgunner" with the 101st Airborne Division at Phu Bai.

"As the months went by, he saw four close friends die in combat," MacPherson wrote. "The final death changed him irrevocably. Michael Murphy was his last and closest friend. Hit by enemy fire but still alive, Murphy fell out of the gunship before Erikson could catch him, just as the helicopter was taking off. The others in the gunship had to hold Erikson back. He tried to fling himself out to save his friend. Later that day, they brought Michael Murphy's body back to the base camp. Erikson was given his friend's unopened mail. With trembling fingers and sobbing, Erikson opened the letter from Murphy's wife. She was ecstatic, and she had written her husband the good news. Michael Murphy had just become the father of a boy."[481]

Back in the U.S., Erikson could not deal with the trauma he had endured. He attempted suicide four times. After going to the VA for treatment, MacPherson said, he began collecting 100 percent disability payments for "psychoneurological disorders." Then one day his wife came home to find her husband's dead body in a closet. He was kneeling, hanging from a rope tied to a five-foot-high clothes pole. He left behind a lavender plastic VA medical identification card. Vietnam had taken another life.[482]

I obtained Erikson's death certificate and discovered that his name was actually Edward Robert Erickson. According to his military records, Erickson did not even join the military until six days before his nineteenth birthday, hardly making him eligible to be in Vietnam when he was eighteen, as he contended. Erickson served in Vietnam from October 20, 1969 to October 5, 1970, as a machinist with the Headquarters Company of the 159th Aviation Battalion, not a doorgunner on a gunship with the 101st Airborne Division. His record showed no Air Medals, no Air Crewman Badge, no Combat Infantryman Badge, and no Purple Hearts.[483]

Erickson claimed his "last and closest friend" Michael Murphy died in Vietnam on the same day he received mail from his wife proclaiming that he had become a new father. Four Michael Murphys died in Vietnam. One was a Marine, which excludes him from being the man in Erickson's story. Two of the others died before Erickson arrived in Vietnam. The fourth Michael Murphy, who was killed during the time Erickson was serving in Vietnam, was an Army infantryman, an "11 Bravo rifleman," not part of an aircrew or helicopter battalion. That Michael Murphy died of wounds inflicted by shrapnel from an exploding mortar in a ground fight—not in a helicopter from gunfire. This Murphy could not have received mail from his wife the day he died saying that his son had been born. Murphy was single.[484]

Maybe Erickson, a ninth-grade dropout, made up stories to tell his family about why his life was such a failure. After his suicide, a *Newsday* reporter repeated them; in turn, MacPherson used Erickson to show how the horror of Vietnam was driving veterans to suicide. No one checked the records.

Anecdotal evidence like this gets cited as "proof" that Vietnam veterans have killed themselves in record numbers. In a nationally disseminated news story, Steve Bentley, then head of a VVA committee on suicide, described the attempted or successful suicides within a few months of five Vietnam veterans treated at the Togus Veterans Administration Hospital in Maine. Although Bentley was careful to say that many factors figure into the decision to commit suicide, the impression left was that combat trauma from Vietnam compelled all these men to kill themselves.[485]

But an examination of the men's military records revealed that the facts weren't as Bentley portrayed them. One of Bentley's examples, William Harrington, who held a dozen police at bay for an hour while he threatened to kill himself with a hunting knife, was a veteran of Korea, not Vietnam.[486]

Another veteran named Bruce Allen, who shot himself in the head, had served in Thailand, not Vietnam, as an Air Force munitions maintenance man.[487]

Veteran Robert A. Daigneau shot and killed five people, then committed suicide after being released from a hospital where he had been treated for PTSD. Daigneau indeed had served in Vietnam. But as a carpenter, not a combat soldier.[488]

Of the men Bentley cites, only two could be described as combat veterans of Vietnam—Dave Garland and Michael "Mickey" Obrin—and both had financial and marital problems, as do many non-Vietnam veterans who kill themselves.[489]

Certainly Vietnam veterans commit suicide. In every population, a certain number of people are going to kill themselves, just as a certain number are going to die of cancer, heart disease, brain tumors, and leukemia.

Suicides even occurred during the war. Over the ten-year period of the war, out of 2.7 million who served in-country, 384 men killed themselves in Vietnam. That's actually a lower suicide rate than their stateside peer group.[490] And it's far lower than the number of Army personnel in the European theater during World War II who committed suicide. During the five years from December 7, 1941 to June 30, 1946, at least 1,257 American servicemen in Europe committed suicide.[491]

Statistically, a certain number of veterans could be expected to commit suicide during the years after the Vietnam War. I'm sure some struggled with memories of the war; others battled the foibles and failings of their lives. The question becomes: Is the suicide rate for Vietnam veterans significantly higher than that for their peers who did not go to Vietnam?

On September 2, 1990, a syndicated column by Jeff Zaslow of the *Chicago Sun-Times* included a letter from a woman who identified herself as a psychiatric nurse in a VA hospital. She was responding to another letter bemoaning the difficulty women have finding men because so many died in Vietnam. Zaslow had responded that Vietnam casualties amounted to just three-tenths of one percent in her age group, so the war could not be the reason she couldn't find a good man.

"One statistic you left out of your calculations is the number of Vietnam vets who've killed themselves," the nurse wrote." If you check it out, you'll find that more than twice as many vets have died by suicide since the war as were actually killed in Vietnam."[492]

Zaslow pointed out that the suicide rate of Vietnam veterans in a 1988 study by the Centers for Disease Control was estimated to be .13 percent, within the range (.09 and .16) of suicides committed by the general population. The study Zaslow referred to had been published in 1988, well before the air date of "The Wall Within." It determined that in the years since the war about nine thousand Vietnam veterans—not one hundred thousand—had committed suicide. But CBS chose to rely on other less reliable studies, wildly exaggerating the issue to squeeze the most mileage possible out of their "trip-wire" vets hiding in the woods.

Perhaps CBS felt that anecdotal reports of high levels of suicide among vets put them on solid ground. After all, VA counselors had told them numerous stories about vets killing themselves. Reporters and authors accepted the connection as fact.

But why? The answer goes back to Jay Lifton and the creation of PTSD.

The Rumor Mill

The idea that Vietnam veterans had unusually high rates of suicide began circulating soon after the war. In May 1970, *Life* magazine did a story on the filth, neglect, and overcrowding at the Kingsbridge VA hospital in the Bronx. Bobby Muller, a paralyzed veteran who later became head of the Vietnam Veterans of America, was one of nine patients in the hospital's spinal cord injury service. In an interview years later, Muller said five patients killed themselves and four were suspected suicides. "I am the only one left," Muller said.[493]

But the men were not identified, making it impossible to verify Muller's story. As Lifton and antiwar activists who became Vet Center counselors promoted the idea that most Vietnam veterans suffered from PTSD, they promoted the concept that many were suicidal.

As early as 1982, the unfounded myth of high suicide rates was refuted by the general counsel of the House Armed Services Committee and the Disabled American Veterans (DAV). But the myth persisted, repeated in media accounts without thorough examination by reporters. In 1991, Richard K. Kolb, director of publications and public affairs for the VFW, called the reports of high suicide rates among Vietnam vets the "most damaging and unfounded myth of the postwar period."[494]

Periodically, pseudo-science reinforced the fiction. In 1986, the prestigious *New England Journal of Medicine* published a "special article" titled "Delayed Effects of the Military Draft on Mortality." Called a "randomized natural experiment," the study examined death records between 1974 and 1983 of 14,145 California and Pennsylvania men involved in the lottery system, which determined who would be drafted from 1970 to 1972.[495]

The *Journal of Medicine* article, reported in the mainstream press as "Viet-Era Draftees' Suicide Rate High" on March 6, 1986, in the *Washington Post*, was the first to "scientifically" link the anecdotal relationship between service in Vietnam and subsequent deaths from suicide. The study was highly touted, praised as "ingenious" by physician Lawrence Kolb in an *NEJM* editorial.[496]

"Military draftees who served in the Vietnam War era are as much as 86 percent more likely to die by suicide than their peers who did not serve, and as much as 53 percent more likely to die in motor vehicle accidents, a major study reports today," wrote Christine Russell in the *Post*. The numbers, if true, constituted a bona fide epidemic.[497]

"We are looking at an expression . . . of the very serious long-term effects that this experience in Vietnam had," said Dr. Norman Hearst, a professor at the University of California at San Francisco, who was coauthor of the study. "They are just as much casualties of the Vietnam War as those on the battlefield. We owe it to these people to do everything we can to help them."

Hearst said his study validated the stories of high rates of PTSD among Vietnam veterans by taking advantage of a "very large randomized natural experiment"—the military lottery system based on birth dates. But what did the study actually show? "The group of men with birth dates that made them eligible for the draft had a higher mortality rate than the group with birth dates that exempted them from the draft." The research did not examine military records to show if the men *actually served in the military, much less in Vietnam.*

On April 6, the *Washington Post* published a fierce response written by James Webb, Secretary of the Navy under President Ronald Reagan. A Marine officer in Vietnam, Webb had been awarded the Navy Cross, Silver Star, and two Bronze Star Medals for heroism. After the war he gained recognition as an attorney, author, and lecturer.

"Viet Vets Didn't Kill Babies, and They Aren't Suicidal," read the headline. Webb ripped the study apart, pointing out that the research failed to identify any of those studied—men born from 1950 to 1953, who died in California and Pennsylvania between 1974 and 1983—as either veterans or nonveterans. They were "draft eligibles" or "draft exempts."

"It ignored the fact that very few of these men would have served in Vietnam," Webb said. Even if someone was "draft eligible," that was no guarantee he would actually pass the physical exam, be inducted, finish basic training, then be assigned a combat job in Vietnam.[498]

The "experiment" was hardly "scientific," but Webb's dissection of the seriously flawed study did not slow down the suicide myth. And neither did a press release by the Vietnam Veterans' Leadership Program, a Washington, D.C.-based organization of prominent Vietnam veterans. They pointed out that the *total* number of suicides for *all men* aged twenty to thirty-four for the decade from 1968 to 1978 does not equal the number of men who died in Vietnam.

The idea of Vietnam veterans' high suicide rates grew so pervasive that in 1988 researchers at the Center for Environmental Health and Injury Control examined various mortality studies of Vietnam veterans and used them to estimate the actual number who had committed suicide since the end of the war. The researchers traced the genesis of the myth that more Vietnam vets had died at their own hands than during the war and its path through the media. They presented their conclusions in a paper given at a meeting of the Society for Epidemiologic Research in June 1988.[499]

The authors said that reports of large numbers of suicides among Vietnam veterans first began to appear in 1980. They cited *Disabled*

American Veterans, a manual by Jim Goodwin on the treatment of posttraumatic stress disorder that included the statement that more Vietnam combat veterans had committed suicide since the war than were killed in Vietnam. That was followed in 1981 by a story in the *Seattle Times*. Reporter R. Anderson wrote that since their return from Vietnam "more than fifty thousand veterans had committed suicide."

A story in *Discover* magazine in June 1985 pegged the suicide toll at fifty-eight thousand. The next year brought *Facing the Wall*, by Duncan Spencer, which pushed the suicide figure up to sixty thousand or more, a number repeated in the 1987 book *Unwinding the Vietnam War*, edited by Reese Williams.

During a *60 Minutes* segment called "Vietnam 101," aired on October 4, 1987, a lecturer in a college history course on the war asserted that more than one hundred thousand Vietnam veterans had committed suicide. That was followed in 1988 by "The Wall Within," in which Rather contended that between twenty-six thousand and one hundred thousand suicides had occurred among Vietnam veterans, "depending on what reputable source you believe."

But the paper by the researchers at the Center for Environmental and Injury Control contended that despite wide dissemination through the news media, the reports on the high rate of Vietnam veteran suicides were not based on data from actual records of mortality among Vietnam veterans.

"If claims that fifty thousand Vietnam veterans had committed suicide were accurate, then 101,718 suicides would have occurred among other men in the [Vietnam veterans birth cohort]. By implication, the risk of suicide for Vietnam veterans during the period 1966–1985 would have been 6.6 times the risk encountered by the peers in the general U.S. population.

"Our estimates indicate that fewer than nine thousand suicides occurred among all Vietnam veterans at a time when there were claims of at least five times as many such deaths. We found no evidence to confirm the large numbers of suicides that have been reported in the print and broadcast media," the authors concluded.[500]

Veterans from World War II are more than three times as likely to commit suicide as Vietnam veterans. Americans sixty-five and older make up only 13 percent of the population but account for about 20 percent of all suicides. Figures from the National Center for Health Statistics released in the early 1990s showed that the suicide rate for men more than sixty-five, the group at highest risk for suicide, was 41 deaths per 100,000. That's far more than the next highest risk group, 25.1 per 100,000 for men from age 25-44. Neither group includes most Vietnam vets, who by 1994 were 40 to 55 years old.[501] (I estimate that Vietnam veterans' suicide rate falls between 12 to 14 per 100,000, based on the Centers for Disease Control study.)

The ever-ballooning false statistics came from a handful of studies on mortality and from a vigorous lobby attempting to obtain funding for veterans' treatment programs, leaping on data that seemed to prove their contentions without examining the numbers too closely.

The Vietnam Experience Study by the Centers for Disease Control compared the health of 9,324 Vietnam veterans to 8,989 non-Vietnam veterans thirteen years after the war. The research revealed that during the first five years after they served in the war, Vietnam veterans had a suicide rate slightly higher than non-Vietnam veterans. But the increase was considered statistically "nonsignificant." The numbers of suicides were few, and because of possible inaccuracies in reporting suicide, the category had been broadened to include accidental poisonings and ill-defined or unknown causes of death. During the succeeding years, there was virtually no difference between the two groups. (Although ironically, over time, both groups of veterans had a *lower* mortality rate than nonveterans, logical because many with serious health or mental problems are not accepted for military service.)[502]

In the largest study to look at suicide among Vietnam veterans to date, investigators for the Department of Veterans' Affairs examined the causes of death of twenty-four thousand U.S. Army and Marine Corps Vietnam veterans. The "Mortality Study of Vietnam War Veterans," reported in the May 1988 *Journal of Occupational Medicine,* compared records of 24,235 U.S. Army and Marine Corps Vietnam veterans with those of 26,685 non-Vietnam veterans.

Potential study subjects were veterans reported to have died as of July 1, 1982. The veterans were randomly selected from the VA Beneficiary Identification and Record Location System (BIRLS). A study by the National Academy of Sciences indicated that the names of at least 94 percent of all deceased Vietnam-era veterans identified through independent means are in BIRLS.

Military service information was obtained from personnel records and the cause of death from death certificates. The study was restricted to ground troops who served in the U.S. Army or Marine Corps from July 4, 1965, to March 1, 1973. (More than 80 percent of those who served in Vietnam were ground troops.)

The military personnel records for 75,617 potential study subjects were requested from the NPRC in St. Louis; 22,332 veterans were found ineligible. The final sample consisted of 52,253 men who died between July 4, 1965, and July 1, 1982, or approximately one third of all deaths that had occurred among Vietnam veterans who had served in the U.S. Army or Marine Corps.

Not only did the researchers find that suicides are not elevated among Vietnam veterans, they also found a 7 percent *lower* risk of suicide among Vietnam veterans than among veterans who served elsewhere during the war. Although researchers agreed that suicides tend to be underreported on death certificates, nothing indicated that they are underreported for Vietnam veterans but not for non-Vietnam vets.

For a 1990 study, researchers at the Washington, D.C., VAMC teamed up with the Los Angeles County Medical Examiner/Coroner's office and attempted to compare the risk for suicide between Vietnam veterans exposed to combat and those who were not exposed. The object was to test the idea that the symptoms of PTSD suggest that those who experienced combat are more likely to kill themselves.

Using the files developed in the Vietnam Veterans' Mortality Study, the authors examined the military duties of thirty-eight genuine Vietnam veterans who committed suicide and compared them to the duties of forty-six Vietnam veterans who died in motor vehicle accidents. They examined toxicology reports, police reports, and suicide notes. Using military occupational specialty codes and interviews with relatives, they attempted to assess the soldier's level of exposure to combat.

The findings: Those who served in combat-related jobs were not more likely to commit suicide than those who did not, and the psychological profile of the Vietnam veteran who commits suicide does not vary substantially from that of the non-Vietnam veteran who kills himself.[503]

But the myth persists, resurfacing every time a reporter on deadline searches a database looking for statistics on Vietnam and suicide. Tom Zucco, a writer for the *St. Petersburg Times*, dragged out the inaccurate statistics during the Gulf War. "Since the war ended in 1975, more Vietnam veterans have committed suicide than were killed during the war—at least fifty-eight thousand," Zucco wrote in a 1991 story called "Aftereffects to Touch Soldiers for Long Time."[504]

Even when a real Vietnam veteran kills himself for reasons unrelated to Vietnam, the press cannot resist the temptation of making a connection. Robson James Mabry, a Vietnam veteran in Tampa, Florida, was found at the foot of a Vietnam War memorial, shot in the head and clutching divorce papers. He was wearing a camouflage jacket and his Bronze Star Medal.

Mabry clearly was upset about an upcoming divorce. "You can rule out anything psychological," said a spokesman for a hospital where Mabry had been treated for minor surgery. "He was never treated for posttraumatic stress disorder."

Although there was no evidence of PTSD—no bizarre behavior, no testimonies from friends that Mabry had been haunted by Vietnam, nothing—the reporter quoted an activist who used the erroneous statistics contending that nearly a million Vietnam vets have PTSD.[505]

And the story's headline on the page where the story continued? "Vet may have suffered from postwar stress."

14

An Army on the Streets

Homelessness

THE CAMERA followed as a hulking black man made his unsteady way down West Ninety-sixth Street, an upper middle-class neighborhood in New York City. Larry Hogue grimaced and kicked at cars, tossed garbage, glared at passersby, all the while arguing with an internal tormentor.

"They call him the "Wild Man of West Ninety-sixth Street," intoned narrator Lesley Stahl, reporter for *60 Minutes.*

The story, which first aired December 12, 1992, described how for years Hogue had terrorized this area of the upper west side of Manhattan, his behavior growing ever more bizarre and menacing. He had destroyed property, set fires under cars, and once threatened to roast a woman's dog and eat it. He assaulted a teenage girl, punching her in the stomach, then throwing her in front of an oncoming truck. She survived only because a quick-thinking driver slammed on the brakes in time.

The residents of West Ninety-sixth repeatedly tried to get Hogue off the streets. He broke a stained glass window at the First Church of Christ Scientist, which cost an estimated twenty-two thousand dollars, and caused about eight thousand dollars worth of damage to cars on or near Ninety-sixth Street. Arrested more than thirty times, Hogue had served at least six terms in prison. But laws that protect the mentally ill repeatedly dumped him back into their neighborhood. Diagnosed as a paranoid schizophrenic, Hogue was only dangerous when he used illegal drugs. A few hours or days in detox, and he was no longer a threat—until he hit the streets again. Stahl interviewed police officers and residents who were convinced it was only a matter of time before Hogue killed himself—and maybe someone else.

"He told psychiatrists that his mental problems started after he was hit in the head by a propeller blade while serving in Vietnam," Stahl said. "Every month, he gets three thousand dollars in veterans' benefits, which he picks up at a local bank." That's an income of thirty-six thousand dollars a year, but Hogue was often homeless because he spent his money on cocaine and alcohol.[506]

The conclusion: Because of his "violent outrages," Vietnam vet Larry Hogue was a walking "time bomb."

Before Hogue's saga was picked up by 60 Minutes, the story first appeared in a small community weekly, the Manhattan Spirit. The sordid tale was then seized on by The New York Times and the Wall Street Journal. The papers described him as a Vietnam veteran who suffered "flashbacks" prompted by exposure to the toxic chemical Agent Orange and a head injury while in the Navy.[507]

The epitome of a pervasive image of Vietnam veterans, Larry Hogue was homeless, drug-addicted, alcoholic, and unemployed. Menacing and unpredictable, probably suffering from PTSD, Hogue did and saw things in the war that made it impossible for him to hold a job. Inevitably, he turned to alcohol and drugs to numb the memories.

Of all the mental images of Vietnam veterans in the American psyche, the homeless vet prevails because it is so frequently reinforced. Everybody who lives in a large city has seen bums at street corners holding signs that say something like "Vietnam Vet: Homeless, Please Help." In Missouri, a panhandler became a fixture along the Interstate 270 corridor in north and west St. Louis. He often wore a sign that proclaimed "Injured Vietnam Veteran: Will Work for Food."

For years, whenever I visited relatives in Nashville, I noticed a similar man at a corner near the Catholic Cathedral. Husky, unshaven, with dirty blond hair and greasy clothes, he usually held the same sign: "Viet vet. Hungry, homeless. Won't you help? God Bless."

Homelessness among veterans is nothing new. Typically dislocated from hometowns, forever changed by their experiences, some veterans since the Civil War have returned from battle only to end up on the streets. In 1932, an estimated fifteen thousand World War I vets who came to be called the Bonus Army camped out in Washington, D.C. In the midst of the Depression, they were homeless and jobless, and they demanded government help. The bedraggled army proved so embarrassing to President Herbert Hoover that he ordered Gen. Douglas McArthur to use U.S. troops in armored cars to roust them.

But World War II and Korean vets were never associated with homelessness the way Vietnam veterans have been. "Veterans, mainly from the war in Vietnam, in many American cities make up close to 50 percent of all homeless males," wrote author Peter Marin in The World on January 25, 1987.[508] He did not cite the source of his statistics. Neither did writer Laura

Palmer, whose syndicated column *Welcome Home* concentrates on Vietnam veterans. She took on the issue of homelessness in a column which ran February 13, 1989. "There are about 250,000 homeless Vietnam veterans nationwide," said Palmer. If true, that would mean that *almost 8 percent* of those who served in the war were homeless, an astonishingly high figure.[509]

Some have attributed homelessness among Vietnam veterans to economic conditions that are unique to them. "Vietnam veterans are the last trained and often the least qualified, and they're displaced sooner than their nonveteran peers," said Paul Egan of the Vietnam Veterans of America in a *Veteran* magazine story on homelessness in February 1989. (*Veteran* is published and distributed by VVA.) "What are available to these people now are minimum-wage jobs in the service industry."[510]

Vietnam veterans are "particularly vulnerable" to becoming homeless, said Steve Bentley, then chairman of the VVA's committee on PTSD and substance abuse, in the same story. A disproportionate number of people from ghettos and poor regions fought in the war, Bentley told the reporter, and many of them started off at a disadvantage before going into the service. "Many of these soldiers hoped that their military service would teach them marketable job skills, offer education opportunities, and boost them out of poverty," he said. But the most significant reason Vietnam vets end up on the streets, according to Bentley and other activists, is not the economy but PTSD, that internal bomb ticking inside all Vietnam vets that one day—for unpredictable reasons—detonates.[511]

"In the eighties, a vast number of Vietnam vets in their middle thirties suddenly broke down [as a result of PTSD] and found themselves on the streets, leaving behind them, in their free-fall into isolated madness, mortgages and jobs and heartbroken families," wrote journalist Paul Solotaroff. His story "Exiles on Main Street," published in *Rolling Stone* magazine June 24, 1993, examined the issue of homelessness, focusing on a shelter in Boston established by Ken Smith, a Vietnam veteran and activist for the homeless.[512]

Smith and other homeless advocates push the idea that hundreds of thousands of Vietnam vets are among the dispossessed who have no place to live, no job, and no hope. Anywhere from two hundred thousand to four hundred thousand Vietnam veterans are homeless at any given time, these advocates say, usually when asking for greater funding for homeless shelters and other programs.

The homelessness rhetoric is further buttressed by stories and photographs in newspapers or television reports that coincide with a "hook" day, like Veterans' Day or the Fourth of July. Over Memorial Day weekend in 1991, a Florida photographer named Lynn Sledki took a photo that was picked up by the Associated Press and carried in newspapers around the country. The poignant picture depicted a man sleeping on a beach in Miami as an American flag fluttered above him. The words "homelessness" and "Vietnam veterans" are scrawled on the flag.

"Vietnam veteran Cecil Dula, forty-one, sleeps on the sand at Miami Beach, Fla., this weekend amid holiday visitors," read the caption in the *Wichita Falls Times,* one of the papers which printed the picture in Texas. "Dula wrote a message defending homeless veterans like himself and recently carried the flag on foot from Pompano Beach, Fla. to Miami Beach."[513]

Washington Post writer Laurie Goodstein went to a homeless shelter for four hundred veterans in Queens to gauge their reaction to the Gulf War. "Half of the shelter's residents served in Vietnam, many in combat," she wrote. "Thirty percent served before or after Vietnam." She trotted out the usual Vietnam stereotypes: The guy at the door singing out "Incoming!" every time the door opened, other men diving under their beds to escape nightmares.[514]

Small mishaps and strange tales of life in the city add to the homeless lore. In April 1989, police officers in Austin, Texas, heard screams for help emanating from a garbage truck stopped at a light about 2:30 A.M. Under six feet of trash, they fished out forty-three-year-old Michael Badial. A homeless alcoholic, Badial apparently had fallen into a Dumpster to fish out some cans while drinking with friends. Badial called the experience "scarier" than his "two combat tours in Vietnam."[515]

Homeless, drug-addicted, alcoholic, unemployed, and unemployable. The image of Vietnam veterans as a major segment of this pathetic population is so pervasive, so thoroughly supported by statistics, so logical, it must be true. Right?

Unless you look a little closer.

The first homeless story I followed up was about Michael Badial, the alcoholic who tumbled into the Dumpster in Austin. Despite an exhaustive search through military records, I could find no evidence that a Michael Badial had ever served in the armed forces, much less Vietnam.

The same was true of Cecil Dula, the homeless man on Miami Beach. I located the photographer who had snapped his picture and explained that Dula was not a Vietnam veteran. "Well, I just took the picture," Sledki said. "He told me he was a vet."

Charles Logan, forty-three, of Ferguson, Missouri, was convicted of robbing a service station in Bridgeton of three hundred dollars in May 1993. According to a story in the *St. Louis Post-Dispatch,* Logan had five prior felony convictions. His familiarity as "injured Vietnam veteran" to motorists along the interstate where he frequently panhandled led to his arrest after police released a composite drawing of the man who held a service station employee at gunpoint.

Logan told police he posed as a Vietnam vet injured by Agent Orange. He admitted he was not a veteran, but he said the ruse was very successful at bringing in donations from sympathetic bypassers. With his substantial earnings, he could afford to stay at a motel for twenty-six dollars a night and buy crack cocaine. "I don't need to work while there are fools out there who will give me money," Logan told police after his arrest.[516]

After the Gulf War had come and gone, I visited Nashville and noticed that the man who always stood near the Catholic Cathedral had changed his sign, presumably to keep up with the times. "Desert Storm Vet. Hungry, Homeless. Won't You Help? God Bless."

Panhandlers' signs and arresting photos of sadsacks who claim to be veterans are one thing. But what about Larry Hogue, the homeless, scary Vietnam veteran whose story appeared in *The New York Times*, the *Wall Street Journal*, the AP, UPI, Reuters, and on *60 Minutes*—all among the world's most prestigious press outlets?

Military records show Larry Hogue joined the Navy in September 1963, and was stationed at Great Lakes, Illinois. Later, he served on the aircraft carrier USS *Lake Champlain* where he suffered an accidental head injury during a training exercise in the Atlantic. He was honorably discharged in March 1964. Hogue's record revealed he never served in Vietnam or its waters.[517]

How did his identification as a Vietnam veteran begin? Apparently the small paper that broke the story identified him as a Vietnam soldier, but then realized its mistake and made a correction in a later edition. But when *The New York Times* reporter repeated the error, other newspapers picked up the mistake and regurgitated it.

New York Times reporter Mary Tabor, who had written several stories about Hogue, told me they were aware of the error; the *Times* was no longer referring to him as a Vietnam veteran. But she was not interested in writing anything further about him. I never saw a *Times* correction.

I started looking for a New York-area reporter who had written about military issues and found Christopher Ruddy, then a writer for a small conservative weekly called *The Guardian*. Ruddy had done stories about the PBS documentary on black U.S. troops who had "liberated" Buchenwald and Dachau concentration camps. The film was based on a book called *Liberators: Fighting on Two Fronts in World War II*. The 761st Armored Battalion had fought well in World War II, more than proving themselves as among America's best fighting men, but the story of them liberating Buchenwald and Dachau was fiction.[518]

On July 23, 1993, *The Guardian* printed Ruddy's story about Hogue headlined "What's the Vietnam Connection?" pointing out the *Times'* mistake in its depiction of him as a Vietnam vet.[519] Columnist Eric Breindel at the *New York Post* picked up the Hogue misidentification story as well. "Tall Tales and Lies about Larry Hogue," headlined his column on August 5.

"Agent Orange? Propeller blade? Who cares?" Breindel wrote. "The point of the media elite is that Larry Hogue's problems were created by a U.S. military misadventure, not by the reckless 'deinstitutionalization' policy foisted on American society by civil libertarians. [That] took mentally ill people out of hospitals—where they belonged and were getting actual help—and threw them into the street. Not a happy fact with which to conjure. Far better to blame Vietnam."[520]

A few weeks later, *60 Minutes* rebroadcast the Hogue piece. Lesley Stahl updated her segment, pointing out that Hogue had been imprisoned and repeating the claim that Hogue suffered his injury in Vietnam.[521] (Surely somebody at *60 Minutes* reads the *New York Post*.) A year later, in July 1994, UPI released another story about Hogue being arrested again and recommitted to a psychiatric hospital after being discovered with crack vials on the upper West Side. Again, Hogue was called a Vietnam veteran.[522]

Over the years, a biased press and thousands of panhandlers, addicts, malingerers, and losers eager to blame their problems on their status as victims of an unjust war have conspired (unwittingly perhaps) to create the national belief that homelessness is widespread among Vietnam veterans.

Few ask the question: Is this really true?

Homeless in America

No social issue defines the 1980s more than homelessness: In the midst of plenty, activists claimed, millions were slipping into poverty so bleak they were literally living on the streets, the hobos of yesteryear now derelicts sleeping on grates, couples sleeping in their cars, whole families living in boxes on downtown city streets.

In their 1982 book *Homelessness in America: A Forced March to Nowhere*, Mitch Snyder and Mary Ellen Hombs estimated that between two and three million people were without homes—one out of every one hundred Americans. Snyder, a homeless man turned activist, did much to put homelessness on the front page of newspapers everywhere when he staged a hunger strike while camped out in front of the White House.[523] (Snyder, who had a criminal record and had abandoned a young wife and family, was *not* a veteran but gave that impression because he habitually wore a faded Army fatigue shirt.)

Three million, four million—statistics and predictions about homelessness fluctuated wildly throughout the decade. Those numbers come from people with agendas.

In 1984, a study by the Department of Housing and Urban Development put the number of the nation's homeless much lower, between 250,000 and 350,000. The Urban Institute four years later concluded that the number of homeless was between 567,000 and 600,000, higher than the HUD study but still significantly less than three million.[524] Not long after that survey, the New York-based Partnership for the Homeless estimated the overall homeless population at two million and rising fast.[525] Who was right?

One of the first attempts to actually count the homeless is chronicled in *Down and Out in America: The Origins of Homelessness*, a 1989 book by Peter H. Rossi.[526] A professor at the University of Massachusetts and author of a study published in 1986, Rossi counted heads of homeless people on the streets in Chicago on two separate nights.

The earlier HUD study had estimated there were nineteen thousand homeless people in Chicago. The count by Rossi and his associates found only twenty-five hundred people in the city's homeless shelters and on the streets. Using those figures, he estimated that the number of homeless in Chicago, and probably around the rest of the country, was probably only one-tenth of HUD's 1984 estimate. That estimate, in turn, was only about one eighth of the "two to three million" figure tossed about by people like Snyder.

During the 1990 census, the federal government attempted to actually count how many people were living on the streets of America on one night. They found 228,621—less than 0.1 percent of the total U.S. population, a figure homeless advocates immediately denounced as "bogus."[527] Mitch Snyder actively opposed the homeless census. His organization planned demonstrations on the night of the count to protest "a politically motivated campaign" to "trivialize the homeless issue."

Maybe he was afraid that empirical data would prove that he had been inflating the numbers for years. Snyder later admitted before his suicide that he plucked the three million figure from thin air after being pressured by journalists to quantify the problem. By then, the issue had settled into bickering over the numbers—statisticians contending that the numbers were much lower, and activists complaining that heartless bean counters were missing large portions of the homeless population.

The Homeless, a 1994 book by sociologist Christopher Jencks, showed how difficult it is to define, much less count, the homeless. What if someone can't afford his own place and is bunking with a relative? What about people who have been evicted, are homeless for a while, then move into another place within a month? He concluded that during any week in March 1990, about three hundred thousand Americans were homeless—meaning they slept either in shelters or in public places. He contended that only one-fifth of the homeless are families with children; the rest are single males.[528]

But the reality never seems to catch up to the rhetoric. In 1994, the federal government designated a massive $1.7 billion plan to eliminate homelessness.

Whatever the true numbers, the issue of homelessness has been used by liberal activists to breathe new life into the political battles of the 1960s, according to a 1993 book called *A Nation in Denial*, by Alice S. Baum and Donald W. Burnes.[529] And veterans' groups have seized on the issue of homelessness as a way to lobby for increasing government funding of veterans' programs. For both groups, Vietnam veterans proved useful tools. The more activists could show that Americans who had served their country were among the down-and-outers, the more they could whip up a level of sympathy among a public wearied by compassion fatigue.

Clearly, many of the homeless were living on the streets because of their own individual failures rather than sheer poverty or lack of low-income housing. Numerous studies reveal that, in general, homelessness involves personal disability. One study in Baltimore indicated about three-quarters of the homeless suffer from mental illness, alcoholism, drug abuse, or some other mental or physical handicap; most possess less than an eighth-grade education and a lack of work history, or are older than sixty-five. Almost half of those studied had a combination of these problems.[530]

In his book, Rossi described how the homeless of today are different from the homeless of fifty years ago. The homeless in the past were older, mostly single white men, often alcoholics, who survived doing day work and living in flophouses and cubicle hotels. Today, most of the homeless are those who have abused drugs and alcohol, or have come into contact with mental health institutions or the criminal justice system. Forty-five percent have criminal records. In other words, many are addicts, criminals, or the mentally ill who have worn out their welcome with family and friends and become homeless when they have no one else to turn to. Marshaling sympathy for people who have ended up on the streets because of a drug or alcohol habit, because they can't follow society's rules, can be difficult.

But Vietnam veterans—well, that's different. The prevailing attitude is that an unjust war ruined these men's lives. It's not their failure, it's PTSD. It's Agent Orange. It's drug and alcoholic addictions brought on by Vietnam trauma. As city dwellers grow weary of putting up with the army of the homeless apparently permanently encamped on their streets, the contention that many are Vietnam veterans injects a note of civic duty and patriotism into the discussion.

The relevant question becomes how many Vietnam vets are really on the streets? Is homelessness really more of a problem for Vietnam veterans than their peers who did not go to Vietnam?

Patriots on the Streets

On "The Wall Within," Dan Rather proclaimed that "one out of three homeless men is a Vietnam vet." His figure was clearly absurd by any massaging of the numbers. Studies by the VA indicate that one-third of homeless men are veterans—veterans of *all* wars, not unreasonable given the fact that about 40 percent of adult males in the general population were veterans in the 1980s. Activists contend that more Vietnam veterans than veterans of World War II, Korea, or peacetime service end up on the streets. But their proof is based on little more than stereotypes. As the VVA's Bentley told *Veteran* magazine: A disproportionate number of people from ghettos and poor regions—those most at risk for homelessness—fought in the war.

But as we pointed out earlier, the Vietnam-era military was *not* disproportionately minority or the poor. And about 80 percent of the troops in Vietnam had a high school diploma or above at the time of their service, which alone makes them less likely to become homeless. (In World War II, only 45 percent held a high school education or higher.)

The median age for the homeless population in one study was twenty-six. Since most Vietnam veterans are now forty-five to fifty-three years old, and fewer than one-tenth of those under thirty are veterans today, it's difficult to imagine how large numbers of Vietnam veterans make up the homeless population.

In one of the few attempts actually to count the number of homeless Vietnam veterans, the state of Missouri convened a distinguished panel to investigate the problem within its borders. After an exhaustive search, the panel concluded that the number of homeless Vietnam vets was too small to warrant a special agency. They did, however, conclude that Vietnam vets had a *higher* employment rate than their peers who didn't serve in the military—making them less likely to be homeless.[531]

Despite the image that Vietnam veterans suffer massive problems of unemployment, they are *more likely* to have a job than other males in the economy, veteran or civilian, according to a 1994 study done by labor economist Sharon Cohany for the Department of Labor. Based on data from the previous year, Cohany's study showed that the national unemployment rate was 6 percent for men eighteen and older. The rate for Vietnam-era veterans was 5.0 percent, but only 3.9 percent for Vietnam vets. An earlier study indicated that the rate was the same for vets who saw or did not see combat. The unemployment rate for all veterans was 4.9 percent.[532] How can a population with such a low unemployment rate spawn high numbers of homeless?

The Homeless Chronically Mentally Ill Program, started in 1987 by the VA, operates in forty-three VA medical centers in twenty-six states. But the program, like the others geared toward the homeless throughout the country, cannot be relied on for accurate measures of the number of Vietnam veterans who are homeless either, for one simple reason.

Nobody checks military records.

Anecdotal Evidence

In the autumn of 1988, after the Texas memorial fund-raising group put the granite tablets with the names of all the state's Vietnam KIAs on display in Dallas, we asked police patrolling Fair Park to include the area in their security patrols. We wanted to make sure the tablets were not chipped or vandalized. One day, I struck up a conversation about Vietnam veterans with two officers walking their beat in the park.

"I'll tell you one thing, almost every wino and homeless guy on the street we pick up is a Vietnam veteran," said one officer, a woman who was in her late twenties. She was deadly serious.

Taken aback, I asked her why she thought they were Vietnam vets. "Well, because they say they are," she said.

"Do you ever check their military records?" I asked.

No, she said, shaking her head. Dallas police routinely check criminal records on homeless people picked up for some wrongdoing but not military records. "But why would someone say he's a Vietnam vet if he's not?" she asked, clearly puzzled.

From the police to homeless shelters to VA hospitals—estimates of homeless Vietnam vets are based on homeless people representing themselves as Vietnam veterans. Reporters doing stories on the homeless listen to their war stories, dutifully write them down, and rarely check military records to verify that they are true. They often identify their subjects only by first names or pseudonyms, making it difficult for others to verify their tales.

A rare exception illustrates my point. In 1993, I received a call from Bill Marvel, a *Dallas Morning News* writer who was working on a story about a homeless man nicknamed Patch, homage to the black eye patch he always wore. Marvel was suspicious because Patch, an alcoholic whose real name was Donald Cederburg, described himself as a former Marine fighter pilot in Vietnam, an airline captain, private aviation instructor, credit investigator, carpenter, cook, and handyman—an impressive list of occupations. Too impressive.

Marvel verified that Cederburg never worked for Northwest Airlines, as he claimed. The reporter wanted to know how to find the man's military record and heard I might be able to help. Because reporters typically can obtain records faster than other researchers, I explained where he could send an FOIA request.

As Marvel suspected, Cederburg's military record revealed that he had been in the Marines, but he never had served in Vietnam or had risen above the rank of lance corporal. He had been discharged after a long series of stays in the hospital.[533] Perhaps Cederburg was an alcoholic before he ever entered the military. But I'm sure shelter workers and homeless advocates all over Dallas believed, before the story ran on May 25, 1993, that poor pathetic Patch had been driven to drink by his experiences in Vietnam. Marvel checked the records because Patch's story seemed particularly hard to accept.[534]

Most other reporters don't seem to have that objectivity. A great example: New laws aimed at getting the homeless off the streets in San Francisco and Berkeley prompted a segment on *Eye to Eye with Connie Chung*, broadcast on April 14, 1994. Two social workers were shown attempting to help a homeless man named Gary Moon, who lived on the streets of Berkeley, find a place to stay at the VA hospital.

The reporter described Moon, a scraggly-looking man who dressed in a camouflage field jacket, hat, and sunglasses, as a "highly decorated Vietnam vet." The social workers took him to several VA facilities, but after putting his name into the computer, employees refused Moon a place to stay—clearly an example of the Department of Veterans Affairs' indifference to the plight of homeless Vietnam vets, the program implied.[535]

Several things about this program infuriated me. One, Moon said he liked living on the streets. He didn't *want* these social workers' help.

Number two: The implication that a VA hospital was a Motel 6.

Number three: How did they know Gary Moon was a "highly decorated Vietnam vet?" Because he told them he was. I could find no military records that indicate Gary Moon ever served in the armed forces.

Do not misunderstand me. Homeless Vietnam veterans—and veterans from World War II, Korea, and Desert Storm—live on America's streets. (In April 1991, a homeless man arrested for sleeping in a city park in San Francisco was discovered to be a deserter from the Coast Guard during the Korean War—AWOL for more than forty years!) Joining the military does not make anyone immune to substance abuse, mental illness, or criminality. But true homelessness, whether of a nonveteran or any veteran, usually is associated with a failed life, not military service.

Another example, from a 1992 issue of *Veteran* magazine: Homeless, living in a Washington, D.C., shelter, veteran Ralph Ray had extensive experience in using computers but refused to take any job paying less than fifty thousand dollars as beneath his dignity.

"Uncle Sam taught me how to get high, how to smoke, how to steal, how to kill and maim, how to have a total disregard for life," said Ralph

Ray, who claimed he was a Marine in Vietnam. But is Ray's fate really the fault of the government? *Veteran* pointed out that he had been dishonorably discharged for running a credit scam after returning from Vietnam but while still in the military.[536] Vietnam taught him to steal? Yeah, right.

Director of the Department of Veterans Affairs, Jesse Brown, has done much to perpetuate the prevailing attitude that large numbers of veterans are homeless. A Vietnam veteran, Brown has long been an activist for the powerful veterans' lobby. He often repeats the unfounded statistic that there are 250,000 homeless Vietnam veterans. In the fight for government funding, the squeaky wheel gets the grease.

In 1993, the VVA launched an initiative called The Homeless Veterans' Task Force to develop a plan of action to address needs of homeless veterans. "Recognizing the unique problems regarding the issue of homelessness among veterans and their families, we will work with federal, state, and local agencies and organizations to implement 'continuum of care' programs to address those unique problems," the proposal said. "Further, given that approximately 30 to 40 percent of all homeless are veterans, VVA insists a fair and equitable share of all private and public resources be devoted to veterans and their families."[537] In other words, "we want more."

Veterans certainly deserve benefits. But the VVA, Brown, and other homeless advocates have contributed to the creation of an image that has now found its way into the movies. The 1993 film *The Saint of Fort Washington* featured actor Danny Glover as a homeless Vietnam veteran. Once middle class, he ends up on the streets after his business fails; he becomes a savvy panhandler.

Ken Smith, founder and director of a homeless shelter for veterans in Boston, has also done much to institutionalize the issue—and has personally profited from it.

I first heard of Smith on a segment of *Geraldo*, which aired May 27, 1988. The show was heavily advertised as featuring homeless Vietnam vets, although only a few of the veterans on the show said they had been in Vietnam.

"We concur that 80 to 90 percent of most Vietnam veterans have reintegrated into society," Smith said. "I just think that the American people were never told that a big percentage of the homeless are veterans, and I think that that's our job here today, to bring that message across to the people who watch this program." At the core of Smith's mission are Vietnam veterans who suffered combat trauma so devastating they end up on the streets.[538]

Over the next few years I saw stories on Smith in *The New York Times*, *Parade* magazine, and *Rolling Stone*. Boyish and intense, Smith has a bullet-headed charm and a no-nonsense approach to getting the homeless off the streets: detox, clean up your act, follow the rules, and find a job. His results were admirable.

But after years of researching Vietnam veterans, I already knew that Vietnam vets are not over-represented among the homeless. I couldn't help thinking, *Here is a guy who has formalized the idea that there are thousands of Vietnam vets on the streets, and he has been anointed to save them, if only we give him taxpayers' money.* I did not have any reason to doubt Smith's sincerity, but I felt strongly that he was reinforcing a negative image that hurts all Vietnam vets.

His clout continued to grow. His shelter was designated a "Point of Light" by President George Bush in 1990. Smith spoke at the Republican National Convention two years later, with veterans from the shelter leading delegates in the Pledge of Allegiance at the opening ceremonies, as they did at the Democratic National Convention.

And in late 1994, Smith led a contingent to Washington, D.C., to lobby for more funding to help homeless vets. By that time, Smith's organization had received millions of dollars in federal grants and had enlisted the social elite of Boston, including the Kennedys, to further his cause. In the spring of 1995, his story appeared in *The House of Purple Hearts*, a book by Paul Solotaroff that all but anointed Smith for sainthood.[539]

Smith's history illustrates perfectly the mixture of self-interest, do-goodism, and outright lies at the heart of the homeless Vietnam vet issue.

Saint Smith

From the moment Ken Smith hit Vietnam, he descended into a hell of gore, drugs and betrayal. A "hot-burning" teenager from Rhode Island, dedicated to rolling joints and talking parochial school girls out of their panties, Smith enlisted in February 1971, so patriotic he rejected "an automatic exemption" as the only son in his family.[540]

Smith told Solotaroff he trained as a combat medic and was assigned to a light infantry brigade in I Corps, "where the action was as fierce and breathless as the weather." He was made a squad leader and for weeks after arriving in Vietnam, Smith and his unit were sent out on ambushes, essentially as bait to draw fire from the NVA, who would then be battered by American artillery. In one operation, Smith said, he was hit by a piece of shrapnel in the leg.

"Naturally, of course, none of us got a Purple Heart for it," Smith said. "More than half the crap that went down in combat was never recorded—and, over and over, the VAs used that trick to deny benefits to these guys."

Smith and his crew endured a ten-day "mind-fuck" in the bush, fragged and outfoxed by a ghost contingent of the Cong. Then Smith and the other men of Delta Company, carried into a supposedly easy mission by a handful of choppers accompanied by heavily armed Cobras, blundered into an attack on VC, a frenzy in which they destroyed everything in sight, including little children.

Medic Smith reacted in horror and raced around to save the twenty-five children caught in the gunfire, "performing heroic medicine, clamping arterial gushers with one hand and tying off gunshot trauma with the other." Smith and his squad were left to bag up the bodies, loading them into a Chinook. "From that day forth, nothing mattered anymore, nothing lived in his heart but the memory of those kids."

Devastated, Smith, remembering the horror of My Lai, wrote to Ted Kennedy, reporting all the details of what he had seen—leaving out, of course, all of the names. He refused to rat on fellow soldiers, even war criminals.

His contempt for the military and America firmly in place, Smith dabbled in dope and the black market. "Of all the thousand things he abominated about 'Nam, none burned him more than its bristling economy of lies," Solotaroff wrote.

Smith claimed that the most intense period of the war for him occurred in the spring of '72, the famous Easter offensive, with fighting stretching from Da Nang to Dong Ha. His squad was airlifted north to Quang Tri to meet entire North Vietnamese battalions coming across the "Zee" (the demilitarized zone). For three days and three nights, he and his men fought their way from building to building, attempting to take back the airport tower.

On day four, Smith and his squad were in a convoy heading south to Da Nang, amid streams of refugees fleeing the enemy. In all the madness, an American artillery round exploded in the midst of the caravan, spewing shrapnel and body parts, throwing him to the ground. He saw three armored personnel carriers on fire and raced to pull two burning men from the wreckage. All around, men were bleeding and dying—killed by their own side. After the chaos subsided, Smith and his company were assigned the gruesome task of bagging and tagging the bodies.

Two days later, as he dug a trench above the Dong Ha River, a Huey swooped in. Smith's tour was up. He climbed aboard the helicopter and caught another in Quang Tri. Unbathed, still dressed in blood spattered fatigues he had worn for six days, Smith was given a first-class ticket on Pan Am and was soon aboard a plane headed for Oakland, California. During the twenty-two-hour plane ride, he relived all the horror of the Easter Offensive, getting high on "fat blunts of opiated dope."

Back in the United States, Smith started dealing drugs and smuggling families of IRA refugees into America. When those illegal pursuits fell apart, he became a hard-charging, workaholic manager at a chain of steak restaurants. The company rewarded his toil by promoting him to regional vice president. But Smith quit, so "full of poison and hatred" caused by the war that success was "like a shovel in the back of the head."

In Boston, Smith went back to the work he was meant to do since 'Nam —driving an ambulance, addicted to the adrenaline rush of saving lives. "Man, the energy of being first on the scene of an accident, cutting some kid out of a pileup or screaming off with a serious burn victim—*that's* what I'd been missing since the day I left the 'Nam."

But the thrill of driving an ambulance did not ease Smith's nightmares, his terrifying flashbacks to Vietnam. He gobbled speed to cope, working double shifts to escape his internal demons. Then one day, walking along the Charles River, he was hit by the "mother of all flashbacks," remembering kids screaming, the smell of flesh burning, the deafening sound of incoming. He fell to the ground and puked his guts out.

Smith tried to check himself into a VA hospital but was instead given a prescription for Valium and an appointment to see a psychiatrist in three weeks. He found himself at the Brighton Veterans' Center, a community drop-in counseling clinic. Therapy with a group of other combat vets saved his life.

After almost two years of group therapy, Smith hooked up with two other veterans, Peace Foxx and Mark Helberg, and began life anew. He cut back his hours as a medic, took courses to become a nurse, and married.

But about six months after his therapy group broke up, he and Helberg made a pilgrimage to The Wall in Washington, D.C., where they broke down and cried for hours. When all the tears were gone, what they saw was shocking. Thirty or so men, living in makeshift shelters in the park, all wearing the 'Nam look—the jackets, the pins, the patches. Decorated war heroes, they were living like bums.

Outraged, Smith realized he must save his "brothers." Rebuffed by the VA in their efforts to open a shelter for the homeless, Smith and his compadres traveled around the country, developing a database of homeless vets from Detroit to San Diego. By 1989, they could call on hundreds of "Vietnam vets" to demonstrate at the VA or march on the governor's mansion at the drop of a hat, a great maneuver to garner press attention. "Ex-Marines, SEALs, Army Rangers," decorated war vets, eating out of Dumpsters, sleeping with rats, Smith cried. How could America be so cruel to its hometown heroes?

An aide to Congressman Joe Kennedy, a member of the Veteran Affairs Committee, told Smith and crew about the Stuart B. McKinney Act for the Homeless. (In 1990, Joe Kennedy made homeless veterans his priority issue. "Over 50 percent of those adult males that are homeless are not only veterans," Kennedy said, "but half of them are Vietnam veterans." Perhaps he obtained those absurd numbers from Smith!) The regulation allows any abandoned or underutilized government building to be appropriated by nonprofit organizations for use by the homeless.

Smith thought big; he applied to take over a $20 million building, once a VA clinic, in the heart of Boston. On January 2, 1990, he signed a six-month, one-dollar-a-year lease on the property, which became the New England Shelter for Homeless Veterans.

Smith persuaded playwright David Mamet to help the cause by writing a play, then staging a benefit performance with Hollywood luminaries like Al Pacino, Michael J. Fox, Christopher Walken, and Lindsay Crouse. *Sketches of War*, brought in a quarter-million dollars for Smith's cause and firmly established the shelter as a favorite charity of Boston's power players. That was soon followed by a $2.3 million HUD grant to remodel the building, and from there, the money poured in. Pacino even wrote a check for new showers.

As the shelter became a magnet for sparse government funds, it also became a model to be copied in other cities. Smith, with his stories about being a combat medic and a ready pool of "foot soldiers" to put at the beck and call of friendly politicians, evolved into perhaps the leading advocate for homeless veterans in the United States. The core of his constituency? Vietnam vets. Or at least people who claim they are Vietnam vets.

"This ain't my job, it's my mission—a red-hot op to bring 'em all back home," Smith has said. "There's half a million vets out there, what I call our stateside MIAs, most of 'em the sick and wounded from 'Nam, and neither me or Mark or anyone else here is gonna quit until the last one is present and accounted for."

In his book about the homeless, Solotaroff said he was aware that, even though they wear field jackets and tell war stories, some "Vietnam veterans" are pretenders. "Check the discharge papers on all those guys telling war stories, and you'll find a third of them never got within twenty klicks of a firefight, and another third did their entire tour in Dusseldorf or Fort Dix," Solotaroff said. But Solotaroff apparently didn't check Smith's own military record, although the advocate's heroic story anchored his book.

According to his military record, Kenneth Smith, born January 22, 1952, enlisted in the Army in Providence, Rhode Island. (As to Smith's claim that he rejected an automatic exemption for only sons, there was no exemption for that reason during the Vietnam era.) Smith entered basic training in February 1971, and arrived in Vietnam in August 1971, when the decision had already been made to withdraw American troops. Most unit commanders at this time considered their primary job to be to protect their position and their area of operation from any unnecessary casualties. They were not using their troops as "bait" to draw enemy fire.

Burkett's recruit photo, shaved head and all. My mother cried when she saw this one.

Burkett in Officer Candidate School at Aberdeen Proving Ground, Maryland. A bachelor with a convertible and no place to go, but a war.

Burkett learning to drive a tank. Notice how all other vehicles have avoided the area.

Burkett in OCS. They can shave my head, shout at me, control my life, but getting me off a golf course is a different story.

Lt. Burkett at Ft. Hood, Texas field exercises trying to look like he knows what he is doing.

Lt. Burkett teaching the troops at Ft. Hood, Texas to fire a "bazooka." The war effort was in obvious jeopardy.

Often we could not find the enemy, but we wanted to make sure they could find us. Camp Frenzell-Jones, home of the 199th Light Infantry—Vietnam.

Sometimes the war got serious. Lt. Burkett in a Chinook on the way to a 199th fire support base.

Lt. Burkett posing for the folks back home during my stint as a ready reaction rifle platoon leader.

The piece of shrapnel that almost mated with my head

This is not spring break, but Cam Ranh Bay. Not all of the war was hell.

Craig Hansell / U.S. Army Photo

Father Angelo J. Liteky, chaplain of the 199th
Lt. Infantry, was awarded the Medal of Honor
for action on December 6, 1967.

B. G. Burkett, self-proclaimed
winner of the 1968 Saigon Open. I
have played on better courses.

B. G. Burkett home from the war
and ready to make his first million,
or at least eat a hot meal and find a
flush toilet.

President George Bush and Co-Chairman B. G. Burkett at the dedication of the Texas Vietnam Veterans Memorial. It is the only Vietnam memorial dedicated by a U.S. President.

The Texas Vietnam Veterans Memorial dedicated Veterans' Day November 11, 1989.

My parents, Helen and Bernie Burkett, shortly after my father was commissioned an officer during World War II.

Capt. Joseph C. McConnell, the leading jet ace of the Korean War. He became a boyhood idol for me after my father introduced us.

My friend and an American hero, Harry Horton, shortly after he graduated from Officer Candidate School. Harry was posthumously awarded a Silver Star while serving with the 25th Infantry Division in Vietnam.

Col. Francis S. "Gabby" Gabreski, America's highest scoring living ace, is from Oil City, PA, my mother's birthplace. A boyhood hero of mine, I was awestruck when I met him in Dallas a few years ago.

USAF Photo

Col. Bill Daniel, a friend and golfing buddy of my father, is a World War II ace.

A1C John L. Levitow, Loadmaster of an AC-47 gunship, is the only USAF enlisted man to receive the Medal of Honor in the Vietnam War. He is also one of two Jewish serviceman to be so honored.

USAF Photo

Col. Robert Howard, one of the most highly decorated veterans of the Vietnam War. His decorations include the Medal of Honor, the Distinguished Service Cross, the Silver Star and eight Purple Hearts.

Collection of Richie Burns

Green Beret Roy Benavidez went to the aid of his encircled comrades and for his heroics was awarded the Medal of Honor by President Reagan.

Air Force Col. George E. "Bud" Day, a former POW, was awarded the Medal of Honor, the Air Force Cross and two Silver Stars for Vietnam. He was also a pilot in the Korean War, and a Marine in the Pacific during WW II.

USAF Photo

Award winning host of the Wheel of Fortune TV show Pat Sajak, is a Vietnam veteran.

Col. Guion S. Bluford, Jr., America's first black astronaut in space, flew F-4's for the Air Force in Vietnam.

Actor Dennis Franz, three time Emmy winner on the TV show NYPD Blue is a Vietnam veteran.

Gen. Daniel "Chappie" James, Jr., the first black officer to achieve four-star rank, was a combat leader in the Vietnam War.

Charles E. "Chuck" Yeager, the first man to fly faster than the speed of sound is a Vietnam veteran who flew B-57's in the war.

USAF Photo

Congressman Sam Johnson (R-TX) is a highly decorated Air Force fighter pilot and a former POW of the Vietnam War.

Roger Staubach, Heisman Trophy winner, two time Super Bowl champion, is also a Navy Vietnam veteran.

Congressman James Walsh
(R-NY) pinning some of the
nation's highest decorations for
valor on phony Vietnam
veteran, Dave Goff. After I
exposed Goff's deception in
Reader's Digest, he was
convicted in Federal Court.

Some claim Jesus L. Garcia is
the most decorated Hispanic
of the Vietnam War. Not if
he takes off the bogus
decorations he is wearing,
including the Distinguished
Service Cross.

Nationally, hundreds of
newspapers depicted Roni
DeJoseph of Brooklyn, NY as
a Marine veteran of Vietnam.
I could find no evidence
DeJoseph served in Vietnam,
or any branch of the U.S.
Armed Services.

TV anchorman Dan Rather as a Marine recruit shortly before the Corps dropped him from their rolls.

A.W. "Bud" Porter, commander of the Port Townsend (WA) American Legion Post claimed to be a Navy Seal who was awarded a Silver Star. Porter's military record revealed he was never a Seal, nor was he awarded a Silver Star.

Bogus Medal of Honor recipient David Wilk addressing an audience at the Dallas VA hospital where he was honored as the keynote speaker.

Stephen T. Banko III, of
Buffalo, NY, displaying his
Vietnam decorations, including
the Distinguished Service
Cross. Many claim Banko is the
most decorated Vietnam
veteran of New York State.
They have been duped. Much
of Banko's heroism has been
manufactured, including
his DSC.

Jack Maslin of Delaware
displaying the medals awarded
for his Vietnam service,
including the Distinguished
Service Cross. He was actually a
clerk who was awarded no
valorous decorations.

Jack Maslin, several years later, as a
member of the Delaware Air National
Guard. Although he is still wearing
bogus medals, he is now considered
one of the most decorated veterans on
the Delaware Guard.

Lt. Cmdr. Larry Sherman Jacobs of Utah, in his official Navy photo, wearing the SEAL Trident, Navy Cross, Silver Star, and other awards from Vietnam. Jacobs, who did not serve in Vietnam, was not a SEAL, nor did he receive decorations for valor.

Frank Dux, whom Jean-Claude Van Damme immortalized in the movie *Bloodsport*, wearing bogus medals.

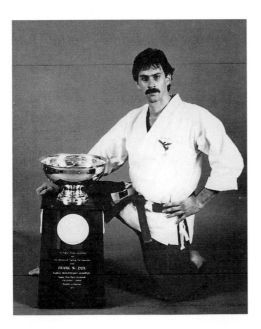

Frank Dux, who duped Judith Regan of ReganBooks into publishing his bogus "true story," *The Secret Man*. The martial arts trophy allegedly won in a "world championship" was made in North Hollywood, near Dux's home.

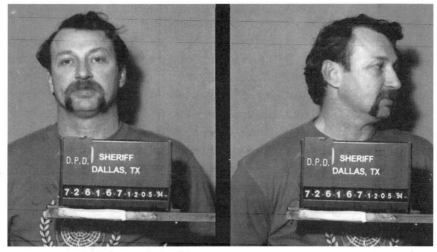

John Woods of Dallas, Texas, Vietnam Veterans of America Chapter President and National Committee Chairman, in an all too familar pose for the Dallas Police.

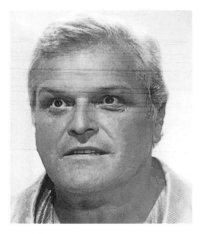

Actor Brian Dennehy has claimed he was wounded in Vietnam while serving there as a Marine. Dennehy's military record shows his only overseas assignment was Okinawa. He was never wounded in combat.

Shelby Stanton, author and historian, in full regalia. Stanton claimed two tours in Vietnam, with accompanying combat exploits. Stanton's military record revealed he never served in Vietnam.

Capt. Lance P. Sijan was posthumously awarded the Medal of Honor for actions while a POW of the North Vietnamese. He is the only Air Force Academy graduate to be so honored.

Capt. Steven L. Bennett was posthumously awarded the Medal of Honor for saving the life of the Marine passenger in his OV-10 when it ditched at sea. The Navy honored Bennett by naming a ship after him, the USS *Steven L. Bennett,* the only USAF pilot to be so acclaimed.

A1C William H. Pitsenbarger elected to stay with the wounded rather than save his own life. He became the first enlisted man to be awarded the Air Force Cross. (posthumously)

Assigned to an infantry company of the 198th Brigade, Smith's job when he first arrived in Vietnam was ammo bearer. In October, his duty assignment changed to rifleman. Smith did not become a squad leader until March 17, 1972—only eleven days before he left Vietnam, when the war was winding down. His unit provided security for Da Nang; it was not engaged in heavy combat.[541]

His record listed a National Defense Service Medal, a Vietnam Service Medal, and the Vietnam Campaign Medal. Despite his lurid tales of going on search-and-destroy missions, the record indicated that Smith has no Combat Infantryman Badge, awarded to those with an infantry MOS who face the enemy in combat. And although he contended he was a combat medic, not a rifleman, and painted vivid pictures of his attempts to save wounded Vietnamese children and soldiers, Smith received no Combat Medic's Badge.

If Smith had been a medic, he would have undergone training at Fort Sam Houston in Texas, where all Army medics are trained. His record listed an assignment to Fort Dix for Advanced Individual Training in infantry, not Fort Sam Houston.

Smith's elaborate narrative of the 1972 Easter Offensive veers into preposterous fantasy. In the last twenty-eight days he was in Vietnam—March 1 through 28—records of I Corps show that only two Army personnel died of any cause in two unrelated incidents.[542] American combat troops, pulling out of Vietnam, were nowhere near the fighting; only U.S. advisors to the ARVN and aircrew were at risk. And Smith rotated back to the states on March 28, 1972—*two days before* the onset of the Easter Offensive, which began at noon on March 30. By April 2, when Smith claimed he was "dug in" at the battle at Dong Ha, going "building to building with 'em, working our way to the tower in one monster firefight," Smith had already been shipped out of Vietnam.

And Smith's tale of being abruptly plucked out of the field by a Huey and sent home in filthy fatigues was absurd. Even if he had been in the field, the military typically pulled people out a month or so before their DEROS. The military bureaucracy needed time for medical checkups and all the paper work to be completed before shipping the soldier home. But I know where Smith found that departure scene. It came straight out of the movie *Platoon*.

When I obtained Smith's record I realized, "Here's a guy who has lied extensively about his background, and who is receiving millions of dollars a year in government money." I began checking further into his history and discovered that Smith had been convicted of a felony.

In 1978, Smith was charged with stealing two thousand dollars in receipts from the steak house he managed in West Springfield. (So it wasn't problems in "handling success" that ended that job.) Less than two months later, authorities in Miami charged Smith with credit card fraud. Both charges were later dropped. But in 1988, Smith pleaded guilty to federal mail fraud for his activities as a manager of a boiler-room operation selling copy machine toner at inflated prices.[543] He was sentenced to five years probation.

This is the man the government, the Kennedys, and other donors entrusted with more than $20 million to run a homeless shelter? Despite all that funding, under the leadership of Smith, who makes sixty-five thousand dollars a year in salary plus a fifteen thousand dollar travel allowance, the center had run almost continuously in the red since its inception. The shelter owed at least four hundred thousand dollars to major vendors, including the local water and sewer company. In the audit period ending June 30, 1994, the shelter's general fund balance had a deficit of $129,083 despite revenues of $4 million. At the same time, the shelter had a negative balance in its checking account of $53,848.[544]

The shelter appeared to be double-dipping. Federal grant money went to pay a sixteen thousand dollar water bill, but when Massachusetts authorities asked for a breakdown of the shelter's expenditures, the shelter included that same water bill in the accounting of state funds. And a food service contract paid a Boston caterer fifty-five thousand dollars for meals on numerous days when a local restaurant was donating meals.[545]

Smith lied about his military record and told absurd stories about his time in Vietnam to build up his reputation as a traumatized vet helping the homeless. Why?

Maybe the answer was in Solotaroff's book.

"Let me tell you a secret about homelessness in America—it's turned into a cozy little business for a lot of people," Smith told Solotaroff. "The money's not bad, especially at the executive level, and nobody expects a goddamn thing from you; just keep *some* of those crazy bastards off the streets at night and maybe mop the shelter out once or twice a week." Of course, he did not mean dedicated people like himself.

Smith and his supporters can point to all the homeless they are getting off the street; up to fifteen hundred a year pass through the shelter. Many undoubtedly go on to find jobs, to remake their lives. But instead of saying that he was a Vietnam vet who saw little combat, who smoked opium, and sucked down speed, who dealt dope and committed fraud—Smith foisted a con job on the American public by claiming that he and most of the homeless vets in the shelter are burned out combat vets haunted by nightmares from Vietnam. I suspect that most of those in the shelter are about as real as the five other "homeless Vietnam vets" whose stories are told by Solotaroff in *The House of Purple Hearts*.

Only one of them was identified by his full name: Richard Morgan Haudel, who maintained he ended up homeless after years of dealing with the anguish lingering from Vietnam. In and out of reform school since age fifteen, Haudel said he had gone to Vietnam in 1966 with the 173rd Airborne, III Corps. He disobeyed orders, went AWOL, but was so dedicated in combat that when he returned, his commander put him on point, and he was so heroic he was awarded a Bronze Star Medal and a second Purple Heart with Oak Leaf cluster.

Haudel told Solotaroff that he and his squad destroyed villages because Army intelligence said they were hostile. Six months into his tour, Haudel said his unit murdered an old man in a village, "slaughtering him like a pig because he couldn't tell him where the Cong were."

Finally, Haudel had had enough of the war. He refused to bear arms; he refused to make reveille; he refused to salute.

The military's response was to throw him in a stockade made out of Conex containers, steel boxes used to transport cargo, keeping him sealed up in more than one hundred-degree heat with only a canteen of water. The MPs brought him out only to beat him with hoses. After ten days, they asked Haudel if he had changed his mind about fighting. He said no and requested conscientious objector status. Back to the steel container. This sequence occurred five times, until Haudel fell apart.[546]

Right before they were going to ship him home, Haudel told Solotaroff, he was visited by the brigade command sergeant major, the "highest ranking NCO in the United States." A World War II hero and Medal of Honor recipient, the man sat down with Haudel and talked father-to-son. The sergeant major told him he had the greatest admiration and respect in the world for Haudel's refusal to fight, and if he changed his mind about leaving the Army, he would give him a job driving a Jeep for a colonel. But if he did not change his mind, Haudel would be dishonored, discredited, and discharged. (A senior NCO would be more likely to kick his butt from Da Nang to Saigon.)

But Haudel rebuffed the "bribe." Shipped back to Oakland, he was drummed out of the military for refusing to get a haircut and possession of a joint of marijuana—given a dishonorable discharge, no back combat pay, no rank, no medals.

Solotaroff wrote: "And, in its consummate expression of martial loathing, the Army even contrived to lose his records, effectively telling him and anyone else who asked: Richard Morgan Haudel never happened."

The lament that "the military lost my records" is, as we've noted, a common ploy by fakers and con artists pretending to be veterans. While not commonly known, proof of military service exists in several archives. One of the first administrative duties of the military is to notify the VA that a man has entered the service. If the veteran ever received a dime in pay, payroll rosters show that fact. If he, like all recruits, received inoculations the first day of basic training, it was recorded. If his sergeant hated his guts and filed charges against him for insurrection, or if the veteran was court-martialed for unspeakable war crimes, a record was made of it. Whether Haudel was in the military one day or ten years, he would have a record.

Despite all my efforts, I was unable to find a shred of evidence that Richard Morgan Haudel—"homeless Vietnam veteran"—was ever in the military. I wonder what I would learn about the other homeless vets that Solotaroff has given pseudonyms? But people like Haudel will continue retailing their improbable war stories to gullible writers who will—in spite of the vast amount of evidence to the contrary—in turn perpetuate the myth that hundreds of thousands of Vietnam vets are homeless.

The myth was given new life by the Gulf War. "Like Vietnam veterans, Gulf veterans have high rates of homelessness and joblessness," read the caption of a photo at a homeless shelter. The photo accompanied a story by Eric Schmitt, which ran on May 28, 1995, in *The New York Times*. In the wake of the bombing of the federal building in Oklahoma City, perpetrated by Timothy McVeigh, an Army sergeant in the Gulf War, Schmitt wrote a story regurgitating all the myths about veterans and homelessness. He cited statistics supplied by the National Coalition for Homeless Veterans, an advocacy group, that 271,000 veterans are estimated to be homeless and said that 55 to 60 percent are from the Vietnam era.[547]

The Dallas Morning News ran a series in April 1995 on the twentieth anniversary of the fall of Saigon. In a story about what has happened to Vietnam vets since they returned home, they repeated the same inaccurate statistics. And what was the front-page picture accompanying the story? A homeless man identified as Larry Douglas King, a Marine veteran of the Vietnam War who has panhandled on the streets of San Francisco since 1976. I could find no record that anybody by that name ever served in the U.S. Marine Corps.[548]

The VA now operates ninety centers serving homeless veterans nationwide; federal spending for these facilities grew from $32 million in the early nineties to $75 million in 1996. In other words, the problem is getting bigger, not smaller, even though the number of veterans is shrinking. And, inevitably, these programs use "traumatized" Vietnam vets to gain public support. Although most of these veterans are addicts, citing the horror of war sounds better than saying they ended up on the streets because they guzzled alcohol or shot heroin. And it perpetuates the libel of a generation of veterans.

In November 1996, just in time for Christmas charity giving, the International Union of Gospel Missions released its findings that one of every three homeless men is a veteran. Conducted at 133 shelters nation-wide, the union survey found that 34 percent of the 10,400 men seeking shelter were military veterans. And of course, it was played as a Vietnam War issue.

"The scars of Vietnam still are not fully healed for many veterans," said the Rev. Stephen E. Burger, executive director of the organization. "Large numbers of Vietnam veterans, unable to cope with the posttraumatic stress of their wartime service, continue to come through our doors."[549] The myth of the homeless vet rolls on, recycled by the elite media, with no end in sight.

If PTSD, with its attendant suicide and homelessness, is the root of the "Vietnam veteran's syndrome," then the trunk of the tree is the tragic hero. Just as wannabes go to elaborate lengths to show themselves as vic-tims, they resort to extraordinary measures to prove they are heroes, awarding themselves medals given by the military to recognize bravery in combat, decorations men have paid for with their lives.

That fuels what could be called—instead of the House of Purple Hearts—the "Flea Market" of Purple Hearts.

PART III

Stolen Valor

15

The Purple Heart Flea Market

IN 1987, TRUCK DRIVER Gary Cartwright of Chicago crashed his eighteen-wheeler into a bridge abutment, suffering serious injuries. Claiming the wreck occurred because the tires were defective, Cartwright sued Goodyear Tire Company. At trial, in addition to testimony about tire defects, truck speed, and skid marks, the plaintiff's attorney led his client through a recital of his life history in order to show the jury Cartwright's sterling character and how badly the crash had damaged him. Cartwright testified that his military background included counterinsurgency and "black-ops" training, followed by a tour in Southeast Asia. The jury was given the impression that Cartwright was a genuine war hero who risked his life for America on clandestine operations so secret they were still classified nearly twenty years later. The jury returned a verdict awarding Cartwright $9 million and his wife an additional $2 million for loss of consortium.

Lawyers for Goodyear believed the verdict was exorbitantly inflated because the jury was moved by Cartwright's tales of perilous war experiences. When Goodyear's insurance company decided to appeal the verdict, they brought in an attorney named Frederic Weber, who happened to be a Vietnam veteran. Assured that Cartwright was an authentic hero, the attorney asked about the military decorations Cartwright had received and learned that Cartwright had testified he had turned down the Medal of Honor "because he was just doing his job."[550]

Shocked that someone would turn down such a prestigious award, Weber asked to see the document that backed up Cartwright's incredible claim and was shown a letter purporting to be from "The Department of Awards and Commendations" of Fort Morris, Maryland, signed by a lieutenant general. The letter to "Capt. Gary J. Cartwright," purported to be a description of his awards and decorations. It described him as "Ranger, Counter Terrorist Specialist, Counter Guerrilla Warfare Specialist. Long Range Recon (sic) Patrol, H.A.L.O. Jump Specialist, Expert Sniper Warfare Specialist, Expert Demolition Specialist, Light and Heavy Weapons Specialist, Expert Medic Combat, Radio Operator, Radio Repairman Field, Light Aircraft Pilot." Cartwright, clearly a Special Forces master warrior, "last served with the Delta Force, Fort Bragg" as the "unit team sniper commando."

The letter said that Cartwright had received the Silver Star, Bronze Star Medal with two oak leaf clusters, Purple Heart with oak leaf cluster, Army Commendation Medal, South (sic) Vietnam Service Medal, South (sic) Vietnam Medal of Valor, National Defense Medal, and eleven letters of commendations. It added that Cartwright had been recommended for the Medal of Honor and recommended twice for the Distinguished Service Cross. "Capt. Cartwright submitted letters stating he would not except (sic) them."

Capt. Cartwright, the document said, had been again recommended for the Medal of Honor for action on July 29, 1974. The recommending officer's name was redacted, but in any case he was "K.I.A. two weeks after he submitted this report." Here's the citation for Cartwright's amazing heroism, errors and all:

"Major _____ stated in his report that on 29 July 1974, you [Cartwright] exposed yourself several times to enemy weapons fire. He stated that four times you exposed yourself to rescue wounded personnel from his downed C&C helicopter. In this time you were wounded twice yourself and that you refused medical attention. Plus you killed four enemy personnel in hand to hand combat to keep them from taking _____ prisoner. He then stated that you destroyed the helicopter and took him to safety. You then lead your men in a attack on enemy positions. In which you personally destroyed three bunkers and two mortar teams, plus killed at least thirty enemy personnel. You then saw too the medical care of the wounded and their evacuation. You still refused medical attention till all your men were taken care of, and the rest of your men and you were flown out of the area. Then medical aid was able to be given to you after you had passed out from the lack of blood and your wounds. Your men told the medic who was treating you, if you died, he would too."

The letter concluded by asking the self-effacing Capt. Cartwright that if he didn't want to "except" the Medal of Honor, to write a letter and have a "Notoriety Public" stamp it. "Capt. Cartwright it is hoped that you will except (sic) the award by the Awards and Commendations Staff. Because Capt. Cartwright we feel that you deserve this award for your courage and bravery for what you did that day. You showed the highest degree of a U.S. Army soldier."[551]

Attorney Weber immediately recognized as fraudulent the extraordinary letter, typed in the wrong format and marred by misspellings and grammatical errors. As a former member of an admiral's staff, Weber knew that no such letter came from the office of anyone of flag rank. The attorney immediately contacted the Department of the Army, which confirmed the letter was a fake.[552] There is no Fort Morris, Maryland, nor is there a lieutenant general in charge of such a facility. Then the lawyers obtained Cartwright's official military record. Cartwright had been a clerk-typist who never rose above the rank of private at Fort Bragg and never served overseas.[553]

Confronted with his falsehoods during a second deposition, Cartwright continued to maintain he was involved in "counter-guerrilla activities" in Southeast Asia, but he refused to name the country because the location was still "classified." When asked about the military documents putting him at Fort Bragg, Cartwright testified that was a cover to hide his true assignment, which was top secret. But Cartwright's answers revealed he possessed only superficial knowledge about actual operations in Southeast Asia. And when asked about his awards and decorations, Cartwright claimed that when he left Southeast Asia, he was given a new uniform on which his medals had already been placed.[554] (After his second deposition Cartwright posted a notice at his paint-ball war-game club that he needed to talk to somebody with experience in Green Beret operations during the latter part of the Vietnam War.)

The attorneys for Goodyear filed an appeal. Their logic was simple: If Cartwright had lied about his military background, had he perjured himself on the stand in other ways, by lying about the way the accident had happened? (The case is still pending.)

Cartwright's embellishments and hero letter had helped net him a whopping $11 million. He may have been using that document to impress gullible people for years. But many of those who claim covert or heroic actions in Vietnam present authentic medals and official-looking documents, including DD-214s, to support their claims. Some have license plates on their cars that indicate they are former POWs or recipients of the Purple Heart or Medal of Honor. Others have medals framed and mounted in their offices to impress those who don't realize such things can be purchased at almost any sizable flea market and through collectors catalogs, as can other military paraphernalia and "in-country" mementos.

A cursory look at one of these categories—military license plates—shows how easily these "authenticators" are obtained. From Maine to California, forty-nine states issue personalized military license plates. Some identify the driver as a Vietnam veteran, the recipient of the Purple Heart, a Disabled American Veteran, or a Medal of Honor winner. The plate issued most frequently is the POW plate. (Only Hawaii and the District of Columbia do not issue a POW plate.) In Texas, the fee for some plates is an additional ten dollars; but the extra fee for the Purple Heart and Pearl Harbor plates is only three dollars. And the recipient actually saves money because the much higher motor vehicle registration fee is waived altogether. The only documentation required to receive such a plate is a photocopied DD-214. (Getting such a plate can lead to other little bonuses like free state hunting and fishing licenses and reduced property taxes. In some states, a disabled vet plate gets you handicapped parking, even if the disability is PTSD.)

The easiest way to spot phonies is to look at how many decorations they claim. Many impostors award themselves entirely too many medals and ribbons, some incompatible with their alleged military service—like a Marine boasting a Combat Infantryman Badge. (A Marine receives not a CIB but a Combat Action Ribbon.) And their decorations often seem to multiply over time.

One Vietnam veteran in Texas is an avid volunteer for veterans' causes. He claimed he had been shot in the head in combat, but his military records listed no Purple Heart or wounds. Every time I saw the man, his collar rank insignia escalated. First, he was wearing the chevrons of an E-6, then a first lieutenant, then a captain. The last time I saw him, he was wearing the single silver star of a brigadier general. (According to his record, his actual last rank in the military was an E-4, making him an enlisted man, not an officer, and his "wound" had been a stroke-like brain seizure that resulted in his being medevacked out of Vietnam.)

And an inordinate number of pretenders claim to be members of elite forces: Green Berets, SEALs, CIA, or other intelligence operatives assigned to supposed covert operations like the Phoenix Program. (Myths about the Phoenix Program—which was neither secret nor run by Americans—continue to flourish, despite well-researched books like *Ashes to Ashes*, by Dale Andradé.)[555]

As someone who never displayed his medals and decorations until my sisters sneaked them from a drawer and had them mounted as a Christmas present, it took me a while to realize how easily military awards and decorations can be fabricated, and how often they are used to deceive. Audacious phonies can even fool the military's own record keeping system.

Bits of Cloth and Metal

To paraphrase Napoleon, "Men fight for bits of ribbon and metal. If I had enough bolts of fabric, I could rule Europe."

Military decorations go back eons. Among active-duty military personnel, much depends on maintaining the integrity of medals and decorations, which are often used to determine who gets promoted and who gets choice assignments. Take two equally qualified candidates in line for a promotion. The one who has a superior war record definitely has a leg up.

Gen. George Washington set up America's first formal system of recognizing individual acts of gallantry during the Revolutionary War. He designed an award of purple cloth in the shape of a heart. Washington made the first presentation of the Badge of Military Merit to three soldiers of the Continental Army on August 7, 1782, for "singularly meritorious action." The medal later became known as the Purple Heart, given not for valor but for wounds in combat—the one decoration every sane serviceman tries to avoid.

All military personnel who are wounded or killed by enemy action are eligible for the Purple Heart. Those who are victims of accidents, self-inflicted wounds, or friendly fire are not. Commanders sometimes make exceptions. In 1951, actor James Garner received a Purple Heart after being shot in the buttocks when his unit in Korea was fired on by the pilot of a U.S. jet who thought the Americans were Chinese troops. In a case like that, few commanding officers are going to make the distinction between friendly and enemy fire.

Since Washington's day, medals and decorations have inscribed histories of duty, patriotism, heroism, and sometimes plain luck—both good and bad—across the chests of American men and women who have served their country. When I was growing up on Air Force bases, I could read the story of a man's service in the hieroglyphics of his decorations. While some decorations remain constant throughout wars—such as the Medal of Honor and the Purple Heart—each war also has its own medals, such as the World War II Victory Medal. A recent addition inspired by the bravery of men captured in Vietnam, the POW medal denotes someone captured and held by the enemy. American military personnel may also receive decorations from foreign governments, such as the Belgian Croix de Guerre in World War II.

The Medal of Honor is America's highest decoration for combat valor. Authorized by the president himself, the decoration is given for "conspicuous gallantry and intrepidity at the risk of life, above and beyond the call of duty, in action involving actual conflict with an opposing enemy force." Created for the Civil War, the Medal of Honor has since been awarded to 3,409 U.S. military men. (During World War II, 465 men were presented with the Medal of Honor; in Vietnam, 239 men received the award.) The MOH often comes at a high cost. Two-thirds of them have been awarded posthumously. As of January 1, 1997, there were 170 living Medal of Honor recipients.

For the impossible, one receives the Medal of Honor. For the almost impossible, the Distinguished Service Cross or the Navy and Air Force Crosses. These are indisputable proof that you performed with valor at great risk to yourself. "Sir, I'd rather be a second lieutenant with a DSC than a general without it," said George Patton in 1918. In Vietnam, the Distinguished Service Cross was given out relatively rarely. Only about a thousand of the more than 2.7 million troops who served in the Vietnam War received a DSC.

The DSC requires approval by the soldier's entire chain of command and brings immediate respect among members of the armed forces. Occasionally, a high-ranking officer has received the Distinguished Service Cross for doing an excellent job while in a combat command, but lower-ranking officers and enlisted men have to perform extraordinary heroics in combat to receive this decoration.

Silver Stars are awarded only for actions in combat; most of those who receive a Silver Star suffer wounds in the process. Receiving a Silver Star requires witnesses and significant substantiation of valor. Far more common are Bronze Star Medals; more than one hundred thousand of these medals were awarded in Vietnam. Most were given not for valor but for meritorious service and achievement in the combat zone. (Even I received a Bronze Star Medal for meritorious service!) Some support troops could earn two or three meritorious Bronze Star Medals without ever going on a combat mission if they transferred to other units within the course of their one-year tour.

Recipients of some medals are eligible for other perks. For example, a Medal of Honor recipient receives a small monthly cash bonus and free transportation for life on government planes and ships, if the space is available. If the Medal of Honor recipient's children are qualified, they receive automatic appointments to the military service academies. In their home states, Medal of Honor recipients can apply for special car license plates. When they die, they can be buried at Arlington National Cemetery. Enlisted recipients of the Medal of Honor, the Army Distinguished Service Cross, the Navy Cross, and the Air Force Cross receive a 10 percent increase in retirement pay.

While it has become fashionable in some quarters to wear full-size medals on a fatigue jacket or a suit coat, active duty military officers wear miniature decorations and awards on their mess dress uniforms. President Lyndon Johnson wore an enameled Silver Star Lapel Pin while in the White House. How he "won" the Silver Star generated some controversy.

As a congressman during World War II, Johnson volunteered for the Navy and received a direct commission as an officer. On a fact-finding tour in the Pacific, the congressman from Texas was sitting as a passenger in a transport plane when the aircraft was buzzed by a Japanese Zero. The plane took no hits and doubt later surfaced that the Zero actually shot at the American aircraft. But Congressman Johnson, always looking for a political edge, pressured commanders to award him the Silver Star. Johnson was the only one on board the aircraft that day to receive a valorous decoration. LBJ's Silver Star was real, but the bravery was artificial.

I mention LBJ to show the distinction between sham medals and pretend bravery. Most people in the military know of soldiers who performed heroically but whose courage and sacrifice went unrecognized. I remember as a child reading a story in *Life* magazine in which a former Russian officer, an advisor to the Chinese army during the Korean War, told how a single American GI stalled an entire division of Chinese troops chasing retreating Americans by covering a narrow mountain pass with devastating rifle fire. Perched high on a ledge, the soldier was protected from the Chinese troops' return fire. Ultimately, the Chinese killed him by using artillery to blow down part of the ridge. The unnamed soldier received no medals and died unrecognized by either side, but his actions probably saved thousands of American GIs. Whenever I visit the Tomb of the Unknown Soldier in Arlington, I think of him.

Certified Heroes

In Vietnam from 1962 to 1973, the military officially awarded 220,516 Purple Hearts. According to standing Navy policy, sailors and Marines who received their third Purple Heart could leave the country. But in 1967, the Marines changed that policy because of the resulting increase in self-inflicted superficial wounds, which drained needed manpower, and stopped awarding the medal for a minor wound even if the Marine received medical treatment.

Since the war's end, several thousand belated Purple Hearts have been awarded by the services to Vietnam veterans. Many requests are for injuries that most troops would never have mentioned in Vietnam for fear of being ridiculed by their peers. Those are typically denied, as are requests for Purple Hearts from service personnel who contracted malaria or were severely sunburned.

Other requests for belated Purple Hearts are more creative. More than ten years after the war, an Army medical officer requested a Purple Heart because his hands suffered severe rope burn when he slid down a line from a helicopter to the ground to prepare litters for the wounded to be lifted out. He argued that his hands required medical attention, and if the enemy had not shot the soldiers he was helping, he would not have suffered the painful abrasions. The Army denied his request. The Navy received a late request for a Purple Heart from a Vietnam veteran who contracted a severe case of foot fungus, and another requested the medal for contracting venereal disease from an "enemy agent." The Navy rejected both requests.[556]

How a soldier, sailor, or Marine receives a valorous medal essentially hasn't changed since the Civil War. One way is from the bottom up. For example, a soldier is with a platoon in the field. The North Vietnamese start pouring over his platoon's perimeter. He's screaming orders, dragging wounded, saving people—being your basic hero. The next day an "after-action" report by his commander will describe the soldier's bravery. The other men who saw the events will be motivated to nominate the hero for recognition. The recommendation goes up the chain of command and is either approved or denied. The "top-down" process occurs when higher-ups—the company or battalion commander—nominate him. Aware that something heroic has happened, his superiors interview witnesses and nominate the soldier, sailor, or airman for a medal.

The system is open to a certain amount of back scratching. Say a platoon fights a battle. People fight; some die. The platoon leader wants a Silver Star, and he lets the platoon sergeant know that the way the sergeant can earn his own Bronze Star Medal is to authenticate his superior's heroism. Except for outright fabrication, this is usually not an official cause of concern. Whatever the medal, there has to be a recommendation by the command authority and supporting evidence. The higher the decoration, the more stringent the requirements for supporting documentation.

A certain unified spirit pushes the process forward. Valorous decorations bring honor to the unit. Each unit holds in high esteem its "writer"—the man or woman who crafts documents recommending decorations. Typically, it's somebody in the personnel section, anyone from a creative private to a captain with a master's degree in English, assigned the job because of his writing skills. A well-crafted recommendation for a decoration, including proper grammar, punctuation, and spelling, stands a better chance of being approved than one poorly written. No matter how creative the "writer," there are always gatekeepers, most often lifers who do not want to see the medals system diluted.

For much of the history of the military, the procedure to award medals was manual, not a computerized process. Even now, when computers handle much of the process, it's heavily dependent on honesty. For the clever and committed, the system is easy to manipulate, a reality that often surprises those not familiar with the military.

Prior to World War II, each Distinguished Service Cross actually had a number engraved on the back that could be traced to the recipient. But that was changed because the sheer numbers of DSCs awarded made the numbering system hard to manage. World War II saw massive hordes of troops fighting along broad fronts stretching from the Pacific Islands and the Philippines to Italy and Africa. As medals proliferated, and as the authority to issue them multiplied, the system became harder to regulate. During Vietnam, for example, four different Army commands had the authority to issue the Distinguished Service Cross at varying times.

Many veterans have claimed to be the "most decorated" serviceman of the Vietnam War, meaning they have the largest number of medals. Others have said they were the "most highly decorated," meaning they have the most coveted medals. The military has no scoring system, nor does the armed service validate such a designation.

My research indicates that if there was a "most highly decorated" serviceman during Vietnam, two candidates are George "Bud" Day and Robert L. Howard.

Day, an Air Force colonel, endured a torturous sixty-seven months as a POW after his F-100F was shot down over North Vietnam. Day's decorations include the Medal of Honor, the Air Force Cross, two Silver Stars, the Distinguished Flying Cross, and three Purple Hearts. All of these decorations were awarded in Vietnam, although Day is also a Marine veteran of World War II and an Air Force veteran of the Korean War.[557] Howard, a Green Beret, was awarded the Medal of Honor, the DSC, a Silver Star, a Bronze Star for valor, three Army Commendation Medals for valor, and eight Purple Hearts. Their decorations rival those of Audie Murphy, whose legendary exploits during World War II are well-known.

After the recommendation for a particular decoration has been made, and the witness statements have been taken, the medal endorsement then goes up the chain of command for each level commander's approval. Ultimately, all recommendations for medals require the approval of the commanding general of the division or similar Navy or Air Force echelon. The DSC, Air Force Cross, Navy Cross, and the Medal of Honor have to be reviewed at an even higher command.

James F. Hollingsworth and Thomas H. Tackaberry had been awarded the DSC in previous wars only to each be awarded two more in Vietnam. And they called Vietnam the war without heroes!

The only real confirmation that an Army or Air Force veteran has been awarded any given medal is not his discharge papers or DD-214 but a "general order" attesting to that fact, which is placed in his individual file. No central clearing house exists where all genuine general orders are computer indexed. (The only service to have done that is the Navy.) General orders can be doctored or created from scratch; only those with a working knowledge of the medals system and how general orders are issued can tell a real one from a fake.

After the bravery has been documented, the general order awarding the medal is issued. Typically, most commanders want to make a show of the valor that has occurred in their units, making a presentation of the award and its documentation as soon after the action as possible. During wartime, the commander might visit the hospital once a week with a photographer and a public information officer and personally hand the medals to wounded soldiers in their beds.

Occasionally, a worthy serviceman will be medevacked home before receiving his decoration. The personnel clerk will make a note that the soldier did not physically receive the medal. He might get the decoration within a few days of returning home, or he may not receive it until years later when a congressman or another high-ranking civilian may present the medal to him.

All valorous awards, complete with blank citations to be filled in by the recipients, can be easily obtained by collectors from mail-order catalogues. Federal law used to require that transactions for U.S. medals be in the form of a trade, forcing buyers to include the "trade" of a postage stamp along with the price. Those rules were relaxed in 1993. Now all awards except the Medal of Honor can be bought and sold freely. A full-sized Distinguished Service Cross can be purchased for $125, a Navy Cross for $155, a Silver Star for $47, and a Purple Heart for $44. (In 1995, a wealthy Palm Beach couple provoked the wrath of Florida veterans when they threw a lavish, military-themed birthday party for their six-year-old son, complete with a presentation of a real Purple Heart, bought from a catalog.)[558]

While in recent years there has been much concern over the "inflation" of medals, the Department of Defense has kept a tight rein on the Medal of Honor, which must be approved by the president. A new law has substantially stiffened the legal penalty for fraudulently claiming and wearing the Medal of Honor. But despite its rarity and the extraordinary level of heroism required to receive the Medal of Honor, the nation's highest decoration, is still popular with fakers. It is still possible to obtain the MOH from collectors or at gun shows, flea markets, and estate sales. TV producers for *20/20* for my segment on sham Vietnam veterans bought a Medal of Honor for $350. Because of the widespread sale of counterfeit Medals of Honor, the federal government began an investigation of thirteen companies and individual dealers. In 1996, after an undercover agent bought two illegally-manufactured Medals of Honor from a dealer, a company called H.L.I. Lordship in Long Island, New York, was charged with selling the medals illegally. Executives of Lordship admitted selling three hundred unauthorized Medals of Honor for a total of $22,500 to collectors and memorabilia shops in the early 1990s and agreed to plead guilty to a misdemeanor federal charge.[559]

One of the buyers, Florida resident Jackie Albert Stern, begged a federal judge for forgiveness for buying one of the medals for five hundred dollars in 1986 and posing as a Medal of Honor recipient. Stern, a retired bread-truck driver, admitted he never served a day in combat. "My actions were stupid and pitiful," Stern said. "My intent was personal and selfish. I wanted my children to love and respect me and to believe their father was a hero."[560]

Medals fraud succeeds because skeptics are usually too polite to challenge liars. If a man has the citation and the framed medal on his wall, few dare to question its validity. And many wannabes prop up their image with displays of other items that "prove" they were war heroes: green berets, unit patches, old uniforms, insignia rings for SEALs and Lurps, guns, knives, gear, Montagnard bracelets, dog tags, and other memorabilia, all available through the free market. Ads in military magazines offer the replacement of "lost documents," such as citations for Silver Stars and Purple Hearts, by a graphic artist, complete with a description of the heroic action, ready for mounting and framing.

Trust Me, I'm a War Hero

During his presidency, Ronald Reagan once gave a speech that included a moving story about a posthumous Medal of Honor recipient in World War II, a pilot who went down with his plane after his gunner was trapped and the rest of the crew had bailed out of the aircraft. But the only place this heart-rending act of bravery occurred was in Hollywood, in a movie called *A Wing and a Prayer.*

When it comes to the Medal of Honor, good actors abound, like Guadalupe Gonzales.

When general contractor Gonzales appeared at business meetings in the uniform of an Army brigadier general, combat boots on his feet and Medal of Honor around his neck, corporate executives invariably were impressed. General Gonzales told them he was in the process of retiring from active duty after serving in the military thirty-one years. During those years he had served in Special Forces and as a Ranger in Vietnam, and had received the Medal of Honor, a Silver Star, and three Purple Hearts.

With his retirement coming up, Gonzales established a company called Inca Continental Corp., based in Wanamaker, Indiana. In 1993, Gonzales attended a meeting with execs from Taco Bell and its parent company, PepsiCo Food Systems, in preparation for his bid to install new equipment in company buildings. He won a contract worth nearly $2 million based on his apparent standing as a brigadier general. During the two-year period ending May 1995, PepsiCo paid Inca Continental $1.7 million in construction contracts.

Indiana businessman Allen Kirkendall had been persuaded to go into partnership with Gonzales because of his prestigious military career. But Kirkendall became suspicious that Gonzales was not what he claimed.

Kirkendall sent me a picture of Gonzales in full uniform. He clearly was a phony from the way his various medals, badges, and ribbons were misplaced. Gonzales had not received the Medal of Honor or any of the other medals he claimed. He had not served with Special Forces, or in Vietnam. In fact, Guadalupe Gonzales had never served in the military at all.

Kirkendall broke off his association with Gonzales and called PepsiCo to report that Gonzales was not a general and that they should investigate his credentials. PepsiCo called the Army's Criminal Investigation Division in Laguna Niguel, California, and in 1995 a CID agent began looking into Gonzales' background. The investigator taped a conversation with Gonzales bragging about his military career. After obtaining a warrant to search Gonzales' home, CID officers found an Army dress green uniform with a star on each shoulder and the Medal of Honor ribbon.

In Los Angeles, Gonzales was arrested and charged with two counts of impersonating a brigadier general as a ruse to obtain the $1.7 million contract from PepsiCo. Gonzales apparently had started pretending to be a general a decade earlier. But his deception went far deeper.[561]

"Since his arrest, I have been contacted by a number of people who have alleged to have been deceived, conned, lost money, jobs, and careers [due to Gonzales] over the last decade," Kirkendall wrote in a letter to the court, asking the judge to impose a stiff sentence. "When I have asked why they didn't turn him over to the authorities, all replied they had tried going to the FBI, State Police, and CID, but to no avail. The authorities replied that because of his age and because it was a civil matter it didn't merit further investigation." The case apparently had been assigned earlier to a CID investigator in Indianapolis, but because impersonating a general was only a misdemeanor, they dropped the investigation.[562]

"I feel that unless you are harsh with your sentencing," Kirkendall said, "Gonzales and others like him will continue to dishonor the medals, uniform and the memory of the men and women who have died and served our country."

Gonzales pleaded guilty but did not really admit wrongdoing. He told the court that he had acquired the nickname "General" and over the years had come to live the part. Gonzales could have been sentenced to six years in prison and a five hundred thousand dollar fine. Instead, the judge gave him thirty days in a federal halfway house, 750 hours of community service, a $2,250 fine, and three years probation. Oh, and while he was on probation, the judge ordered, Gonzales must "refrain from dressing like a soldier."

Here Comes the Judge

The gold star-shaped medal hung from a blue star-studded ribbon, carefully framed and displayed on the wall of Circuit Judge Michael O'Brien's office in Kane County, Illinois. A pamphlet in the judge's chambers described how, as a Navy reservist aboard a ship off the coast of Lebanon in 1958, O'Brien received the nation's highest award for valor by staying at his gunner's position and throwing live ammunition overboard after the vessel had taken a hit.

In 1992, Judge O'Brien requested information about special honorary license plates identifying himself as a Medal of Honor recipient. O'Brien submitted documents to the Illinois Department of Veterans' Affairs attesting that he had received the Medal of Honor and asked what additional proof he needed to provide. In response, the director of the Illinois VA asked Harold "Hal" Fritz, a Peoria man who had been awarded the Medal of Honor in 1969 during the Vietnam War, to verify whether O'Brien qualified for the plates.

At the time, there were only 190 living recipients of the Medal of Honor. Fritz looked on the official Medal of Honor list. O'Brien was not one of them. His tale of heroism sounded pretty implausible as well. Lebanon in 1958? Fritz found out that no Medals of Honor had been awarded between 1953 and 1964. Fritz told the director of the Illinois VA that O'Brien was an impostor and heard no more about the case.

But O'Brien's ruse did not unravel publicly until two years later. In October 1994, Fritz heard that "Medal of Honor" recipient Judge Michael O'Brien was scheduled to speak at a veterans' rally for the reelection campaign of Illinois Gov. Jim Edgar. Angry that O'Brien "had prostituted the whole award system," Fritz called the Department of Defense and the Department of the Navy and reported O'Brien's fraud. Confronted, the fifty-seven-year-old judge admitted the medal was counterfeit. O'Brien had been in the Naval Reserves for eight years, but there was no combat, no heroism.[563]

"I was trying to live out a fantasy," O'Brien said. He blamed his deception on an "emotional breakdown." But later, in a letter of apology to all the judges of the Sixteenth Judicial Circuit, O'Brien attributed the lie to alcoholism. O'Brien claimed that in 1992, as a recovering alcoholic, he suffered a relapse that sent him to the hospital. "During this time, for reasons not fully understood by me, I requested special plates from the Secretary of State. The papers that I submitted on behalf of the application were prepared many years ago as a fantasy when I was an active alcoholic in private practice."[564]

O'Brien contended that during the week he asked about the special Medal of Honor license plates, he did some other "strange things," such as sending a letter to the Illinois Supreme Court and asking for autographs of the justices. After going into the hospital, O'Brien said, he was diagnosed as suffering from "posttraumatic stress syndrome." Exactly what caused his alleged PTSD was not defined.

The judge staunchly maintained that he had never spoken publicly about the medal or boasted of the decoration in campaign literature. But for fifteen years, O'Brien certainly had led others to believe that he was a hero. "I've seen enough and heard enough that I believe it," another circuit judge told a news reporter. "I have always understood (O'Brien) won the Medal of Honor."

After being caught, O'Brien returned not one but two bogus Medals of Honor to the Medal of Honor Society in North Carolina. One even had been engraved with O'Brien's name on the back. The Department of the Navy announced that it planned to seek criminal charges against the judge. O'Brien clung to his defense that "alcohol" made him pose as a combat hero. "I wonder how that excuse held up in his courtroom for bad check writers, auto thieves, child and wife abusers," one commentator wrote wryly.

Although exposed as a liar, O'Brien refused to resign from office. When O'Brien announced his intention to run for another term as judge in 1996, he was told by the Kane County Republican Party that he could not run under the party banner, and if he ran as a member of another party, the party intended to "blow him out of the water." O'Brien finally resigned rather than face possible criminal charges of official misconduct for using Sixteenth Judicial Circuit Court stationery to apply for special Medal of Honor license plates.[565]

In 1994, Andy Rooney did a story on *60 Minutes* exposing a handful of wannabes who claimed they were Medal of Honor recipients. One of those Rooney exposed was Alan Lorinth, who said he had received a Medal of Honor after a stint as a POW in Vietnam. He had not been a POW nor had he received the medal. Lorinth had been a driver for a chaplain in Vietnam. Another impostor, John Michael Ianone, a Pittsburgh oil man, contended he had received the Medal of Honor in Vietnam. Ianone had never served in the military.

And then there was Lucille Hewitt, a sweet little old lady and self-proclaimed Medal of Honor recipient from World War II. Asked to lead a parade in Kern, California, Hewitt backed out when she heard Rooney wanted to ask her about the medal. (Only one woman has received the Medal of Honor: Mary Walker, a civilian doctor in the Civil War.)

In the last thirty-five years, Mitchell Paige, a Medal of Honor recipient and member of the Legion of Valor, has discovered well over one thousand Medal of Honor pretend "heroes" who somehow obtained the actual medal. He believes that at least three thousand others exist. One reason: Very few American citizens can name even one or two actual recipients (and today probably half of those would name the fictitious character Forrest Gump instead of real heroes Audie Murphy and Fred Zabitosky).

The VA itself is so indifferent to this fraud that phonies can gain legitimacy by their association with this government agency. David Wilk of Dallas, who claimed that he was awarded the Medal of Honor as a Green Beret in Vietnam during 1969–1972, wore the distinctive star-shaped medal and blue ribbon around his neck as he gave the keynote speech at the Dallas Veterans Affairs Medical Research Day program in 1996. "This is given to me for all those who didn't get it," Wilk said modestly.

David Wilk has much to be modest about. His military record shows that he enlisted in 1972, was not a Green Beret, and his only overseas assignment was as a truck driver in Germany.[566] And the name of David Wilk is not on the list of the men who received the Medal of Honor in Vietnam—a list made even shorter by the fact that 148 of them received the nation's highest military honor posthumously. (See Appendix I.)

Like Judge O'Brien, the motivation of most Medal of Honor pretenders seems to be that they are living out their fantasies. The motivations of others who go to elaborate lengths to award themselves the country's highest medals and decorations are often more complicated.

16

Fudging the Records

OVER AND OVER, I have been asked how phonies are able to fool so many people, including government officials and experienced journalists. Not content just to tell war stories, many wannabes authenticate their heroism by hanging forged certificates on their walls, wearing and displaying medals and ribbons they never earned, buying fake ID cards, and doctoring DD-214s. Counterfeit records can be used to totally deceive not only trusting friends and family but also lawyers, judges, government bureaucrats, even military personnel.

But some dishonest veterans go even farther, fraudulently altering their military records at various levels within the government archive system. Personnel clerks can be bribed to insert counterfeit documents into files. In fact, some impostors actually are former clerks who doctored their own records. Anybody with a tenth-grade education and the desire to polish his credentials as a warrior can circumvent the rules.

When a serviceman leaves his unit, he's given a large sealed manila envelope containing his personnel file and any general orders issuing awards and service badges, and told to deliver that file intact to his new unit. Breaking the envelope's seal is a court-martial offense. But a determined wannabe can steam the flap open or buy a replacement envelope and slip in altered documents making himself a war hero.

In the late 1980s, while compiling the list of KIAs for the Texas Memorial, I needed to know which Texans had been posthumously awarded the Distinguished Service Cross, but the Army could not tell me. The Army had no centralized list of all the DSC recipients. Army medals experts guessed that about 850 men had received the award during the Vietnam War.

One Army official mentioned that publisher Paul D. Stevens had done in-depth research in Army archives to compile a list of DSC recipients for a book. Stevens, who had already published books on the Navy Cross and the Medal of Honor, wasn't finished with his research, but he was far along in compiling a list of DSC recipients. He sent me copies of about 450 general orders awarding the DSC in Vietnam.

General orders are the official documents which award various military awards and decorations. From the ones Stevens sent me, I was able to pull out the posthumous awards and match them to my Texas casualty list. (At least fifteen Texans had posthumously received the DSC during the Vietnam War.)

Col. Al Gleim, a retired Army officer now deceased who was considered one of the nation's experts on military awards, had just started researching Distinguished Service Crosses awarded during Vietnam, painstakingly examining unit histories, trying to ferret out individual recipients, cross-checking them against general orders.

All general orders issued by a unit have three levels of identification that can be used to detect fakes: the unit issuing the decoration, the date the general order is issued, and the general order number. One simple way to check a general order's authenticity is to review the calendar. Typically, general orders were not issued on Sundays, even in Vietnam. And some decorations are only authorized at certain levels of command. A Distinguished Service Cross cannot be issued by a division; the DSC must be issued by an Army-level command. (A Silver Star can be issued at the division level.)

If a fabricated general order conforming in appearance to a regulation document is somehow placed in a man's official military file, only rarely will the fraud be caught at any of the soldier's successive units. Most commanders don't know how to cross-reference a general order. Besides, they have much more pressing business. The presumption is honesty and integrity. Who would steal the valor of men who fought and often died for those medals?

Men like Boyer Westover, Jack Maslin, Benjamin Ricciardi, and Larry Jacobs.

Dear LBJ

"Dear President Johnson," wrote Mrs. Kenneth Westover Wills of Lower Yoder Township, PA, in 1969. She asked LBJ to expedite the award of the Medal of Honor to her beloved son Sgt. Boyer Westover.

Mrs. Wills enclosed a clipping from her hometown newspaper describing how young Westover had received numerous awards for heroism in Vietnam, including the Distinguished Service Cross, two Silver

Stars, two Bronze Star Medals for valor, two Air Medals for participating in more than fifty airmobile combat assaults, three Purple Hearts, the Army Commendation Medal, and the Vietnamese Cross of Gallantry with Palm. Courageous Westover also had been recommended for the Medal of Honor. If he received the MOH, Sgt. Westover would hold every major valorous award that could be bestowed by the United States Army for action in combat.

The clipping described how the twenty-one-year-old Westover received the DSC for action on April 28, 1967. The news account, drawn from a press release, described the young Westover's awesome tenacity, skill, and courage in the face of certain death.

Westover had been a member of a fourteen-man patrol with the 2nd Battalion, 27th Infantry "Wolfhounds" of the 25th Infantry Division. During a night ambush operation in the Ho Bo Woods of Vietnam, a reinforced company of Viet Cong attacked.

"The patrol leader and his radio operator were killed almost immediately, and the small force was rapidly overcome by panic," the release said. "Although not the senior man, Sgt. Westover assumed command without hesitation and quickly organized his men into an effective fighting unit.

"Maneuvering the platoon to a nearby bomb crater, Sgt. Westover established a perimeter and then repeatedly exposed himself to hostile fire as he crawled from position to position, redistributing ammunition, and encouraging his men.

"Realizing the need for artillery support, he left his position of relative safety and ran through a murderous hail of fire to the point where the radio operator had fallen. Finding two VC trying to disentangle the radio from the dead man's body, Sgt. Westover killed them both with his shotgun.

"Grabbing the radio and returning to his platoon's position, he was engaged by three more VC. Westover killed the enemy, but not before he had been shot five times in the legs," the news release said.

Despite his wounds, Westover used the radio to direct devastating artillery fire into the enemy positions until the radio was destroyed by a grenade. After a nine-hour break in the fighting, the perimeter's weakened flank was penetrated by an enemy assault. Roused from semiconsciousness, Westover struggled valiantly to the center of the attack. "While fully exposing himself to enemy fire, he succeeded in killing at least twelve VC, and almost single-handedly blunted the assault."

With fewer than a third of his men alive, Westover clung to consciousness throughout the night despite a torrential monsoon and constant attacks by the VC. "I was so exhausted," the news release quoted Westover as saying, "that I couldn't see more than a few feet. All my friends were dead or dying, but I kept telling myself that I was too damn proud to die in this mudhole. That single thought kept me from blacking out, and as long as I was conscious, I was determined to stay alive."

Only four men of the original patrol were still alive when they were finally rescued by an armored relief element; two died before reaching the hospital. Searchers found sixty-eight VC bodies, and evidence that more had been dragged away. The next day, in a Saigon hospital, Westover was presented the Silver Star for heroism by Gen. William Westmoreland. A DSC was later approved for the same action. The account said that Westover was recommended for a direct commission to lieutenant, a promotion the modest Westover refused to accept.

After seven months in the hospital, Westover returned to combat duty, assigned to a long-range patrol detachment of the 173rd Airborne, assuming command of a five-man reconnaissance team. "He led his team on thirty-one missions into enemy territory and compiled a fantastic record of enemy kills before again entering the hospital for a series of operations on his legs."

When he left the hospital, with only eighteen days remaining on his tour, Westover decided to take out one last patrol on a "top secret mission." His "conspicuous gallantry" on this mission resulted in his second Silver Star—and the recommendation for the Medal of Honor.

Westover, leading a patrol to rescue a downed pilot, silently entered an enemy camp, eliminated a sentry with a knife, located the wounded captive, and carried him back to the perimeter. Unable to slip the injured man past the guards, Westover entered an NVA bunker, killed two enemy troops in hand-to-hand combat, carried out the pilot, and for an hour directed murderous concentrations of artillery and air strikes into the area.

But as the extraction helicopter made its approach, the team was suddenly taken under heavy automatic weapons fire by a far superior NVA force. Ordering his men to rescue the pilot, Westover and "Pfc. Parker" stayed behind. "With complete disregard for his own life, Sgt. Westover fearlessly stood his ground against an overwhelming number of enemy with no other motive than to preserve the lives of his men."

After Parker was hit by machine-gun bullets, Westover called in artillery and used the barrage as a cover to reach the wounded man. "Treating him with a superior knowledge of first aid, Sgt. Westover then used his own body as a shield to drag the man through a withering rain of fire to a deserted enemy bunker, killing ten NVA before running out of ammunition."

Grabbing more ammo, Westover continued to kill enemy soldiers until he was wounded by a series of grenade explosions. Bleeding profusely in several places and in severe pain, he fired into the charging enemy until an allied relief force arrived in the area. "Total body count for the operation was set at 172. Of these, Sgt. Westover personally accounted for at least thirty-one of the confirmed kills," the release said.

The sergeant's humble comment: "It's not hard to be a hero when the only alternative is having your ears dangling from Chuck's [the VC] belt, or watching your best friends get blown apart. In this case we had even more at stake. That pilot would have been in Hanoi within a week, condemned to stare at four walls till his brain turned to mush. I had the power to abandon the mission—I declined. As far as I'm concerned, there was no alternative."

Westover returned home to much acclaim. But his mother was concerned because he had not yet received his well-deserved Medal of Honor. "My son has no idea that I would write to you, but as his mother, I think he is an example of the fine young men that America is still producing in spite of the hippies and draft card burners," Mrs. Wills said to LBJ in her letter. With the long, laudatory story that had appeared in the Johnstown *Tribune-Democrat*, she enclosed a photo of Westover from the front page of *Stars and Stripes*.

A White House inquiry was launched. Maj. Gen. Kenneth Wickham had the unpleasant task of writing back to Mrs. Wills. "After a thorough investigation, including an inquiry to the commanding general, United States Army Vietnam, no evidence could be found that Boyer has been recommended for award of the Medal of Honor," Wickham said.[567]

What the letter did not say is that the investigation revealed that despite the general orders in Westover's file awarding him multiple valorous decorations, the only personal award he was actually entitled to was the Army Commendation Medal. Westover was not a combat soldier, but he was an enlisted man in the Public Information Office of the 173rd Airborne Brigade. A PIO lieutenant described Westover as a writer and photographer for his entire tour in Vietnam. Westover had never accompanied a patrol on missions, and the only time he had received medical attention was for an upset stomach.

How did Westover pull off this elaborate fraud? Public information personnel typically gather general orders after awards were issued to help them write news releases for the soldiers' hometown papers. "All indications are that Sgt. Westover, being knowledgeable of award order formats and having access to PIO releases on exploits of other personnel, formulated episodes with himself as the main character and then published appropriate award orders for these actions showing himself as the recipient of the award," the investigative report said. Westover had dropped himself into several actual experiences of the Lurps of the 173rd Airborne Brigade.

If the hoax ended there, Westover's vivid imagination and creative attempt at fashioning himself into a hometown hero might elicit little more than a chuckle. But once denied his Medal of Honor, Westover did not give up. In the late eighties, Westover found a job with Sharp and Dunnigan, a publisher in Chico, California, as a researcher for a book on the Distinguished Service Cross. Company president Paul Stevens believed Westover had received the DSC and numerous other decorations. Westover began doing research for the publisher in the Awards and Decorations Office of the Army at the Pentagon.

Westover then used fraudulent credentials to gain admittance to the Legion of Valor. His application passed through their stringent screening process. The group—combat veterans who have received the Medal of Honor, DSC, Navy Cross or Air Force Cross—then elected Westover to their board of directors! The public information clerk finally had become enthroned as an official hero.

The fraud was discovered only when medals expert CWO William Thayer, then principal fraud investigator in the Military Awards Branch of the Army's Personnel Command, became suspicious. Despite being unmasked once, Westover had persisted until he succeeded in deceiving high-level experts on awards and decorations and had been given the stamp of approval by the Legion of Valor. Westover was booted out of his job as well as the Legion of Valor.[568]

Fraud at the National Guard

After the 20/20 broadcast about my work, a member of the Delaware Air National Guard contacted me, expressing suspicions about his unit's own "Vietnam War hero," a man whose uniform was peppered with some of the Army's highest decorations.

Air Force Tech. Sgt. Jack Maslin, an NCO in charge of security air police with the Delaware Air National Guard, had served one tour in the Army during the war. A full-time employee of the National Guard, a military force controlled in peacetime by the state of Delaware under the command of the governor, Maslin was probably its most highly decorated member. He proudly wore the Army Distinguished Service Cross, Silver Star, Bronze Star Medal, Combat Infantryman Badge, and Purple Heart with two oak leaf clusters, all from his year in Vietnam.

I received anonymously in the mail a picture of Maslin wearing numerous full-size medals, including the Distinguished Service Cross. But Sgt. Jack Maslin was not on the list of recipients of the DSC.

His military record confirmed that Maslin was a Vietnam veteran and, on the surface, appeared to support some of his other claims of glory, giving him a Silver Star, Bronze Star Medal, CIB, and a Purple Heart. However, a close analysis of Maslin's record called those and many of his other claims into question. Somehow, documents in Maslin's official file had been significantly altered.[569]

Maslin enlisted in the Army on April 14, 1970, at the age of twenty-three. His record indicated that after initial training, Maslin spent the period from June 19, 1970, to September 1, 1970, at Airborne, Ranger, and Special Forces schools. Training that usually takes up to two years Maslin somehow miraculously completed in just three months. And Maslin's elite combat assignment after completing all these highly competitive schools, grooming him to be a skilled combat soldier with Special Forces? The record indicated Maslin was made a supply clerk at a basic training school at Fort Dix. That raised my eyebrows.

The record of Maslin's time in Vietnam indicated that he yo-yoed from the mundane to the elite. Sent to Southeast Asia in March 1971, Maslin first was assigned to an artillery battery as a supply clerk. A week later, Maslin suddenly leaped into the field as a Lurp with Company P, 75th Infantry "Brigade." (Whoever doctored the record obviously was not aware the 75th Infantry [Rangers] maintained the old designation of regiment, not brigade.)

Three months later, in June 1971, Maslin went back to being a supply sergeant in the artillery battery. But a combat hero such as Sergeant Maslin obviously wasn't content with such an assignment. In September 1971, Maslin served as a Green Beret "rifleman, forward observer" with 5th Special Forces—for a grand total of one month. That assignment is clearly impossible, not only because "rifleman, forward observer" is an incorrect entry for Special Forces, but because 5th Special Forces left Vietnam as a command months earlier, on March 1, 1971. (I doubt Special Forces was turning supply clerks into Green Berets any more than Air Force cooks were suddenly being called on to serve as pilots.) Maslin completed the remainder of his Vietnam tour as a supply sergeant with his old artillery battery—Svc. Battery, 8th Battalion, 4th Artillery, leaving Vietnam in October 1971. But that unit left Vietnam August 31, 1971. Maslin rotated back to the states as a supply sergeant and was discharged in 1972.

What an incredible tour of duty: assigned as a supply clerk three times, with stints as a Lurp and a Green Beret, coming home with a Distinguished Service Cross, a Silver Star, a Bronze Star Medal, and multiple Purple Hearts—all in a seven-month tour. How could Hollywood possibly have chosen Rambo over Sgt. Jack Maslin?

The record was clearly bogus. Maslin's claims to other awards and decorations proved as flimsy as his career as a war hero. His record abbreviated the Silver Star as "SSM," for Silver Star Medal, instead of the proper abbreviation "SS." The block for wounds reads, "Arm Right Arm, Forearm," an improper spelling, calling his Purple Heart into question.

Also in his file was a Special Order supposedly awarding a Bronze Star Medal with V device to Maslin and another man for valor shown while on patrol in Quang Tri Province, RVN.

"Above mentioned soldiers did distinguished (sic) themselves while under fire from a hostile enemy force," the citation read. "Above did, at risk of life, in complete disregard of their own safety, did assault the enemy's automatic weapon position. Completely destroying the enemy's position, killing 4 (four) enemy soldiers. Their action rallied the spirit of their pinned down team members. Thus eliminating the hostile threat. Their action is in keeping of the highest degrees of heroism and are a credit to their unit and their country."

But this document, replete with typos and grammatical mistakes, is clearly fraudulent. For example: Valorous decorations correctly are issued under a "general order," not a "special order." Medals for bravery are given for a specific action on a specific day. Instead of "date of action," Maslin's citation erroneously showed "dates of service," from March 26, 1971 to June 30, 1971. And the order is dated May 26, 1971—a full month *before* June 30, when these courageous actions supposedly occurred. The special order awarding Maslin a Combat Infantryman Badge on June 29, 1971, makes the same mistakes.

Maslin had used the fraudulent military record to curry attention and favor as an employee of the Delaware Air National Guard, in effect becoming the base's resident Vietnam veteran war hero. In 1994, I sent all of this information to Maj. Gen. George Hastings, commander of the Delaware Air National Guard.[570] General Hastings appointed someone to investigate my charges. I was not the first skeptic to call Maslin's "military fruit salad" into question. Five years earlier, a civilian Ranger organization had rejected Maslin's application for membership because it contained material about his accomplishments and recognitions that were suspected to be false. The Rangers made their suspicions known to Maslin's commander.

On September 25, 1989, a Colonel Dugar and Lt. Col. James F. Waehler, staff judge advocate, had brought Maslin in for an interview. According to a memo by Waehler, Maslin was advised by the two that nothing in his record appeared to justify the DSC, Silver Star, or the two oak leaf clusters for the Purple Heart—all of which he was wearing on his uniform. Nor did there appear to be anything in Maslin's record to support his entitlement to wear the Parachutist Badge, the Special Forces "Rocker," the Diving Badge, and a number of other badges on his uniform.

Maslin's explanations for the discrepancies covered all the bases. Maslin complained that he had been engaged in an ongoing battle with the Ranger organization since its founding in 1985 and that "one or more individuals were attempting to get even with him." His military records were in disorder, Maslin maintained in a written response, for a variety of reasons, including all of the following:[571]

1. Because he had been engaged in a number of sensitive missions as a member of Special Forces, Maslin's records did not fully and accurately reflect his military duties.

2. A fire at the Army Personnel Records Center destroyed some of his records.

3. For some bizarre reason, Maslin didn't have a "201 file" (his personnel file) when he left the Army, and he never received his pay for his last six months of service.

4. Maslin left active duty without a lot of friends. He had turned down a job with the military he should have accepted, and he had been advised at the time that he would suffer repercussions because of that. "He believes that some individuals are now attempting to undermine and hurt him because of the enemies he made while in the service."

5. Maslin had suffered several difficult divorces, including a particularly nasty one in 1978. One day Maslin had come to pick up his children only to discover his soon-to-be ex-wife out on the driveway burning his military decorations and records. Maslin was able to rescue only a few of the records from the pyre.

Maslin persisted that he was entitled to every one of the considerable ribbons and badges that he was wearing on his uniform that day. Waehler pointed out to him that fraudulently wearing military decorations was a serious offense, punishable under the Uniform Code of Military Justice. The meeting ended with Maslin promising to make an effort to provide documentation for the ones in question by October 13. Maslin apparently presented documents covering everything but the DSC. Not trained in evaluating military records, the investigators merely ordered Maslin to stop wearing the DSC. He complied and nothing more was done.

All that had happened long before I became involved. Confident that daily duty rosters could place Maslin continuously in his supply clerk's job in Vietnam, I told the general's investigators how to obtain the rosters. But evidently they could not be bothered. Despite all the documentation I supplied that Maslin's record was bogus, making him subject to prosecution for fraudulently wearing military decorations, Hastings merely ordered him not to wear three minor decorations and badges. Revealing the unit's heroic "poster boy" as a charlatan would have embarrassed everyone involved. Even while the investigation was going on, Maslin was chosen to represent the unit in ceremonies. Outrageously, during one such ceremony, when the body of a Vietnam MIA was returned to the Dover, Delaware, mortuary, the wannabe Maslin was designated to present the American flag to the family.

I sent my information to the governor of Delaware and a reporter who covered the National Guard for a local paper. The governor's office's merely accepted Maslin's command's response that the matter had been settled. The reporter said he would look into Maslin's background but seemed reluctant to make waves. Sometimes fakers reach such levels of official acceptance that exposing them is virtually impossible.

Frustrated by the lack of response in Delaware, I sent the material to the Air Force inspector general in the Pentagon, which elicited a quick investigation. Their findings were forwarded down the chain of command, which meant they could not be ignored again. Court-martial proceedings were filed against Maslin. However, to avoid the public embarrassment of a trial, the Guard allowed Maslin to resign, thus losing his retirement. Maslin's record was expunged of his bogus medals.

The Green Beret

In the winter of 1989, a battalion commander of the 78th Division of the U.S. Army Reserve made a very special presentation. The commander pinned a Distinguished Service Cross on the uniform of Command Sgt. Maj. Benjamin V. Ricciardi. "Vietnam Veteran Decorated 20 Years Late" headlined a subsequent story in *The Flash*, the newspaper of the division, based in Edison, New Jersey. Accompanying the story was a picture of the tall, rugged, good-looking Ricciardi. Obviously of Italian descent, Ricciardi had a luxurious dark mustache and full head of black hair. He wore the Green Beret of Special Forces and a chest full of ribbons and decorations. The article said Ricciardi did not know he had been awarded the DSC until long after his three tours in Vietnam were just memories.

The story described Ricciardi's incredible heroism in Vietnam. A team leader with the Lurps of the 75th Infantry, Ricciardi was guiding a reconnaissance patrol in Thua Thien province near the Laotian border when they discovered a large cache of enemy ammunition. Hit by intense fire from a North Vietnamese force using mortars and automatic weapons, the Americans were vastly outnumbered. "Rapidly assessing the situation, Sergeant Ricciardi fearlessly raced across the fire-swept terrain as he consolidated his positions," read the citation supposedly awarding Ricciardi's DSC. He then led a squad to provide cover while others in his unit destroyed the enemy supplies.

Despite a severe wound to the right thigh, "with complete disregard for his own safety and against seemingly impossible odds," Ricciardi rallied his troops into a defensive perimeter and began to direct "withering fire" on enemy positions. Only then did Ricciardi allow himself to be treated by medics. "By his inspiring leadership, indomitable fighting spirit, and daring actions, he undoubtedly saved the other members of the patrol from injury, capture, or possible death," the citation said.

Ricciardi told the *Flash* reporter that he had left the Army shortly after his heroic actions on November 16, 1969. Aware that he had been given the Bronze Star Medal for valor for the action, Ricciardi said he didn't realize that award had been upgraded to a Distinguished Service Cross until 1989. "To me it was an everyday job," Ricciardi said. "I did what I had to do to keep alive and to keep the men on my team alive." He was "amazed and honored" when he found out about the DSC.

From this account, Ricciardi's military career seemed truly remarkable. Ricciardi had attended Ranger School, Special Forces Medic's Course, Jungle School, and many other Special Forces schools. Over three tours with Special Forces in Vietnam, Ricciardi had been awarded thirty medals: The DSC, a Bronze Star Medal for valor, an Army Commendation Medal with V device, a Purple Heart, Combat Infantryman Badge, the Vietnam Cross of Gallantry, and many others. After the war, Ricciardi joined the reserves. A firefighter and paramedic in Newark, New Jersey, the award made reservist Ricciardi one of the most highly decorated Vietnam veterans in the state.[572]

What happened a few months after the ceremony was not in the newspaper. Military police arrested Ricciardi for switching tags on an expensive camera and shoplifting a plastic spittoon and a gun magazine at a base PX.

Facing administrative action and the possibility of being forced from the military only months before he was to receive his "twenty-year" retirement letter, Ricciardi went to Sandra Schoeneman, Ph.D, a clinical psychologist in Larchmont, New York, to explain his "uncharacteristic behavior." She diagnosed him as suffering from posttraumatic stress disorder.

During the impressive ceremony to honor him with the presentation of the DSC, the psychologist wrote in a report to his commander, Ricciardi had suffered from feelings of guilt that he had survived Vietnam and others had not. After the event, Ricciardi began having nightmares, insomnia, hypervigilance, irritability, and increased startle response.

"His nightmares were usually of two particularly troubling war experiences, after which he felt guilty," the psychologist said. "One involved the Vietnamese officer in his group slaughtering the inhabitants of a village for no reason in an operation, and the other involved his killing of an enemy soldier with a knife in a surprise attack. In both nightmares, Mr. Ricciardi dreams that he is killed as well, a manifestation of his feelings of guilt and his need to be punished."[573]

Ricciardi then went with friends to visit the Vietnam Veterans Memorial in Washington, D.C. Already traumatized by the DSC ceremony, Ricciardi was further shaken by the experience of seeing a dead friend's name on the wall. The final blow to his psyche came days later when Ricciardi was chosen to lead an opposing force during an infantry skills training drill.

"He remembers having a set of night goggles like the ones he had in Vietnam," the psychologist's report said. "With the goggles on, he remembered the smells of combat and felt the rush of adrenaline associated with combat. He felt 'wired' and did not sleep all day or all night. [During the training] his group penetrated the [enemy] perimeter three times." For Ricciardi, Vietnam had returned with a vengeance. (Apparently, psychologist Schoeneman did not realize "night goggles" had not been perfected until long after the Vietnam War. A military veteran counselor like Rich Burns would have known that instantly.)

After the night was over, Ricciardi went to the PX for some fruit. Although Ricciardi had twelve hundred dollars in his pocket and three cameras at home, he switched the price tag on a camera, all the time watching himself as if he were on TV, in a surreal "depersonalized" zone. He shoplifted a few items but wasn't arrested until he returned later and bought the camera at the much lower price. The psychologist said the incident had been precipitated by PTSD. Latent since the years of Ricciardi's combat service in Vietnam, the condition had been triggered by the awards ceremony when the DSC was pinned to his chest and exacerbated by the simulated combat drills.[574]

Maj. Gen. Frederick W. Roeder, commander of the 78th Reserve Division, had served in the 101st Airborne in Vietnam. He believed Ricciardi was a real hero. Anxious not to tarnish the combat veteran's sterling reputation, the brass handled the scandal quietly, behind the scenes. Roeder filed an admonishment in Ricciardi's official record. "After review of these matters, I have determined that the offenses here, and the lack of judgment, maturity, and professionalism shown, are sufficiently serious to warrant filing of this reprimand." wrote Roeder.[575]

After receiving only a slap on the hand for the theft, Ricciardi applied to become a member of the Legion of Valor. They recognized him for what he was: A phony. His membership request was rejected.[576]

When medals expert Al Gleim saw a story about Ricciardi's DSC presentation, he went to the National Archives to find more information for the list he was compiling of DSC recipients. In the files, Gleim located General Order 3748, an official document awarding a Distinguished Service Cross to Benjamin Ricciardi for heroic actions in Vietnam, signed by Lt. Gen. Melvin Zais of the XXIV Corps on February 20, 1970.

But Gleim instantly realized something was wrong with the citation. The XXIV Corps was not authorized to issue a Distinguished Service Cross during the Vietnam period. And in December 1970, the last general order number used by XXIV Corps was 1570. General orders are numbered sequentially and chronologically. How could General Order Number 3748 have been issued in February? When Gleim began examining the document, he noticed numerous other little mistakes. Gleim concluded that although the general order awarding Ricciardi a Distinguished Service Cross had somehow been inserted into the official record, the document was completely bogus. Gleim's interest was in legitimate DSC winners, not phonies, so he gave the document to me.[577]

Ricciardi's official military record, which I obtained through FOIA, indicated that he had been a command sergeant major with the 78th Division and had a sterling combat record in Vietnam. The file included a copy of General Order 3748 awarding Ricciardi the Distinguished Service Cross as well as general orders giving him the Silver Star, the Bronze Star Medal, and numerous other medals.[578]

But the DSC was bogus, even though the forged citation was in the file. That raised the question: What else in Ricciardi's military record was fake? Careful cross-checking the file with other Army records indicated that Ricciardi's military heroism existed only on paper.

Ricciardi's record stated that he had been a Green Beret and had attended the Special Forces Qualification Course, Pathfinder School, Airborne School, Special Forces Aidman's Course, and Jungle Expert School. But records at various Army bases where those schools are held revealed that he had not attended any of them. And the dates of various events conflicted. For example, Ricciardi was married in New Jersey *on the same day* that he graduated from Ranger School at Fort Benning—all of which occurred while he supposedly was fighting in Vietnam.

His military record said Ricciardi had earned the master parachutist badge and had participated in two combat jumps, one a mass tactical jump. But only one mass tactical jump occurred during the Vietnam War, on February 22, 1967, by the 173rd Airborne. Ricciardi's record indicated he wasn't in the 173rd Airborne.

General Order 2290 supposedly issued Ricciardi a Bronze Star Medal. But a cross-check with the National Archives indicated that GO 2290 actually awarded an Army Commendation Medal to Le Nghiep, a South Vietnamese Popular Forces soldier.

Despite the vivid language describing his injuries in the citation for the DSC, there was no proof Ricciardi had ever been wounded. (In various documents, Ricciardi claimed that the wound occurred in different years. His injury was not identified to doctors as a war wound until 1983.) The documentation for an Army Commendation Medal for valor likewise did not hold up.

According to the most reliable records, Ricciardi did indeed serve in Vietnam for one tour in the late sixties. But he was not a Green Beret, did not have a combat infantry MOS, and had received no valorous awards. Records show that Ricciardi was a communications specialist—a telephone operator—in a signal battalion with the 101st Airborne.

For years Ricciardi had reaped an advantage over his peers in the New Jersey civil service system, which gives extra promotion points for superlative military records.[579] The alterations of Ricciardi's official record had taken place over eighteen years and had never been discovered until he was "awarded" the DSC and Gleim pulled the general order.

The U.S. Army, informed of Ricciardi's deception, did nothing. I talked to CWO William Thayer, Army fraud investigator, who referred me to William D. Clark, acting assistant secretary of the Army (and son of the legendary Gen. Mark Clark of World War II fame. Both father and son received the DSC.) After I had a conversation with Gen. William Westmoreland about the situation, the Army initiated an investigation of Ricciardi as well as its methods of keeping records of medals. At the conclusion of the investigation, Ricciardi's period of service was determined to be less than exemplary by the commanding general at Fort Leonard Wood. Ricciardi was summarily discharged from the Army Reserves and ruled ineligible for retirement payment.[580]

Reporter Bill Gannon of the Newark, New Jersey, *Star-Ledger* spent eighteen months enthusiastically pursuing the story. After going to court twice to obtain state records on Ricciardi and sending Gannon to Florida, where Ricciardi had retired, editors at the paper killed the story. Their excuse to Gannon was that Ricciardi was no longer a New Jersey resident and no longer was employed by civil service, and a story of this nature could "ruin his life." I wonder if those Ricciardi had stepped over to advance in the civil service with his fictitious hero status would be so charitable.

The Navy SEAL

At the start of the Gulf War, Adm. Margaret Hall, commander of all Navy nurses, needed an officer to take command of 120 nurses to be sent to the Middle East in support of Marine units. She turned to Lt. Cmdr. Larry Sherman Jacobs, a dark-haired, handsome, athletic hotshot in the Medical Services Corps.

Jacobs, an enlisted man who served in the Vietnam War, had risen through the ranks of the Navy. After the war, Jacobs had signed up for the Naval Enlisted Nurse Education Program (NENEP), a college plan for highly motivated enlisted personnel who qualify to become officers. The program provides full-duty pay as well as tuition while sailors attend the college of their choice. A Utah native, Jacobs enrolled at Brigham Young

University. Upon his graduation four years later, Jacobs was sworn in as a Navy officer. Jacobs reported to the fleet to continue his military career.

Jacobs' record was extremely impressive. For his official file, Jacobs made out biographical sheets listing both bachelor's and master's degrees from BYU and his many military awards and decorations. The official photograph in his file depicted Jacobs wearing the Navy Cross, Silver Star, Bronze Star Medal, Purple Heart, Combat Action Ribbon, Navy Commendation Medal, Vietnam Service Medal, Republic of Vietnam Gallantry Cross, Republic of Vietnam Campaign Medal, and the Navy Special Warfare Badge, denoting Navy SEAL status—a list of awards and decorations few of his peers could hope to match. Because of these obvious qualifications, he was chosen to interview enlisted personnel within the command who wished to become SEALs.

Handsome, charismatic, glib, and a war hero to boot, Jacobs was a natural for recruiting. Each spring, the Navy put a big push on enticing young nurses who were graduating from college to "join the Navy and see the world." Jacobs was sent to San Diego on temporary duty to interview prospects. His job included making sure his interviewees saw the finest the Navy had to offer, including the Officers Club.

While on just such tough duty with three young college nurses at the San Diego Naval Station Officers Club, Jacobs caught the eye of a mustang officer named Mike Silva. Silva, dressed in his khakis, was inconspicuous compared to Jacobs in his whites adorned with rows of ribbons. But Silva was a true SEAL hero of the Vietnam War. While an enlisted man, he had served with SEAL Team One and personally knew every SEAL who had been awarded a Navy Cross. Jacobs, he knew, wasn't one of them. (Each SEAL detachment in Vietnam usually was composed of sixty to seventy men; at any given time during the war, there were only a reletively few SEALs in Vietnam. During the decade of the war, only about one thousand SEALs served in Vietnam.)

Approaching Jacobs' luncheon party, Silva engaged Jacobs in a friendly SEAL-to-SEAL conversation. Jacobs' responses were vague, ambiguous, and just flat wrong. Silva quickly realized that Jacobs was not who the decorations on his chest made him out to be.

When Silva left the club, he wrote himself a memo about the encounter and vowed to check it out. But Silva was in the middle of a transfer and without Jacobs' full name or Social Security number, he filed the memo away, intending to take the matter up at his next duty station.

In 1991, the Gulf War broke out, and Silva was assigned to help set up the Navy's medical system in the theater of operations. One of his assigned enlisted men casually mentioned he had previously worked for a Vietnam SEAL at Bremerton, Washington, a commander named Larry Jacobs.

Reminded of his meeting with Jacobs, Silva decided to get to the bottom of the situation.

After completing his assignment and returning from the Gulf, Silva called a fellow corpsman from Vietnam, a naval officer in Washington, D.C., who had access to personnel records. It was quickly ascertained that Jacobs had received no valorous decorations, nor had he served in Vietnam.

In the meantime, Jacobs had deployed to the Gulf War. Navy authorities notified the Marine command in the Middle East, and military officials detained Jacobs. Questioned about the decorations, Jacobs at first steadfastly maintained their legitimacy. But he soon broke down and confessed. Jacobs had actually enlisted in 1974 after the SEALs and all troops pulled out of Vietnam. He had never been a SEAL or earned any valorous decorations. Records indicated the only award Jacobs had received was the Navy Achievement Medal.

Through the grapevine, I heard that Jacobs, stripped of his fraudulent medals and sent back to the jurisdiction of Admiral Hall, submitted his resignation, six months short of the date that qualified him for a retirement pension. Official end of episode.

Curious to know how Jacobs had built an entire career on bogus decorations, I filed an FOIA request for Jacobs' records. But the Navy told me I had to wait until his records were sent to the National Personnel Records Center in St. Louis. (By policy, records are supposed to be sent within ninety days of termination of service.) Months and months passed. Finally learning that Jacobs' records had arrived in St. Louis, I filed another FOIA request. But I received only a few pages of his record, incredible for a man with a twenty-year military career. None of the documents indicated whether he had been retired or forced to resign, information that should have been available under the Freedom of Information Act.

FOIA requests to various Navy bureaus met continued rejection. At that point, a Dallas attorney named Rob Hartmann, a Vietnam veteran, the lawyer for the Texas Vietnam Veterans Memorial, and the son of a two-star admiral, suggested his law firm might get better results. But Hartmann's FOIA requests met with the same dead end. Together we made more than two-dozen FOIA requests of the Navy and received nothing of substance but a letter from a woman in the Navy's awards and decorations office. Clearly the Navy, reeling from the Tailhook scandal, was stonewalling me. Why? Jacobs was certainly an embarrassment. He had passed through four military promotion boards without arousing an ounce of suspicion. I wondered if the Navy cut a deal with Jacobs, offering him a reduced pension if he resigned without a stink.

After consulting with the attorneys, I made the decision to sue the United States Navy, Secretary of the Navy John Dalton, and U.S. Attorney

Janet Reno in federal court for violating my rights under FOIA. Little by little, the Navy has eked out a few documents, including a fuzzy photograph of Jacobs wearing his various bogus decorations. But Navy lawyers have refused to comply with most of my requests, saying that the material is not available. In the meantime, I independently verified that while Jacobs did attend Brigham Young University, he received only a two-year associate's degree, not a bachelor's or master's degree, meaning that even his commission as an officer was based on a fraud. Did the Navy retire Jacobs quietly rather than court-martial him, as he deserved, because a trial would reveal they had a serious problem with their records-keeping system?[581]

On January 5, 1996, I wrote to Adm. Jeremy "Mike" Boorda, Chief of Naval Operations at the Pentagon, and included stories on my efforts to unmask pretenders and the *20/20* tape. I told him about uncovering Jacobs' fraud and how the Navy was stonewalling on his records. At that point in time, the Navy had spent tens of thousands of dollars of the taxpayers' money to defend Jacobs, an individual who any other branch of the service would consider a disgrace. The Navy definitely did not want the Jacobs matter made public. They even refused to tell me whether he had retired or resigned.

Because Boorda had the reputation of being an honest straight-shooter, I presumed that he would be as outraged by the Jacobs' case as I was. "That the Navy would defend this individual is an outrage," I wrote. "If you are aware of this situation and condone it, shame on you. If you are not aware of it, get briefed and do the right thing. Larry Jacobs is a disgrace to every man who wore a Navy uniform and a sacrilege to every man who served in Vietnam, especially those posthumously awarded the very decorations Jacobs claimed as his own."

Boorda did not reply. But I received a letter from Capt. T. J. Connelly, Boorda's staff counsel, that said that it would be inappropriate for Boorda to comment because the matter was under litigation.[582] More stonewall.

I had no idea that Boorda himself had problems with combat decorations; after Vietnam, he had begun wearing combat Vs on two Vietnam-related decorations. The V devices had not been authorized, and Boorda was wearing them in violation of regulations. If he read my letter, I imagine it caused some discomfort.[583]

In May 1996, when his own record came under scrutiny by *Newsweek*, rather than face public humiliation and disgrace, Admiral Boorda committed suicide.[584] I'm sure that there were many things that played into his decision to take his own life, but the controversy about the V devices dramatically showed that to a military man and to a military culture, combat decorations do matter.

Like the tragic story of Admiral Boorda, many veterans have received decorations for exemplary service—some even for battlefield bravery—but for them it's not enough. They feel compelled to add decorations they didn't earn to their rows of ribbons.

Heroes Too Far

For heroism during two tours of duty in Vietnam, Capt. Clyde Bonner of El Paso, Texas, proudly wore a Distinguished Service Cross, Silver Star, two Purple Hearts, and a Combat Infantryman Badge, making him one of the most highly decorated soldiers in the Army.[585] Tragically, in 1972, the twenty-nine-year-old Bonner, who was stationed in Heidelberg, West Germany, was killed in a terrorist bombing of the American military headquarters. The three bombers were eventually caught and convicted, and the fact that Bonner was a major war hero certainly contributed to the stiff sentence given.[586] (They were released in 1992.[587]) There was even a rumor that a building on a U.S. military base was named for Bonner.

But in his research, Al Gleim discovered that Bonner had not received the DSC. The general order for the DSC in Bonner's official file was rife with typos and mistakes; research proved the document was forged. The Army never suspected, but after Gleim and I pointed out the errors, they confirmed Bonner's Distinguished Service Cross was bogus. Bonner had an excellent record, and his other medals were legitimate.[588]

The highly decorated Fred N. "Mad Ranger" Ranck of Wheaton, Illinois, assumed the presidency of the 101st Airborne Division Association in August 1995. The next year, *Static Line*, an Airborne publication, named Ranck its "Man of the Year." But other members of the association began to wonder about Ranck's heroic tales. In Ranck's biography, printed in a book for the 101st Airborne Division's fiftieth annual reunion, he claimed thirty-one decorations, including four Silver Stars, eight Bronze Star Medals, five Purple Hearts, and four Vietnamese Crosses of Gallantry—a highly commendable war record. But some Vietnam veterans in the association thought it impossible Ranck had received so many decorations; infantry officers typically were assigned to combat duty their first six months in-country then reassigned to less hazardous responsibilities for the remainder of their tours.

Ranck's true military record revealed that he had served with distinction in Vietnam and had been awarded one Silver Star, three Bronze Star Medals (all for meritorious service, not valor), and one Vietnamese Cross of Gallantry. But it does not back up his claim to any additional Silver Stars, five additional Bronze Star Medals, or any Purple Hearts.[589]

Another "hero-too-far" lives in New York. Stephen Banko III served two tours in Vietnam through all of 1968 and part of 1969 with the 1st Infantry and 1st Cavalry Divisions during some of the heaviest fighting of the war.

In one five-hour battle, his 125-man company was reduced to fourteen men.

Except the Medal of Honor, Banko received every decoration for combat heroism: the DSC, two Silver Stars, four Bronze Star Medals for valor, four Purple Hearts, Air Medal for valor, Army Commendation Medal for valor, and the Combat Infantryman Badge. At least that's what his resume said.[590]

After Vietnam, Banko became principal speechwriter for the speaker of the New York Assembly. Later, he worked as press secretary during the 1980 presidential campaign of Sen. Edward Kennedy. After that race, Banko signed on as chief of staff for New York State Sen. Anthony M. Masiello's Buffalo office. When Masiello became mayor of Buffalo, Banko went to work as his assistant.[591]

Through the years, Banko has literally built a career out of being the "most highly decorated Vietnam veteran in New York State." His writing about Vietnam and about veterans has appeared in numerous magazines and newspapers, including *The Wall Street Journal*.

In *Eagle*, a magazine "for the American fighting man," Banko wrote about "The Week I Lost Two Cherries." Once in combat as the "FNG" (Fucking New Guy) and once in the bed of a bored and pudgy Cambodian prostitute who ate an apple during the three-minute exercise. Banko's reaction to his first "kill" in combat? He immediately threw up and started crying. (His reaction to the loss of his virginity? The experience was so unpleasant that, for a while, he entertained the notion that he could be gay.)[592]

Since the war, Banko frequently has been involved in veterans' projects and is often interviewed by journalists about various veterans' issues. The tag line for one article he wrote about his reaction to the news of Americans bombing Baghdad during the Gulf War read: "[Stephen T. Banko III] has been awarded every combat decoration except the Medal of Honor and is recognized as New York State's most decorated Vietnam veteran."[593]

Witty, talented, hardworking, Banko *did* receive numerous decorations for combat heroism. Why did he have to gild the lily?

Banko's embellishments started even before he left the service. Shortly after returning to Fort Dix following his first tour in Vietnam, Banko produced a copy of a general order issued by the 1st Cavalry awarding him a Distinguished Service Cross and another document adding a Purple Heart to his swelling cache of medals. The orders were clearly fabricated. He was caught and reprimanded.[594] Banko returned to Vietnam for another tour. After his discharge, he *again* began making the claim that he had received the DSC.

Banko's claims came to my attention, again through Gleim's research on the DSC. I obtained his record through FOIA and it did indeed include a general order giving Banko the DSC.

General Order 971 for the DSC describes how squad leader Sergeant Banko, his platoon under assault, crawled from his position, exposing himself to enemy fire to aid a wounded soldier. When flames from a grassfire engulfing the landing zone threatened both men, Banko "used his hands to beat down the fire and dragged the wounded man to safety."[595] But the document contained numerous errors.

Gleim and I finally determined that Banko *did* receive one Silver Star. Although he claims two, both were for the same action; one Silver Star was rescinded as a duplicate put in by another command.

But Banko did not receive a Distinguished Service Cross. The language of the citation for Banko's sham DSC is startlingly similar to the words used in General Order 1140, issued by the same unit on the same date, awarding the Distinguished Service Cross to another soldier.

General Order 1140 describes a soldier who evacuated all the injured members of his element to a medical evacuation site then rushed to the platoon engaged in the heaviest fighting. He moved among the wounded, treating and carrying them to the evacuation point. Then he moved to the waist-high grass in which several casualties lay ignited in a furious blaze. "Working feverishly, he rescued the men and then used his shirt to beat out the fire before he was forced back by the spreading flames, suffering burns and near exhaustion." Hearing a cry for a medic, the brave soldier again risked withering fire to reach a stricken soldier. Although painfully wounded by an enemy grenade, the man continued to drag the wounded soldier to safety until he finally collapsed.

General Order 1140 bestows the DSC not on Banko, but on Sp4 Walter T. Bahl, a combat medic, for heroism on December 3, 1968, when his company, on a mission northeast of Quan Loi, was ambushed by intense fire from a battalion-sized NVA force hidden in the trees. Bahl received the DSC posthumously, dying in pain trying to save others.[596]

Walter T. Bahl, whose parents still live in Denver, died in near obscurity. Few know of his courage or the anguish of his family. The Bankos of the world flourish by figuratively picking the pockets of the heroic dead.

Ranck, Bonner, and Banko are genuine combat veterans. But somehow they needed more. Perhaps Bonner, at some point between Vietnam and Germany, slipped the false DSC order into his file in order to further his military career. And for years, Banko has capitalized on being "the most decorated Vietnam veteran in New York State," bringing in the veterans' vote for his political employers.

A grateful nation honored Ranck, Bonner and Banko for their courage but should equally heap contempt on them for stealing the valor of men who heroically gave their lives for this country.

Craving the authentication combat medals and membership in elite associations bring, pretenders have managed to worm their way into extremely distinguished company and, as the stories of Ricciardi and Maslin vividly demonstrate, often refuse to back down even when exposed. But some of the most audacious are those who set down their memories of Vietnam in black and white, in books that will be around for generations to come.

17

War Stories and Other Lies

Writers Go to Vietnam

ONE MOMENT he was talking on the telephone. The next, *Boom!*, Dannion Brinkley had been flung back on his bed. The phone receiver, still clutched in his hand, was melted. Struck by lightning during a thunderstorm, Brinkley floated in and out of his body, watching as his wife and friend frantically tried to resuscitate him.

The rescue attempts failed. Brinkley died, and as he died his consciousness saw a tunnel of light drawing him toward it. At the other end he encountered a heavenly creature, a "Being of Light" more beautiful than anything he had ever seen. The entity shimmered as although composed of thousands of tiny diamonds, each emitting the colors of the rainbow, encompassing him in a feeling of deep love and pleasure almost impossible to withstand.

As the Being of Light engulfed him, Brinkley began to reexperience his whole life: His days as a vicious bully on the school ground, and then his experiences performing military and intelligence work in Vietnam. Brinkley found himself back in the muggy, suffocating jungles of Vietnam, doing what he liked to do best—fight. Attached to an intelligence unit operating mainly in Laos and Cambodia, Brinkley did "observation work," reporting on troop movements. But his main job was to "plan and execute the removal of enemy personnel."[597] In other words, he was an assassin.

Now dying, Brinkley found himself experiencing each event from the point of view of those whom he hurt, those he killed. Sent to "terminate" a North Vietnamese colonel with his troops in Cambodia, Brinkley saw himself focusing the crosshairs of his high-powered sniper rifle on the colonel's head as he stood before his unsuspecting soldiers. Brinkley squeezed off a round and watched the colonel's head explode in a pink mist. Now, he felt—not the man's pain—but his "confusion at having his head blown off and sadness as he left his body and realized that he would never go home again."

Sent to "a country bordering Vietnam," Brinkley was ordered to execute a government official who did not share the "American point of view." Unable to line up a clear shot after four days, he and his team finally blew up the rural hotel where the man was staying. Now, under the influence of the radiant Being of Light, Brinkley felt his victims' horror as well as their families' pain, even the loss their absence would make to future generations.

Over and over, Brinkley was forced to see the death and destruction that had taken place as a result of his actions. This was not only in Vietnam but also after the war ended when he smuggled weapons to Central America in his continuing role as a covert operative for the U.S. government.

Chastened, Brinkley vowed to change his life. But he liked being dead; he felt peaceful, harmonious. Brinkley was taken to a place where he saw thirteen Beings of Light, and they revealed to him secrets of the future, wars to unfold, political alliances to be forged. Then the ethereal spirits told him he must return to his body. They gave Brinkley a mission: To build a series of seven rooms, a sort of heavenly stress reduction center where people could come and learn that they are higher spiritual beings. Reluctantly, Brinkley's soul reentered his earthly flesh. And after recovering from the effects of the lightning strike and another near-death experience triggered by pneumonia, he wrote it all down in a book called *Saved by the Light*, published in 1994 by Villard Books, which quickly became a bestseller.

After the phenomenal success of *Saved by the Light*, Bantam Books signed Brinkley to write another book about his divine revelations, committing to a major publicity campaign that included television commercials. Brinkley signed a deal with Fox Television to make a movie of his life and near-death experiences. The film starring actor Eric Roberts aired in late 1995, about the same time that Brinkley's second book, *At Peace in the Light*, was released.

"What I have discovered about Dannion," wrote author James Redfield in the foreword to Brinkley's second book, "is that as incredible as it may seem, he is exactly the person he appears to be. Yes, he used to be an intelligence operative, a background that caused him much agony in his first near-death life review, but which prepared him well for the kind of global-military-economic-cultural analysis that rolls off his tongue as easily as the southern drawl and good-ol'-boy attitude he picked up during his upbringing in South Carolina."[598]

In both books, Dannion Brinkley contended that the story of his life and his encounter with the beyond actually happened, that these events are fact, not fiction. His credibility as a speaker of divine truth, as the chosen one to whom angelic beings reveal great spiritual mysteries, rests on the confidence people have in his veracity about events on earth.

Brinkley claimed he was a Marine Corps sniper, sent to assassinate enemy officers and civilian politicians in Cambodia and Laos. But his military records showed something far different. Brinkley attended college for one year then dropped out in 1969 to join the Marine Corps. Brinkley went through boot camp at Parris Island, South Carolina. He was then shipped to Camp LeJeune, North Carolina, where he completed requirements to be —drum roll please—One Tough Truck Driver.

Not only was Brinkley not a "Marine Corps assassin" in Vietnam, he never left the United States during his eighteen months of service. Records revealed he was assigned to Company A, 4th Marine Transportation Battalion, stationed in Atlanta, Georgia, until his discharge in July 1971. It's likely that he spent most of his time in the military trucking quartermaster supplies like toilet paper and blankets to other Marine facilities. He attended no schools for specialized combat operations, received no medals related to the war.[599]

When Roy Rivenburg of the *Los Angeles Times* questioned Brinkley's tales of heroism, the angelic mouthpiece declined to offer any evidence of overseas duty, saying that the government (of course) was covering up his record because it was classified.[600]

Did Brinkley really encounter heavenly beings who gave him the low-down on the afterlife and events to come? I have no way of filing an FOIA for heaven's records, but my guess is that his tales of angelic encounters are about as real as his stories of military combat. Brilliant marketing by Random House (which owns Villard Books) created a gold mine out of a tissue of lies and an overactive imagination. They should market the book as such.

But Brinkley is simply one of the latest in a long line of authors, journalists, and other peddlers of history who have taken the Vietnam War and twisted it for their own ends. Unfortunately, a vast amount of what has been documented and preserved about the war in the last thirty years— especially in oral histories—is based on information from wannabes and prevaricators.

And this fraud is not limited to writers of pop culture such as Brinkley, whose tales are easy to dismiss by military experts. They include some of the most famous authors whose best-selling books are highly regarded not only as histories of the war but also of the entire Vietnam generation. Some authors claim to write about the war from the combatant's view-point. For an author of military history, combat experience creates an aura of perseverance, endurance, and courage that authenticates the material.

One such historian was the anonymous "Cincinnatus," author of the 1981 book *Self Destruction: The Disintegration and Decay of the U.S. Army During the Vietnam Era*. The book jacket described the author as a "senior field-grade officer" at the Pentagon.[601] The writer, who received wide acclaim for his damning indictment of the Army's performance in Vietnam —which the publishers implied he had personally witnessed—was revealed by Col. Harry Summers (with the help of *Washington Post* publisher and Vietnam veteran Donald Graham) to be Cecil Currey, a chaplain in the U.S. National Guard who had never served in Vietnam.[602]

Writers who do not have direct military experience often see themselves as being conduits for history, talking to those who participated, writing down their stories to preserve and document the history for future generations. But in many cases, they have a political agenda that makes them susceptible to using false information when it suits their purposes. Often these individuals show authors falsified documents, doctored photographs, self-awarded medals, and altered discharge papers to prove their authenticity. Rarely do these authors independently check military records at the National Personnel Records Center in St. Louis. They want to believe; checking records might raise too many red flags.

Many authors, like the previously mentioned Jonathan Shay, avoid those nagging questions by using pseudonyms, first names only, or composite characters. That sets them free to tell the most outrageous tales. Because they don't identify anyone by name, it's hard to check out their claims.

A prime example is *'Nam*, a 1981 book by Mark Baker that sold more than one million copies. A powerful, dramatic telling of the "hell" that was Vietnam, *'Nam* was marketed as a factual oral history, compiled from interviews with more than 150 Vietnam veterans. Although Baker contended that his book was nonfiction, he hedged his bets.

"It must be assumed that included here are generalizations, exaggerations, braggadocio, and—very likely—outright lies," Baker wrote in the introduction. "But if these stories were told within a religious framework, the telling would be called bearing witness. The human imperfections simply authenticate the sincerity of the whole. The apocryphal aspects have more to do with metaphor than with deceit."[603]

Huh? Is that a way of saying, "I was too damn lazy to check whether my sources were telling the truth or not? Besides, does it really matter"?

Yes, the truth does matter! Readers form opinions about reality based on what authors claim is factual. And the reality in Baker's book was dubious. To read Baker's version, drug use, rape of women, throwing prisoners out of helicopters, murdering officers, and wanton butchering of civilians were everyday occurrences in Vietnam. Because the sources are not named, it's impossible to verify most of his information.

Baker quoted a nurse saying she denied civilians medication. "I saw patients being poisoned because we had no beds, and we needed beds for the GIs," the nurse said. An Army veteran claimed that his unit threw so many bodies of the enemy in the Saigon River that they clogged boat traffic. A grunt told Baker he was attacked by NVA wearing UCLA sweatshirts. When? Where? How? Ludicrous on their face, these are stories that cannot be disproved because they are anonymous and ambiguous.

But telling details flag many of the stories as untrue. Baker described the death of "Johnny Kane" who goes into the Marine Corps only to be killed in action. No one named Lt. Johnny Kane died in Vietnam, nor did a Lt. Carver or a Marine enlisted man named Browne, as Baker's sources contended.[604] Were these real names? Baker didn't say.

One man said he was transferred to the 2nd Marine Division in Vietnam. (The Marine Corps 2nd Division did not serve in Vietnam.) Another veteran contended that he and his fellow pilots were twice recommended for Distinguished Flying Crosses for running through a mortar barrage to their helicopters. (DFCs are given only for action occurring in the air, not stumbling across an airfield on foot.) These historical inaccuracies are easy to check.

The most hilarious report in Baker's 'Nam was that of a soldier who claimed he had been within 150 yards of a B-52 strike, so close the concussion "blew all the tubes in the radio and knocked all the buildings down." Well, the radios in use at that time did not have tubes, and anyone that close to a B-52 strike would have been killed or severely wounded. The same veteran described watching shells that sounded like "a subway train pulling into Times Square" fired from the battleship USS Arizona. Obviously, neither he nor author Baker gave a second thought to the fact that the Arizona had been sunk December 7, 1941, and is now at the bottom of Pearl Harbor.[605]

Everything We Had

Even serious, well-respected historians can easily be led astray if they don't bother to check the records in St. Louis (which should be the first step by anyone claiming to be a historian). A case in point is Red Thunder, Tropic Lightning, the story of the 25th Infantry, told as an oral history by author Eric Bergerud, a professor of military and American history at Lincoln University. In his preface, he talks about how, between the records and a large body of oral evidence, he is "immunized from outright falsehood."

"I am a trained researcher and skeptic, but only on a handful of occasions did I decide someone was creating fantasy," Bergerud wrote.[606] To his credit, he does not rely on anonymous accounts, although he changed the names of a few victims.

But Bergerud is not "immunized" from outright falsehood. He liberally quoted a combat infantryman named C.W. Bowman, who told a wildly implausible yarn about his buddy Gary, who stepped on a Bouncing Betty mine while on patrol. The explosion blew off his left leg and shredded his left arm. "They sewed his leg back on, and he's still walking around with a brace and a cane," Bowman said.

Oh, come on. No leg was reattached in Vietnam medical facilities. Even in the 1990s, in the best hospitals in the world, even with a clean cut, reattaching a limb is considered extremely difficult. Digits are often reattached, and other appendages, such as John Bobbitt's now infamous penis, have been sewn back on. But an explosion leaves little more than mush for surgeons to work with.

Bowman also described doing other things that men in the bush wouldn't do, like carrying up to fifty pounds of C4 plastic explosives and an M14 with twenty-two loaded magazines at a time—not including his grenades, a 6omm mortar round stuck in his hip pocket, smoke grenades, CS grenades, at least two canteens, and his C rations.

Bergerud placed Bowman in Vietnam when he was eighteen. But according to his military record, Bowman was a civilian in the states when he was eighteen. His military record indicated that Bowman did not join the Army until he was nineteen and didn't arrive in Vietnam until he was twenty. And although he told Bergerud "Charlie" shot his helmet off his head, grazing his skin and giving him a concussion, his record shows no wounds and no Purple Heart.[607]

When I called Bergerud to express my skepticism, he reacted with belligerence and asked if I was trying to impugn his integrity.

Even authors who are Vietnam veterans can be fooled by pretenders. Journalist Al Santoli, who served two tours in Vietnam, wrote an oral history called *Everything We Had*, interviews with thirty-three American soldiers who fought in Vietnam. One of the first serious oral histories of the war, the 1981 book quickly became a classic, also selling more than a million copies.[608]

Commissioned by the Vietnam Veterans of America (VVA), the book had a political agenda from the outset. The VVA received two-thirds of the royalties. And it seemed intended to further the "veteran-as-victim" strategy of the VVA.

Santoli traveled the country interviewing Vietnam veterans, who were often identified as good sources by VVA officials. One of the subjects was Thomas Bird, a cofounder of the VVA. In 1981, Bird flew to Hanoi with VVA executive director Bobby Muller and, once there, laid a wreath at the mausoleum of Ho Chi Minh. He went on to become a media darling, running the Vietnam Veterans' Ensemble Theater in New York.

Bird told Santoli he served as a rifleman in the 1st Cavalry Division (Airmobile) from August 1965 to August 1966. The book said his unit was overrun during the infamous battle of the Ia Drang Valley in November 1965. "We were air assaulted out of Pleiku to LZ Falcon, and from there we went out on a search-and-destroy mission to find the North Vietnamese who were butchering the hell out of the 7th Cavalry," said Bird in the book.[609] He described in elaborate detail the ensuing firefights.

"As we came into the valley, the first thing that happened was we got some fast fire from the right," Bird said. "This was the first time I had ever been fired on. I froze. I completely froze and dropped behind a tree. The right flank started moving toward the fire, and as that happened, the enemy started dropping mortars in our middle and firing from the left, too. I realized I was supposed to do something, but the only thing I knew how to do was follow the guys around me, and they were meeting fire with fire. But no sooner did they advance toward the fire and widen the perimeter than the enemy started opening up on the left and the rear, so we pretty much stayed where we were, and some guys were returning the fire. They kept popping mortars into our center to keep our perimeter wide—wider than we could defend. It became a battle of trying to get back into a tight perimeter and fight off what was becoming a hell of an ambush."

Surrounded by the NVA, who picked off the wounded, Bird and eleven other men were captured by the enemy. "They were in brown uniforms, and they were all full of leaves, leaves coming out of their pockets, out of their helmets, they were all camouflaged in leaves," Bird said. "One guy had his bayonet out and was ready to fight, but Staff Sgt. Starkweather told him, 'Don't resist.' The alternative to Starkweather was to resist and get killed or don't resist and see what happens. I don't know why he took the gamble because they were just killing. They killed the wounded as they came out of the tree line."

The American captives were tormented and abused for several days. "They dragged a couple of prisoners to trees and tied them up by their necks—not enough to strangle them—with their wrists and ankles still tied together." Bird said. "They kept us apart and wouldn't let us speak to each other. Anytime anyone was caught talking to another prisoner, he got slapped around. I didn't remember anything about the Code of Conduct. I don't remember feeling loyalty to anything."

Bird said one soldier from Maryland named Elvin Evans, was taken off by the enemy never to be seen again. The other prisoners endured slaps on the face, "little taunts in the balls with sticks," and a game where the prisoners "got pissed on."

"A guy took a knife to my throat and pressed enough to puncture the skin," Bird said. "I spent the whole time praying."

Inexplicably, the NVA abruptly abandoned their prisoners one night, leaving them naked and trussed up in the jungle where they were rescued by friendly troops the next day.

His military record revealed that Bird's fanciful tale of being captured was completely fallacious.[610] (And his story about Evans was bogus as well. There are no records of an Elvin Evans who died, was taken prisoner, or is missing in action in Vietnam.[611])

Veteran Dan Cragg had also seen Bird's stories for what they were and exposed him in *The Stars and Stripes* in 1982. Cragg pointed out Bird was a rifleman with a unit that was part of the relief force sent to help the 7th Cavalry, heavily engaged in Ia Drang. But his unit was not overrun by the enemy and had only sixteen men wounded through the entire six-month period from July 1 through December 31, 1965. Both Bird's battalion commander and his company commander confirmed that Bird's stories of the Ia Drang battle and his capture were untrue.[612]

Bird's POW escapade was not the only dubious story in *Everything We Had*. A whole chapter told the saga of Mike Beamon, who described himself as a scout for the Navy SEALs in the Mekong Delta, where—you guessed it—he did covert assassinations of village chiefs as part of the Phoenix Program.[613] I could find no record that anyone named Mike Beamon served as a SEAL, in the Navy, or even in the military, much less as a "Phoenix assassin."

Another exaggerated story in *Everything We Had* was that of Stephen Klinkhammer, an aviation ordnance specialist who said he did a three-and-a-half-month tour of duty on the USS *America* at the tail end of the war. Later, in 1975, as a hospital corpsman, Klinkhammer said he was flown with a surgical team to a carrier off the coast of Vietnam as Saigon fell. Klinkhammer claimed that from the USS *Midway*, he could see the rockets hitting Tan Son Nhut airbase in Saigon.[614]

Saigon is located about twenty miles inland. Klinkhammer would not have been able to see rockets hitting Saigon from the sea. Klinkhammer also claimed that South Vietnam vice president Nguyen Cao Ky escaped from Saigon by flying his own Cessna, loaded with gold bars, to the Midway, on April 30, the day Saigon fell. But Ky actually used a helicopter to fly himself, his family, and other officers of his command to the *Midway* on April 29. Ky's gold bars? Nonexistent.[615]

Through FOIA, I obtained the record for Stephen Phillip Klinkhammer, which revealed he was on active duty from June 30, 1972, to June 1, 1976. He has a Vietnam Service Ribbon, indicating at least one day of Vietnam service. But he has no Vietnam Campaign Ribbon and no Combat Action

Ribbon. And if he had been involved with the rescue operations during the fall of Saigon, "Operation Frequent Wind," Klinkhammer would have received an Armed Forces Expeditionary Medal. His record shows none.[616]

Santoli has readily admitted that he had been taken in by some of his subjects and that he did not check military records. "I guess it never dawned on me that people would lie about this kind of thing," Santoli told me. Although Bird has admitted he made up the story about being a POW, the tale has taken on a life of its own. Without knowing it was bogus, Michael J. Badamo, a skilled writer, relied on the Bird segment of Santoli's book to write a piece comparing the fight of Ia Drang with the battle of Shiloh in the Civil War in June 1992 for *Vietnam*, a history magazine.[617] Bird's story now stands for future generations to read as "fact."

The book *Saigon to Jerusalem* by Eric Lee is the story of Jewish Americans who fought in Vietnam then emigrated to Israel. Lee, an antiwar activist, said in the foreword that he required DD-214s from his sources. "In only one case did I have the feeling that some of what I was being told might be a tall tale and, accordingly, that tale doesn't appear in this book," Lee wrote.[618] Unfortunately, another pretender did end up in Lee's book and a subsequent story in *Vietnam* magazine.

Lee told the story of William Northrop, a Citadel graduate who claimed he was an officer in the 5th Special Forces who served in Vietnam and Laos from February 1967 until he was wounded at the famous battle of Lang Vei a year later. Then a journalist in Israel, Northrop told Lee he used drugs—"speed"—while on patrol in Vietnam. "You bet," Northrop said. "I wouldn't go out without it." He described catching a fifteen-year-old student at a Catholic school in Khe Sanh laying down "mechanical ambushes" that caused some American casualties. Northrop did not shoot the boy; he pushed him into the "MA," which did the job for him. (It should be noted that there was no Catholic school in Khe Sanh.)

Lee quoted Northrop's description of going on cross-border missions into Laos. "There was an artillery regiment of gooners that moved into the C.O. Rock," Northrop said. "We would just infiltrate in, set up mechanical ambushes, booby traps—or call strikes down on them. Claymores, grenades, anything we could lay our hands on. I used to do a real cute trick with detonation." Or they would ambush NVA coming off the Ho Chi Minh trail at night, blasting them with shotguns provided by the Baltimore Police Department. "We'd paint ourselves up real pretty with war paint," Northrop said. "And all of a sudden you jump out of the darkness—my friend, you were the bogey man!"[619]

Northrop's major tale concerned the battle of Lang Vei on February 7, 1968. The fight is well known as the first documented time the North Vietnamese ever used tanks, which overran the Green Beret camp at Lang

Vei. Northrop claimed to be in the middle of the fighting. The Green Berets held their ground against impossible odds. Northrop said he was badly wounded. Virtually every officer at the camp—alive or dead—received valorous decorations. A DD-214 Northrop provided to Lee indicated he was awarded, among others, the Silver Star, Bronze Star Medal with V device, "Croix de Guerre," Air Medal, Purple Heart, Combat Infantryman Badge (second award), "Ranger Badge," and "National Defense Medal."

But Northrop's tale doesn't fit the facts. The battle of Lang Vei is well-documented. Only two Special Forces first lieutenants were present during the attack: Miles Wilkins and Paul Longgrear, both of whom received Silver Stars. According to the historical record, Lt. Northrop wasn't there.

In addition, the Special Forces Association has no record of Northrop. The name William Northrop appears in none of the Green Beret publications issued during the Vietnam War. Although Northrop claimed he was an Army officer from 1966–1969, the officer roster at the Pentagon for those years lists no William Northrop.[620]

Then there's Northrop's DD-214 itself, which is fraught with errors. The most basic mistake is that the document is typed on two different typewriters. No legitimate DD-214 is typed on two typewriters (although some units use DD-214s with preprinted generic material, such as the name of the unit). Northrop's total period of service does not match his entry and discharge dates, and the acronyms and medals are wrong. His record lists his job title as "SF LDR," or Special Forces Leader; no such designation exists. In addition, the military has no decoration called the "National Defense Medal." (It's the National Defense Service Medal). No "Ranger Badge." (It's called a Ranger Tab). To have received a second CIB, as Northrop claimed, he had to receive the first one in Korea, when he was about ten years old.

The Republic of Vietnam had no Croix de Guerre. Northrop could not have completed all the courses he claimed to have attended and still have one year, nine months, and nineteen days overseas. And he could not have served with MAAG-VN, as the DD-214 indicated. The Military Assistance Advisory Group ceased to exist in 1964, long before Northrop claimed he arrived in Vietnam, and was replaced by MACV. These are mistakes that would not be made on a true DD-214.

The Citadel refused to verify whether Northrop graduated or not. According to an arrest record, Northrop had been taken into custody in El Paso in 1974 for illegal importation of firearms. In 1983, another warrant was issued for his arrest in El Centro, California, on charges of grand theft; Northrop was taken into custody in Phoenix, Arizona.

Northrop, who's now living in Oklahoma City, popped up again in July

1996 in *The Dallas Morning News* as the "military advisor" to a woman named Suzanne Migdall, who is writing a book about female Gulf War veterans. He was described by the reporter as a Special Forces Vietnam veteran with "vague CIA and Israeli intelligence associations."[621]

Born on the Fourth of July

Ron Kovic became one of the icons of the antiwar movement when he returned home from Vietnam, paralyzed by a gunshot wound to the spine. In the 1976 book *Born on the Fourth of July*, Kovic painted a powerful portrait of a starry-eyed, guileless teenager sent off by a vicious and lying American government to fight an immoral war.[622] The theme was corruption of an innocent all-American boy by all things he once held holy.

The book became a 1989 film by director Oliver Stone, billed as "a true story of innocence lost and courage found." The movie won eight Oscar nominations. Vincent Canby, movie critic of *The New York Times*, endorsed the film with effusive praise: "May be the final word on Vietnam." That's what many said of Stone's earlier *Platoon*, which portrayed combat soldiers as drug addicts and war criminals.

The book began with Kovic, born on Independence Day, his views of war shaped by a jingoistic Hollywood and television. An enthusiastic Kovic joined the Marine Corps, determined to prove himself a hero. But his zestful patriotism was perverted by the Marines, who turned him into a remorseless killing machine.

Then Kovic was wounded, paralyzed from the waist down by a gunshot wound during a firefight. Impotent, sentenced to live the rest of his life in a wheelchair, Kovic realized that the war was terribly wrong and had to be stopped. Bitter, he became an antiwar activist. At the 1972 Republican National Convention, where he was a vivid symbol of the terrible price of war, he was beaten by fascist police.

Kovic's military records tell a different story. Kovic did serve in Vietnam, as a Marine who did his job well and enthusiastically. He received a Bronze Star Medal for valor, a Combat Action Ribbon, a Purple Heart, the Navy Commendation Medal, and the Vietnam Cross of Gallantry, among other decorations. And he was terribly wounded in combat. I sympathize with him.

But the reality is that Kovic was on his second tour of duty in Vietnam when he suffered his crippling wound. After his first tour, from December 13, 1965 to January 13, 1967, he came home to the United States, safe, whole, and healthy. GIs returning from Vietnam were protected for six months from an involuntary redeployment back to the war zone. Kovic enthusiastically waived this protection.[623]

In fact, Kovic wrote letters *campaigning to be sent back* to Vietnam.

Instead of saying "I did my duty" and serving the rest of his commitment outside the war zone, he begged to be sent back into combat with the 1st or 3rd Recon Battalion.

"I participated in more than twenty-two long-range reconnaissance patrols deep within Viet Cong controlled territory and earned the 'Navy Commendation Medal' for meritorious service as a radio operator with the 1st Recon Battalion, 1st Marine Division in Vietnam from July 1966 until January 1967," Kovic wrote in support of his request on May 18, 1967. "I hold a 8651 'Reconnaissance Man' MOS and also served with 3rd Battalion, 7th Marines participating on seven major operations and twenty-six combat patrols.

"My country calls me again. I am willing, as on my last tour, to give my Marine Corps and my country 100 percent of my abilities and then some. I love my country above all else and am ready now as before to place my life, if need be, at the service of my flag."[624]

When that letter didn't get results, Kovic, then stationed at Cherry Point, North Carolina, filled out another form on June 2, 1967: "During a previous assignment in Vietnam, I participated in numerous reconnaissance and combat patrols, earning the Navy Commendation Medal for my service," he said. "I have a very strong desire to return to this type of duty."

Kovic pleaded to be allowed back into combat. He wanted to be a big war hero, something that soldiers know is a matter of good training combined with blind, dumb luck. He was willing to "place his life, if need be" at the service of his flag. Kovic knew war exacted a terrible price, but as long as he wasn't on the receiving end of that horror, he was gung-ho.

The Marine Corps granted his wish and sent him back to Vietnam on September 12, 1967. When luck turned on him, when that price turned out to be too high, Kovic changed his mind. His writing about what happened to him is dishonest at best and deliberately distorted at worst.

Kovic was not an innocent, naïve boy when he demanded to be sent back to Vietnam. *He had been killing people for a year.* The recommendation for Kovic's Bronze Star Medal described his skillful actions in coordinating armed helicopter fire during fighting from July 2, 1966 to January 13, 1967, which killed numerous enemy soldiers. It's tragic that Kovic is now in a wheelchair, but he was a Marine. Marines kill enemy soldiers. Marines are wounded and killed. There are no guarantees. For Kovic to pretend he was victimized by the American government is an outrage.

When Stone's *Born on the Fourth of July* was released, Kovic praised the movie as an accurate depiction of the horrors he had experienced. "This film is about breaking down walls of ignorance, of lies, of half-truths," Kovic said.

"I'm obviously telling Ron's story," Stone echoed. "I'm not screwing with the facts."[625]

But the movie did not even follow Kovic's book, much less the factual story of Kovic's life. The film depicted Kovic's wrestling coach screaming at his high school athletes like a Marine Corps drill sergeant: "I want you to kill!" But Kovic's book described the man as a "very dedicated" coach, who preached the values of hard work and commitment. Kovic's coach, Al Bevilaqua, read the screenplay and refused to give Stone permission to use his name. "I'm not that type of person," he said later.

In a scene in Vietnam, Kovic went to his major and confessed that he mistakenly killed Pfc. Wilson. "I don't need you to tell me this," the major snapped. "I'll take your head off." In reality, Kovic did tell his major his fears that he accidentally killed one of his own men in the heat of battle, but the officer did not callously dismiss his anguish. He investigated and concluded that it was unlikely that Kovic killed him. The major later promoted Kovic to leader of a scout team.

And Kovic did not visit the family of Pfc. Wilson in Venus, Georgia, and confess his terrible deed, as shown in the movie. There is no Venus, Georgia. Kovic later admitted that scene happened only in a dream.

In the movie, Kovic spoke at a Fourth of July celebration after his return from Vietnam in support of the war but is shattered when he hears a baby cry. The sound flashes him back to Vietnam, prompting him to remember an infant he left behind after mistakenly slaughtering a group of Vietnamese peasants. He can't finish his speech.

This incident was a figment of Stone's over-heated imagination and doesn't appear in Kovic's book. Instead, when Kovic and another disabled veteran participate in a Memorial Day ceremony in his hometown of Massapequa, Kovic wondered why he and the other vet "hadn't even been given the chance to speak."

Police at Syracuse University didn't club the wheelchair-bound Kovic at a 1970 antiwar student strike, where the fiery speakers include Kovic's true love from the prom, now an antiwar leader, and Abbie Hoffman. Not only was there no police violence during that strike, Kovic was never there. Neither was Hoffman. More of Oliver Stone's poetic license. Why doesn't he just admit it?

Even the story of Kovic's terrible injuries was distorted. In the movie version, Kovic is wounded in the heel and goes berserk, spraying lead at the enemy in a rage with little regard for keeping under cover. He's hit again, paralyzed when his spinal cord is severed. In the book, when Kovic is shot in the heel, he realizes the wound will send him home. "I was getting out of the war and I was going to be a hero," Kovic wrote. "I started to get up and a loud crack went off next to my right ear as a thirty-caliber slug tore through my right shoulder, blasted through my lung, and smashed my spinal cord to pieces."

The citation for Kovic's Bronze Star Medal, attested to by witnesses, describes events leading up to Kovic's spine-shattering injury very differently: "Alertly observing a wounded Marine lying in a dangerously exposed area, Sergeant Kovic, with complete disregard for his own safety, began moving toward a wounded Marine and was wounded in the leg. Ignoring his painful injury, he continued his determined efforts to reach the man until he was wounded on two additional occasions and was evacuated."

Kovic acted like a well-trained, loyal Marine—until he made it home.

Vietnam veteran Richard Eilert, author of a book called *For Self and Country*, also suffered terrible injuries in the war when he was hit with a grenade.[626] Eilert lost one leg and the use of the other.

"*Born on the Fourth of July* and *Platoon* share common characteristics," Eilert wrote in 1990. "Both are laced with enough fact to make the stories difficult to refute, while at the same time they are saturated with so much hateful negativism that in the end the proper term to describe them is probably 'propaganda' or 'disinformation.' In the end, both films seem to work most effectively on the guilt of those who did not serve in Vietnam, while at their kindest they disappoint the honest expectations of those who did.

"I, like many who were seriously wounded in Vietnam, have a bone to pick with both Stone and Ron Kovic. It was not easy for any of us. During the time I was hospitalized at Great Lakes Naval Hospital, I was surrounded by some of the most hideously wounded people the war produced. A visitor once commented that it was a miracle many of us survived. I replied that the real miracle was that so many even wanted to survive.

"But there was a camaraderie and acceptance of responsibility in that hospital—and even today among those who have known heavy combat—that curiously seem to have evaded both Stone and Kovic. Men fight wars for each other."[627]

But Stone's version of events in Vietnam is forever enshrined in a book and a movie, starring heartthrob Tom Cruise having a bad hair day. *That's* who people will think of when they think "wounded Vietnam vet," not the many men who were disabled, came home, and rebuilt their lives.

The Maverick

Another good soldier twisted reality to portray himself not as a victim but as a hero in the 1990 book *Maverick: The Personal War of a Vietnam Cobra Pilot*, by Dennis J. Marvicsin and Jerold Greenfield. *Maverick* was picked up by the Military Book Club, sold as a "powerfully authentic memoir of one soldier's duty in Vietnam."[628]

Marvicsin, one of a group called—what else?—"the Assassins," weaves a gripping story of his capture by the enemy after his chopper was forced down.

Injured, he was held in a bamboo tiger cage, pulled by a water buffalo through little South Vietnamese hamlets. Dressed in black pajamas, pissing blood, Marvicsin was displayed like an animal to the villagers who poked at him with sharpened sticks and pelted him with garbage and excrement. After being kept for a month, unable to either stand or lie down in the tiny cage, fearing that any moment could bring death, Marvicsin was abruptly removed from the cage. Trussed up like a chicken, his arms pulled back and lashed to a pole, his NVA captors forced him to walk under his own steam.

But as they tramped through the jungle, American jets attacked, dropping napalm and frying or scattering his captors. In a scene worthy of John Rambo, "Maverick" Marvicsin, still tied up, scurried into the underbrush. But Maverick was not home free. He turned to see one of his captors, the one he called Dopey, with his rifle aimed at the back of his head.

"Dopey, silhouetted in the orange light of burning jungle, lowered his rifle to his side, saluted him, and bolted off down the trail away from the flames, was swallowed up by the forbidding green, was gone."[629]

If that wasn't incredible enough, what happened next was amazingly fortuitous. Given a momentary reprieve from death, Maverick continued to crash through the jungle until he stumbled on a huge clearing teeming with American helicopters, Cobras, "the most beautiful, most moving, most poignant sight that Maverick had ever witnessed. And then they all began shooting at him."

Saluted by an enemy soldier while escaping, shot at by his own troops, who luckily had very bad aim, Maverick survived two tours in Vietnam while those around him succumbed to its death and destruction.

The truth, unfortunately, is more mundane.

Marvicsin is a former Navy enlisted man who became an Army aviator. He indeed survived multiple honorable tours in Vietnam. And he was an excellent helicopter pilot. Heroic, courageous, Marvicsin received a Silver Star, two Distinguished Flying Crosses, a Bronze Star Medal, and two Purple Hearts, showing he was wounded twice.[630]

But Army records show there is nothing to indicate Marvicsin was ever a POW during the Vietnam War. And he is not on the official POW list. Marvicsin was merely one of the thousands of good helicopter pilots whose story was not particularly unusual—until he threw in the juicy stuff about tiger cages, villagers poking sticks and throwing shit at him, and "Dopey" saluting Marvicsin rather than shooting him in the back.

Sometimes publishers make claims for authors in order to sell books. *Before the Dawn* is the 1988 biography of Mickey Block, who served in Vietnam as a crewmember of a PBR river patrol boat, sometimes used to ferry SEALs into combat. Excerpted in *Reader's Digest*, the book was marketed on the cover of the paperback edition as "the powerful true story of a Navy SEAL—from elite training to top-secret missions in Vietnam."[631]

In reading the book, it's obvious that Block never took SEAL training and did not graduate from the various schools that a potential SEAL must attend. Block actually admits that in one sentence in the book. The publishers exaggerated his military accomplishments to sell the book. Then Block began to assume the role. Now Block lectures extensively on his Vietnam experience and does so wearing the Navy SEAL badge lapel pin, which military records show he did not earn.[632]

When Presidio Press, which calls itself "America's foremost publisher of military history," published *Swimmers Among the Trees* in 1996, the book jacket proclaimed author Joel M. Hutchins "a highly decorated SEAL veteran" with five years of service and combat experience.[633] The book described SEAL operations in Vietnam, but Hutchins made a number of major mistakes in the book that no true SEAL would make about weapons and methods of operations. In Chapter 11, "Watching the Trail for SOG," he claimed that SEALs conducted raids against NVA base camps and POW camps within North Vietnam and operated with H'mong tribesman and CIA agents along the Ho Chi Minh Trail. They did not.

According to Hutchins' military record, he did serve in Vietnam but not as a SEAL. Hutchins was a Navy hospital corpsman assigned to Da Nang. He served in the Navy from February 1966 to November 1969, and received an honorable discharge. But his record listed no Combat Action Ribbon, denoting combat in Vietnam. Nor did he receive SEAL training.[634]

After I gave Hutchins' record to Capt. Larry Bailey, USN (Ret.), he wrote a scathing review of the book for the November issue of *Soldier of Fortune*. But Bailey pointed out that Hutchins never actually asserted that he was a SEAL in the book nor claimed to have served in specific operations. After Hutchins' record was brought to its attention, Presidio Press issued a *mea culpa,* taking the blame.

"[The errors] started with a copywriter's assumption and ended up in print without Mr. Hutchins having had the opportunity to correct the record," said Richard Kane, marketing director for Presidio. "The author, however, is not responsible for these errors."[635] Kane said the book was virtually sold out, but it would not be reprinted. (This was after the Military Book Club chose it as a selection.) Still, it's hard to imagine that Hutchins didn't read the jacket of his own book before publication and call someone's attention to the errors.

With another 1996 publication, *Covert Warrior: Fighting the CIA's Secret War in Southeast Asia and China, 1965–1967* by Warner Smith, Presidio Press's claim to be the foremost publisher of military *history* took it on the chin—

and it wasn't because of a copywriter's "assumption" but an author's wholesale prevarications.[636]

Smith, who described himself as a veteran of CIA/Naval Intelligence, wrote of his participation in secret missions for the CIA as a member of a sixteen-man unit known as FRAM 16, which operated in North Vietnam, Laos, Cambodia, Thailand, even mainland China. "There were thousands of battles, skirmishes, and missions in Vietnam, Laos, and Cambodia," Smith wrote. "The ones included in this book are described here because I believe the information should be a part of the documentation of the Vietnam War." And writing the book was also Smith's way of finally dealing with his long-standing PTSD—first understood when he broke down and wept when visiting The Wall.

Among the numerous covert operations Smith claimed his unit undertook was the liberation of twelve American aviators from a prison camp in Cambodia. His small team attacked the camp, overpowered the guards, released the prisoners, and whisked them from the area on CIA helicopters. In another operation, one he described as crucial to the outcome of the war, Smith parachuted into South China alone to reconnoiter a highway used to transport SAMs (surface to air missiles). After killing an enemy truck driver, Smith slithered under the tarpaulin to record the markings on the missiles. Smith trekked miles over the Chinese landscape until he was able to set up an elaborate rig that allowed an airborne aircraft to snatch him off the ground.

The Military Book Club chose *Covert Warrior* as its selection of the month. The book jacket described Smith's missive as "the most remarkable memoir to come out of the Vietnam War." That may be true. It certainly gets high marks for creativity and imagination. According to Warner Lloyd Smith's military record, he was commissioned a Navy ensign on June 14, 1964. As part of his air intelligence officer preparation, Smith entered noncrewmember flight training at the Naval Air Basic Training Command in Pensacola, Florida, on July 6, 1964. He was disenrolled at his own request. Smith received no training in clandestine operations, and his only overseas assignment was at Sangley Point, Luzon, Republic of the Philippines. Smith was an aviation maintenance officer, with the extra duty of treasurer of the officer's mess. His only award was the National Defense Service Medal, and he left the service in July 1966.

But Smith covered his bases, explaining how, while he was in the hospital recovering from injuries incurred on his final mission, he received a thick manila envelope with his records showing incorrect dates of service, that his last duty station was Sangley Point, and listing only the National Defense Service Medal.

"It was part of the reverse 'sheep-dip,' and I was briefly amused at the lengths to which the Company would go to cover my activities over the last eighteen months or so," Smith wrote. (The usual one-size-fits-all explanation: "Of course my military records don't show I was a covert operative! That proves I was!")

Of course, Smith claimed that of his sixteen-man team, only two survived. Besides himself, there was "Robert Gomez," paralyzed as the result of a Claymore mine, "rarely speaking as a result of his wounds and physical anguish." The rest of his team members are given common names and are described in such vague terms that it makes it impossible to verify they really existed.

But Smith's tale was revealed as a fabrication in the details. Just one example: Smith described his convalescence from injuries (suffered during the free-fall from a helicopter into the South China Sea) at Clark Air Force Base hospital. In the curtained-off bed next to Smith is a young Army nurse, who dies of injuries suffered in an enemy ambush of a MASH unit. No such casualty occurred in Vietnam.

Another SEAL book puts all those problems with truth and reality aside right up front. *Mekong! The Authentic Novel of Naval Special Forces in Vietnam*, by James R. Reeves, was marketed by Ballantine Books, a division of Random House, as the "adaptation of the Vietnam experience" of former SEAL James C. Taylor of Harrison, Arkansas. "We chose to present the story through the medium of fiction to avoid difficulties with classified information and to avoid invading the privacy of those whose names and character would be included in a nonfiction narrative: the survivors of SEAL Team One and Boat Support Unit One." But while names, dates, and locations of actions were changed, it is "as true to the actual events as possible. In no instance have the exploits of the SEALs been exaggerated, however."

During Taylor's heroic tour in Vietnam, he was required to shoot a young Vietnamese girl, who turns out to be a suicide bomber. His team killed captured prisoners and smoked dope while on patrol. And of course, when Taylor returned home from the war, he was plagued by flashbacks and nightmares, his long-suffering wife awakening at night to find his hands around her throat.

"*Mekong!* is based on Taylor's story, as told to Reeves in many conversations and taped interviews," says the back cover of the paperback. "Taylor's nightmares and flashbacks have been greatly reduced by the telling of this story." The book was followed by another in 1987: *Covert Actions*, by James C. Taylor and James R. Reeves, a novel of Vietnam "based on the actual experiences of James C. Taylor, a former SEAL and Vietnam veteran." Fictionalized, although to a lesser extent than *Mekong!* this book included five episodes that took place during Taylor's first—and only—tour in Vietnam. "The second tour is completely fictitious," the jacket said.

Well, according to military records, virtually everything in both these books is fictitious except for Taylor's name. James Carl Taylor of Harrison, Arkansas, served in the Navy from April 3, 1969, to April 2, 1973—as a mechanic. His only award was a National Defense Service Medal. Taylor was not a SEAL, nor did he serve in Vietnam or in waters off the coast of Vietnam.

The Clancy Stamp of Approval

Mega-thriller writer Tom Clancy, of *The Hunt for Red October* fame, has built a fortune and a reputation as a novelist with an encyclopedic knowledge of the weapons systems and all things military. In 1991, Clancy hailed the publication of *North SAR* by Navy pilot Jerry Carroll, published by Pocket Books, a division of Simon & Schuster.[637] Carroll and Clancy knew each other well in high school. "This is the best first novel I have ever read," stated Clancy's enthusiastic blurb on the front cover. The book described the exploits of a fictional pilot named Tim Boyle involved in Sea-Air Rescue in Vietnam, a character based on Carroll, a retired Navy lieutenant commander who received a Distinguished Flying Cross.

"This novel concerns the Navy and the Vietnam War," Clancy wrote in the introduction in which he said Carroll had been shot down three times. "Although our country has bad memories of that conflict, those memories result not from what our men did, but rather what was done to our men. Jerry and all the others did not choose to go there. They were sent."[638]

Clancy gave the reader the distinct impression that his friend was a combat pilot in Vietnam, adding much credibility to the authenticity of Carroll's novel. His second book, *Ghostrider One*, also was about Sea-Air Rescue operations in Vietnam.

Sadly, Carroll's third novel, *No Place to Hide*, which continued the saga of Tim Boyle, was published after Carroll's death of heart failure. Clancy wrote an afterword to the book, memorializing his friend.

"He was supposed to be safe," Clancy said. "Almost five thousand hours aloft as a naval aviator, much of that combat time. History will probably take note of what our generation has accomplished. But it wasn't all of our generation. It was actually just a few, many of whom, like Jerry, expressed their devotion in a hot, lonely place called Vietnam." Clancy concluded the book by pointing out that Tim Boyle, the fictional combat Vietnam War hero celebrated in Carroll's books *"is* and always will be Jerry Carroll."[639]

Jerry Carroll was indeed a Navy helicopter pilot. He did receive a Distinguished Flying Cross for a difficult noncombat rescue during the

Grenada conflict. But according to Carroll's military record, he never served in the Vietnam War or Southeast Asia at any time. He was not shot down, nor did he come under fire, as evidenced by the fact that during Carroll's entire career he was never awarded a Combat Action Ribbon, given by the Navy to those who experience combat.[640] Indeed, most of Carroll's flying career was spent in Atlantic Ocean antisubmarine squadrons. Jerry Carroll's imagination may be matched only by Tom Clancy's gullibility. If someone with Tom Clancy's military expertise can be fooled, then anyone can be fooled.

One Tough Marine

In the category of good troops with vivid imaginations is *One Tough Marine* (Ballantine Books, 1993), by Maj. Bruce H. Norton, who has a considerable reputation as the author of authentic war biographies.[641] (Norton is now the director of the Marine Corps Recruit Depot Museum in San Diego, California.)

This best-seller is the biography of Marine Corps 1st Sgt. Donald N. Hamblen. Hamblen fought in Korea, where he had an exemplary military record. But his exceptional career appeared to be cut short when, during a parachute training exercise at Camp Pendleton in 1962, Hamblen fell into a power line carrying sixty-nine thousand volts. Five days later his badly burned left leg was amputated six inches below the knee.

Determined to stay in his beloved Marine Corps, Hamblen went into rehabilitation and learned with the help of a prosthesis not only to walk but also to run and swim again. He convinced the Marine Corps to let him remain in the service if he passed all the physical tests required. Miraculously, he did. At his request, Hamblen was sent to Vietnam and assigned to a Marine detachment assigned to MACV-SOG. Their job was to train North Vietnamese nationals for clandestine operations in both North and South Vietnam.

From here, the book veers into fantasy. Hamblen said that for the next thirty consecutive months, he performed sixty missions, forty of them into North Vietnam on "snatch" assignments. (Since he had one prosthesis for walking and one for swimming, presumably he took his extra leg, swathed in camouflage, strapped to his back.) Hamblen said he was wounded twice on these missions.

No Americans routinely were involved in any clandestine operations into North Vietnam. Almost all of those operations were conducted by North Vietnamese defectors, without any direct participation of Americans. The handful of occasions that Americans did enter North Vietnam were expressly approved by the President of the United States.

(Although MACV-SOG spent nine years trying to infiltrate the North, the operations were a complete failure.)[642]

But even harder to believe was that the Marine Corps would send a one-legged man into combat. When *One Tough Marine* was released, Maj. Gen. John ("Jack") Singlaub, commander of MACV-SOG during part of Hamblen's tour, took offense. Singlaub is unequivocal in his statements about Hamblen, whom he calls an "absolute liar" and his tales of activities in North Vietnam "pure fantasy."

"I seriously doubt that any MACV-SOG subordinate commander would have run the risk of a court-martial of himself to satisfy the ego of a fantasizing Marine even once, let alone the forty times claimed by Sergeant Hamblen," Singlaub wrote. "In short, it didn't happen."[643]

Singlaub's comments were passed through Harve Saal (who has compiled and published a history of MACV-SOG), to Owen Lock, the editor-in-chief at Del Rey Books. (The book was published by Ballantine. Ballantine, Del Rey, Fawcett, and Ivy are divisions of Random House.) Lock had edited Hamblen's book. Lock minimized General Singlaub's objections, saying that Hamblen had buddies who backed up his stories and implying that Singlaub did not know what his own men were doing.

I tracked down Hamblen's chain of command, finding those who were his immediate commanders or those who served with him.

"The book would be better titled 'One Lying Marine,' "said Lt. Gen. Bernard E. Trainor, USMC (Ret.), now director of the National Security Program at the John F. Kennedy School of Government at Harvard University. Trainor was Hamblen's commander for a large part of the time Hamblen was supposedly making incursions into North Vietnam.

"With due respect to Hamblen's excellent Marine Corps record, he certainly exaggerates it in this book," said Trainor. "At no time was Hamblen ever privy to intelligence material received for our operations, nor did he ever know the identity of the targets of the operations. Hamblen's tale of cross-border land operations is ludicrous." He pointed out several technical mistakes in Hamblen's description of the unit's operation. "In short, Hamblen, a very fine Marine with an enviable record, has cheapened and discredited himself and the Marine Corps with a tissue of distortions and lies."[644]

Maj. Pat Carothers, USMC, whom Norton refers to as "Smothers" in the book, was just under Trainor in Hamblen's chain of command. While pointing out several inaccuracies in the book, Carothers completely supports Trainor's analysis. Hamblen's claim to forty missions in North Vietnam "is not based on any truth that I'm aware of in the year that I was there as Chief, Operations and Training (CHOPSTRA)."[645]

W. H. "Duff" Rice, who later became a Marine major general, took command of the unit in August 1967. Hamblen claimed he did not leave the unit until November of that year. But Rice does not remember him; it is highly unlikely for a commander not to remember his first sergeant of four months. "Also, I can unequivocally state that during my watch (1967–68), no U.S. personnel were allowed to go into North Vietnam with our South Vietnamese teams," Rice said.[646]

His records show that Hamblen spent the majority of his time in Vietnam as part of a unit within MACV-SOG whose job was to train North Vietnamese defector volunteers for raids on the North.[647] No American accompanied these raids. During the latter part of his tour, Hamblen was assigned to counsel fellow amputees in a hospital, a noble responsibility but not one that makes a best-seller.

In *Vietnam: The Other Side of Glory*, author and Vietnam veteran William R. Kimball told first-person accounts of thirteen Vietnam veterans, including Capt. David C. Shaffer, former Green Beret, now of Minneapolis, Minnesota. Shaffer claimed he was with the "Special Operations Group" from December 1967, to November 1969. His squad carried out covert counterinsurgency operations "deep in enemy territory for months at a time." Their true identities closely guarded, their orders were to "take no prisoners, leave no survivors." If captured, their government would disavow any knowledge of them. "It was somewhat like *Mission Impossible*— except it was real."[648]

Oh, yeah? The problems with Shaffer's narrative abound. But the very first is that, as I've pointed out before, anyone who was a Green Beret in Vietnam knows that SOG did not stand for Special Operations Group, but Studies and Observations Group.

Another major discrepancy: Before one secret mission, Shaffer claimed, a general gave him a sealed envelope and ordered him not to open the flap until they were twenty-five minutes from their drop-zone. Most Green Berets, if given sealed orders moments before being dropped into enemy territory, would tell the general to go screw himself. (Before a mission, Special Forces troops train intensively, going over and over, in endless, excruciating detail, the plans for the specific operation. As an example, the Son Tay Raid to extract prisoners from North Vietnam was months in preparation.) Shaffer and his men were told to parachute north of the DMZ to destroy an NVA staging camp with the assistance of the Montagnards. (Bogus! If the American military wanted to destroy a staging area, it would send bombers.) Then Shaffer and his team escaped an ambush only by crawling into a VC tunnel system, wriggling more than half a mile to safety. (Ludicrous. Didn't happen.)

Much more entertaining stuff happens in Shaffer's narrative. A six-hundred-pound tiger attacks. The VC capture, kill and mutilate members of their team. Vast numbers of the enemy are killed when Shaffer and his men mine the bottom and bank of a river. But it's all a fantasy, a Hollywood Rambo version of spies and covert operations.

Shaffer even talked like James Bond in this book. "Back in 'Nam, I was a professional with a license to kill," Shaffer is quoted as saying. "I was a seasoned master in the deadly art of stealth and sabotage. I'd learned to live an earshot from death, to hunt humans, to survive off the land by the cunning and resourcefulness of my fine-tuned skills." And, of course, as the highly trained killer he was, Shaffer could not adjust to life after Vietnam.[649]

"The Army could teach you how to waste people with proficiency, but they couldn't teach you how to return home the same way you left," Shaffer told Kimball. "I was an adrenaline junkie, hooked on my own self-induced high. I was addicted to the lethal rush of warfare." Back in the states, he joined an outlaw motorcycle gang, a "tumbleweed existence of violence, drugs, and sex."[650]

I contacted author Kimball about my reservations with Shaffer's story and explained I had been unable to locate a military record for Capt. David C. Shaffer. Kimball readily admitted he believed the story was fabricated. Although he had not gotten Shaffer's real record, he became aware of Shaffer's fabrications after publication. All subsequent printings of his book did not contain Shaffer, Green Beret. The problem is, tens of thousands of copies are still out there, containing more bogus history of the Vietnam War.

The Irregulars

The story of John Gallagher turned up in "Soldiers: A History of Men in Battle," a thirteen-part series by BBC-TV. Gallagher was featured in a segment called "Irregulars," about civilian guerrilla troops and elite units such as the Green Berets. He was the only one quoted about American Special Forces in Vietnam. The narrator described how the Americans tried to win the "hearts and minds" of the aboriginal Montagnards by providing medical treatment. Gallagher described himself as a Special Forces medic.

"My job was what was known as a bush doctor," Gallagher said. "The Montagnards had never seen a doctor. I would take care not only of my twelve-man A-team but of all the villages that were in my area."[651]

Gallagher, a thin-faced man with glasses and black hair, described the exceptional local knowledge and fieldcraft possessed by the Montagnards. "We were on a patrol at night," Gallagher said. "This Montagnard said there was a Viet Cong in a tree about three hundred meters ahead. I looked at this guy and said, 'Sure there is.' I called for a night scope, which makes everything look like daytime. I couldn't see anybody in any tree."

With wonder in his voice, Gallagher told what happened next. "Another guy brought up what's known as an infrared scope, which shows body heat. Again, nothing shows up on the scope. This Montagnard picks up his crossbow, puts an arrow into it, and fires it, and all we hear is a thu-thump. A body hit the ground. He [the Montagnard] said that guy was there for days."

Gallagher's team was later attacked by the Viet Cong while on patrol with Montagnard troops. "We tried to run and they surrounded us, and we had an ensuing gun battle. Two of my team members were wounded. Three Montagnards were killed. They took the Montagnards who were still alive and killed them one by one in front of us, then dismembered the bodies. Then they took the two team members who were wounded and were going to do the same to them. I got them to stop that.

"They held us for forty-seven days. They put us in holes in the ground eight feet by four feet. And that's the way we lived until we managed an escape. During the escape, only seven of us made it. Five were killed."

Gallagher appeared again in *The New Face of War*, a *Time-Life* book.[652] In a chapter called "Special Forces and Missions," Special Forces Sgt. John Gallagher described walking into a Viet Cong ambush: "Taking two of his men, he attempted to outflank the hidden assailants and take them out. [Gallagher] later recalled, 'I got around to the side and pointed my M-16 at them, and this person turned around and just stared, and I froze because it was a boy. I would say between the ages of twelve and fourteen. When he turned at me and looked, all of sudden he turned the whole body and pointed his automatic weapon at me, I just opened up, fired the whole twenty rounds right into the kid, and he just laid there. I dropped my weapon and cried.'"

Open up *The Vietnam Experience*, a book by the Boston Publishing Company. There, in a section called "The Aftermath," was the intrepid Gallagher again. A photo depicted Green Beret John "Doc" Gallagher at a reunion of the Special Forces in November 1984, hugging a man he thought was dead. Gallagher hadn't known whether his buddy Santiago lived or died, but they rejoiced at the reunion. They later visited the Vietnam Veterans Memorial together. "After the Viet Cong had overrun their camp at Dak To during the 1968 Tet offensive, Gallagher had patched up a bullet wound in Santiago's throat and sent him out on a medevac helicopter," the caption said. "Of the twelve men in their unit, Gallagher, Santiago, and a Green Beret named Carter Stevens were the only survivors of the war."[653]

Gallagher really made the rounds. He was portrayed as a medic, Green Beret sergeant, child killer, POW, war hero, the recipient of three Silver Stars, three Bronze Star Medals for valor, three Air Medals, and five Purple Hearts.[654] His Colorado car license plate bore the legend "POW 863." Not only did authors and filmmakers buy his wild stories, Gallagher was even accepted by Special Operations Association (SOA), an organization open only to those in elite units such as the Green Berets and Navy SEALs.

But Gallagher's real military record showed he was a wheeled vehicle mechanic with the Special Forces Group (Reserve), a stateside duty, from June 1968 to June 1976, when he entered active duty. (Note that he didn't go into active duty until well after the war was over.) He then was assigned to Fort Sam Houston for medical specialist training, followed by duty with the 505th and 504th Infantry, 82nd Airborne at Fort Bragg. Gallagher's highest rank was as a specialist five. He had not been a prisoner of war and earned no valorous decorations or Purple Hearts. Gallagher, discharged in June 1980, had not been assigned to a Special Operations unit, nor did he serve in Vietnam.[655]

After finding out Gallagher was a fraud, the SOA kicked him out. Colorado authorities confiscated his "POW 863" plates.[656] But his fantasies live on in the *Time-Life* series, available for generations to come at your local library.

Yet another self-described veteran of the Phoenix Program is Yoshia K. Chee, featured in *Strange Ground: An Oral History of Americans in Vietnam 1945–1975*, by Henry Maurer.[657] Chee also appeared in a *Time-Life*/BBC documentary called "CIA: Phoenix Rising," wearing long black hair and an earring, looking quite the mystical warrior.

Born in Hawaii, the son of a Chinese-American man and a Native American woman, Chee claimed that he joined the Army in 1966 and qualified for Special Forces. Sent to Okinawa, Chee said he was one of two hundred Asian-Americans who trained for membership in a special elite force called Peregrine Group. Only twenty-five finished the grueling program.[658]

"The theory was that being Asians or half-Asians, we would look like the Viet Cong, live like the Viet Cong, and think like the Viet Cong," Chee said on camera. (Only credulous British television producers would mistake Yoshia for a Viet Cong.)

Chee's fourteen-man Peregrine team arrived in-country in late 1967, not long before Tet. They began working in the highlands with the Montagnards. As they adapted to village life, Chee and his buddies also discovered opium. "We started doing unmentionable quantities of the stuff," Chee said.

After Tet, the Peregrine Groups worked mostly on secret missions looking for sympathizers of the Viet Cong in the delta, near the Cambodian border, or inside Cambodia. "We were supposed to grab the Cong suspects and send them back for interrogation," Chee said. "Not many made it back. It was interrogation on the spot." Chee claimed his group was used to settle scores between villages, that he and his men often detained the wrong people and frequently resorted to outrageous forms of torture. "One of the favorite things was popping one of their eyeballs out with a spoon," Chee said. Or they would skin the bottom of the prisoner's feet and beat them with a bamboo rod. They routinely tossed prisoners out of helicopters and took the heads of others.

On missions to find VC, most often they just killed everything in sight. "Anything that moves, you shoot it," Chee said. "It's dark and you don't give a fuck what it is anyway. We had a saying, *Gomen nasai*, which means 'Pardon me.' It comes from the Japanese. Sometimes if there were four houses in a row, and we weren't sure which was the right one, we'd kill everybody in the four houses. It happened all the time." Chee and his men proved they killed their targets by bringing back the enemy heads.[659]

Another of their duties was to destroy Viet Cong hospitals. "The thing was to go in there and get the doctors. Get the nurses. Get the patients, too, fuck it. Anyone in white, you shoot first, any way you want to do it."

During these brutal excursions, Chee and his team were high most of the time on opium and methedrine, a form of speed given to them for endurance. "We had to be stoned," Chee claimed. "I can't see anybody in their right mind doing the stuff I did."

Of course, there were some things even Chee could not tolerate. Once, "lying against a mango tree, smoking a doobie," he saw two ARVN troops about to rape a woman with a pop-up flare. Chee pulled out his sidearm and shot the two soldiers dead.

Chee claimed that on April Fool's Day, 1969, his team—seventeen men in all—was assigned to a secret operation in Cambodia. They were ordered to kill three targets, a sympathizer and two NVA. But word of their mission somehow leaked out. No one but women and children and old men were in the Cambodian village when they arrived. Frustrated, Chee grabbed a baby and held him up by his ankles, threatening to kill the infant unless the mother told them where the soldiers were. She refused.

"Then the major told me to shoot the kid," Chee said. "I would have done it, but the whole thing, something in the back of my mind—I saw this woman's face. And I said, 'Fuck it, you shoot it. It's not going to be on my conscience.' And the guy shot it. He shot the baby." But the mission went from bad to worse. The Americans were ambushed. Fifteen died—everyone but Chee and his best friend. They found the other team members naked and decapitated in the village.

But the carnage was not over. Assigned to command a rifle company of Vietnamese draftees, on Christmas Day, 1969, Chee said he lost forty-two men, including five Americans. "There was supposed to be a cease-fire, but we went out," Chee said. "We ambushed these people first, and all hell broke loose."

During his tour in Vietnam, Chee claimed he was awarded a Silver Star, Bronze Star Medal with V, two Purple Hearts, Vietnamese Cross of Gallantry, and was recommended for the Distinguished Service Cross. But Chee had turned against the war, deciding the North Vietnamese were right and the Americans were wrong.

Of course, after all this trauma, Chee went on an opium and heroin binge. One night, he was in the act of having sex with a whore in Cholon when someone threw two grenades in the whorehouse, and her head was blown away. He went AWOL, developed a three-hundred-dollar-a-day heroin habit, and ultimately received a medical discharge. He returned to America in 1971, plagued by emotional turmoil.

"I was taking a lot of speed. And I had a couple of breakdowns. I would destroy everything in the house." But Chee finally pulled himself together with help from the Veterans' Outreach Centers.

Getting the wrong targets, secret missions, staying stoned, routine torture, killing innocent women and—of course—babies, getting commendations for committing war crimes, a moral epiphany after losing those he loved—all the quintessential myths of Vietnam permeate Chee's stories.

Chee provided few hard details in his ramblings. But those few facts clearly reveal Chee's tales for the fantasies they are. On April 1, 1969, the day Chee claimed fifteen men in his team were killed, casualty records show that twenty-one men died in Vietnam. But only nine died in the same province. And according to casualty reports, the story Chee told about the ambush on Christmas Day, 1969, in which forty-two ARVN and five Americans died, also did not happen.[660]

I was unable to locate any records that anyone named Yoshia Chee ever served in Special Forces or the Army in Vietnam—or for that matter, that Chee ever served in the United States military at all.

The Duke

At age thirteen, he was a nerdy, overweight boy with a terrible self-image. He enrolled in a martial arts class taught by Ninjitsu master Tiger Tanaka, who took the determined young man under his wing. Under Tanaka's tutelage, young Frank William Dux mastered the fine arts of subterfuge, weapons, herbology, and hand-to-hand combat used by the legendary band of secret assassins known as Ninja.

Those skills came in handy later when eighteen-year-old Dux enlisted in the Marine Corps in 1975. He quickly found himself part of a "Special Operations Group," sent on a covert mission into Laos called "Operation Sanction." One of the few survivors of that horrific mission, Dux claimed he "fought his way back into Thailand," returning with "bayonet wounds in the stomach and shrapnel in the back."[661]

During his career as a Marine, Dux claimed to have received the Navy Cross, the DSC, the Silver Star, the Bronze Star Medal, the Navy Marine Corps Medal, the Purple Heart, and a "secret" Medal of Honor, bestowed for a clandestine mission. After the war, "because of his experience and practical knowledge," according to Dux's resume, he "was recruited as a Special Tactic Instructor" and acted as a consultant "to more than twenty-five foreign and domestic police and military agencies," including antiterrorist consultation for Nicaragua. His resume also indicated experience with the FBI and the National Security Agency/Defense Intelligence Agency.

Dux contended he became the first Westerner to win a mysterious, no-holds-barred international tournament of Ninja fighters held every five years called the Kumite and reigned as the undefeated "Full Contact Kumite World Heavyweight Champion" from 1975 to 1980. Some of his records included: most consecutive knockouts, fastest knockout at 3.2 seconds, fastest recorded kick of seventy-two miles an hour, and fastest recorded punch of 0.12 seconds with a knockout. One incredible fighter.

Thanks to Hollywood, the exploits of Frank Dux will live on as long as there are VCRs. "Shidoshi" Dux received national attention when the movie *Bloodsport* starring Jean-Claude Van Damme was released in 1988. Advertised as a true story based on Dux's life, *Bloodsport* followed his training by the Japanese master warrior Tiger Tanaka and Dux's ultimate triumph.

Dux, who also claimed to be the first "non-Japanese martial artist" awarded the title Shidoshi, owned two Ninjitsu studios in California. The success of his studios and the movie gave credence to Dux's boasts that he had carried out covert missions in Southeast Asia. As a former lance corporal in the U.S. Marine Corps, Dux maintained, he was one of the most decorated although "unsung" veterans of the conflict in Southeast Asia, "gaining awards for valor and self-sacrifice in clandestine operations behind enemy lines."

But the *Los Angeles Times* called Dux's exploits into question after the release of the movie *Bloodsport*. Reporter John Johnson pointed out that the trophy Dux said he received after the "no-holds-barred" world championship in the Bahamas had apparently been made in North Hollywood. And a trace of the organization which sponsored the tournament, the International Fighting Arts Association, led back only to Dux. Film producer Mark DiSalle, who had taken the project to Cannon Film Group, defended Dux, saying that his research "definitely convinced" him that Dux's story was true. But even the screenwriter, Sheldon Lettich, acknowledged that Dux's contentions could not be verified. "We were taking Frank on his word," Lettich said.[662]

Dux seemed to have gone to elaborate lengths to create documents to support his story. He showed Johnson an editorial that he said had appeared in the *Washington Star*. The article, written in support of Dux's "testimony" to a House intelligence committee on secret missions in Southeast Asia, purported to quote from a commanding officer's diary: "We're hungry. We're tired. We're all out of ammo. We all might go mad if not for a spunky kid named Duke for short." The "diary" then described how "Duke" crawled into a minefield and rescued—you guessed it—a baby, which he later gave to a Taoist priest. "When we almost gave up, the Duke, by himself, charged the gun. The next thing you know, the Duke was behind the gun, cutting the enemy to pieces. He must have killed a hundred gooks at least. He turned defeat into victory." But Johnson's check of the archives of the *Washington Star* indicated no such article about Dux had ever appeared.

According to Dux's official Marine Corps record, his true military career was far from glorious. Frank William Dux served on active duty in California from June 15 to October 23, 1975—less than six months—when he was honorably released from active duty. (He continued on reserve status until 1981.) Dux's record showed no valorous decorations and no overseas service, nor did he graduate from any of the military schools that are mandatory preparation for clandestine operations.[663]

The record indicated that Dux's predilection for tall tales concerned his superiors so much that on January 22, 1978, while still in the Marine reserves, Dux was referred for psychiatric evaluation. "This individual interviewed because of some bizarre type behavior which centered @ (sic) flights of ideas and exaggerations," the doctor who interviewed Dux wrote in the file.[664] The report said that Dux insisted he was working for an intelligence agency. Dux was then a lowly private in the reserves and not likely to be entrusted with major operations. The doctor diagnosed "problems in adjustment to adult life" and recommended that Dux receive "psychiatric evaluation and/or therapy."

A follow-up medical assessment at a military psychiatric clinic in Long Beach, California, in April of that same year found Dux's mental condition sound, but the medical records repeat that Dux's only intelligence work had been his casual involvement in gathering facts about one person.

While Dux contended that he was wounded in combat, records show no evidence of that; however, they do show that in May 1978, Dux fell from a truck in the motor pool while painting the vehicle. Doctors diagnosed him as suffering "possible muscle strain." (That California motor pool was a long way from the fetid jungles of Indochina.)

When confronted by reporter Johnson, Dux's explanation of the discrepancies was that the military sabotaged his record to discredit his information about clandestine missions. But even the Ninja world called Dux's exploits into question. "There is not (sic) Mr. Tanaka in Japanese history" of Ninja families, said Shoto Tanemura, a Japanese man who is part of an elite group of recognized Ninja masters in the world. Tanemura had never heard of Dux. The name Tiger Tanaka? It apparently came from *You Only Live Twice*, a James Bond novel by Ian Fleming.

Johnson called Dux a "bright but undistinguished young man who, using cleverness and chutzpah, re-created himself as a superhero a decade ago, painstakingly authenticating his new persona with military medals, trophies, and newspaper clippings of questionable origin."

But the exposé of Dux's lies did not make a dent in his sham reputation as a covert operative. He convinced New York editor Judith Regan that he was legitimate. Regan, who made a sizzling reputation in the media world by bringing out books by Howard Stern and Rush Limbaugh, had persuaded media mogul Rupert Murdoch to create an imprint under her name at HarperCollins. In April 1996, ReganBooks published one of its first projects, *The Secret Man: An American Warrior's Uncensored Story*, purporting to be the "true story of the U.S. government's most trusted spy"—namely Frank Dux.

"He was the CIA's finest covert operative," reads the cover, "the subject of the martial arts film *Bloodsport*. A bridge to international organized crime. A legend on both sides of the Iron Curtain, his true identity always concealed from the people he served." And finally, "Truth stranger than fiction."[665]

No kidding.

In this new revelation of himself, Dux painted a picture of an out-of-control, sleazy CIA with accusations of unpunished and unreported killings and implications of cooperation with drug kingpins in South and Central America as well as other countries in Southeast Asia and the Middle East.

Dux claimed he was recruited by CIA Director William Casey for top secret missions. "I demand absolute loyalty," Casey supposedly told him. "I need a ghost. Someone not subject to reports, red tape, even laws. I want a zookeeper, son. A spy for spies. You answer to me, and I mean only me." Casey sent him to assassinate rogue U.S. agents, to work with the Soviets to search for a stolen "bioweapon," and to sabotage oil tanks in Nicaragua.

The climax of the book was the story of Dux's most prolonged mission —his two-year effort to find and assassinate a highly decorated Vietnam veteran-turned-CIA-operative. In Dux's previous representations of himself, he had boasted of his status as a Vietnam hero awarded a "secret" Medal of Honor. In *The Secret Man*, Dux flipped the myth. Now he was the one brutalized by the war, denigrated by the "anti-Semitic" Marine Corps.

And the major villain was a vicious rogue agent who—during his four tours of duty in Vietnam—led a secret life as a war criminal, child slave trader, and serial killer.

The book was given an aura of authenticity with the reproduction of official-looking documents and ID cards that purported to show that Dux not only was a U.S. operative but also was the man known as Soviet Officer "Fedor Nicolayevich Duchovny." One foreword was written by "Maj. Gen. Anatoly Pavlovich Kornienko," who allegedly enjoyed a long career with the Soviet armed forces and provided support to "Officer Duchovny," as Dux was known in his undercover capacity in the Soviet Union. A longer foreword by Cmdr. Larry W. Simmons, U.S. Navy (Ret.), former commander of SEAL Team Five, gave *The Secret Man* an important stamp of approval. After serving almost twenty-eight years in the SEALs, Simmons is a legend. There's even a picture of Simmons and Dux together "talking shop." But the book, like *Bloodsport*, like the Soviet officer "Major General Kornienko," is completely bogus.

In their zeal to release Dux's sensational, bitter "true story" as a covert operative, Judith Regan and her legal advisors apparently did insufficient fact-checking. If they had, they would have discovered the *Los Angeles Times* story challenging Dux's claims. They also would have discovered that the FBI had investigated Dux for fraudulently wearing military decorations, including the Medal of Honor and the Navy Cross, and recommended to the U.S. attorney in Los Angeles that Dux be prosecuted. (He also had been arrested for spousal abuse.)

Shortly after the release of the book, I contacted former SEAL commander Simmons, whose foreword granted Dux's book such validity. Simmons admitted he knew nothing of Dux. An aspiring Tom Clancy, Simmons did a favor for his literary agent, Joel Gotler, who also was Dux's agent. After Simmons' first book was purchased by Simon & Schuster, the agent talked him into writing a short foreword for Dux's book. Simmons asked to read the book, but HarperCollins told him they couldn't show it to anyone until it was published. Simmons dropped the subject and assuming that the book had been checked out by HarperCollins—which, after all, is a major publisher—took thirty minutes to write a generic foreword, with his agent's assurance that it would help his own literary career. "I needed the plug to sell my book," Simmons admitted sheepishly.

Then Simmons was asked to show Dux around the Coronado Island SEAL facility. Although Simmons refused to take Dux to an active duty command, he agreed to set up a tour of the Naval Special Warfare Training Center. Dux brought along a photographer, who snapped pictures of Dux with Simmons. One photo appeared in the book with the caption: "Talking shop with SEAL Team 5" and described Simmons as "Lieutenant

Commander," as if the picture had been taken sometime in the past. (In fact, most of the "commando"-type photos in the book were taken during Simmons' tenure at the center. Dux obtained them from a friend of Simmons, who is making a documentary film on the SEALs.)

When the book was released, Simmons quickly realized from reading the first few chapters that Dux was not an "American warrior" but a brazen liar. Simmons penned a furious letter to HarperCollins. "It has come to my attention that much of the information in [Dux's] book is fabrication and that I have been deceived into lending credibility to this fraudulent book," Simmons wrote. He demanded that his foreword and the photograph be removed from all subsequent printings of *The Secret Man*.[666]

Gen. Norman Schwarzkopf also issued a statement regarding the book, denying Dux's contention that he delivered "intelligence assets" for Schwarzkopf's implementation of a plan to disguise U.S. helicopters as Iraqi copters to penetrate Iraqi airspace during the Gulf War. There was no such plan, Schwarzkopf said.[667]

Casey, conveniently, is dead and could not protest Dux's portrayal of him. But Dux clearly never even met Casey; he described the CIA director as a "short, balding old man with white tufts of hair in disarray around huge ears." Working with Casey all those years, Dux apparently never noticed that Casey was more than six feet tall.

But another player in the book—retired Maj. Gen. John. K. Singlaub—is very much alive and was furious at Dux's depiction of him. Dux described Singlaub as heading the Phoenix project, "known for bordering on excess and used techniques that in some quarters might be classified as war crimes. One practice described to me left a strong impression: booby-trapping flashlights with C-4 explosive and leaving them alongside trails. Of course, kids and civilians often found them before the 'bad guys.' I didn't like that."

While a colonel, Singlaub was commander of the Studies and Observations Group. He was never involved with Phoenix, an entirely separate project, and he strongly objected to Dux's implication that he condoned atrocities. Singlaub's attorney sent a letter to HarperCollins, demanding that the book be withdrawn.[668] The publishers defended Dux, pointing to a book called *Soldier*, by Anthony Herbert, which painted Singlaub as the conniving head of a rogue counterterrorist agency. But if they had made even a slight effort at checking his information, they would have discovered that Herbert's book has been thoroughly discredited.[669]

Other mistakes, contradictions, and just plain fabrications abound in Dux's book. *Well, so what?* seemed to be the attitude of the people at Harper-Collins. If the book depicts lying, murderous government officials, evil military operatives, war crimes, atrocities, and Vietnam, well—"everybody" knows that's what it was really like, and anyone who disputes that view is an apologist for the establishment. And that's what people like Dux count on.

Real Hero, Phony Writer

Texas author Pete Billac wrote *The Last Medal of Honor*, the story of MSgt. Roy Benavidez.[670] At the time Benavidez was the last Vietnam veteran to be awarded the Medal of Honor. He was seriously wounded while on a mission in Vietnam. Left with only a Bowie knife and a bag of medical supplies, he rescued a besieged Green Beret detachment and a downed helicopter crew. He's a legitimate hero. (On July 10, 1998, President Clinton awarded the Medal of Honor to Navy Corpman Robert R. Ingram for action on March 28, 1966.)

Benavidez has said he chose Pete Billac to write his biography because he was enthralled with Billac's own tales of multiple heroics as a Navy SEAL in Korea and a Green Beret in Vietnam. On publicity flyers, Billac has described himself as a gifted athlete, with more than 150 trophies for boxing, swimming, tennis, golf, football, track and field, skydiving, hot-rod racing, karate, and spearfishing—and the recipient of degrees from Tulane University in geology, physics, and chemistry.

During his stint in the military, Billac supposedly retrieved guided missiles and astronauts from the water for the government. "He also served more than seven years as a mercenary in such places as Biafra, Rhodesia, Bay of Pigs in Cuba, and two years in Laos and Cambodia with Delta and SEAL teams," said one of his flyers.[671]

After the war, he not only wrote screenplays for television, he also worked as a Hollywood stuntman. And he has owned "real estate companies, nightclubs, a string of art galleries, an uptown modeling studio, a salvage diving company, a charter airline, and a coconut plantation in Mexico. His books include *How Not to Be Lonely Tonight*, *How to Handle a Macho Man*, and *The Annihilator*, a book about the Mafia, for Swan Publishing Company, which is owned by Billac.

Whew! What a guy!

I did not investigate all of Billac's boasts, but I did file an FOIA request for his military records. Billac served in both the Army and the Navy, with very unspectacular tours of duty. In the Navy, Billac was your basic seaman, serving from May 13, 1951 to September 25, 1956.[672] So much for being a SEAL or underwater demolition expert.

In the Army, he served at a NIKE site (an antiaircraft missile station) as an enlisted man, not as a colonel in the Green Berets, as he has claimed. His active duty Army career lasted less than two years, from October 15, 1956, to July 23, 1958. (Delta Force didn't begin until the 1970s.) Billac's record indicated no overseas assignments whatsoever.

Jailbird

Some authors turn to creative writing about the war because they have considerable time on their hands.

In early 1991, I was alerted by retired Col. Jack Abraham, president of the Special Operations Association, about a book called *Slow Dance on the Killing Ground* (Alpha Publications, 1990), by Lenox Cramer.[673]

"For some grunts, 'Nam was hell—for others, it was home," read the front cover of the paperback, a direct ripoff of Rambo. And the back cover: "The story is true—the ops, the engagements, and the death. The names have been changed to protect the innocent—and the guilty."

The book purported to be the "true" experiences of Cramer performing clandestine operations as a Green Beret in Southeast Asia, specially trained in martial arts. (Cramer's previous book was called *War With Empty Hands: Self-Defense Against Aggression*, also published by Alpha.)

Cramer's sensational experiences of war included a hair-raising tale about his unit's ambush in South China of a Chinese train carrying nerve gas into North Vietnam. *South China?* Needless to say, Abraham suspected that Cramer's fantastic tales were bogus.

Reprinted in the front of the book—clearly an effort to show that the author was a genuine war hero and the story was real—was a purported copy of the author's DD-214, showing work with Special Forces with the name whited out. The form indicated that the writer had received a Distinguished Service Cross, a Silver Star, two Bronze Star Medals for valor, five Purple Hearts, and a Combat Infantryman Badge. But numerous typing and record-keeping errors made it easy to see the document was a crude forgery.

Working in conjunction with Abraham of the SOA, I began tracking down information about Cramer. The book said that Lenox Cramer was a *nom de guerre*; I wanted to know the author's real name. Alpha Publications would not tell me.

The SOA kept after the publisher. Finally, in a letter to Colonel Abraham, John Staub, director of Alpha Publications, explained that the author's real name was Michael Erik Cramer and enclosed his DD-214. "I would appreciate being kept informed of your finding," Staub wrote. "If the author has misrepresented himself to us, we would have to take the necessary legal actions since this would be a breach of contract."[674]

Cramer himself, hearing about the questions, wrote a letter to Abraham, contending that his book was based partially on actual experience and in part on stories related to him by participants. "I was unsure of what might still be classified, so to be safe in that regard, and again for the sake of 'dramatization,' I altered the who, what, when, and where significantly," he wrote. I'll say.

He also explained why he could not use his real name. To his embarrassment, he was incarcerated in the Kentucky State Prison and had been since February 1978. "When threatened, I reacted the way I'd been trained," Cramer wrote. "Unfortunately, it was in the wrong country at the wrong time."[675]

A light clicked on in my head. I checked with the prison. They had Lenox Cramer, not Michael, in jail. The prison personnel people gave me his biographical data. I checked St. Louis and located a record for a Lenox Cramer. His Social Security number was the same as the number of the Lenox Cramer in prison. Bingo! Cramer had contended to the publisher that Michael was his real name so that nobody would check the military record for Lenox.

The record indicated that Cramer had never been a Green Beret. He was a clerk-typist and his only overseas assignment was in Germany. His service was marred by several AWOLs and charges of possession of amphetamine and a pipe with marijuana residue, and the wrongful possession of a switchblade knife. He had been court-martialed out of the service.[676]

Abraham wrote back to Alpha Publications with this news. Despite his earlier letter pledging to take action, Staub was indifferent. He was satisfied with Cramer's explanations that his clandestine missions were classified, and besides, Alpha had sold the paperback rights to Avon Books.

An editor at Avon readily admitted they did not verify that Cramer had served in Vietnam. He even laughed about it. Avon packaged *Slow Dance on the Killing Ground* as fiction completely based on the "true life" of Lenox Cramer. Talk about having your cake and eating it, too.

When I found out Cramer was in the Kentucky State Prison, I did not think to ask why he was incarcerated. In 1994, when Tom Jarriel of *20/20* decided he wanted to use Cramer's story, his producers checked with the prison system. They quickly informed me that he had been convicted of the brutal and sadistic murder of a hitchhiker. But they also found out Cramer was no longer on the prison rolls. When the producer told me this, I managed a weak laugh. "You're going to have me on national television exposing a murderer who is now out there and free!" I said.

"Don't worry, your murder will make a great ending to our story," the producer joked. But the next day, *20/20* located Cramer. He had been sent to Florida to stand trial for killing two people in a contract hit. I was substantially relieved to find out that Mr. Cramer would be incarcerated for a considerable amount of time.

Cramer agreed to an on-camera interview with *20/20*. It turned out that Cramer had been the star of a creative writing class in prison. He had built a reputation as a martial arts expert in his previous books, then totally fabricated his persona as a Green Beret in Vietnam. But when confronted with his real record, Cramer refused to 'fess up. Why should he? He can make big bucks sitting in prison, spinning ludicrous tales about Vietnam and selling them to gullible publishers.

Valentine's Day

The Phoenix Program: A Shattering Account of the Most Ambitious and Closely Guarded Operation of the Vietnam War (William Morrow and Company, 1990) by Doug Valentine, is a more scholarly version of clandestine operations.[677] But his book has about as much to do with the real Phoenix Program as Cramer's Green Beret fantasy.

The Phoenix, or Phung Hoang Program, was designed to root out the infrastructure of the Viet Cong, the South Vietnamese guerrilla Communists who were supporting the aim of the North Vietnamese to conquer the South. Valentine painted Phoenix as the "CIA's bloodiest reign of terror," a government-sponsored "murder for hire" and "assassination" program in which Americans tortured, killed, and imprisoned anyone suspected—however remotely—of being associated with the Viet Cong, including families, supporters, and innocent bystanders.

One of Valentine's main characters was Elton Manzione, supposedly a Navy SEAL who trained Vietnamese friendlies to make raids with "Nasty-class" PTF boats on North Vietnamese shipping and coastal installations. Manzione said he worked in a "hunter-killer" team. He was the first person to answer an ad Valentine placed in a Vietnam veterans' newsletter asking for interviews with people who served with the Phoenix Program.

As part of a secret operation, which preceded the Phoenix Program, Manzione was aboard one of two Nasty-boats that raided two North Vietnamese islands in the Tonkin Gulf in 1964. But North Vietnamese PT boats spotted them, and the chase was on. During the pursuit, Manzione and his clandestine compadres inadvertently led the enemy boats into the path of patrolling American destroyers doing standard duty in the gulf. The North Vietnamese mistakenly believed that these destroyers were part of the attack and attacked the USS *Maddox*.

This is no insignificant tale. Manzione was claiming responsibility for an epic event, what came to be called the Gulf of Tonkin incident, which effectively precipitated America's deeper involvement in the Vietnam War. President Lyndon Johnson immediately ordered air raids on North Vietnam, the beginning of the direct participation of American troops in the Vietnam War.

Manzione described in loving detail stories of his gruesome covert operations, which included killing children and removing the livers from the bodies of dead enemy soldiers. He and his fellow SEALs were told to ignore the rules of engagement.

Remorseful, Manzione turned on the military, on his country, denouncing "American imperialism," speaking out against the "misdeeds of the CIA." He joined the Vietnam Veterans Against the War.

His reason for talking to Valentine: "This story needs to be told because the whole aura of the Vietnam War was influenced by what went on in the 'hunter-killer' teams of Phoenix, Delta, etc. That was the point at which many of us realized we were no longer the good guys in the white hats defending freedom—that we were assassins, pure and simple."

Valentine swallowed all this hook, line, and sinker.

I checked for the military records of Manzione and his fellow SEALs named by Valentine: John Laboon, Eddie Swetz, and Kenneth Van Lesser. Laboon, Swetz, and Van Lesser had served stints in the Navy, but none was a SEAL, and none had Vietnam service. Van Lesser did not enlist until 1977.

But the only military record I could find for an Elton Manzione belonged to a man who served during World War II.[678] And according to historical accounts of the Gulf of Tonkin incident, Valentine's version is inaccurate. No Americans participated on the Nasty-boat raids into North Vietnam before, during, or after the Gulf of Tonkin incident.[679] Valentine attributed the creation of Phoenix to Col. Dang Van Minh. But Minh had nothing to do with Phoenix; Minh was working as a translator for the Americans during that period.

Valentine admitted in his book that there was no record of Elton Manzione ever serving in Vietnam, but the writer was predisposed to believe him because he had discovered that his own father's military records had been deliberately altered to show the older Valentine had not been interred at a Japanese prison camp during World War II. That episode became the basis of Valentine's book, *The Hotel Tacloban*, another book which has been criticized as based on faulty history. Valentine offered no explanation for the fact that none of the other men named by Manzione had served in Vietnam. All sheep-dipped, presumably. (Valentine also relied on the previously mentioned Mike Beamon for information: " 'Sometimes we'd go out with a whole pack of mercenaries,' recalled Mike Beamon. 'They were very good going in, but once we got there and made our target, they would completely pillage the place. It was a complete carnival.'"[680] I could find no record that Beamon served in Vietnam.)

Active duty officer Navy Cmdr. F. C. Brown, who served two tours of duty in Vietnam, took Valentine to task on the historical inaccuracies in a review that was printed in the *Foreign Intelligence Literary Scene*, a publication of the National Intelligence Study Center, in 1993.[681] Valentine's response was a postcard: "What's the color of horseshit? What's the color of cowshit? What's the color of bullshit? Brown! Brown! Brown!"[682] Apparently Valentine doesn't take well to bad reviews or other criticism.

But Valentine and others who present their fanciful, distorted versions of history should not take offense when truth is demanded.

A more accurate and reliable book on the Phoenix Program is *Ashes to Ashes*, by Dale Andradé, a researcher at the U.S. Center for Military History.[683] Although widely believed to be a super secret American operation to assassinate thousands of Vietnamese civilians who were part of the Communist political infrastructure, in reality Phoenix was a public program announced at a press conference by a South Vietnamese government official, analogous to a U.S. Justice Department task force on drugs. Americans aided and supported the operations, but the actual activities were carried out by South Vietnamese. The purpose of Phoenix was to identify and apprehend the political leaders of the Communist movement in the South, not to assassinate them. A live captive with information about the system, his peers, supporting personnel, his orders, and future strategies was much more valuable than a dead Communist.

As one can imagine, when cornered, many of these terrorists did not surrender peacefully. They were heavily armed and usually traveled with entire squads of combat armed troops. Many of them died in ensuing firefights. There is no doubt there were abuses in the program; personal vendettas among the Vietnamese could be settled by identifying an adversary as a Communist political cadre to the Phoenix operatives. But it was not a program of widespread terror and assassination as often depicted. After the war, the North readily admitted that the most effective operation ever mounted against them was the Phoenix Program because it disrupted their entire organization.

Despite the accurate information available about Phoenix, it continues to be a source of fascination for wannabes who use it to fuel their written fantasies of covert operations.

Presidential Politics

Another creative writer, whom veteran journalist Alan Dawson has dubbed "my favorite flake," is Scott Barnes, an Arizona dress shop owner whose ludicrous lies may have changed the course of American history. He somehow managed to seize the ear of Dallas billionaire Ross Perot during his 1992 presidential campaign. In May 1992, Perot had the support of 37 percent of voters responding to presidential polls. But when Barnes told Perot he had been hired by the Republicans to tap his phones and to smear his daughter Carolyn, using doctored photographs to portray her as a lesbian in order to disrupt her August wedding, Perot called off his campaign.

Perot-gate was just one of many bizarre events in the topsy-turvy world inhabited by Barnes. In 1985, ABC News bought Barnes's assertion that he had been hired by the CIA to assassinate a Honolulu businessman; the network later was forced to retract the story.[684]

A self-described former intelligence operative, over the years Barnes has claimed to have been an Army MP, a Navy SEAL, a Green Beret, a CIA assassin, and a DEA agent. He is best known for contacting POW-MIA groups, claiming sightings and escapes of men still missing in Vietnam and asking for money and other help to stage rescue attempts. (That's apparently how he met Perot, who is known for his interest in the POW issue.) In 1987, Barnes claimed he was taken deep into Cambodia by the Khmer Rouge, where he saw weapons and munitions supplied by the U.S. defense attaché's office in Bangkok. A BBC "documentary" featured Barnes hooked up to an apparatus dispensing sodium pentathol, presumably to ensure that he was telling the truth, spinning tales about POW rescue attempts.

Barnes wrote a 1987 book called *BOHICA*, billed as "A True Account of One Man's Battle to Expose the Most Heinous Cover-Up of the Vietnam Saga!"[685] The title is an acronym that stands for *Bend Over, Here It Comes Again.*

In the book, Barnes described his involvement in a 1981 U.S. government-sanctioned operation called Grand Eagle with retired Army Lt. Col. James "Bo" Gritz, supposedly organized to investigate reports of live POWs in Laos. Barnes claimed he swam across a river from Thailand to Cambodia and photographed an American POW. He located other POWs in Laos but received orders from the CIA to assassinate them. The bottom line: The U.S. government not only knowingly abandoned POWs, it wanted them killed when their presence became known.

The book included copies of Barnes's DD-214, his security clearance papers allowing him to do top-secret work for the Defense Investigative Service, and other papers purporting him to be involved in "clandestine" work in Vietnam as well as alleged CIA assassinations and U.S. aid to the Contras.

Despite Barnes's braggadocio, he has never produced a single shred of convincing proof for his stories. Barnes created enormous dissension among POW-MIA activists. The National League of Families, the only organization composed of family members of those still unaccounted for in Indochina, accused him of exploiting the issue for personal gain (he had persuaded the wife of POW Charles Shelton to mortgage her house to pay his legal bills) and released a response to Barnes's book.[686] They pointed out that the border between Cambodia and Thailand has no river and that on the day Barnes claimed he crossed the alleged river into Thailand, he was observed in the U.S. embassy cafeteria.

Although his book includes a document purported to be Barnes's

DD-214, military records show Barnes was never involved in Special Forces or intelligence operations, nor did he ever serve in Vietnam. In reality, Barnes enlisted on August 21, 1973, and was discharged on December 19, 1974. Barnes served as a security guard in a detention facility at Fort Lewis, Washington. But after only sixteen months of a thirty-six-month commitment, Barnes was given an early discharge for "failure to meet acceptable standards for continued military service." Although his records are not specific, that kind of a discharge could have been the result of several things: poor attitude, lack of motivation, lack of self-discipline, inability to adapt socially or emotionally, or failure to demonstrate potential for promotion. In other words, Barnes was a screw-up.[687]

He had not been employed by the DEA, the CIA, the FBI, or the DIS, had no top-secret security clearance, and had not conducted government investigations. Barnes received no training as an investigator, secret agent, or spy. And his claims about locating POWs and seeing MIAs in Southeast Asia were as bogus as his alleged military career.

After interviewing Barnes as a possible guest for *Nightline*, journalist Ted Koppel called him a "pathological liar." But Col. Joseph A. Schlatter, chief of the special office for Prisoners of War and Missing in Action at the Defense Intelligence Agency, said it best in a letter to the National League of Families.

"In conclusion, Barnes's book *BOHICA* is nothing more than a collection of his fantasies and the fantastic tales he has been peddling for years," Schlatter wrote.[688]

Despite all the documentation challenging Barnes's veracity, he still manages to grab national attention. In mid-1995, Barnes turned up again, under investigation by the FBI as the alleged source of a fabricated letter faxed to Rep. Robert G. Torricelli (D-NJ) on National Security Agency stationery. The letter accused two U.S. Army officers of destroying records linking American government operatives to two murders in Guatemala. The FBI subpoenaed Barnes's telephone records after learning he had called Torricelli's office, the office of White House Chief of Staff Leon E. Pannetta, and the National Security Council, no doubt spinning new tales of intrigue.

The Mob and the War Hero

When Dominick Montiglio agreed to turn state's evidence against one of the bloodiest mob gangs in New York history, writers Gene Mustain and Jerry Capeci, well-known investigative reporters who cover organized crime for the *New York Daily News*, found a great source of information. In their first book on John Gotti, Mustain and Capeci had mentioned Montiglio briefly, as a "thief, loan shark, and drug addict." When the reporters began work on a book about the crime family headed by Montiglio's uncle, which killed more than two hundred people, FBI agents told them more about Dominick, describing him as an incredible war hero, a Green Beret who had fought in 'Nam. Montiglio had tried to use his experiences in the war to forge a new path, but then he fell under the spell of his murderous uncle, a captain in the notorious Carlo Gambino organized crime family who had raised him after his father left Dominick's mother.

The reporters spent hundreds of hours interviewing Montiglio for their 1992 book, *Murder Machine: A True Story of Murder, Madness, and the Mafia*, published by Penguin Books, which detailed the bloody exploits of the Roy DeMeo gang, vicious killers who not only killed their enemies but also cut them up into small pieces. The star witness who helped the government put them behind bars? Dominick Montiglio.[689]

This was Dominick's story. He grew up in Brooklyn. Although his father was a veteran of the Army Air Corps named Anthony Santamaria, from the time he was four years old, Dominick had been raised by Nino Gaggi, who ran a widespread mob operation for Gambino. Later, Dominick took his stepfather's last name. Handsome, with a good singing voice and a yearning to go into show business, Dominick was graduated from MacArthur High School in 1965 only to find his music career at a dead end.

The Vietnam War was heating up; a friend told Dominick about an elite group of warriors called the Green Berets who were fighting communism in Southeast Asia. The group sounded heroic and patriotic. On impulse, determined to become a Green Beret, Dominick joined the Army, a move that infuriated his uncle. If he was going to fight and die, Uncle Nino raged, he should fight for the Family, not America.

But Dominick never wavered. He progressed through basic and advanced infantry training, then he was accepted for Airborne and Ranger School at Fort Benning, Georgia, the next step toward becoming a Green Beret. Sent to the elite John F. Kennedy Special Warfare Center at Fort Bragg, North Carolina, he was cross-trained in two specialties—light weapons and silent warfare—and earned his Green Beret. (In reality, there was no training in "silent warfare.")

Two months after arriving in Vietnam, he rescued a fellow Green Beret hit by a sniper. Dominick shot the enemy soldier dead and dragged the wounded soldier to safety. For his heroism, Dominick received the Silver Star and later earned a Bronze Star Medal for valor for "saving a patrol from an ambush and helping to destroy a machine-gun nest while under heavy fire." After his first tour of duty ended, Dominick then volunteered for Long-Range Reconnaissance Patrol duty. The Lurps worked in close-knit, six-man teams. After his second year was up, Dominick volunteered for a third tour to be with them. In the summer of 1967, Sgt. Montiglio, just twenty years old, returned to the Central Highlands of Vietnam, where his unit was based near Dak To.

Late that summer, some of the worst fighting of the war broke out. About twelve thousand North Vietnamese army regulars had massed in the jungle west of Dak To. In the brutal artillery assaults and ground fire, his 173rd Airborne infantry company was reduced from 164 to 44 men. Dominick said he and others were sent into "mobile morgues" to identify parts of their dead buddies by the only remaining identifiers—their tattoos. Haunted by the images of dismembered bodies, he was wracked by his guilt at having survived the horror. Dominick told Mustain and Capeci how he received the Distinguished Service Cross in a battlefield ceremony that included an eerie tribute to the dead, with 126 empty pairs of combat boots lined up in neat rows. But the worst was yet to come.

That November, Dominick said, his six-man LRRP team was sent to scout a hill near the Cambodian border known as Hill 875. The enemy soldiers had retreated into Laos and Cambodia, and American commanders felt an NVA remnant was holed up on the hill, guarding the retreat. On November 18, 1967, the LRRP team's tenth day on patrol of the hill, Dominick, the "point man," came around a bend and saw a series of man-made steps running up the trail. The team followed the steps to an empty bunker connected to tunnels burrowed deep within Hill 875. Based on the Lurps' intelligence, commanders sent about five hundred American troops into the area. Although running low on food and water, Dominick's team was ordered to stay in place halfway up the hill.

But the next day brought a bloodbath that later become known as the Battle of Dak To. The NVA decimated the companies sent to pursue them. With Hill 875 under North Vietnamese control, the Lurps were not only stranded, they also were trapped by the enemy. The moans of fellow soldiers dying drifted up the hill. Montiglio and his fellow Lurps hid for two days. On the morning of the third, with their supplies used up, the six-man team was forced to move out. They fought their way down the hill until their ammo was virtually gone.

On November 22, 1967—the day before Thanksgiving—a rocket-propelled grenade attack exploded around them. Exhausted, dehydrated, Dominick tried to take cover. But a hand grenade exploded nearby, shredding his back and shoulders and knocking Dominick unconscious. The next thing he remembered was waking up in a military hospital two weeks later. The NVA had inexplicably melted away, allowing the LRRP team to escape with their wounded. His team had killed approximately fifty enemy soldiers during their escape down the hill. Montiglio spent several more weeks in the hospital. In early 1968, he left Vietnam for Fort Bragg. Told by a doctor that he could not parachute again because of a knee injury on Hill 875, Dominick angrily changed his decision to make the Army a career. He was discharged on December 16, 1968—but even before he left the military, Dominick began having flashbacks of combat. At a dance with a girlfriend, he saw the room explode, body parts flying everywhere.

Back in the states, Dominick married and moved to California, determined to stay out of the family business of organized crime. But after another failed stab at the music business, he returned to New York. Slowly, Dominick found himself drawn into the illegal end of Nino Gaggi's business—and into the killings. At the same time, he also began experiencing more flashbacks and nightmares of Vietnam. Dominick finally went to the VA for help. A VA doctor diagnosed him as suffering Vietnam "delayed stress syndrome." As he sank deeper into organized crime, Dominick began dealing drugs, eventually fleeing New York for Sacramento, only steps ahead of murderous rivals.

There, Dominick started going to a Vietnam Veterans' Center, attending therapy and eventually becoming a counselor for men who were still troubled by the war. He used the VA diagnosis of war trauma to qualify for welfare. But, although Dominick had left New York, he could not leave the Family. Arrested on an extortion charge while visiting New York, Dominick met with prosecutors from the office of Rudolph Guiliani, who had just been appointed U.S. attorney. Facing twenty years in prison, Dominick agreed to testify in a major racketeering case against his uncle and other relatives. In exchange, he would be given a new identity in the federal witness protection program. Guiliani's office issued a seventy-eight-count RICO (organized racketeering) indictment against Paul Castellano, Nino Gaggi, and twenty-two other crew members and associates of the crime family. In a press conference, Guiliani described the case as the "most important chapter" in the history of the federal government's war on the Mafia.

On December 4, 1985, *The New York Times* ran a story about the scheduled appearance that day of the case's star witness, Dominick Montiglio—describing him as a Vietnam veteran, loanshark collector, and drug dealer who had agreed to testify against Castellano and Anthony (Nino) Gaggi. Only days later, Castellano was gunned down in the street; Gaggi was convicted of conspiracy. A juror later wrote in a newspaper column that if not for Dominick's testimony, the panel would have acquitted his uncle.

After the RICO trials were over, Dominick pleaded guilty to murder, attempted murder, robbery, extortion, loansharking, and drug dealing. "I have found Dominick to be forthright and honest in all the dealings I have had with him," one of the task force investigators told the judge. Given five years probation, Dominick disappeared into the witness protection program.

That case and the Gotti case to follow cemented the tough-on-crime reputation of Rudolph Guiliani, later elected mayor of New York City. Prosecutor Walter Mack snared a big job on Wall Street. In the epilogue to *Murder Machine*, Mustain and Capeci acknowledged a "special debt" to Dominick Montiglio, who made his national television debut in disguise on the TV show *A Current Affair*. One of the only witnesses still alive, he talked about the trauma of testifying against his uncle. "I'd rather do three more tours in 'Nam," Dominick said on camera. He later appeared on a Fox Television documentary about his life in the Mafia.

I heard about *Murder Machine* when a Green Beret saw me on television discussing the bogus Vietnam vet phenomenon and called to tell me he thought that Dominick Montiglio was a pretender. I read the book and quickly formed my own suspicions. Montiglio said he had entered the Army at age eighteen, then went through jump school, Ranger School, and Green Beret training—a two-year sequence that makes him at least twenty by the time he arrived in Vietnam. But Montiglio described himself as returning for his *third* year-long tour in 'Nam as a "twenty-year-old sergeant." How was that possible?

When Montiglio entered the witness protection program, his personal military file was reconstituted under a new name, making it impossible to verify much of his story. But other records could be checked. No one by the name of Dominick Montiglio had ever been awarded a Distinguished Service Cross. A check with the Ranger School showed that no one named Montiglio had attended or graduated from that training from 1966 through 1968, nor was Montiglio a member of the Special Forces Association.

And the historical record also cast doubt on Montiglio's tales. According to the 1993 book *Dak To* by Edward F. Murphy, the infamous battle on Hill 875 did not happen the way Montiglio described. Montiglio claimed the fight was triggered when the LRRP team for which he was "point man" bumped into a large North Vietnamese force entrenched on the hill, subsequently trapping the LRRP team for several days as the battle raged.

But the battle of Dak To was actually triggered by a Green Beret, who instantly realized the indigenous force he was leading was completely outgunned by enemy troops. The Green Beret put out a call to the 173rd Airborne, which rushed infantry companies to the scene. A ferocious battle erupted, causing substantial casualties on both sides. Although the men of the 173rd Airborne LRRP company individually volunteered almost to a man to be sent back to their former infantry companies to serve as riflemen, all their requests were denied. The commanding officers sent the

Lurps to patrol other areas vulnerable to attack, which could result in the Americans being outflanked. At no time did the Lurps participate in the battle itself.[690]

Montiglio had fabricated the entire story, convincing not only his buddies in the Mafia, but the NYPD, the FBI, the U.S. Justice Department, federal prosecutors, and two expert investigative crime reporters that he was a major war hero—adding substantial credibility to his testimony. The government used a master fabricator as its star witness, then hid him in the witness protection program, obliterating any way to trace his real military record, and paid for him to start a new life. (Ironically Walter Mack, the prosecutor, had been a Marine Corps company commander in Vietnam.)

In 1995, after confirming that Montiglio had lied about his military experiences, I contacted reporter Jerry Capeci and told him my suspicions about Montiglio. Impatient, Capeci said he was on deadline and promised to call me back. He never did. But a call to his coauthor, Gene Mustain, elicited a totally different reaction. Mustain was curious and wanted to know more. I gave him a rundown of my evidence, and he agreed to check his sources. Over the next few months, we exchanged dozens of calls.

Mustain and Capeci had interviewed Montiglio for days. The FBI agents regarded him as a war hero, providing a strong stamp of authenticity. Montiglio also had documents and photos of himself in Army uniforms and jungle fatigues in what looked like Southeast Asia. His records were unavailable; but I heard about a reunion of the Lurps with the 173rd Airborne, who had served during the time period described by Montiglio. Mustain, determined to find out the truth, paid his own way to the reunion held in August 1995, at the Riviera Hotel in Las Vegas. At the reunion, Mustain interviewed the men about the battle of Hill 875 and confirmed that none of them had participated as Lurps. He met eight veterans who should have known Montiglio; none remembered him or recognized his picture.[691]

Mustain now realizes that Montiglio completely fabricated his stories of heroism in Vietnam. As an investigative journalist, he is embarrassed—and angry. "I've been a reporter for twenty-five years," said Mustain. "I always have my antenna up for phonies and frauds. I had no reason to doubt that he was anything but authentic. If it wasn't the truth, he did a masterful job of fooling not just us but the U.S. government. They came to a conclusion that he was truthful, and he was their key witness in this big case."[692]

Was Montiglio ever in Vietnam or even in the military? Only the federal government knows, and they've made sure that none of the rest of us ever will.

What Montiglio proves is that a man with a limited education, a vivid imagination, a streak of chutzpah, and heroic tales about the Vietnam War can fool the Mafia, the authorities, and anybody else. Worse, Montiglio equated the role of Mafia foot soldier—a participant in racketeering, drug-dealing, and murder—with heroic Vietnam service, and nobody thought this was inconsistent.

Vietnam Goes to College

One of the most prominent speakers at a conference at Texas Tech University on the Vietnam War in 1996 was Dr. Larry E. Cable, a professor of history at the University of North Carolina-Wilmington. Cable, who has written a handful of books on counterinsurgency, was an eccentric figure in jeans, sweatshirt, Indian turquoise jewelry, with a flowing mane of brown hair that reached his waist.

Despite his unusual appearance, more new-age hippie than military spit-and-polish, his reputation as an expert on counterinsurgency was impeccable. For years, Cable has lectured on covert operations at some of the most prestigious military institutions in the country—West Point, the U.S. Naval Academy, the U.S. Air Force Academy, the Marine Corps Command and Staff School at Quantico, and the U.S. Air Force Special Operations School. Cable had been chosen Lecturer of the Year by both U.S. Air Force and the Marine Corps schools and is featured in the official publication of the Army's Special Forces at Fort Bragg.

Although a Ph.D., Cable's expertise drew on his own experiences in the Vietnam War. In fact, Cable's status as a Vietnam covert operative gave him vital credibility when he began to publish his theories on counterinsurgency. Indeed, Cable presented himself as a sort of super spook. He claimed that during a tour of duty as a Marine in 1965–66, he advised the "Quang Ngai Special Platoon," which he described as a CIA-backed paramilitary force, and later the Quang Ngai Provincial Reconnaisance Units, (PRUs). He was not only effective but also was an honorable leader. Cable boasted that the South Vietnamese units with which *he* worked "never engaged in any abuses of the population because he led them directly and prevented the abuses," unlike other American advisors who were ineffective and whose forces committed atrocities.[693]

But Cable's stories conflicted with accounts of many other PRU advisors. Bob Wall, the CIA officer in charge of paramilitary programs in Quang Ngai during 1966, and Rudy Enders, the CIA's senior advisor in I Corps from 1966 to 1969, both said they had never heard of Cable and that there was no such unit as the "Quang Ngai Special Platoon."

I could find no record that Larry E. Cable ever served in Vietnam, the Marines, or in any branch of the U.S. military. Authorities at Shimer College in Illinois, where Cable claimed to have earned an undergraduate degree, said he dropped out his sophomore year and did not return to graduate.[694] Aware that Cable often lectured at many military schools, I contacted the

U.S. Air Force Special Operations School at Hurlburt Field, Florida, and alerted them about his misrepresentations. Authorities there investigated my charges and confronted Cable, who declined to provide documentation of his Marine Corps service. The professor was removed from the list of lecturers. Officials at the Marine Corps Command and Staff School heard about Cable's expulsion from the Air Force school and contacted me. They undertook their own investigation and determined Cable had not served in the Marine Corps. Confronted, Cable again refused to provide proof of his service. He no longer lectures at the Command and Staff School.

I sent my information about Cable to Dr. James Leutze, Chancellor at the University of North Carolina-Wilmington. I did not receive a reply. Cable, however, abruptly announced his resignation.[695]

In 1991, *60 Minutes* aired a segment called "Vietnam 101," about a class in the religion department of the University of California at Santa Barbara. The class had grown from a handful of students in 1979 to the most popular course not only on campus but also possibly the most heavily attended college class in America, with as many as fifteen hundred students each semester signing up.[696]

Presented by a religion professor named Walter Capps, the course featured the history of the war in Vietnam as presented by individuals who had been there. "Healing"—of the veterans, of a generation, of the entire country—is a common theme. Often the stories are so emotional, the speakers so overwhelmed by their memories, the class seems to be like an eight-hundred-member encounter group, with everyone in tears.

The lecturers have included everybody from Sen. Robert Kerrey, Medal of Honor recipient, to B.T. Collins, the Green Beret who headed the effort to build a California Vietnam veterans' memorial. But a virtual legion of average soldiers and airmen tromped through Capps' classroom to tell their stories to nineteen and twenty-year-olds who know little about Vietnam beyond what they had seen in the movies *Platoon* or *First Blood*.

Some of the speakers' stories seemed so crazy—emphasizing atrocities and amazing heroics—that I suspected many of the presenters were not Vietnam veterans at all. In 1990, I called Professor Capps, and he readily admitted that on a couple of occasions he had heard that some of the stories might not be accurate. He personally had never checked his speakers' military records. But Capps assured me that all of those he allowed to speak came to him with good referrals.

In 1994, a member of the Special Forces Association, an unofficial historian of the Special Forces, sent me a tape of former Green Beret Dan Gisel making a presentation to this class. Capps' class had grown in prestige to such an extent that the course was being shown on the National Educational Television Network and piped through cable systems in major metropolitan areas around the country. The Special Forces veteran had heard of my interest in false history and wanted to point out another outrageously ludicrous story being foisted on naïve and impressionable college kids.

Like many others, Gisel had visited the class out of curiosity and then had signed up to attend. After that, he returned each year as a guest speaker.

Gisel's presentation began with a Vet Center employee reading a citation for the Distinguished Service Cross given to Green Beret Dan Gisel for heroism in Vietnam. In full Special Forces regalia—green beret, uniform, full-sized decorations including the DSC and Silver Star—Gisel took the lectern.

Dramatically, Gisel told how he and other members of Green Beret team A-342, along with nearly four hundred South Vietnamese troops and their families, were attacked on June 9, 1965, at a Special Forces base in the Central Highlands by more than fifteen hundred enemy soldiers. Assault after assault hit the camp. The firefight raged for fifteen hours. When his commanding officer was killed, Gisel assumed command.

Air strikes finally made it possible for helicopters to evacuate the survivors. The enemy had killed some two hundred Vietnamese troops and members of their families. Twenty Americans were killed or wounded—one of the highest losses Americans had suffered in a single day up to that point in the war.

Although he didn't say so outright, he was describing the infamous battle of Dong Xoai. As Gisel told of fellow Green Berets who died, leaving him one of the few survivors, he seemed to choke up, pausing as if fighting back tears. Hollywood casting agents would have been impressed. Capps certainly was. At the end of the tape, the professor came out and praised Gisel as a hero, thanking him for sharing his compelling story. The bookend comments by Capps and the Vet Center employee authenticated Gisel's tales.

"I just tell the kids how the thing evolved as the firefight continued, how I reacted to the fact of losing so many of my friends," Gisel told the *Dallas Morning News*, which ran a story about the course. "I remember more about it each time I tell the story. I guess that's just because I tried to put all that stuff out of my mind for so many years."[697]

This was really an easy one. In the aftermath of the battle of Dong Xoai, Americans were awarded two Medals of Honor and three DSCs. Gisel described a Lt. Williams who received the Medal of Honor. Lt. Charles Williams did, in fact, receive the Medal of Honor after Dong Xoai. But Gisel didn't receive the Distinguished Service Cross, as he claimed. He wasn't even there.

Gisel's military record indicated that at the time of the battle of Dong Xoai, Dan Morris Gisel was a military policeman in Japan. Not until almost a year later, in April 1966, did Gisel set foot in Vietnam—as an MP security guard at a large communications facility at Qui Nhon. Gisel received no valorous decorations nor was he a Green Beret.[698] In other words, Gisel's story was a hoax.

Realizing from our first conversation that the professor didn't seem particularly concerned with the veracity of his participants, I didn't contact Capps. But when 20/20 came knocking on my door for stories about impostors, they gravitated to Gisel for two reasons: the outrageous nature of Gisel's lies, and because they had a full hour of pure cinematic prevarication on national television. The producers called Gisel at his home in Coeur d'Alene, Idaho, and asked if correspondent Tom Jarriel could interview him. Gisel readily agreed.

Before talking to Gisel, Jarriel interviewed Jim Taylor, a medic with the Green Berets that terrible day. "I knew every man on the team, and he wasn't there," Taylor said. "None of us ever heard of him." Taylor provided a picture of the twelve-man team.[699]

Jarriel skillfully led Gisel into a journalistic ambush. Gisel recounted his tales of heroism at Dong Xoai for an hour before Jarriel brought the hammer down. He showed him Taylor's picture of the real Green Beret team at Dong Xoai.

"Do you see your picture here?" Jarriel asked.

Gisel squinted and put on his glasses. There was a long, awkward silence.

"No, I do not," Gisel said.

"Can you explain your absence in this picture?" Jarriel asked.

"No, I cannot," said Gisel, breathing heavily and looking like a deer caught in the headlights.

The interview ended. As the two camera crews started packing their bags, Gisel's wife ran around the house, screaming at them. *How dare they impugn her husband's reputation!* Gisel just sat, as if in a state of shock. His lies were going to be exposed on national television.

Gisel had worn full-size military decorations in violation of federal law. I talked to agents from both the Justice Department and the FBI, but medals violations are not a high priority of an overworked judicial system. They declined to do anything.

When 20/20 rebroadcast the story in May 1995, the producer called Capps, who was later elected to Congress, and the university for a comment. They had only one thing to say: Gisel was no longer lecturing at UCSB.[700]

I'm not aware of any reprimand or any changes being made in screening course participants. Gisel had been a linchpin of this class for a decade. My guess is that in the years since the course started, literally dozens of pretenders have presented bogus history of the Vietnam War to thousands of impressionable college students. These liars will go on telling their fables. And young adults will go on believing that they heard the truth about the war.

But two well-known writers—Randy Shilts and Shelby Stanton—have reached far more people than all those in Capps' classes over the years combined. Both have distorted history in different ways. One to promote a political agenda and the other to promote himself.

18

The Historian and the "Gay Beret"

WRITERS who claim to write history or journalism bear a special burden: They must do meticulous research, be faithful to the historical record, and tell a good story. Their work, if done well, can stand for generations as a beacon of truth to those who want to understand our world and its upheavals. But those who have an agenda to promote or an ego to stroke can do an enormous disservice—setting in stone attitudes and beliefs that can be difficult for those who come behind them with more meticulous methods to dislodge. Nowhere is this more true than with writing about Vietnam.

The Historian
In the world of Vietnam military history, one of the best-known names is Shelby Stanton. Often presented as the foremost historian of the Vietnam War, Stanton has written eleven books on the war. As a definitive expert on the war, Stanton has lectured at the Canadian Military War College. A senior editor at *Vietnam*, a history magazine, Stanton was appointed Distinguished Adjunct Fellow at the Center of Strategic and International Studies in 1986, and was hired by the U.S. Department of Defense to write an analysis of exposure of troops in Vietnam to Agent Orange. His first book, *Vietnam Order of Battle*, outlined the entire structure of the U.S. military in Vietnam, unit by unit, from 1961 through 1973, and is now considered a classic.[701]

But Stanton is peculiar among historians: He was there. Not only was he there, Stanton boasted combat experience in Vietnam. As one of his book jackets pointed out, Stanton "served six years on active duty during the Vietnam War as a paratrooper platoon leader; a Ranger advisor to the

Royal Thai Army Special Warfare Center at Lop Buri, Thailand, and a Special Forces long-range reconnaissance team commander." He went through Airborne school, Ranger School, Special Forces School, and scuba school, retiring after being wounded in action.[702]

In "Project 404," a section of *War in the Shadows*, a book in the *Time-Life* series on the Vietnam War, Stanton described his clandestine work. As a lieutenant with the 82nd Airborne at Fort Bragg, Stanton was a supply officer providing equipment to the 5th Special Forces group when he was summoned by a Special Forces lieutenant colonel.

"You're just the right size and Ranger qualified," the old Southeast Asia hand told Stanton, who is five foot five. The Army had insisted on a waiver of his height before commissioning him as an officer. "We need small Americans like you for a special recon mission overseas," the officer said. "After all these years fussing with camouflage, we finally realized that the VC were getting our teams because they could spot tall Americans."[703]

It was an offer Stanton could not resist. Given top-secret training, Stanton was then sent to Thailand with the 46th Special Forces Company and attached to "Project 404." As part of an eight-man recon team, Stanton went into the jungle planting electronic sensors in Laos. He also performed underwater scuba missions in the Mekong River in Vietnam for MACV-SOG and ran interdiction missions in Cambodia.

But Stanton was wounded by shrapnel during a night rocket barrage in February 1973, making him one of the last casualties of the war. His severe war wounds forced him out of the service.

His numerous hazardous missions were represented among Stanton's many medals, which included the Bronze Star Medal for valor, for services while with Project 404; an Air Medal, for combat insertion into Cambodia in 1973; the Purple Heart, for wounds suffered in combat on February 5, 1973, at Vien Pou Khe, Laos; the Vietnam Service Medal with one star, and the Vietnam Campaign Medal with device, both of which indicated service in Vietnam. He also received the Cambodian National Defense Medal, a decoration given to only a handful of Americans, usually Special Forces, involved in clandestine training missions inside Cambodia.

After the war, Stanton attended Louisiana State University Law School, but his true love was writing about the war. Even when he was editor of the *Law Review* and writer and producer of the Law School Senior Play, Stanton was finishing up his first book, *Vietnam Order of Battle*. When he went to work for Exxon, he continued to write.

In addition to his prodigious output, what set Stanton off from his peers who were also attempting to set down the war's history was his incredible access to military records. He seemed to be able to find photos, files, and top-secret documents no one else could locate. From his first book, published in 1980, to his subsequent histories of the Green Berets and Rangers, Stanton's ability to provide incredible detail about his subjects distinguished his books from all others.

And the fact that he was there made a difference not only in his writing but also in his stature as an authority. He wasn't some wimpy academic. He was a rough, tough Green Beret, one of the elite. In the *Time-Life* series, Stanton wrote about his thrilling rescue of the crew of a CIA plane that had gone down in Laos.

It happened during his stint with "Project 404." Stanton led an eight-man team of Americans, Thai warriors, and Meo hill tribesmen. "Armed to the teeth," they moved at night, laying electronic sensors along the Ho Chi Minh trail to provide intelligence about troop movements. In December 1972, his team received a radio message that an Air America plane, supplying the CIA's war in Laos, had crashed. His team, sent to rescue the wounded pilot and copilot, was attacked while securing the aircraft. As the firefight escalated, Stanton radioed for rescue aircraft. A four-man Loach helicopter raced to their aid, its miniguns pinning down the enemy until a larger aircraft could scoop up Stanton's platoon and the crew. Years later, Stanton, an accomplished artist, painted a picture to accompany his writing that was as detailed as a photograph, down to the serial code XW-PDJ on the tailboom of the downed CIA aircraft.

Stanton's scuba team was sent on another rescue mission. A training plane that had been sabotaged crashed in the Mekong River. Although the pilot was killed, Stanton's team was sent to retrieve the plane's engine. This time, the only enemy they encountered were some mud wasps.

Clearly Stanton understood not only the experience of combat but also the excitement and terror of clandestine missions. The Green Berets, the Rangers—the elite units—loved the man who promoted their glorious history.

When I began buying books about Vietnam, I naturally turned to Stanton for the "real" history of the war. He was the acknowledged expert. But I had become the world's biggest skeptic—generally suspicious of anyone pushing wares based on their combat experience. A Ranger, a Green Beret, and an Airborne trooper? It seemed all a little too heroic for a five-foot-five asthmatic.

I asked one of my "Vietnam grapevine" friends on the East Coast if he knew Stanton. The friend admitted that Stanton was the most unlikely candidate for the tales of daring he told. Stanton claimed that, in addition to participating in clandestine operations in Thailand, Laos, and Cambodia, he had been part of Command and Control Detachment North, a command unit for MACV-SOG Green Berets in Vietnam.

When I filed an FOIA request for Stanton's record, I expected to find out he had exaggerated his exploits a little. You know—war stories. But what came back surprised even me.

Stanton, although a Green Beret and Ranger, had claimed he spent two years in Southeast Asia planting sensors along the Ho Chi Minh trail and performing underwater scuba missions in the Mekong River, that he was attached to MACV-SOG, ran interdiction missions in Cambodia, fought in Vietnam, and was wounded in Laos. But Stanton's official military record showed that most of his Army service was spent behind a desk assigned to ordinary administrative matters. In December 1972, Stanton was sent from Fort Bragg to Thailand, where he went to work as the administrative officer for a Special Forces training detachment in Lop Buri, 150 kilometeres north of Bangkok, far from the war zone. A year later, he returned to Fort Bragg. There was nothing in the file to indicate Stanton ever was stationed in Vietnam, Laos, or Cambodia, nor did he perform covert operations.

Portions of Stanton's military record, including the section outlining his awards and decorations, appeared to have been altered. The record indicated he was entitled to the CIB, as well as the Vietnam Service Medal and Vietnam Campaign Medal. But he had not been in Vietnam. How was that possible?[704]

Stanton's company commander in Thailand, former Capt. Henry "Hank" Newkirk, is now a mortgage banker in San Antonio. Newkirk confirmed that Stanton had not participated in any combat operations, let alone a battle in Laos, and that no one in his unit qualified for the CIB. As his company commander, Newkirk would have known if Stanton had been pulled out to do a clandestine mission. In Southeast Asia, Stanton was already a budding military historian. He was designated to order supplies, draw up the charts, and maintain records for the unit.

In later years, as a member of the Military Order of the Purple Heart, Stanton often pointed to a large piece of shrapnel on his desk at home and told visitors that the chunk of steel had ended his military career. Over the years, he has given two different dates and three different locations for his wounds. But Newkirk said that Stanton was not wounded while under his command; no one under his command in Thailand had been injured by enemy fire.[705]

A CID investigation later indicated that Stanton did receive a Purple Heart. How he earned the decoration is open to question. However, it wasn't in a battle at Nam Yu, Laos, as Stanton has contended in the past. Apparently Stanton was driving in a Jeep to bring back Thai soldiers when a round exploded near the road. Stanton either fell out of the Jeep or the concussion knocked him out of the vehicle, injuring his leg and back. He was put in for a Purple Heart and received it in Thailand. (Although Stanton claimed it was a serious injury, his military records showed no period of hospitalization.)

In any case, the shrapnel on Stanton's desk had nothing to do with his "war wound." It was given to him by a Green Beret who is still in the military. And the injury had nothing to do with him being forced to leave the military. Stanton was medically retired for asthma.

Obtaining Stanton's official record was just the beginning of a prolonged and peculiar tale. Not long after I received it, Col. Harry Summers Jr., USA (Ret.), editor of *Vietnam* magazine and distinguished fellow at the Army War College, wrote an editorial in the August 1992 issue boasting that the magazine's review board was scrupulous about keeping inaccurate history out of the magazine. "Not one of our almost two hundred authors has ever sold us a bill of goods," Summers wrote, adding that he and his editors could tell phonies in "the first three sentences."[706] Summers had written the foreword of Stanton's *The Rise and Fall of an American Army*, praising him as a "Vietnam combat veteran decorated for valor and now retired as a result of wounds suffered on the battlefield. "

Unable to resist, I wrote Summers. Not only had they bought a "bill of goods" the previous month (in a story by Michael J. Badamo who resurrected Tom Bird's fake POW tale from *Everything We Had*), his senior editor was a pretender. I pointed out that Stanton had never served in Vietnam, and he wasn't retired for wounds. "Not only can't you or anyone else tell a phony in the 'first three sentences,' neither you, nor I, can tell in the first three decades of personal contact," I wrote.

Shocked at this accusation, Summers told me it couldn't be true. But he confronted Stanton, who ultimately admitted that he had not been retired for wounds suffered in combat. Not too many issues later, Shelby Stanton's name disappeared from the *Vietnam* masthead. "Our readers keep us honest," is now the magazine's credo.

Although I had never visited Stanton's home in Bethesda, Maryland, two people who had been there told me that his house and garage were jammed full of file cabinets and boxes that overflowed with government documents and photographs—original military records about the Vietnam War that should have been housed in the National Archives. One active duty officer was stunned to see that Stanton had original files on nearly one thousand men still missing in action in Vietnam.

Another saw in Stanton's files reports of the Army investigations of every lost helicopter in Southeast Asia, along with gruesome photographs; files of every Chieu-Hoi (amnesty) poster issued; pay records and ID cards of every Special Forces detachment in Vietnam; photos of ships and Vietnamese ports. Stanton had thousands of documents, original military records. That was why his writing was so detailed, so accurate, so impossible for anyone else to duplicate.

I had swapped data about Stanton, including his military record, with several other researchers. His record made its way to Susan Katz Keating, a reporter for the *Washington Times*. When I heard she was working on an exposé of Stanton, fearful that Keating's article would prompt Stanton to destroy historically important documents, I immediately notified the National Archives. They in turn alerted the Secretary of Defense and the Justice Department, which started an investigation of possible criminal activity, including theft of government property, forgery of government records, fraud, and possession of security-classified records in violation of federal law.[707]

Keating's first story on Stanton, entitled "Tin Soldier? Shelby Stanton's War," appeared on July 23, 1992.[708] Stanton seemed to have a hard time sticking to his story. He told Keating varying tales about his own family—that he was an only child, then that a brother was serving time for a felony at Fort Leavenworth. (He's also said that a brother was killed in Vietnam.) He claimed that he worked as a lawyer for Exxon and was fired for refusing to falsify Indian oil leases, but a spokesman for the company said that Stanton was fired "for cause" from a low-level job.

Col. Broadus Bailey Jr., who ran Project 404 from 1972–74, when Stanton was supposedly involved, told Keating he did not remember Stanton. Despite Stanton's official written "history," Project 404 was neither secret nor involved in planting electronic sensors. Started in 1966, it performed routine advisory tasks for the Laotian military.

"We were not involved in planting listening devices," Bailey told Keating. "That is absolute nonsense. It's balderdash. It's absurd. The people I had were communicators and advisors. We had no combat reconnaissance role at all." No "Project 404 Team" would have performed any rescue operations of a CIA aircraft. On top of that, there was no record of any light aircraft crashing in Laos in December 1972, when Stanton claimed his heroic rescue occurred.

Stanton had written in the past that he was a "small, weak Ranger" who barely made it through the arduous training only to be plucked from obscurity and trained in clandestine combat operations where he excelled. But Keating's interviews revealed that Stanton was not the sort of officer who would ever be chosen for such an intense, highly skilled job. Stanton was a disaster even in training for combat.

An Army officer was designated Stanton's buddy in Ranger training to help him through the program. "He was totally out of place in a Special Forces unit," said the officer, who is still on active duty and couldn't speak for attribution. At one point in an endurance exercise, sent into the mountains of Georgia, Stanton fell apart on the third day of a snowstorm. "He just started bawling," the officer said. "He wouldn't stop. I told him to get ahold of himself. I threw a poncho over him so no one would see him."

There is nothing wrong with being short or being unable to complete the rigorous, extremely difficult training required of Rangers or Special Forces. The military needs intellectual skills as well. Stanton had those in abundance, but he lied about his Army service to pump up not only his ego but also his reputation as an author of military histories.

When confronted with the discrepancies in his record by Keating, Stanton tried to evade the issues. "I don't have to defend myself," he snorted. "It's like Jesus. People nail me on a cross. They can accept my words or not put money down and buy my books. I'm a modest and humble person." Didn't she see, Stanton insisted, that his own record did not matter?

Stanton's reputation as a military scholar rests on the belief among his readers that he is presenting not fantasy but facts. When pressed by Keating to explain his fanciful tales of combat and clandestine operations, Stanton's response was *so what*?

"Okay, so I exaggerated a few things," he said. "Everyone exaggerates their war record. I exaggerated the Air America thing. Okay, let's say it never took place. So what?" But when Keating pointed out that such "exaggerations" could cast suspicions on the rest of his work, he backtracked.

"I did not say it did not happen. I might have exaggerated the fact that it happened in December 1972. You're trying to reconcile everything with every single thing. What difference does it make if I say it took place in November, December, January, or April?"

Well, what difference does it make if D-Day took place on June 6, 1944? In Stanton's own introduction to *Rangers at War*, he offered this nugget of wisdom: "Military history cannot become anchored on fabled exaggerations."[709]

Over the next two years, it emerged that not only had Stanton managed to gain possession of thousands of government documents, he also had made several outrageous attempts to sell them back to the government.[710] (After I notified the National Archives about the documents, three different agencies began investigating Stanton: U.S. Army Criminal Investigation Division, the Defense Criminal Investigative Service, and the FBI.) Among the documents Stanton held were:

- What one military historian described as "the Holy Grail of MACV-SOG," a top-secret one-hundred-page book "that all military historians want to get their hands on." The book describes classified operations of MACV-SOG, covering operations in Vietnam, Laos, and Cambodia. Few copies were ever made.
- Grisly photographs of crash sites and investigative files on air crashes in Vietnam in which several Army generals died.
- Official photographs showing military activities along the Ho Chi Minh Trail, apparently retrieved from the bodies of enemy soldiers.

- Payroll cards for undercover agents for the Army's 5th Special Forces Group, many believed still alive and living in Southeast Asia.
- Documents concerning American defectors working with the Viet Cong.[711]

The investigation confirmed that the records came from a U.S. Army Intelligence unit and should have been forwarded to the National Archives at the end of the war. Although they could not pin down exactly when the records had been diverted, Stanton had worked on an Agent Orange study for the government in the late 1980s. The report theorized that Stanton might have slipped the documents into his briefcase a few at a time and taken them home.[712]

On August 20, 1992, two FBI agents talked to Stanton at his home. He admitted that he used these records to write his books. He claimed that he first saw the documents at the National Archives in 1984–85, when he referred to them while writing *Green Berets at War*. But miraculously, in late December 1987, the documents were delivered to his house, wrapped in plain brown paper and with no return address. Stanton had no idea who would do such a thing. He used them in the writing of *Rangers at War*. Stanton conceded it was a "lapse in judgment" to keep the files for so long and to use classified documents without permission. The next day he consented to a search of his house, which uncovered more photographs, government documents, and other war memorabilia. A week later, Stanton confessed to a CID agent that he was not being "completely truthful" about how he had gotten the documents, but he declined to explain further.

In 1992, while researching Stanton, I contacted Owen Lock, military editor at Random House. I told him of my research on fakers, hoping to sell him on the idea of publishing my book, and mentioned Shelby Stanton and his manufactured claims of heroism. There was dead silence on the other end of the phone. Lock was in the process of publishing a paperback of Stanton's book on the Rangers under the Ivy label.

Lock couldn't believe that Stanton was not a Vietnam combat veteran, so I sent him Stanton's military record. Ivy published the book anyway. In a later conversation with Lock, his only comment was, "We no longer deal with Shelby Stanton." But the Ranger book still is being sold by Ivy.[713]

The fallout from Stanton's deceit is enormous. He produced entire books, plagiarizing virtually verbatim from government documents and other people's writings with no accreditation or acknowledgment. For years, he's cited documents supposedly in archives that other researchers are unable to find. They are no longer there. What is real and what is not real in Stanton's "histories"? How can anyone know? "Stanton has lied so often he doesn't remember the story he last told," one Army investigator handling his case said.

The point is, once you know a historian has deliberately fabricated a single "fact," his work is rendered, if not invalid, then at least questionable. History demands accuracy.

Army CID spent two years and tens of thousands of dollars preparing the Stanton investigative report and presented it to the U.S. Attorney's Office, which assured investigating officers they would see action. But federal attorneys ultimately declined to prosecute Stanton.

So Shelby Stanton is free to continue writing his version of history, perhaps based on more files he "forgot" to turn over. Those he gave to the government measured about seven linear feet. But one man who saw Stanton's home estimates that he actually possessed up to two hundred linear feet of government documents. Where are they now?[714]

The "Gay" Beret

During the height of the Clinton controversy over the military's proposed "don't ask, don't tell" policy, *People* magazine came out with a story about gay soldiers in February 1993. Gerald L. Rosanbalm was the only homosexual veteran in the story claiming Vietnam service.[715]

Homosexuals have served in the military as long as nations have had armies. When I was in the Army, they stayed in the closet. I read the *People* magazine story with suspicion, not because I don't think homosexuals have soldiered well, but because I'm naturally wary of anyone promoting an agenda.

Rosanbalm, a New York stockbroker, sent me his resume. I made an FOIA request for his military record, then discovered Rosanbalm was a dominant figure in a book called *Conduct Unbecoming: Gays and Lesbians in the U.S. Military* by acclaimed San Francisco journalist Randy Shilts.[716]

Shilts had written a best-seller about the AIDS epidemic, *And the Band Played On*, which became a movie for HBO. He spent five years researching the 784-page *Conduct Unbecoming*, which received national acclaim as a well-documented study of the many homosexual men and women who have served their country in uniform and the military's efforts to ferret them out. Shilts significantly expanded on the tale Rosanbalm told *People* magazine, that of the "love story" between an officer named Gerald Rosanbalm and an enlisted man named Donald Winn, who became one of the "many gay men" whose names are on The Wall in Washington, D.C.

But if the rest of the book is as "well-documented" as this ridiculous fantasy, Shilts did a disservice not only to the military but also to the gay community.

Here's the story Rosanbalm told Shilts and *People* magazine:

As an Army intelligence officer in Vietnam assigned to the "top-secret" Phoenix Program, in mid-1966, Lt. Jerry Rosanbalm was stationed in

Saigon, where the gay lifestyle thrived, unaffected apparently by the bothersome reality of the war. At night, Rosanbalm cruised the bar of the Continental Hotel, the Pasteur Baths, and Tu Do Street for homosexual sex. On the evening in 1966 that Vice President Hubert Humphrey visited the president of Vietnam at the Presidential Palace, across the street at a luxurious villa a very different type of party was happening. Servicemen in drag, wearing exquisite gowns and wigs, strolled into the villa, past the unsuspecting brass arriving in limousines at the palace. The next morning, some of those same drag queens appeared, sans their female finery, at intelligence briefings for Humphrey and other military higher-ups. At least that's the story Rosanbalm told.

A tall, dark man from Southern California, Rosanbalm had enlisted in the military and attended basic training at Fort Ord. That's where Rosanbalm met Donald Winn, a sandy-haired, blue-eyed, all-American boy from Eureka, Kansas. It was a case of opposites attracting. Rosanbalm had to sneak out of his barracks at night to have sex with Winn, always making sure he was back before the dawn bunk check.

Rosanbalm applied for OCS and was accepted. But he and Winn maintained their relationship, determined to spend the rest of their lives together. They both received orders to go to Vietnam at the same time. During a week's leave in San Francisco, as they both prepared to ship out from Fort Ord, Rosanbalm bought a pair of wedding bands, which they exchanged in a mock ceremony. They wore the rings on their little fingers as a sign of their love. A letter Winn wrote Rosanbalm in Vietnam included a picture of himself in a green beret and depicted him wearing the gold band. "Jerry, notice it is where it has been since you saw me last and it will stay there," Winn wrote on the back of the snapshot.

For Rosanbalm, life in Saigon was exhilarating. He briefed colonels and generals on intelligence garnered through the Phoenix Program during the day, and at night, enjoyed the wild gay subculture. He even played tennis with General Westmoreland. But Rosanbalm felt deeply conflicted, knowing that if the Army ever found out the truth about his sexual orientation, his military career would be ruined.

And the guilt-ridden Rosanbalm battled his conscience about being an REMF (Rear Echelon Mother Fucker), the derogatory term combat soldiers used for people who sat in nice air-conditioned rear bases while they fought the enemy. Many of his peers from OCS had been killed. So in late 1967, Rosanbalm happily accepted a riskier reassignment to a spy job at Quang Nagh, "a remote outpost near the Laotian border." (No such town exists. In the later paperback of Shilts' book, the spelling of the name was changed to Quang Ngai, and its location is moved to "near the Cambodian border.") His new assignment, monitoring enemy traffic on the Ho Chi Minh trail in Laos, could be hazardous.

Given a new identity as a "civilian soil expert" and the undercover name "Jerry Rusk," Rosanbalm gathered daily intelligence for headquarters in Saigon. Set up in a four-bedroom colonial villa with a large staff of servants, Rosanbalm managed a number of undercover operatives whom he paid from a hidden cash drawer in his study.

The situation was not ideal. Rosanbalm wanted to bring his lover, Winn, to Quang Ngai for a visit. Nobody there was supposed to know his real identity, so Winn had to think of a ruse allowing him to take R&R at a little outpost on the Laotian border. A plan was worked out; Winn was scheduled to arrive in late January.

But all hell broke loose in the form of the 1968 Tet Offensive. Rosanbalm awoke one morning to hear mortar and artillery rounds bombarding Quang Ngai. The handful of "Red Cross nurses," bedded down in his living room, were terrified. Rosanbalm frantically called Da Nang for help, but none was available. The VC and NVA were attacking not only his station but also American bases all across Vietnam.

At daylight, although the fighting continued, Rosanbalm led the nurses as they sneaked out of the villa and worked their way to what he called the "citadel." Only twenty minutes later, the NVA captured and killed his entire staff and their families. Determined to fight back, Rosanbalm rounded up a group of South Vietnamese troops and led them in an attack on the local high school, where a large group of Communist troops had taken over. Before he was wounded, Rosanbalm shot a number of Viet Cong.

Amid furious fighting, ducking machine gun fire, Rosanbalm raced across a courtyard to reach other wounded soldiers, his injured right arm dangling uselessly at his side. He felt a heavy impact on the back of his head, a burning sensation in his back, and another in his shoulder. Shot six times, Rosanbalm crumpled to the ground. In incredible pain, he wondered if he was dying. Then Rosanbalm heard a familiar, beloved voice.

Miraculously it was Winn, who had arrived in Quang Ngai just in time to find the town under attack. Rosanbalm watched as his lover leaped through a hole in a wall, coming to save him, only to be cut down by machine gun fire. The two men lay yards apart, both seriously wounded. That was the last time Rosanbalm ever saw Winn alive. Medevacked out, Rosanbalm underwent extensive surgery in Japan. Rosanbalm was later transferred to Germany as a military intelligence officer. But when he was caught in bed with another man, the "homophobic" American military ended his illustrious career.

Rosanbalm had heard Winn died that day in Quang Ngai. But years later Rosanbalm found that was not true. Winn had recovered from his wounds, then returned to Vietnam only to be killed in action on January 1, 1971. His name was inscribed on the black granite of the Vietnam Veterans

Memorial. "He was a very good soldier, and he loved me very much," Rosanbalm told Shilts.

In recounting this story, Shilts and Rosanbalm made Donald Winn the only known homosexual killed in Vietnam, a gay hero in a green beret. Shilts did not bring Winn out of the closet; he yanked him out of the grave. And Rosanbalm portrayed himself as a sterling and valiant homosexual soldier, unfairly treated by a bigoted and ruthless Army.

Rosanbalm appeared on national television to tell his Vietnam love story and the saga of how he was unfairly hounded from the military. Sam Donaldson, on ABC's *PrimeTime Live*, hailed Rosanbalm: "Capt. Jerry Rosanbalm was a decorated veteran of the Vietnam War stationed in Munich when the CID (military investigators) broke down his door to catch him in bed with another man, a Czech national."[717]

But the story sounded dubious to me, mainly because it was full of easily identifiable falsehoods. For example, Rosanbalm said Red Cross nurses stayed at his villa on the eve of the Tet Offensive. No Red Cross nurses worked in Vietnam. And a search of the casualty records revealed that only one Donald Winn died in Vietnam—of a heart attack in his barracks on January 1, 1971.[718]

The story that emerged from military records was quite different from the one that Shilts told. Apparently Rosanbalm concocted the entire tale to present an episode of heroism and love by homosexuals in Vietnam.

According to his record, Rosanbalm enlisted in 1965 and was commissioned a second lieutenant on January 13, 1967. He said he arrived in Vietnam in August 1967 and was assigned to the J-2 staff headed by Robert W. Komer, whom he described as "ambassador for the State Department." But Komer was not part of the State Department; he was the deputy commander of MACV.

"I know who I worked with," Komer said. "A major, a colonel, and a civilian secretary." He had no recollection of 2nd Lieutenant Rosanbalm.

Rosanbalm claimed he "set up the ICEX (Operation Phoenix) for the State Department" and received special recognition for his intelligence work from LBJ in 1968. A second lieutenant set up Phoenix? Not likely. Besides, Phoenix was not the responsibility of the State Department. One of the principal architects of the Phoenix Program, besides Komer, was the late William E. Colby, onetime Saigon CIA station chief and later director of the Central Intelligence Agency. Before his death, Colby confirmed that he did not know Rosanbalm.

Rosanbalm claimed he was later a team chief attached to the 513th Military Intelligence Group in Quang Ngai Province, where he monitored traffic on the Ho Chi Minh Trail in Laos as well. But the 513th was not based in Vietnam; headquartered in Obursel, Germany, the 513th never conducted operations in Southeast Asia. And according to Dr. John

Finnegan, an Army historian, Army intelligence did not monitor traffic on the Ho Chi Minh trail. That was the job of the Air Force, and they did that from Thailand, not Vietnam.

According to military documents, Rosanbalm first was assigned as a training officer in the 525th Military Intelligence Group. (That group was not involved in Phoenix.) Two months later, he was reassigned as an Army intelligence officer, acting as liaison with military intelligence and field troops. In January 1968, he was transferred to the 149th Military Intelligence Detachment at Quang Ngai.[719]

According to his records, Donald Dean Winn did not enter the Army until April 1967, *two years* after Rosanbalm claimed they met. Winn and Rosanbalm were not in basic training at Fort Ord together. Winn trained at Fort Leonard Wood. Rosanbalm said Winn served in the infantry and indicated that he was a Green Beret. He was neither in the infantry nor a Green Beret. Winn's record revealed he was an Army combat engineer.[720]

In one interview, Rosanbalm claimed the two men were in OCS together until Winn washed out. But Winn was a high school dropout with low scores on Army tests. He was admitted to the service as part of "Project 100,000." No one admitted under Project 100,000 ever entered OCS. In any case, by the time Winn entered the service, Rosanbalm was already attending OCS. Records show that at no time were Winn and Rosanbalm stationed at the same camp together.

Despite Rosanbalm's amazing tale about Winn leaping through the breach in a wall at Quang Ngai, Winn was not shot in the head. He was never even wounded. His heart weakened by a childhood bout of rheumatic fever, Winn succumbed at age twenty-six to cardiac arrest — brought on by exhaustion and the oppressive Vietnam heat — in his barracks at Quang Ngai on January 1, 1971, long after Rosanbalm had left Vietnam.

Winn's family in Kansas was outraged by the book. At the time Winn died he was engaged to be married. Certainly there are homosexuals who marry, who deny their sexual orientation. But Donald's lone-surviving family member, a brother named David Winn, insisted that Donald was not homosexual.

"There was no way that boy was gay," David Winn said. "He loved girls and dated plenty of them." His friend Bob Love, also of Eureka, served with Winn. He remembered Winn as a gregarious young man who had many girlfriends. Donald's former fiancée Margie Lawrence had the flag that had covered Winn's coffin at his funeral. "Donald Winn was all man," she said.

The bottom line: Military records show no connections between Donald Dean Winn and Gerald L. Rosanbalm — either in time, assignment, or place.

One of Rosanbalm's immediate commanders in Vietnam was Lt. Col.

Robert B. Annenberg, U.S. Army (Ret.). In a lengthy letter, Annenberg made it clear that Rosanbalm was not the hero he portrayed himself in Shilts' book.[721]

"Rosanbalm was the goofball of the Vietnam War!" Annenberg wrote.

Annenberg was the person who set up cover identities for his intelligence officers. "Rosanbalm may have well been documented [as] 'Jerry Rusk'—I don't recall," Annenberg said in the letter. "But he was certainly not a 'civilian soil expert for the Dept. of Agriculture.' If I had proposed such a silly cover my superiors in Saigon would have disapproved the proposal immediately and probably sent me to the hospital for a mental evaluation. Most of our covers involved work with refugees.

"Rosanbalm was not set up in a four-bedroom colonial villa with a large staff of servants," Annenberg said. "Most living arrangements were austere. I recall rather cramped conditions. As for the 'large staff of servants,' that would have violated operational security as the office was part of the living arrangement."

Annenberg pointed out that most enemy activity in I Corps was in the north, not near Quang Ngai, a small provincial capital near the coast of the South China Sea. (Because Khe Sanh had been under continual attack, a collection team had to be relocated to Quang Tri.)

"For weeks [prior to the Tet Offensive] we had been reporting regimental sized infiltration across the DMZ and into the A Shau Valley, where build-ups and fortifications had become very sophisticated, with high-tech antiaircraft batteries which all but eliminated friendly probes/observations," Annenberg said. "By contrast, enemy units operating near Quang Ngai were mainly local force battalions, farmers by day and soldiers by night. Their capability was severely limited compared to what was going on up north. As the New Year's holiday Tet approached, an American operation nicknamed 'Ali Baba and his Forty Thieves' developed detailed 'early warning' information of a planned attack at Quang Ngai.

"The S-2 alerted the 2nd ARVN Division at Quang Ngai, and other friendly units were placed on full alert by 31 January 68. A 'Ruff Puff' unit [civilian irregulars] in Son Tinh (about six kilometers north of town) was overrun but was later returned to friendly control by 2nd ARVN.

"Intelligence personnel at Hue, to the north, engaged in combat. The team chief in Hue took a rocket round, which blew a hole in the wall of his house. He died of a rifle shot to the neck. Another team member in Hue was captured and marched off to the A Shau—barefooted. I myself was trapped in a small compound with several others and fought off the enemy for five days, until being rescued by a Marine tank unit from Phu Bai on 5 Feb 68." Intelligence personnel at Hue took heavy casualties—seven of thirteen were captured or killed.

"That is why the Shilts account of heavy fighting in Quang Ngai seems so phony," Annenberg said in his letter. "Shilts wrote 'a column of North Vietnamese regulars put a rocket through his compound wall and captured and killed Rosanbalm's entire staff and their families.' That never happened. If it had happened I would have heard about it and had to write after-action reports for weeks. In short, enemy attacks against Quang Ngai were a complete failure. There was no large-scale fighting in the town."

The night the Tet Offensive started, Rosanbalm did not grab his guns and escort Red Cross nurses to safety at the "citadel." (Remember, there were no Red Cross nurses in Vietnam.) In fact, when the attack began, enlisted personnel could not find Rosanbalm.

"When Tet broke out, Rosanbalm's duty was to be in an office communicating intelligence," Annenberg said. "But no one knew where he was." Rosanbalm had left the enlisted personnel to fend for themselves.

After daybreak, Rosanbalm was located in a field hospital, having been wounded in the middle of the night in an outlying area where his commanders felt he had no official business. Although Rosanbalm later received a Purple Heart, Annenberg wasn't the one who recommended the decoration.

Rosanbalm's absence from his post endangered the lives of thousands of Americans depending on him to disseminate intelligence information. "His desertion of his team members at a critical time during Tet constituted dereliction of duty," Annenberg said. But by this time Rosanbalm had been evacuated to the United States. A court-martial would have been an administrative nightmare. Therefore, an angry Annenberg simply gave Rosanbalm a poor officer efficiency report (OER), a document more interesting for what it said between the lines than outright.

"There were indications that Lt. Rosanbalm tended to overreact under conditions of stress, and on one occasion this resulted in a decrease in operational security," Annenberg wrote. "I do not think he has the temperament for operational intelligence assignments, particularly ones on which he cannot be closely supervised. Thus it is recommended that he be considered for cross-training into a related specialty or assigned to duties wherein his activities can be closely supervised."[722]

The poor OER was the kiss of death for any officer hoping to make Army intelligence a career. "The efficiency rating I gave Rosanbalm captured the essence of the man, a loser who was unfit for duty in MOS 9668 (intelligence)," Annenberg said.

After his wounds healed, Rosanbalm was transferred to an intelligence unit in Munich, Germany. Within months, Rosanbalm was again in deep trouble. Brig. Gen. Robert Williams (Ret.), then in charge of intelligence operations, was notified that Rosanbalm, billeted across the street from

Group Headquarters, was "shacked up" with a Czech national, having homosexual relations intermittently during working hours as well as at night. The Czech was suspected of being an agent for the Communists.

"I am sure that I asked for evidence, reported the case to U.S. Army Europe, and set the wheels in motion to remove him from the theater, although I'm sure this decision was made in Heidelberg by U.S. Army Europe," Williams said. "We knew little about the Czech or about Rosanbalm's other friends, and in those days we often hustled possible security cases out of Europe."[723]

Rosanbalm claimed that on March 19, 1969, as he lay in bed with Karel Rohan, American CID agents burst in his apartment and dragged them naked out of the bedroom. Rohan gave a statement that he and Rosanbalm had repeatedly engaged in "anal and oral sodomy," a crime in those days. Rosanbalm was hustled out of Europe. Fearful that intelligence matters could be divulged in any court proceeding, the military's solution to the problem of Rosanbalm was to medically retire him for his wounds suffered during his "disappearance" during the Tet Offensive in Vietnam.

I told some mainstream reporters about what I had discovered in Shilts' book, but nobody would touch the story. Shilts was an icon; calling his work into question wasn't worth the inevitable hassle. The only one who would raise the questions about the book was Chris Ruddy at the *New York Guardian*.[724] The story was then picked up by an odd media trio: the *New York Post*, a newsletter put out by Accuracy in Media, and that bastion of free speech, the *National Enquirer*.[725]

The only mainstream media publication to criticize Shilts' book was the *Wall Street Journal*, in a scathing editorial written by former Navy Secretary John Lehman, who had intervened to change the implementation of a policy during the Carter presidency to expel soldiers who had merely "a propensity" for homosexuality. Shilts distorted his position but never interviewed Lehman.[726]

Lehman accused Shilts, who was gay, of using "anonymous sources" and "gifted fabulists" to exaggerate the presence of homosexuals in the military. He pointed out that Shilts accepted as fact a spurious story about gay discos on board aircraft carriers, something Lehman somehow missed in his twenty-five years of service on carriers.

In the paperback edition of *Conduct Unbecoming*, Shilts made reference to the furor I had created over Rosanbalm. "When [Rosanbalm] refused to turn over his war records to an extreme right-wing magazine, the *New York Guardian*, the publication asserted he had never been in combat and had never had a relationship with Don Winn," Shilts wrote. "The magazine hoped to make a splash with its 'revelation,' but Rosanbalm's genuine records showed he had been truthful, and the story never went beyond the tabloid *National Enquirer*."

That was not true and Shilts knew it. Shilts refused to address the glaring discrepancies between his story and the official documents beyond the lame excuse that someone must have tampered with Winn's records. He contended that his accounts were "buttressed by exhaustive documentation and on-the-record interviews." (It's worth pointing out here that Shilts's "on-the-record" source for the story of Army officers cross-dressing at a party held at a villa across the street from the Presidential Palace was none other than the prevaricating Gerald Rosanbalm.)

But Shilts had announced he had AIDS and was dying. None of his peers was prepared to take him to task. (He has since died.)

"Gee, could there be two Donald Winns?" was Rosanbalm's only response when it was pointed out to him that he could not have met Donald Dean Winn in basic training or OCS. Well, only one Winn's name is listed as a casualty of the Vietnam War. Rosanbalm then said he had AIDS and was too sick to answer questions. Both he and Shilts refused to release the photo of Winn wearing the alleged "wedding ring" to compare to known photographs of Winn.

Donald's brother David remembered getting a call months before the release of the book from a private investigator from Oklahoma City who said he wanted to determine who was left of Donald Winn's family. The investigator said the inquiry had to do with a book, but he refused to give more details. Could Rosanbalm have plucked a name from the casualty records and hired a detective to determine if Donald Winn would be a "safe" man to use in the hoax?

I don't know if Shilts initially knew Rosanbalm was lying, but it's hard to believe a journalist of his international acclaim was that naïve or stupid. Maybe Shilts, like so many authors, hoped that by not looking too closely at the facts, a tale he hoped was true could become reality. Certainly weaving a spectacular Vietnam homosexual love story with two gay heroes under fire was a major selling point of this book, which now has been optioned as a movie. But the bottom line: Shilts wrote a fabricated story about Winn's sexual preference, about his character, for his own financial gain.

In perpetrating this fraud, Shilts robbed Winn of something important. This farm boy, a guy with Heartland of America stamped all over him, died in obscurity in the service of his country. No one acclaimed his Vietnam service. Now, thanks to Shilts, he's the only "known homosexual" on the Vietnam Veterans Memorial.

Shilts and Rosanbalm stole something from David Winn that can never be replaced: The memory of his brother. Winn was outraged that Shilts and Rosanbalm had painted his brother as someone who cheated on his fiancée with another man.

"He fought for our country," David told a reporter, tears in his eyes. "They took my brother off The Wall."

19

The Minority Myth

Blacks in Vietnam

THE CAMERA panned across the weed-choked vacant lots and wire fences surrounding a dilapidated school in northeast Philadelphia. "They came from the farms and from the ghettos, from high schools like this one, Thomas Edison in Philadelphia," said a voice-over by producer and author Wallace Terry. For a 1986 segment called "The Bloods of 'Nam" of the public television show *Frontline*, the program described Edison as a school that lost fifty-four of its students to Vietnam, a casualty rate far higher than any other high school in America.

"They didn't have the money to sit out the war in college or leave the country," Terry intoned. "They joined the armed forces, they got drafted, many of them never came back."[727] Black Vietnam veterans were shown talking to Edison's predominantly black student body about the war. The overall impression was that this ghetto school sent its poor black students to Vietnam to be used as cannon fodder.

Like *Bloods*, Terry's 1984 best-selling oral history about blacks in Vietnam, the *Frontline* segment made the strong argument that blacks died in numbers far exceeding their representation in the population, an assumption during the late 1960s that made opposing the war an important part of the civil rights movement.

"In the heat of the civil rights and black nationalist movements, black soldiers were accounting for more than 23 percent of American fatalities in Vietnam," said the book jacket, "although blacks comprised only 10 percent of America's population."[728]

Early reports in the popular press supported the idea that blacks were more likely than whites to receive combat assignments in the Army and were more likely than whites to be killed in action in Southeast Asia. Now this documentary was saying this black high school had lost more soldiers than any other high school in the country. I wanted to know if that was true, so I called Edison High School.

Several teachers at Edison, which was all-male until 1979, told me that many of the boys did not have fathers. So the instructors—many of whom were veterans of World War II or Korea—tried to instill in them a sense of pride and patriotism.

"Many of us had encouraged the teenagers to join the military as a way out of poverty," assistant principal Ronald Kender told me.[729] He had been a teacher in the 1960s, when Edison was what one alumnus later described as a "blackboard jungle," a place where "Joe the Cop" patrolled the hallways and schoolyard, ready at a moment's notice to intervene in any gang fight.[730]

Later, when some students died in combat and the tide of popular opinion turned against the war, many of the teachers felt guilty. To memorialize the KIAs, the Edison school community gathered the names of those boys who died in Vietnam by word of mouth and local advertising. The names were engraved on a large bronze plaque, which was mounted in a place of honor at the school: "Share Your Image with These Fifty-Four Young Americans, and You, for Whom They Fought, Honor Their Sacrifice."

I sent FOIA requests for the records of every man from Edison High School who died in Vietnam, then obtained most of the students' pictures from the school's yearbooks. In his haste to use Edison as a symbol for his premise that blacks died in disproportionate numbers in Vietnam, Terry apparently neglected to check the high school's rolls or military records. In the sixties, the student population of about 2,200 at Edison was around 60 percent black and 40 percent white. Of the fifty-one records of those killed that I was able to obtain, twenty-seven were black and twenty-four were Caucasian—approximately the same percentage as the school's enrollment.[731] And the image that these men were all killed fighting the enemy wasn't exactly true. Several of Edison's dead were victims of friendly fire and vehicle accidents. One was stabbed to death during a barroom brawl between a group of Americans and several Vietnamese. One died of drowning while taking a bath in a river; another was killed when he fell out of a truck.[732]

The school is now 77 percent Hispanic, and the principal is Raul Torres, the brother of Army Sgt. Robert Torres, a 1965 Edison grad who died in the Tet Offensive. Ironically, the valedictorian of Edison High School in 1995 was a Vietnamese refugee named Triu Nguyen, born in 1975, the year of the fall of Saigon.

Using Edison to make a case that blacks died in disproportionate numbers was misleading, but so were many of the statistics on black KIAs cited by Terry—statistics which are accepted and repeated by most of those who write about blacks and Vietnam. The supposedly high black casualty rate is used as proof of America's racism and immorality in pursuing its objectives in Vietnam.

Terry claimed that in the early years of the fighting, blacks made up 10.5 percent of the American population, but represented up to 23 percent of the fatalities, making them over-represented both in combat and in the number of KIAs of the war. In reality, although blacks as a group represented 10.5 percent of America's population during the Vietnam era, African-American males accounted for 13.5 percent of draft-aged males in America during those years.

During the ten-year period of the war, 7,257 African-Americans died in Vietnam, or 12.5 percent of the KIAs, slightly under their proportion in the population of draft-aged males. (Eighty-six percent of those killed were Caucasian; 1.5 percent were of other races.) An examination of the casualty records indicates that the highest rate for black servicemen was 16 percent in 1965, and almost all of those killed were volunteers in elite units, not reluctant draftees involuntarily assigned to combat units. Black casualty rates dipped under their proportion in the population in most other years. In 1969, the war's peak, black deaths accounted for 11.4 percent of the total.[733]

Blacks were not in Vietnam because an evil government drafted them out of the ghettos to use as cannon fodder; they were there because of the courage and patriotism of young black men, despite the fact they lived in a country where they frequently experienced racism. The early units to go into the war were elite troops of the Marine Corps, the Special Forces, and the 173rd Airborne, units almost exclusively populated by highly motivated volunteers—including higher proportions of blacks. Seventy-five percent of blacks who served in Vietnam volunteered to go. In fact, blacks tended to volunteer for combat at *higher rates* than whites. Twenty blacks received the Medal of Honor; almost one hundred received the Distinguished Service Cross.

But the image that the poor, the black, and the extremely young suffered the highest casualty rate continues to be perpetrated by the selective use of statistics and misleading anecdotal evidence.

Bloods

In his best-selling book *Bloods*, Terry told a story about a sixteen-year-old black Marine from a poor and broken family in Brooklyn, whom he described as the youngest American soldier to die in Vietnam, killed in combat in Quang Tin Province.

"He had lied about his age to join the Marines and thereby earn money to help support his mother," Terry said. "I vowed then that one day I would see between the covers of a book the story of the sacrifice of such young men and others in the rice paddies of Vietnam."

It's a sad tale of a poor disadvantaged youngster so desperate to help his family he goes to war and dies. But casualty records show no sixteen-year-old soldiers of any race in any branch of service died in Vietnam. Terry said the boy lied about his age. Could he have been listed as seventeen? Twelve seventeen-year-olds died in Vietnam, including three Marines. But all the seventeen-year-old Marines who died were Caucasian.

In fact, of the eleven black Marines from New York State who died in Quang Tin Province, one was eighteen, one was nineteen, and the rest were in their twenties.[734] While Terry's story made an eloquent statement about the victimization of young ghetto blacks, records show the incident of the sixteen-year-old casualty could not have happened as he described.

Throughout *Bloods*, Terry gives the oral histories of about twenty African-American GIs in Vietnam. Many are men who performed heroically and patriotically in Vietnam, like Capt. Joseph B. Anderson Jr., who described himself as an "absolute rarity in Vietnam," a black West Pointer commanding troops. His company was the subject of an Oscar-winning French documentary called "The Anderson Platoon," which noted that the American Army in Vietnam was probably the first in the history of the world that did not just take what it wanted. "If we wanted to eat off the land, we would buy a chicken or a pig," Anderson said. When his troops went into villages, they did not burn them down but set up their medics to treat the local people.

Anderson lost only one man to the enemy during his first year in Vietnam. "In two tours, I just did not experience any atrocities," Anderson said. "Sure, you shot to kill. But personally I did not experience cutting off ears from dead bodies or torturing captured prisoners." Even in his second tour he saw little drug use in the field.

Like Anderson, most African-American soldiers did their duty as they saw it, winning the admiration of their commanders and their peers. However, a handful of the vets in Terry's book perpetuated the negative myths of Vietnam veterans, describing black soldiers in Vietnam not only enduring rampant racial discrimination and harassment but also routinely committing outrageous atrocities with no consequences. An examination of the men's military records shows they are guilty not only of exaggeration but also of outright fabrication.

Sp4 Haywood T. "The Kid" Kirkland said he was a recoilless rifleman in the 4th and 25th Infantry Divisions, and that as a member of a long-range reconnaissance patrol, his team burned down fifty to seventy-five villages.

He claimed he witnessed his peers push Vietnamese prisoners out of helicopters and mutilate corpses. Following the war, Kirkland began a life of crime; he ended up in prison after robbing a mail truck with some buddies. Kirkland blamed his criminal actions on Vietnam.

Kirkland's record indicated he was a light-truck driver in a headquarters company; nothing in his file indicated he was a Lurp or saw any combat. Kirkland did receive an Army Commendation Medal, but for merit, not valor. His record listed no awards or badges indicating he was a combat soldier.[735]

Sp5c. Harold "Light Bulb" Bryant of East St. Louis, Illinois, told Terry about his year in Vietnam as a combat engineer with the 1st Cavalry Division—probing for and blowing up mines, disarming booby traps. Later in his tour, which lasted from February 1966 to February 1967, Bryant served as "point man" for a squad somewhere in the Central Highlands. He and a team were "dropped into Cambodia" to help retrieve a helicopter that had been shot down. Bryant repeated for Terry the usual litany of atrocities: GIs torching villages, mutilating enemy bodies, raping women, throwing prisoners out of helicopters, and torturing prisoners with electric wires.[736]

He described in vivid detail the death of his "best friend" in Vietnam, a black man named James Plummer from Cincinnati. They were both twenty and liked jazz. Bryant said Plummer was killed when a mortar round blew up a nearby ammo dump.

"His head was gone, both his legs from about the knee down were gone," Bryant said. "One arm was gone. The other was a stump left. The rest of it we really couldn't find, 'cause that one mortar round, it started the ammo dump to steady exploding."

Bryant, who later became a counselor at a Vet Center, told Terry of visiting the Vietnam Veterans Memorial in Washington, D.C. and seeing his friend's name. "When I saw Plummer on the memorial," Bryant said, "I kind of cried again."

But his military record showed that Bryant's primary Army MOS was "76P20," making him a "stock control and accounting specialist." His record indicated that Bryant took an eight-week Pioneer (combat engineer) course, and he did perform some duties as a Pioneer when he first arrived in Vietnam. But during most of his Vietnam tour, Bryant was a dump-truck driver. His record listed no valorous decorations, no Purple Heart, and no Combat Infantryman Badge, making his tales of being dropped into Cambodia and torturing prisoners dubious at best.[737]

And the death of his buddy? The only James Plummer who died in Vietnam was thirty-three years old—a white guy from Hardin, Illinois. He died of an illness several months after "Lightbulb" Bryant left Vietnam. (Of the nine Plummers killed in Vietnam, three were black. None of them matches the description of Plummer given by Bryant.)[738]

In *Bloods*, Sp4 Richard J. Ford III, from Washington, D.C., said he served as a Lurp with the 25th Infantry Division from June 1967 to June 1968. Ford told Terry that he shot a woman, an old man, and a little girl and that his buddies killed a dozen or so other old people and little kids who would not vacate a village. Ford also contended that in the field, most of his fellow soldiers stayed high smoking opium. He told a story of Americans playing the game "Guts," which basically amounted to the vicious torture and disembowelment of an NVA soldier.[739]

But Ford's record confirmed he was not a Lurp. He served as a fire crewman and a rifleman in the 4th Infantry for four months (from August 1967 to November 1967). The rest of his year in Vietnam was spent as a rifleman in Company C, 54th Infantry, an infantry company used for security duty at rear-area bases in Tuy Hoa and Cam Ranh Bay. And although Ford said he was wounded three times and received two Bronze Star Medals for valor, his record listed no valorous decorations, no wounds, and no Purple Hearts.[740]

During his tour, Ford claimed, a black man in his unit named Louis Ford from New Orleans was killed by a sniper; his death caused a fellow soldier to break down. No Louis (or Lewis) Ford is listed as a casualty of the war. The only combat casualty with that last name from Louisiana was Bob Joe Ford, who died December 21, 1969, long after Richard J. Ford III had left Vietnam.[741]

We enter the realm of wild fantasy in *Bloods* with the story of Air Force Staff Sgt. Don F. Browne, who told Terry he served in Vietnam as a member of the 31st Security Police Squadron at Tuy Hoa from November 1967 to early January 1968, and then as a security guard at the American Embassy in Saigon from mid-January to November 1968.

Browne's narrative has him arriving in Saigon in the middle of the Tet Offensive (which began on January 31, 1968). He and other security guards were ordered to go into the embassy and clean out six Viet Cong who had penetrated the main building called the Chancery. He and his team worked their way from the top floor down to the bottom; Brown threw a grenade in a corner, and his buddy "Brute" wasted a Viet Cong in black pajamas hiding behind a desk. "By the time we got down to the lobby, the five [the other team] killed were all stretched out in a row, lined up like ducks," Browne said.[742]

But Browne's own record and the historical archives show none of this occurred.

According to his military record, Browne arrived in Tuy Hoa on January 13, 1968—eighteen days before the Tet Offensive. Browne spent his entire tour in Tuy Hoa, with no detour for assignment to Saigon guarding the American embassy.[743]

Even if he had been there, no Air Force security forces were involved in the protection of the embassy. Although Browne claimed his team had an office in the basement of the American embassy, that would have been difficult. The embassy doesn't have a basement. And the VC sappers attacking the embassy did not wear black pajamas.[744]

Although a dispatch by reporter Peter Arnett told the world that the Viet Cong had successfully entered the embassy—painting the picture that the nerve center of American operations in Vietnam had been captured—military sources told reporters repeatedly that no enemy soldiers ever entered the building. Although a small VC sapper unit killed several MPs on the grounds and were in turn killed by remaining U.S. personnel, they never entered the building. Several Viet Cong had been killed at an adjacent office building, but none was found in the embassy.[745]

In any case, the MACV headquarters at Tan Son Nhut, not the American embassy, was the heart of America's military command. But over the next few days, the supposed "capture" of the American embassy became the quintessential symbol of America's military setback in the Tet Offensive.

Another tale in *Bloods* was even more ridiculous.

"I went to Vietnam as a basic, naïve young man of eighteen," said Sp4 Arthur "Gene" Woodley Jr., whose nicknames were Cyclops and Montagnard. "Before I reached my nineteenth birthday, I was an animal. When I went home three months later, even my mother was scared of me."[746]

Woodley's stories in *Bloods* are relentlessly grim. Woodley told Terry that on patrol in the jungle, he encountered a wounded soldier whose maggot-infested body had been mutilated and staked out in the sun by the VC. The man begged Woodley to shoot him. "I just pulled the trigger," Woodley said. "I canceled his suffering. We buried him. Very deep. Then I cried."

Woodley claimed that he collected about fourteen ears and fingers from dead enemy corpses. "With them strung on a piece of leather around my neck, I would go downtown, and you would get free drugs, free booze, free pussy because they wouldn't wanna bother with you 'cause this man's a killer." Yeah, right. If a soldier did this in any unit I belonged to, he would have been thrown in Leavenworth. (Even more ludicrous to any GI who served in Vietnam is the idea of free sex. Sex was certainly available, but Vietnamese prostitutes had wholeheartedly embraced the concept of capitalism.)

He claimed he was dropped into North Vietnam on a reconnaissance mission, where he suffered shrapnel wounds. And when his team went out on a POW snatch in June 1969, Woodley said he stepped on a punji stick, which went through his boot into his foot. For his service during the war, Woodley claimed he received five Bronze Star Medals for valor—a record of heroism that makes his atrocity stories even more horrible, especially because of the way his character was corrupted.

Terry also featured Woodley as a centerpiece of the *Frontline* segment "The Bloods of 'Nam." For PBS, Woodley elaborated on the tales he told in the book.

"It wasn't like World War II, it was like no other war, because we fought behind bushes, we fought like animals," Woodley said on camera. "We became animals a lot of us, a lot of us stayed animals, a lot of us are still animals. I had a collection of twenty-five, twenty-six ears and fingers that I wore to the field and downtown, because it was a part of your manhood. It was a part of that war mentality." (Notice that his collection of body parts had escalated.)

Woodley may have been an "animal" before he was nineteen. But he was not in the United States Army at the time. Woodley did not even enlist until after his nineteenth birthday. He didn't arrive in Vietnam until after he turned twenty.

According to his record, Woodley served as a Lurp and a Ranger in the 173rd Airborne in Vietnam. But he did not serve with the 5th Special Forces, as he contended. And Woodley's record showed no Purple Hearts and no valorous combat awards.[747] Maybe Terry could give him five Bronze Star Medals for a "five-star performance."

Terry has built a career out of claiming blacks were victimized in Vietnam. And the myths nourished by books like *Bloods* continue. In 1995, the movie *Dead Presidents* regurgitated Terry's distortions and ratcheted them up a notch, portraying the war as "an endless series of atrocities" committed by a crazed band of black Marines. (Often, when blacks have been portrayed in Vietnam movies, it has been as cowards (*Platoon*), as shuffling, lazy orderlies (*Born on the Fourth of July*), or as not particularly bright (*Forrest Gump*). Screenwriter Michael Henry Brown and filmmakers Albert and Allen Hughes, the twin brothers who created the hit movie *Menace II Society*, based *Dead Presidents* on the life of Haywood Kirkland, a featured source in *Bloods*.

The movie followed a Marine named Anthony Curtis (based on Kirkland) and his platoon in Vietnam. Curtis volunteers for reconnaissance patrol and serves two hellish tours that must reckon as the most unrelenting combat inferno in the history of war. In *Veteran* magazine, critic Marc Leepson described the Vietnam scenes as among the "goriest ever put on celluloid"—dwelling on the battlefield carnage and the crazies, such as the guy in Curtis' platoon who lovingly carries the head of an enemy soldier around for a few days.[748]

Back in the United States, Kirkland's real robbery of a mail truck in which no one was hurt is transformed by the filmmakers into a grisly explosion of blood and death. ("Dead Presidents" is a slang term for paper money.) Instead of showing Kirkland winning early parole and turning his life around—as he did—the movie portrays the character Curtis throwing a temper tantrum in court and being shipped off to prison in a sulk, a seething black cauldron of violence doomed to wreak havoc on society if ever allowed back on the streets.

What black fifteen-year-olds who go to the movies believe about Vietnam is now enshrined in *Dead Presidents*. And they will never know the truth: Kirkland wasn't even a combat rifleman; he was a light truck driver in a headquarters company.

Racial Politics and the VC

During the war, North Vietnamese radio broadcasts harped on the assassination of Dr. Martin Luther King to goad blacks into deserting. The savvy Viet Cong also attempted to exploit differences in American troops' skin color in their propaganda.

One day during my tour, the Vietnamese housegirls came into our barracks. "VC come last night," one sister told me, meaning the Viet Cong had paid a visit to her hamlet.

"Shoot anybody?" I asked.

"No shoot," she shook her head. "Just talk."

"What did they talk about?" I asked.

The women pinched their skin. "VC no white," one sister said. "We no white. You white." I realized the VC came to give the villagers their standard speech on racism.

"What do you think about that?" I asked one sister.

She laughed. "When Trung Uy Burkett come in, Adams jump up, salute." She meant that Private Adams, my driver (who was black), saluted me, 1st Lieutenant Burkett. That fit in with the VC's teaching: Blacks acting subservient to whites.

"General Davison come in, Trung Uy Burkett jump up, salute." There were peals of laughter all around. Brig. Gen. Frederic Davison, commander of our brigade, was black. I was subservient to him. The VC's argument about whites and nonwhites did not win over the house sisters.

But race played a big role in the way Vietnam was perceived both during the war and after it ended.

A section on Vietnam in a book called *Blacks in America's War*, by Robert W. Mullen, concentrates on racism in Vietnam and antiwar sentiment among blacks in America. "During the course of the Vietnam War," Mullen said, "the majority of Afro-Americans and most Afro-American political groups opposed the war, seeing it as a waste of black youth, a waste of resources that could be better used to ameliorate the conditions of America's poor, and often a racist war against a colored people struggling for self-determination."[749]

Somehow, in all the rhetoric, the remarkable record of honor and achievement black servicemen earned in Vietnam has been transformed into a national dishonor.

What's most striking about black participation in Vietnam is how different it was from World War II, when blacks were segregated in all-black units and, with a few exceptions, not allowed into combat. African-American troops primarily performed manual labor and stevedore-type jobs. While stories about racial strife in Vietnam received front-page play, the racial conflict among troops in World War II was rarely mentioned in the press.

Few know about incidents like the one that occurred in June 1943, at Bamber Bridge in Lancashire, England. A race riot broke out after some white MPs tried to roust some black American soldiers from a local pub after closing time. One black soldier was killed and four others were wounded by gunfire. Several MPs suffered broken bones. After the riot was quelled, about thirty-five black soldiers were tried for mutiny; twenty-eight were found guilty. One defendant called the courtroom scene a "kangaroo" trial; the lone black officer in the unit was never asked to testify.[750]

Race problems among American troops in England persisted throughout the war. In February 1944, serious fighting flared between black and white soldiers of the 82nd Airborne Division stationed at Leicester. And in October 1944, an English woman was killed in the cross fire between black and white troops near Newbury, Berkshire.

Such incidents forced the military to address the continuing problems of segregation, unfair treatment, and poor leadership for black units. After World War II, black leaders lobbied the military to allow blacks into more combat roles. By the time Vietnam rolled around, blacks were a major force in elite units composed of volunteers, such as the Airborne and the Marines. In Vietnam, African-Americans constituted up to a fourth of some elite units. That resulted in the outcry early in the war that the brunt of the combat effort fell disproportionately on blacks.

But data for the entire war shows there was no significant relationship between race and getting sent to Vietnam or an assignment to combat arms, according to a 1993 study for the Population Research Institute at The Pennsylvania State University.[751] The study of enlisted men, called "Who Fought in Vietnam? An Analysis of Combat Exposure Risk," by researchers Cynthia Gimbel and Alan Booth, examined several studies of black participation in the war and concluded that the research did not support the idea of disproportionate African-American service during the war, the idea that African-Americans had higher levels of combat exposure, or that they suffered higher casualty rates.

Their research indicated that black draftees had a significantly lower risk of being given a combat arms assignment than did white draftees. African-American draftees were more likely than whites to be assigned low skill service jobs, such as food service, general duty including laundry and graves registration, and general supply. "There are twice as many African-American draftees in these jobs than one would expect based on the marginal distribution," say Booth and Gimbel.

But blacks were being represented among the officer corps in increasing numbers. More than two hundred blacks were graduated from the service academies during the Vietnam War. Black officers in Vietnam commanded white troops, unheard of in World War II. Several blacks I knew in Vietnam were senior officers. Frederic Davison, my general, was the first black promoted to general in a combat zone. Both my company commander and battalion commander were black. And two fellow platoon leaders were black. Charles Calvin Rogers, an African-American Army captain, was given command of a battery in the artillery. Rogers, one of twenty blacks who received the Medal of Honor in Vietnam, became a two-star general.

And an African-American Army officer from the Bronx named Colin Powell commanded an infantry company. Powell loved the camaraderie and the discipline of the military from the moment he joined ROTC as a college freshman. He quickly knew he wanted to make the military his career. "You could not name, in those days, another profession where black men routinely told white men what to do and how to do it," Powell said.[752]

In fact, Vietnam was central to Powell's success. He went there first as an advisor in 1962, an assignment given to young hotshots. During the Vietnam era, Powell has said, it was an advantage to be black. "It was in the military that blacks were able to show their equality long before other areas opened up—we were able to show that we could serve as well as white men —and die as well as white men," Powell said years later.

And they endured captivity as well. In October 1965, Maj. Fred V. Cherry, USAF, was the pilot of an F-105 Thunderchief fighter bomber on a mission to destroy a surface-to-air missile installation northwest of Hanoi when he was shot down. He became the forty-third American captured in the North and the first black. Cherry ultimately became one of the most highly decorated blacks in Vietnam. For his war service, Cherry received the Air Force Cross, Silver Star, two Bronze Star Medals, Distinguished Flying Cross, and two Purple Hearts.

Held captive seven and a half years, Cherry was tortured by the North

Vietnamese to "encourage" him to broadcast orders to the "bloods" fighting in the South, urging them to desert or lay down their arms. Although he was beaten three times a day and kept in solitary confinement almost two years, Cherry refused.

His cellmate for a part of his captivity, a white Navy flyer named Lt. Porter A. Halyburton tried to keep Cherry alive—feeding him, bathing him. Halyburton counted up one day; Cherry had ten significant wounds on his body. Still, Cherry would not give in to the North Vietnamese demands. Separated, Cherry and Halyburton later were released at the same time in 1973. Cherry credited "Hally" with keeping him alive, just one example of how some blacks and whites in Vietnam came to depend on—and care about—each other.

For Terry's segment on *Frontline*, Cherry and Halyburton told their emotional stories of being captured—and of the day the North Vietnamese came in and told Halyburton to get his gear, he was moving. "And we couldn't believe it," Cherry says. "Good Lord, I've lost everything if I lose Hally. But they took him away and I was left. It was at night, and that was the most lonesome night I ever spent in my life."

The camera shifted to Halyburton. "I knew that it was not going to be good," he said. "And I was really heartbroken."

Wallace Terry: "Why?"

"Because I had grown to love him," Halyburton said.

Beyond Vietnam

Fred Cherry is now a business and marketing consultant in Maryland. Robert L. Mountain, another vet featured in *Bloods*, is chief of prosthetics, Department of Veterans Affairs Medical Center in Chicago.[733] Despite all the problems black men faced in the Vietnam-era armed forces—and continuing racism in American society—studies show that black servicemen who served in Vietnam have done as well as or better than those who didn't.

By the end of the war, there was one black admiral in the Navy, three black generals in the Air Force, and twelve black generals in the Army. After the war, the black Vietnam-era officer corps made amazing strides toward creating a more egalitarian military. More than one hundred black officers who served in Vietnam have attained general officer or flag rank since the war ended. An estimated three hundred black officers who served in Vietnam will attain general officer or flag rank throughout all of the armed services before they retire.

An African-American pilot named Daniel "Chappie" James Jr. was a member of the nation's first group of black fighter pilots, the "Tuskegee

Airmen." A hot pilot in the Korean War, James was also a Vietnam veteran, assigned to Ubon Royal Thai Air Force Base in Thailand in 1966. He flew seventy-eight combat missions over North Vietnam. On one mission led by James, the American fighters shot down seven enemy MiG-21s, the highest total single-day air loss inflicted on the North Vietnamese during the war. In 1975, President Gerald Ford authorized the promotion of James to four-star grade. He became the nation's first black four-star general, assigned as commander in chief NORAD/ADCOM, Peterson Air Force Base, Colorado. As such, he had operational command of U.S. and Canadian strategic aerospace defense forces.

What's less well known is that his son, Daniel James III is also a Vietnam veteran. An Air Force officer, James III served two tours in Southeast Asia. After leaving active duty in 1978, he became an airline pilot and joined the 182nd Fighter Squadron of the Texas Air National Guard. In November 1995, Texas Gov. George Bush helped Col. Daniel James III put on one of the stars worn by his famous father as he was promoted to brigadier general and named commander of the Texas National Guard.[754]

In Vietnam, Lt. Col. Roscoe Robinson Jr. was the first black to command the 2nd Battalion, 7th Cavalry. During the postwar years, Robinson worked his way up the ranks to become the Army's first four-star African-American general. And Colin Powell, told in 1972 by the Army to apply for a place as a White House Fellow, rose quickly to national prominence, serving eventually as national security advisor to President Reagan and chairman of the Joint Chiefs of Staff. In 1996, Powell was seriously considered as a candidate for president. Although he declined to run, it is certain that Powell will continue to play a role in national politics.

One of four blacks to graduate from West Point in 1965, Art Hester served in Vietnam as an Army lieutenant. In 1969, the Army sent him to Stanford University to study industrial engineering. He earned a master's degree, then returned to West Point as an admissions officer. After retiring from the service as a lieutenant colonel, Hester joined General Motors, becoming the second black to be named general manager of a GM assembly plant.

Other successful black Vietnam veterans in business include former Gen. Hugh Robinson, president of Dallas-based Cityplace Development. In Vietnam, Hugh Robinson served as executive officer of an engineering group and worked his way up the ranks to Army major general.

William S. Norman, who joined the Navy after earning a degree from college, served two tours in Vietnam and was appointed assistant for minority affairs to chief of naval operations Adm. Elmo Zumwalt. After the military, Norman joined the marketing department at Amtrak, eventually becoming executive vice president and second in command. Norman led the effort to renovate the ornate Union Station in Washington, D.C., and launched an aggressive marketing campaign that put the nation's railroad back on track.

The first black Marine to command a detachment at sea and to lead a company-sized infantry unit in combat, Jerome Gary Cooper also became the first black to reach flag rank in the Marine Corps. In Vietnam, he received the Bronze Star Medal, two Purple Hearts, and three Vietnamese Crosses of Gallantry. Brigadier General Cooper later became commanding officer of the 4th Force Services Support Group in Atlanta. Later, as vice president of an engineering firm, Cooper ran for public office and was one of the first African-Americans elected to the Georgia legislature. Cooper later was appointed to the governor's cabinet.

Lt. Gen. Julius Becton, a Vietnam veteran, is now head of the District of Columbia public school system. Maj. Gen. Charles Hines, a military police officer in Vietnam, is now president of Prairie View A&M University. Lt. Gen. Calvin Waller was deputy commander to General Schwarzkopf in the Gulf War.

For all the false rhetoric about the war taking the heaviest toll on African-Americans, it was in Vietnam that black soldiers had a chance to prove the leadership skills that had been there all along. It's a shame that what most people will remember about blacks fighting in Vietnam are the negative images from despicable movies like *Dead Presidents*.

20

Baby, You Looked Like the Cong

Women and Vietnam

ARMY NURSE 1st Lt. Sharon A. Lane enthusiastically reported for duty at the 312th Evacuation Hospital at Chu Lai, South Vietnam, on April 29, 1969. The facilities were not primitive. Each of the nurses had a room in newly built quarters. But the hospital constituted little more than Quonset huts connected by a rampway. Constantly assaulted by the noise of F-4s flying in and out of a nearby airstrip, Lane and the other nurses worked twelve-hour shifts, six days a week, a grueling schedule.

The hospital had a ward for Vietnamese civilians as well as several for American troops. Like most new personnel, on her arrival Lane was given the unpopular assignment of nurse on the Vietnamese ward, where many of the civilians had diseases that compounded any war wounds. That ward was not on the sewer system, and many of the Vietnamese didn't know how to use the "honey buckets" provided for human waste, so the ward always reeked of urine and excrement. After a few weeks, Lane was scheduled to be transferred from the Vietnamese ward to one treating American soldiers, but she chose to remain there to take care of sick and wounded children.[755]

Because the area around the 312th Evacuation Hospital was often pelted by rockets, the nurses learned to grab their flak vests, helmets, and bunker bags and head for the bunkers when they heard the sound of incoming rounds. One of Lane's last letters home to her parents, written on June 4, 1969, said that her unit had just reached a milestone by treating its ten-thousandth patient since arriving in Vietnam the previous September. "Start 'nights' tomorrow so don't have to get up early tomorrow," Lane wrote. "Nice thought. Still very quiet around here. Haven't gotten mortared for a couple of weeks now."[756]

466

At about 7 A.M. on the morning of June 8, just before the end of Lane's long shift, the enemy launched four to six rounds of 122 mm rockets at the sprawling Chu Lai facility. Although most of the rockets went wide, one landed just outside the Vietnamese ward. Shrapnel injured twenty-five patients and killed a Vietnamese child. Sharon Lane was trying to move patients to a safer area when a jagged piece of shrapnel from a rocket ripped through a Quonset hut wall and hit her in the throat, severing her aorta and killing her almost instantly. Nurse Lane died less than a month before her twenty-sixth birthday; she had been in-country only forty-five days.

Her name is engraved on Panel 23W, line 112 of the Vietnam Veterans Memorial. A road at Fort Belvoir, Virginia, is named for her, the only road at the installation named either for a woman or a Vietnam veteran. A life-sized statue of Lane in Army uniform stands in the courtyard of Aultman Hospital in Canton, Ohio, the hometown where she attended nursing school. And a recovery suite at Fitzsimmons Army Medical Center in Denver, Colorado, is named in her honor. Posthumously awarded the Purple Heart, the Bronze Star Medal for valor, and the Vietnamese Gallantry Cross with Palm, Lieutenant Lane was the only American military woman killed by enemy fire during the ten long years of the Vietnam War.

Although nurse Sharon Lane was the only female combat death, seven other American nurses died in Vietnam of accident, suicide, and stroke, and are listed on The Wall as casualties of the war:

- 2nd Lt. Carol Ann Drazba, twenty-two, and 2nd Lt. Elizabeth Ann Jones, twenty-two, killed February 18, 1966, in a noncombat helicopter crash. Both Drazba and Jones had been in Vietnam 128 days.
- 1st Lt. Hedwig Diane Orlowski, twenty-three, and Capt. Eleanor Grace Alexander, twenty-seven, died November 30, 1967, also in a noncombat plane crash. Orlowski had served almost a year in-country—307 days; Alexander had been in Vietnam 177 days.
- 2nd Lt. Pamela Dorothy Donovan, twenty-six, died July 8, 1968, a victim of suicide, after less than three months in-country.
- Lt. Col. Annie Ruth Graham, fifty-one, died August 14, 1968, of a stroke. Graham had 272 days of service in-country.
- Capt. Mary Therese Klinker, twenty-seven, an Air Force nurse, died on April 9, 1975, in a noncombat plane crash while trying to evacuate Vietnamese orphans; she had five days total duty in Vietnam.[757]

Other American women died in Vietnam. The Red Cross lost five workers during the war: two men and three women. The men were killed when their Jeep hit a land mine. The three women—Hanna E. Crews,

Virginia Kirsch, and Lucinda J. Richter—died of noncombat-related factors. A female photojournalist was killed when she stepped on a land mine. There is one woman missing in action: Dr. Ardel Vietti, a surgeon with the Christian and Missionary Alliance, who was taken prisoner by the Viet Cong in 1962.[758]

Despite the deaths noted here, statistically, American female military personnel were safer in Vietnam than driving America's highways or living alone in Washington, D.C. They typically served on very secure bases, where most medical facilities were located. China Beach is a prime example. But that doesn't mean they didn't endure hardships and stress. Living in a tropical country surrounded by overheated and oversexed GIs should have qualified them for combat pay.

Women and War

Women have always been a part of America's war efforts, although they were not formally incorporated into the U.S. military until World War I, when thirty-four thousand women served, mostly in the Nurse Corps. Of those, ten thousand were sent overseas. Thirty-eight American service-women died during that war, for the most part during the 1918 worldwide flu epidemic.

During the four years of American involvement in World War II, about 350,000 women served in the military, primarily in administrative positions. (About sixty-eight thousand were nurses.) Women in that war often faced danger from combat. Army nurses went ashore on D-Day in North Africa. Two hundred nurses died in World War II, including six killed in a German bombing attack on a hospital at Anzio beachhead in 1944. Four of the nurses who survived Anzio received the Silver Star for bravery, the first women to ever receive that combat decoration.

In the Pacific, the Japanese captured eleven Navy and sixty-six Army nurses on Guam and on Corregidor; they spent thirty-seven months in POW camps. (Despite claims to the contrary, no American military women were POWs in Vietnam.)

Korea also saw a strong contingent of females who served in the American military. At the peak of the Korean War, about forty-six thousand women were on active duty; while no nonmedical female personnel were allowed to serve in Korea, five hundred to six hundred served in Korea in MASH units, in evacuation hospitals in-country, on Navy hospital ships in Korean waters, and on Air Force medical evacuation aircraft.[759]

Lane was one of about 261,000 American women who served their country's military in some capacity during the Vietnam era. About 7,500 women—5,000 Army, 2,000 Air Force, 500 Navy, and 27 Marines—served in-country. Of those, 90 percent were nurses; others worked as clerks, medical technicians, and in administration. Maj. Evelyn Foote served as a public relations officer with the Army in Vietnam; after the war, she rose in rank to brigadier general and commanded MP units and served as post commander at Fort Belvoir, Virginia. Other women worked in military intelligence as photo interpreters and as advisors to the South Vietnamese Women's Army Corps.

An additional twenty-five hundred women worked in Vietnam as civilian clerks and secretaries for various government agencies. About 650 worked as American Red Cross "Donut Dollies." The Red Cross had about seventeen recreation centers and clubmobile units staffed at any given time by these young, college-trained women who traveled around the country entertaining American servicemen in "audience-participation recreation programs"—meaning they joked, played games, and sang songs with the soldiers.

Like Sharon Lane, every one of the American military women in Vietnam had volunteered for the armed forces. Typically, they were officers and older than the average enlisted man. Many of the women wanted to take advantage of the opportunities the military offered, such as training and travel. Some joined to escape a bad personal relationship or to leave home. Once in the military, two-thirds volunteered to go to Vietnam despite the dangers of being in a war zone.[760] They put up with the heat, the stench, the fear, and the boredom.

Despite the perception that nurses were in the thick of the fighting, braving combat conditions every day, there were virtually no nurses on the battlefield with combat units. Tet was the exception. (Women nurses in World War II, when hospitals moved with the front, actually served closer to the scene of carnage than did women in Vietnam.) And only a small percentage of the nurses in the hospitals were actually operating-room nurses. Most nurses who served in Vietnam worked on wards changing bandages, giving medication, charting treatment, and helping GIs write letters home. There was nothing more inspiring to the men in Vietnam than American nurses. A wounded soldier felt better just being able to hear and see a nurse who reminded him of his sister, his wife, his fiancée, his mother.

Female Vietnam veterans deserve recognition as much as the men who served. Like male Vietnam veterans, female Vietnam vets also faced disapproval and ostracism when they arrived home from their tours of duty. An officer who served as a nurse in the war told me that after she received her commission, she flew home on leave. Beaming with pride, wearing her father's old second lieutenant bars, she walked into the civilian airport in San Antonio to catch the plane. But as she stepped into the ticket line, a male antiwar protester spat in her face. While she stood there in shock, the man laughed and walked off. What makes the memory especially sour for her: The couple of dozen men in the ticket line looked away as she stood in embarrassment, spittle dripping from her face. She later served a tour of duty in Vietnam, but her longest-lasting impression of the war was the episode in the San Antonio airport.

Many nurses in Vietnam were like Kathy Lynn Emanuelsen, who joined the military to follow in the footsteps of her mother, an Army nurse during World War II, and her father, an infantryman. She arrived in Vietnam in 1969, at the 12th Evacuation Hospital in Cu Chi, the base camp for the 25th Infantry Division. The medical facility was a series of Quonset huts with a helipad, an emergency room, an X-ray unit, preop ward, operating room, recovery room, and a quasi-intensive care unit. The camp also had wards for Vietnamese citizens, tropical diseases, and POWs. The facility had between fifteen and twenty doctors, and twenty-four to twenty-eight nurses, as well as numerous medics, corpsmen, and other support personnel.

Emanuelsen spent about a month in the recovery room/burn unit, then the rest of her tour in the emergency room, working a twelve-hour shift. "The first time someone arrives with their leg off, femur hanging amid shreds of tissue, you do want to get sick," Emanuelsen has written. "War is horrible. I had seen enough in the first month, so by the time [the Tet Offensive] arrived, I was somewhat adjusted to the carnage."[761] To deal with the horror, she said, everyone relied on that peculiar form of black humor known to all those in a war zone.

When mortar rounds exploded near the hospital, the medical staff was forced to crawl around on the floor to attend to the wounded. The most common injuries they treated were fragmentation wounds from stepping on mines, then gunshot wounds, then shrapnel wounds caused by grenades and mortars. Emanuelsen said they always had the supplies they needed, although at times they ran low on blood.

But—just like the men—female Vietnam veterans are often portrayed as "hero-victims." Victims not only of the psychological trauma of war, but Agent Orange, sexual harassment, and rape committed by those they were there to save.

The television show *China Beach* shed some light on the life of nurses in Vietnam, but only now, with the creation of the statue of female nurses in Vietnam at the Vietnam Veterans Memorial in Washington, are they finally getting the recognition their devotion and hard work deserves. Their trailblazing efforts have led to the current acceptance of women in the all-volunteer armed forces, as vividly demonstrated in the Persian Gulf with Operation Desert Storm.

Still, just as misconceptions about male Vietnam veterans abound, with the dawning of the politically correct era, women's service has been distorted as well. The bronze sculpture of women nurses at The Wall, dedicated in 1993, is far more heroic than the nearby statue of the three male GIs. The women's statue, by sculptor Glenna Goodacre, portrays three nurses, one with arms reaching up as if to accept casualties from a helicopter, one who appears to be preparing medical supplies, and another cradling a man as if he has just been shot and has fallen into her arms in the midst of battle, an image reminiscent of the Madonna cradling the dying Christ. The only problem with this very inspiring work of art is that its message is not accurate.

The media regale us with stories of nurses caring for unending streams of GIs as they lay dying, of nurses standing ankle deep in blood in the operating room only steps away from the combat zone. For example, "How to Bandage a War," a 1993 *New York Times Magazine* story by Laura Palmer, discussed female nurses coping with PTSD after the trauma of holding innumerable soldiers in their arms as they died—trauma which later triggered depression, alcoholism, promiscuity, and violent rages. (The story included a quote from a friend of nurse Diane Orlowski, saying that her plane had crashed after being hit by enemy fire. Records show the aircraft crashed in a noncombat situation.)[762]

But Vietnam casualty records show that almost all the men killed in Vietnam died in the field, not in the hospital. Of those wounded men who lived long enough to reach a hospital, only 1.2 percent died, testimony to the dedication and skills of the combat medics as well as the doctors and nurses in the field hospitals. Only about twenty-five hundred men died in hospitals in Vietnam.[763]

The most severely wounded soldiers were treated, stabilized, and "packed for evac"—immediately taken to more sophisticated hospitals in the Philippines, Guam, Japan, or stateside. But even if all those who died in a hospital succumbed while in Vietnam, that works out to less than one man per three nurses, fewer deaths than an emergency room nurse might see on a hot summer Saturday night in New Orleans. While they had to cope with the psychological stress of seeing young men seriously wounded, the image that women suffered the same traumas and dangers that combat soldiers in Vietnam experienced is not accurate.

But that reality doesn't stop the myth makers. Lynda Margaret Van Devanter, an ex-Army nurse, told a gruesome tale of her one-year tour in Vietnam in her 1983 best-seller *Home Before Morning: The Story of an Army Nurse in Vietnam.*[764] Written with Christopher Morgan, Van Devanter's book was the first about the war by a female veteran. The paperback rights sold for more than one hundred thousand dollars, and CBS optioned the story for a TV movie starring Sally Field.

An antiwar activist and self-described "professional veteran," Van

Devanter served in the early 1980s as women's director of the Vietnam Veterans of America. In 1982, she traveled to Hanoi with VVA President Bobby Muller. That same year, Van Devanter and Muller, a disabled Vietnam veteran and antiwar activist, did a lecture tour of college campuses funded by *Penthouse* magazine. Writer Dan Cragg caught one of Van Devanter's lectures and described her as "a cross between a blood-flecked Medea mourning the deaths of her 'children' and a burned-out sixties liberal bemoaning the good old Kennedy years and the Great Society killed by Vietnam."[765] Describing all the nasty things that happen to young men in war, like "losing your family jewels," Van Devanter delivered what Cragg described as "virulent antiwar, antimilitary propaganda designed to make us reject the principle of service to country."

Home Before Morning told the story of Van Devanter, who arrived as a twenty-two-year-old nurse in Vietnam in June 1969, and was assigned first to the 71st Evacuation Hospital and later to the 67th. A naïve and patriotic Catholic girl, she was quickly disillusioned by exhausting seventy-two-hour work shifts. She described "falling into an almost deathlike sleep at the operating tables." Van Devanter and her fellow nurses worked under a continuous barrage of enemy rocket attacks on a ceaseless stream of dying men, all the while standing in a muck of blood and mud "reminiscent of a fifties horror film." To Van Devanter, Vietnam was an unending, hellish chaos of blood, horror, and insanity.

It's hard to tell if Van Devanter and her fellow nurses suffered a bigger toll due to the difficult work or the heavy drinking and drug use after shift's end: "We partied as hard as we worked," Van Devanter said. "And when we slept it was frequently because we passed out from too much alcohol or too much exhaustion." She gave explicit details of her long affair with a married surgeon and portrayed some other nurses as lesbians.

Disillusioned with the war, Van Devanter took part in the "John Turkey" movement, a tiny band of active-duty war protesters at the hospital. At the end of her year-long tour, twenty-three-year-old Van Devanter returned home embittered and angry, a psychological war casualty. She disintegrated into sexual promiscuity, alcoholism, and depression. After losing a series of nursing jobs, Van Devanter went on welfare, then married and divorced. Finally diagnosed by a counselor who specialized in veterans' problems as suffering from PTSD, Van Devanter began writing the book as therapy.

How accurate is *Home Before Morning*? Van Devanter told a reporter that the first day she arrived in Vietnam, one of the nurses in her unit was killed by the enemy.[766] The only woman killed by the enemy, Sharon Lane, died about the time Van Devanter arrived in Vietnam, but Lane's death occurred at the 312th Evacuation Hospital, not the 71st, where Van

Devanter was based. Van Devanter has admitted that she suffered large periods of amnesia of her time in Vietnam. And all the names in Van Devanter's book have been changed, making verification of her story impossible.

Nora Kinzer, special assistant to VA Administrator Harry Walters, challenged the book on a TV talk show. "Lynda Van Devanter herself has said on numerous occasions that the image of the Army nurse is either lesbian or whore," Kinzer said. "I am upset that such an image is portrayed in her book."

Some nurses, including one of Van Devanter's roommates in Vietnam, supported her version of events. But other female Vietnam veterans blasted it as a historically-inaccurate distortion, more a diatribe reflecting Van Devanter's antimilitary views than a responsible depiction of a nurse's life and work in Vietnam.[767]

Robb Ruyle and his wife, Lynne Morgan Ruyle, both served at the 71st Evac Hospital from early 1969 to early 1970; they were there when Van Devanter arrived and when she left. Both sat down with Van Devanter and shared their memories before she wrote the book. "Lynda took our information, our stories, our memories of an intense, exhausting, occasionally terrifying, but very fulfilling year in a superbly functioning medical unit, along with the recollections of many others, and turned them into a trashy work of fiction," said Ruyle. "A lot of what she describes as fact in her book simply did not happen, and those episodes which did happen were distorted to make Lynda the central character in them, even if she was really nowhere around when or where they actually occurred."[768]

Col. Mary Grace, a nursing supervisor who served at the 71st Evac with Van Devanter, also found the book less than accurate. "I certainly don't recognize (the incidents in the book)," Grace, chief nurse at an Army hospital at Fort Bragg, NC, told the *Washington Post*. "I'd say she's been watching too much *M*A*S*H*."[769]

Reviewing the book for the *Washington Times*, Joanne K. Webb, an Army nurse in Vietnam, Germany, and the United States, pointed out that Army hospital statistics do not support Van Devanter's contention that the nurses were brutally overworked. (Joanne Webb is married to James Webb, author and highly decorated Vietnam vet who wrote the best-selling Vietnam novels *Fields of Fire* and *A Sense of Honor*.)

Hospital records revealed a "steady, but manageable workload" that was actually decreasing during Van Devanter's tour. The Army eliminated 105 of the 305 beds at the 71st Evac facility near Pleiku where Van Devanter worked as a general duty nurse from June 1969 to March 1970.[770]

Webb cited a quarterly hospital report issued February 14, 1970, documenting the "continued lull in enemy activity in the area for most of the period, reduction in the number of Vietnamese hospitalized, and a concerted effort to keep down the census in order to maintain the capability of handling an unexpected mass casualty situation." In the three-month period from November to January, the hospital received only 401 men wounded in action.[771]

Hospital reports showed that the average surgical caseload was four per day, Webb said. The hospital was never more than 50 percent full, and the death rate was less than one per day. In the 71st Evac's worst month—June 1969—there were 346 surgical cases, or about twelve operations per day divided among several physicians, far less than the daily surgical workload in a community hospital in America. Van Devanter arrived in Vietnam during the middle of June and worked the last two weeks of that month. After that, the load grew lighter.

"This is not to say that a mass casualty situation was not a possibility," Webb said. "But rather that it was not a daily or even a frequent occurrence, as the book's reference to a 'never-ending flow of casualties' suggests."

1st Lieutenant Van Devanter transferred to the 67th Evacuation Hospital in Qui Nhon on March 1, 1970. She worked there as a surgical nurse for three months until June 5, 1970, when she departed Vietnam.[772] The former head nurse at the 67th Evac was upset by Van Devanter's portrayal of the nurses' social lives. "Lynda's exaggerations and the negativism of her book distress me terribly," said retired Col. Edith Knox. "This book makes us look like a bunch of bed-hopping, foul-mouthed tramps."

Webb was concerned that the public would see Van Devanter's story as universal of women nurses in Vietnam. "It was not easy for military nurses to carry the burden of an unpopular war as well as the innuendo of having been a woman in a war zone," Webb wrote. "We do not see in Van Devanter's tale the quiet dedication and humility with which they provided the best medical care in the history of war. Nor do we see the great friendships that carried many women through the experience without mental deterioration and still give them support today. We see a shattered woman, telling a histrionic untruth."

Van Devanter's book started a victimization trend that continues. In a 1995 television broadcast commemorating the fiftieth anniversary of D-Day, the emcee paid homage to female Vietnam veterans, saying they suffered as much as the men: "Like the returning soldiers, many of the women brought their ghosts home with them: their nightmares, the flashbacks, difficulties with jobs and relationships. Some women turn to alcohol and drugs, even suicide. [Some] have never told anyone of their agony and to deny the experience, to deny the pain, means never to grieve, never to heal." Van Devanter now is head of the VA's outreach for women, extending PTSD therapy not only to female veterans but the wives and children of male veterans.

But I'm betting more nurses are like Emanuelsen, who also served at the height of the war. She said she coped by focusing on the living, the men they saved. "That wall in Washington would be double in size if it wasn't for the medics, the dustoff choppers, and everybody who gave so much of themselves," Emanuelsen said. "These were human beings in a very inhuman place, trying to do the best they could." She does not feel victimized. "I was not angry about my time there. I had my successes and failures. But I did my very best."[773] After her discharge from the Army, Emanuelsen received a master's degree and has published three books on respiratory disease and critical-care nursing.

Despite the negative images such as those promulgated by Van Devanter, female Vietnam veterans blazed a path for military women today. Many women who served in Vietnam made the military a career. Brig. Gen. Hazel W. Johnson is a Vietnam veteran, as is Brig. Gen. Sherian Grace Cadoria, who served as protocol officer, Qui Nhon Support Command, from 1968 to 1969.[774] Always important to the military, women became more directly integrated into the armed services after the Vietnam War, when Congress dissolved the Women's Army Corps, and women were assigned to all the Army's branches except infantry, artillery, and armor. It's estimated that one of every eight new recruits is a woman. Women served in Panama, Grenada, and Operation Desert Storm, flying helicopters, toting M-16s and doing just about everything that men did— including dying in combat. During the Gulf War, for the first time in U.S. military history, six American enlisted women were killed in action, and two female soldiers were held as POWs. Today, women serve in all four branches of the military, except in direct combat roles, and it is probably only a matter of time before those units open to them as well.

That new-found respect for female veterans is probably a major reason phony female Vietnam veterans occasionally pop up.

Equal Opportunity Fakers

In the files of the Special Warfare Public Affairs Office in Coronado, California, home of the Navy SEALs, are photographs of women wearing Navy uniforms with the SEAL Trident. But female "SEALs" are fakers. No woman to date (Demi Moore in *G.I. Jane* notwithstanding) has graduated from the SEAL qualification course and become a SEAL. In the special warfare community, women are still restricted to support and administrative jobs.

While legitimate women veterans are fighting to gain recognition of their contribution as nurses, clerks, and technicians in the war, they are also represented on the flip side of the story: female wannabes.

- "My nightmare is a river of red running into an ocean of red and it never stops, and it's blood." This gruesome image is from a story in the *Rocky Mountain News* about former Army nurse Ann Funck telling a tenth-grade high school class about her experiences in Vietnam.

  Funck, a founder of the Denver chapter of the VVA and a specialist in veterans' issues for then-Sen. Gary Hart, wanted the kids to know the truth about Vietnam. She described the "roaches and maggots streaming from the wounds" of the men she treated in a combat hospital in 1967. Almost twenty years later, Funck claimed, she still had nightmares about those "rivers of blood." She also denounced the American government for refusing to press for the release of the "hundreds" of U.S. troops "still enslaved" in Southeast Asian prison camps.

  Although the story ran on April 1, 1985, it was not intended as an April Fools joke but as a discussion of high school history lessons, which often don't include the Vietnam War.[775] Ann Funck appeared three years later in the *Dallas Times Herald*, in a story by columnist Ann Zimmerman about the effort to build a statue honoring the women who served in Vietnam. Funck had moved to Dallas and became involved with the local chapter of the VVA. Funck again lamented the streams and seas of blood and moaned bitterly about her nightmares generated by service as an operating room nurse in Vietnam.

  "I had seen dead people before," Funck said, "but they were all whole. I had never seen them in pieces before. If there was a large battle in our area, we would have hundreds of guys on cots screaming, waiting for us to sort out the bodies as we decided who lives and who dies. A lot of combat vets have said to me, 'You had it rougher than we did.'"[776]

  Funck felt that female Vietnam vets should be recognized. "Our fight was to keep these men alive," she said. "The statue of three fighting men was supposed to represent all of us. It doesn't." She described visiting the Mall in Washington and seeing a man with a scar on his neck. She told the startled man he still had a bullet in his hip. Funck knew because she was the one who had pieced him back together.

  I filed an FOIA request for Funck's record and received word there was no record that Ann Funck had ever served in the military. But you have to be careful when researching the records of women; their names may change when they marry and divorce. More research revealed Funck had served under the name Karen Ann Cowles. Her record revealed she was not a nurse. She had served in the Army from January 24, 1966 to August 23, 1966—all of seven months—as a dentist's assistant. She never left the United States. According to the code used to describe "reason for discharge," the unmarried Funck had become pregnant.[777]

I gave the record to some local Vietnam veterans who were upset by the wild stories she was telling. It made its way to the local VVA chapter. When Funck asked for permission to speak at a local Vietnam conference, she was confronted by Joe Testa, the president of the local VVA chapter, with her military record. *Permission denied.* Can't have prevaricators mucking up the Vietnam story. (The irony was that Testa, who did speak at the conference, also was a liar.)

Funck disappeared from the Dallas vet scene. Ironically, the next time she popped up, in a *Dallas Morning News* front-page story in 1993, she had a whole new persona, as the founder of the American Indian Student Association at Texas Woman's University. She was pictured using a smudge stick of sage, sweetgrass, and cedar to "bless" books donated to the Pine Ridge Indian Reservation in South Dakota. This time she described herself as a premed student, adopted as an infant by a Lakota Sioux family.[778]

• Television camera crews and satellite trucks invaded the quiet northeast Texas ranching community of Bogata in 1992, when state health counselor Dona Spence reported that six of the town's 198 students at Rivercrest High School were infected with the AIDS virus—a dramatic and frightening allegation in a small town where everybody knows everybody. An AIDS rate six times the national average? How could that be possible?

But that wasn't all. Not only had the teens from the high school tested HIV positive, Spence said, she was counseling about thirty other HIV-positive teenagers from that rural corner of Texas.[779]

The ensuing uproar sparked stories about Spence, who described herself as a former Army nurse with combat experience in Vietnam, in publications as diverse as *People* magazine and *The New York Times*, on network news programs, and on tabloid television shows such as the *Maury Povich Show* and *Sally Jesse Raphael*.

The firestorm of publicity stunned the town of Bogata, population 1,421. People from Bogata complained that others were shunning them, calling their home "AIDS town." When the school's girls' basketball team took the floor at the high school in nearby Paris, Texas, their opponents chanted, "HIV, HIV, HIV!" Two other schools refused to allow their junior varsity teams to play the Rivercrest Rebels at all.[780]

But as the news media chased the story, it evaporated into smoke and mirrors. Issues of confidentiality made details impossible to prove, but there was no evidence the town had even one teen with AIDS.

Questions about Spence's credentials began to surface. When hired by a state health agency in May 1990, she had told officials she served as an Army nurse for seventeen years and had completed two tours in Vietnam at a military hospital in Saigon. Spence claimed she had achieved the rank of captain and received a Purple Heart after being wounded by a piece of shrapnel when somebody "tossed something that exploded over the wall outside while I was helping with a gurney." Spence gave a document backing up her claim of a Purple Heart to a reporter for *People* magazine.

But Dona K. Spence wasn't registered as a nurse in Texas or California, where she had previously lived, and her military records indicate that she served in the Air Force from November 1972 to April 1973, and in the Army, from April 1981 to March 1982. In neither service was she a nurse. Spence worked as a medical laboratory specialist and achieved only the rank of private first class. She was stationed in Monmouth, New Jersey, not South Vietnam.[781]

During interviews by the media, Spence blamed the discrepancies on misreadings of her resume and confusion caused by medication she was taking for breast cancer. Although she continued to insist that the thirty-six HIV positive cases existed, a Texas Health Department probe found no evidence her stories about teens with AIDS were true. Spence had perpetrated a disturbing hoax that victimized an entire community. Some speculated that she made up the story to win grants for a clinic she wanted to open in a nearby town.

- When patients at VA hospitals throughout Texas competed in the "Heroes and Holidays" art contest sponsored in 1991 by the American Legion, the only female among the ten winners was veteran Johnnie Rainwater. The contest asked patients to create images for Christmas cards sold by the Legion to raise money for veterans' benefits and youth programs. Rainwater's creation was "Angel of Joy," a beautiful depiction of a winged being in blue, green, and white chalk on black paper. On the inside, in addition to a scripture verse, was a description of Rainwater's heroic service in Vietnam.

"E-7 Rainwater was a courier for the 525th Military Intelligence during the Vietnam conflict," the card said. "She was wounded at Chu Lai and received her second Purple Heart and her Bronze Star

Medal in action near Pleiku. Rainwater is an outpatient at the VA Medical Center in Houston and works as a volunteer seven days a week in the Nursing Home Care Unit."[782] A story about Rainwater in the *Dallas Times Herald* reiterated her status as a decorated Vietnam vet.[783]

On February 27, 1992, I called Johnnie Rainwater at the hospital and had a delightful conversation. Rainwater said she had signed up in 1986 as a volunteer for the VA, discovered she had PTSD, and began undergoing counseling in the VA outpatient clinic.

Her Vietnam experience was quite colorful. Rainwater told me she had served thirty-six months in Vietnam from 1969 to 1972, as a military intelligence courier in Saigon and as an operative in the Phoenix Program. She said she had been engaged twice to men in Vietnam: once to a journalist who was killed in Cambodia and then to a colonel who was missing in action. Rainwater claimed that Lt. Sharon Lane, the only woman killed in action in Vietnam, was her best friend and that the two women had grown up together. Tragically, Rainwater had been with Lane on the day she was struck by shrapnel and had watched her friend die.

Rainwater confirmed that she had indeed received a Bronze Star Medal for valor as well as a Purple Heart for injuries she suffered when a tire blew out on a Jeep in which she was riding. Five others were killed, Rainwater said, and she had been knocked out. She was discovered twelve hours later, lying unconscious only six feet from a Viet Cong trail. Her injury was so severe doctors had to implant a titanium plate in her head. After a six-month recuperation at a hospital at the Presidio in San Francisco, Rainwater said, she was sent back to Vietnam. The conversation told me quickly that Rainwater might be a gifted artist, but she was not a Vietnam veteran.

Years earlier, Rainwater had turned up in Portland, Oregon, seeking counseling at a VA center. Then thirty years old, Rainwater told doctors that she had been attacked on the Ho Chi Minh Trail, captured, and taken prisoner. Her life was in disarray, and she often embroiled compassionate acquaintances in her histrionics, which included factitious seizures and multiple conflicting medical symptoms. An essay Rainwater wrote about her "return" to Vietnam demonstrated either incredible literary skill or that she had no qualms about plagiarizing.

I obtained Rainwater's military record through an FOIA request. Rainwater was indeed an Army veteran; she served under the name Juanita Olvera for a time in Korea. But she had never served in Vietnam and was never a POW. Rainwater was a clerk-typist.[784]

Rainwater popped up again in 1995 when a writer in Houston submitted a story about the female intelligence operative to Col. Harry Summers, editor of *Vietnam* magazine. Suspicious that such a remarkable story had never before been told and alerted to the issue of wannabes after the Bird and Stanton affair, Summers called me to ask the legitimacy of her story and gave the writer my phone number. The writer was chagrined that she had been fooled. Rainwater was a major character in a play she had written and was staging about female veterans.

• In 1994, medical illustrator Anne Label returned to Vietnam to make peace. The wife of a Southern California neurosurgeon, Label said she had worked as an Air Force medic at a U.S. field hospital in Vietnam in 1970. Her fiancé, an Air Force flier, was lost in combat. After months of tending soldiers without limbs or hands, writing their letters home, she suffered a nervous breakdown.

Sent home, she resigned from the military and locked away her past, not even telling her husband that she was a veteran until after they were married. Guilt-ridden, Label decided to journey back to Southeast Asia, pledging to give one thousand dollars a month to a school in Hue in an effort to heal her emotional scars from the war.

Reporter Richard A. Serrano for the *Los Angeles Times* chronicled Label's return to the country of her torment, a visit meant to be a soul-cleansing experience. Near China Beach, she bought a string of two thousand dog tags of missing American GIs for twenty dollars from a woman who claimed she was the daughter of a dead Viet Cong commander. Led one night to a very small village, she was taken to what the villagers described as a burial grave near the site where a U.S. helicopter had crash-landed during the war. There, she was given a decaying skull; inside the eye and nose cavity were a chain and dog tag belonging to Marine E.A. Baker. Label was exhilarated.[785]

But when Label turned over her shocking evidence about MIAs to a career Army field investigator in Ho Chi Minh City, she was met with disinterest. Forensics revealed that the skull was Mongoloid, not Caucasian. And as for the dog tags, she was told that they were manufactured by the thousands for sale to naïve Americans. None of the dog tags was of use in documenting what happened to any American MIAs or POWs. Angry that her "evidence" was dismissed so lightly, Label returned home to Southern California and became heavily involved in veterans' issues. She even obtained a license plate for her car identifying her as a "NAMVET."

Reporter Serrano quoted Tony Diamond, head of BRAVO—the

Brotherhood Rally of All Veterans' Organizations—as supporting Label's efforts. "I believe her story because of the sincerity I feel in her," he said. "Let me tell you: Her word is enough for me."

"The truth, like so much that haunts the debate over whether Americans were left behind in Southeast Asia, will probably never be told," concluded reporter Serrano.

But the truth is available for a reporter who wants to check the facts. Another *Times* reporter who had served in Vietnam was skeptical when he read the story. For starters, he found the "NAMVET" license plate was issued to a man in Northern California, not Label. The reporter read about me in *Texas Monthly* and called for help in getting Label's military record.

Label's name had changed by marriage, but by tracing her Social Security number, I finally located her military record. Anne Label had served in the Air Force under the names Anne Cecilia Caro and Anne Cecilia Dulaney. She had enlisted in the Air Force as an airman basic in July 1970; her active duty ended November 22, 1971. She was not a medic, and her records show she never served in Vietnam.[786]

Despite proof that Label had made up her tales of trauma in Vietnam, the higher-ups at the *Los Angeles Times* decided not to print a correction. Their apparent reasoning: Label was delusional and to call her story into question might be too traumatic.

"It's Contagious"

Women are more likely to be the victims of impostors—the men they love —rather than fraudulently claim Vietnam service themselves. After the *20/20* program aired in 1994, I was inundated with letters. Almost half were from women involved with abusive males who claimed they were traumatized Vietnam veterans. These men excuse their anger and violent behavior by telling their women that "Vietnam made me do it." Like Steve Southards, who told Dan Rather he tried to strangle his mother one night "because she looked like VC," these men use Vietnam as a pretext for losing their jobs, for taking drugs, for beating up their wives and girlfriends.

The story usually goes like this: She sympathizes when her husband, lover, or boyfriend whimpers about how Vietnam screwed him up. She believes the stories about covert operations and clandestine heroics. She covers up for his alcoholism or battering, believing that it's all because of Vietnam. Still, even the most loyal woman has to begin to wonder when she repeatedly is awakened by her man's hands clamping around her throat. He always apologizes. "Baby, I thought you were the Viet Cong," he moans in repentance.

Crazed Vietnam vets terrorizing their women has become such an issue that several popular books have taken up the cause, like *Recovering From the War: A Woman's Guide to Helping Your Vietnam Vet, Your Family, and Yourself*, by Patience H.C. Mason.[787] Therapists have begun treating "Vietnam wives" for suffering from "contagious PTSD." That's a potentially huge market.

And that's not all. "Veterans with PTSD have children with PTSD," according to Juanita Davis, the clinical coordinator for the Indianapolis Vet Center.[788] And Charles R. Figley, who has long worked with PTSD and Vietnam veterans, discovered another group with contagious PTSD: counselors. In 1995, Figley published a book called *Compassion Fatigue: Coping with Secondary Stress Disorder in Those Who Treat the Traumatized*.[789] (Soon someone will have a book out about treating the grandchildren of Vietnam vets with PTSD!)

The VA has set up a system to treat these women, using taxpayer funds. Is this phenomenon really contagious PTSD or a reaction to abuse suffered at the hands of someone with "factitious" PTSD? Therapists almost never verify military records, so they have no way of knowing.

In her 1988 book *Vietnam Wives*, psychologist Aphrodite Matsakis, Ph.D., presented stories told by women living with abusive men who traced their trauma to the war. Matsakis described how the Vietnam wife normally arranges her domestic life around her husband's frames of mind, always on guard against his violent or angry explosions. The couple's sex life may be apathetic or even nonexistent. "Being the wife of a veteran usually means I function like a single parent," says "Melanie," described as the wife of a combat vet and mother of three children.

"I am responsible for almost every detail of my children's lives. I am also responsible for most of the details of my husband's life. When my husband is in a good mood, he vacuums, does the dishes and irons my blouses. But I never know how long his moods are going to last. I wish I could socialize and do more for myself. [but] I have to think twice before I leave the kids alone with my husband. I do everything for everybody else. I don't do anything for myself because that would be selfish. No one ever says 'thanks.' Sometimes I feel so unappreciated that I want to run away from home."

Many of the husbands' tales told in the book are highly improbable, but they are impossible to trace because Matsakis used only pseudonyms. Still, the impostors are easy to spot if you know the reality. For example, Matsakis described two husbands—Bob and Fred—who claimed they were POWs.

"Anna Marie" was married to "Bob," supposedly a POW for nine months. "He saw every horror imaginable and *later inflicted those same horrors on as many VC as he could find*," Matsakis wrote. (Emphasis added.)

"Wives and girlfriends of veterans who were sexually abused during the war are particularly sensitive to the fact that their veteran's memories may be exceptionally intrusive and troublesome," she wrote. "What they may not know, however, is that their veteran may withdraw sexually because he is plagued by sadistic thoughts. These sadistic thoughts may arise, in part, from an urge to retaliate against his abusers. For example, Fred *was sexually abused by Viet Cong guards* during his six months as a POW. After he was released, *he sought to kill his abusers, but they could not be found.*" (Emphasis added.)[790]

Fact number one: Not a single POW in Vietnam reported sexual abuse. Vietnamese society is extremely reticent about sexual matters; that did not enter into their very inventive torture techniques. And fact number two: While Bob claimed he returned to the field to inflict horrors on VC, and Fred allegedly hunted for his abusers to seek revenge, *no freed POWs were ever returned to duty in the war zone.* Official MACV policy was to remove any POW from the Southeast Asia theater as soon as possible after escape or release. Prisoner of war Col. Nick Rowe wanted to return to combat after his release, but he was forbidden to do so.[791]

Writer Malcolm McConnell wrote Matsakis to ask her about these and other discrepancies. She wrote back that the people in her book were not specific patients but composites of all her cases. Composites? Is that psychologist talk for, "I made 'em up"?

"It's no surprise that sexual abuse of POWs isn't recorded because of a) shame, b) fear of ridicule, c) denial of the event," Matsakis wrote. "There were also POWs who were significantly injured but a) downplayed their injuries so they could go on fighting or b) were told they'd 'get over it' on their own. Obviously the injuries were not debilitating enough to prohibit movement, but they were significant enough to leave deformities, which I have seen with my own eyes.

"I've been with the VA since 1971—some twenty years—and I can count the 'fakers' on one hand. They are so obvious it's pathetic. The men I refer to as POWs in my book were in such obvious psychic torment, came for help, received and asked for no money from [the] VA, were frightened of therapy, there is slight chance they 'faked' it."[792]

But how does she know this? Matsakis did not independently check official military records of her clients' husbands to verify these stories. Even the most naïve therapist must realize that money is not the only goal of many fakers: The "obvious psychic torment" enables them to manipulate and control others and gives them a convenient—even heroic—explanation for their failed lives.

Matsakis clearly believes she can discern the truth better even than military psychiatrists who examined POWs after their release. As Pankratz has demonstrated, doctors are fooled all the time. Just because a patient shows a scar or seems in obvious psychological distress, that doesn't mean he or she is telling the truth! And how does Matsakis know that her patient isn't already 30 percent service-connected, trying for 100 percent, unless she reviews the file?

The theory that PTSD is contagious makes it possible for women, like men, to claim the condition as a criminal defense. A 1994 case in southern Louisiana illustrates the ever-expanding phenomenon.

Vietnam veteran Buck Pugh and his wife Joyce lived in a remote area of Sabine Parish, Louisiana. Buck was a "go-getter." Every morning he drove his wife to the shop where she worked as a waitress, then in the afternoon he would "go get her." A Vietnam veteran, Buck had few friends. His yard was ringed with trenches covered with pieces of tin, much like those dug by soldiers in Vietnam. Detectives later learned that Buck had gone to a VA hospital for numerous tests. Although counselors had recommended that he return for treatment of PTSD, he didn't accept therapy.

When Buck disappeared on Thanksgiving Day 1994, Joyce first told authorities he had gone hunting. A neighbor attested to the fact that Buck was an excellent marksman, a dead shot when it came to deer. But when Buck did not return, Joyce offered another explanation: Buck had gone to Haiti to work a construction job. Authorities finally found Buck—buried in a grave in the couple's yard.

Detectives arrested Joyce and charged her with murder. They determined that during an argument in their front yard, Joyce had shot her obese husband four times. But at 280 pounds, her husband was too big to move. Joyce tied a rope to her husband's hefty corpse, then pulled him with their van until his body dropped into one of the trenches in the yard. She covered him with six to eight inches of dirt and leaves, then filled the hole with eighteen inches of Sackrete.

When her husband's body was discovered, Joyce contended that when she returned on Thanksgiving from visiting her mother, Buck had threatened her with a weapon. For years, he'd suffered from PTSD, which caused him to beat her. Therefore, she had PTSD, and when he terrorized her with a gun, she lost control and shot him dead.

Half the community sided with Joyce; the other half thought she was guilty of premeditated murder. Although detectives saw no bruises or marks indicating she had been abused, a Sabine Parish grand jury declined to indict Joyce. Twice. Could hardly blame the girl, married to that crazy Vietnam vet.

Buck Pugh indeed served in the Army in Vietnam—as a truck driver.

The Serial Wife Killer

Bogus Vietnam vets can make their women's lives a living hell—and worse. Premier crime writer Ann Rule told the story of one such pretender in her 1993 book *A Rose for Her Grave*.

For years, Seattle resident Randy Roth regaled his third wife with horrific stories about serving in the Marines in Vietnam, yarns that explained
why he suffered such terrible nightmares, why he woke up screaming so
many nights. His war memories were so painful, Roth could only bring
himself to speak of them haltingly.

Roth claimed he had been in a Special Forces unit, on a team of ten
highly trained men sent on missions so secret there was no record of them.
His squad, Roth contended, was forced to kill a whole village of women
and children in Vietnam. On one mission, Roth claimed he was so badly
wounded he had been admitted to a special hospital for ninety days.

Although the war had been horrific for him, Vietnam obsessed Roth. He
often wore camouflage fatigues during the year and his dress uniform on
patriotic holidays. Military magazines littered the house. Roth had a little
personal shrine in a hallway at home, showing a photo of himself in his
dress uniform and a bronze plaque for "valor" inscribed to Sgt. R.G. Roth.
He insisted his young sons watch the movies *Platoon* and *Hamburger Hill*. To
help her understand the terrible reality of Vietnam, Roth showed his wife
scrapbooks filled with gruesome pictures, some of corpses lying in ditches
in Vietnam. Roth also gave her an oral history book about Vietnam,
claiming that the authors had interviewed him. The book described a living
hell.

His third wife was lucky. Randy merely divorced her. She discovered
Roth had pushed his second wife off a cliff only weeks after insuring her
life. He later drowned his fourth wife, who was also heavily insured.

She was stunned to learn that Roth graduated from high school three
months after American troops were withdrawn from Vietnam in March
1973. He had been in the Marines all right, but in late 1973 and 1974. His only
duty overseas was in Okinawa, where he was a file clerk, a bizarre echo of
David Goff, the phony clandestine operative from the state of New York.[793]

Most of the women who have contacted me for help are involved with
fakers who have not sought press attention. These men are content to use
their stories to manipulate their loved ones, family, and friends. I've chosen
a few of their stories that are representative.

Great Expectations
Single after a difficult divorce, Sally Randall[794] was interested in dating
again but concerned about sharing private information about herself with
men she did not know. After being assured their careful screening eliminated "undesirables," Randall paid twenty-five hundred dollars in
December 1992, to sign up with Great Expectations video dating service. A
subsidiary of Houston-based Great Southern Video, Inc., Great
Expectations has forty-six offices in major U.S. cities and Mexico City. A TV

infomercial claimed Great Expectations is the "world's oldest and largest video introduction service" and promised that "at Great Expectations you know everything about [dates] up front." It sounded like an easy and safe way for Randall to meet suitable suitors.

On March 15, 1993, Randall met Travis Dean Crawford, another Great Expectations client, when he chose her video. Crawford seemed like a man of impeccable moral character: His profile sheet said he had been a Green Beret in Vietnam, a military instructor at West Point, a graduate with bachelor's and law degrees from Northwestern University, a former IRS agent, and an employee of the Small Business Administration. After a whirlwind courtship that lasted a month, Randall married forty-six-year-old Crawford, who assured her that he was so deeply religious that they had to be wed to live together.

But after only four months of marriage, when her new husband was arrested by the Secret Service, Randall found out to her shock that nothing she believed about Crawford was true. Crawford had a long string of aliases: Travis Hooper, Travis Nix, Edward Finnegan, Dean Crawford, and Travis Hernden. He had been married not once, as he had said on his profile, but four times—and not to the Dallas woman he said was his former wife.

Crawford possessed no college degrees; he had dropped out of the ninth grade and falsified his college transcripts. His claim that he had worked as an IRS agent for eight years was also a lie. A trainee, he had been forced to leave the IRS after six months when the agency discovered he had falsified government forms to get the job. The same thing happened with the SBA job.

Although Crawford claimed he was wounded fighting valiantly as a Green Beret in Vietnam, his military record revealed that Crawford was actually an Army cook at Fort Stewart, Georgia, during the war. In 1985, Crawford was court-martialed by the Army in Germany for passing 143 bad checks totaling $52,593 on a worldwide spending spree while AWOL. He was sentenced to five years in Leavenworth Prison and dishonorably discharged.[795]

Crawford pleaded guilty in 1993 to federal charges of credit-card fraud and making false statements to a government agency and was sentenced to five years in federal prison.[796] During his eighteen-month incarceration, he filed documents with the VA attempting to obtain disability payments for "bipolar disorder," a diagnosis a doctor had given Randall after she sought medical treatment during her experience with Crawford.[797]

Randall, who obtained an annulment after Crawford's arrest, said that during the four months they were married, he spent all her life savings—$203,400—and incurred substantial debts in her name. She filed a lawsuit against Great Expectations, alleging deceptive trade practices by leading her to believe that its screening process eliminated people like Crawford from its database.⁷⁹⁸

The Child Molester

After the *20/20* story ran, I received a letter from a woman in Madison County, Illinois, begging for my help. A Green Beret who had fought in Vietnam had recently been charged with committing a crime against a member of her family. "There are so many missing pieces to this puzzle," said Barbara Harris.⁷⁹⁹ "Please call me immediately if you can."

A veteran named Louis Paul Rolofson Jr. had come into the lives of Barbara Harris and her two sons in 1994. Harris was divorced, and the boys' father had limited contact with the sons. Befriended through her church by Rolofson, a retired banker, she was thrilled to have such a "man's man," the "Christian version of John Wayne," as an influence on her impressionable boys.

Rolofson said he had been a Green Beret in Vietnam. He regaled the boys, particularly her younger son, then ten, with amazing stories of military prowess. The youngsters were enthralled. So when Rolofson volunteered to take them on outings, Harris agreed. Rolofson seemed so responsible, so religious, that in August 1994, when the retired banker offered to take the boys on an overnight trip with a church group to Grant's Farm and Six Flags, Harris readily acquiesced.

But after the trip, Harris discovered from her ten-year-old son that Rolofson had asked him to come to his bed and take his clothes off. The "Vietnam Green Beret" then committed a sex act with the child. His older brother was asleep and heard nothing. The mother was devastated. On the telephone, she confronted Rolofson. "It wasn't planned," he admitted. "It just happened."

After his arrest, Rolofson changed his story, claiming that nothing unseemly had occurred; he had only given the boy a backrub to console him because he missed his mother. He insisted that the little boy had made the molestation story up because he was angry and jealous of Rolofson. Character witnesses from his church came forward to insist that Rolofson could not have committed such a heinous act.

When Harris talked to the prosecutor, she was concerned. Investigators had found no criminal record for Rolofson nor had they attempted to get his military record. She was worried that he would get off lightly for his crime—even if he was convicted. After all, it was the word of a ten-year-old against the testimony of a Green Beret war hero who had made a career in banking. Whom would the jury believe?

This one really made me mad. Here was a man using his tales of bravery in Vietnam to earn the trust of little boys in order to molest them! I told the prosecutor Teresa D. Brown how to get his military record, and while I was at it, I ran a search of Rolofson's criminal history. Rolofson had been convicted of misappropriation of funds in 1973 and bank embezzlement in 1975. He had been sentenced to three years in prison.

At the trial, which was held in September 1995, Rolofson took the stand. He talked about his distinguished career in the financial world. Although the prosecutor was prohibited from asking him about any prior criminal record, she managed to show the jury that his banking career was less than sterling.

When the defense attorney asked Rolofson about his military record, he repeated the story he had told Harris and her boys about his leadership as a Green Beret in Vietnam. The prosecutor then presented him with his real military record, which showed that he had served two years of active duty from 1966 to 1968 but he was not a Green Beret, nor had he served in Vietnam. His only overseas assignment was Korea. As a rifle platoon leader, his performance was called into question, and his commanding officer took the unusual step of requesting that Rolofson be denied a virtually automatic promotion, a sure sign of a troubled military career.

"This officer is not recommended for promotion to the grade of first lieutenant because he has, as of this date, failed to indicate that he is in fact qualified to be a second lieutenant," said his superior officer on an officer efficiency report dated December 21, 1967. "During my tenure as battalion commander, he has been relieved from his assignment as battalion adjutant due to his gross incapacity to satisfactorily perform his duties."[800]

After his fabrications were revealed so dramatically, the jury knew whom to believe. Rolofson was convicted of aggravated criminal sexual assault and sentenced to eighteen years in prison.

"Dear Mr. Burkett: I'm just taking a few minutes to thank you for your part in convicting my son's molester," Harris wrote the day after his conviction. "Without your help, we would not have had his criminal records— or his military records. As you know, they both revealed vital information. Now, Louis R. Rolofson Jr. has been exposed for what he truly is—a fraud, a liar, and a child molester."

Of all those deceivers I have exposed, Rolofson made me the angriest. I can't help but wonder if Rolofson has been using those fake stories of heroism in Vietnam to impress—and molest—young boys for years.

Baby, Are You VC?
Terri Stout introduced her new boyfriend to her father in 1985. "Dad, this is Jerry Kullman. He's a Vietnam veteran." Although she did not know much about the Vietnam War—she was only twenty and Jerry was thirty-eight— Terri had been raised to revere veterans. Terri's uncle had been severely

wounded in World War II. Some might dishonor Vietnam vets, but not her family. Terri's father grabbed Kullman's hand and pumped it.

"Son, bless your heart for serving your country," he said.

Terri and Jerry had met two years earlier when living in adjoining apartments in Rancho Cordova in Northern California. They didn't like each other at first. For two years, they traded barbs. But one night, during a fight with her boyfriend, Jerry heard the commotion and came to Terri's rescue. Soon, they were inseparable and began living together.[801]

Terri soon realized that Jerry was still deeply obsessed with the war. One night, he insisted that she go with him to see the newly released movie *Platoon*. In the middle of the film, he began sobbing loudly. In the parking lot after the movie, Jerry collapsed on the back of his pickup truck, tears in his eyes.

"There are things you have to know," he said. He began telling her about his harrowing experiences in Vietnam as a crypto-courier, ferrying encoded messages from the states to high-ranking people in the field. But he was also involved in other secret operations. He had been dropped into the jungle to commit heinous executions of Viet Cong men, women, and—of course—children.

That night, Jerry talked of field-stripping cigarette butts, of eating jungle vegetation and bugs to survive, of trying to think and smell like the "Cong." Once left behind at a rendezvous point after a surprise attack by "Charlie," he played dead. But the worst was clutching his friends when they were hit by enemy fire, holding them as the men bled to death. On return trips to the states, Jerry often was assigned to accompany planeloads of body bags back home.

Terri was stunned, but she had no reason to doubt his stories. After the movie, Terri finally persuaded him to come to bed. But at 3 A.M. Terri was awakened by Jerry, who was quivering and shaking, gripped in the throes of a nightmare. "I let them down!" he moaned, crouching in the corner of the bed. "I let them die!" She soothed him, assuring him that he had done all he could, then held her lover's trembling body until he finally went back to sleep.

The nightmares came two or three times a week. One night, she woke to find his hands around her throat. "Fucking Cong! Fucking Cong!" he screamed as he choked her. She flailed at his hands, trying to make him let go, yelling, "Stop it! Jerry, it's me! Stop!" He finally awoke and begged her forgiveness. The next morning Terri went to work, wearing a scarf to cover the bruises around her throat. Over the next eight years, she frequently was forced to wear high necklines, long sleeves, and scarves to hide the bruises where Jerry pummeled her during his nightmares about Vietnam. Often, she needed all her strength to remove his hands from her neck.

Terri supported them, working first at a title company, then as an executive secretary. During their first two years together, Jerry worked a total of six months. The same thing happened every time. For a while the boss and other employees adored him. Everybody wanted so much to help him out, they would bend over backward for him. But typically, by the end of the month, Jerry was fired or quit in a huff. The conflicts were never his fault. Vietnam was to blame.

Although her father staunchly defended him, Terri's sisters didn't like Jerry at all. They were upset when Terri and Jerry married.

"Terri, the guy is nuts," her sister Deborah often said after hearing about something strange Jerry had done. Bob, her brother-in-law, who had been a paratrooper in Vietnam, pointed out that Jerry seemed to have the wrong dates for various battles. That gave her pause. Jerry had told her a story about running up a hill with an American flag. The scenario sounded suspiciously like the battle of Iwo Jima in World War II. But Terri brushed off their suspicions.

Jerry's family confirmed that Jerry had been in 'Nam, but they knew very little about his war experiences. After months of not hearing from him, his mother and father had contacted a commander at Beale Air Force Base, where he had been stationed before shipping out to Vietnam and asked him to contact Jerry.

Jerry wrote them from Vietnam, via an APO address, saying that he wanted no contact with them. The terrible things he was being required to do in the war went against the moral foundations they had instilled in him, Jerry said. They did not hear from him again until he returned home from Vietnam. He seemed deeply troubled.

"When you got married, we knew you were either a saint or insane," one in-law told Terri. She was beginning to wonder which was true.

Not long after their wedding, Terri asked Jerry for his discharge papers to complete application forms for a business loan. She had another motive —to get him some help at the VA. "I burned it all," he said. "My dog tags, my uniforms, my discharge papers, my ribbons and medals, everything. It was too painful to have around." That explained why he had no memorabilia from the war, no pictures, nothing.

Her brother-in-law Bob urged her to talk to Jerry about attending a veterans' support group. But Jerry refused. "It brings back too much of the past," he told Terri.

When they were living together, Jerry told her that the stress and strain he had gone through had rendered him sterile. He frequently complained about headaches and other ailments he said were brought on by Agent Orange. After he became convinced he had a brain tumor, Terri paid for a brain scan. Doctors found no tumor. Terri urged him to take advantage of his veteran's benefits and go to a VA hospital for treatment of his various ailments, but Jerry refused. He wanted nothing to do with the VA or any government agency.

In 1989, it became apparent that Jerry was not sterile. Terri became pregnant and had a baby girl, who was followed by a sister in 1991. But fatherhood did not seem to help. If anything, Jerry's behavior grew progressively worse. He spent the days indoors with the blinds closed so that no one could spy on him, watching war movies.

After the couple had been together six years, Jerry's sister took Terri aside. Married to a psychologist, the sister suspected Jerry might have post-traumatic stress disorder. She pressed some brochures into Terri's hands and urged her to coax Jerry to go to the VA for help.

Terri began reading the pamphlets on PTSD. They described Jerry's symptoms perfectly: nightmares, flashbacks, hypervigilance, alienation from society. Unable to hold a job. Inability to get along with people or to connect with significant others. But Jerry refused to go to counseling.

One night, they were watching *Hamburger Hill*, a very realistic movie about the spring of 1969, when troops with the 101st Airborne Division in Vietnam tried to take a heavily defended summit known as Hill 937 from the NVA. A platoon of infantry grunts made eleven assaults over ten days. Men were chopped to pieces, the casualty rate mounting to such heights that 937 was dubbed "Hamburger Hill."

As they watched, Terri held Jerry on the couch, in case the memories were too much for him to handle alone. But during the middle of the movie, she heard a few lines of dialogue that Terri knew she had heard before. She realized with a shock: *Jerry had told that story, line for line, as if it had happened to him.* She looked at the man she had lived with for almost seven years. She had no idea who he was.

Late that night, she urged him again to go to the VA for counseling. Again, he refused. "I'm beginning to think that Bob is right about your Vietnam stories," she flung back at him. He slapped her face. "Don't ever doubt what I did," he snarled. "I've seen more men die than you ever knew." He grabbed her by the hair and kicked her down a flight of stairs, then started to come down after her.

Terrified, Terri scrambled into the kitchen, grabbed a cast iron skillet pan and waited behind a door. When he came down the stairs, Terri brought it down hard on his skull. Jerry collapsed. At three in the morning, she packed up her belongings and her two crying daughters and left him.

Her dad was upset when he heard Terri had filed for divorce. "He fought and nearly died for his country," her dad said. "You can't leave him now. You've got to stick it out." But Terri refused to back down. Enraged, Jerry announced that he wanted custody of the children. His attorney filed papers accusing her of being a drug addict and of dealing drugs through her office at the title company. Although the charge was untrue, Jerry called the president of her company and told him that she had used drugs and had stolen office equipment, humiliating Terri and making her fear for her job.

Pending the outcome of the judge's decision about Jerry's charges that she was an unfit mother, she was advised by her attorney to give custody of the children to Jerry. Terri found herself in a walking nightmare. Jerry had manipulated the system so that she was the villain. For two months, she had to go through court-ordered drug testing in order to prove that she was not a drug addict. Finally, after all the tests showed up clean, she welcomed her two daughters back home with hugs, tears, and fears for the future.

In the midst of the battle over her children, Terri's father continued to defend Jerry. When Jerry fell into the "hog" on his lumber mill job and was injured, her father asked Terri to take her estranged husband back.

There was no way she could ever return to Jerry, Terri told her father.

"I guess I'll have to take care of him then," her dad said.

"Dad, you have to make a choice," Terri replied, looking at her father. "It's Jerry or me." Her dad looked stoic. "I guess I have to take care of Jerry," he said. "I can't abandon him after all he's been through." For months, her father nursed Jerry back to health, refusing to speak to his own daughter, who could not believe her father had chosen Jerry over her.

One day, as part of the divorce process, Terri met with a court investigator who was preparing documents to determine permanent custody arrangements for the children. Terri and Jerry each had to write a narrative of what had happened in their marriage. She wrote about his nightmares, about him attacking her because of "the Cong." About the assassinations, the covert operations, the men he held as they died.

The investigator read the document, then looked at her and said, "Your husband was never in the war."

"Yes he was," Terri said.

"He told me that you were psychotic and insane, that you had all these delusions about him and the Vietnam War," the investigator said. "Where did you come up with all this?" The investigator looked at Terri with a mixture of disbelief and curiosity, as if the young woman was explaining that a UFO had swooped down and abducted her.

Terri could not understand what the investigator was saying. Jerry told the investigator that Terri made up all the stuff about Vietnam? About attempting to strangle her in bed, mistaking her for the Viet Cong? It slowly dawned on Terri: The investigator, the woman making decisions about her children's future, thought *Terri* was the crazy one, not Jerry.

The more she tried to explain, the more skeptical the investigator looked. Determined to get custody of the kids, to beat her at all costs, Jerry had come up with a brilliant strategy. *Deny everything. Say it's all a figment of Terri's imagination.* The sheer audacity of his tactic took her breath away. The next day, she went to work depressed and worried about the custody situation.

That morning, her boss brought in a copy of that latest issue of *Reader's Digest*, which contained a story about my research into phony traumatized veterans.

"This is Jerry!" Terri realized after she read the details about David Goff. Shaking, crying, she realized that she had a way of proving for once and for all the truth about Jerry's experience in Vietnam.

She wrote to *Reader's Digest*, and the magazine put her in touch with me. I filed an FOIA request for her husband's file. When the documents arrived, Terri was stunned to find out the truth.[802]

Gerard Kullman had entered the Air Force in October 1966 and left four years later, his military career completely undistinguished, even mediocre. After basic training, Kullman was stationed at Beale Air Force Base in Marysville, California. He worked as a security guard and a clerk. Jerry was not a covert assassin, he never held friends in his arms as they died, he did not accompany their bodies home. And he never set foot in Vietnam.

There was a sign that the military recognized Jerry's emotional instability. Under "assignment limitations" was the notation: "Not to be assigned duties involving nuclear weapons."[803]

Jerry had created a persona out of whole cloth, feeding on movies and myth to manipulate her and terrorize her. He had lived as an unwanted, dishonored, dysfunctional Vietnam veteran for years, but he was a fraud.

Terri made copies of Jerry's military record and sent them to everyone who knew them. Then she took a copy of the record to her parents' home. Jerry had healed but still declined to work. Father and daughter hadn't spoken in months.

"Dad, you need to read this," she said. "It's Jerry's military record."

As her father read the handful of papers, a tear trickled down his face. Jerry had taken advantage of his patriotism and sense of duty in an obscene parody that belittled all those who did serve honorably. Broken-hearted, he asked for Terri's forgiveness.

Terri regained custody of her children and remarried. Jerry Kullman is still trying to get sole custody of their daughters. He is now receiving welfare benefits because he cannot work. Jerry Kullman now denies he ever claimed he served in Vietnam.

21

Bogus Guests at the Hanoi Hilton

FOR SEVERAL YEARS, David Fletcher had heard amazing stories about Donald R. Liston from friends in Stanfield, a small Arizona community south of Phoenix where they both lived. Actively involved in the POW-MIA movement, Liston, a former Green Beret sergeant, toured the state, giving speeches, spending his own money to set up a yearly reunion of Vietnam veterans called "Firebase Phoenix." Well-known and highly respected as a hero of the Vietnam War, Liston told people he had been a POW who had been nominated for the Medal of Honor. Fletcher had heard about all Liston had suffered as a captive of the North Vietnamese, and he was impressed.[804]

In the hierarchy of Vietnam War victimhood, the POW is the ultimate hero/victim, a status that ranks above even a battle-scarred combat veteran. John Rambo was a POW; and in *First Blood*, the viewer glimpsed agonizing torture of prisoners in flashback scenes. In the sequel, Rambo is sent to rescue long-forgotten POWs from the North Vietnamese. The image is that POWs not only suffered more than anybody, they demonstrated courage far beyond that of most soldiers. The prisoner of war survived the horrors of combat until he was captured and then was starved, beaten, and tortured, yet still persevered.

What came to be known as the 4th Allied POW Wing—an unofficial unit formed among American POWs in North Vietnam—is probably the most decorated unit in the annals of American warfare. (The POWs in Vietnam received more decorations during their captivity than all POWs did in all previous wars combined.) To declare yourself a member of this elite group is to automatically anoint yourself a highly decorated combat veteran. Most of those captured were men in the thick of combat, on the point of the spear: fighter pilots, helicopter pilots, combat soldiers—the risk takers. To Fletcher, Liston was one of those men.

During an encounter at a swap meet, Fletcher and Liston talked about common interests such as tanning snake skins. Invited to his home, Fletcher heard more of Liston's story. A Vietnam veteran himself, Fletcher was captivated. Fletcher's war, which had been uneventful, paled in comparison to Liston's experience in Vietnam. Liston's story had appeared in the local newspaper, and a singer named Jim Walktendonk had even written and recorded a ballad about Liston's exploits in Vietnam.

THE BALLAD OF DON LISTON

Don Liston heeds the warning 'round about Christmas Eve.
He checks into the V.A. where he's locked up and not allowed to leave.
In 'Nam he rescued 6 POWs but in the end was captured, too.
Well he paid the price so dearly.[805]

Liston admitted to Fletcher, an aspiring author, that a director had wanted to make a movie of his story, but the proposal had been thwarted by artistic differences. Impressed by Liston's self-deprecating modesty, inspired by his heroic tale, Fletcher asked Liston if he would collaborate on a book with him. Liston agreed hesitantly, although he warned Fletcher that some veterans might say his stories were "bullshit." Others, jealous of his heroism, might try to discredit him. But Liston had the papers to prove all his stories were true.

One night, as they began to outline the book, Liston produced numerous papers, certificates, forms, letters, and pictures from a battered olive-drab field pack. There was Liston's DD-214, confirming his status as a Special Forces sergeant, combat medic, and intelligence specialist. The form described his many wounds and had been stamped POW-MIA VIETNAM. Other documents were awards for the Silver Star, Bronze Star Medal, and five Purple Hearts, and other letters of commendation. Liston had certificates showing he had been graduated from the Airborne course at Fort Benning, Georgia; Intelligence School at Fort Huachuca, Arizona; and from the MACV Special Warfare Training Center of the 5th Special Forces Group in Vietnam. Others certified that Liston had qualified as an "advanced scuba diver" for Special Forces, had successfully completed the reconnaissance team leader's course, the Ranger Qualification School, the Pathfinder course, and was a member of a Special Forces "A" Team in Vietnam. He even had certificates showing he had completed Vietnamese Language School and sixty hours of training in spoken Chinese-Cantonese.

Several documents were stamped "SECRET." One was apparently an after-action report from the Military Assistance Command, Vietnam. It referred to the extraction of American POWs from Laos and requested the Medal of Honor for two MIAs, including "Sergeant Liston."

Another was on the letterhead of the "War Department, Military Intelligence Division" of MACV-SOG. This paper confirmed that Liston was an MIA and would receive the Silver Star for the mission on which he disappeared. "Due to the surreptitious goal of this mission, and its' (sic) location, we have denied the CMH (Congressional Medal of Honor) award at this time," the document said. "Although your two MIAs have went (sic) beyond the 'call of duty' We (sic) wish not to raise any questions of possible violations of the Geneva Convention Accords in respect to this type of mission at this time."

Liston even produced copies of a diploma from the University of Missouri showing he had earned an associate of science degree in behavioral psychology and another degree from the University of Kansas for a bachelor of science degree in criminal law.

Fletcher worked for eight months recording Liston's memories of the war, then began putting them down on paper. Under Fletcher's gentle prodding, Liston recalled more and more details of his tour in Vietnam. Reliving his experiences clearly took a toll on Liston. Symptoms of PTSD seemed to emerge as the two men covered the most traumatic periods, like the execution and mutilation of his buddy Sergeant Gator by the Viet Cong. Liston's family seemed to be genuinely distressed; they had never heard the stories in such depth.

Inspired by the movie *Green Berets*, Liston had enlisted in the Army in 1967. (Oops! The movie didn't come out until 1969.) After basic training, he was accepted for Special Forces school. Intense and brutal training as a Ranger, Pathfinder, and Green Beret followed, then Liston was sent to Vietnam in 1968. Liston found himself at base A-108, ironically the very base used as a model for the gung-ho movie that inspired him to join Special Forces.

As a combat medic, Liston's duties included winning the hearts and minds of the locals as well as being a member of an A-Team on missions to extract POWs. On one such mission, a punji stake impaled his leg and left a gaping hole about a half-inch in diameter. Despite excruciating pain, Liston continued on with the mission. He later received the first of his five Purple Hearts.

According to Liston, atrocities were committed by both sides in Vietnam. His squad routinely cut off enemy soldiers' ears to prove body count. Some American soldiers took enemy fingers as well, wearing the severed digits on dog tag chains around their necks. "The ears and fingers obtained became a way to gauge the efficiency and productivity of the top workers," Liston said. "They became the BMWs, the Rolexes, the Porsches, the yuppie status symbols of the war zone."

In December 1968, Liston's A-Team and a support group of ARVN were assigned a dangerous covert mission: to rescue six American prisoners held captive by the Viet Cong in Laos. The mission was so important the A-Team's leader, Capt. Harold W. Kroski, went along. Simply getting to the encampment took a terrible toll; one man was bitten by a Malayan pit viper and almost instantly died. The men were forced to make repeated stops to remove leeches from their skin after river crossings. But when they finally located the enemy base, the Americans and their allies decimated the enemy in a horrendous firefight, freeing the six emaciated American POWs.

While loading a helicopter with the prisoners and surviving members of his A-Team and the ARVN, Liston and his captain were forced to remain behind to provide covering fire. Pursued by the infuriated Viet Cong, the two split up, planning to rendezvous at an alternative landing zone. Liston never made it.

Enemy soldiers captured Liston and stuffed him into a bamboo "tiger" cage suspended in chest-high water. Tortured and interrogated daily, Liston suffered broken fingers when he refused to answer the questions posed by his captors. The enemy knew he was somebody special; they had found his green beret. But Liston was determined not to let them discover he was an intelligence officer. He informed his captors that he was with the 7th Cavalry under the command of Gen. George Armstrong Custer.

Undaunted by his injuries, determined to escape, Liston ducked beneath the surface of the river at night, holding his breath while he chewed on the softer bamboo underwater. "The time I was able to stay under the water, along with the time I could remain under without the guard noticing my absence from sight, limited the attempts that I could make," Liston said. "As the night wore on, the chances grew as the guard became tired. Carefully keeping an eye on the guard, I would slip under the water to gnaw at the bamboo."

After seventeen days of hard chewing, Liston created a hole large enough to accommodate his body. One night, he wriggled out of the hole, losing his boxer shorts, his last article of clothing. Naked, Liston slipped into the river and traveled for three days in the dense jungle before being found by American troops. Battered and filthy, Liston was recognized as an American only after the grime was washed from his arms to reveal Airborne, Green Beret, and Pathfinder tattoos.

Liston's injuries were his ticket home. But after recuperating at a military hospital in Japan, Liston insisted on returning to Vietnam to provide vital information for the rescue of Captain Kroski, who apparently had also been captured by the Viet Cong. Before Liston could lead the mission, however, the American camp was overrun by the enemy in the now infamous Tet Offensive of 1968. Shot five times, Liston was the only survivor of his twelve-man team. A bullet lodged permanently between his heart and spine, Liston abandoned all hope of rescuing Captain Kroski and returned home to America.

But Liston's trials had just begun. Even as he was carried off the medical airplane at the airport, Liston could hear protesters screaming "baby killer" and could see them spitting at him. Not long after his arrival in the United States, several men obviously with the CIA visited him to warn that he was to disavow any knowledge of missions to Laos. If Liston decided to blow the whistle, the men insinuated, his records would be altered to discredit his accusations. Given a medical discharge, Liston suffered a final indignity: During the mustering-out process, he was told he owed the government seventeen days' pay for AWOL—the time he spent in a tiger cage lowered into a river in Laos!

Not until years later did Liston, then a shift sergeant for the Phoenix Police Department, really begin to suffer the effects of PTSD. On Christmas Eve, 1980—the anniversary of his capture—Liston went berserk while on duty, firing his gun into the air and attacking fellow officers, ranting and raving all the while about Vietnam. The episode, Liston claimed, made the front page of the local newspaper.

In a lockdown unit of the VA hospital, Liston was served with divorce papers. When he recovered enough to leave the hospital, Liston moved to rural Stanfield, where he ran the Hidden Valley Oasis cafe. But Liston continued to be plagued with flashbacks and nightmares of Vietnam. Only a PTSD therapy group calmed the demons. Liston turned those demons into something positive, becoming a staunch supporter of the POW-MIA movement.

After months of work, Liston's amazing saga was down on paper. Fletcher was proud of the finished manuscript, which they called *Chieu-Hoi: Surrender with Open Arms*.[806] The Vietnamese phrase symbolized Liston's surrender to the American infantry he came upon after his escape from captivity, as well as his surrender to the nasty treatment he received from the government and the VA after his return from the war. Fletcher sent the manuscript to the William Morris Agency with hopes of making a sale to a publisher. He also mailed a copy to John Del Vecchio, the award-winning novelist, who took the time to read it, point out apparent errors, and to suggest Fletcher do some more research.[807]

Nonplussed, Fletcher asked Liston to address some of the discrepancies. Liston dismissed them as the result of blackouts or memory loss caused by trauma. But the more Fletcher researched, the more Liston's astonishing story unraveled. Fletcher discovered there was no front-page news story about "Police Sergeant Liston" going berserk. Indeed, there was no record that anyone by the name of Liston had ever been hired by the City of

Phoenix in any capacity. The VA hospital where Liston claimed he was hospitalized on a locked ward had no secure units at the time he was supposedly treated. And by examining military records, Fletcher learned that Liston would have had to spend three years and ten months in training in order to gain the different skills he claimed. How was that possible? By his own admission, Liston had been sent to Vietnam only eighteen months after he enlisted.

Finally, after investing months of his life on the project, Fletcher obtained Liston's real military record, which revealed his tale was all a fantasy. Liston had not been a combat medic and intelligence officer with Special Forces in Vietnam. He had been an Army supply clerk. Liston had received a Purple Heart for wounds sustained when driving a truck filled with supplies, but he had received no valorous decorations. Out of a total of twenty-three months in the military, Liston spent only three months in Vietnam. Liston never reached the rank of E-5, or sergeant. The highest rank he attained was a temporary designation of E-3. After the war, Liston had not worked as a policeman. He had worked as a jail guard and as a security guard for a local supermarket chain.

Devastated, Fletcher realized all his work was for nothing. How could he have been so completely suckered? Fletcher had been in Vietnam himself. But then he realized that Liston had fooled official organizations, which had included Liston in their lists of POWs. He thought back to his many conversations with Liston and the man's vivid reactions to the traumatic "memories."

"He is so convinced that his exploits are authentic he has no trouble convincing the listener as well," Fletcher says. "He lives his imaginary life as fully as you or I live ours." Fletcher remembers a conversation he had had with Liston early on in which Liston tried to explain why he was dedicating his life to the issue of POW-MIAs.

"I'm fortunate to be in the position of respect to where people will take the time to listen to what I have to say," Liston told him. "If I were only a private or a clerk they wouldn't be as prone to take the time to hear what I have to say."

And, of course, he's right. No reporter would listen to Liston's stories if he did not talk about atrocities. No writer would want to do a book about Liston unless he could regale readers with stories about escaping the enemy by chewing through bamboo tiger cages, an image, by the way, straight out of the movie *The Deer Hunter*. In order to feel that his story of Vietnam mattered, Liston had to appropriate the stereotypes and clichés peddled by filmmakers and the media. He had to make himself the ultimate hero-victim or no one would give a damn.

Return of the POWs

Of those captured by the Viet Cong or the NVA, sixty-four Americans died in captivity. Before 1973, about one hundred POWs were released in dribbles. The bulk of POWs were returned as a consequence of the cease-fire agreement with North Vietnam; 566 military and 25 civilian captives were released in February and March 1973 as Operation Homecoming, part of the negotiated settlement ending American involvement in the war. Twenty-four prisoners were released after 1973. Throughout the war, only thirty-four POWs successfully escaped.

When the POWs returned home in early 1973, they received a hero's welcome. Interviewed by the national media, they were wined and dined at the White House and were guests of honor at parades in their hometowns. Frankly, other Vietnam veterans felt a tinge of resentment when they thought of the contrast in the way POWs came home versus the way they returned to the states.

POWs of World War II or Korea were not considered heroic by their status as prisoners. Typically, throughout military history, being captured has not been considered an honor. Captives usually surrender rather than fight to the death. (About 125,000 American troops became POWs in World War II.) It was official military policy that POWs were not eligible for valorous awards while in captivity because they were not in combat.

But the courageous resistance of American POWs in North Vietnam led to the creation of the POW Medal. When first proposed, controversy surrounded the medal. The old guard in the military resisted the idea of a POW medal because the idea brought to mind soldiers giving up, throwing aside their weapons when faced with an enemy onslaught. "Why fight and die when I can throw my hands up and get a medal?"

In fact, in Vietnam many troops died because they refused to surrender. Those who were captured were usually alone or in small groups—pilots, crews of planes, small teams on reconnaissance patrol—groups so small and lightly armed that when confronted with a superior enemy force, resisting was suicidal.

Another difference: During World War II, few POWs were kept in captivity longer than two or three years. Most of those captured in Europe were held less than a year. Even the longest held POWs in World War II were captive for only three-and-a-half years. But during the war in Vietnam, which lasted ten years, American POWs were held an average of five years. It's widely believed, even among Vietnam veterans, that Everett Alvarez, who later became undersecretary of the VA, was the longest held. That unfortunate honor actually goes to a Green Beret named Capt. Floyd Thompson, who was held by the enemy for nine years. (Thompson retired from the Army with the rank of colonel at age forty-eight. He received the

Distinguished Service Medal for "truly magnificent powers of faith, physical endurance, and trust in the nation during years of almost unfathomable deprivation and hardship.") But even Thompson was not the first American serviceman captured. That dubious distinction belongs to Army Maj. Lawrence R. Bailey, captured in Laos on March 23, 1961, and released seventeen months later.

Despite the Communists' attempts to use them for propaganda purposes, almost all members of the 4th Allied POW Wing consistently resisted. Some were held in bamboo cages, others in caves. The ones taken north were held in jails and other buildings constructed in the French colonial era. But all suffered starvation diets, psychological and physical torture, and solitary confinement. Many, such as Vice Admiral Stockdale and Sen. John McCain, spent years in complete isolation. But the POWs were incredibly resourceful. When isolated, they found ways to communicate with tap codes and hand signals. When the North Vietnamese moved them into large dormitory-like cells, they set up a college of sorts with POWs who had advanced degrees or specialized skills teaching the others courses in everything from astrophysics to beekeeping. One Air Force captain, who had done a tour of duty in Europe, taught wine appreciation, complete with imaginary "tastings" from rusty tin cups.[808]

Many POWs came home to dramatically changed circumstances and initially had a slightly higher divorce rate than other veterans. During those years that her husband was a prisoner, the wife was forced into the role of provider and head of household. Some POWs reported very bitter relationships with their spouses on their return. Everett Alvarez' wife divorced him while he was held captive. Fred V. Cherry's wife had a child with another man and pocketed all his pay while he was a prisoner. (Cherry sued the Air Force for mishandling his funds, some $150,000, and won.)

To maximize both their supposed heroism and victimhood, wannabes latch onto stories like that of Stockdale, McCain, and Alvarez. But fake POWs are actually easy to identify.

Two or three months after I obtained the official casualty computer tape for Vietnam, I heard that there was a list of every man taken captive. Even if a man was held for less than twenty-four hours, if a POW returned alive, he was on that list. My request for the POW computer tape sent the military personnel office into another flurry of discussion about whether it was classified or public. They finally decided I could have the tape with all private information redacted.

About the same time that I received the prisoner computer tape, I read a story in the *Fort Worth Star-Telegram*, prompted by the capture of some Americans by the Iraqis during the Gulf War, about John Kennelly, a former Vietnam POW who worked for Bell Helicopter. His story echoed many of the themes lifted from books and movies that are common to phonies. Kennelly said he was on a secret mission when captured. He claimed he and his troops were marched through villages and displayed "like animals." Other POWs died off until only Kennelly and another man were left. After a year of brutal captivity and near starvation, the two men escaped, making their way south with the VC in hot pursuit. (Pretenders often say they "escaped;" that explains why they did not come out in a well-publicized prisoner exchange.) But the two escapees were not so starved that they didn't have superhuman strength.

"During those days my buddy killed eighteen with his hands, stones, or sticks," Kennelly told the reporter. "I managed to kill fourteen."[809] His buddy was killed by automatic fire on the morning of the fourth day. Kennelly managed to evade the attack and by chance ran into some Americans.

Totally bogus. I checked the POW list and Kennelly's name was not on it. I contacted the *Star-Telegram* reporter who said the American Ex-POW Association had referred him to Kennelly because he was a member and lived near Fort Worth.

Sally Morgan, the woman who ran the office of the American Ex-POW Association in Arlington, Texas, had been incarcerated as a child when the Japanese overran the Philippines during World War II. The association has about twenty thousand members and extends its affiliation to POWs from all wars. By 1990, only about 160 Vietnam POWs had become members. To outsiders, membership in the American Ex-POW Association, with its official-looking ID card, is a verification of someone's claim of POW status. Until 1986, you could become a member by referrals from other members. After that, the group began requiring more documentation of POW status. But that evidence could include anything from photographs (simple to doctor) or VA forms. Those are easy to obtain because clerks at some VA facilities stamp documents "POW" at veterans' self-reports and don't verify records.

I told Morgan that Kennelly wasn't listed among the POWs during Vietnam. "What list?" she asked. "We didn't know there was a list." I sent the organization a printout of the official Vietnam POW roster, explaining that it could be used not only to weed out the pretenders but also to recruit members.[810]

In return, Morgan sent me a list of her Vietnam POW members. After volunteering to verify their records, I filed FOIA requests for the records of John Texas Kennelly Jr. and the other association members from the Vietnam War, asking specifically for their status as POWs. (Personal military records may or may not show POW status.)

Kennelly's record revealed he had served as an aircraft mechanic in

Greenland during the late fifties and in Okinawa during the early 1960s. He had never served in Vietnam.[811] Confronted by the association board and asked for documentation of his POW status, Kennelly resigned from the group.

As the files of the others trickled in, the astonishing truth emerged: Almost 30 percent—one third—of the alleged members supposedly held captive in Vietnam had not been POWs. Some of them had conned a newspaper reporter, then used the reporter's subsequent story to qualify for membership. Others had gone to the VA and gotten a VA claim card stamped "POW" or a "POW" sticker on their medical records papers.

A Tennessee resident named Roger D. Dinsmore claimed he had been with 5th Special Forces and had been held captive in Cambodia during the Vietnam War. Papers Dinsmore had submitted to the American Ex-POW Association included a VA medical record with a POW status sticker checked "Vietnam." But Dinsmore's military record indicated that he served as a carpenter with an engineering battalion in Vietnam, not Special Forces, and was never a POW.[812]

Another association member, Jerry W. McCall of Bloomfield, Missouri, had "Former POW" license plates on his car. McCall's application claimed he had served with "Second Special Operations" and had been held captive in "jungle camps along the Ho Chi Minh Trail." His military record showed McCall served in Vietnam as an ammo bearer and security guard. He was never a POW.[813]

One phony POW had started two chapters of the American Ex-POW Association in a western state. His own daughter turned him in as a fake. A VFW state commander asserted that he was a Marine POW who escaped; he wasn't. The biggest surprise: One of the pretenders was not only a life member of the American Ex-POW Association, but also the vice commander of the Texas chapter. Texas POWs had elected a faker as their second highest-ranking officer.

The Flag on Pork Chop Hill

Archie Launey of Port Arthur is often described as the "second most decorated" veteran in Texas—recipient of the Distinguished Service Cross, four Silver Stars, two Bronze Star Medals, seven Purple Hearts, Master Parachutist Badge, two Combat Infantryman Badges, Soldier's Medal, and numerous other decorations. (That list alone was enough to make me suspicious.)

Launey, who said he retired from the Army as a major, has held numerous positions of honor in veterans' groups throughout the "Golden Triangle," the oil-producing and refining region of East Texas near Beaumont. Launey frequently talks to schools and civic organizations about the "true history" of the Vietnam War. When reporters in the area write stories on veterans' issues, they often call Launey for a quote.

A twenty-one-year veteran, Launey likes to say he survived not one but two "undeclared" wars, with two tours of duty in Korea and three tours in Vietnam. "Archie is our war hero," one local veteran told a reporter for the *Orange Leader*. "He captured the flag on Pork Chop Hill."

Launey maintained that in 1951, his first year in the Army, he fought in the infamous battle for Pork Chop Hill in Korea and personally rescued the American flag that flew atop that bloodstained ridge. (That battle was actually fought in 1953.) Encased in glass, streaked with the dried blood of two soldiers killed trying to keep it from hitting the ground when the pole was shattered by bullets, the tattered banner hangs on the wall of the building where the Archie Launey VVA Chapter 348 meets.

"We got overrun by North Koreans and Chinese," Launey told one reporter. "The flag was on a pole we'd made from a small tree. The pole got shot down, and the flag started falling." The soldiers tried to keep the cloth from being desecrated by falling in the dirt and were shot dead. "After we repelled the enemy, my C.O. told me to get rid of the flag, so I folded it up and put it in my field pack."[814]

Not long after that he was ordered from the front with no explanation. Launey was field-commissioned from sergeant first class to second lieutenant in front of the brass.

Saying he was trained as a paratrooper and Ranger, Launey claimed that during Korea he served "with intelligence." After going on recon patrol, he often came back and gave "suggestions about what we should do to stop enemy advancement." But Launey's arrogant C.O. refused to listen to him. The commander insisted on following channels, "maybe even all the way back to Washington like they did in Vietnam, every time, and by the time the OK got back to us, it was too late, hordes of them were all over us," Launey lamented. "A lot of lives could have been saved if he had just taken my advice."

That problem was magnified in Vietnam, Launey contended. By the time he arrived in Vietnam, Launey had been promoted to captain. He told a reporter that every proposed move had to be sent "through the CIA and they'd sift it, and it'd usually go all the way back to Washington and come back to us in five or six days. That was too late, of course—the VC was gone by then."

In Vietnam, Launey said he worked with "Command Control North," doing reconnaissance all over—the Mekong Delta, Pleiku—pulling ambushes in North Vietnam and Laos. Launey was assigned in 1962 to equip and train the "Kah mountain guards" (sic) in Laos. "But they wouldn't listen to me or do anything I told them to unless I would accept one of the girls as a bride." That arduous duty accomplished by Launey, the Kah tribe worked hard to learn. "All I had to do was give the word, and they would have died for me," Launey said. "They were beautiful people."[815]

But Launey refused to tell the reporter some of his worst memories of the war. Those supposedly occurred when he was with Special Forces and were "still classified."

Launey's POW experience was described in the American Ex-POW Association's newsletter in November 1990. The article told how he and eight other men on a reconnaissance mission were captured in Yangdok, Korea on November 1, 1952. Taken to Kangdong, Launey was kept in solitary confinement. He and ten other prisoners later escaped, hidden from a military convoy by a Korean family.

The organization's newsletter pointed out that Launey's military records did not indicate he was ever a prisoner of war. His evidence was a letter his mother received while he was a prisoner.[816] The story created a controversy within the organization. Some Korean War POWs were skeptical. And there was another bizarre twist to the story. Another Beaumont-area man named Sidney LaFleur, who wore the green beret of Special Forces, had joined the ex-POW organization at Launey's referral. LaFleur claimed he had been a prisoner of the North Vietnamese for ten months and eight days—and that Launey had rescued him in Vietnam.

Pork Chop Hill? Training the "Kah"? A Korean POW rescuing a Vietnam POW? There were a few too many coincidences in Launey's story. The Ex-POW group gave me a copy of Launey's DD-214. Those discharge papers revealed that Launey had been a member of Army Special Forces, medically retired as a major. According to the document, Launey had received the DSC, five Silver Stars, three Bronze Star Medals, eight Purple Hearts, and more. Launey had attended schools or training in Military Intelligence, Guerrilla Warfare, Martial Arts, Demolition, Medical Chief Aid Man, Light Weapons, Psychological Warfare, and Communications.

Not convinced, I filed an FOIA request for Launey's true military record. The one he submitted to the ex-POW group had been significantly doctored, to say the least. The record indicated that Launey served in the Army from April 1952 to December 1955 and was discharged as an E-2, not a major. For part of that time, Launey had been assigned to an Army engineering utility company as a telephone lineman in Korea. There was no evidence he was in military intelligence or Special Forces, and I could find no records to indicate he was ever a POW. Despite his boast that he was the "second most decorated veteran in Texas," records show the only awards Launey received were the standard service campaign ribbons and a Parachutist Badge. Although Launey received a general discharge, he had a record of repeated AWOLs, totaling 232 days.[817]

In many ways, Launey's manufactured DD-214 was hilarious. The Army has never had such training course titles as "Guerrilla Warfare," "Demolitionist," or "Martial Arts." For Launey to have received a Combat Infantryman Badge with two stars, he would have had to fight in three wars: World War II, Korea, *and* Vietnam. "Lt. J.E. Pinker," at Fort Bragg, signed Launey's general discharge in 1955; he was still a lieutenant and signing discharge papers in 1972 for the same man, only now he was at Fort Hood.[818]

Launey's war stories had been buttressed for years by his buddy Sidney LaFleur, who claimed that Launey had saved his life in Vietnam. Launey in turn bolstered LaFleur's stories of heroism as a POW in Vietnam. But LaFleur was as deceitful as Launey. The DD-214 Sidney R. LaFleur submitted to the POW association bore a striking resemblance to Launey's. As a supposed member of Special Forces in Vietnam from January 1, 1958, to March 23, 1962, LaFleur had also taken nonexistent "Guerrilla Warfare" and "Demolitionist" training. The record also described LaFleur as a prisoner of war from May 10, 1961, to March 18, 1962, in Hanoi, North Vietnam, and listed the awards he received as Silver Star, Bronze Star Medal for valor, CIB, and two Purple Hearts.

But military records show that LaFleur served in the regular peacetime Army from September 12, 1955, to February 15, 1957. His records were among those burned in the fire at the St. Louis NPRC in 1973, but in the officially reconstructed records (based on VA documents and pay records, among others) there is nothing to indicate he ever served with Special Forces or received any valorous decorations. Not only does LaFleur's name not show up on any POW list, he had left the Army before the war in Vietnam started.[819]

Based on the military records from St. Louis, the American Ex-POW Association booted Launey and LaFleur from its rolls.[820] After I showed them how easy it was for impostors to obtain a purple VA card designating POW status, the organization decided no longer to accept them for membership qualification. I gave the association the military records of other fakers, but I don't know what the organization did about most of them. They needed members, and scrutinizing the military records too closely might result in a lot of the supposed prisoners from World War II being kicked out as well.

The POW-MIA Cottage Industry

Pretend POWs pop up frequently not only in news reports but also in books and films. They frequently repeat the misinformation about POWs spread by the press. Another claim popular with impostors is that they — incredibly — escaped, invariably killing enemy soldiers in the process. But official policy of the 4th Allied POW Wing discouraged escape attempts because the North Vietnamese retaliated by torturing those left behind. And some American POWs were so ill or injured, more abuse could easily kill them. The chances of success were deemed too minimal for the price.

Numerous MIA/POW claimants bolster their bogus identities through lobbying state and national legislatures about "bringing our boys home," demonstrating by staging hunger strikes or living in bamboo cages. They align themselves with the POW-MIA advocates who contend that there are still American POWs in Southeast Asia.

As of June 1996, 2,153 men were still listed as missing in action—1,608 in Vietnam, 461 in Laos, 76 in Cambodia, and 8 in China. At the end of the war, approximately 1,100 were declared "killed in action/body not recovered." Since then, the remains of 430 men have been returned.[821] (The Korean War, fought for three years, resulted in 8,200 men still missing in action; 77,000 U.S. soldiers are still unaccounted for after World War II, a figure that exceeds by 20,000 the total number of Americans killed in Vietnam. All were presumed dead a year and a day after they disappeared.)

Years after the Vietnam War ended, Lt. Col. Walter Stueck, USAF (Ret.) described an unofficial policy in his squadron for pilots to sign forms indicating whether they wanted to be listed as killed in action or missing in action if their planes went down, a practice fairly standard among all units. If a pilot was listed as killed in action, his paychecks sent home ended. If he was listed as missing, his family continued to receive the husband's full pay and benefits. Not surprisingly, many pilots indicated they wanted to be designated MIA. So even if his plane was observed hitting a mountain or going down in the sea with no sign of the pilot or crew ejecting, they often were officially listed as MIA.

The U.S. military is aware of about three dozen MIAs who might possibly still be alive, although the chances are extremely remote. Almost certainly wounded during capture, they had to survive the rough transit to North Vietnam. They lived in an extremely dangerous and unhealthy environment, suffering torture, malnutrition, and exposure to disease. It's very unlikely that any have survived for the last twenty-five years.

But a cottage industry has sprung up to exploit the issue by raising the hopes of families with MIAs with counterfeit photographs and sham "sightings." Two excellent books lay to rest the notion that American troops are being held against their will in Southeast Asia: *Prisoners of Hope*, by Susan Katz Keating,[822] and *Inside Hanoi's Secret Archives: Solving the MIA Mystery*, by Malcolm McConnell.[823]

McConnell and I first met in 1993 when we exchanged information about Larry Pistilli, a California resident who claimed he had been a POW in North Vietnam. Because Pistilli was a member of the American

Ex-POW Association, I already had his military record, which I faxed to McConnell. Within a few days the writer was in my office in Texas, combing through my files.

Pistilli is liberally quoted in a book called *Soldiers of Misfortune* by James D. Sanders, Mark A. Sauter, and R. Cort Kirkwood.[824] The authors describe Larry Pistilli as a Marine working special classified missions, the kind where you have "no ID, dog tags or other identification." In the fall of 1965, on his way back to base after completing a clandestine mission in South Vietnam, Pistilli saw a group of nine Marines pinned down by Viet Cong forces. Because of heavy mortar fire, Pistilli waved off a chopper that came to evacuate the wounded. When a mortar blew up nearby, Pistilli sustained a concussion and shrapnel wounds. After Pistilli regained consciousness, VC hauled him off to an interrogation camp between Dong Hai and Ron Ron in North Vietnam.

For several pages, the authors described what Pistilli saw at the interrogation facility: English-speaking Soviet and Red Chinese interrogators, not North Vietnamese, were running the prison camp. At their hands, Pistilli endured a month of "expert Communist interrogation and torture." He and the prisoners had only one future: "China, Soviet Union, or die."[825]

Several captives were selected to be taken north by the Red Chinese. But Pistilli and three other Americans staged a daring escape, commandeering a truck and driving until an axle broke. They continued south on foot until "the North Vietnamese finally caught up to us but lost in some frantic hand-to-hand combat." Farther south, Pistilli and his group eventually stumbled into some friendly troops who took them back to an Army post in South Vietnam. There, the Americans separated the men and took them each to a "classified debriefing," in which techniques used were similar to the Communists, only for a shorter period of time, "to ensure the person being questioned revealed all classified information that he had given to the enemy."

Pistilli, the authors contend, had been taken to a camp that was preparatory to being taken to China, Russia, or even East Germany, and interrogated by Soviet and Red Chinese officers. After escaping, he was sworn to secrecy about his exploits. His colorful tale was actually cited as *proof* of Soviet abduction of American POWs in testimony before a Senate committee.

Was Pistilli a reliable source? Was he even a POW?

Pistilli, an Illinois native, often showed others a letter from Otto Kerner, the governor of Illinois, dated February 5, 1966, shortly after his supposed escapade. "I would like to take this opportunity to express the gratitude of the people of the State of Illinois for your courage and heroism as a prisoner of war," the letter said. "Your courageous escape has been read into the records of the State Legislature here in Springfield. We look forward to your quick and safe return to the Great State of Illinois." Pistilli sent the American Ex-POW Association the letter as proof of his POW status. But a search of the Illinois State Archives revealed no such mention of Pistilli's heroics.[826]

According to Pistilli's military record, he served with the regular Army as a specialist fourth class from June 10, 1964 to May 31, 1970. A communications man, Pistilli was not Special Forces qualified, and he did not participate in secret missions. Pistilli's only overseas tour was in Korea, not Vietnam. And Pistilli most emphatically was never a POW.[827]

The authors of *Soldiers of Misfortune* never bothered to check his record. Yet Pistilli's tale is still being cited as reliable evidence that many American POWs were taken to the USSR and Eastern Europe.

Bamboo Cages and Bugs for Dinner

The tales of deprivation and degradation recounted, usually tearfully, by pretend POWs can elicit sympathy, admiration, and often money.

In 1983, John Maughn turned up at the Veterans' Counseling Center in Atlanta. A former prisoner of the Vietnam War, he told such vivid stories of his five-and-a-half years in captivity in North Vietnam that counselors cried. Sympathetic Vet Center workers helped Maughn find a place to live and eased the way for him to obtain a ten thousand dollar loan to get back on his feet.

For four years, Maughn continued to weave his tales of torture and debasement at the hands of the enemy. He ran up debts of more than thirty thousand dollars. Finally, local veterans' doubts overcame their sympathy for the former POW. They took their suspicions to local law enforcement authorities.

Sure enough, Maughn had been a prisoner—of the State of Georgia. He had been in jail for auto theft during some of the time he claimed he was being tortured in Southeast Asia. Charged with illegal possession of a firearm, he was again returned to Georgia's custody.[828]

Some fake POWs target a larger audience. In 1987, an Oregon man named Thomas A. Clift set off on a walk across America to bring attention to Americans still being held as POWs in North Vietnam. Traveling from town to town, Clift visited the offices of local newspapers, regaling reporters with his experiences as a POW, the only survivor of a ten-man patrol attacked by NVA troops in 1966. The papers dutifully printed stories of his ordeal and noble crusade.

Many local veterans and veterans' groups donated money or goods to help him along. The Holiday Inn in Odessa, Texas, gave him a room. The Permian Basin VVA Chapter gave him one hundred dollars, as did an

American Legion Post in El Paso. But veterans in the Texas panhandle grew suspicious. Clift's stories sounded a little too good to be true.

Then someone checked. Clift was not a POW. He wasn't even Thomas A. Clift. He was actually William George Clift; Thomas was his brother. When Thomas was contacted, he said he had been trying to track down William for two years. "He's always one step ahead of me," Thomas Clift told a reporter. "I've been to lawyers, judges, mental health (officials), trying to get help."[829]

William Clift had served in Vietnam, but he was not in combat, nor was he a POW. Upon his return to the states, Clift spent five years in the Oregon State Penitentiary for felonies committed after the war.

Clift had violated no law in posing as a POW. But members of the National League of Families of American Prisoners of War and Missing in Action in Southeast Asia were upset that Clift and others like him were sending out misinformation about efforts to recover servicemen's remains.

Alleged covert operations often play a large role in ersatz POW stories. Russell Mullen of Berkley, Michigan, a staff sergeant with a U.S. Air Force Security Squadron, said he became a POW when his aircraft was shot down on a secret mission near the DMZ. Mullen told a reporter for a local paper that two of the six men in his crew died in the crash. The survivors destroyed the aircraft, then Mullen and another man set off on foot to make their way out of the jungle. Unfortunately, they ran into a Viet Cong patrol, which took them prisoner.

For eighty-seven days, Mullen said, the two prisoners moved with the patrol across the DMZ into Cambodia. (Cambodia is actually hundreds of miles from the DMZ.) When an American aircraft flew over and "dropped smoke, normally an indication that an air strike would follow," the VC patrol panicked and ran, allowing Mullen and his fellow airman to over-power their guards and escape.

"We ran for three days," Mullen said, "and then we ran into American troops. They kept us in 'Nam for a couple of weeks then sent us home."[830] For his efforts in Vietnam, Mullen claimed he received a Distinguished Flying Cross, a Bronze Star Medal, an Air Medal, and two Purple Hearts. After the war, Mullen served as a board member with the POW Committee of Michigan. At a special ceremony in Lansing, Mullen received a POW medal from Michigan's governor.

However, a member of the POW Committee of Michigan grew suspicious and launched a private inquiry into Mullen's status. Mullen was not a POW at any time during the Vietnam War, confirmed Charles F. Trowbridge Jr., deputy chief, Special Office for Prisoners of War and Missing in Action at the Defense Intelligence Agency.

"You might note that many individuals posing as former PWs claim that

they were on so-called 'secret missions' and the records of their imprisonment were destroyed/altered/classified, etc.," Trowbridge wrote in 1990 in
response to a request for information about Mullen's status as a prisoner.
"This is not the case; there are no 'secret' PWs. Complete lists of former
U.S. servicemen held in Southeast Asia are publicly available."[831]

The Black Beret

At age eighteen, Robert Mitchell asserted, he became a member of the
Navy's "Black Berets," an elite group of highly trained guerrilla warfare
specialists whose mission was very basic: Search and destroy. During a two-
year tour, Mitchell said, he was involved in more than three hundred
combat missions. After being captured, Mitchell claimed he spent 108 days
as a POW before he was able to escape.

In 1984, Mitchell and other members of a VA PTSD therapy group in
Wisconsin talked about their experiences on *First Camera*, an NBC network
show which aired on Sunday nights. (Mitchell's story also appeared in the
Beloit *Daily News*.)

When he returned from Vietnam, Mitchell struggled to hold a job.
"With me, I'd get paranoid," Mitchell said. "I'd think everybody was out to
get me. So I'd quit and find a new one." Mitchell's PTSD was diagnosed in
1981 after he went hunting in the woods near his home alone and disappeared for three-and-a-half weeks. He said being in the forest and handling
a gun brought flashbacks of Vietnam. When found, he was fifty miles away
and had forgotten who he was and how he came to be there. "Who are
you, lady?" Mitchell asked one woman only to learn she was his mother.

Mitchell had married a year after the war; and not until he was diagnosed as suffering from PTSD did his wife discover her husband had been a
POW. The news was a shock and a relief. "It made me see why he acted the
way he did," his long-suffering spouse said. Mitchell spent seventeen weeks
in the VA Hospital in Tomah, reliving his Vietnam trauma and going to
group therapy with other Vietnam veterans.[832]

About a month after the article ran in the *Daily News*, Managing Editor
Bill Barth wrote a follow-up. After receiving calls alleging that Mitchell's
story was fabricated, the newspaper did an independent investigation.
Mitchell had not been a prisoner of war. He had not served with the "Black
Berets." Mitchell's stint in the Navy consisted of duty aboard the USS *Mt.
McKinley*. His only Vietnam service was from June 29, 1966, to July 6, 1966—
less than a month—when the *Mt. McKinley* was stationed off the coast of
Vietnam. Mitchell never took part in any land-based combat missions in
Vietnam. Despite the fact that he had not been in combat, Mitchell had
been officially diagnosed as having Vietnam-induced PTSD at the VA
center in Tomah.[833]

Escape Artists

Escape is a common theme in fraudulent POW stories.

At a Minnesota Twins baseball game in 1987, Minnesota Gov. Rudy Perpich honored four Vietnam veterans with proclamations declaring the first week of May to be named in their honor. Two—Thomas Curtis and David Weiss—had been POWs during the war.[834] A follow-up story in the *Minneapolis Star Tribune* by columnist Robert T. Smith described how they had been captured.[835]

Oakdale veteran Thomas Curtis had served as a lance corporal in Marine reconnaissance, the "elite" of the Corps' ground fighters. Curtis said he was on a classified mission eight miles inside Laos when he and four other Marines were captured by NVA troops. Stripped, blindfolded, and bound with wire, they were stuffed in a steel box with one slit for air. For two months, they were allowed out of the stifling box only intermittently for a few moments. Given only a cup of rice every other day, Curtis lost sixty pounds during the ordeal. But he was not too weak to fight back. Curtis managed to free himself from his bindings and "garroted three guards with a wire." The four men escaped, traveling by night and hiding by day in the jungle. Dressed in black pajamas, they were mistaken for the NVA and nearly shot by Americans. Curtis said he received the Vietnamese Cross of Gallantry for his heroism, then he returned home where his parents knew nothing of his capture.

Although they did not serve together, Dave Weiss claimed he had a similar experience as a Green Beret medic "attached" to the 3rd Marine Division. Weiss said he and nine Marines were captured in February 1968 by the Viet Cong and kept in "tiger cages" in a prison camp in the DMZ.

When one captive died, the VC left his body there for three days until the other prisoners finally persuaded a guard to remove the corpse. When the guard opened the cage door to comply with their request, Weiss killed the enemy soldier with his bare hands. Weiss and the rest "grabbed rifles and shot their way out of the POW camp." A few days later they were spotted by an Army helicopter and rescued.

After the war, both men studied nursing and ended up in the St. Paul area. Curtis and Weiss both joined VFW Post 5555. Curtis became senior vice commander of the group in 1988, the year Weiss was the post's POW-MIA chairman, a position Curtis had previously held. As the grand marshal of the 1988 Loyalty Day parade in Richfield, Minnesota, Curtis was quoted in a news story about the POW-MIA issue. "My time in the box was a walk in the park compared to those guys who are still there," Curtis told the reporter.

But records show neither Curtis nor Weiss was ever a POW. Curtis served as a motor vehicle operator with Company B, 7th Marine

Transportation Battalion in Vietnam during 1969, not with the 3rd Battalion, 3rd Reconnaissance. Personal American decorations Curtis received were the National Defense Service Medal and the Vietnam Service Medal (no Combat Action Ribbon). And according to his records, Curtis was court-martialed for four violations of military law that occurred on August 8, 1969: AWOL, exceeding the speed limit at Quang Tri Combat Base, transporting more than four passengers in a quarter-ton Jeep, having a person on the hood, and reckless driving. Your basic dumb stunt. Curtis was assigned to be a dispatcher for the rest of his time in Vietnam.[836]

According to military records, David William Weiss was not a Green Beret. He served in Vietnam as an Army medic during 1967–68, not the Marines. During his tour, Weiss said he received a Silver Star, Bronze Star Medal, the Soldier's Medal, and two Purple Hearts from shrapnel that still remained in his legs. Weiss's record lists a Bronze Star, a Soldier's Medal, Vietnamese campaign medals and a Sharpshooter (Rifle) Badge. He was not a POW.[837]

Although many of these fictitious POW stories are blatantly preposterous, often no one is willing to call their bluff. That's what people like Gary Locks count on.

Air Force Reserve Lt. Col. Gary L. "Lucky" Locks received acclaim as a Vietnam War hero as a civilian employee in the B-1 Bomber Systems Program at Wright-Patterson Air Force Base in Dayton, Ohio. And his combat heroics indeed seemed the stuff of the movies, full of close escapes and intrepid nerve. Locks told several versions of the story. Here's one:

Assigned in 1968 to a mission that flew into Laos to drop phosphorous markings on North Vietnamese supply vehicles, Locks was forced to take over the aircraft's controls when ground fire knocked the pilot unconscious. Using the plane as a kamikaze weapon while executing a crash landing, Locks sheared off the heads of two Viet Cong soldiers with the aircraft's wings. Locks said he was then captured and subjected to "extreme torture"—tied to a stake while his wrists were slowly cut during interrogation. After seventeen days of captivity, Locks escaped from his bamboo cage by chewing through his bindings and ran into the jungle. Only a thousand yards from the Viet Cong camp, he stumbled into a five-man U.S. Army patrol. Although exhausted and injured, Locks demanded that they give him an M-16 and accompanied them back to the camp, where he exacted revenge by killing all nine enemy soldiers.[838]

His heroism made for a great feature story in his hometown paper in 1989, the year Locks led the Memorial Day parade in Fairborn, Ohio.[839] He could have gotten away with telling his ludicrous stories for years but for one small error. On May 17, 1990, in order to legitimize his stature as a suffering Vietnam veteran and former POW, Locks submitted to the Board of Correction of Air Force Records the claim that he was a wounded combat veteran and former POW, and as such was entitled to the Purple Heart and Prisoner of War Medal.

That request might have gone unnoticed except that at the same time, Locks applied for a top executive post with the Senate Select Committee on POW-MIA Affairs in Washington, D.C., in 1992. The application triggered scrutiny of his military records. Those indicated that Locks had not been shot down or taken prisoner and had spent his time in the military as a maintenance officer at bases in the United States.[840] In January 1993, Locks stunned his fellow workers and his community when he pleaded no contest to federal charges that he falsified his military records.

John Reed of Louisville, Kentucky, claimed that in Vietnam he served as a doorgunner on a helicopter and twice had been shot down by the enemy. The second time, the Viet Cong captured him and other crew members and held them prisoner for "five months, eighteen days, and twenty-two hours" before they were rescued by South Korean troops.

"We lived in cages twenty-two inches wide and thirty-two inches deep," Reed told the *Louisville Record*. "They put guns to our heads, pulled their triggers and laughed."[841]

Even more traumatic than his capture was an incident that happened in March 1965 before he was taken prisoner. It occurred while Reed and other soldiers were resting at a base camp after a twenty-eight-day operation in the jungle.

The soldiers had been required to turn in their weapons when returning to base camp. One night, an eleven-year-old Vietnamese girl the men had befriended came into their tent carrying a hand grenade, and Reed was forced to kill the little girl to stop her attack. Many years later, Reed was plagued by memories of that incident as well as nightmares in which he saw the faces of American soldiers left behind in rescue attempts because overloaded helicopters had no room for them.

All the trauma of Vietnam tormented Reed, who said he returned to the United States only forty-eight hours after being released by the Viet Cong. "I came back home and lived in a tree," Reed told the newspaper: "My mother thought I was looney. I stayed in the tree because I felt safe there. In the jungle we always slept in trees and never near our helicopters because they were the first things to get hit." Reed lost his job as a union ironworker. He and his wife divorced. When the nightmares grew unbearably intense and reality became distorted, Reed sought counseling, joining a therapy group with nine other Vietnam "combat veterans" which met at Life Spring Mental Health Center in Jeffersonville, Indiana. Dr. William Dinwiddie, a therapist on the staff of Life Spring Mental Health Center, told the Louisville *Record* that Reed suffered from PTSD.

Almost every cliché of Vietnam victimhood permeated Reed's story: Being forced to kill women and children, kept in a tiny bamboo cage and tortured by the enemy, forced to abandon comrades, tormented after his return to America by nightmares and flashbacks.

Military records revealed that Reed enlisted in the Army on March 12, 1965, and served almost all of 1966 in Vietnam but not as a helicopter doorgunner. Reed's MOS was light vehicle driver, and he was assigned to the 63rd Transportation Company at Phu Bai. Discharged December 19, 1966, there is no record that Reed was ever captured or experienced combat.[842]

A last comment from Reed: "There's a big difference between Vietnam era vets, Vietnam vets, and Vietnam combat vets," Reed told the Louisville *Record*. Apparently, he felt that difference keenly.

Give Peace a Chance

Vietnam vet and former medical corpsman Joel "Doc" Furlett regaled students at a high school in Spokane with harrowing tales of being held for thirty-nine months as a POW at Son Tay prison outside Hanoi. Furlett said his captors knocked out his teeth with their rifle butts and had his kneecaps ripped off to keep him from escaping. His first thirty-three escape attempts failed. But he was determined. The thirty-fourth bid succeeded when Furlett crawled through the jungle to safety, pulling a wounded buddy on his back.

For his heroics in Vietnam, Furlett said he received the Navy Cross, three Silver Stars, two Bronze Star Medals and seven Purple Hearts. But Furlett was bitter: Not only had he been tortured and held captive by the enemy, Furlett said he also had been poisoned by America with its Agent Orange.

Well-known in the Spokane area as a Vietnam veterans' activist, Furlett told his stories from a wheelchair. He would proudly pull his war medals from a bag, then hint darkly at a conspiracy by the federal government and major chemical companies who were out to discredit or hurt him because of his activism on behalf of Vietnam vets. Furlett described being shot at during a ceremony at the Washington Vietnam Veterans Memorial by two people—a VA employee and a sinister agent for a chemical company. The conspiracy was so big, so pervasive, that not only were the VA and law enforcement agencies covering up the plot, Furlett contended, newspaper files also had been changed to erase all mention of Furlett's shooting.

But a story by Jim Camden, a reporter for the Spokane *Spokesman-Review*, exposed Furlett as a fraud.[843] I helped Camden obtain Furlett's record, which indicated he served a year in the Navy at the Great Lakes Naval Training Center in Illinois as an apprentice seaman before his discharge in 1968. The only decoration Furlett received was the National Defense Service Medal. Furlett was never a POW, nor had he ever served in Vietnam.[844]

Lawyer Kitt Horne of San Diego felt so strongly about the threat of nuclear weapons that he dug into his closet for boots that had been returned to him on his release from a POW camp in Vietnam to participate in a peace march across America. Horne told Karine Schomer, who wrote about the peace march for the VVA's *Veteran* magazine in June 1986, in a story headlined "Viet Vets Walk Point," that he had served two tours of duty in Vietnam between 1973 and 1975 with the 5th Special Forces Special Operations Group (MACV-SOG). After a stint as a POW from July to December 1975, he was awarded the Medal of Honor.[845]

"We're not left-over hippies from the sixties," said Horne. "We're not a bunch of bitter vets striking out against our government and society. We're vets who served very loyally and are very proud and are simply saying that this nuclear insanity can't go on. We represented the military proudly, and now we represent peace just as proudly."

Horne was one of sixty Vietnam veterans who announced they were dedicating a year of their lives to march from Los Angeles to Washington, D.C., as part of the "Great Peace March for Nuclear Disarmament." As head of "security," Horne was in charge of maintaining order. His status as a POW and Medal of Honor recipient lent stature to the whole effort.

But the march fizzled by the time the fourteen hundred participants hit the California desert—about as long as it took veteran Dan Cragg to notify *Veteran VVA* that Horne's claims were untrue. Cragg pointed out that the 5th Special Forces Group had been withdrawn from Vietnam in March 1971, and MACV-SOG had terminated its operations there on April 30, 1972. There was no record that Horne had ever been a POW, or that he had received the Medal of Honor.[846]

It Just Snowballed

The commander of the Sangamon County Inter-Veterans Council in Illinois, Navy Vietnam veteran Robert "Doc" Brehmer proudly drove a van with Ex-POW license plates. Another of Brehmer's cars had plates that read "USN LT1."

Brehmer publicly wore the Navy Cross, the Distinguished Service Cross (an Army decoration), Navy and Marine Corps medals, Bronze Star Medal, Combat Action Ribbon, Purple Heart with two oak leaf clusters, the Legion of Merit, and a variety of other decorations.

In order to qualify for the numerous posts he held at various veterans' organizations, Brehmer proffered documents showing that he was a Vietnam combat veteran and former prisoner of war who had been wounded in action three times. After eleven years in the U.S. Navy, Brehmer said he had retired as a lieutenant in the medical services corps. During his military service, Brehmer claimed he earned a master's degree in hospital administration from Duke University. Brehmer worked as a security guard for the city of Springfield's Department of Public Affairs, a job in which designation as a Vietnam vet might come in handy.

But his military career was a tissue of lies, woven with the help of a fake DD-214 he bought for one hundred dollars. Brehmer's real military record showed that except for a seven-month cruise to the Mediterranean, his duty in the Navy Medical Corps from 1970 to 1977 was spent in the United States. Brehmer was not wounded in action and never rose above petty officer. Brehmer was never a POW, nor did he serve in Vietnam.

Brehmer's fraud was exposed by a Vietnam vet named Rich Luttrell, who asked for my help in looking into Brehmer's claims. I told him how to obtain Brehmer's records, and Luttrell passed them on to a reporter, who confronted Brehmer.

Brehmer confessed his pretense started when his veteran friends began joining the new VFW post in the area. Because he had not served in Vietnam, Brehmer was not eligible to join. Brehmer could not tell his buddies that the Vietnam War stories he had told for years were lies, so when a guy he knew only as "Roger" offered to sell him a counterfeit document at a veterans' event, Brehmer jumped at the opportunity.

But there was a big problem with the document: Except for the name, all the facts had been filled in. So Brehmer had to adjust his age, and even changed his birth date on his driver's license to conform to that on the fraudulent DD-214. Brehmer started adding awards and decorations to his phony form to keep up with his friends who were sending off for awards they had not previously known they were entitled to receive.

"It was like a snowball," Brehmer said after resigning from various veterans' groups. "Either you go with the snowball, or you get run over by the snowball. I had to keep up the façade until I couldn't take it mentally or emotionally any more."[847] (Brehmer was one of the few pretenders I have ever encountered who actually apologized in writing after his fraud was uncovered.)

Museum-Quality Mendacity

In 1988, when Stan Bozich, director of Michigan's Own, Inc., a military and space museum, met former Staff Sergeant Randy G. Brock Jr., he was impressed. Brock, then thirty-seven, was the most decorated Army enlisted Vietnam veteran in the state of Michigan.

Brock had enlisted at age seventeen, and after more than eight years in the Army, he had been awarded more than fifty medals, including the

Distinguished Service Cross, Silver Star, Bronze Star Medal for valor, Soldier's Medal, and seven Purple Hearts. As an official Michigan hero, Brock served as grand marshal in local parades and gave speeches to the VFW and other organizations about his exploits in combat as a member of Special Forces. Wounded seven times in combat, held as a POW for twenty-nine days, Brock had been involved in a clandestine operation in Vietnam that earned him the DSC.

After their meeting, Bozich asked if he could display Brock's uniform, green beret, and medals at the military and space museum. Located in Frankenmuth, Michigan, the museum specializes in the preservation and presentation of military paraphernalia of Michigan's war heroes, especially those who have earned the Medal of Honor, the DSC, the Navy Cross, or the Air Force Cross.

Brock agreed, but said he first had to obtain certain medals he had been awarded but never received, such as the DSC, to complete his uniform before it could be properly displayed. Brock sent off for the medals and after receiving them, shipped them pinned to his uniform to the museum. He also provided copies of official documents proving his training in Special Forces and Ranger School, his DD-214, which listed all his awards, and the general order citations for the combat decorations. Brock's uniform, medals, and green beret were placed in a case, along with his dog tags and a religious medal he had carried into combat with him.

Not long after Brock provided the items to the museum, he was featured on the front page of the local paper in Westland, Michigan. Brock told the paper he received the DSC for rescuing men who were pinned down: "I went after them, shooting my way to get them out." The accompanying picture showed Brock in a business suit, one side of his chest covered with full-sized medals.[848]

Still, Bozich thought it strange that every time he saw Brock, his medals seemed to proliferate. The last time he saw him, Brock was wearing "HALO Wings," indicating a high altitude parachute jump with a low altitude opening. Bozich couldn't say Brock did not do such a thing, but he knew Brock didn't have that award when he first saw him.[849]

A few years after Brock's military memorabilia went on display, several members of a Michigan chapter of the Special Forces Association came into the museum to see Brock's collection. They took one look at the case and went straight to Bozich, complaining that Brock was not a member of Special Forces.[850]

Brock was going around Michigan speaking at VFWs about his combat exploits. He had provided his uniform, medals, and green beret to a museum exhibit to enshrine his heroism. Brock had somehow obtained a VA form showing that he had seen combat, had been exposed to Agent

Orange in Vietnam, and had been held prisoner by the North Vietnamese from September 25 to October 29, 1972.

Brock's true military record indicated that he had been a military aidman in Vietnam. But he was not a member of Special Forces. He had not taken Ranger training. And he had not been a POW.

Sorting fact from fiction in the case of Brock was more complicated because his official military record contained documents which were apparently altered. The copy from the National Personnel Records Center on the surface appeared to confirm that Brock had received a Distinguished Service Cross—a claim that was false because he had no valid general order. The paper looked official, but it listed a division not authorized to issue a Distinguished Service Cross. A Silver Star appeared on his records, but the general order supporting it contained numerous typos, the mark of a crude forgery. Chief of U.S. Army POW-MIA Affairs, Lt. Col. J.G. Cele, confirmed Brock had never been a POW.[851]

Brock had applied for membership in the Legion of Valor, which is open to recipients of the Medal of Honor, of the DSC, the Air Force Cross, and the Navy Cross. The organization's staff, realizing his Distinguished Service Cross was not legitimate, had rejected him.

When confronted by Bozich, Brock did not admit anything. He just sent Bozich a money order and a demand that all his paraphernalia be returned to him, which the museum gladly did. In a letter to Bozich, Brock claimed that two years earlier he had stated he did not want his uniform in the museum but was outvoted by his family. "I further stated I was tired of the way I was being treated by Veterans' Organizations, meaning they showed me off like a whore and bragged about my being in their organization but never listened to what I had to say," Brock wrote. "This is the reason I dropped my life membership with the DAV, VFW, MOPH, POW-MIA and the VVA organizations. I am just tired of proving to every person that is jealous, envious or that is down right mean that I have over fifty decorations and that I have proof of each and everyone [sic] of them.

"For my own piece [sic] of mind I will say what General McArthur said, 'Old soldiers never die, they just fade away.' All I what [sic] is to be left alone by everyone."[852]

Green Berets in Cages

In a frame in his office, Vietnam veteran Roger Elton Watson exhibited his many awards and decorations from his time in Special Forces during the war. A civil service employee with the Department for Employment Services for the state of Kentucky, Watson was certainly highly decorated. The frame included the Distinguished Service Cross, two Silver Stars, two Bronze Star Medals, two Purple Hearts, the Army Commendation Medal, the Combat Infantryman Badge, the POW Medal, and several others. Watson's car bore POW license plates.

Watson's tale appeared in the *Kentucky New Era* for a Veterans' Day story that ran on November 12, 1984. The paper is published in Hopkinsville, near Fort Campbell, the home of the 101st Airborne Division. An accompanying picture showed the Distinguished Service Cross superimposed over a photo of Watson.

Watson claimed that as a Green Beret he had served back-to-back tours in Vietnam from 1968 to 1971. Most of that time Watson was on reconnaissance patrols; their duty was to observe NVA troop movements and strengths, measuring the enemy's supply, water, and ammunition situations.[853]

During his last patrol across the Vietnamese border into Laos, his platoon was ambushed by the Viet Cong. Watson and his men were forced to spend six grueling months in a crude Viet Cong prison camp. After an altercation with a guard, Watson spent forty-eight days in a cell measuring only five by five feet, his right arm broken, and in agonizing pain.

One night, Special Forces troops borne by helicopters overran the prison camp, rescuing Watson and the other twenty-eight Americans being held captive. Packed away at his home was a souvenir from that terrible time: The yellow, blue, and red Viet Cong flag that flew over the prison camp, which he had remembered to grab after the firefight that ensued.

Briefly hospitalized, Watson returned to the battlefield, assigned as second-in-command at a Special Forces camp in Dong Xoai, south of the border with North Vietnam. On June 9, 1971, a Viet Cong regiment attacked the base. But Watson could not communicate with the commanding officer; the radio linking them had been destroyed.

Watson ran across an open area toward the commander's location, taking shrapnel wounds in the right leg. As enemy troops scaled the walls of the compound, the commander was seriously wounded, putting Watson in charge. Heroically, Watson was herding South Vietnamese soldiers into their defensive positions, trying to reach the communication bunker to call in air support, when a rocket-propelled grenade shattered a nearby tree. Watson took more shrapnel in his thigh, left leg, stomach, and right arm. But he still fought.

Although Watson said he remembered little of the rest of the fourteen-hour firefight, Watson handed the reporter the citation he had received when he was awarded the Distinguished Service Cross for heroism after being thrust into the position of commander. "[Watson] destroyed an enemy machine gun with a 3.5-inch rocket launcher, pulled an injured soldier to safety, coordinated air attacks from ship-based Navy bombers and took charge of the relief and evacuation of the camp once gunfire had slowed enough that American helicopters could land," the citation said. Watson said he spent most of the next year in hospitals. At Fort Bragg, as his stretcher was being moved from the bus to the hospital, anti-war protesters showered him and other wounded soldiers with garbage.

With the date he gives, Watson was claiming he was involved in the famous battle of Dong Xoai, the same battle in which Dan Gisel pretended to have fought and received a DSC. (Was this a standing-room-only battle or what?) In addition to getting the facts all wrong, Watson's story about being returned to duty as second-in-command at Dong Xoai after being rescued from a prison camp could not have happened.

Watson's true military record indicated that he spent a year in Vietnam. But he was not a Green Beret. After a brief stint as an ammo bearer, Watson was assigned as a chauffeur, then as a stock control and accounting specialist, and finally, as company clerk. Watson's rank had not risen above specialist fifth class. His record showed a Bronze Star Medal for merit (not valor) and a Combat Infantryman Badge, but no DSC, no Silver Stars, and no Purple Hearts. And, of course, Roger Elton Watson was not a POW.[854]

What was most astonishing about this story is that Watson lived near Fort Campbell, but no active duty or retired military personnel in the area called his hand on this ludicrous tale. Even after he was exposed, Watson continued his charade. Five years after completing my initial research on Watson, a medals expert called me with the news that Roger Watson had sold a friend an alleged Viet Cong flag for three hundred dollars. Watson no longer was claiming just a DSC. He was now telling people he had received the Medal of Honor and was showing people a counterfeit general order as proof.

What made me most angry: The action that Watson claimed earned him the Medal of Honor really did occur. The Medal of Honor claimed by Watson actually was awarded to Lt. Charles Q. Williams, a courageous Green Beret who fought and was wounded at Dong Xoai.[855]

Honoring the Flag

Occasionally, fakers entangle even high-ranking military officers like General William Westmoreland in their charades, providing prestigious validation for their lies.

During a ceremony on September 18, 1994, to honor POW-MIA Day, retired U.S. Army Lt. Col. John Murray made a special and unexpected presentation to a New York VVA chapter. Murray came forward with a tiny American flag no bigger than an index card, mounted in a beautiful frame.

As a POW in Vietnam, Murray said that the flag had been the only thing that inspired him and fourteen other Americans held captive by the North Vietnamese to live. Murray had made the symbol from a piece of his clothing, staining the cloth red with his own blood and blue with the juice of berries the captors fed them. Every day he raised the flag on a bamboo stick so that he and the other POWs could pay their respects. At night, Murray hid the flag from his captors by inserting it into his rectum.

Since his release from captivity, the flag had remained wrapped in wax paper, stuck away in a strong box for twenty-five years. Murray now wanted it to do some good for others.[856]

Murray, who wore a black eye patch and a chestful of medals on his uniform, looked every inch the retired lieutenant colonel. About two years earlier, he had moved to a rural area of New York, getting deeply involved in veterans' issues. Murray told those he met various stories. He had been a military intelligence officer—or maybe with U.S. Army Airborne Rangers —in Vietnam before he was captured. Some people learned that Murray had received a medical discharge from the Army after being diagnosed with cancer caused by Agent Orange, which had cost him his eye. Others were given the impression the injury was caused by shrapnel in Vietnam.

In October, Murray invited General Westmoreland to the Poconos area of Pennsylvania for a "watchfire" ceremony to commemorate the missing in Vietnam. Murray had often told others that Westmoreland was his "mentor" in Vietnam. The general's willingness to come seemed to back up Murray's story.

Murray obtained a permit for the event to be held on National Park Service grounds in an area called Smithfield Beach. Westmoreland, who has made special efforts to appear on behalf of Vietnam veterans, was the guest speaker at the ceremonial fire, attended by about two hundred veterans. Murray stood before the general and saluted him proudly. After the general's speech, the bonfire was lit, followed by the playing of taps and a rifle salute. All who attended agreed the ceremony was quite poignant. Murray was the hero of the day.

But Murray's charade unraveled that night when his Lincoln Continental swerved on a Pocono Township road and hit a utility pole. Charged with driving under the influence of alcohol and a drug, later described as an antidepressant, Murray could produce no driver's license. When police asked Murray's date of birth, he gave not one but three dates.

Police could not verify his military status or even Murray's real name. He had two Social Security numbers. Five days after his arrest, Murray confessed that he was an impostor. His war hero past was a masquerade. He had never been a POW. He had never even served in the military.

An investigation revealed that the imposing former officer was really John M. Murray, a resident of Corning, N.Y. Murray said he wore the eye patch as the result of injuries suffered when he was beaten by a coworker. He reportedly had received an $89,000 settlement as compensation.[857]

When his deceit was revealed, Murray was indicted on federal charges of impersonating an officer, using fraudulent identification, and making false statements to obtain a government permit. Murray did not seem to understand the impact his lies had on those who believed in him. "I only wanted to help," he said. He later pleaded guilty to falsifying a government permit and was sentenced to spend a few weeks in a halfway house.

Infuriated about the hoax, Westmoreland admitted that some of the things Murray had told him about Vietnam didn't quite ring true. "But I was there for four years and we had troops there for ten," Westmoreland said. "What he told me could have been true when I wasn't on the ground." Westmoreland assumed Murray was legitimate because he was there as Murray's guest.[858]

Others were more blunt about their opinion of Murray. "I've heard a lot of people say they'd like to take that flag and put it back where it came from," said Chief Park Ranger Doyle Nelson. But Nelson pinpointed Murray's appeal. "When you were around him, you wanted to believe him."

The President's Guest

During the 1992 presidential campaign, Vietnam veteran Ronald Patrick Murphy attended a speech by Democratic candidate Bill Clinton at the University of Nevada at Las Vegas. In a crowd of seventy thousand, Murphy caught Clinton's attention because he was wearing a military veteran's cap.

At the time, Clinton was struggling with his image as a draft dodger, someone who had not only avoided the military but also had made numerous derogatory remarks about the armed services, even protesting in London against American participation in the Vietnam War. During his speech, Clinton took the opportunity to single out Murphy, making the point that although he, Clinton, had protested the war, he supported the veterans who had fought in Vietnam.

Murphy asked Clinton for help. Unemployed, without health insurance, Murphy said he was unable to prove eligibility for desperately needed VA health care. Murphy gave Clinton his Vietnam Service Medal and asked the presidential hopeful if he was elected not to forget Vietnam veterans. Cameras rolling, Bill Clinton and Ronald Patrick Murphy embraced and wept together. "I would rather have your name on the presidential ballot than on the Vietnam wall," Murphy told him.[859]

This encounter was not as spontaneous as it appeared on camera. Clinton's staff had been notified that Murphy wanted to give him the medal. The dramatic scene worked beautifully. Newspaper stories that followed described Murphy as a former POW, a Vietnam veteran who had been wounded in action. Murphy claimed he had served in the Army for fourteen years, including two tours in Vietnam as a communications advisor in intelligence. He was getting 20 percent disability, but wanted his rating level upgraded. He had been diagnosed as a paranoid schizophrenic, but Murphy insisted he instead suffered from PTSD, induced by spending twenty-seven days in captivity at the hands of the North Vietnamese. Murphy claimed that after his escape from the North Vietnamese he returned to the United States where he was arrested by the Army and charged with espionage. The charges were later dropped but had traumatized him still further.

On reading about their meeting, I talked to Murphy, who said he had been wounded in Vietnam and had received a Purple Heart.[860] After his encounter with the candidate, Murphy had received a hand-written letter from Clinton, who said he was very moved by Murphy's gift of the Vietnam medal. "I will honor it and your service," Clinton wrote. "I will also do all I can to see that your government keeps its commitments to people like you. Hang in there!"[861]

The newly-elected president proved as good as his word. Shortly after the inauguration, Murphy's disability compensation for PTSD was upgraded from 20 to 60 percent. In addition to VA benefits of $693 per month, he was also eligible for $782 in Social Security.[862] (It apparently went up still farther. The VA later verified that Murphy had been pronounced 100 percent disabled, but the spokesman could not tell me what condition Murphy suffered. Although eligible for $1,930, Murphy was receiving $1,841 a month until the amount of a lump sum he received at discharge was recovered.[863])

After his election, Clinton created the "Faces of Hope," a group of forty-six Americans who had inspired his campaign and invited them to dinner at the White House. Murphy was one of them. Gearing up his reelection efforts, Clinton held a reunion dinner for the "Faces of Hope" in June 1995. Again, Murphy was at the table.

I hope the other forty-five "Faces of Hope" stories are not as bogus as Murphy's tale. According to Murphy's record, he was not involved in intelligence, he was not wounded, and he was never a POW. Ronald Patrick Murphy served two tours in Vietnam—as an ADP (data processing) repairman. In those days, data processing equipment was highly sensitive to dust and dirt, which meant the equipment was kept in secure, air-conditioned buildings.[864]

The Commander-in-Chief of the U.S. Armed Forces had bought a bill of goods.

PART IV

Victims and Heroes

22

The Myth of Agent Orange

IN THE EARLY EIGHTIES, when journalist Jon Franklin was assigned to cover the emerging story of how Agent Orange had poisoned millions of Vietnam veterans, he was ecstatic. As a science writer for the *Baltimore Evening Sun*, he had already won a Pulitzer Prize in 1979 for a story about brain surgery. He would receive another Pulitzer in 1985 for a series of articles about brain chemistry. But Franklin was sure that Agent Orange would be the pinnacle of his science-writing career.

Unlike many journalists, Franklin had experience in the military. In 1959, he joined the Navy and served eight years, mostly as a Navy journalist. Stationed on an aircraft carrier carrying nuclear weapons during the Cuban Missile Crisis, Franklin said the realization that the United States and Russia had teetered on the brink of nuclear war turned him into a "peacenik" overnight. He became involved in the peace movement within the Navy. "In those days, it was a big deal just to say you didn't think that mutually assured destruction was necessarily the right way to think about things," Franklin says.[865]

After his honorable discharge in 1967, Franklin joined the growing American antiwar movement. "I liked the idea of 'make love, not war,'" says Franklin. He went to college, where he marched against the war and against Dow Chemical because the company was manufacturing napalm being used to kill the Vietnamese. Antiwar protesters were also criticizing the military for using herbicides in Vietnam to defoliate the jungles, comparing herbicides to the use of nerve gas and claiming that America was destroying the jungles of South Vietnam and that they would not grow back for a thousand years. That made sense to Franklin. Caught up in the rebellion and paranoia of the times, he believed that the government, like anybody over thirty, was not to be trusted.

Franklin then turned an interest in science and nature and his experiences as a military journalist into a writing career. Influenced by the caustic work of writer H. L. Mencken as well as Rachel Carson's 1962 book *Silent Spring*, Franklin began writing groundbreaking stories on the environment and medicine. The fledgling environmental movement was gathering strength, pushing the idea that chemical pollutants in low doses could devastate human health and endanger the earth. Franklin remembers attending a 1974 press conference when the American Cancer Society announced that 95 percent of all human cancers are environmentally caused. "I bought it," Franklin says. "Although in hindsight we were bloody fools. They didn't have a shred of evidence."

When American involvement in Vietnam ended, many of those who had protested the war turned their efforts to activism on the behalf of veterans of the war. One of them was Maude DeVictor, a Chicago woman who worked for the Benefits Division of the VA and was also involved in the black power movement. She began reporting that many of the soldiers returning from the war had disturbing but similar health problems. An ambitious TV reporter named Bill Kurtis did a special program built around DeVictor's contentions. "Agent Orange, the Deadly Fog," aired on WBBM, a CBS affiliate, in March 1978, and pinned the blame for a wide variety of health problems on a herbicide used in Vietnam that contained the chemical dioxin.[866]

The story percolated for a while as fears of dioxin grew. Environmentalists claimed that dioxin was the most dangerous chemical known to man, particularly hazardous because it did not exist in nature, and thus humans had never developed a detoxification system to protect themselves from its contamination. "The idea developed in our culture that just a tiny bit of chemical would do you in," Franklin says. "By the time the Agent Orange thing hit, we could find chemicals in parts per billion. It became possible to run a story that said we found dioxin in just about anything. The public was getting bombarded with the impression that they were taking in all these trace chemicals. What the public didn't realize—and I didn't either, until later—is that we also have defense mechanisms against the chemicals."

When dioxin was discovered in a landfill on Love Canal in New York, the ensuing panic led to the evacuation of an entire neighborhood. The same thing happened at Times Beach, Missouri. By 1980, whenever Vietnam veterans—men then predominantly in their late twenties and early thirties—became ill with cancer or their children were born with birth defects, the afflictions were attributed to Agent Orange.

Assigned to write about Agent Orange, Franklin also shared the popular fears. In hearings in Congress, activists charged that children of Vietnam veterans had an extraordinarily high rate of birth defects, about 1.5 percent, and that vets were dying of cancer at an alarming rate—not to mention the explosions of violence, the heart palpitations, the brain tumors. The irony was inescapable. These soldiers had survived combat in Vietnam only to be killed by their own military's chemical warfare.

The sad story of Admiral Elmo Zumwalt had all the elements of a Shakespearean tragedy. As the commander of all naval forces in Vietnam, Zumwalt was instrumental in ordering the use of Agent Orange along the rivers of Southeast Asia where his son Elmo III, a naval officer, patrolled. When his son was diagnosed with cancer, and his grandson was born with brain damage, Zumwalt became convinced that he was responsible for their ordeal. Not only had we sent our sons to war and told them not to win, we also had poisoned them. (Elmo Zumwalt III died in August 1988 at age forty-two of non-Hodgkin's lymphoma.) And the American government was refusing to acknowledge its responsibility to these men, claiming that their diseases and birth defects could not be traced to the herbicide. "I gathered about me that righteous fervor that is the armor of the crusading reporter, and I went to work," Franklin later wrote.[867]

Franklin teamed up with an investigative reporter named Alan Doelp. Their assignment was ideal: They could take as much time and spend as much money as they needed to research and write the story, an incredible luxury for newspaper reporters. "Nobody, but nobody, gets that much time and money," Franklin says. "I was basically ready to lynch Dow Chemical," the primary manufacturer of Agent Orange.

The journalists worked on the story for eight months. A stickler for accuracy, Doelp insisted on tracking every piece of information to its source. "The first step was obvious," Franklin later wrote. "Veterans' groups were leveling all sorts of charges against Dow Chemical and the military. My first step was to verify that those charges were legitimate. I wasn't looking for, or expecting, proof. In matters environmental, truth is so complex that proof of anything can rarely be established. But I was, in good journalistic conscience, obligated to investigate accusations before legitimizing them in the *Evening Sun*."[868]

As award-winning journalists, they had access to the most brilliant scientific experts in the country. One of the first charges Franklin set out to confirm was that Vietnam veterans had fathered hundreds, even thousands of seriously deformed children. Franklin found out that the normal rate of birth defects is 2.1 percent of all live births. If a million men served in Vietnam, and if each had one child upon returning, they would be *expected* to father numerous deformed children—more than twenty thousand.

Franklin found no indication that the rate of birth defects for the children of Vietnam veterans was any higher than normal.

He then interviewed people who believed they were victims of Agent Orange. One Vietnam veteran, involved in a mammoth lawsuit against the government and chemical companies, told Franklin that Agent Orange had made him "too nervous to work." The veteran described how in Vietnam he had been sprayed with an orange powder. Another said Agent Orange made him too lethargic and lazy to work and remembered how he had been in a tank column when orange powder came drifting down on them. In fact, most of the veterans Franklin interviewed, including a number who had been quoted in *The New York Times* and the *Washington Post*, remembered orange powder or orange liquid. Franklin knew the herbicide was a colorless liquid and was called Agent Orange because it had been shipped in metal drums painted with an orange stripe.

Other "victims" blamed their wife-beating, alcoholism, unemployment, and child abuse on Agent Orange. They quoted various scientific studies but never could seem to put their hands on them. They assured Franklin that he could easily find the research papers. "Or I could do what other reporters were doing, which was taking the veterans' word for it," Franklin says. When he tried to document statements other reporters printed about various scientific studies, the sources always said they heard the information from someone else. It was like playing a giant game of gossip.

Franklin spent more than a week pulling technical papers from the University of Maryland medical library and the National Library of Medicine archives. He compiled a stack of material about two-feet high and began the "tedious, but enlightening" process of plowing through the accumulated scientific literature.

He discovered that dioxin was essentially an industrial waste product, created during the manufacture of trichlorophenol (TCP). In turn, TCP was a component of a number of chemicals, including 2,4,5-T, which was mixed with 2,4-D to make Agent Orange. Some of the Agent Orange used in Vietnam had been contaminated with five parts per billion of dioxin; much of the herbicide contained far less. Once sprayed over the Vietnamese jungle, the herbicide's concentration of dioxin was diluted still further, to a few parts per quadrillion. When the first studies on Vietnam veterans and Agent Orange were attempted, there were only three laboratories in the country capable of testing for such incredibly minute concentrations.

Calling the scientists who had authored the papers most quoted by self-proclaimed Agent Orange victims confirmed Franklin's growing suspicion that the case against the chemical was "at best highly speculative." The experts pointed out that dioxin had been around a long time. Finding the chemical in the body fat of a veteran was "more a tribute to the sophistication of scientific instruments than to the dangers of dioxin." One scientist boasted: "Give me enough money and I'll find anything in anything. We're getting that good!"

The only disorder that the scientific studies could positively link to Agent Orange was chloracne, a pernicious skin rash that develops immediately after high exposure to dioxin by the reaction of certain fat cells to highly chlorinated hydrocarbons. Some of the scientists complained scornfully to Franklin that their work was being distorted, that veterans' activists and self-serving politicians were using the fears of dioxin to further their own causes. The hue and cry over dioxin did not reflect the scientific reality, they told Franklin. One scientist even took a day off from work to explain to Franklin the scientific principles needed to make sense of the toxicology reports, beginning with the maxim that "the dose makes the poison." Other scientists showed the writer why, biologically, toxins rarely damage sperm. In mammals, sperm are manufactured constantly, unlike eggs.

But none of the scientists would speak out. Some told Franklin they were afraid of being harassed by the growing Agent Orange movement. Others just didn't want to get involved. A few frankly admitted that, with federal grant money drying up, they hoped to obtain funds to study dioxin. And there was another sentiment at play. Almost all the scientists sympathized with the Vietnam veterans, feeling that they had been mistreated by their government and deserved help.

Frustrated, Franklin began researching tropical diseases and stress reactions to combat to see if they explained the veterans' symptoms. He and Doelp began writing stories about Agent Orange syndrome; unable to tie the symptoms to dioxin, the articles were less than earth shaking. But as Franklin grew more skeptical, the Agent Orange story erupted around him. Other reporters plastered unsubstantiated charges on the front pages of their newspapers. Fear spread that not only were Vietnam veterans victims of the insidious chemical dioxin, average Americans also were succumbing to the chemical's sinister effects. A cluster of mysterious brain tumors in Pennsylvania was attributed to dioxin; none of the reporters bothered to point out that scientists had known for years that brain tumors, leukemias, lymphomas, and Hodgkin's disease occur in clusters.

Franklin grew increasingly frustrated. Veterans charged that the government was engaging in a "conspiracy of silence." Every time he seemed to have his hands on definitive evidence that Agent Orange was the culprit, the "proof" evaporated like mist in the jungle. Veterans told him to go talk to a scientist who had shown that tiny amounts of dioxin had caused a wide range of diseases in laboratory animals. But when Franklin tried to trace him, he found the scientist had left his university under a cloud of suspicion over disbursements of his grant money. Veterans said he had been framed; Franklin knew only that once again he had come up with nothing.

Slowly, Franklin realized that while he had approached the Agent Orange phenomenon from a scientific point of view, the story really was not about science. He began to wonder if he was witnessing a modern witch-hunt. "The veterans I talked to represented the range of human personalities and capabilities, but they had one thing in common," Franklin wrote. "They had been ill-used by their government, and they had as a result incurred an abiding suspicion of it. They were perfectly willing to believe that the politicians who sent them to Vietnam were capable of poisoning them while they were there and denying it when they returned.

"They also saw scientists as a monolithic force, a force capable of large-scale conspiracy, a group of faceless intellectuals who would, naturally, share the government's interest in obscuring the facts. The civilians who joined the Agent Orange movement came from many backgrounds, but they, too, from housewives to maturing hippies in Oregon, shared that fierce distrust of government. They also shared a distrust of chemicals, pernicious chemicals that could not be seen, touched, or tasted that were poisoning us all and causing an epidemic of cancer."[869]

The only epidemic of cancer Franklin could find that was supported by hard statistics? Lung cancer—caused not by Agent Orange or other exotic chemicals, but almost certainly by smoking.

The last straw came later when Franklin ran into one of his best sources, a scientist who, after demanding anonymity, had privately told Franklin that Agent Orange syndrome was a hoax. The scientist was in Washington negotiating for a major government grant. When Franklin asked what the grant was for, the researcher tried to change the subject. Finally the scientist confessed: The grant was to investigate the effects of Agent Orange on a specific organ system. Defensive, the scientist explained he had lost his earlier grant. He had children to feed, a mortgage to pay, a laboratory to keep running. The money was there for the taking.

In frustration, Franklin turned to other stories. He left the newspaper to write a book. Still the dioxin story mushroomed. Despite the spectacular lack of evidence, Agent Orange has become firmly entrenched as the cause of a wide variety of health problems among Vietnam veterans and their offspring, used by veterans' activists to further their demands of monetary compensation from the government.

The Pulitzer Prize-winning reporter had seen the story of his career disappear into that strange world where "a lie is a sort of a myth, and a myth is a sort of a truth," he said, paraphrasing Cyrano de Bergerac. Seeing other reporters buying into the myth created a profound loss of confidence in his profession. Franklin was even accosted in his own newsroom by several reporters who loudly accused him of taking bribes from Dow Chemical.

"The Agent Orange story was a myth created by a group of Vietnam-era protesters, seized upon by Vietnam vets, and disseminated by the press," Franklin said. "That discovery and the more shocking discovery that my colleagues (in the press) didn't care much about the truth of the matter and had never bothered to look into the substance very deeply, changed my life."[870] Franklin left journalism for academia, becoming the dean of journalism at Oregon State University.

The myth of Agent Orange added yet another significant layer to the victimhood of Vietnam veterans. Poisoned by our own military, sent to fight a war with our hands tied, Vietnam veterans now had to face the terror of imminent death from within. The image of the diseased body as well as the broken spirit is now inextricably bound up with the image of the Vietnam veteran.

Looking at how the myth began provides a fascinating glimpse into the coalescing of the antiwar movement, the scare tactics of the environmentalists, and the politics of victimization.

Herbicidal Warfare

Early in the war, the United States offered an unusual weapon to South Vietnam in its fight against the Communist-backed Viet Cong. Chemicals would be used to defoliate strategic areas of the countryside, denying the insurgents the cover of jungle vegetation for the movement of supplies and troops, to expose VC bases, to destroy crops, and to discourage ambushes. Defoliation wasn't a new idea; the tactic had been used in Malaysia in the late 1940s and during the French Indochina War in Vietnam. Prime Minister Ngo Dinh Diem supported the proposal. In December 1961, the Air Force initiated Operation Ranch Hand in Vietnam. Ranch Hand was a unit composed of Air Force personnel from the Special Aerial Spray Flight—which sprayed insecticide to control malaria-carrying mosquitoes—as well as airmen experienced in the use of an ungainly twin-engined cargo aircraft called the C-123.

The 1,265 "cowboys" of Ranch Hand became legendary in Vietnam as the Air Force unit most fired on by the enemy. They became known as fliers with "balls of steel" because they cruised C-123 aircraft at about 150 miles an hour—near stall speed—just above treetop level, often with wingtips no more than fifteen to twenty feet apart. The extremely low speed and altitude routinely exposed the unarmed and unarmored aircraft to enemy gunfire. In 1966, nearly one-third of all C-123 defoliant sorties suffered ground fire hits. The two units involved in Ranch Hand were the most highly decorated Air Force squadrons of the war—not the hot jet pilots who flew to Hanoi or the pilots of the Big Boys (B-52s) who dodged surface-to-air missiles over North Vietnam.

The most celebrated Ranch Hand aircraft was named "Patches," in honor of the myriad bullet holes in the aircraft's metal skin. By the time the plane was retired to the Air Force Museum at Wright-Patterson Air Force Base, Patches had been hit by more than eight hundred rounds of enemy fire. But many of the "cowboys" couldn't be patched up. The Air Force's first combat deaths in Vietnam came in 1962 when a Ranch Hand C-123 was shot down, and three crewmen were killed. In all, twenty-five Ranch Handers died in Vietnam.

The cowboys partied as hard as they worked. Ranch Hand celebrations —which took place for just about any reason—were legendary in Vietnam, mainly for their extravagant alcohol consumption and generally raucous nature.

Over the ten years of the war, Operation Ranch Hand sprayed about eleven million gallons of Agent Orange on the South Vietnamese landscape. After 1965, most of the herbicide used was a 50/50 mixture of 2,4-D and 2,4,5-T. (The herbicide was called "orange" in Vietnam, not Agent Orange. That sinister-sounding term wasn't coined until the mid-1970s.)

Other herbicides were used in Vietnam as well: Herbicide White, Blue, Purple, Pink, and Green, again derived from the colored stripe painted on the fifty-five-gallon shipping drums. And they were effective. Admiral Zumwalt, who ordered the defoliation of riverbanks, deemed the Ranch Hand mission a success. "There's no question, in so far as the Navy is concerned, that it was effective," Zumwalt said. "Very rapidly after its use, the enemy was driven from just a few feet away from the boats to several hundreds of yards away. And the casualties, which had been running at the rate of 6 percent a month, were reduced to less than a percent a month. On balance, we saved many more lives than will be lost as a result of Agent Orange."[871]

The herbicides were nothing new. Considered safe and effective, they had been used throughout the world for twenty years by farmers and to control weeds and unwanted vegetation along highways and power-line rights of way. The herbicide labeled orange was deemed the most effective in controlling the "broadleaf" vegetation common to Southeast Asia. (The dioxin itself had no effect on the plant. Dioxin was a by-product of the manufacturing process of the herbicide, which killed the leaves.) Although activists later claimed that Agent Orange "destroyed the land" or turned the countryside into a "moonscape," that was not accurate. The herbicide basically turned the leaves brown so they shriveled up. Most trees were not killed by the herbicide, only "de-leafed." Regrowth occurred rapidly in the hot and humid climate of Indochina, sometimes only six weeks after spraying.

Another misconception about Agent Orange is that the area sprayed would be left "dripping" with the chemical, or that the clothing of people inadvertently caught in the spray would be "soaked" with herbicide. The spray equipment on the aircraft used by the Ranch Hand was calibrated to spray at a rate of three gallons per acre.[872] Maj. Jack Spey, USAF (Ret.), a former Ranch Hander, points out that this is the equivalent of 0.009 of an ounce of liquid per square foot, or nine-thousandths of a whiskey shot glass, hardly enough liquid to saturate the ground or drench a person's clothing.

When sprayed on dense jungle foliage, less than 6 percent of the herbicide released from the Ranch Hand aircraft ever reached the ground. Spray tests showed that 70 percent of the herbicide settled and remained on the upper branches and leaves of the trees. Typically, ground troops didn't enter a sprayed area until four to six weeks after the mission and the leaves were defoliated. Because most of the Agent Orange used in Vietnam contained a scant 0.0002 of 1 percent of dioxin—and scientific research has shown that dioxin degrades in sunlight after forty-eight to seventy-two hours—troops' exposure to dioxin was infinitesimal.

Organic chemists know that dioxin has existed in our environment even before humans appeared on the earth; it's a natural by-product of combustion, such as forest fires, and is also created in nature by the action of enzymes in soil. Auto exhaust is a source of dioxin, as is the smelting of copper.

Concern arose over the herbicides in the sixties for several reasons. Herbicides were being used to destroy crops to deny food to the enemy, but this tactic also hurt civilians—not exactly conducive to winning "hearts and minds." And although there was no scientific evidence that exposure to the herbicides harmed humans, the North Vietnamese were able to use the spray's plant-killing properties to scare the civilian population.

In 1969, a civilian study linked high rates of birth defects in animals with 2,4,5-T and 2,4-D (not dioxin). Although the herbicidal program was effective—and certainly saved American lives—controversy over its use resulted in the shutdown of the Ranch Hand program in April 1970.

A 1978 study, in which rats fed high doses of dioxin developed liver cancer, gave dioxin the reputation as the "most toxic substance known to mankind." Fears were growing about the insidious dangers faced by the public from "toxic" chemicals in even small doses. In 1979, a Boston television station broadcast "A Plague on Our Children," linking 2,4,5-T spraying to health problems in Oregon. That same year, KRON-TV in San Francisco aired "The Politics of Poison," about the battle over what "values will prevail in this chemical age."[873] The "documentary" posed the premise that Americans were receiving tiny doses of dioxin, called "a synthetic chemical so powerful an ounce could wipe out a million people."

The reports were triggered by a single study in the Alsea, Oregon, area which linked women's miscarriages and spraying of 2,4,5-T. The EPA issued an emergency suspension of the herbicides' use in the rangeland and rice fields. But the study had not undergone the peer review process, and in the months after publication, at least eighteen reviews of the methodology concluded the research was seriously flawed—the data did not support a link between any spraying and miscarriage.

The "experts" made it sound as if tiny amounts of dioxin would soon wipe out mankind. That fear was legitimized by the federal government in 1982 when the Environmental Protection Agency, responding to the activists' alarms, ordered the evacuation of Times Beach, Missouri. The government bought out the property owners for about $40 million and closed off their 480-acre neighborhood after dioxin-contaminated oil was sprayed on area roads.

By 1982, thirty-six government-sponsored research projects on dioxin had begun and more were in the pipeline. "Dioxin can cause severely adverse health effects, and death, at the lowest dose imaginable. Millions of pounds of the two ingredients of Agent Orange are still being sprayed, despite the enormous harm they are known to have caused to human health, wildlife, and the environment," said a story in *The New York Times* in 1983. The message was clear. As they grew older, many Vietnam veterans with health problems began to look to their experience in Southeast Asia to find a possible cause.

Hollywood took up the issue in movies such as *Unnatural Causes* and *My Father, My Son*, which portrayed the defoliation operation in Vietnam as a sinister mission spreading death and disease. Veterans' organizations such as the American Legion and the Vietnam Veterans of America latched onto Agent Orange as grounds for lobbying Congress for more funds for Vietnam veterans.

The feeling of the times was captured brilliantly in a 1983 documentary called *The Secret Agent* by Jacki Ochs. "The tale of military and industrial collusion which allowed America to unleash the toxic defoliant dioxin, or Agent Orange, on the world is one of such premeditated evil," said the *Village Voice*. "We follow a trail from Vietnam vets contaminated during the war, to cool apologists in corporate boardrooms, to mothers of dioxin-deformed children, in a calm panorama of an international crime now seeking moral and economic redress in American courts."[874]

"I Died in Vietnam, But I Didn't Even Know It"

The publication of *Waiting for an Army to Die*, by Fred A. Wilcox in 1983, was hailed as an important and frightening call to arms, comparable to *Silent Spring*, the ecological alarm that had ignited the environmental movement two decades earlier.[875] Wilcox had been a long-time activist of the left. His first book had been a primer and source book for antinuclear activists. Now he targeted yet another invisible terror.

The primary evidence used by Wilcox to convince readers of the terrifying effects of Agent Orange were anecdotal stories about sick and dying veterans. Their situations are indeed sad; the premature deaths of young people from disease are always tragic. But in any large population, a certain number of people are going to succumb to cancer and other diseases at an early age. Name a cancer and somewhere a Vietnam veteran suffers from it. Proving exposure to some substance doesn't mean that the substance caused the disease. Any honest scientist will confirm that only large epidemiological studies can do that.

Wilcox "proved" his thesis through stories about men like Paul Reutershan, founder of Agent Orange Victims International, who filed a $10 million claim against Dow Chemical and two other manufacturers of Agent Orange. "I died in Vietnam, but I didn't even know it," Reutershan told a shocked audience on the *Today* show in the spring of 1978. Only twenty-eight, Reutershan died of abdominal cancer on December 14, 1978.

But what did his death really prove? Reutershan had testified before Congress that Agent Orange was so potent that "within two days [it] could topple a hardwood tree 150 feet tall."[876] (The herbicide defoliated leaves, it did not kill trees.) Wilcox described Reutershan as a helicopter pilot who flew "almost daily" through "clouds of herbicide" being sprayed from planes.[877] However, Reutershan's military record indicated that he was an enlisted man, not a commissioned or warrant officer, a prerequisite for being a pilot. In Vietnam, Reutershan served as a helicopter mechanic.[878]

Typically, mechanics had flight time in helicopters, but it's absurd to think that a helicopter pilot would intentionally fly in the wake of an Air Force C-123 spraying herbicides. All the spraying was done at a slow speed and at an extremely low level, which would unnecessarily expose the chopper to ground fire. Another factor to consider—diesel fuel was mixed with Agent Orange for weight and consistency and would have coated the windshield of any following aircraft, effectively blinding the pilot.

Another veteran activist named by Wilcox was Ed Juteau, vice president of Agent Orange Victims International. Juteau blamed his lymphatic cancer on Agent Orange.[879] Juteau's military record revealed that he served a tour of duty in Vietnam as an inventory management specialist at Cam Ranh Bay Air Base—not a job likely to bring him into contact with much Agent Orange. Cam Ranh was a giant, enemy-free sandbar and was not in need of defoliation.[880]

A leading character in Wilcox' book was Joe Naples, a Vietnam veteran who attributed his son's birth defects and his own memory lapses, dizziness, headaches, stomach aches, and sensitivity to light to his exposure to Agent Orange in Vietnam.

Wilcox described Naples as a Navy SEAL who spent three years in Vietnam, "mostly involved in reconnaissance, setting up ambushes, intercepting gun runners and tax collectors." Naples said he was wounded three times and was with the "very first group, or one of the first" to enter Cambodia in 1966, four years before the war "officially" spread to that country. Naples contended that as a SEAL he often had been dropped off at ambush sites and spent hours lying in foliage drenched with Agent Orange.

"It would actually be comin' down on us." Naples said. "I spent a lot of time on my stomach in 'Nam and in and out of the water that would have contained the stuff either from direct spray or runoff. You'd bathe in a bomb crater, so you'd be drinkin' it. You'd be takin' a bath in it. You'd wash your clothes in it."[881]

Naples told Wilcox he was having a hard time getting a service-connected disability because he could not obtain the records of his three years in Vietnam—sound familiar?—which could prove he had been exposed to the herbicide. He and his wife said they suspected that because they were pressing the issue, their phone was bugged. Naples claimed he had seen government cars with men inside taking pictures of their house with telephoto lenses.

I don't know why Naples had a problem getting records showing he served in Vietnam; I was able to obtain them through FOIA. They show Joseph C. Naples was a Navy enlisted man who served from January 29, 1964 to November 27, 1967. A fine seaman, he received a Bronze Star Medal for valor, a Navy Commendation Medal with Combat "V" device, a Combat Action Ribbon, and a Purple Heart.[882]

But Naples was not a Navy SEAL. Assigned to the USS *Northhampton* as a mess cook, Naples volunteered in January 1966 to be retrained in small boats, which ultimately led to an assignment in Vietnam. He remained on the U.S. West Coast for the entire year of 1966. Naples could not have entered Cambodia in that year as he claimed, unless that was the name of his favorite Oriental restaurant in San Diego.

Naples served in Vietnam for ten months, from February to November 1967, not three years, as he said. That time was spent as a crew member of River Flotilla One in the Mekong Delta, assigned to one of the larger gun boats in the force known as a Monitor. Naples said he spent a lot of time on his stomach in Vietnam, implying that he was low-crawling through enemy territory in the jungle. Given his true assignment, I suspect that the only significant amount of time he spent on his stomach was in his bunk on the boat. Naples was wounded in July 1967, but not seriously enough to be evacuated or even hospitalized. He left Vietnam in November 1967, the end of his enlistment.

The rest of *An Army Waiting to Die* is a hodgepodge of unprovable allegations, insinuations, and assumptions that don't hold up to serious scrutiny. Most articles and books about Agent Orange suffer from the same problems. Reporters often don't do the very basic step of checking military records to find out if their subjects are telling the truth about their experiences.

The misinformation about the herbicidal missions was repeated by reporters, even when patently ridiculous. One veteran describing his experiences to a reporter remembered that a tanker plane flew six hundred feet above him, spraying an "umbrella of mist on the trees below — and into the helicopter onto [him]." (Ranch Handers did not spray at six hundred feet.) The widow of a veteran who claimed Agent Orange caused his disease reported: "Dioxins are what they sprayed in Vietnam. They make plants grow so fast they explode, so when it gets into humans, it must do much the same."[883]

In March 1981, the *Los Angeles Times* reported the story of thirty-two-year-old ex-Marine James Hopkins, who drove a Jeep through the glass doors of a VA facility and shot the place up. The headlines tied his health problems and subsequent despondency to Agent Orange exposure in Vietnam. When Hopkins committed suicide with an overdose of liquor and sleeping pills a few months later, the news reports, of course, connected the suicide of the "heroic Marine" and Agent Orange. But several months later, the *Times* ran a story quoting Hopkins' ex-wife, sources at the VA, and the Marine Corps, who pointed out that Hopkins was not a former Marine, nor was he a Vietnam vet.

About the same time, a veterans' group organized a protest demanding research into the long-range effects of exposure to Agent Orange. One of the coordinators of the protest was a wheelchair-bound Vietnam veteran who said he had been crippled by an enemy's bullet. The veteran actually had been shot in 1972 while AWOL when he tried to hold up a liquor store. He admitted the attempted armed robbery but said he had no memory of the incident due to "induced psychotic amnesia" caused — of course — by Agent Orange.

In 1990, Dallas newspapers told the tragic story of Judge Charles N. "Nick" Lundy, who desperately needed a liver transplant. Lundy's political resume said he was a former Special Forces captain, a Green Beret who received two Bronze Star Medals for valor, an Army Commendation Medal, a Combat Infantryman Badge, and the Parachute Badge. Lundy attributed his ill health to his exposure to Agent Orange while he was on missions in the field. Lundy described being covered with a white dust that did not easily wash off and was noticeable in food and water.[884] (Reporters did not point out that Agent Orange did not leave a white dust.)

Lundy suffered from fatigue, headaches, rashes, and benign tumors; he underwent forty surgeries, hundreds of hospital stays, and spent thousands of dollars on doctors bills. After a bout with Hepatitis B, Lundy received an emergency liver transplant. But the transplant could not save him; Lundy died at age fifty-one. Although his death certificate stated that the cause of death was adult respiratory distress syndrome, the attending physician stated his belief that Lundy had been heavily exposed to Agent Orange during the Vietnam War. "He was killed in the war—it just took him twenty-three years to die," his wife Peggy told reporters.[885]

But Lundy's military record showed he was not a Green Beret captain in Vietnam. Lundy served a tour of duty in 1967–68 as an officer in an armored unit.[886] His primary duty would have placed him in a tank, which put several inches of steel between him and the outside environment. Tanks did not travel in heavily foliated areas, where Agent Orange was used, but typically stayed on flat, hard ground or paved roads. (For a portion of his tour, Lundy served in a mobile advisory team.) While Lundy's death is certainly tragic, there is nothing in his record to indicate he was exposed to any significant level of Agent Orange—as his comments about a "white dust" and a flavor noticeable in food and water reveal.

Henry "Sonny" Kinsey of Coeur d'Alene, Idaho, told reporters that he was a Vietnam veteran suffering from the effects of Agent Orange exposure during a stint in the U.S. Navy Seabees. After being diagnosed with cancer, Kinsey's left leg had been amputated below the knee. Kinsey said Agent Orange also caused his emphysema, osteoporosis, osteoarthritis, nerve damage, an ulcer, and chloracne, and that four of his children suffered from birth defects. In the late 1980s, Kinsey began a wheelchair journey to various towns from Texas through South Dakota. A companion who described himself as a Vietnam POW announced to local veterans' organizations and reporters news of Kinsey's pending arrival. Kinsey rolled into town in his wheelchair, wearing Vietnam campaign and service medals and a cap that said "Vietnam Vet and Proud of It." He gave interviews to local reporters about how he had been poisoned by Agent Orange and was trying to raise money and awareness to get help for Vietnam veterans. Often, the local vet groups took up a collection or gave him a charitable donation from chapter funds. After all, he was fighting their fight.

But Kinsey's military record indicated he joined the Navy in May 1970 and was stationed at Port Hueneme, California, until April 1972, when he entered the inactive Naval Reserve. During his active duty, Kinsey served in a construction battalion. There's no indication he ever served in Vietnam.[887] In 1989, I passed Kinsey's record on to a Dallas veteran, who let other veterans' groups in the state know that Kinsey was pulling a lucrative charade. Shortly thereafter, Kinsey disappeared from the Texas scene.

In August 1990, Kinsey again popped up in the press when he began traveling by wheelchair from Spokane to Washington, D.C. He carried an American flag and a sign that read, "American Vets Marching On Washington, D.C. Agent Orange. Radiation. We are Dying. Donations Needed." Kinsey told reporters he hoped to meet with President Bush and members of Congress about his plight and to push for help for other veterans who received little help from the VA. "When I was in a combat hospital in 1971, I was on oxygen, and I had to get out of bed to change my own sheets," Kinsey told one reporter. At a VA hospital the year before, he said, "I laid in my own bloody sheets for eleven days before they changed them."[888]

Kinsey cut his trip short after newspaper stories about his journey through South Dakota came to the attention of Bruce "Brad" Bradfield in Dallas, then president of the Dallas VVA Chapter, who called his bluff by giving reporters copies of Kinsey's military record. Kinsey's response was that he always told people he was a Vietnam-*era* vet and he had been exposed to Agent Orange in Japan as a Navy Seabee while mixing the herbicide "by hand" with creosote to treat timbers for a Marine base (ludicrous, of course, unless his commander was worried about weeds growing out of telephone poles).[889]

But, like a bad penny, Kinsey kept turning up. In 1992, Kinsey testified before a prestigious National Academy of Science Committee, which was mandated by Congress to examine the effects of Agent Orange. There was obviously insufficient scrutiny of those accepted for testimony.

Men like Kinsey and Naples spread the irrational panic about Agent Orange, leading to stories like one in *Rolling Stone* magazine that said "the effects of dioxin on humans have been *documented* by veterans." (Emphasis added.)[890] While many legitimate veterans who did not exaggerate or lie about their service sincerely believed their health problems were caused by Agent Orange, that belief has not been backed up by scientific studies.

The Facts About Dioxin

Just how dangerous is dioxin?

Dioxin indeed can be hazardous, as author Michael Gough, one of the federal government's premier experts on the chemical, pointed out in his 1986 book *Dioxin, Agent Orange: The Facts*.[891] Formerly with the Office of Technology Assessment, Gough said that dioxin given in large doses to laboratory animals can cause cancer, spontaneous abortions, and birth defects when the female animal is exposed. And the chemical can cause skin disorders—mainly an acne-like rash called chloracne—in humans who endure heavy exposure.

But Gough and other experts point out that injecting rats with massive doses of any chemical cannot be a comparable measure to humans receiving very low amounts. Scientific studies of industrial accidents in which the victims were heavily exposed to dioxin show no evidence the chemical causes *any* long-term health problems in humans.

An industrial accident in northern Italy in 1976 exposed several thousand people—including children, pregnant women, and the elderly—to dioxin. Follow-up examinations found no excess birth defects or reproductive failure, even at the high doses they received.[892]

In 1984, a study published in the *Journal of the American Medical Association* reported that workers contaminated with dioxin in a 1949 manufacturing accident developed no more life-threatening problems in the next thirty-five years than workers who were not exposed. They revealed no higher rates of cancer, heart or liver damage, nerve problems, kidney damage, reproductive problems, or birth defects. However, they did have higher rates of chloracne and digestive tract ulcers, both treatable conditions.[893]

Another study done for the CDC's National Institute for Occupational Safety and Health examined the health records of 5,172 workers in chemical factories where dioxin wastes were produced as a by-product. There was no higher incidence of stomach, liver, or nasal cancers, nor were there higher rates of Hodgkin's lymphoma or non-Hodgkin's lymphoma as predicted by those who claim dioxin is deadly.[894] Five years of studies in Missouri related to exposure at Times Beach found no significant chronic disease caused by environmental dioxin exposure.[895]

"As far as we know," said Elizabeth M. Whelan in her 1993 book *Toxic Terror*, "no human has ever died or become chronically ill from environmental exposure to dioxin in the United States."[896] President of the American Council on Science and Health, Whelan said fears that dioxin is the "deadliest" chemical known to mankind were based on animals exposed to large doses of the chemical and inaccurate scientific extrapolations from those studies. When a lab rat is fed a huge dose of a chemical, its liver cannot filter the toxin; the animal's cells are forced to replicate at very high rates, multiplying the chances of natural mutation and triggering cancer. But it's the size of the dose and not the chemical that is to blame, Whelan said.

In September 1987, scientists at the CDC told key Agent Orange advisory committees in the administration and Congress that they could not proceed with a major, congressionally mandated study on the effects of the herbicide on soldiers in Vietnam because they were unable to find soldiers with significant levels of exposure. That conclusion was based on a pilot study to determine whether enough troops with high exposure to the herbicide could be identified from military records for a large-scale study. (Other studies have shown that Vietnam veterans have levels of dioxin *slightly* lower than their peers who did not serve in Vietnam.)

"This study has demonstrated that, for most of the ground troops, the exposure was not significant," said Dr. Vernon Houk, assistant surgeon general and director of the CDC's Center for Environmental Health. "I'm quite sure there were some individuals, such as Chemical Corps workers, who were exposed. But this study shows it is not possible to get a sufficient number of exposed people through military records to do a meaningful study of ground troops."[897]

Of course, veterans' activists jumped on this research. John Terzano, then president of the Vietnam Veterans of America Foundation, insisted the conclusion proved only that the methods the CDC explored for doing the study would not work, not that it was impossible by other methods. Politics, not science, gained the upper hand. Legislation was introduced in both houses of Congress that year to compensate Vietnam veterans exposed to Agent Orange.

In 1988, the CDC's Vietnam Experience Study (VES), which used military records to locate veterans, compared about nine thousand men who served in Vietnam to veterans who had served elsewhere. Their level of exposure to dioxin was assessed, and they were given medical and psychological examinations, a reproductive outcome assessment, and a mortality assessment. The study showed that few except those whose jobs included handling herbicides were exposed to significant levels of dioxin. Only 4 percent of the veterans examined had dioxin levels above eight parts per trillion. Blood tests revealed that only two of the nine thousand Vietnam veterans examined had been abnormally exposed. (The CDC in Atlanta in recent years has determined that the average American's blood contains four to seven parts per trillion of dioxin, the background level resulting from the natural environment.)[898]

The VES study revealed there was little difference in the Vietnam and non-Vietnam veterans in incidence of chloracne-like lesions. (Experts have found that dioxin-associated chloracne becomes evident shortly after exposure, not years later.) And Vietnam veterans had no higher incidence of five types of cancer, including soft tissue and other sarcomas, Hodgkin's disease, nasal and nasopharyngeal cancer, and primary liver cancer. In fact, veterans who served in the area of highest Agent Orange exposure were at the lowest risk for non-Hodgkin's lymphoma; Navy men who had served in areas far away from Agent Orange use showed the highest incidence of this disease.

The only significant differences in the health of the two groups: The Vietnam veterans had more hearing loss and lower sperm concentrations.

But the study reported that Vietnam veterans and non-Vietnam veterans had fathered similar numbers of children, and children of Vietnam veterans were no more likely to have birth defects recorded on hospital birth records than non-Vietnam veterans, consistent with the findings of three epidemiological studies conducted since 1981.

Almost a decade after the closing of Times Beach, Missouri, Vernon Houk, who as a CDC official had urged that the town be evacuated, admitted he had made a mistake. Houk said in 1991 that he and others had seriously overestimated the hazards of dioxin a decade before. "I would not be concerned about the levels of dioxin at Times Beach," Houk said.[899] Of course this was long after the Environmental Protection Agency had begun a $200 million cleanup project of Times Beach.

The *New England Journal of Medicine* in February 1991 reported a study of five thousand chemical industry workers exposed to dioxin over forty years. Only those with dioxin levels *five hundred times* higher than normal showed an excess risk of cancer, and even then the increase was deemed "slight."

But that same month, due to political pressure from veterans' activists, the House and Senate unanimously ratified a decision by the VA to categorize two types of cancer as service-related disabilities resulting from exposure to Agent Orange. The legislation made almost four thousand veterans and survivors eligible for benefits at a cost to the taxpayer of more than $13 million—all despite the fact that there was no valid scientific evidence to back up the link between the herbicide and the diseases. However, Congress consistently has ignored the scientific studies by its own agency, the CDC, in favor of the dubious science touted by the activists using Agent Orange to promote their own agenda.

In the last twenty years, more than $400 million has been spent on studying the effects of dioxin, only to come up empty. But as journalist Jon Franklin pointed out, "proving" cause and effect in environmental issues is often difficult. For two decades, the outcome of poorly designed studies of dioxin and Agent Orange have been touted as "proof" that the chemical causes everything from memory loss to brain tumors. Studies that find no connection between illness and dioxin are dismissed by activists as *prima facie* evidence that the government or chemical companies are covering up something. More studies are demanded.

But it's clear that many of those claiming Agent Orange exposure caused their diseases clearly were not even exposed to significant amounts of the herbicide. What has scientific research shown about those who clearly were? By far, the definitive epidemiological study of the effects of Agent Orange on Vietnam veterans has been the twenty-year Air Force Ranch Hand study.

The Cowboys of the Ranch

Military aviators wish to project a macho image, and the pilots and crew of Ranch Hand were no exception. In response to the antiwar protesters back home who were screaming about Agent Orange, the Ranch Handers developed an initiation rite for new arrivals: Each had to drink a cup of the herbicide. The veterans drank right along with the new man and kept a tally of all they drank. Some estimated they ingested a gallon of the stuff. At their reunions years later, Ranch Handers sported T-shirts that said things like "Retired Tree Killer" and "I Drank Agent Orange."

Chemical cocktails aside, of all the American troops in Vietnam, the Ranch Handers had the most contact with Agent Orange. Most of the airmen in Ranch Hand were exposed to the herbicide up to twelve hours a day, five to six days a week for at least a year. Although they were supposed to wear protective clothing, the Ranch Handers often wore cutoff fatigues or boxer shorts and tennis shoes when making spraying runs instead of putting on the hot, encumbering garb. During the slow, low-level flights, the crewmen often stood in the open cargo bay doors, covered in a fine mist of Agent Orange.

The exposure became particularly acute when the aircraft took enemy fire; the C-123 had the consistency of a full beer can. Rounds easily pierced the large bladders filled with Agent Orange, spewing it throughout the aircraft, drenching the crew as they attempted to plug the holes. The herbicide often spilled onto the decks of the aircraft, and the crew completed the mission, which typically lasted several hours, saturated in the chemicals. The average Ranch Hand aircrewman was exposed to thousands of times the dose of herbicide that the typical ground-pounder encountered entering a sprayed area later.

When concerns arose about Agent Orange, the Air Force School of Aerospace Medicine's epidemiology division at Brooks Air Force Base in San Antonio began a long-term $120 million study of Ranch Hand personnel in 1978. Using military records, the study's creators tracked down those "cowboys." Of 1,206 eligible members of Operation Ranch Hand, 1,174 agreed to participate. The research protocol for the Air Force Health Study was submitted to various scientific bodies for review before the research began to ensure that the results would be statistically valid.

The first physical examinations on the study participants began in 1982, and were scheduled to take place in the first, third, fifth, tenth, fifteenth, and twentieth years. Since the research started, the men have undergone four rigorous examinations at the Scripps Clinic and Research Foundation in La Jolla, California, and at the Kelsey-Seybold Clinic in Houston, Texas. In addition to physical and psychological examinations, the veterans' past and current medical records are reviewed, as are the medical records of children fathered by Ranch Handers. A control group closely matched for age, race, military occupation, lifestyle, and personal habits was also subjected to rigorous examinations. The only difference between the two groups was that more Ranch Hand participants smoked.

Initial blood serum analysis indicated that the airmen in Ranch Hand had "clear and meaningful dioxin exposure," an average of about forty-seven parts per trillion, with the highest about 617 parts per trillion, or anywhere from 10 to 150 times the exposure of the average American. But according to medical records, none had heavy enough exposure to cause chloracne either during or after their tour of duty.

The first reports showed that ten to fifteen years after their exposure, the health of the Ranch Hand group was normal. No excess cancers. No excess heart disease. No excess alcoholism. The only difference was that Ranch Handers suffered 50 percent more basal cell carcinomas, a type of skin cancer that rarely spreads, is relatively easy to treat, and which is generally believed caused by exposure to the sun, not dioxin. Most newspapers did not run this story, and those that did minimized its significance.

In 1987, the second stage of the study, which examined the health of 1,016 Ranch Handers and 1,293 controls, showed the same results, although the difference in skin cancer between the two groups was decreasing with time as more men in the control group developed carcinomas.

After four examinations and more than a decade of study, the mortality rate of the Ranch Hand group continues to be the same as the control group—*which is actually lower than the mortality rate of the male population of the nation.* The reproductive outcome of the Ranch Hand children is essentially the same as the children of the comparison group. There are no major differences between the two groups with a couple of exceptions. Ranch Handers were found to have slightly more deaths due to digestive system disease attributed to alcohol abuse. (Perhaps that legendary partying finally caught up with them.) And the Ranch Handers recently have shown a small but statistically significant increase in the frequency of diabetes, thus far medically unexplained but perhaps also due to alcohol abuse.[900] Future examinations will look closely to see if that difference is real or a statistical aberration. The study will conclude in the year 2002.

Some veterans' advocates have tried to discredit the Air Force Health Study, arguing that the Ranch Hand group was not the appropriate population to examine. But if any exposure to dioxin caused health problems, those who were most heavily exposed would surely be the first to exhibit those disorders.

But a compelling reason—beyond that of the paranoia many people feel about chemicals of any kind—pushes Agent Orange as the killer of an Army. And, predictably, that reason is money.

The Agent Orange Lawsuits

In 1979, a small group of Vietnam veterans who felt Agent Orange had caused a wide variety of health problems, including cancer, birth defects, and nerve disorders, filed a class-action lawsuit in federal court against Dow Chemical Company, a major manufacturer of Agent Orange. The lawsuit was later expanded to include six other companies that manufactured the herbicide for the American military.

After five years of legal maneuvering and discovery, a trial date for the class-action lawsuit called *U. S. Veterans vs. Dow Chemical* was set for May 1984 in the Eleventh District federal court in Brooklyn, New York, before Judge Jack Weinstein. Just hours before the trial was to begin, the plaintiffs' lawyers and the lawyers for the seven chemical companies settled out of court. Without admitting liability, the chemical manufacturers agreed to create an indemnification fund of $180 million; in return, the plaintiffs agreed that no veteran would ever be able to bring another Agent Orange suit. Both sides, perhaps, were motivated by fear.

The plaintiffs' attorneys were aware of a previous case involving the harmful effects of herbicides 2,4-D and 2,4,5-T, which had been heard by the Supreme Court of Nova Scotia in 1982. The Canadian case had been filed in an effort to prohibit the use of the herbicides to control unwanted weeds in commercial forest areas of Nova Scotia. The scientific evidence regarding the two chemicals presented to the court was in large part the same evidence that would have been presented to Judge Weinstein in New York.

The presiding Canadian judge ruled that no scientific evidence had been presented that the two herbicides harmed humans. "The totality of the evidence in this regard does not even come close to establishing any probability, let alone a strong probability, of risk to health to warrant the granting of injunctive relief," the Canadian judge said. "I am satisfied that the overwhelming currently accepted view of responsible scientists is that there is little evidence that, for humans, either 2,4-D or 2,4,5-T is mutagenic or carcinogenic and that TCDD (dioxin) is not an effective carcinogen, and further, that there are no-effect levels and safe levels for humans and wildlife for each of these substances."

Like his Canadian counterpart, Judge Weinstein's comments after the 1984 settlement in New York made it clear that he saw no scientific support for the allegation that the herbicides caused serious health problems.

"The most serious deficiency in plaintiffs' case was their failure to present any credible evidence of a causal link between exposure to Agent Orange and the various diseases from which they are allegedly suffering—which ranged from baldness to the most serious cancers," Weinstein remarked. "The unfounded and speculative assumption underlying the testimony of plaintiffs' experts had no probative value whatsoever. No rational jury could conclude that exposure to Agent Orange caused the alleged injuries."

Even though there was no hard evidence that Agent Orange caused disease, the chemical companies paid millions of dollars. But settling out of court eliminated the risk of an even larger judgment against them by a scientifically illiterate jury sympathetic to the plight of "victimized" Vietnam vets. This payment was, in effect, a relatively inexpensive insurance premium that equaled less than three day's revenue of the companies involved.

Regardless of the reasons for the defendants' settlements, the lawyers for the plaintiffs still were looking out for their own fees. Victor Yannacone, another lawyer involved in the class action suit, has remarked that Stanley M. Chesley, the lawyer who entered the lawsuit late and negotiated the settlement on behalf of the veterans, was quoted as saying: "Yannacone, you don't understand the purpose of personal-injury litigation. Its purpose is to create a fund to produce attorneys' fees." (Chesley has denied making the comment.)[901]

When the plaintiffs' lawyers asked Judge Weinstein for legal fees totaling $26 million from the settlement, the judge turned them down, giving them only 7.5 percent instead of the 30 to 40 percent contingency fees they usually collect. "I'm not going to reward attorneys for bringing a case that has no merit," Weinstein said. "Given the fact that I find and have found that you've shown no factual connection of any substance between the disease and the alleged cause, I do not believe it desirable to encourage cases like this." Still, Chesley's firm was awarded $525,000 in fees and expenses for less than a year's work.[902]

Agent Orange and the VA

In response to the concerns over Agent Orange, the VA began offering free medical screening to all veterans who served in Vietnam. Slowly, the VA has added various disorders to its list of disabilities eligible for free treatment and monetary compensation. These now include: chloracne, porphria cutanea tarda (a urinary tract disorder), non-Hodgkin's lymphoma, and some soft tissue sarcomas.

Some in Congress have demanded blanket compensation for all veterans who served in Vietnam, regardless of their exposure to Agent Orange or the medical evidence about dioxin. But early in the debate, the Heritage Foundation pointed out the danger of that thinking. "By awarding compensation to veterans, irrespective of the medical evidence, the legislation threatens to undermine the foundation of veterans' benefits: the notion that eligibility for treatment of compensation derives from reasonable medical evidence indicating that the illness or injury was a consequence of military service," said a 1984 Heritage Foundation paper.[903] "Should this standard be undermined, the veteran's compensation system could become as vulnerable to political manipulation as other entitlement programs, allowing claimants with sufficient political clout to win benefits regardless of the merits of their case." And that is what has happened.

By the late eighties, the settlement fund from the class action suit had grown with interest to $240 million. The payoff was divided into two programs. The Agent Orange Veteran Payment Program distributed money directly to veterans or their survivors. In 1989, veterans who filed requests for Agent Orange compensation began receiving payments of anywhere from $256 to $12,800. Families of veterans who died of certain illnesses could receive $340 to $3,400. The other program was the Agent Orange Class Assistance Program, which distributed grants to groups assisting veterans and their families. By 1994, all but $21 million had been claimed.

Today, the VA spends millions of dollars of taxpayers' money on compensation and treatment of disorders supposedly stemming from exposure to Agent Orange—money chasing a myth.

Still, the studies go on. In 1992, the Institute of Medicine undertook a mammoth project to receive testimony and examine all the research to date on Agent Orange. The gargantuan effort involved examining the protocol, sample populations, and methods of virtually hundreds of studies involving herbicides and dioxin. The results were published in 1995 as a hardback book called *Veterans and Agent Orange: Health Effects of Herbicides Used in Vietnam*.[904] Exhaustive, this 789-page report inundates the reader with information. But when it came to the bottom-line, the authors hedged their bets.

"As in science generally, studies of health outcomes following herbicide exposure are not capable of demonstrating that the purported effect is impossible or could not ever occur," the authors said. "Any instrument of observation has a limit to its resolving power, and this is true of epidemiological studies as well. Hence, in a strict technical sense, the committee could not prove the absence of any possibility of a health outcome associated with herbicide exposure. Nevertheless, for some outcomes examined for which there was no evidence consistent with an association, there was limited or suggestive evidence consistent with *no* association, and the committee was able to conclude *within the limits of the current resolving power of the existing studies* that there is no association with herbicide exposure." (Emphasis in the original.)[905]

The report did point out that only some of those who served in Vietnam were exposed to Agent Orange, and of those, the exposure level is usually not known. Regardless of the effect that herbicides might have on cancer incidence, many veterans can be expected to be diagnosed with cancer; and some cancers are so rare that even among all Vietnam veterans there will be too few cases for reliable studies. So far, the epidemiological studies of Vietnam veterans have shown no higher mortality rates due to cancer.

The few exceptions were non-Hodgkin's lymphoma, Hodgkin's disease, and soft tissue sarcoma, which the authors concluded had a positive association with exposure to herbicides. But although the limited studies of Hodgkin's disease in Vietnam veterans tend to show elevated risks, all but one have been deemed statistically insignificant. And, as the report pointed out, soft tissue sarcomas (STS) are very rare. In the twenty years of follow-up of the Ranch Hand group, only one has died of STS; although one was diagnosed with non-Hodgkin's lymphoma, he did not die of the disease. A pretty weak link. Over and over, in looking at various types of disorders, the report concluded, "it is not possible for the committee to quantify the degree of risk likely to have been experienced by Vietnam veterans because of their exposure to herbicides in Vietnam."

Ironically, although the VA has for years claimed that Agent Orange was a disease-causing chemical, it wasn't until 1995 that the department banned the use of 2, 4-D, which contains 50 percent Agent Orange, as a weedkiller at its medical facilities.[906]

Surely, after millions of dollars and a decade of research, if there was an Army "waiting to die," it would have gotten really ill by now. But Vietnam veterans are no sicker than those who didn't go to Vietnam. After all the hullabaloo over Agent Orange, perhaps they can be forgiven if they think they are.

The Myth Marches On

Although Agent Orange was the first mass tort lawsuit, the concept of litigation blackmail is now deeply imbedded in the American legal system. Although there has yet to be published a single peer-reviewed study that supports the central allegation behind the lawsuits involving silicone breast implants—that the implants cause disease—the manufacturer Dow Corning has been driven into bankruptcy.

Journalists perpetuate these medical myths through their own profound ignorance of science, Jon Franklin says. He points to a study done at the Columbia University Graduate School of Journalism, one of the most elite institutions in the profession: 57 percent of the student journalists believed in ESP, 57 percent believed in dowsing (the trade of "water witches"), 47 percent believed in aura reading, and 25 percent believed in the lost continent of Atlantis.[907] In another poll of managing editors at newspapers, Franklin said, two-thirds thought humans and dinosaurs lived at the same time and that there was a "dark" side of the moon on which light never fell. When a reporter for the *New York Times* wrote about the hysteria surrounding dioxin, Franklin saw him come under attack by many other publications, including the *American Journalism Review*.

Franklin says that the public's willingness to believe that the United States poisoned its soldiers in Vietnam with Agent Orange and that scientists aided in the cover-up, marked a sea change in the way Americans think. A profound suspicion and fear of science, government, and technology has been so deeply embedded in our culture, no amount of testing and longitudinal epidemiological studies can ever convince the public that it *didn't* happen, that Agent Orange is no more deadly in the doses most soldiers received than water. The human mind seeks cause and effect. When a young person is struck down by illness, by disease, by abnormality, people look for reasons. As Franklin said: "Apocalypse sells!" And so the Agent Orange myth tramps on, now firmly ensconced in the media and the minds of Americans.

In June 1996, President Clinton announced that his administration was extending veterans' compensation (for Agent Orange) to all Vietnam troops who in the future contract prostate cancer. This broad new benefit —for a disease that as many as one out of five men will contract in their lifetime—was bestowed despite the fact that a National Academy of Sciences panel found only "limited suggestive evidence" that exposure to Agent Orange might be a cause. Even a Department of Veterans' Affairs task force could say little more than "the credible evidence for an association was at least equal to the credible evidence against."

The announcement came while Clinton was facing a flap over his lawyer's attempt to cite the Soldier's and Sailor's Civil Relief Act in his defense against the lawsuit charging sexual harassment by Paula Corbin Jones. His aides defended Clinton's decision, saying that it was based on the merits and was not politically motivated. An editorial in the *Washington Post* called the merits "shaky at best."[908]

After that announcement, VA benefits were extended to the offspring of Vietnam vets who were born with spina bifida, a congenital birth defect. Although there is no evidence of a disproportionate incidence of spina bifida among children of Vietnam veterans, Agent Orange had made the generational leap.

Offering monthly compensation for such a common illness as prostate cancer is yet another example of how politicians pander to the veterans' lobby using the sham Agent Orange issue.

But it is easy to start a myth and almost impossible to stop one, as we're discovering with the so-called "Gulf War Syndrome." The proponents of the "cover-up" theory concerning illnesses afflicting troops who served in Operation Desert Storm evoke the specter of the alleged "cover-up" regarding Agent Orange.

One "victim" of Gulf War syndrome who has been quoted extensively in the press and featured twice on *60 Minutes*, is Brian Martin, head of an activist group called International Advocacy for Gulf War Syndrome.

Martin has testified before Congress, claiming to be afflicted with a long list of disorders, including lupus, which rarely affects men, and daily bouts of heaving up "fluorescent" vomit during physical training after the war.

"Thus we are dealing with a man who insists both that his vomit glows and that he had a squad leader, a platoon leader, and a company commander who heartlessly insisted that he do physical training 'every morning' for ten months, knowing that 'every morning' he would end up in the hospital with IV tubes in his arms," said medical writer Michael Fumento. "Yet extraordinarily, no reporter before me ever relayed this information to his readers."[909]

Fumento pointed out that John Hanchette, a Pulitzer Prize winner with Gannett News Service, has written more articles on Gulf War Syndrome than any other national reporter. But in his coverage of Martin's symptoms, "Mr. Hanchette not only reduced Mr. Martin's symptom list to a handful, omitting the glowing vomit, but also made the dubious but authoritative-sounding claim that the symptoms were confirmed by 'federal medical exams.' Yet Mr. Martin's doctors told me that some of the illnesses Mr. Hanchette says are in their records haven't been experienced by *any* of their Gulf vet patients."

What really happened in the one hundred-day Middle East war? Was it inoculations, chemical weapons, flea collars, combat stress? So far, the studies have shown that the illnesses suffered by gulf vets cover a wide variety of symptoms and medical diagnoses—about what would be expected from a population of about seven hundred thousand troops. In clinical studies of gulf veterans, psychiatric disorders account for the largest category of diagnosis. As Jim Schnabel, a science writer based in London has pointed out, there are hardly any reports of "mystery illnesses" among gulf veterans of other countries. "Perhaps this is because this syndrome hasn't had as much play in the foreign media," Schnabel wrote. "Perhaps another reason is that, thanks to Vietnam and Agent Orange, Americans share a deep belief in the possibility of mysterious and delayed postwar ailments."[910]

Before the Vietnam veteran generation has died, whether of accident, disease, or old age, the price of this paranoia will cost America hundreds of millions of taxpayer dollars.

23

The VVA
Vietnam Victims of America

WHEN Joe Yandle and Eddie Fielding drove up to the liquor store in Boston that June evening in 1972, they were looking for quick drug money. The two men had pulled half a dozen stickups already that day. Yandle, frantic for his next heroin fix, sat in the car as getaway driver while Fielding went inside. Within moments, Fielding came running out and jumped in the car. "Get the fuck out of here!" Fielding yelled. "I just had to shoot the dude!" Behind them, proprietor Joseph Reppucci, a sixty-five-year-old man with two teenage sons, lay dead on the floor of Mystic Liquors.

Fielding claimed Reppucci, who was working two jobs to make extra money for his family, had lunged for the weapon and the gun had gone off. Their take? Only ten dollars. Not to be deterred, Yandle and Fielding robbed several more establishments that night.

Caught, Fielding and Yandle were convicted of murder. Although Fielding pulled the trigger, both men received the same punishment: life in prison without possibility of parole. For years, it seemed Yandle would spend the rest of his life in custody. But that was before the Vietnam Veterans of America (VVA) jumped in, and the "Free Joe Yandle" movement gathered momentum. Stories about Yandle's ordeal in Vietnam — what he had endured and had been forced to do — began to appear in the press.

Yandle claimed Vietnam had been so traumatic he turned to heroin to dull the horrors of combat. Back home, the drug was the only thing that could help him cope with the flashbacks. His desperate need for a fix led to Reppucci's murder. Veterans' advocates made the connection. If Yandle had been properly diagnosed at the time, his defense would have been obvious: PTSD, not recognized officially until 1980. *Boston Globe* reporter

Kevin Cullen and Mike Wallace at *60 Minutes* took up Yandle's cause; Yandle's supporters began pressing the governor of Massachusetts to commute his sentence.

Yandle told reporters a compelling story. This account is drawn from various interviews he has given different publications.

He grew up in a blue-collar family in Charlestown, where he played hockey as a teen. But, in January 1967, to escape an unhappy home life, seventeen-year-old Yandle enlisted in the Marine Corps. Less than a year later, Yandle was sent to Vietnam, where his first assignment was to retrieve bodies still caught in barbed wire. "It was my first taste of death and what war is about," Yandle said.

Assigned to "Alpha Company, 1st Platoon, 9th Marines" (sic)—called "the walking dead" for their short life expectancy—Yandle said that just after the start of the Tet Offensive on January 31, 1968, his company was moved from Con Thien to Hill 861 North, outside the village of Khe Sanh, to relieve the 26th Marines.

According to Yandle's various descriptions of events, he was claiming that he fought in the now-infamous battle of Khe Sanh, a relentless siege by the enemy that lasted seventy-seven days. He and a fellow Marine named Dusty supposedly were standing guard at Hill 861 when all hell broke loose.

"We were up against the 304th Battalion (sic), North Vietnamese," Yandle said. "They spent a couple of days softening us up with rockets and mortars. They came after us about two o'clock in the morning and overran our flank." (Perhaps Yandle was referring to the NVA's 304th Division.)

Yandle could see fellow Marines falling, dying all around him. When Yandle turned and looked at Dusty, his face was gone. But Dusty wasn't dead; he kept trying to jam another clip into his rifle. Yandle tried to drag the man to safety, but a mortar round broke his grasp. Dusty was not a regular in his unit. Although Yandle did not even know his full name, he blamed himself for not saving him.

"I've struggled with the idea of being a coward, even though I understand there was nothing I could do," Yandle said. Hit by shrapnel, which gouged out pieces of his face and backside and knocked him to the ground, littered with the dead and dying, Yandle was finally medevacked out, not knowing Dusty's fate.

"Man, I was scared to death," Yandle told *Boston Globe* columnist Mike Barnicle in February 1994. "I still get shaky today just thinking about it."[911]

Hundreds of Marines died in the battle of Khe Sanh, but thousands of the enemy were killed. The siege added to the legend of the Marine Corps' ability to take on incredible odds and prevail, as had the battles of Tarawa and Iwo Jima a generation before. Today it is considered one of the most important engagements of the Vietnam War. For a Marine to say he was at the battle of Khe Sanh is to convey instantly that he performed heroically and survived the worst carnage of the Vietnam War.

Despite the horror, Yandle volunteered for another year in Vietnam. Still, the fear never went away. To deal with his terror, Yandle started using dope, working his way up from smoking pot to smoking heroin. "I was always waiting to die—waiting for a sniper, a booby trap, a mortar shell—something," Yandle said. "The only way I thought I could deal with it was heroin. I didn't want to think about that boy I thought I had left to die."[912] He later received a Bronze Star Medal for valor for saving another "grunt" to add to his two Purple Hearts.

After Vietnam, Yandle returned to Charlestown with "a fistful of medals" and a three-hundred- to five-hundred-dollar-a-day drug habit. He could not hold a job. His first marriage fell apart. Yandle claimed he wanted treatment for his addiction, but the VA substance-abuse programs had long waiting lists. He and Fielding, both "drug-sick," stuck up Mystic Liquors.

Convicted of the murder of Reppucci and sentenced to life without parole, Yandle continued to use and sell heroin even inside prison. Before his incarceration, he had met Jan Estelle; although they had used drugs together, she sobered up after his arrest. She gave him an ultimatum; quit using drugs or she would never see him again. That got his attention. Yandle went into counseling and kicked his heroin habit. He earned an education while a convict and led programs like Toys for Tots. In 1978, he cofounded American Veterans in Prison and was eventually elected president of the state Council of Vietnam Veterans of America. Before Massachusetts clamped down on programs allowing inmates furloughs, Yandle successfully completed twenty such overnight excursions outside prison walls, working with severely retarded children and doing other good deeds.

Although he was behind bars, Jan showed her support in 1975 by marrying him in a ceremony in a prison chapel. Yandle's wife and his lawyer Joseph Shea then began a campaign to win his release from prison. Those who joined the effort included clergymen who had befriended him, his former substance-abuse counselor, and teachers who helped him earn two college degrees in prison.

Boston Globe reporter Kevin Cullen began writing a series of stories about Yandle's crime and punishment, always referring to Yandle as a "decorated Vietnam veteran." He interviewed Yandle and his wife, who had borne a child conceived during one of her husband's furloughs. Yandle pleaded for his release on the grounds that he should be allowed to go home to his wife, his young son, and stepson. The classic model prisoner, Yandle expressed sorrow for Reppucci's death.

In 1991, the Massachusetts pardons board unanimously recommended the release of Yandle, then forty-six, saying he had worked to better himself. But the prosecutor in the case disagreed.

"The Reppucci family thinks it's outrageous, and I think it's outrageous, that a convicted murderer can be allowed to father children while on furlough, then use it as a mitigating factor to win his release," said Middlesex District Attorney Thomas F. Reilly. "Mr. Yandle wants what he deprived the Reppuccis of—a family life."[913]

Reilly pointed out that Yandle wasn't merely a getaway driver. Before the night Reppucci died, the pair had pulled a two-week string of robberies. The two alternated sticking up stores and driving the getaway car. In some of the robberies, Yandle had pointed a gun at the clerks' heads. And although Yandle had told the press his drug problems began in Vietnam, he actually had started using heroin at age fifteen, before he entered the military.[914]

Gov. William Weld declined to recommend the commutation of Yandle's sentence after meeting with Reppucci's family. Weld had championed efforts to strip prisoners of privileges such as furloughs and was obviously concerned that being perceived as soft on crime could backfire, as had the notorious Willie Horton furlough for former Gov. Michael S. Dukakis's 1988 presidential bid.

But then the powerful national media took up Yandle's case. In February 1994, *60 Minutes* reporter Mike Wallace broadcast a story called "The Getaway Drivers," comparing the cases of Joe Yandle, Vietnam veteran-turned-criminal, and Katherine Ann Power, antiwar protester-turned-criminal.[915] Power had finally surfaced after years underground to face criminal charges in the murder of a Boston policeman killed during a 1970 bank robbery. She had driven the getaway car in that crime, committed to raise money to further the antiwar effort. While Yandle, a two-tour "war hero," was condemned to spend the rest of his life in a maximum-security prison, Power was given only five years, a virtual slap on the hand. Wallace found an unlikely Yandle supporter in police Sgt. Claire Schroeder, the daughter of the police officer murdered by Power and her cohorts.

Yandle contended that his addiction was caused by PTSD, but at a commutation hearing he made little of his war service. "The only thing you could say is that your job as a grunt was to kill people," Yandle said. "I didn't want that in the record. The only thing PTSD connotes is being crazy. People think if you suffer from it, you are permanently damaged psychologically. I didn't want to open that door with the parole board."[916]

But the Vietnam Veterans of America (VVA) was not reluctant to use PTSD as an issue. In May 1994, the board of the VVA took the unprecedented step of asking all its state councils and chapters to encourage their members to lobby Governor Weld to recommend to the Governor's

Council, which has final approval on all such decisions, that Yandle's sentence be commuted. Weld's office was inundated with letters. Still, Weld resisted making a decision until one of his aides visited Yandle in prison and reported back to the governor, recommending mercy.

"While the crime can never be excused, Joseph Yandle went to serve his country in Vietnam," the anonymous aide told the *Boston Globe*. "He returned a scarred man, and he has served a lengthy prison sentence. It is time for the Governor's Council to consider commuting him."

In May 1995, after putting off a decision for four years, Governor Weld, under pressure from the VVA, the *Boston Globe*, and Mike Wallace, finally recommended Yandle's release based in large part on the contention that his Vietnam service and PTSD were at the root of Yandle's crime. Weld mentioned that he was particularly impressed with the large numbers of letters he received from other Vietnam veterans.[917] (Perhaps he did not realize that many of those letters were from incarcerated prisoners who belonged to VVA prison chapters.) His recommendation was approved a month later by the Governor's Council. Shortly after that, *60 Minutes* ran its third piece on the issue, with an update from Wallace on the news of Yandle's commutation.

On October 11, 1995, Joseph Yandle walked out of prison, a free man. Everyone, except the heartbroken Reppucci family, felt good about the decision. After all, Yandle was a decorated war hero who had suffered enough.

But Yandle's true military record is far different from his tale of valorous victimization. His supporters, the VVA, Mike Wallace, and the governor were conned by a man who saw that his only way out of a lifetime in prison was to lie about suffering combat trauma in Vietnam, to play the role of the traumatic war hero numbing the horrors with drugs.

Joseph Russell Yandle wasn't an eighteen-year-old Marine hero thrown into combat in Vietnam, a two-tour grunt picking the dead off barbed wire and desperately trying to rescue a dying buddy at the fierce battle of Khe Sanh. Yandle's military record revealed that he was twenty years old when he was sent overseas in September 1968. The battle of Khe Sanh had ended by March 1968—six months *before* Yandle left his comfortable base in Yorktown, Virginia—so he could not have been at Hill 861 during that terrible fight.

In fact, according to his military record, Yandle *never* served in combat. He *did not* receive a Vietnam Service Medal or Combat Action Ribbon. He *did not* receive a Bronze Star Medal for valor or two Purple Hearts. And he *was not* wounded in combat.

Yandle did not serve *even one tour in Vietnam*, much less volunteer for a second tour. Assigned to the 9th Marine Amphibious Brigade in Okinawa as a supply administration clerk, Yandle worked his way up to administrative manager. After a year of arduous overseas duty filling out forms, Yandle was back in Kansas City, Missouri.[918]

His record does indicate a period of AWOL. Was that related to a heroin addiction? The record doesn't say. If Yandle was using heroin in Okinawa, a huge strategic facility more than a thousand miles from Vietnam, it was not to "dull the horrors of combat," as he claimed. Maybe to spice up the boredom.

Neither Kevin Cullen at the *Boston Globe* nor Mike Wallace at *60 Minutes* ever questioned Yandle's claim that he was at the battle of Khe Sanh nor his insistence that his heroin use stemmed from combat trauma. Their preconceived ideas about Vietnam veterans were so entrenched, they accepted that a Vietnam War hero could be both a drug addict and a murderer. They made Yandle a poster boy for Vietnam PTSD without ever conducting basic journalistic fact-checking and ultimately helped put a convicted murderer back on the street. Even Boston University gave Yandle, a murderer serving life without parole, $17,000 in scholarships enabling him to receive two college degrees. I wonder how much scholarship money the university offered Mrs. Reppucci, struggling to educate her two sons after Yandle and his partner killed her husband? While Joe Yandle enjoys his freedom with his family, Joseph Reppucci's two sons continue to mourn the death of their father.

But Governor Weld did not request Yandle's commutation until the VVA asked its members to write on his behalf. Yandle's case is a classic example of how the VVA—the only congressionally chartered organization exclusively for Vietnam-era veterans—has built a political platform on the continuing assumption that Vietnam veterans are victims not only of the war but also of the Iron Triangle: Congress, the VA, and other veteran's organizations like the American Legion. Even though Yandle was reluctant to proclaim himself a casualty of PTSD, knowing such a claim could not withstand careful scrutiny of his military record, the VVA was not.

The organization's clout in Washington belies the fact that *most* Vietnam veterans are not members of the VVA. Only a tiny percentage of combat vets belong to the organization. How, then, does the VVA set the legislative agenda for a generation of veterans? The answer lies in the politics of victimhood.

The Antiwar Connection

Few of those who belong to the VVA realize that its roots lie in the antiwar movement, beginning with the tiny but vocal group called Vietnam Veterans Against the War, which formed in 1967 after a group of six veterans met while marching in an antiwar demonstration. Involved in most major antiwar activities, the VVAW pushed the agenda that American troops routinely perpetrated atrocities in Vietnam and conducted the "Winter Soldier Investigation" in Detroit in 1971.

"The crimes against humanity, the war itself, might not have occurred if we, all of us, had not been brought up in a country permeated with racism, obsessed with communism, and convinced beyond a shadow of a doubt that we are good and most other countries are inherently evil," said VVAW executive secretary Al Hubbard at the Detroit hearings.[918] (Remember Hubbard? He claimed he was an Air Force officer in Vietnam who was wounded. Not only was Hubbard not an officer, he wasn't wounded, and he was not a Vietnam veteran.)

The organization's main goal, according to cofounder Jan Barry: To make America realize "the moral agony of America's Vietnam War generation," which he said was a choice between "to kill on military orders and be a criminal, or to refuse to kill and be a criminal. One cannot participate in the Vietnam War without being at least in complicity in committing war crimes."[920]

Barry served as a radio mechanic very early in the war (under the name Jan Crumb), before America committed a large number of combat troops. His biggest moral dilemma may have been whether to have his eggs scrambled or fried each morning.[921]

But the VVAW's "Dewey Canyon" demonstrations with camouflage-clad veterans hurling their hard-earned medals at the White House powerfully symbolized the group's philosophy and certainly influenced many who thought that all the men they were seeing were indeed real Vietnam veterans. (At one such demonstration a rumor floated around that only 30 percent of the veterans were Vietnam veterans, probably a good guess. "Only 30 percent of us believe Richard Nixon is president," replied one antiwar veteran.)[922]

This radical group embraced a paraplegic Vietnam veteran named Robert O. Muller, who had been a first lieutenant in the Marine Corps. Muller had served as company executive officer and weapons platoon commander of a company in the 3rd Marines, located in 1968 a few miles north of Cam Lo at Firebase Charlie-2.[923]

In early 1969, battalion headquarters assigned Muller to temporary additional duty with the ARVN, over the protests of his commanding officer, Lt. Col. J. M. Hargrove, who regarded him as a very competent, aggressive, and professional officer and didn't want to lose him. During Operation Maine Craig, Hargrove received word through Regimental Headquarters that Muller had been killed while serving as an advisor to the ARVN. Much later, Hargrove learned Muller had survived but was paralyzed from the neck down. While he led an assault against the Viet Cong, a bullet struck

Muller in the chest and severed his spine. Twenty-three-old Muller woke up on the USS *Repose*, a hospital ship, where he learned his war wound sentenced him to a life in a wheelchair.

Life magazine did a dramatic cover story in May 1970, exposing the terrible conditions in a rat-infested, poorly staffed Bronx VA hospital where Muller was a patient. Photographed with eight other disabled Vietnam vets, Muller has said that he was the only survivor of that group.

Muller is quoted in a book called *The Wounded Generation* about the terrible trauma he endured "in that shithole VA hospital where I was put in bed with fucking drunks and derelicts and degenerates and old fucking has-beens."[924] That experience galvanized Muller's rage into protest.

"I am bitter because I put my faith, my allegiance in my government," Muller said. "I'm bitter because I gave to my country myself, 100 percent, and they used me. They used me as a pawn in a game and for that reason I am bitter."[925]

Although Muller has said his festering anger did not result from his being shot, it's difficult to imagine him joining the antiwar movement had he not been paralyzed. His words are reminiscent of another paraplegic victim of the war, Ron Kovic, who was a gung-ho Marine until he paid a terrible price for his competence and enthusiasm for combat. Both Muller and Kovic *volunteered* to join the military, *volunteered* to go into the Marines, and *volunteered* for combat duty. There were at least seventy-five hundred other equally disabled Vietnam veterans. Few joined the antiwar movement.

While his fellow GIs were still fighting in Vietnam, Muller appeared in the antiwar documentary *Hearts and Minds,* which portrayed the North Vietnamese as underdogs struggling for peace and justice. Muller began working with the VVAW, speaking at protests, staging demonstrations, becoming a spokesman and a very visible symbol for the antiwar movement.

The *Life* magazine piece led to the first of his five appearances on the *Phil Donahue Show.* On TV, Muller effusively praised Jane Fonda: "Phil, I think Jane Fonda epitomizes what being an American citizen is all about. It's involvement with what we're doing as a country, not only domestically but around the world. There is a woman who has taken a position that is based on principle and belief. Whether it's right or wrong is obviously for debate. She has gotten into the process, and she has made a commitment to be a player. That is patriotism. A lot of Vietnam vets will respect the fact that she took a difficult position and she advocated the truth."[926]

Muller participated in antiwar demonstrations staged by the VVAW in Washington, D.C., in the spring of 1971. "Every single Vietnam veteran that I knew was a member of VVAW," Muller said. "I did not know a Vietnam veteran who was not in great sympathy with what we were going through collectively, most notably in public here in '71, with throwing the medals back."

But when he caught political flak, Muller backtracked, saying he had never officially joined the group. John A. Lindquist, a national officer of the VVAW, indicated Muller was indeed a member of the VVAW. "He [Muller] used to belong to our organization," Lindquist wrote in December 1980, "but he resigned when he found out we weren't going to back candidates for government. He had himself in mind at that time, and we feel that he still has his own personal aspirations at heart."[927]

But Muller said he became disillusioned with the antiwar group after the VVAW was taken over by the Revolutionary Communist Party. He fell into despondency and turned to drugs. Meeting his future wife helped him to overcome the debilitating depression and drug addiction. As legislative director of the Eastern Chapter of Paralyzed Veterans of America (PVA), Muller returned to college and earned a law degree.

By 1973, all American combat troops had been withdrawn from Vietnam; two years later, Saigon fell to the Communist North Vietnamese. Muller dedicated himself to fighting for recognition of the rights of Vietnam veterans. But fighting for people to honor and respect Vietnam veterans proved frustrating. In an interview for *V.F.W. Magazine*, Muller cited a Harris Poll as reporting "the majority of Americans believed those who served in Vietnam were suckers and heroin addicts who killed women and babies."[928] (He didn't point out that one of the groups primarily responsible for that image was the VVAW.) The VA's expenditures had shifted in recent years to providing care for nonservice-connected ailments. He wanted to change that, to focus the VA's attention away from its geriatric treatment of the aging warriors of World War II to better care for Vietnam veterans with service-connected disabilities and disorders.

In February 1978, with forty-two thousand dollars in seed money from the PVA, Muller incorporated the Vietnam Veterans' Coalition. A few months later he changed the name to Council of Vietnam Veterans. Established veterans' groups resented the upstart CVV. By the end of the first year, while Muller had generated a lot of press, he had little to show for his efforts at lobbying Capitol Hill.

Wilbur Scott, in the *Politics of Readjustment*, described what happened next. Phil Geyelin, an editor at the *Washington Post*, urged Muller to shift his efforts from a lobbying group to a membership organization. Politicians understand votes; Muller needed to show he could generate support that translated into political clout. Perhaps more importantly, Geyelin recommended that Muller concentrate not only on Vietnam veterans' benefits, but also on the overall "Vietnam experience." That would accomplish two things: It would create a "more sympathetic environment" for veterans of the war and raise the "level of discussion."

So in June 1979, Muller changed the name of his group to Vietnam Veterans of America and began recruiting members, promoting the VVA as "the only national, exclusively Vietnam-era veterans' organization in America." But attracting Vietnam veterans was tough, especially because he continued to identify himself with the antiwar movement and the earlier VVAW. Muller continued to insist that the antiwar group represented the mainstream of Vietnam vets.

"I think it's remarkable that the VVAW still stands to this day, in my opinion, as the only viable representation of the Vietnam veteran community," Muller said in *The Wounded Generation*, a 1981 book by A.D. Horne. "There has not been another organization that has been able to say and speak with any authority that it represents a broad base of Vietnam veterans."[929]

But as Dan Cragg, a Vietnam veteran and contributing editor to the *National Vietnam Veterans' Review*, has pointed out, the idea that the VVAW ever enjoyed a "broad base" of support among Vietnam veterans is a myth. "Out of a total Vietnam-era veteran population of nine million potential members, the VVAW, even at the zenith of its activism, is estimated to have enjoyed a membership of only around seven thousand," Cragg said. How many were actually Vietnam veterans is anyone's guess.[930]

A political consulting firm in New York drew up a VVA master plan in 1979, showing Muller how to build his organization. "Robert O. Muller must meet immediately with Bob Guccione and Hugh Hefner," the plan advised. "These two magazines [*Penthouse* and *Playboy*] can be instrumental in raising funds, developing membership, and increasing public awareness in VVA's efforts."[931]

The consultants also advocated that Muller meet "immediately" with antiwar activists such as Jane Fonda, Jon Voight, and Ed Asner. "Each of these personalities should be asked to indicate the method of assistance they consider most appropriate," the firm said. "They should also be asked to put the VVA in contact with not fewer than five of their colleagues." A major entertainment industry fund-raising event should be scheduled for June 1980 in either New York or Los Angeles, the master plan said. "This could be a musical concert, benefit performance, or cocktail dinner party. The goal must be to raise funds *and* add some glamour to the VVA."[932]

Fonda acknowledged Muller's request with a check for five hundred dollars. (Muller later provided technical assistance on her 1978 film *Coming Home*.) But "considering her unpopularity with most Vietnam veterans, was it proper that the VVA even ask her for the money in the first place?" asked Cragg. Muller's response to those who raised the issue at a meeting of the Buffalo VVA Chapter: "It may seem unconscionable to you. I don't deal with membership. The only function I have with the organization is to raise money."

Few Vietnam veterans knew that Muller lectured on campuses with the film *Heroes*, a "documentary" that depicted Muller and other Vietnam veterans protesting the war by throwing their medals over the White House fence, and film clips comparing combat in Vietnam to fighting in El Salvador.

Sponsored by *Penthouse* magazine, the lecture/film series traveled the country, accompanied by Muller and "combat nurse" Lynda Van Devanter, national women's director of the VVA. The film's left-wing stance on foreign policy and military issues certainly did not represent the attitude of the majority of Vietnam vets. "The filmmakers kept asking me did I feel any guilt over what I did in Vietnam," said David Christian, a decorated Army officer and founder of United Vietnam Veterans Organization, who appeared in the film. "I said, 'What guilt? I'm proud of what my men and I did in Vietnam.'"[933]

By 1981, Muller had emerged as the self-proclaimed national spokesman for Vietnam veterans, despite the fact that his group had only eight thousand members. And of those, most were probably not in-country Vietnam veterans. Membership was open to all "Vietnam-era" vets, as well as their "associates," meaning anyone who wanted to join. Muller was extremely successful in persuading members of the arts and entertainment industry that the VVA was actually helping Vietnam veterans. That year, musicians Bruce Springsteen, Pat Benatar, and the Charlie Daniels Band performed concerts benefiting the VVA. (In fact, for the fiscal year ending April 1982, 77.5 percent of the VVA's revenue came from such special events; membership dues brought in only 1.4 percent of revenue.[934])

Muller brought the confrontational style of the antiwar movement to the VVA, taking stances on issues that inevitably were at odds not just with the VA and Congress but the traditional veterans' organizations as well. The VVA's liberal philosophy on social issues flew in the face of the old-timers' mom-pop-and-apple-pie conservatism. Agent Orange played a key role in winning recruits for the VVA, which demanded that the VA extend a "presumption of service connection" to those claiming chemical exposure as it had to veterans exposed to radiation. "Now, like a hidden bomb on a long-delayed time fuse, Agent Orange diseases are erupting in the bodies of veterans and their children. Liver cancer, chloracne, soft-tissue sarcomas and other hideous diseases," read one VVA fund-raising letter in the 1980s. However, the VVA's demands for funding of readjustment programs while opposing a pension bill for older veterans won the group no allies.[935]

But the VVA succeeded in establishing a fundamental principle of veterans' benefits: When there is a question about a claim, the veteran should be given the benefit of the doubt. That simple concept has given rise to the absurd situation that prevails today with literally hundreds of millions of dollars in benefits going to malingerers.

If Muller had focused on veterans' benefits, the VVA might have become the grassroots organization he envisioned. But he could not resist dabbling in foreign policy. In December 1981, Muller shocked and outraged Vietnam veterans nationwide when he and a delegation from the VVA made a pilgrimage to Hanoi to meet with representatives of the Communist government of Vietnam. The invitation to visit Vietnam came after Muller met in London with the Vietnamese ambassador and told them he wanted the VVA to be the "first delegation of former American troops to return to Vietnam" to address veterans' concerns about Agent Orange and MIAs.

The VVA leader's stated motive was to open a "dialogue" with the Vietnamese Communists about POW-MIA issues and the effects of Agent Orange, to conduct talks on a "veteran-to-veteran" basis. Of course, the Vietnamese used the VVA leaders to promote their own agenda.

Muller helped their propaganda efforts by agreeing to visit the tomb of Communist tyrant Ho Chi Minh, laying a wreath inscribed: "With respect, from the Vietnam Veterans of America." A fifty-minute documentary film of the six-day trip called *Going Back: Return to Vietnam*, was shown on public television stations.

"These are the people we were wasting," Muller said in Hanoi. "A couple of years ago you'd have gotten medals for wasting 'em. Now we're sittin' down and they're feeding us dinner. I like 'em. They're nice people."

Muller talked about how America's schoolchildren are incredibly ignorant of the "facts" about the Vietnam War, then appeared to learn for the first time that American aircraft engaged in dogfights with enemy pilots over North Vietnam. He and another VVA official marveled at the skill of the enemy pilots, their dedication to their cause.

At the tomb of Ho Chi Minh, Muller gushed: "You do have an immediate sense of respect, I can tell you that, too. Cannot help but have respect for the man." To *New York Times* correspondent Bernard Weinraub, Muller marveled: "You visit Ho Chi Minh's two-room wooden-frame house and you see two phones, one to the Army and one to the Air Force, and that's how he carried on the war against us. It knocked me out. It was so incredibly basic."[936]

At a "rap session" in Saigon, Muller told his Vietnamese hosts: "You relate to maybe a square mile of territory, live in these little hooches, take care of your little fields of rice and then all of a sudden out of the skies come these bombs, come helicopters and the soldiers. The violence and insanity of it, that gets me so. It's not even open to discussion. Like we try and argue with these people that there was some legitimacy to our being here. Forget it! You can't look at them in the face and advance that proposition without feeling stupid about it. There's no way you can justify it."

Except perhaps by pointing out that his hosts and their predecessors had massacred hundreds of thousands of fellow Vietnamese because they refused to give up their freedom and religion for the glories of communism. Muller announced at the end of the film that he would use the VVA's clout to make a direct appeal to Vietnam veterans to pressure the U.S. government to give Hanoi foreign aid. "Believe me," Muller said, "I consider myself very much a patriotic American."[937]

Certainly many Vietnam veterans felt differently. "I feel you are a total disgrace!" author Albert Santoli, saying he represented the attitudes of seven veterans' groups, shouted at Muller during a post-trip news conference. Even representatives of the Agent Orange Victims International and the National League of Families of American Prisoners of War and Missing in Southeast Asia denounced the trip. Coast-to-coast, Vietnam veterans were furious that Muller and his cronies had laid a wreath on the tomb of Ho Chi Minh in their name, with no consultation of the VVA membership.

Because the VVA has always been reluctant to permit an audit of its membership statistics, it's unknown how many people resigned from the organization after Muller's homage to Ho Chi Minh. All 250 members of the Contra Costa VVA Chapter of Santa Cruz, California, reportedly resigned. Nineteen chapters were dropped from the rolls of the VVA and its foundation between August 1981 and July 1982.

At a lecture at Niagara Community College in Buffalo, New York, after the Hanoi trip, Muller called the National League of Families an "irresponsible organization." When asked about the Vietnamese accountability for resolving the POW-MIA issue, Muller refused to hold them responsible: "I'm more concerned with our government's accountability and with our government's conduct in understanding what happened and making sure that some of the things that happened in Vietnam don't happen again than I am in terms of the accountability of the North Vietnamese or the Viet Cong."[938]

After all these outrageous quotes and acts, Muller blamed the VVA's difficulties in recruiting on Vietnam veterans' reluctance to band together because of their extreme negative image. "People think we're all junkies, psychopaths, killers of women and children—or worst of all, suckers for getting stuck in a lousy war," Muller said in the May 17, 1982, issue of *Newsweek*. It appears not to have dawned on Muller that Vietnam veterans just did not care to join *his* organization.

Most Vietnam veterans actually felt good about their service. A 1980

Lou Harris poll of Vietnam combat veterans showed that 91 percent were glad they served their country; 74 percent enjoyed their time in the military, and 70 percent would serve again, even knowing the result of America's failed foreign policy.[939]

In 1982, Muller returned to Hanoi to discuss Agent Orange. A Hanoi daily newspaper, announced his arrival this way: "Following the request of the Vietnam Veteran Association of America, a delegation of representatives of that organization led by its president, Mr. Robert Muller, arrived in Hanoi to work with the national committee to investigate the effects of U.S. chemical warfare in Vietnam. The purpose of the delegation's visit is to gather information about the effects of chemical warfare in Vietnam in order to denounce it before public opinion."[940] In effect, Muller was equating the use of the herbicide Agent Orange with the use of deadly chemical weapons—tricothecene mycotoxins or "yellow rain"—then still being used by the Vietnamese against the Cambodians and Laotians.

Determined to practice foreign policy, despite the fact that the VVA obviously has no such mandate, Muller generated controversy when he announced the VVA was getting involved in negotiating with the Vietnamese and Cambodian governments to recover the remains of missing servicemen, a measure the VFW publicly opposed. The VFW national commander wrote Muller asking him to stop his involvement in the POW-MIA issue.

Muller did not limit his meddling in foreign policy to Southeast Asia, sending a VVA envoy to Nicaragua in 1982 at the invitation of the "Nicaraguan Peace Committee." The envoy's mission was to study the relationship between the "Vietnam Experience" and American foreign policy in Latin America. The trip was set up by two officials of the U.S. Peace Council, an arm of the Soviet-front World Peace Council.

The fallout from those efforts and the trips to Hanoi created internal rifts in the organization. Former insiders filed complaints with the IRS charging Muller with failure to report hundreds of thousands of dollars coming into the VVA's coffers from donations by entertainers and Muller's fees from lectures. Santoli and others gave the IRS internal documents showing that from 1979 to 1981, the VVA had reported that its assets were less than ten thousand dollars. But documents filed during the same period with the VA, in an effort to obtain accreditation, the VVA had claimed it had collected more than $250,000. Muller accused Santoli of "betrayal," saying his actions were motivated by a dispute over royalties from the book *Everything We Had.*[941]

"I'm not doing this for the money," Santoli said. "I will give the money to somebody else, but Bobby Muller must be stopped. Every dime he takes, every time he goes on TV or makes a speech he is taking something away from the veterans of Vietnam who deserve more than to finance an organization that exists solely to boost Bobby Muller's ego."[942]

A few years later, Muller and the VVA arranged for a commercial venture between the VVA and Vietnam's Communist government—setting up tours of Vietnam for Vietnam veterans, including "trips for former grunts down the Ho Chi Minh Trail and into the vast tunnel complex from which Viet Cong guerrillas once battled them," according to *Newsweek*. This despite the fact that refugees who valued their freedom were still fleeing the repressive regime and that thousands of our former allies were still interred in slave labor "reeducation" camps.

About the same time, the Vietnamese government announced it might turn over the remains of three missing Americans to the VVA. In March 1984, the National League of Families reported that the family of the only identified individual adamantly opposed the VVA's involvement and had asked Muller to stop interfering. The VFW agreed. "The League's report outlines how VVA's involvement with the Vietnamese government is a clear hindrance to speedy recovery of remains and resolution of the POW-MIA issue," said a letter from Clifford G. Olsen, national commander of the VFW, to the VVA. "I strongly urge you to step aside to permit the Vietnamese to turn over the remains of the identified American to the U.S. government in accordance with his family's request. I further urge you to terminate this hindering relationship with the Vietnamese Communists and to join, in full support, with the National League of Families and the U.S. government's efforts to resolve the issue of the POW-MIA as quickly as possible."[943]

In the early 1980s, the VVA began angling for approval as the only congressionally chartered Vietnam veterans' organization. A 1982 policy statement by the VVA had the audacity to suggest that the continued success of the organization would "have meaning for the more than 2,800,000 American immigrants from Vietnam." The suggestion that I, an American citizen—and the millions of other citizens who served—are "immigrants" from Vietnam was outrageous and just one more absurd example of how out of touch the VVA was from the vast majority of Vietnam vets.

The VFW actively opposed this federal charter because of the statements and actions of the VVA's national executive leadership. "The VVA has done nothing of substantive benefit for the Vietnam veterans that it purports to represent," wrote the VFW's Olsen to members of Congress. "In fact, our Vietnam veterans have been disgraced and dishonored by the VVA's shameful relationship with the Communist governments of Vietnam and Kampuchea [Cambodia]. Their involvement with the Vietnamese Communists also has interfered with the U.S. government's effort to resolve the status of our men still missing in Southeast Asia and has resulted in unnecessary delays in the return of remains. We believe these activities should be condemned not condoned by the Congress.

"We find it necessary to depart from our long-held policy of not commenting on the granting of federal charters to veterans' groups and urge in the strongest terms that you not support the award of a federal charter to the Vietnam Veterans of America Inc. Such an award, in our view, would only bring discredit upon the Congress."[944]

Clearly, Vietnam veterans were not flocking in droves to join Muller's organization. In 1983, after five years of recruiting, out of a potential membership of nine million Vietnam-era veterans, the VVA had only 12,500 members. Nor did the VVA provide services to a sizable number of veterans. In September 1986, the VVA announced its merger with the United Vietnam Veterans Organization (UVVO), a move that could catapult their membership to sixty thousand overnight. But long-standing antipathy between the groups undermined the union. The majority of the UVVO chapters refused to comply with the merger.

Despite the VVA's small numbers and the fact that numerous questions had been raised about how the organization spent its money, in 1986 the Judiciary Committee of the United States Senate endorsed the VVA's effort to become the first—and only—federally chartered group to represent veterans of the Vietnam War.

But whom does the VVA really represent? And are the group's leaders really Vietnam vets?

Was He Just Acting?

Nearly seven hundred members, honorees, and their supporters crowded into the ballroom of the Hyatt Regency in Burlingame, California, for the 1991 Vietnam Veterans of America National Convention, where the organization was holding a gala to honor Vietnam veterans for their work in the arts.

One honoree could not be there to receive the plaque recognizing his outstanding service as a Vietnam vet: Character actor Brian Dennehy, who played Rambo's antagonist in *First Blood*. Dennehy was on location making a movie. He sent a telegram thanking the VVA for its honor. Remember Dennehy? He never served in Vietnam.

But certainly one organization that wouldn't acknowledge a faker is the VVA. When pretenders in their upper ranks are brought to the attention of the group's leaders, they deal with them only reluctantly. (Indeed, the VVA seems to promote wannabes to ever higher levels of responsibility.)

Some years ago, the VFW, faced with membership eligibility challenges, began verifying membership qualifications by requesting service information from the National Archives. However, when the same process was offered to the VVA, Wayne Smith, then membership director, declined to pursue it. (Perhaps he did not want the VVA to check records too closely. Smith is a real Vietnam veteran. But civilian criminal records show he also is a convicted killer.[945] His troubles may even have begun while in the service; he was sentenced to hard labor for going AWOL.[946])

During the eighties, Muller and his board of directors honed their recruitment strategy, focusing on combat vets. "What we find is that the guys who tend to relate more to what we do and what we are as an organization are the guys who saw combat," Muller said. "That's the core group that I think has the greatest potential for us to reach. I've got to tell you there is no comparison between the service of that combat soldier and the one that was never involved."

In a 1979 speech to veterans in Sonoma, California, Muller blasted VA administrator of veterans' affairs Max Cleland, a triple amputee, because he was not wounded in combat. Cleland was a general's aide in Vietnam. (He is now a U.S. senator from Georgia.) "This joker got off a helicopter, saw some grenades standing on the side, went over, picked one up, examined it, and it went off," Muller said. "I think that makes a statement in itself."[947]

Muller is a combat veteran, of course. But while Muller denounced Cleland, he rarely expressed any interest in the true credentials of those surrounding him, invariably veterans with no combat experience or those who had an annoying tendency to exaggerate or lie about their combat experience.

In fact, Muller's first legislative director worked for an amnesty group and had never served in the military. Another early administrator for the VVA, John Terzano, was a former president of the VVAW. He served in the fleet, well away from the ground fighting. Terzano's "combat duties" aboard ship? Storekeeper. You know, the guy who hands out the towels, toothpaste, and toilet paper.

Larry E. Mitchell, the VVA's director of minority affairs in the early 1980s, signed a letter to "brothers, veterans, and former prisoners of war," supporting Muller's trip to Hanoi, referring to himself as a former captain in the U.S. Army 5th Special Forces Group and a former POW.[948]

Mitchell had been hired by the VVA not long after *Time* magazine featured him as an ex-Army officer, former POW, and promising young veterans' activist. In the story, Mitchell claimed the war was just one atrocity after another. In the story that got him the VVA job, *Time* quoted Mitchell: "You never saw the enemy. That was the most frightening part. Even though you shot thousands of rounds, you never saw no bodies but those of your friends." After his first tour in 1965, Mitchell said he returned for a second tour in 1967, this time as a lieutenant assigned to a combat unit.[949]

One day, on a search-and-destroy mission in the Central Highlands, Mitchell's platoon approached a village and began to draw fire. They were searching house to house when a movement caught Mitchell's eye, "I just turned and fired a full clip. Then I looked. It was a woman, maybe eight months pregnant. The burst had taken her right across the midline. The fetus was hanging out." The reporter describes Mitchell's voice as "halting and husky" in the telling of this atrocity. "I was so cold about it. When we were adding up the dead, I counted the fetus. It was a body." (This *mea culpa* makes Mitchell the quintessential baby killer.)

Mitchell contended he spent the rest of his tour lurching between an alcoholic haze, "drinking a fifth a night," and the "surreal alertness of hunt-and-kill missions." At the end of this tour, he was captured by the Viet Cong and held two-and-a-half years. Abruptly freed in 1971, he came home to a hostile New York City, pushed around by police who thought he held up a service station. Fed up, he signed up to fight as a mercenary with guerrillas in Angola. "This time," Mitchell said, "I was the Viet Cong."

It's a fascinating tale, but completely bogus. Military records show that Mitchell was not an officer in the Regular Army, the Army National Guard, or the U.S. Army Reserve in 1967–70. No records indicate he was ever with 5th Special Forces. Nor was Mitchell ever a prisoner of war. (I was unable to locate a military record for Larry Mitchell because his name is common. It was difficult to trace his record with any degree of certainty, but it is easy to document what he didn't do.)

Only after Cragg and others raised questions about his background did the VVA confront Mitchell. Unable to verify his assertions about his war service, Mitchell was fired.[950]

Michael Harbert, an executive with a consulting firm, was a member of the VVA board of directors.

Harbert went to Hanoi with Muller in 1981, where they toured the "U.S. War Crimes Museum" (actually the Central Military Museum), which had exhibits of wrecked U.S. planes and a MiG-21 fighter flown by the Vietnamese. Harbert claimed he was an ex-sergeant who had flown forty-seven missions over Vietnam during 1967 and 1968. Here's the transcript of an exchange between Harbert and Muller in the museum:[951]

"These things," Harbert said, pointing to a MiG-21, "could fly circles around the F4s."

"Get outta here!" Muller said. "How could they have better weaponry than we had?"

"Cause they had better pilots," Harbert said.

"Don't tell me they had better pilots!" Muller said.

"Better pilots, and this is a better aircraft than the F4," Harbert said.

"It's a fighting machine," Muller said.

"Oh, ho, ho!" Harbert replied. "It was more the people in it were fighting machines, too. I mean, really dedicated fliers."

Film of the Hanoi trip portrayed Harbert crying, apparently overcome with emotion, amid the wreckage of U.S. Air Force planes.

"All of the emotion and all of the fear of my forty-seven missions came back in the space of about five minutes," Harbert later said. "It ganged up on me, so to speak. I had fantasies that they were going to take me prisoner because I was in the Air Force and flew in bombing missions over the North." Harbert said the sight of craters in the rice paddies made him realize he was "directly responsible not only for the loss of life but also for the damage to property and everything else that had been put upon those people." As the perpetrator of those war crimes, he had "great difficulty" accepting what he had done. "To see it from a slow-moving plane, as opposed to seeing it at four hundred or five hundred miles an hour, at ten thousand or fifteen thousand feet, was too real to me."952

That day inside the "war crimes" museum, Harbert said, had caused him to flash back to Vietnam. "Suddenly I was back on my last combat mission after the Long Binh [sic] Bridge, over the Red River," Harbert said. "I closed my eyes, and I was right back in the AWACS, directing an air strike. And the MiGs are in the air, and the surface-to-air missiles are after us. And hearing the explosions."

Remember Harbert? He was a major fixture of the VVAW who claimed he was a combat pilot. He wasn't.

Thomas A. Bird, cofounder of the VVA and a member of the board of governors, also flew with Muller to Hanoi in 1981 and led a subsequent trip to Communist Vietnam. Bird was featured as one of the Vietnam veterans in *Everything We Had*, the book by Santoli that was a project of the VVA. You will recall that Bird told Santoli that he and eleven other men were captured in November 1985 by the North Vietnamese when the NVA overran his unit in the Ia Drang Valley. But he fabricated the story about being a POW. Challenged, Bird 'fessed up and resigned from the VVA board, but still retained a position as head of a VVA committee.

The VVA's official explanation for Bird's fable was hilarious. "Because of his response to the provocative actions of some war protesters, Tommy entered a program to help with his readjustment," read a statement by Rick Weidman, membership services director of the VVA, published in *Stars and Stripes*. "He helped himself through this period by creating an account of being held as a POW for thirty hours."953 (The "readjustment program" probably was a group therapy session at a Vet Center!)

Struggling to build up their membership, the VVA broadened their recruitment strategy, seeking new members in prisons, sweeping into their ranks ex-cons and criminals, drug addicts and alcoholics. In an attempt to be allowed to raise charitable donations by appealing to federal employees, the VVA's legislative liaison John Terzano wrote this explanation of those served by the organization: "Many receive treatment, care, rehabilitation, and counseling and would be described variously as criminals, released convicts, persons who abuse drugs or alcohol, persons who are otherwise in need of social adjustment and rehabilitation, and the families of such persons." In his plea, Terzano repeated—and inflated—the Vietnam veteran myths.

"In World War II, the average age of American combat troops was twenty-six, and average exposure to enemy fire was six weeks. In Vietnam, a U.S. soldier's average age was nineteen, and combat exposure was fully fifty-two weeks. Vietnam combat veterans have a higher arrest rate and are the most frequently convicted. The suicide rate for Vietnam veterans is historically higher than for their nonveteran peer group. Between seven hundred thousand and eight hundred thousand are suffering from PTSD." And on and on and on.

Why? In the new corollary to the "squeaky wheel gets the grease" adage, he who is dysfunctional gets the cash.

In 1982, VVA director Bobby Muller took up the cause of Peter Krutschewski, an oil executive who had been a helicopter gunship pilot in Vietnam. Charged with smuggling fifty-seven thousand pounds of marijuana and hashish, Krutschewski pleaded not guilty, arguing that Vietnam "delayed stress syndrome" forced him to turn to crime. A federal judge found he made $1.5 million smuggling and invested some of the money in his oil business, Fairway Petroleum, which just happened to be a major financial contributor to the VVA in 1981. Muller referred to Krutschewski as the "Audie Murphy of Vietnam," a man who had set an exemplary example for his fellow veterans. But Krutschewski, a good helicopter pilot, bore little resemblance to World War II hero Murphy. An adrenaline junkie, Krutschewski loved the thrill and the money of smuggling dope. Although the jury found him guilty, and he was sentenced to serve ten years in prison and pay a sixty-thousand-dollar fine, lobbying efforts by the VVA paid off. The judge ruled him eligible for a reduced sentence and immediate parole consideration.[954]

My experience with the VVA did not begin until I was involved with raising money for the Texas Vietnam Veterans Memorial. I had refused to join because many of the leaders of the VVA had been active in the VVAW, and I felt they had betrayed the rest of us. I don't know *any* Vietnam veterans who joined or were even slightly sympathetic to the VVAW. GIs were dying in Vietnam while these men were doing the propaganda work of the North Vietnamese. Although they claimed they were not against the troops, just against the war, their chanted rhetoric of "bring our brothers home" rang false. Why did they put on the Winter Soldier "investigation," projecting the image of American combat soldiers committing atrocities as a standard policy?

When I was fund-raising for the memorial, I often received information about the VVA, including membership rosters, from friends around the country. I obtained the membership roster of a VVA chapter from a friend from another state. I had assumed all members of the VVA were veterans who served in Vietnam. With a shock, I realized immediately in looking at one list that about one-third were not Vietnam veterans and didn't claim to be. According to the VVA's membership rules, you don't have to be a Vietnam veteran to be a full-fledged voting member. You could have been a clerk who never left Fort Bragg. In addition to Vietnam-*era* vets, associate members did not even have to be in the military, just sympathetic to the cause.

To figure out just what percentage of that chapter were really Vietnam veterans, I sent off for the military records of those who claimed they had been in Vietnam. About 20 percent were pretenders. Only about half of the VVA chapter's entire roster were actually Vietnam veterans. And of those who had been in Vietnam, many had inflated their service, claiming medals and status they had not earned.

Remember Ann Funck and one-time chapter president Joe Testa of the Dallas chapter? Testa had a criminal record, indicative of the VVA's active recruitment of jailed inmates. The VVA is the only federally chartered veterans' service organization that extends the privileges of its membership to felons and those with dishonorable discharges. They make it especially easy for those in the government's custody: Dues are waived, and the application form even has a place to put your inmate number. Each year, the VVA recognizes the "incarcerated member of the year."

One ex-convict who rose in the VVA's ranks was John Woods, who founded the first "incarcerated" chapter in Texas while an inmate at the Federal Correctional Institution in Texarkana on drug and firearms charges during the 1980s. After his release from prison, Woods became an outspoken advocate for troubled Vietnam veterans who claimed they had been driven into crime by PTSD and Agent Orange. He testified on their behalf before the U.S. Senate Veterans' Affairs Committee and the U.S. House of Representatives, speaking of his own wartime trauma, which had led to his term in prison.

In 1988, Woods was appointed executive director of the Vietnam Veterans' Resource and Service Center (VVRSC) in Dallas to help veterans obtain VA benefits and services. A story about Woods in *The Dallas Morning News* called him a "ballpoint guerrilla," a "point man in near-daily firefights," the "Vietnam Veterans of America's answer to Rambo in Texas."[955]

"His motivation comes from personal experience," wrote reporter Steve Levin. "Four times he has had surgery to remove tumors he believes are related to his exposure to the defoliant Agent Orange in South Vietnam as a member of the Coast Guard." The only thing vets needed to do at Woods' center was show an ID with a picture and a DD-214. "That's the only hoops we make people jump through," Woods said.

The impression is that Woods is a dedicated Vietnam vet who has suffered much. But Arthur John Woods' military record revealed something else. After dropping out of the eleventh grade, Woods served in the Coast Guard as a seaman apprentice for one year, from October 1970 to October 1971. The closest he came to the Vietnam War was a short cruise to Honolulu.[956] Although Woods signed up for a four-year tour, he was discharged early, declared "unsuitable for military service" after repeated abuse of drugs aboard the Coast Guard cutter *Mellon*.[957]

Woods progressed from smoking marijuana to taking hits of LSD, then became addicted to heroin, suffering three separate drug overdoses during his one year of military service. He has been arrested fourteen times for charges including homicide, robbery, assault, theft, stolen vehicle, dangerous drugs, and weapons violations, and convicted of three felonies. His first arrest and conviction came when Woods traded VA medication to an undercover police officer in San Antonio shortly after his release, against medical advice, from a VA medical center in Houston.

"You glorify these guys, but you never check them out," I told *Dallas Morning News* reporter Bruce Tomaso, who had come to interview me about the memorial. "What do you mean?" he asked. I showed him Woods' record. Tomaso wrote a copyright story in the paper exposing Woods, who admitted he had allowed people to assume he was a combat veteran.[958]

After his exposure, four members of the center's board of directors resigned, including Howard Swindle, an assistant managing editor of *The Dallas Morning News*. Swindle is a Vietnam veteran and the author of a nonfiction book about an ex-soldier haunted by PTSD who goes on a bank-robbing spree. (Ironically, the previous executive director of the Vietnam Vets Resource and Service Center was Steve Nail, a Vietnam veteran, convicted kidnapper, bank robber, and VVA member. A judge allowed Nail to leave jail early after lobbying by VVA members, who claimed combat stress drove him to commit crime.)

After the initial uproar and his *mea culpas*, Woods began to backtrack, saying he had never told people he was a Vietnam veteran. "There is no difference between combat veterans and good people," Woods told the *Morning News*. "Just because you're a combat veteran doesn't make you a good advocate. I'm probably the most effective advocate in this country."[959]

Although Woods attempted to dodge responsibility, the week of the newspaper story a fund-raising letter from the center had called Woods a "Vietnam veteran, U.S. Coast Guard." Woods had told Teri Butler, the widow of a dead serviceman and a board member of the center, that he was a Vietnam veteran. And Woods had told others variously that he had been a—you guessed it—"secret assassin" in Vietnam and that he had been on "secret" missions on Coast Guard boats taking the herbicide Agent Orange up the Mekong Delta.

Woods was scheduled to testify as an expert witness that week at a congressional panel meeting on the operation of the Dallas Veterans Administration Medical Center. If the reporter had not obtained his record, would Woods have come clean?

But the disclosure of his military record didn't slow his rise in the VVA. A few months after Tomaso's report, Muller sent Woods on a "mission of mercy" to Vietnam. Incredibly, the state leaders of the Texas VVA "cleared" Woods of allegations he lied about his war record, apparently because no one came forward with a formal complaint, and he had not falsified his record to obtain employment or government benefits.

Woods' ascent into the upper echelons of the VVA was only stalled a short time. In 1991, Muller designated Woods the VVA's National Liaison to Veterans Incarcerated. (One of Woods' predecessors was fellow convict Wayne Smith.) In the ultimate irony, Woods was elected president of the Dallas VVA Chapter, and for a ceremony on Memorial Day in 1994 he played host to General Westmoreland. Some VVA members insist Woods suffers tumors caused by exposure to Agent Orange. It must have occurred in Honolulu harbor.

The VVA's willingness to embrace anyone who agrees with the "Vietnam-vet-as-victim" agenda has created some strange situations. In 1993, three candidates ran for national VVA president. One, former membership chairman Wayne Smith, had been convicted of manslaughter after killing a man in Rhode Island. (His record also indicated disciplinary action while in the military.) Another candidate campaigned from his cell at the Ohio State prison, where he was incarcerated for murder. And there was incumbent James L. Brazee Jr., a lawyer whose only Vietnam experience consisted of twenty-one days of temporary duty assignment on a legal case.[960]

What a Hobson's choice: Two convicted killers and a lawyer.

Before the election, a technicality disqualified Smith, who had been fired from his job at the VVA and had gone to work at the National Vietnam Memorial Fund.[961] That left the incarcerated vet and Brazee. Not too incredibly, the lawyer was reelected VVA president. One of Brazee's first moves after being reelected was to form a national VVA task force on homeless veterans. "Homelessness is *one of the most important issues facing VVA*, as it cuts across many of the things concerning veterans," said Randy Barnes, the head of the new task force. (Emphasis added.)[962]

The Missouri VVA chairman during this period of time, Chris Davis, was also a convicted felon, serving time for committing a series of robberies with a group of "young, black, angry Vietnam vets" in 1971. In his last robbery, a police officer was killed. Davis received two life terms, plus fifty-seven years. In prison, Davis became involved in the VVA and eventually was chosen head of the Missouri delegation. Meetings of the state VVA board had to be held in the prison.

This is the best the VVA can do? The VVA's aggressive agenda pushing Vietnam veterans as victims ensures that most real Vietnam veterans look elsewhere for their advocates. What's astonishing is that congressmen and other political leaders take them seriously at all.

The Future of the VVA

In 1990, the VVA boasted 35,820 members, less than 1 percent of Vietnam-era vets. That year, they counted 13,165 terminated members, most likely people who failed to pay their dues, a mere twenty dollars a year. The next year, an independent audit indicated that the organization's financial picture was bleak, with expenses far outstripping income. The VVA fought tooth-and-nail for its congressional charter, contending that they had an agenda far different from the World War II veterans' agenda. They are right. These other veterans' organizations have enough pride not to let criminals and those with dishonorable discharges become members. They don't want to be sullied by association. Not so the VVA.

Here's a perfect example of the VVA's desperation: Vietnam veterans had a lower rate of dishonorable discharges than did their peers who did not go to Vietnam. But that's not the message the VVA sends the public. To build their audience, one of the VVA's primary objectives is to help less-than-honorably discharged veterans like Joe Testa get their "bad paper" upgraded so they can obtain VA benefits. The military had standards and adhered to them. You either maintained them or you were disciplined. If you did not fulfill your end of the bargain, why should you profit?[963]

The VVA's roots in the antiwar movement and its continuing obsession with victimization is reflected in its house organ, *Veteran* magazine. Few issues go by without a story about Agent Orange, PTSD, POW-MIAs, homelessness, suicide, unemployment, incarceration, disability pensions, mistreatment by the VA, and demands for more services. Dysfunction creeps into every subject, even something like coverage of the tenth anniversary of the fall of Saigon.

"For years, veterans were ignored as unwanted relics of a lost war," wrote Myra MacPherson in the May 1985 issue of *Veteran*. "There was a moment in America's conscience—since the opening of the memorial in 1982—when the public seemed ready to understand veterans and those among them who had real problems—posttraumatic stress disorder, Agent Orange, job and benefit concerns, VA health care."[964] Are those issues real for most Vietnam veterans? Aside from VA health care, I don't think so.

The VVA's litany of victimization has continued until now. Even true believers tire of this diet of dreariness. "I'm compelled to admit that I'm sick and fed-up of reading about PTSD," wrote subscriber Stephen D. Lutz of Portage, Michigan, in a letter to the editor for *Veteran* magazine. "Why not do some articles on everyday, nearly normal people? I'm sure if one looked hard enough, everyday, family oriented 'Nam veterans could be found. I'm tired of reading about drugs, alcohol, and suicide."

And Kenneth R. Furhman of Buffalo, N.Y., who described himself as a career airman and a three-tour veteran of Vietnam: "Month after month, all I read in your news magazine is PTSD trouble, alcoholism, substance abuse, rage, guilt, pain, and 'damn the VA.' Let's have fewer articles on the pain and suffering of those who couldn't hack it, and let's have more about those who could—or else how will the rest of us know that we're still 'normal'?"

"The only people who seem to get into print are those negative people who snivel about their Vietnam experience," wrote another. "What about the vast majority who served our country in Vietnam and who came home and resumed our lives, and we did not blame everything that happened to us on Vietnam?"

Feeding at the Tax Trough

In January 1993, the *VVA Veteran* magazine reported that its legal services department had helped a Vietnam veteran whose disability claim had been denied—because his record showed no combat medals, no combat MOS, and no significant "stressor"—to obtain compensation. The veteran claimed his PTSD had been triggered by the death of his platoon sergeant, who had been killed during an ambush, but he could remember him only by his nickname. The VVA service representative reviewed the names on The Wall and found a sergeant with a similar name. Thanks to the VVA, the VA accepted the man's death as a stressor and granted the veteran's compensation request.

Was the veteran's claim real or bogus? It's impossible to tell, but thousands of pretenders have stories like his.

In 1994, the VVA succeeded in introducing into Congress an amendment to a comprehensive legislative crime package that requires penal authorities to identify veterans among the incarcerated to give them the benefits they deserve.

"We won," declared John Woods, the Texas pretender who noted that the VVA had pushed for the measure since he became liaison to incarcerated vets three years earlier.[965] Will the prisons actually obtain military records and verify that the inmates who say they are veterans truly are entitled to benefits? Since the VVA does such a poor job at this for its own leaders, careful screening seems unlikely. The potential costs, not to mention the security problems, of having guards taking prisoners who claim they are veterans to VA facilities to be interviewed for their benefits are enormous, as are the expenses incurred by the filing of claims and attempts to upgrade disability ratings. And for those who need help in pursuing those benefits, the VVA provides aggressive advocacy through its Legal Services Program.

In 1995, the VVA issued a series of resolutions at its annual convention. Included were: a call for more money to be spent on Agent Orange research; a study of female Vietnam veterans' health problems (i.e., PTSD, Agent Orange); employment training for Vietnam vets; inclusion of veterans in affirmative action programs; obtaining discharge upgrades for Vietnam veterans; the repeal of laws limiting veterans' benefits to incarcerated criminals; setting up a VA diagnostic and forensic unit to provide an evaluation, at the request of a veteran or his counsel, of any role PTSD may have played in a veteran's criminal conduct; extending Vet Center outreach activities to incarcerated vets; and a general expansion of the Vet Center program.

"Hundreds of thousands of veterans and their families suffer severe psychological and emotional difficulties related to the veteran's military service," said the plank on PTSD and the VA. It cited the absurdly inflated figures of the National Vietnam Veterans' Readjustment Study and proclaimed the VA's response "woefully inadequate." The VVA resolution called for—of course—more money to treat these fictional vets by expanding the specialized inpatient PTSD units and PTSD clinical teams.[966]

Even within the system, however, there's been criticism of VVA's approach to treating PTSD. "As a clinical psychologist specializing in the treatment of posttraumatic stress disorder of Vietnam veterans, I find Muller's suggestion of encouraging veterans to get together and talk about their war experiences or problems of readjustment irresponsible and criminal," said Dr. Tom Williams in a letter to the editor of Newsweek in 1982. "These leaderless groups tend to exacerbate PTSD rather than alleviate the symptoms and have, in my opinion, led to suicide, family disruption, and further isolation of the veteran from society."[967]

The VVA, while claiming to be the spokesman and friend of Vietnam veterans, has actually done more damage to their public image than any other group in America. They've made patriotic and honorable men appear to be whining welfare cases, men who have no pride in their service, and men who can find nothing better to do with their lives than bellyache about what an immoral government did to them.

But for every so-called Vietnam vet wearing dirty fatigues and a "thousand-yard stare," myriad real Vietnam veterans have gotten on with their lives. Most Vietnam-era veterans, those with honorable discharges and no criminal records, refuse to join VVA.

They have voted with their feet and found groups where the agenda is support for all veterans and not a propaganda campaign for "victims." By 1982, seven hundred thousand Vietnam-era vets had joined the American Legion and five hundred thousand had joined the VFW. Vietnam-era vets now make up 25 percent of the membership of each of the three big veterans' organizations: The Disabled American Veterans (DAV), the VFW, and the American Legion.

By 1995, three Vietnam veterans had served as commanders of the VFW. That same year, after fifteen years of recruiting, the VVA had only about forty-five thousand members. The VVA's number of actual Vietnam veterans is probably twenty-five thousand or fewer.

Considering their history, the VVA leaders' contention that they represent the views of the majority of Vietnam veterans borders on the farcical. They don't, and the probability is they never will. But the press, politicians, and policy makers will continue to pay deference to the VVA in the mistaken belief that they represent true Vietnam vets.

24

America's Wailing Wall

We few, we happy few, we band of brothers,
For he to-day that sheds his blood with me
Shall be my brother.

WILLIAM SHAKESPEARE
King Henry V
Act IV, Scene III

SINCE ITS DEDICATION in 1982, the Vietnam Veterans Memorial in Washington has become our national wailing wall, a place of pilgrimage for veterans and nonveterans alike. The most popular memorial in the nation, it averages more than ten thousand visitors a day.

Some come alone to weep, to seek a measure of comfort, to confront their memories. Others, at the urging of counselors who advise them not to face The Wall by themselves, band together with other veterans to make the journey. They huddle in clusters, some quietly remembering and recognizing their friends' sacrifices, others seeking solace for wounds that occurred long ago but feel as raw as if they happened yesterday. Many leave bits of themselves—flowers, medals, boots, records—items as diverse as the people who died and those who lost men they loved.

The long, wing-shaped wedge of black granite, engraved in chronological order with the names of the 58,209 dead, is a powerful acknowledgment of the price paid by those who served in Vietnam. Anyone who was in-country knows his or her name could have been engraved in that implacable stone. But like the rest of the history surrounding Vietnam veterans, The Wall is a fusion of reality and myth, of truth and fantasy. Its importance lies in the names of those who died serving their country when so many others abstained. Unfortunately, around that essence of strength, respect, and honor a facade of sham and fakery has risen—the inevitable pigeon droppings on a monument to sacrifice.

The Dead

The story told by the black chevron of The Wall begins at panel 1E, located at the bottom of the hill where the wings meet, with the name Maj. Dale R. Buis. Buis, an Army advisor to the ARVN 7th Infantry Division at Bien Hoa, was in the mess hall watching a movie—*The Tattered Dress*, starring Jeanne Crane—on July 8, 1959, when six Viet Cong attacked with machine guns. Buis and Master Sgt. Chester Ovnand were killed, as were two Vietnamese guards and a small Vietnamese boy whom Buis had befriended.[968]

First Buis, then Ovnand. Thousands of names march across the reflective black granite out to the far-flung ends of the V, then come back and end on Panel 1W, with the names of Richard Rivenburgh, Walter Boyd, Andres Garcia, Elwood E. Rumbaugh, and Richard Vande Geer, the last to die in 1975 retaking the USS *Mayaguez*. The first and the last, the Alpha and the Omega, the story of a generation of men who died not for philosophy or ideology as much as they died for each other.

Because the killed-in-action are listed in chronological, not alphabetical order, visitors hoping to find a particular person can check the electronic guide at the entrance or locate one of the telephone book-sized directories listing all of the names alphabetically.[969] But it's impossible to tell from the listing or tracing the name with your fingertips the cause of each person's death. A helicopter crash, a firefight, a grenade attack?

The Meaning of the Wall

The curious collection now kept at the federal Museum and Archeological Regional Storage (MARS) began not with an official government program but by an impromptu decision by a park maintenance foreman named Tony Migliaccio. He and his crew were cleaning up after the dedication in 1982 when someone called Migliaccio over. The worker pointed to some unusual items—a Purple Heart, a scuffed pair of jungle boots, a framed photo of a '55 Chevy, a teddy bear—that had been left among the litter at the base of The Wall. They obviously had been placed there deliberately, perhaps by grieving family members or former soldiers in homage to their buddies in arms. Migliaccio was touched and told his crew to save the items. Those really weren't the first items to be left at the memorial. On the day that the foundation was poured, a man came along and tossed his dead brother's Purple Heart from Vietnam into the wet concrete to be buried there forever. Now people come at all hours of the day and night. They take rubbings of names. They take pictures. And they leave small bits of themselves behind.

Crosses, earrings, a locket, panties, love letters, baby pictures, a high school yearbook. The crew picks it up, and does the same the next day, and the next, stowing the objects in cardboard boxes in a tool shed. After two years, the National Park Service made the collection official. Every day, volunteers wearing white gloves now pick up and catalog each item, marking it with the date and a number denoting the order in which it is retrieved.

Dog tags, medals, C-ration cans, baseballs, a ceremonial sword, a gun belt, a VA-issue wooden cane, hundreds of pairs of combat boots. The items are stored in a cavernous warehouse where the temperature is kept at a constant 66 degrees. Dark plastic sheets cover the windows to keep out damaging sunlight. The volunteers pick up everything that is left that is not perishable, no matter how seemingly trivial or incomprehensible, and seal it in a plastic bag, acid-free boxes, or airtight metal cabinets for posterity. Some items, such as an old M-14 rifle, its wooden stock carved with the words "USMC, Chu Lai, 1965-66," seem instantly significant to the collectors.

Many visitors leave photographs. One of a dead VC. Snapshots of men in fatigues. A picture of a pretty young girl, signed "To Dad."

Notes, poetry, prayers, letters to dead buddies, apologies, songs. "If anyone knew or served with my brother in the Marine Corps . . ." They write to express their feelings, to say what they've longed to say for years, to put down burdens carried long distances. "I miss you so much! I've looked for you so long. How angry I was to find you here—although I knew you would be. I've wished so hard I could save you." They write to remember and they write to forget. "Cary, I'll always love you. Linda."

A McGovern button, a Dionne Warwick album, a roll of GI toilet paper, a can of beer, a tiny bottle of Jack Daniel's. The items are logged into a government computer and preserved forever. Although the collection is not now open to the public, it may some day become the focus of a Vietnam War museum. The unorthodox store of items is unique in that no "expert" has decided what should be included, just a long stream of visitors, mourners, and pilgrims, coming to pay their respects. And it shows profoundly that the country needed a place to honor its dead from the war.

But even though The Wall has provided a measure of dignity and honor to Vietnam veterans, it also has come to possess the strange ability to magnify negative stereotypes.

It started with the proliferation of nearby booths selling Vietnam memorabilia, T-shirts, books, and kitsch like Montagnard bracelets and dog tags. Shoppers could buy illicit unit patches, replicas of medals, and T-shirts with macho messages: "Rangers—Mess with the Best—Die like the Rest." Belt-buckles with a replica of Hart's "Three Soldiers" statue. Stained glass windows, baseball caps, posters, bandanas, whiskey decanters, engravings, clocks, coins, even rectangles of black granite engraved with the name of your choice. There seemed to be nothing that could not be turned into a souvenir of The Wall.

A group of Ohio veterans who called themselves "Freedom Birds" wangled permission from the Vietnam Veterans Memorial Foundation to sell T-shirts bearing the image of the "Three Soldiers" statue. They sold thousands of eight-dollar shirts, but the VVMF made no money from it. "It just didn't turn out right," said Jan Scruggs, the veteran who instigated the creation of the memorial. "These guys came to D.C., used the copyright and sold sixty thousand [shirts], and we never got one red penny."[970]

Some quick-buck hustlers didn't even bother to sell anything. They turned The Wall into an opportunity to panhandle. Men in military garb put out large glass jars adorned with a photograph of a POW in a cage and a sign that read, "Help Bring 'Em Home!" The implication was that donations would help bring home still-captive prisoners of war. People routinely dropped spare change and dollar bills in the jars as if donating to a church collection to feed the hungry. Other panhandlers in fatigues just put out a can and solicited donations for whatever.

The commercialization of The Wall created a carnival atmosphere around what was meant to be a somber monument to sacrifice, like money-changers in the temple. Some protested the presence of these private commercial outlets on government property. The vendors fought back, claiming that banning them would violate their rights to free expression—slogans on T-shirts, apparently.

But most were concerned about their right to make money. In her 1995 book on POWs, Susan Katz-Keating estimated that Ted Sampley, chairman of The Last Firebase, an activist POW-MIA organization, earned nearly $2 million over three years from his T-shirt concession near the memorial. He kept his costs low by using volunteer workers.

The National Park Service finally managed to limit the flea-market atmosphere. When a 1995 court order from U.S. Judge Harold Greene ruled that the only items that could be sold are books, newspapers, pamphlets, buttons, or stickers pertaining to a political cause, workers drove dump trucks onto the Mall and collected all the tables and wooden stands abandoned by the merchandisers. Sampley accused the Park Service of deliberately attempting to "get rid of the veterans who set up vigils around the memorials. They know these vigils are financed through the sale of T-shirts." Sampley's Last Firebase and six other groups challenged Greene's ruling and succeeded in getting another federal judge to declare the ban on T-shirt sales unconstitutional. So a handful of booths remains, protected by the First Amendment.[971]

Inevitably, like a shining light attracts bugs, The Wall has become a veritable beacon to all the whiners and wannabes who see it as a place of validation for their exaggerated and fabricated stories of heroism and trauma. Veterans band together and journey to Washington to confront their memories. Remember "The Wall Within"? Dan Rather brought his crew of embellishers to Washington to stand before the memorial and offer up contrived stories of grief.

Counselors began bringing groups of PTSD patients to The Wall. *Life* magazine did a cover story for November 1992 on one such group pilgrimage. "The Wall is like a Rorschach test," said one VA psychologist quoted in the story. "It allows people to project onto it whatever it is that they're carrying around." While I'm sure some of these pilgrims are hurting vets, many others are fabricators, if my research involving PTSD programs at the VA is any indicator.

There are so many wannabes that, inevitably, they end up not only in newspaper and magazine photographs, which are ephemeral, but also in picture books that will last for generations. One example: On page thirty-eight of the 1993 *Life* book called *The Wall: A Day at the Vietnam Veterans Memorial*, is a poignant photograph of a medal-bedecked man in jungle fatigues, weeping on a group-therapy bus trip to the memorial. He's wearing the Silver Star, Soldiers Medal, master jump wings, air assault badge, and a mixed bag of other medals and decorations from the Army, Navy, and Marines. He's clearly a phony, as his jumble of awards reveals. He's even wearing a "V" device (signifying valor) on his Meritorious Service Medal, a decoration given only for noncombat service![972]

One of the most famous images of the post-Vietnam veteran world adorns the cover of an acclaimed coffee table book called *The Wall*, a collection of photographs by Sal Lopes and sixteen other photographers. The picture by Seny Norasingh shows Gary Gene Wright Jr. wearing fatigues and a boonie hat festooned with decorations and unit pins, his chest adorned with Vietnam ribbons, his hand pressed against the black granite wall. Atop one shoulder sits Wright's small son, who is kissing one of the engraved names. It is the name of Wright's father, Col. Gary G. Wright, an Air Force pilot missing in action in Vietnam. The image is of one Vietnam vet reaching out to another, a son grasping for his dead father, a grandson paying homage to the grandfather he will never know. (This powerful image, which is sold in photography galleries, also appeared on the cover of a *Newsweek* issue called "A Celebration of Heroes" on July 6, 1987, and on ABC's news program *Nightline*.)[973]

Gary Gene Wright Jr.'s story is told in *Shrapnel in the Heart*, a book by columnist Laura Palmer. Only ten when his father was shot down over Vietnam in 1967, Gary followed in his dad's footsteps. The book states that he joined the military when he was seventeen. Stationed off the coast of

Vietnam on the USS *Oriskany* from 1973 to 1975, loading ordnance onto planes and working on maintenance, Gary suffered back injuries that partially disabled him. On one arm he wears an MIA bracelet; on the other, a watch that says "Vietnam Vet and Proud of It."[974]

Col. Gary Wright, the father, was indeed shot down over Vietnam and remains missing in action. But after a search of military records, I could find no indication that his son, Gary Gene Wright Jr., was a Vietnam vet—or indeed ever served at all in the military.

Another photograph in *The Wall* was taken by Sal Lopes of Sgt. Major Charles "Chuck" Eatley, often called the sergeant major or the "grandfather" of The Wall. A veteran not only of Vietnam but also of World War II and Korea, "Top" Eatley began hanging out at the memorial after its creation.[975]

As a former Green Beret and highly decorated Vietnam veteran, Eatley commanded much respect from younger vets, who often told reporters they served with him during the Vietnam War. During events at The Wall, Eatley usually wore "tiger" fatigues, a green beret, and his numerous medals in miniature: Silver Star, Bronze Star Medal, CIB for three wars, and two Purple Hearts among them. Eatley told how he served in the Phoenix Program and did clandestine operations for the Green Berets and with MACV in Vietnam. But Eatley's story was especially tragic; he said he had lost his legs to cancer "caused" by Agent Orange in Vietnam.[976]

But even that couldn't get him down. "If they gave me back my legs, I'd go back again," Eatley said in another book called *The Vietnam Veterans Memorial*, a photography book by Michael Katakis.[977]

By virtue of hanging around the memorial, Eatley became a spokesman for Vietnam veterans, interviewed by reporters on issues like flag burning and Agent Orange. He organized the first twenty-four-hour vigils on the Mall to remind visitors to the memorial of those still missing in Southeast Asia. At his death in 1989, Top Eatley was mourned as the tough, battle-hardened sergeant major Green Beret by an audience full of veterans wearing green berets, black berets, blue berets, and jungle hats. A fund was created to memorialize him that in part will be used to honor the top Green Beret of the year.

But, according to his military record, Eatley was not the Green Beret war hero he portrayed himself as. Eatley did serve in three wars: the African-Italy campaign in World War II, Korea, and Vietnam. But while he received a Combat Infantryman's Badge and a Purple Heart in Korea, his record shows no Silver Star or Bronze Star Medal for valor from any war. (Nor did he have CIBs or Purple Hearts from World War II and Vietnam.)

In none of those periods was Eatley a Green Beret. Eatley was not Special Forces qualified nor did he serve in the Phoenix Program. Eatley

served in Vietnam for ten months during 1963–1964 in an advisory group—
well before America's full combat participation and long before Agent
Orange was heavily sprayed. But his close identification with The Wall
made him a spokesman for suffering Vietnam vets.[978]

Facing The Wall, another popular picture book about the Vietnam
Veterans Memorial, featured several phonies, including previously mentioned Bill Callahan, the "Green Beret" who ran from Florida to New York
to publicize the issue of POW-MIAs. (He was really a carpenter in
Vietnam.) Another photograph depicted a man named Anatol Konenenko
on crutches, wearing a cap emblazoned with the word Vietnam and a
kitschy Vietnam T-shirt that reads: "Rice Paddy Daddy Sez. Willie Peter
Will Make You a Believer. Sin Loi NVA."[979]

The caption described Konenenko as a POW-MIA activist from
Philadelphia known as "Gimp" because both of his legs were paralyzed in
Vietnam in 1969, and noted that "Willie Peter" or white phosphorous, is
"the most dreaded antipersonnel weapon of the war. A single shell throws
thousands of phosphorous particles; the burn cannot be extinguished."
The words leave the impression that Konenenko was paralyzed by
white phosphorous while serving in Vietnam. But according to the military
record of Anatol Kononenko (his name was misspelled in the book), he
served 11 months in Vietnam as an infantryman. The record shows no
Purple Heart for wounds; the only physical disability noted was a dislocated elbow.[980]

Inevitably, on Memorial Days and Veterans Days, photographers gravi-
tate to The Wall or its smaller replica, which travels around the country, for
appropriate images they can send to the nation's newspapers. The more
the veterans at the memorial represent the stereotypes—homeless, traumatized, crazy—the more likely they are to be photographed. On
Memorial Day, 1996, *The Dallas Morning News* ran a huge front-page color
photograph of a man named Roni DeJoseph, a scraggly veteran dressed in
a boonie hat and fatigues, weeping in anguish, his face pressed to the black
plexiglass surface of The Wall's traveling replica. "Reflecting on the
Fallen," was the headline, and the caption described DeJoseph as a U.S.
Marine veteran who fought in Vietnam. The Associated Press photograph
appeared in numerous other papers around the country.

But DeJoseph, from Brooklyn, New York, was wearing a camouflage
BDU jacket first issued in 1983, a commercially-manufactured bush hat, a
full-color 3rd Marine Division patch not authorized for wear after 1947 (and
not worn on camouflage in any case), and a pin for the 1st Reconnaissance
Battalion, part of the 1st Marine Division, not the 3rd. A search of military
records revealed that DeJoseph had never served in the Marine Corps or
any other branch of the service.[981]

Unfortunately, The Wall's perpetuation of the stereotypes will continue. A program called "In Memory" now allows friends and family to memorialize veterans who served and returned home "only to die as a result of their tour in Vietnam"—meaning they died of Agent Orange exposure or "physical or emotional wounds suffered in Vietnam." The program places information about the veteran, including photos, letters, and information about their service, in a leather bound volume at the memorial. It also places a copy of that information in a sealed envelope to be left at the memorial, where it will be collected by a Park Service Ranger and placed in the permanent archive. Now that should be a fascinating collection.

The Contrition "Rag"

In recent years, the *mea culpas* have trickled in as people reexamine their beliefs about the Vietnam War and its veterans. The most notorious is by Robert McNamara, one of the architects of the war, in his book *In Retrospect: The Tragedy and Lessons of Vietnam*, who 'fessed up that the whole thing was a big mistake.

But perhaps the most astonishing act of repentance is that of folksinger "Country" Joe McDonald, who has created a memorial to the war dead from Berkeley, California, the site of perhaps some of the most vehement anti-Vietnam War demonstrations in America.

Country Joe and the Fish performed the "I-Feel-Like-I'm-Fixin'-to-Die Rag," which became a singalong antiwar ditty. McDonald wrote the catchy song in 1965; an estimated five hundred thousand sang it along with the band at Woodstock in 1969. "One, two, three, what are we fighting for?" His tune became an anthem for a generation, all the more powerful because of its upbeat melody and rhyming lyrics.

The oldest of three children, McDonald came from a family of radical activists. His parents named him after Joseph Stalin. He was living in Berkeley during the war when the City Council voted to stop saying the Pledge of Allegiance at its meetings, and antiwar demonstrators chanted "Ho, Ho, Ho Chi Minh." A building near the Berkeley campus was adorned with the words "Go Ho Chi Minh," and it was not unusual to see someone on the campus waving a Viet Cong flag. But McDonald, a twenty-three-year-old Navy veteran when he wrote the song, later had some regrets, particularly over such lyrics as, "Be the first one on your block / To have your boy sent home in a box."

In the 1980s, McDonald went public with the fact that he was a veteran (although he did not serve in Vietnam), and began thinking about reconciliation. He was troubled by the hypocrisy he saw when Berkeley activists collected money for the leftists in Central America but ignored the homeless in Berkeley's parks. In 1995, McDonald told *People* magazine that after the war ended, he realized his sympathies lay with the veterans who were treated with such contempt by activists in Berkeley.

"Blaming soldiers for war is like blaming firefighters for fire," McDonald said. "There are no bad guys. There are just victims on both sides."[982]

To make amends, twenty years after the end of the war, McDonald kicked off a campaign to raise money for a memorial to the twenty-two KIA from Berkeley. The monument, which McDonald designed, includes an interactive computer site with photos and memorabilia of those who died. It will also include a bronze plaque to be mounted in the city's Veterans' Memorial Building. "The healing is still going on," he said at the unveiling of a temporary plaque. "It may take the rest of our lives."

Everyone was surprised when Country Joe's memorial triggered no protest marches. But some things will never change. Berkeley being Berkeley, a letter writer compared honoring Vietnam veterans to honoring Nazi soldiers.

Visiting the Wall

The controversy surrounding the building of the Vietnam Veterans Memorial left me with a great sense of frustration. The monument's creation hasn't changed America's perception of Vietnam veterans. Although it signaled long-due honor, the memorial also magnified the negative clichés. Because America has never united around a single vision of the Vietnam War, the controversy over The Wall became just another firefight in an unending battle.

I had no burning desire to see the memorial. While cochairman of the Texas Vietnam Memorial, I had for months researched the names on The Wall. I had gained a familiarity with their backgrounds and history that would make a visit to the memorial anticlimactic. One of the strange outcomes of my research was the discovery of twenty-five names of men on the Wall, like Timothy Honsinger, who actually had survived the war. Another seven were fictitious; they turned out to be misspellings of real names already on The Wall. Finding these thirty-two errors actually made me feel as if I had lessened the grief of America by an ounce.[983]

In the spring of 1989, when I visited the White House to coordinate President Bush's attendance at the dedication of the Texas Vietnam Veterans Memorial, I finally visited the site. Almost reluctantly, I walked from the White House to the Mall simply out of a sense of honor and duty.

Although sunny, the spring day held a slight chill. A handful of booths and tents manned by those selling T-shirts, books, and bumper stickers clustered around the entrance to the site. Some tables featured large glass containers proclaiming, "A POW Never Has a Good Day," beside photos of American POWs supposedly still suffering in North Vietnamese prisons.

The jars were stuffed with one-dollar bills. Behind the tables were bearded, longhaired men garbed in camouflage fatigues adorned with combat patches. To the visitors walking past, they were just one more proof of the stereotypes of Vietnam veterans.

A slow stream of people flowed down the concourse. A thin slice of The Wall started to my left and, as we walked, the granite panels appeared to grow. It seemed as if we were walking into a sepulchre, as the lines listing the names of the dead multiplied from panel to panel. Wisps of cumulus clouds floated in reflection over the lustrous black granite. A graying woman knelt in grief in front of one black panel. A man in uniform held up a teenager so she could rub a pencil over a paper held against an engraved name. Another man simply stood, rooted to the ground, tears streaming from his eyes. Strangely, it was as if their very real sorrow was simply part of the show at America's grimmest tourist attraction.

The uniformed Park Service personnel did their jobs quietly and efficiently, helping individuals find certain names, assisting with rubbings, reciting the history of The Wall. But those whose names are etched there seemed incidental to the process. Somehow, even the respectful silence seemed out of place. We were the rock and roll generation. Those songs of the times blared out all over Vietnam and kept us believing there was a world out there to which we would return, a world where we could claim our piece of the future. I think those on the memorial would vote for rock and roll background music, not silence.

Watching the ebb and flow of those visiting The Wall that day, dropping their change in the jars, buying the T-shirts, I realized that most of them didn't see what I saw. When those tourists looked up at the imposing black granite, they saw an almost endless list of America's victims.

I wished for the courage to stop the hushed parade and shout: "Victims? These men and women weren't victims. They were the best and brightest of my generation. They were warriors, patriots. Some of them were heroes!

"You see that name right there? That's Bobby Stryker. When his Army unit was ambushed he threw himself on a Claymore mine just as it detonated, saving six of his wounded friends. They gave him the Medal of Honor.

"And this one? This is Jimmy Cruse, a corpsman who ran under enemy fire to give aid to two wounded Marines. They gave him the Navy Cross. He was one of the Navy's finest. And here is Greg Clement. Greg carried two wounded men to safety only to die as he tried to rescue a third. He was awarded the Army's Distinguished Service Cross.

"Here! Tiago Reis. He died while repeatedly dragging his wounded buddies to safety. He brought honor to the Corps that awarded him the Navy

Cross. A Marine who lived and died knowing the meaning of 'Semper Fidelis.'"

"This one? William Pitsenbarger, the first enlisted man to be awarded the Air Force Cross. Bill volunteered to be lowered from a rescue helicopter to aid wounded on the ground. He helped recover nine injured men. When the enemy attacked, Bill Pitsenbarger elected to stay with the remaining wounded rather than leave with the helicopter.

"Victims? Heroes! Ladies and gentlemen, heroes!"

On The Wall are the names of 148 men who were awarded the Medal of Honor, 43 who were awarded the Air Force Cross, and 176 who received the Navy Cross for heroism; and 385 of those who died were awarded the Army's Distinguished Service Cross. Thousands were posthumously awarded the Silver Star or Bronze Star Medal for valor. These men wouldn't want our pity; they would want our respect.

But, of course, I didn't shout any of this, but simply observed in silence the ritual procession as it passed the mute names. These true heroes of America remain virtually anonymous while thousands of liars and phonies, celebrated in the media, have stolen the valor of the dead to claim as their own.

Unfortunately, we live in a world in which sometimes black is white, falsehood is truth, and cowardice is courage. These dead men and women exist in a state of conspicuous oblivion. Their names are all there, but nothing else. The honor and esteem afforded other generations of America's warriors have been denied them. No one spotlights their courage or tells epic tales of their valor and sacrifice.

Yet men like Dave Goff of Syracuse, New York, can blacken their reputations by claiming he was an assassin who killed political officials and was subjected to electric shock treatments by military superiors. The reward for his lies was to have a congressman pin a Distinguished Service Cross on his chest and others to honor him as "Veteran of the Year."

Or Stephen Banko of Buffalo, New York, who pilfered the heroism of Walter Bahl, killed in action on December 3, 1968. Banko has been proclaimed the "most decorated Vietnam veteran of New York State" by the press, while Bahl is simply a name on the Wall.

Or Professor Larry Cable of the University of North Carolina, who created a lucrative lecture career by fabricating a story of serving as a Marine in Vietnam. The more than fourteen thousand Marines whose names are etched in granite would not find his charade flattering.

Or Benjamin Ricciardi of Newark, New Jersey, whose forged heroism allowed him to receive extra civil service points, advancing him ahead of his peers. He now enjoys a comfortable retirement in Florida, bought by the bravery of those killed in action.

Or William Northrop of Oklahoma City, who received acclaim in books and the press for his courage at Lang Vei, supposedly decorated with a Silver Star defending those casualties listed on Panels 37 and 38 E. If these dead could bear witness, they would loudly proclaim, "No, no, he wasn't with us!"

Or Ronald Murphy of Las Vegas, a phony POW who enhanced the presidential campaign of a Vietnam War resistor, rewarded with dinners at the White House, and heralded as a hero in the press. The stark black panels carry the names of sixty-four POWs who died in captivity. Their children now pay taxes that are forwarded to Murphy for his VA disability compensation, payments facilitated by a grateful president.

And finally, Joseph Yandle of Massachusetts, a drug addict, robber, and convicted murderer, glorified by Mike Wallace and the *Boston Globe*. They were all too willing to broadcast Yandle's lies of having fought courageously at Khe Sanh. These journalists should read the more than 262 names of men killed in the fighting at Khe Sanh and contemplate the insult and denigration they heaped on these heroes by mentioning Joe Yandle's name in the same breath.

The Wall is many things to many people, but for me, it is not a place where I found much truth and justice.

I'm often asked, "Why are you doing this?" Most who ask do not understand and consider my research a compulsion that has no meaning. I have no good "sound bite" answer. I know only that I am compelled to draw attention to the truth about Vietnam veterans and to do otherwise would be a violation of some personal code of conduct.

The first question is usually followed by a second. "What do you want?" I have thought long and hard about that one. Do I want something? The question is usually asked in such a tone that I know the inquisitor considers my "irrational" behavior to be the prelude to a demand—a demand like a kidnapper or a terrorist might make. Why would I have gone to all this trouble if there was no demand? On reflection, I know they are right. I do want something.

I want an apology.

In the past, America has expressed regret for diplomatic indiscretions and military blunders. It has asked forgiveness of Native Americans and enemy and friendly nations. Three and a half million Americans—our Vietnam veterans—have been unjustly disparaged, ridiculed, and offended: An expression of regret is appropriate.

I want an apology from America to every man and woman who served in Vietnam and to every family who lost a son or a daughter, an apology not for their service or their loss, but for the indifference and disrespect heaped on Vietnam veterans, living or dead, after the war.

The dictionary defines an apology as a "statement of acknowledgment expressing regret or asking pardon for a fault or offense." Yeah, I want an apology from America. Not for myself but for Connie Wright, who lost two sons. And for Allen Clark, who lost both legs at Dak To. And for Tim Honsinger, who kept protecting his friends even after his arm had been blown off. And to the family of Harry Horton, who knew before it happened that he would give his life for America. An apology not for their loss —there is no compensation for that—but for the lack of honor and respect, both of which were owed but withheld.

It would be nice if the apology was in the form of a joint resolution of Congress and read by the President of the United States at the Vietnam Veterans Memorial on an appropriate date. It matters little if the president is a war hero or a draft dodger. Others could be invited to participate: Jane Fonda, Tom Hayden, and Joan Baez come to mind, as do members of Congress and the Joint Chiefs of Staff of the period, not to mention Ramsey Clark and Robert McNamara.

Present to accept the apology could be the living Medal of Honor recipients from Vietnam. Guests of honor could be the next of kin of the men and women on The Wall.

For my part, I hope on that day to be on a picnic with my family in the park, kicking a soccer ball with my daughter, enjoying my freedom as an American, bought and paid for by men better than I, some of whom I once had the privilege to know.

Postscript

Stolen Valor is my personal memorial to those who gave their lives in Vietnam. May it stand as a beacon of truth about them and all those who fought in the war as long as there are men who honor courage, fidelity, and patriotism.

B. G. BURKETT
DALLAS, TEXAS

Heroes of the Vietnam War

"War is an ugly thing, but not the ugliest of things; the decayed and degraded state of moral and patriotic feeling which thinks nothing worth a war, is worse. A man who has nothing which he cares more about than he does about his personal safety is a miserable creature who has no chance at being free, unless made and kept so by the exertions of better men than himself."

JOHN STUART MILL

Appendix I: Medal of Honor
Appendix II: Distinguished Service Cross
Appendix III: Navy Cross
Appendix IV: Air Force Cross

Prisoners of War

Appendix V: U.S. Military Prisoners of War Returned Alive

• Posthumous Award

Appendix I

Medal of Honor: Vietnam War

- Adams, William E.
- Albanese, Lewis
- Anderson, James, Jr.
- Anderson, Richard A.
  Anderson, Webster
- Ashley, Eugene, Jr.
- Austin, Oscar P.
  Baca, John P.
  Bacon, Nicky Daniel
  Baker, John F., Jr.
  Ballard, Donald E.
- Barker, Jedh Colby
- Barnes, John Andrew, III
  Barnum, Harvey C., Jr.
  Beikirch, Gary B.
- Belcher, Ted
- Bellrichard, Leslie Allen
  Benavidez, Roy P.
- Bennett, Steven L.
- Bennett, Thomas W.
- Blanchfield, Michael R.
- Bobo, John P.
  Bondsteel, James Leroy
- Bowen, Hammett L., Jr.
  Brady, Patrick Henry
- Bruce, Daniel D.
- Bryant, William Maud
  Bucha, Paul William
- Buker, Brian L.

- Burke, Robert C.
- Capodanno, Vincent R.
- Caron, Wayne Maurice
- Carter, Bruce W.
- Cavaiani, Jon R.
  Clausen, Raymond M.
- Coker, Ronald L.
- Connor, Peter S.
- Cook, Donald Gilbert
- Creek, Thomas E.
- Crescenz, Michael J.
- Cutinha, Nicholas J.
- Dahl, Larry G.
- Davis, Rodney Maxwell
  Davis, Sammy L.
  Day, George E.
- De La Garza, Emilio A.,
  . Jr.
  Dethlefsen, Merlyn Hans
- Devore, Edward A., Jr.
- Dias, Ralph E.
- Dickey, Douglas E.
  Dix, Drew D.
- Doane, Stephen Holden
  Dolby, David Charles
  Donlon, Roger Hugh C.
  Dunagan, Kern W.
- Durham, Harold
  Bascom, Jr.

- English, Glenn H., Jr.
- Estocin, Michael J.
- Evans, Donald W., Jr.
- Evans, Rodney J.
  Ferguson, Frederick
  Edgar
- Fernandez, Daniel
  Fisher, Bernard Francis
  Fitzmaurice, Michael
  John
- Fleek, Charles Clinton
  Fleming, James P.
  Foley, Robert F.
- Folland, Michael Fleming
  Foster, Paul Hellstrom
  Fox, Wesley L.
- Fratellenico, Frank R.
- Fournet, Douglas B.
- Fous, James W.
  Fritz, Harold A.
- Gardner, James A.
- Gertsch, John G.
- Gonzalez, Alfredo
- Graham, James A.
- Grandstaff, Bruce Alan
- Grant, Joseph Xavier
- Graves, Terrence
  Collinson
- Guenette, Peter M.

Hagemeister, Charles Cris
- Hagen, Loren D.
- Hartsock, Robert W.
- Harvey, Carmel Bernon, Jr.
Herda, Frank A.
- Hibbs, Robert John
- Holcomb, John Noble
Hooper, Joe R.
- Hosking, Charles Ernest, Jr.
Howard, Jimmie E.
Howard, Robert L.
- Howe, James D.
- Ingalls, George Alan
Ingram, Robert R.
Jackson, Joe M.
Jacobs, Jack H.
Jenkins, Don J.
- Jenkins, Robert H., Jr.
Jennings, Delbert O.
- Jimenez, Jose Francisco
Joel, Lawrence
Johnson, Dwight H.
- Johnson, Ralph H.
- Johnston, Donald R.
- Jones, William A., III
- Karopczyc, Stephen Edward
- Kawamura, Terry Teruo
Kays, Kenneth Michael
- Kedenburg, John J.
- Keith, Miguel
Keller, Leonard B.
Kelley, Thomas G.
Kellogg, Allan Jay, Jr.
Kerrey, Joseph R.
Kinsman, Thomas James
Lambers, Paul Ronald
Lang, George C.
- Langhorn, Garfield M.
- LaPointe, Joseph G., Jr.
Lassen, Clyde Everett
- Lauffer, Billy Lane
- Law, Robert D.
Lee, Howard V.
- Lee, Milton A.

- Leisy, Robert Ronald
Lemon, Peter C.
- Leonard, Matthew
Levitow, John L.
Liteky, Angelo J.
Littrell, Gary Lee
Livingston, James E.
- Long, Donald Russell
- Lozada, Carlos James
- Lucas, Andre C.
Lynch, Allen James
Marm, Walter Joseph, Jr.
- Martini, Gary W.
- Maxam, Larry Leonard
McCleery, Finnis D.
- McDonald, Phill G.
McGinty, John J., III
- McKibben, Ray
- McMahon, Thomas J.
McNerney, David H.
- McWethy, Edgar Lee, Jr.
- Michael, Don Leslie
Miller, Franklin D.
- Miller, Gary L.
Modrzejewski, Robert J.
- Molnar, Frankie Zoly
- Monroe, James H.
- Morgan, William D.
Morris, Charles B.
- Murray, Robert C.
Nash, David P.
- Newlin, Melvin Earl
- Noonan, Thomas P., Jr.
Norris, Thomas R.
Novosel, Michael J.
- Olive, Milton L., III
- Olson, Kenneth L.
O'Malley, Robert E.
- Ouellet, David G.
Patterson, Robert Martin
- Paul, Joe C.
Penry, Richard A.
- Perkins, William Thomas, Jr.
- Peters, Lawrence David
- Petersen, Danny J.
- Phipps, Jimmy W.
- Pierce, Larry S.

Pittman, Richard A.
- Pitts, Riley L.
Pless, Stephen W.
- Port, William D.
- Poxon, Robert Leslie
- Prom, William R.
- Pruden, Robert J.
- Rabel, Laszlo
- Ray, David Robert
Ray, Ronald Eric
Reasoner, Frank S.
- Roark, Anund C.
Roberts, Gordon R.
- Robinson, James W., Jr.
- Rocco, Louis R.
Rogers, Charles Calvin
- Rubio, Euripides
- Santiago-Colon, Hector
- Sargent, Ruppert L.
Sasser, Clarence Eugene
- Seay, William W.
- Shea, Daniel John
- Shields, Marvin G.
- Sijan, Lance P.
- Sims, Clifford Chester
- Singleton, Walter K.
- Sisler, George K.
- Skidgel, Donald Sidney
- Smedley, Larry E.
- Smith, Elmelindo R.
Sprayberry, James M.
- Steindam, Russell A.
- Stewart, Jimmy G.
Stockdale, James B.
- Stone, Lester R., Jr.
- Stout, Mitchell W.
- Stryker, Robert F.
Stumpf, Kenneth E.
Taylor, James Allen
- Taylor, Karl G., Sr.
Thacker, Brian Miles
Thornton, Michael E.
Thorsness, Leo K.
Vargas, M. Sando, Jr.
- Warren, John E., Jr.
- Watters, Charles Joseph
- Wayrynen, Dale Eugene
- Weber, Lester W.

Wetzel, Gary George
- Wheat, Roy M.
- Wickam, Jerry Wayne
- Wilbanks, Hilliard A.
- Willett, Louis E.
Williams, Charles Q.
- Williams, Dewayne T.

Williams, James E.
- Wilson, Alfred M.
- Winder, David F.
- Worley, Kenneth L.
Wright, Raymond R.
- Yabes, Maximo
- Yano, Rodney J. T.

- Yntema, Gordon
Douglas
Young, Gerald O.
- Young, Marvin R.
Zabitosky, Fred
William

Appendix II

Distinguished Service Cross: Vietnam War

Abernathy, Joe V.
Abood, Edmund P.
Adderly, Tyrone J.
Adkins, Bennie G.
Aguirre, Jimmy
- Alamo, Gabriel R.
Allen, George C. D.
Allen, Hulon C., Jr.
Allen, Lawrence W.
- Allen, Terry D., Jr.
Alley, Lee B.
- Alvarado, Leonard L.
Ames, Lawrence J.
Anagnosotopoulos,
    James
Anderson, Anthony C.
- Andrade, Kenneth S.
Archibald, Robert S.
Arment, Dixon G.
Armstrong, Lester
Armstrong, Robert E.
- Aronhalt, Charles E., Jr.
- Arsenault, Richard R.
- Bahl, Walter T.
Bahnsen, John C.
Bailey, Henry M., Jr.
Bailey, Otis J.
Bailey, Stephen F.
Baker, Eldon L.
Baker, Walter E.

- Baldwin, Norman E.
- Ballard, Mel R.
Banks, Charles J.
Barela, Felix R.
Bargewell, Eldon A.
- Barker, Jack L.
- Barnard, Richard G.
Barnes, Brice H.
- Barrios, James
Barrow, Robert H.
    (USMC)
Bartley, Julius I.
- Baxter, Bruce R.
Baxter, William P.
Beach, Martin
- Beagle, Howard E.
- Bechtel, Herbert J.
Beckstrom, Donald R.
- Beers, Jack B.
- Bell, Christopher
- Bell, Lewis D.
Benedict, Calvert P.
- Bender, Gernot
Benson, John O.
Bercaw, William E.
Bernardo, Peter R.
Bessinger, Terry B.
Bias, Ronnie E.
Bieri, Leon D.
Biggin, Donald M., Jr.

Binkoski, Victor R.
- Birchim, James D.
Birmingham, John
Bissell, Norman M.
Blair, John D., IV
- Blakely, William
Blanford, Raymond V.
Blanks, Boots C.
Blaz, Juan
Bledsoe, William H.
Bleskan, Ralph J.
Blunt, Stanley A.
Boedecker, Billy E.
Boice, Craig H.
Bolin, Harold E.
Bondsteel, James A.
Borck, Keith R.
Boris, Timothy D.
- Borja, Domingo R. S.
- Borowski, John C.
- Bosworth, Richard L.
Bott, Russell P.
Bouchard, Thomas D.
Bowers, Charles J., Jr.
Bowlin, Calvin J.
- Bowman, David W.
- Bowman, Joseph B.
Boyd, Charles N.
Boyington, Jerry J.
Bradsell, Peter

- Brady, Joseph M.
Brady, Patrick H.
- Bragg, Fred G., Jr.
Branham, Steven R.
Braun, Conrad D.
Breed, Rolla M.
Breland, Artis, Jr.
- Brenner, Kenneth J.
Brewer, Garry D.
Brindel, Charles L.
Bridges, James A.
Briscoe, Charles H.
Brock, Bobby Q.
Brock, Don E.
- Brophy, Daniel R.
- Brown, Charles
- Brown, Fred E.
Brown, Herman Lee
- Brown, Joel A.
Brown, Lester W.
- Brown, Richard
- Brown, Robert A., II
Brown, Walter R.
- Brucker, Leslie L., Jr.
Buchanan, Michael D.
- Bullard, Karl L.
Bullard, Thomas E.
Burbank, Kenneth R.
- Burke, Kevin G.
Burnett, William D.
- Burns, Darrell E.
Burrow, George D.
Bustamante, Manuel C.
- Butts, Lonnie R.
- Byrd, Guy A.
Cain, Jerry A.
Calhoun, Johnny C.
- Caliboso, Robert M.
Campbell, Darrell W.
- Campbell, Keith A.
- Canavan, Martin J., Jr.
Caristo, Frederic J.G.
- Carlson, Gary W.
Carmichael, Patrick S.
Carnes, Edward L.
Carpenter, Michael F.
Carpenter, William S., Jr.
Carr, Donald F.

Carrizales, Daniel A.
- Carroll, Robert H.
Carter, Dennis H.
- Casey, Maurice A.
Cartherman, Robert T.
Cavazos, Richard E.
  (OLC-Kor.)
Cecil, Gerald T.
Chamberlain, Craig R.
- Chamberlain, Henry
Chapman, Leslie A.
Charles, Paul D.
Chatelain, Ronald M.
Chedester, David G.
- Chervony, Eddie E.
Childers, Richard L.
Childress, Raymond D.
Chirichigno, Luis G.
- Chock, Linus G. K.
Chrietzberg, Randolph T.
Christian, David A.
Cizmadia, Joseph
- Clark, Douglas M.
Clark, Michael D.
- Clay, Charles E.
Clayton, Jerry D.
Clemmons, William A.
- Clement, Gregory C., Jr.
- Cline, Paul H.
- Cobb, Hubbard D.
- Cochran, Robert E.
- Cody, William D.
Coehlo, Antonio J., Jr.
- Coffroth, Alfred P.
- Coleman, Donald H.
- Collazo, Raphael L.
- Collier, Noah C.
Collins, Kenneth G.
Colon, Hector E.
Comer, Billy R.
Comerford, Steven W.
- Conde-Falcon, Felix M.
Conner, DeForest S.
- Conner, Eugene J.
- Connors, David T.
- Contreras, Albert, Jr.
- Conway, James B.
- Copas, Ardie R.

Cotto, Perex E.
Cover, Winston A.L.
Cox, Timothy, J.
- Coyle, Garry
- Coyle, James M.
Cozzalio, Alan A.
Crabtree, Ormand B.
Crain, Carroll V.
Crews, Gary E.
- Crow, Edward D.
- Crowell, Roger B.
Crowley, Fred R. (USMC)
Cruz, Enrique C.
- Culpepper, Allen R.
Cundiff, Brian H.
Cunningham, John H.
- Cunningham, Larry L.
- Curran, John D.
D'Avignon, George C.
Dabney, James F.
- Dacey, Bertrand J.
- Dahr, John W.
Daly, Jerome R.
- Daniel, Robert G.
Darnell, John E., Jr.
Daugherty, Milton C.
- Davan, Benedict M.
David, Kenneth J.
Davidson, Donald F.
Davidson, Thomas A.
Davis, Eugene R.
Davis, Leroy L., Jr.
Davis, Mitchell
Deane, John R., Jr.
Deane, John R., Jr. (OLC)
Deibert, Charles L.
Delavan, Patrick N.
Deleo, Joseph D.
- De Marchi, Frank, Jr.
- Dempsey, Jack T.
Dempsey, Michael O.
- Denisowski, Stanley G.
Dennard, Danny
- Denney, William H., Jr.
- Dent, William L.
Dettman, Douglas A.
Dentinger, David D.
DePuy, William E. (OLC,

WWII)
Devlin, Gerard M.
- Dexter, Herbert J.
Diamond, James A.
Dietrich, Frank L.
Dimsdale, Roger
- Dingman, Milfred H.
Dinkins, Clifford
- Dixon, Patrick M.
- Do, Van Tan (Viet)
Dobbins, Raymond H.
- Dobrinksa, Thomas L.
Doezema, Frank, Jr.
- Dolan, James E.
Dolbin, Douglas R.
Dorch, Michael E.
Dorland, Gilbert
D'Orlando, Michael
- Douglas, Clark R.
- Downing, Lester E.
Dozer, Robert L.
- Drake, Steven C.
Duffy, John J.
- Dunlop, Johnston
- Dunsmore, Leo P.
Duran, Jesus S.
- Durand, Dennis C.
Dydasco, Vincente T.
Edwards, James L.
- Eisenhour, James D.
Elliott, Artice W.
Emerson, Henry E.
Emerson, Henry E.
  (OLC)
- Enners, Raymond J.
Esher, Brian R.
- Estrada, Esteban P.
Eszes, Joseph W.
- Eutsler, John W.
Evans, Bill D.
Evans, Daniel E.
- Evans, Donald P.
Evans, Donald R.
- Evans, Jerry D.
- Ewing, Jerry L.
- Factora, Douglas G.
Falck, Douglas M.
- Faldermeyer, Harold J.

Fanesi, David
Fant, Ernest L.
- Farmer, Neil P.
Farrelly, Hubert
Favreau, Robert A.
Feinberg, Mark M.
- Ference, Edward P.
Ferguson, Kenneth D.
- Ferguson, William G.
- Fergusson, Robert C.L.
- Fesken, William P.
Fiack, Paul
Fields, Elija
- Fields, Lloyd, Jr.
- Figueroa-Melendez,
  Efrain
Fitzpatrick, James M.
Fleener, Larry D.
Fletcher, Larry A.
Floody, Harold V., Jr.
- Floyd, Alvin W.
- Floyd, Robert G.
- Fontaine, Michael A.
Ford, Ruben H.
- Foreman, James L.
Fraker, William W.
- Franklin ,Eugene D.
- Franklin, James A.
- Freppon, John L.
- Frericks, Louis W.
Friedrich, Robert L.
Friend, Richard E.
Fry, Jerry R.
Fugere, Oliver J., Jr.
Fujii, Dennis M.
Fuller, Sherman G.
Fulton, William B.
Furlong, James J.
Furrow, Gail W.
- Gabrys, Stephen M.
Gallo, Joseph A., Jr.
- Galloway, Sam H.
- Gandy, Michael L.
Garcia, Candelario
Garcia, Edward
- Garcia, Gregorio M.
- Garcia, Joseph A.
Garrett, Chester

Garza, Andres
Gasdek, Garry D.
Gaskin, Gordon W.
George, Robert A.
- German, Bromley H.
Getz, Charles E.
Gibson, Samuel T.
- Gilbert, James C.
- Gipson, Robert P.
Glemser, James P.
- Glenn, Richard J.
- Glines, Allen B.
Godlewski, Larry E.
- Godsey, James F.
- Godwin, Harry M.
Goff, Stanley C.
Gorman, Paul F.
- Gorton, Gary B.
Gourley, Guy H.
Graham, Michael F.
Grant, Gerald V.
Green, Alex C.
Green, Daniel R.
Green, Gerald D.
Green, Jeffrey S.
- Green, Jimmie R.
Green, Richard A.
Greene, Stanley E.
Greer, Earl D.
- Gregory, Bob L.
Griggs, Leslie D.
- Grigsby, Joe W.
Grimm, Michael C.
Grimmer, Jack E.
Grof, Robert L.
Grogan, Timothy J.
Gross, Lynn J.
Guevara, Jesus J.
Gutierrez, Andres
Guy, Cornelius, Jr.
Hackworth, David H.
Hackworth, David H.
  (OLC)
Haig, Alexander M., Jr.
- Haines, John L.
Hale, Richard M.
Hales, James P., III
- Haley, Patrick L.

- Hall, Billie A.
  Hall, Sequoyah
  Hamilton, George E.
- Hamilton, Gilbert L.
  Hammer, Martin J.
- Hammersla, James
  Hand, Michael J.
- Hardison, Robert S.
- Hardy, Herbert F., Jr.
- Harper, Tony
  Harr, Gerry A.
  Harrell, Rohnie
  Harris, James A.
- Harris, Roy C., Jr.
- Harrison, Paul J.
  Harvey, Thomas H.
  Haszard, Sidney S.
  Hattersley, Roger K.
  Haupt, Earl C., III
  Hay, John H., Jr.
  Hayden, Philip P.
- Haynes, Freddie N.
  Haynie, Harris R.
- Hays, John H.
  Hazel, Richard L.
  Hazelip, Charles R.
  Healy, Paul V.
  Heaps, George H.
- Hellenbrand, David P.
  Helmick, Robert F.
  Helvey, Robert L.
  Henderson, Donald L.
  Hendrick, Richard A.
- Hennessy, Daniel A.
  Henry, Jeffery J.
  Hepp, Ferdinand
  Hering, Gregory D.
  Herrera, Fernando Q.
  Hetzler, Walter G.
  Hewitt, Melvin R.
  Hightower, Thomas K.
  Hill, James H., Jr.
- Hill, Richard G.
  Hitti, John L.
  Hoang, Cha Ly (Viet.)
  Hofstrom, William R.
  Hogan, John
  Holbrook, Mark L.

- Holland, Carlton J.
- Holland, Charles J.
  Hollingsworth, James F.
    (OLC, WWII)
  Hollingsworth, James F.
    (2nd OLC)
  Hollis, Emmett A.
  Honeycutt, Weldon F.
  Hook, William W.
  Hopkins, Perry C.
  Hopkins, Ronald J.
  Hopper, Paul W.
  Horn, William W.
- Horst, Robert L.
- Houston, John L.
  Houthoofd, Charles
  Howard, Robert L.
  Hudson, Claude K.
- Hudson, Joseph W.
  Huggins, Charles R.
  Hughes, George W.
- Hunsley, Dennis R.
  Hunt, Tom C.
  Hurtt, Michael J.
- Hutchinson, Robert S., II
  Iacovacci, John H.
- Igoe, William J.
  Ireland, Daniel L.
  Isaac, Jesse A.
  Isenhart, Wilson J.
- Jablonski, John A.
  Jackson, Warren G.
- Jackson, William
  Jaeger, Thomas W.
  James, Kirk J.
  Jarman, Jeffery G.
  Jenkins, Wilbur G., Jr.
- Jobst, Kurt K., Jr.
  Johndro, Dana A.
  Johnson, Dallas, W.
- Johnson, Dean R.
  Johnson, James H. (LTC)
  Johnson, James H. (Sp4)
  Johnson, Jesse L.
  Johnson, John C.
  Johnson, Larry
- Johnson, Peter W.
  Johnson, Richard H.

  Johnson, William D., Jr.
  Johnston, John R., Jr.
  Jonas, Spencer, W.
- Jones, Dennis K.
- Jones, Gary C.
- Jones, Horatio L.
  Jones, Kyle D.
  Jones, Malvin E.
- Jordan, Daniel W.
- Jordan, Orval C., III
  Joubert, Donald L.
  Judkins, Roy
- Justiniano, Victor A., Jr.
- Kaneshiro, Edward N.
  Kasun, David R.
- Kauhaihao, John K.
  Kays, Kenneth M.
  Kelley, Gordon F.
- Kelley, Jerry C.
- Kelley, William F.
- Kelly, Charles L.
  Kelly, Donald W.
  Kelly, Ross S.
  Keltner, Neil L.
  Kemmer, Thomas
  Kendall, Joe A.
  Kennedy, Alton R.
  Kennedy, Herman J.
  Kennedy, Leslie D.
  Kent, Alan
- Kernahan, Gregory P., Jr.
  Kerns, Raymond A.
  Kettles, Charles S.
- Kiger, Dennis D.
  Kimura, Donald K.
- King, Larry D.
  Kingston, Robert C.
  Kizirian, John
- Kline, James J.
  Klinger, Vernon L., Jr.
- Klug, Herbert W.
- Knadle, Robert E.
- Knight, Peter S.
  Knight, Robert C.
  Kopsolias, Lester
  Korte, Chelse C.
- Koski, Richard A.
- Kotrc, James C.

Kratzer, William M.
- Kreckel, John W.
- Krupinski, Raymond J.
- Kunz, Anthony E.
Kurz, Alfred
Kyles, Bobby W.
- Laier, Stephen E.
Landry, Robert M.
- Lane, John T.
- Lasater, Luther M.
Lawrence, Stephen E.
Lawrence, William, Jr.
Lawton, John P.
- Lechuga, Martin
Ledbetter, William C., Jr.
Ledfors, Frederick D.
- Lehew, Donald L.
Lemonds, Gary L.
Leonard, Ronald R.
Lepeilbet, Andrew R.
Lewis, John J.
- Lhota, Robert
- Liebespeck, James W.
Lindemann, Edward W.
Lindsay, David J.
Lindsay, James J.
Lines, William, Jr.
- Link, John F.
- Little, William F.
- Litwin, Robert R.
- Loback, Thomas J.
Loftus, Robert
- Loncon, Larry J.
- Lopez, John E., Jr.
- Lopez, Manuel T.
Lose, Charles R.
Loucks, Jerry T., Jr.
Luong, Phan-Ngoc (Viet)
Lutchendorf, Thomas E.
Lynch, Eugene M.
- Lytton, Balfour O., Jr.
Mace, James E.
- Maddox, Julius
Magouyrk, James R.
Malachi, Ronald E.
- Malave-Rios, Abelardo
Maloney, George A.
Maloney, Robert W.

- Mangan, Michael R.
Manglona, Martin A.
Manley, Glen R.
Mansfield, Gordon H.
Marecek, George
Mari, Louis A.
Marinacci, Jack L.
Marinovich, Branko B.
Mark, Marion L.
Marshall, Carl B.
- Martin, Donnie J.
- Martin, Larry
- Martin, Linwood D.
Martin, Roy D.
Matz, William M., Jr.
Maus, William C.
Mayer, Frank H.
- Maynard, Thomas H.
Mayor, Robert G.
McAfee, Jerry D.
McBee, James M.
- McBride, Morris R.
McCaffrey, Barry R.
McCaffrey, Barry R.
   (OLC)
- McCain, Michael C.
- McCarthy, John E.
McCarthy, Thomas V.
- McCarthy, Thomas W.
McClean, Michael A.
- McCoig, Donald B.
McCollum, Timothy P.
- McCrary, Douglas M.
McDermott, John K.
McDermott, Michael A.
McDermott, Michael A.
   (OLC)
McDonald, Charles A.
- McDonald, Martin T.
McDougald, Lacy, Jr.
McEnery, John W.
McGinnis, Edward G.
McGowan, Arthur J., Jr.
McGowan, Robert S.
McGuire, Ray D.
- McHugh, John J.
- McKibben, Larry S.
- McKinsey, Gerald L.

McNamara, Laurence V.
- McNeil, Harold L.
McNichol, John Q.
- McQuade, James R.
McQuiston, Hugh J., Jr.
- McSwain, Baynes B., Jr.
Meade, Wendell T.
Meadows, Richard J.
- Meara, William D.
- Mears, Guy L.
Meloy, Guy S.
Menetrey, Louis C.
Merkerson, Willie, Jr.
Michienzi, James A.
Middleton, John C.
Miles, Martin C.
Miller, Phillip L.
Miller, Richard L.
Miller, Robin K.
Miller, Tommy L.
Millsap, Walter G.
Minarta, John D.
Mines, Ernest G.
- Minogue, Thomas
- Mitchell, Thomas P.
- Moehring, Dean W.
- Moncavage, David J.
Monnick, Edward W., III
Montgomery, Donald B.
- Moore, Charles T.
- Moore, Dennis F.
Moore, Douglas E.
Moore, Harold G., Jr.
Moore, Joseph W.
Mordue, Norman A.
Morgan, Michael J.
Morris, Melvin
Morris, Wayne H.
- Moses, Walter L.
- Mousseau, Lloyd F.
Mueller, Arndt L.
Mullen, William J., III
Murphy, Kenneth E.
Murphy, Robert C.
Murray, Michael J.
- Murrey, Tracy H.
Myers, Richard J.
Nedolast, Daniel A.

- Neely, Dan L.
  Nelson, Charles E.
- Nelson, Hugh R., Jr.
- Nelson, Larry D.
- Nelson, William D.
  Newman, James T.
  Nicholas, Glenn R.
  Nichols, Philip L.
  Nicol, Lon D.
  Noel, John M.
- Noeldner, Daniel M.
  Northrup, Ralph A.
  Nowicki, James E.
- Nunez, Rudolph A.
- Nussbaumer, Steven O.
- Nutt, Walter
  Nutter, Raymond T.
- O'Brien, Terence D.
  O'Claire, Richard D.
  O'Connell, Terrence M.
  O'Connor, Oscar L.
  O'Dell, Eugene J., Jr.
- O'Kusky, Henry J., Jr.
  O'Neill, Daniel L.
  O'Quinn, Donald L.
- O'Reilly, Anthony
- O'Sullivan, Christopher J.
  O'Sullivan, John I.
  Oakland, Patrick
  Ogas, Fred , Jr.
  Okamoto, Vincent H.
  Oliver, J.L.
- Oquendo, Fruto J.
  Orsini, Donald A.
  Ortiz, Raymond
  Otis, Glenn K.
  Otis, Malcolm D.
- Overweg, Roger D.
- Pagan-Lozada, Wilfredo
  Palmer, Harold T., Jr.
- Paonessa, Michael D.
  Parker, George W.
  Parker Jesse J.
- Parker, Otis
  Parrish, Andrew W.
  Parrish, Richard
  Patterson, James H.

  Patton, George S.
  Patton, George S. (OLC)
  Payne, Keith (Aust. Army)
  Payne, Patrick J.
  Peacock, Mickey K.
  Pearson, Samuel L.
  Pease, Thomas S.
  Peck, Millard A.
- Peda, Robert C.
- Pederson, Roger A.
  Peoples, Leon
- Perez, Daniel F.
  Perez, Joseph M.
  Perry, Michael P.
  Phifer, William
- Phillips, Henry R.
  Phillips, Richard H.
- Pickard, Alfred
- Pierce, Bernard L.
- Pina, Frank D.
  Piper, John D.
  Pittman, Homer L., Jr.
- Plato, Robert D.
- Polusney, James F.
  Ponder, Billy W., Sr.
- Pongratz, Ronald E.
- Poole, Thomas D.
  Porter, Alfred L.
  Poutrain, Jean D.
  Powell, Thomas E.
- Powers, Francis E., Jr.
- Price, Arnold W.
  Primmer, Frank G.
  Pritchard, Paul M.
- Proffit, John B.
  Pruitt, James N.
  Pryor, Robert D.
  Puckett, Ralph, Jr. (OLC-Kor.)
  Quamo, George
  Queen, William R.
- Quinn, Richard F.
  Radcliffe, Ronald A.
- Ragin, William D.
- Ramirez, Lorenzo, Jr.
  Ramirez, Ramiro
- Randall, Michael E.

  Ranger, Michael B.
  Rankin, Howard F.
- Rarrick, John E.
  Rasser, Gary V.
  Rau, Raymond R.
- Ray, William E.
- Reeder, Philip D.
- Rees, Richard M.
  Reeves, Thomas M.
  Reinburg, John E., III
- Reiter, Clyde A.
- Renteria, Rudolph S.
- Reyes, Thomas G.
- Rhodes, Donald
  Rice, Robert C.
  Rich, David F.
- Richardson, Roy L.
  Richardson, William R.
  Rickman, William M., Jr.
  Rider, Archie A.
  Ridley, Mark T.
  Riley, Ronald J.
  Rinaldo, Richard J.
  Ring, George M.
  Rios, Alfred R.
  Rios, Ricardo L.
- Roberts, Marvin J.
- Robinson, Calvin
- Robinson, Melvin C.
  Robinson, John R.
- Robison, Donald R.
  Rock, Paul J.
  Rodela, Jose
  Rodrigues, Francisco
- Rodriguez, Reinaldo
  Rodriquez, Enrique P.
- Rogan, James P.
  Rogers, Bernard W.
  Rogers, James D.
  Rogers, Robert B.
- Rollins, Dale F.
  Romero, Artenio, Jr.
- Roniger, Junior F.
  Rose, Gary M.
- Rose, Onsby R.
  Ross, Edgar A.
- Roush, William W.

- Roush, William W. (OLC)
- Rouska, Dennis L.
  Rowland, John R.
  Rowser, Preston
  Rozelle, Joseph H.
  Rubin, Kenneth E.
- Rucker, John W.
- Rushing, Gary G.
- Russell, Gregory A.
  Sabalauski, Walter J.
- Sabel, Joel M.
  Sackett, William P.
- Sanchez, Thomas J.
  Sanders, Horace G.
  Sanders, James R.
- Sanderson, Jack
- Santa Cruz, Jose A
- Sanzone, Robert B.
- Saracino, Frank D., Jr.
- Sauble, Thomas E.
- Sauls, Robert N.
  Savage, Clyde E.
- Scarborough, Edmund B.
  Scher, Donald M.
  Schoch, Nicholas W.
  Scholtus, David
  Schlottman, James
  Schroeder, Donald B.
- Schubert, Joel L.
- Schultz, Robert W.
  Schungel, Daniel F.
  Schweitzer, Robert L.
- Schwellenbach, Gary R.
- Scibilia, Robert P.
  Scott, James A. (CSM)
  Scott, James A., III (Cpt)
  Scott, Jon E.
- See, Otto W.
- Seibert, Richard J.
  Sellers, Richard D.
  Sergent, Orville W., III
  Severson, Daniel J.
- Severson, Paul R.
- Shaffer, Earl T.
  Sharpe, Merle J.
- Shaughnessy, Edward J.

- Shaw, Clarence L.
- Shaw, Gary F.
  Shaw, William F.
  Shea, Thomas
- Sherrill, James J.
  Shortman, Phillip V.
- Siders, Marvin I.
  Silverstein, William I.
- Simmons, Burnell
  Simons, Arthur D.
  Simons, James P.
- Simpson, Michael P.
  Sincere, Clyde J., Jr.
- Sizemore, Clarence
- Skaggs, Lonnie G.
- Smith, Avery G.
- Smith, Jack
  Smith, James H.
- Smith, Lynn H.
  Smith, Mark A.
  Smith, Norwood W., Jr.
  Smith, Patrick R.
  Smith, Paul F.
  Smith, Ralph
- Snell, Robert N.
  Snoddy, Harold M.
  Snyder, Robert A.
  Soppe, Ronald J.
- Sosa, Aristides
- Sowell, Ronald
  Spackman, Philip L.
  Speers, Max D.
- Speer, Richard M.
  Spence, Richard G.
  Sperling, Richard A.
  Spinaio, Edward W.
  Spitz, James D.
- Springer, Charles A.
- Sproule, William C., Jr.
- Squires, David R.
  Stahl, Leonard C.
- Stahl, Phillip T.
  Stark, Peter M.
  Starr, William J.
  Steeley, Noble L.
  Steffensen, Dennis C.
- Steimel, Gregg F.
- Steinberg, George C.

- Steiner, Mark S.
  Steinman, Jackie W.
  Stephens, Rufus
- Stevens, Forestal A.
  Stevenson, Robert D.
  Stewart, Harvey E.
- Stewart, Samuel R., III
- Stigall, Arthur D.
- Stoflet, Michael H.
- Stone, Byron C.
- Stone, James M.
- Stone, Raymond E., Jr.
  Stowell, Robert D.
- Street, Brent A.
  Stuart, Richard
- Sturdivant, Jasper D.
- Swann, Johnnie D.
- Swanson, Jon E.
  Sweet, Richard S.
  Swenson, Robert L.
- Swoveland, William A.
  Sydnor, Elliot P., Jr.
  Sykes, Larry W.
  Szyiback, Clarence
  Tackaberry, Thomas H. (OLC-Kor.)
  Tackaberry, Thomas H. (2nd OLC)
  Taft, John K.
- Tasker, James B.
- Taylor, James E.
  Taylor, James R.
  Taylor, James T., Jr.
  Taylor, Lawrence R.
  Taylor, Ronald S.
- Taylor, William E.
- Techmeier, Larry L.
- Teevens, Richard P.
  Terry, Gilbert N.
  Terry, Ronald T.
- Theriault, Samuel S.
- Thomas, Joseph B.
  Thomas, Richard A.
  Thomas, William C.
  Thompson, Byron, W.
  Thurman, Jerry W.
- Tierney, Brian E.
- Tiffany, David L.

Tilley, Leonard W.
• Tillquist, Robert A.
Tissler, John G.
Tolson, John J., III
Tomcik, Dennis C.
Tomcik, Dennis C.
 (OLC)
Tomlinson, Raymond
 F. R.
Tomlinson, William
Tonsetic, Robert L.
Toomepuu, Juri
Totten, Clifford R.
Townsend, Samuel W.
Trent, Herman L.
Trinkle, Patrick M.
Tucker, Gary L.
• Turnbull, Robert C.
Tusi, Ronald L.
Twiford, Larry M.
Underwood, Victor C.
Urban, Dale A.
Valor, Frank
• Van Deusen, Frederick F.
• Van Poll, Hubert C.
• Vann, John P. (U.S.Civ.)
Vaughan, Denny R.
Vernon, Charles E.
Vessey, John W.
Viau, Wallace E.
• Vickers, Roger L.
Villanueva, David O.
• Villarosa, Paul H.
Villarreal, Raul
• Villasenior, Gonzalo
• Vinassa, Michael G.
Voiles, Lanny
• Volner, John D.
• Wagner, Grey H.
Wagner, Louis C.
Waite, Raymond F.
• Walden, Darrell E.
Walden, Jerry T.

Waldron, Adelbert F.
Waldron, Adelbert F.
 (OLC)
Waldrop, Andrew H., Jr.
Walkabout, Bill B.
Walker, Dennis K.
Walker, Frank J.
Walker, Robert H.
Walker, Wesley F.
• Walker, William W.
Wall, Lee O.
• Waller, Casey O.
Wallin, Dennis G.
• Walsh, David W.
Wanat, George K., Jr.
Wandke, Richard D.
• Ward, Tom
Ward, William H.
• Ware, Keith L.
Warren, Thomas E.
Wasco, Joseph , Jr.
Washington, Johnny L.
Watts, Albert R.
• Waycaster, Richard L.
• Waymire, Jackie L.
Webb, Francis R.
Weedmark, James A
• Wellman, Kenyon G.
Wessel, Leon M., Jr.
West, Hugh M.
West, Thomas E.
Westfall, Ronald K.
Wetzel, Allan R.
Weyand, Frederick C.
• Whalen, Michael C.
Whitaker, Ira E.
White, Gerald J.
Whitehead, John B., III
Whitehead, Rudolph L.
Whitted, Jack G.
Wickward, William J.
• Wideman, Elvin J.
Wijas, Rodney J.

• Wilcox, William E., Jr.
• Wilderspin, Vernon C.
Wilhelm, Jerald W.
Williams, Felix E.
• Williams, Harold D.
Williams, Jack L.
Williams, Jack L. (OLC)
• Williams, Lester , Jr.
Williams, Michael J.
• Williams, Ralph L.
Williams, Robert R.
Williams, Roger A.
Williamson, Ellis W.
• Williamson, Robert J.
• Wilson, Gerald L.
Wilson, Lee E.
• Wilson, Richard L.
Winland, Floyd
• Winningham, Clifton
• Winston, Alvester L.
Wishik, Jeffrey
• Witherspoon, Thomas,
 Jr.
Wolford, Grover
• Wolter, James J.
Wood, Daniel
Woods, James O.
Woods, Luther L.
Worbington, John H.
Worley, Morris G.
Wright, Larry D.
• Wright, Leroy N.
• Wright, Robert C.
Wright, Robert L.
Wright, Ronald J.
Wroblewski, Frank M.
Wymer, Merrill F., Jr.
Yearta, Jesse L.
Yost, Burrwood , Jr.
Young, Ronald R.
Zauber, Jeffery F.
Ziobron, Edward C.
• Zerr, Kent M.

Appendix III

The Navy Cross: Vietnam War

- Abrams, Lewis H.
  Abshire, Bobby W.
- Abshire, Richard F.
- Adams, John T.
  Adams, Laurence, R., III
  Ajdukovich, George
  Alfonso, Vincent
  Allen, Yale G.
- Almeida, Russell V.
  Alspaugh, Timothy D.
  Ambrose, Gerald D.
- Amendola, Willet R.
  Anderson, John J.
  Armstrong, Russell P.
- Arquero, Elpidio A.
- Ashby, James W.
- Aston, James M.
- Ayers, Darrell E.
  Back, James B.
  Badnek, Samuel J.
- Baggett, Curtis F.
  Bailey, Walter F.
  Baker, Harold L.
  Baratko, Robert E.
  Barber, William B.
  Barnes, Robert C.
  Barnett, Robert L.
  Barrett, James J.
  Barrett, John J.
  Baskin, Richard W.

Batcheller, Gordan D.
Bateman, Kent C.
Bell, Van D., Jr.
  (2nd Awd-Kor.)
- Beaulieu, Leo V.
  Bay, Tran Van (Viet.)
- Bendorf, David G.
- Benoit, Francis A.
  Benoit, Ronald R.
  Berger, Donald J.
  Binns, Ricardo C.
  Bird, William C.
- Blann, Stephen
- Blevins, Thomas L., Jr.
  Blonski, Thomas J.
  Bogan, Richard E.
  Brady, Eugene R.
  Brandtner, Martin L.
  Brandtner, Martin L.
  (2nd Awd.)
- Brantley, Leroy
- Brindley, Thomas D.
  Brown, Charles E.
- Brown, David H.
  Browning, Randall A.
- Bryan, Charles
  Bryant, Jarold O.
  Buchanan, Richard W.
  Bull, Lyle F.
- Burke, John R.

Burnand, Robert W., Jr.
Burnham, Thomas R.
Burns, Dewey R., Jr.
Burns, Leon R.
Busey, James B., IV
Caine, Lawrence B., III
- Calhoun, John C.
- Cameron, Kenneth R.
- Campbell, Joseph T.
  Canley, "J" "L"
- Carroll, James J.
  Carter, Marshall N.
- Casebolt, Henry C.
- Casey, Michael J.
- Casey, Robert M.
- Casey, Thomas M., Jr.
  Castillo, William
- Cavanaugh, Thomas J.
  Cheatham, Ernest C., Jr.
  Cheatwood, Paul R.
  Christensen, Paul K.
- Christman, William J., III
  Christmas, Goerge R.
- Cisneros, Roy
  Clay, Raymond D.
  Claybin, Edward A.
- Cobb, Paul F.
- Cochran, Robert F., Jr.
  Coffman, Clovis C., Jr.
  Coker, George T.

Collins, Bryant C.
Compton, Bryan W., Jr.
Cone, Fred "J"
Confer, Milton W.
Conklin, Richard F.
• Connell, James J.
Connelly, Matthew J., III
Cook, Clarence L.
Coolican, James J.
Corsetti, Harry J.
• Cousins, Merritt T.
• Covella, Joseph F.
Cover, Robert L.
Cox, Charles J.
• Crawford, Charles H.
Crockett, Joseph R., Jr.
• Cruse, James D.
• Cummings, Roger W.
Cunningham, Randall H.
Curley, Ronald T.
Curtis, Russell W.
Dalton, Robert G.
Danner, David J.
Dannheim, William T.
• Danrell, Dana C.
• Davis, Dennis D.
• Dawson, John R.
• Day, Edward
De Bona, Andrew D.
Dengler, Dieter
Denton, Jeremiah A.
De Planche, Mark B.
Devries, Marvin H.
• Dickson, Edward A.
• Dickson, Grover L.
Dillard, Henry C.
Dinsmore, Harry H.
Dittman, Carl R.
Donaldson, Billy M.
Donovan, Joseph P.
Donovan, Joseph P. (2nd
    Awd.)
• Dorris, Claud H.
• Dowd, John A.
Downing, Talmadge R.
Driscoll, Thomas B.
Driscoll, William P.
• Duff, Barry W.

• Duncan, Richard W.
Dutterer, Carroll E., Jr.
Eades, Lawrence M.
Ebbert, Terry J.
Edwards, Craig A.
Eggert, Lowell F.
Ennis, Joseph J.
Enoch, Barry W.
Ensch, John C.
Estrada, Manuel A.
• Evans, Richard A., Jr.
Fairfield, Rupert E., Jr.
• Fante, Robert G.
• Federowski, Robert A.
Feerrar, Donald L.
Felton, Samuel L., Jr.
• Finley, Michael P.
• Fisher, Thomas W.
• Fitzgerald, William C.
• Floren, Jimmy E.
• Ford, Patrick O.
Fowler, Earl W.
• Frederick, John W., Jr.
• Freund, Terrence J.
Fryman, Roy A.
• Fuller, John L., Jr.
Fuller, Robert B.
• Galbreath, Bobby F.
• Gale, Alvin R.
Gallagher, Gary G.
Gallagher, Patrick
Gallagher, Robert T.
Gates, Michael L.
• Gauthier, Brian J.
• Gerrish, Alan R.
• Getlin, Michael P.
Gibson, George R.
Gilleland, Richard M.
• Gillespie, Martin L., Jr.
• Gillingham, Richard K.
Gillotte, Kevin
Gomez, Ernesto
Gonzales, Daniel G.
• Goodsell, William J.
• Grant, Gollie L.
Gray, George E.
Green, John S.
Green, Maurice O.V.

Gregory, Robert B., Jr.
Gresham, Michael E.
Gresko, Richard W.
• Griffith, John G.
Grimes, Paul E., Jr.
Groce, Donald B.
Grosz, Nicholas, H., Jr.
Guarino, Timothy S.
Guay, Robert P.
Guerra, Victor J.
Hall, Michael R.
• Halstead, Lee M.
Hampton, Gregory O.
• Hancock, Eugene S.
Hanson, Anthony C.
Harrington, Myron C.
• Hartsoe, David E.
Hayenga, William E., Jr.
Hayes, Daniel J.
Hazelbaker, Vincil W.
Helle, Ronald B.
Henderson, Billy K.
Hendricks, Robert L.
Herbert, Robert S.
• Herrera, Felipe
• Herron, Lee R.
Hickey, William L.
Hilgers, John J. W.
• Hill, Lamont D.
Hoapili, John
• Hodgkins, Guy M.
Hoff, John R., Jr.
Holmes, Billie D.
Holmes, Walter C.
• Honeycutt, James E.
• Hopkins, Michael E.
Houghton, Kenneth J.
House, Charles A.
• Howard, Billy
• Howell, Gatlin J.
• Hubbard, Robert W.
Huffcut, William H., II
Huggins, Michael A.
Huges, Stanley S. (2nd
    Awd.-Kor.)
Hunnicutt, Hubert H.,
    III
Hunter, Charles B.

Jaehne, Richard L.
James, Alan C.
• Jmaeff, George V.
Johnson, James L., Jr.
• Johnston, Clement B., Jr.
• Jones, Phillip B.
• Joys, John W.
• Judge, Mark W.
• Kaler, Richard D.
• Kaufman, David M.
• Keck, Russell F.
Kelley, Edwin C., Jr.
• Kelly, James R., III
Kelly, Robert A.
Kemp, Marwick L.
• Kenison, Benjamin A.
Kennedy, Johnnie M.
Keys, William M.
Kinnard, Donel C.
• Koelper, Donald E.
• Kollmann, Glenn E.
Koontz, Leonard
Korkow, Kenneth A.
Kowalyk, William
Krueger, Roger W.
• Kuzma, Marc J.
Lain, Bobby D.
Lankford, Albert J., III
La Pointe, Alvin S.
La Porte, Alfred P., Jr.
• Laraway, William D.
Larsen, David R.
• Lauer, Charles R.
Lazaro, Lawrence J.
• Leal, Armando G., Jr.
Lebas, Claude G.
Ledbetter Walter R., Jr.
Ledford, Kenneth, Jr.
   (USA)
Lefler, Alan C.
Leftwich, William G., Jr.
Lewis, David H.
Linder, James B.
• Lineberry, Jerry E.
Livingston, Lawrence H.
Long, Melvin M.
Lopez, Jose G.
Lopez, Steven D.

• Loweranitis, John L.
Lowery, Steven M.
Lownds, David E.
Luca, Joseph
Lumbard, Donald W.
• Lunsford, Glen T.
• Mack, Francis W.
MacVane, Matthew C.
Malone, George M.
Mann, Bennie H., Jr.
Marlantes, Karl A.
Martin, Cecil H.
• Martin, Raymond C.
Mayton, James A.
McAfee, Carlos K.
McCauley, Bertram W.
• McCormick, Michael P.
McDaniel, Eugene B.
McDaniel, James V.
McDonald, Thomas C.
McEwen, Robert M.
McHenry, William D.
• McKeen, Gerald C.
McKeown, Ronald E.
McRae, Arthur G.
• McWhorter, James E.
• Meier, Terrance L.
• Mendez, Angel
• Mercer, William I.
• Meuse, John R.
• Meyerkord, Harold D.
• Milius, Paul L.
Miller, Cleatus A., Jr.
Mitchell, Robert G.
Moe, Robert F.
Moffit, Richard E.
Monahan, Frederick G.
• Monahon, Robert
Montgomery, Robin L.
Moore, Freddie L.
• Moore, Ronald A.
Mosher, Christopher K.
• Muir, Joseph E.
Mulloy, James E., Jr.
Murphy,David R.
Murphy, James E.
Murray John D.
• Myers, William H.

Neil, Michael I.
Nelson, James R.
Noel, Thomas E.
Noon, Patrick J., Jr.
• Norris, James A.
Norton, John J.
Norwood, George O.
Oakley, John L.
O'Connor, Martin E.
O'Kelley, John W.
• Orlando, Samuel G.
Palmer, Frederick F.
Panian, Thomas C.
Parrott, Lee R.
Paskevich, Anthony, Jr.
Pate, James W., Jr.
Peczeli, Joseph S.
• Peters, William L., Jr.
• Peterson, Dennie D.
Phelps, John G.
Phillips, John C.
Piatt, Louis R.
• Pichon, Louis A., Jr.
Pierpan, Herbert E.
• Pitts, Roy E.
• Popp, James A.
Porter, Robert O.
Poulson, Leroy N.
• Powell, Charles T.
• Powell, Richard L.
• Powers, Trent R.
Prendergast, Francis S.
• Quick, Robert L.
• Ralya, Warren H., Jr.
• Rash, Donald R.
• Ray, Darrell T.
• Reid, John M.
• Reilly, Donald J.
• Reilly, James R.
• Reis, Tiago
Reynolds, Marvin D.
Rhodes, Francis E., Jr.
Richards, Thomas A.
Riensche, Harold A.
Ripley, John W.
Rivera, Jose L.
• Rivers, Jettie, Jr.
Roberson, James J.

Robinson, David B.
- Rodrigues, Joe G., Jr.
Rogers, Gerald W.
Rogers, Raymond G., Jr.
Roland, John R., Jr.
Roller, Robert T.
Rollings, Wayne E.
Romine, Richard E.
- Rosenberger, Roger D.
Ross, David L.
Rudd, Donald L.
- Rusher, Robert C.
Russell, Timothy W.
Russell, William E.
Rusth, John E.
Sadler, Charles D.
- Sampson, Gerald H.
- Sanders, Thomas
- Sargeant, George T., Jr.
- Schley, Robert J.
Schreiber, Klaus D.
Schunck, Henry M.
Scott, Donald W.
See, Roger D.
Sexton, Charles T.
Sexton, Harry E.
Sexton, Merlyn A.
Shepherd, Burton H.
- Sherman, Andrew M.
- Sipple, Conrad A.
- Sirousa, Michael A.
- Skibbe, David W.
Skweres, Jeff C.
Slater, Albert C., Jr.
Slater, Robert M.S.
- Sleigh, Duncan B.
Sliby, Dennis M.
Smith, Chester B.

- Smith, Homer L.
Smith, Ray L.
- Snyder, Stephen F.
- Soliz, Thomas
Sotomayor, Miguel A. Rivera
- Spark, Michael M.
Sparks, Neil R., Jr.
Speer, Paul H.
- Spicer, Jonathan N.
- Srsen, Steve A.
- Stahl, Mykle E.
Starrett, Edward F.
Stayton, Norman B.
- St. Clair, Clarence H., Jr.
- Stewart, Michael E.
Stockman, Robert D.
Stone, Guy E.
Strode, Gerald M.
Stuckey, James L.
Sullivan, Daniel F., Jr.
Sullivan, George R.
Taft, David A.
- Taylor, Jesse J.
Thatcher, Charles D.
- Thomas, Michael H.
Thomas, Robert J.
Thompson, Brock I
Thompson, Clinton W.
- Thompson, Jerrald R.
Thompson, John C.
Thompson, Robert H.
Thoryk, Barry L.
- Thouvenell, Armand R.
- Timmons, James M.
Tonkyn, Michael S.
- Trent, William D.
- Truett, Quincy H.

- Tycz, James N.
- Tyrone, Willie D.
Underwood, David F.
- Valdez, Phil I.
Vampatella, Philip V.
Vancor, Norman W.
Van Kiet, Nguyen (Viet.)
- Vasquez, Jesus R.
Verheyn, David A.
Walker, James R.
Wallace, Ernie W.
- Ward, James "C"
Warren, Roger O.
- Webb, Bruce D.
Webb, James H., Jr.
Weise, William
Weseleskey, Allen E.
Westin, Brian E.
Westphal, Warren R.
Wiant, Jeffrie E., Jr.
Widger, Robert I.
- Wilhelm, Mack H.
- Willeford, Franklin P.
Williams, James E.
Williams, Lloyd T., Jr.
Williams, Robert S.
Wilson, Willis C.
- Wirick, William C.
Woods, Lloyd
Work, Warren A., Jr.
Wynn, Edward H.
- Yarber, Vernon L.
- Yates, John Charles
Yordy, Charles R.
Young, William D.
Young, William H.
Zacharias, Jerrold M.
Zinser, Harry J.

Appendix IV

Air Force Cross: Vietnam War

Adams, Victor R.
- Allee, Richard K.
Allison, John V.
Armstrong, Larry D.
- Atterberry, Edwin L.
Backlund, Donald R.
Baer, Allan R.
- Baldwin, Robert L.
Beale, Robert T.
Black, Arthur N.
Bode, John R.
Boyd, Charles G.
Boyd, William, Jr.
Brickel, James R.
Brims, Richard C.
- Britt, Aquilla F.
Britton, Warner A.
Broughton, Jacksel M.
- Brower, Ralph W.
- Bucher, Bernard L.
Burroughs, William D.
Caldwell, William R.
Campbell, Jesse W.
Campbell, Thomas A.
- Carroll, John A.
Carter, William R.
Cherry, Fred V.
Clarke, Colin A.
Clay, Eugene L.
- Cobeil, Earl G.

- Cody, Howard R.
- Collins, Willard M.
- Conley, Eugene O.
Conran, Philip J.
- Cooper, William E.
Corder, John A.
Courtney, Terence F.
Curtis, Thomas J.
Dallman, Howard M.
Day, George E.
Dayton, Thomas
Debellvue, Charles B.
DeTar, Dean E.
Donelson, Nicholas J.
Donohue, Frederic M.
Dorsett, Tracey K., Jr.
- Draeger, Walter F., Jr.
Damesi, John A.
Damesi, John A. (OLC)
Engle, Charles E.
Eppinger, Dale L.
- Etchberger, Richard L.
Etzel, Gregory A. M.
Feinstein, Jeffrey S.
Feuerriegel, Karl T.
Finck, George C.
Firse, John A.
Fish, Michael E.
Fleener, Delbert W.
Flynn, John P.

Francisco, Michael C.
Funderburk, Leonard J.
Gamlin, Theodore R.
Gibson, James K.
Gilroy, Kevin A.
Gonzales, Leonard A.
Green, Joe B.
Griggs, Jerry M.
Gruver, John C.
Guarino, Lawrence N.
Gustafson, Gerald C.
Guy, Theodore W.
Hackney, Duane D.
Hackney, Hunter F.
Hall, James H.
- Hamilton, John S.
Harding, James C.
Harp, Tilford W.
Harston, Jon D.
Henning, Hal P.
- Hickman, Vincent J.
Hoggatt, Ralph S.
- Holland, Lawrence T.
Hopkins, James R.
Horinek, Ramon A.
Hudson, Jackson L.
Hunt, Russell M.
Jeannotte, Alfred J., Jr.
Johnson, Harold E.
Kalen, Herbert D.

Kasler, James H.
Kasler, James H. (OLC)
Kasler, James H. (2nd
 OLC)
Kennedy, Leland T.
Kennedy, Leland T.
 (OLC)
Kent, Nacey, Jr.
• Killian, Melvin J.
• King, Charles D.
Kirk, Thomas H., Jr.
• Knight, Roy A., Jr.
Koeltzow, Paul F.
Lackey, John E.
• Leetun, Darel D.
• Lielmanis, Atis K.
• Lukasik, Bernard F.
Madden, Joseph B.
• Maisey, Reginald V., Jr.
• Martin, Duane W.
• Martin, William R.
Marx, Donald L.
Mason, Larry B.
• Maysey, Larry W.
Maywald, Phillip V.
• McAllister, William W.
McCarthy, James R.
McGrath, Charles D.
McInerney, James E., Jr.
McKnight, George G.
McTasney, John B.
Mehr, Richard L.

• Mitchell, Carl B.
Mize, John D.
Mongillo, Paul J.
• Moorberg, Monte L.
Nagel, Richard A., Jr.
Newman, Thomas A.
Norris, William C.
Olds, Robin
Olsen, Don P.
O'Mara, Oliver E.
Orrell, Bennie D.
Parr, Ralph S.
Personett, Joseph A.
• Pitsenbarger, William H.
• Pogreba, Dean A.
Poling, Richard L.
Price, Donald S.
Purser, Rowland W.
• Richter, Karl W.
Risner, Robinson
Risner, Robinson (OLC)
Ritchie, Richard S.
Robinson, William A.
Robinson, William P.
• Ronca, Robert F.
Rowan, John M.
• Schaneberg, Leroy C.
• Schmidt, Norman
Schurr, Harry W.
• Scott, Travis H., Jr.
• Sellers, Jerry A.
Sellers, Kenneth H.

Shannon, Fred
Shaub, Charles L.
Smith, Donald G.
Smith, Robert W.
Smith, Ronald E.
Smith, Rowland F., Jr.
Smith, Weston T.
Stevens, Donald D.
Stocks, Bruce D.
• Storz, Ronald E.
Stovall, Dale E.
Talley, Joel E.
Titus, Robert F.
Trautman, Konrad W.
Traynor, Dennis
 W., III
Tsouprake, Peter
Turner, Robert E.
• Weatherby, Jack W.
Wells, Norman L.
Whatley, Wayne N.
White, Robert M.
• Whitesides, Richard L.
• Wilke, Robert F.
Williams, David H.
Wofford, Travis
• Wood, Patrick H.
Worrell, Rowland
 H., III
Wright, Garth A.
Wright, LeRoy
York, Glen P.

Appendix V

Vietnam War U.S. Military Prisoners of War Returned Alive*

Abbott, Joseph S., Jr.
Abbott, Robert Archie
Abbott, Wilfred Keese
Acosta, Hector Michael
Agnew, Alfred Howard
Agosto-Santos, Jose
Aiken, Larry Delarnard
Albert, Keith Alexander
Alcorn, Wendell Reed
Alexander, Fernando
Allwine, David Franklin
Alpers, John Hardesty, Jr.
Alvarez, Everett, Jr.
Anderson, Gareth Laverne
Anderson, John Thomas
Anderson, John Wesley
Anderson, Roger Dale
Andrews, Anthony Charles
Angus, William Kerr
Anshus, Richard Cameron
Anton, Francis Gene
Anzaldua, Jose Jesus, Jr.
Archer, Bruce Raymond
Acuri, William Youl
Astorga, Jose Manuel
Austin, William Renwick, II
Ayres, Timothy Robert
Bagley, Bobby Ray

Bailey, James William
Bailey, Lawrence Robert, Jr.
Baird, Bill Allen
Baker, David Earle
Baker, Elmo Clinnard
Baker, Vito
Baldock, Frederick C., Jr.
Ballard, Arthur T., Jr.
Ballenger, Orville Roger
Barbay, Lawrence
Barnett, Robert Warren
Barnett, Thomas Joseph
Barrows, Henry Charles
Bates, Richard Lyman
Baugh, William Joseph
Bean, James Ellis
Bean, William Raymond, Jr.
Bedinger, Henry James
Beekman, William David
Beeler, Carroll Robert
Beens, Lynn Richard
Bell, James Franklin
Berg, Kile Dag
Berger, James Robert
Bernasconi, Louis Henry
Biss, Robert Irvin
Black, Arthur Neil
Black, Cole

Black, Jon David
Blevins, John Charles
Bliss, Ronald Glenn
Bolstad, Richard Eugene
Bomar, Jack Williamson
Borling, John Lorin
Boyd, Charles Graham
Boyer, Terry Lee
Brady, Allen Colby
Branch, Michael Patrick
Brande, Harvey Gordon
Braswell, Donald Robert
Brazelton, Michael Lee
Breckner, William John, Jr.
Brenneman, Richard
   Charles
Brewer, Lee
Bridger, Barry Burton
Brigham, James
Brodak, John Warren
Brown, Charles Arthur, Jr.
Brown, Paul Gordon
Browning, Ralph Thomas
Brudno, Edward Alan
Brunhaver, Richard Marvin
Brunson, Cecil Hugh
Brunstrom, Alan Leslie
Buchanan, Hubert Elliott

*Department of Defense list provided to NAM-POW, Inc.

614

Budd, Leonard R., Jr.
Burer, Arthur William
Burgess, Richard Gordon
Burns, Donald Ray
Burns, John Douglass
Burns, Michael Thomas
Burroughs, William David
Butcher, Jack Meyring
Butler, Phillip Neal
Butler, William Wallace
Byrne, Ronald Edward, Jr.
Byrns, William Glen
Callaghan, Peter Alfred
Camacho, Issac
Camerota, Peter Paul
Campbell, Burton Wayne
Carey, David Jay
Carlson, Albert Edwin
Carpenter, Allan Russell
Carpenter, Joe Victor
Carrigan, Larry Edward
Cassell, Harley Mac, Jr.
Cavaiani, Jon Robert
Cerak, John Paul
Certain, Robert Glenn
Chambers, Carl Dennis
Chapman, Harlan Page
Charles, Norris Alphonzo
Chauncey, Arvin Roy
Cheney, Kevin Joseph
Chenoweth, Robert
    Preston
Cherry, Fred Vann
Chesley, Larry James
Chevalier, John Russell
Chirichigno, Luis Gerardo
Christian, Michael Durham
Cius, Frank Edward, Jr.
Clark, John Walter
Clements, James Arlen
Clower, Claude Douglas
Coffee, Gerald Leonard
Coker, George Thomas
Collins, James Quincy, Jr.
Collins, Thomas Edward,
    III
Condon, James Carroll
Conlee, William Walter

Cook, James Raymond
Copeland, H.C.
Cordier, Kenneth William
Cormier, Arthur
Coskey, Kenneth Leon
Crafts, Charles Earle
Craner, Robert Roger
Crayton, Render
Crecca, Joseph, Jr.
Cronin, Michael Paul
Crow, Frederick Austin, Jr.
Crowe, Winfred Douglas
Crowson, Fredrick Hugh
Crumpler, Carl Boyette
Curtis, Paul P.
Cusimano, Samuel Bolden
Cutter, James Dickinson
Daigle, Glenn Henri
Daly, James Alexander, Jr.
Daniels, Verlyne Wayne
Daugherty, Lenard Edward
Daughtrey, Robert Norlan
Davies, John Owen
Davis, Edward Anthony
Davis, Thomas James
Day, George Everette
Deering, John Arthur
DeLuca, Anthony
Dengler, Dieter
Denton, Jeremiah Andrew,
    Jr.
Despiegler, Gale Albert
Di Bernardo, James Vincent
Dierling, Edward A.
Dingee, David Burgoyne
Dodson, James E.
Donald, Myron Lee
Doremus, Robert Hartsch
Doss, Dale Walter
Doughty, Daniel James
Drabic, Peter Edward
Dramesi, John Arthur
Driscoll, Jerry Donald
Drummond, David Ian
Duart, David Henry
Dunn, John Galbreath
Dunn, John Howard
Dutton, Richard Allen

Eastman, Leonard Corbett
Eckes, Walter W.
Elander, William James, Jr.
Elbert, Frederick L., Jr.
Elias, Edward Knight
Elliott, Artice Weldon
Ellis, Jeffrey Thomas
Ellis, Leon Francis, Jr.
Ensch, John Clyde
Estes, Edward Dale
Ettmueller, Harry
    Lawrence
Everett, David Anderson
Everson, David
Fant, Robert St. Clair, Jr.
Fellowes, John Heaphy
Fer, John
Finlay, John Sewart, III
Fisher, John Bryant
Fisher, Kenneth
Fleenor, Kenneth Raymond
Flesher, Hubert Kelly
Flom, Fredric Russell
Flora, Carroll Edward, Jr.
Flynn, John Peter
Flynn, Robert James
Forby, Willis Ellis
Ford, David Edward
Fowler, Henry Pope, Jr.
Francis, Richard Logan
Frank, Martin Stanley
Franke, Fred Augustus W.,
    Jr.
Fraser, Kenneth James
Friese, Laurence Victor
Frishman, Robert Franchot
Fryett, George Fredrick, Jr.
Fuller, Robert Byron
Fulton, Richard Joseph
Gaddis, Norman Carl
Gaither, Ralph Ellis, Jr.
Galanti, Paul Edward
Galati, Ralph William
Gartley, Markham Ligon
Garwood, Robert Russell
Gauntt, William Aaron
Geloneck, Terry Mercer
Gerndt, Gerald Lee

Gideon, Willard Selleck
Gillespie, Charles R., Jr.
Giroux, Peter James
Glenn, Danny Elloy
Glenn, Thomas
Goodermote, Wayne Keith
Gostas, Theodore William
Gotner, Norbert Anthony
Gough, James Wayne
Gouin, Donat Joseph
Graening, Bruce Allen
Granger, Paul Louis
Grant, David Brian
Gray, David Fletcher, Jr.
Greene, Charles Edward, Jr.
Gregory, Kenneth Ray
Grigsby, Donald Edward
Groom, George Edward
Gruters, Guy Dennis
Guarino, Lawrence
    Nicholas
Guenther, Lynn Ellis
Guffey, Jerry Lester
Guggenberger, Gary John
Gurnsey, Earl F.
Guttersen, Laird
Guy, David S.
Haines, Collin Henry
Hall, George Robert
Hall, Keith Norman
Hall, Thomas Renwick Jr.
Halyburton, Porter Alexand
Hamilton, Walter D.
Hanton, Thomas John
Hardman, William Morgan
Hardy, William H.
Harker, David Northrup
Harris, Carlyle Smith
Harris, Jessie B. Jr.
Hatch, Paul G.
Hatcher, David Burnett
Hawley, Edwin Alexander
    Jr.
Hayhurst, Robert Edward
Heeren, Jerome Donald
Hefel, Daniel Henry
Hegdahl, Douglas Brent

Heilig, John
Heiliger, Donald Lester
Helle, Robert Ray
Henderson, William Joseph
Henry, Lee Edward
Henry, Nathan Barney
Herlik, Querin Edward
Hess, Jay Criddle
Hestand, James Hardy
Hickerson, James Martin
Higdon, Kenneth Hill
Hildebrand, Leland Louis
Hill, Howard John
Hinkley Robert Bruce
Hiteshew, James Edward
Hivner, James Otis
Hoffman, David Wesley
Hoffson, Authur Thomas
Horinek, Ramon Anton
Horio, Thomas Teruo
Hubbard, Edward Lee
Hudson, Robert Markham
Hughes, James Lindberg
Hughey, Kenneth Raymond
Hunsacker, James
Hutton, James Leo
Hyatt, Leo Gregory
Ingvalson, Roger Dean
Iodice, Frank C.
Jackson, Charles Allen
Jackson, James Elex, Jr.
Jacquez, Juan L.
James, Charlie Negus, Jr.
James, Gobel Dale
Jayroe, Julius Skinner
Jeffcoat, Carl Herbert
Jeffrey, Robert Duncan
Jenkins, Harry Tarleton, Jr.
Jensen, Jay Roger
Johnson, Bobby Louis
Johnson, Edward Robert
Johnson, Harold Eugene
Johnson, Kenneth Richard
Johnson, Richard Edgar
Johnson, Samuel Robert
Jones, Murphy Neal
Jones, Robert Campbell

Jones, Thomas Nelson
Kari, Paul Anthony
Kasler, James Helms
Kavanaugh, Abel Larry
Keirn, Richard Paul
Kernan, Joseph Eugene
Kerns, Gail Mason
Kerr, Michael Scott
Key, Wilson Denver
Kientzler, Phillip Allen
Kirk, Thomas Henry, Jr.
Kittinger, Joseph W., Jr.
Klomann, Thomas Joseph
Klusmann, Charles F.
Knutson, Rodney Allen
Kobashigawa, Tom
    Yoshinisa
Kopfman, Theodore Frank
Kramer, Galand Dwight
Kramer, Terry Lee
Kroboth, Alan Joseph
Kula, James David
Kushner, Floyd Harold
Labeau, Michael Harold
Lamar, James Lasley
Lane, Michael Christopher
Larson, Gordon Albert
Lasiter, Carl William
Latella, George Francis
Latendresse, Thomas B.
Latham, James Downs
Lawrence, William Porter
Lebert, Ronald Merl
Leblanc, Louis Edward, Jr.
Lehnrn, Gary
Lehrman, Ronald John
Lengyel, Lauren Robert
Lenker, Michael Robert
Leonard, Edward Watson,
    Jr.
Leopold, Stephen Ryder
Lerseth, Roger Gene
Lesesne, Henry Deas
Lewis, Earl Gardner, Jr.
Lewis, Frank Douglas
Lewis, Keith Herbert
Lewis, Robert, III

Ligon, Vernon Peyton, Jr.
Lilly, Warren Robert
Lockhart, Hayden James, Jr.
Logan, Donald Karl
Lollar, James Leon
Long, Julius Wollen, Jr.
Long, Stephen Glen
Low, James Frederick
Luna, Jose David
Lurie, Alan Pierce
MacPhail, Don Allen
Madden, Roy, Jr.
Madison, Thomas Mack
Makowski, Louis Frank
Malo, Issako Faatoese
Marshall, Marion Anthony
Martin, Donald Eugene
Martin, Edward Holmes
Martini, Michael Robert
Marvel, Jerry Wendell
Maslowski, Daniel Francis
Masterson, Frederick James
Mastin, Ronald Lambert
Matagulay, Roque Santos
Matheny, David Paul
Matsui, Melvin Kazuki
Mayall, William Thomas
Mayhew, William John
McCain, John Sidney, III
McClure, Claude Donald
McCuistion, Michael K.
McCullough, Ralph
　　William
McDaniel, Eugene Barker
McDaniel, Norman A.
McDow, Richard Henry
McGrath, John Michael
McKamey, John Bryan
McKnight, George Grigsby
McManus, Kevin Joseph
McMillan, Isiah
McMorrow, John P.
McMurray, Cordine
McMurray, Frederick
　　Charles
McMurry, William G., Jr.
McNish, Thomas Mitchell

McSwain, George Palmer,
　　Jr.
Means, William Harley, Jr.
Mechenbier, Edward John
Mecleary, Read Blaine
Mehl, James Patrick
Mehrer, Gustav, Alois
Merritt, Raymond James
Metzger, William John, Jr.
Meyer, Alton Benno
Miller, Edison Wainwright
Miller, Edwin Frank, Jr.
Miller, Roger Alan
Milligan, Joseph Edward
Mobley, Joseph Scott
Moe, Thomas Nelson
Molinare, Albert R.
Monlux, Harold Deloss
Montague, Paul Joseph
Moore, Dennis Anthony
Moore, Ernest Melvin, Jr.
Morgan, Gary Lee
Morgan, Herschel Scott
Mott, David Phillip
Mullen, Richard Dean
Mulligan, James Alfred, Jr.
Murphy, John Stanley, Jr.
Myers, Armand Jesse
Myers, Glenn Leo
Nagahiro, James Yoshikazu
Nakagawa, Gordon Ross
Nasmyth, John Heber, Jr.
Naughton, Robert John
Necoquinones, Felix Viador
Nelson, Steven D.
Neuens, Martin James
Newcomb, Wallace Grant
Newell, Stanley Arthur
Nichols, Aubrey Allen
Nix, Cowan Glenn
Norrington, Giles Roderick
Norris, Thomas Elmer
North, Joseph S. Jr.
North, Kenneth Walter
Nowicki, James Ernest
O'Connor, Michael Francis
Odell, Donald Eugene

O'Neil, James William
Ortiz-Rivera, Louis Antonio
Osborne, Dale Harrison
Osburn, Laird Pearson
Overly, Norris Miller
Padgett, James Phillip
Page, Jasper N.
Paige, Gordon Curtis
Parrott, Thomas Vance
Parsels, John William
Peel, Robert Delayney
Penn, Michael Gene
Perkins, Glendon William
Perricone, Richard Robert
Peterson, Douglas Brian
Peterson, Michael Terry
Pfister, James F., Jr.
Pirie, James Glenn
Pitchford, John Joseph, Jr.
Pitzer, Daniel Lee
Plumb, Joseph Charles, Jr.
Polfer, Clarence Ronald
Pollack, Melvin
Pollard, Ben Marskbury
Potter, Albert J.
Prather, Phillip Dean
Price, Donald Eugene
Price, Larry Donald
Profilet, Leo Twyman
Pryor, Robert James
Purcell, Benjamin Harrison
Purcell, Robert Baldwin
Purrington, Frederick
　　Raymond
Pyle, Darrel Edwin
Pyle, Thomas Shaw, II
Quinn, Francis
Raebel, Dale Virgil
Randall, Robert Irving
Rander, Donald J.
Ratzlaff, Brian Michael
Ratzlaff, Richard Raymond
Ray, James Edwin
Ray, Johnnie Lynn
Rayford, King David, Jr.
Reeder, William Spencer, Jr.
Rehmann, David George

Reich, William John
Reynolds, Jon Anzuena
Riate, Alfonso Ray
Rice, Charles Donald
Ridgeway, Ronald Lewis
Riess, Charles Francis
Risner, Richard F.
Risner, Robinson
Rivers, Wendall Burke
Robinson, Paul Kurtz, Jr.
Robinson, William Andrew
Rodriguez, Ferdinand A.
Roha, Michael Robert
Rollins, David John
Rose, George Alan
Rose, Joseph, III
Rowe, James Nicholas
Rudloff, Stephen Anthony
Ruhling, Mark John
Rumble, Wesley Lewis
Runyan, Albert Edward
Russell, Kay
Rutledge, Howard Elmer
Sandvick, Robert James
Sawhill, Robert Ralston, Jr.
Schierman, Wesley Duane
Schoeffel, Peter Vanruyter
Schrump, Raymond Cecil
Schulz, Paul Henry
Schweitzer, Robert James
Schwertfeger, William
    Ralph
Seeber, Bruce Gibson
Seek, Brian Joseph
Sehorn, James Eldon
Sexton, John Calvin, Jr.
Shanahan, Joseph Francis
Shankel, William Leonard
Shattuck, Lewis Wiley
Shepard, Vernon Clark
Shingaki, Tamotsu
Shively, James Richard
Shore, Edward R.
Shumaker, Robert Harper
Shuman, Edwin Arthur, III
Sienicki, Theodore Stanley
Sigler, Gary Richard
Sima, Thomas William

Simms, Harold Dean
Simonet, Kenneth Adrian
Simpson, Richard Thomas
Singleton, Jerry Allen
Smith, Bradley Edsel
Smith, Dewey Lee
Smith, Donald Glen
Smith, George Edward
Smith, Mark Allyn
Smith, Philip Eldon
Smith, Richard Eugene, Jr.
Smith, Wayne Ogden
Sooter, David William
Souder, James Burton
Southwick, Charles Everett
Sparks, John George
Spencer, Larry Howard
Spencer, William Alfred
Sponeyberge, Robert David
Spoon, Donald Ray
Springman, Richard Harold
Stackhouse, Charles David
Stafford, Hugh Allen
Stark, William Robert
Stavast, John Edward
Sterling, Thomas James
Stier, Theodore Gerhard
Stirm, Robert Lewis
Stischer, Walter Morris
Stockdale, James Bond
Stockman, Hervey Studdie
Storey, Thomas Gordon
Stratton, Richard Allen
Strickland, James Henry, Jr.
Stutz, Leroy William
Sullivan, Dwight Everett
Sullivan, Timothy Bernard
Sumpter, Thomas Wrenne,
    Jr.
Sweeney, Jon Martin
Swindle, Orson George, III
Tabb, Robert Ernest
Tallaferro, William B.
Talley, Bernard Leo, Jr.
Talley, William Hansen
Tangeman, Richard George
Tanner, Charles Nels
Taylor, William Brooks

Tellier, Dennie Andrew
Temperley, Russell Edward
Terrell, Irby David, Jr.
Terry, Ross Randle
Tester, Jerry Albert
Thacker, Brian Miles
Thomas, William Edwin, Jr.
Thompson, Dennis L.
Thompson, Floyd James
Thompson, Fred Neale
Thornton, Gary Lynn
Thorsness, Leo Keith
Tinsley, Coy Richard
Tomes, Jack H.
Torkelson, Loren Harvey
Trautman, Konrad Wigand
Triebel, Theodore Wallace
Trimble, Jack Randolph
Tschudy, William Michael
Tyler, Charles Robert
Uyeyama, Terry Jun
VanLoan, Jack Linwood
VanPutten, Thomas Harry
Vaughan, Samuel Richard
Vavroch, Duane Paul
Venanzi, Gerald Santo
Vissotzky, Raymond Walter
Vogel, Richard Dale
Vohden, Raymond Arthur
Waddell, Dewey Wayne
Waggoner, Robert Frost
Walker, Hubert Clifford, Jr.
Walker, Michael J.
Wallingford, Ken
Walsh, James Patrick, Jr.
Waltman, Donald Glenn
Wanat, George Karp, Jr.
Ward, Brian Hayden
Warner, James Howie
Watkins, Willie Arthur
Webb, Ronald John
Wells, Kenneth Roth
Wells, Norman Louross
Wendell, John Henry, Jr.
Wheat, David Robert
White, Robert Thomas
Wideman, Robert Earl
Wieland, Carl Thomsen

Wilber, Walter Eugene

Williams, James Wesley

Williams, Lewis Irving, Jr.

Wilmouth, Floyd Allen

Wilson, Glenn Hubert

Wilson, Hal K., III

Wilson, William Wallace

Winn, David William

Womack, Sammie Norman

Woods, Brian Dunstan

Woods, Robert Dean

Wright, Buddy

Writer, Lawrence Daniel

Young, James Faulds

Young, John Arthur

Young, Myron Alvin

Yuill, John Harry

Ziegler, Roy Esper, II

Zuberbuhler, Rudolph Ulric

Zuhoski, Charles Peter

Zupp, Klaus H.

Notes

Chapter One: A Year in Vietnam

1 Now Ho Chi Minh City.

2 Award of the Silver Star: "Horton, Harry W. Jr., 2d Lt, Inf. USA, Co D, 3d Bn., 22d Inf, 25th Inf Div. For gallantry in action: Second Lieutenant Horton, distinguished himself by heroic actions on 22 December 1967, while serving as platoon leader with Company D, 3d Battalion, 22d Infantry on a combat operation in the Republic of Vietnam. Lieutenant Horton's platoon was pinned down when Company D came under intense fire from an unknown enemy force. With complete disregard for his own safety he exposed himself many times to the enemy while trying to move his men into better fighting positions. As the battle raged Lieutenant Horton soon realized that it was imperative that the enemy bunker be subdued. Rather than call on one of his men to risk his life by charging the bunker, Lieutenant Horton elected to make the move himself. Charging the bunker under withering fire from automatic weapons, he came to within 10 meters of his goal before he was mortally wounded. Refusing to let a medic come to his aid he again started to move toward the bunker. Again the enemy opened fire killing him. Lieutenant Horton's personal courage and outstanding leadership are in keeping with the highest traditions of the military service and reflect great credit upon himself, his unit, the 25th Infantry Division and the United States Army.

3 Master Sergeant Ray A. Bows, U.S. Army Ret., *Vietnam Military Lore 1959–1973* (Hanover, Massachusetts: Bowe & Sons Publishing, 1988), pp.156–162. Camp Frenzell-Jones, 199th Infantry Brigade Base Camp, Long Binh, Bien Hoa Province, was named on September 28, 1967, for Herb Frenzell and Billy C. Jones, assigned to Company A, 4th Battalion, 12th Infantry, 199th Light Infantry Brigade. Privates Frenzell and Jones were killed when their patrol was ambushed by well-entrenched Viet Cong forces on January 21, 1967. To draw enemy fire away from his pinned-down patrol, Frenzell left his position hidden in a tree line and ran across an open field, shooting his own weapon while his fellow soldiers got to cover. Hit in the chest, Frenzell's body

dropped into the marsh. Jones crawled through heavy enemy fire to help his friend. Though Frenzell was dead, Jones dragged his body for two hours as the embattled patrol made its way to a helicopter landing zone. When another soldier was hit by enemy fire, Jones lowered Frenzell's body and went to the wounded man's aid. A single enemy gunshot struck Jones in the head. Their names are inscribed side-by-side on the Vietnam Veterans memorial on the east wall, panel 14E, line 62 and 63. Both were awarded the Silver Star for valor.

4 Every major unit in Vietnam had its own newspaper, and there were several Army magazines for the troops.

5 The Brigade newspaper, *Redcatcher!*, quoted one of the survivors, who spoke of Liteky with awe. "As everyone crawled and ran during the battle, Chaplain Liteky walked through the woods with the shrapnel and bullets cutting down trees all around him," said lst Lt. Wayne Morris, a platoon leader from Oak Ridge, Tennessee. "He would not take cover, and I never saw him try to protect himself. Later, while talking to the men who were left, I found they had the same story. He just seemed to be everywhere during the battle, and his actions and presence awed and inspired myself and my men. God only knows how many men we would have lost if he had not been there risking his life over and over again to get them out." Story by lst Lt. Michael D. Swearingen Jr., "Medal of Honor for Chaplain," *Redcatcher!* December 15, 1968, p.1. Wayne Morris, the platoon leader quoted, received the Distinguished Service Cross for his heroism in that battle.

6 My father, Bernie Burkett, was the true golfer in the family. A three-year letterman at Pennsylvania State University, he was elected captain in 1938 and played in the NCAA tournament every year of his college career. Ultimately, as an amateur, he would win almost one hundred golf tournaments, including the Bermuda Amateur, the 2nd Air Force Seniors (six times), and the Dallas County Senior Four-Ball. In April 1983, *Golf Digest* wrote a story about my father as the only man in the history of golf who had made holes-in-one in five different decades. Before his death in 1994, he scored another in a sixth decade. He considered his grandest golf feat scoring four consecutive eagles in a tournament.

7 Although golf was a central athletic focus of my family life, I was introduced to many other athletic pursuits at a young age. I was voted most valuable player of my Little League conference. At age fourteen, allowed to enter the air base rifle tournament, competing against many combat veterans, I placed third. In high school, I lettered in baseball, basketball, track, and golf. However, it was in basketball that I excelled. My senior year at C.E. Byrd High School in Shreveport, La., I played for the legendary coach Scotty Robinson, who would go on to fame in the college and professional coaching ranks. We won thirty-two games, and I was named to the All-City and All-District teams. At Vanderbilt I lettered three years on the varsity golf team, and was voted to the all-star intramural football team.

8 Bill Davidson, *Jane Fonda: An Intimate Biography* (New York, Penguin Books, 1991), p. 160.

9 A study of helicopter casualties taken from the Vietnam casualty master computer tape shows that about 3,100 died in combat-related helicopter crashes compared to 2,200 who died in noncombat-related crashes. Altogether, almost 10 percent of those who died in Vietnam were killed in helicopter-related incidents.

10 *Newsweek*, March 10, 1969. The battle involving these two towns was also described in *Newsweek* by correspondent Kevin Buckley, who reported that Tam Hiep was

reduced to rubble. I drove through the town several days after the firefight. While a number of the buildings were destroyed, Tam Hiep continued to be a thriving center of activity. Our "house girls" lived in Tam Hiep. They heard the noise but were unaware of the battle raging in the vicinity. It hadn't interrupted their daily activities.

Chapter Two: Welcome Home, Baby Killer

11 John Wheeler, *Touched With Fire: The Future of the Vietnam Generation*, Franklin Watts, Inc., New York, 1984, p. 104. Allan Bakke, a Marine veteran of the Vietnam War, was denied admittance to medical school at the University of California at Davis. He sued on the grounds of reverse discrimination [Regents of the University of California vs. Bakke]. He prevailed and was admitted when the Supreme Court ruled on June 28, 1978, that setting a quota was unconstitutional. What was never fully explored by the press or the courts was that two members of the Admissions Board felt strongly that a Vietnam veteran should not be allowed to be a doctor.

12 When veterans allow their memberships to lapse, many veterans' posts pay their dues to keep their membership figures up. It's the number of members that give these organizations political clout. Because membership rosters list the post address for the lapsed members, an inordinate number of the envelopes were delivered to the post address.

Chapter Three: Will the Real Vietnam Vet Stand Up?

13 I discovered a treasure trove of information about the Vietnam Killed-in-Action (KIA) while researching the names to be engraved on the Texas memorial. We wanted to show the names of the killed and missing in action alphabetically, along with their branch of service, rank, date of birth, and date of death. But when I asked about an accurate list of the Texans who died—from Bill Aadland to Carl Zywicke—the memorial group did not have one. I could find no official list of KIAs broken down by state. (Since only names are engraved on the national memorial, we could not use that list.)

After a wild goose chase through the Department of Defense and various military offices, I discovered that all the information I was looking for was in the electronics branch of the National Archives in Washington. That office had a list of every single Vietnam casualty. There was only one catch. There was no hard copy. Everything was on mainframe computer tape. The information had never been given out to the general public and was unavailable. I asked if the data was classified.

"Well, no one's ever asked us for it before," the woman said. She told me that if I made a request for the data under the Freedom of Information Act (FOIA), which applies to material collected by all federal agencies, they had to address the issue of whether the KIA tape was available to the public.

I knew about FOIA from talking to someone at the National Archives. The process seemed like something used only by investigative reporters for the *The New York Times*, not private citizens. But the archives official sent me a pamphlet explaining the procedure and in early 1987, I sent in a formal FOIA request for the tape. After a few weeks, they approved my request. For about $100, I could have the tape, with certain information barred from release by the Privacy Act deleted.

After receiving a round tape the size of a dinner plate in the mail, I took it to a Vietnam veteran who happened to be working in one of the mainframe computer rooms at a local corporation at night. The computer had excess capacity and he wangled permission to work with the data during the system's free time. We downloaded the whole tape into the computer and discovered an astonishing amount of information. The archives had deleted a few items, such as next-of-kin, but many other facts—date of birth, date of death, age, marital status, race, service, hometown—were listed for every one of those killed or missing in action in Vietnam, a sample of over 58,000.

14   The Army lost 496 second lieutenants, compared to 1,018 captains, 254 majors, and 117 lieutenant colonels.

15   Paul Fussell, *Wartime* (New York, Oxford: Oxford University Press, 1989), p. 52.

16   *Washington Times, Insight* magazine, March 19, 1991.

17   During World War II, 50 million men were registered with the draft, 20 million received draft notices, but only 10 million qualified and were inducted.

18   Once training facilities were completed later in the war, volunteers were no longer accepted and all induction was handled by Selective Service.

19   Harry G. Summers Jr., *Vietnam War Almanac* (New York: Facts on File Publications, 1985), p. 146.

20   Ibid., p. 108.

21   Tom Wolfe, "Art Disputes War: The Battle of the Vietnam Memorial," *Washington Post*, October 13, 1982, pp. B1, 3.

22   Bob Baker, "Staying Behind Now Catches Up," *Los Angeles Times*, February 22, 1988, p. A-1.

23   Mark Helprin, "I Dodged the Draft and I Was Wrong," *The Wall Street Journal*, October 16, 1992.

24   Our 199th commander demanded conscientious objectors pull all the same duty as other soldiers, which included perimeter guard. Not wanting to send men out without weapons, the commander and the C.O.s compromised. They would carry baseball bats. Fortunately, none had to test his batting prowess against an enemy with an AK-47.

25   Myra MacPherson, *Long Time Passing: Vietnam and the Haunted Generation* (Garden City, New York: Doubleday and Company, Inc., 1984) p.132.

26   *VVA Veteran*, April 1990, p. 11, quoting Department of Defense Report on Project 100,000.

27   George Q. Flynn, *The Draft: 1940–1973*. (University Press of Kansas, Lawrence, Kansas, 1993), pp. 31–32. *VFW Magazine*, "Vietnam Warriors: A Statistical Profile," March 1993.

28   *Redcatcher!* March 15, 1969, quoting a Department of Army news release. Seventy-nine percent of all Vietnam veterans had at least a high school degree. The draft brought in large numbers of college graduates."

29   Flynn, *The Draft: 1940–1973* (University Press of Kansas, 1993), p. 234.

30   Ibid., p. 235.

31   Christian G. Appy, *Working Class War: American Combat Soldiers and Vietnam*, (Chapel Hill: University of North Carolina Press, 1993.)

32   John F. Guilmartin Jr., Lt. Col. USAF (Ret), "America in Vietnam: A Working-Class War?," *Reviews in American History*, June 1994, pp. 322–326. Guilmartin relied on analysis of Department of Defense casualty records by researcher Bill Abbot, "Names on The Wall," *Vietnam*, June 1993.

33   Department of Defense casualty records, FOIA request by B. G. Burkett. According

to a demographic "State of the Jewish World" report issued during the World Jewish Congress held in January 1996, the percentage of Jews in the United States dropped from a post-World War II high of 4 percent to 2.3 percent. *Religion News Service*, January 27, 1996.

34   David Epstein, "Jewish Vets Not Fond of Jane," *Washington Times*, September 4, 1989, p. E-5.

35   William F. Buckley Jr., "Rich Man, Poor Man, and the Vietnam War," *Washington Post*, November 1, 1992, p. B-4.

36   Arnold Barnett, Timothy Stanley, and Michael Shore, "America's Vietnam Casualties: Victims of a Class War?," *Operations Research*, Vol. 40, No. 5, September-October 1992, pp. 856–866.

37   By enlisting in the Marine Corps, McLean had followed the example set years earlier by his step-father, actor Jimmy Stewart, who suspended his acting career to serve as a bomber pilot for the Army Air Corps in WWII and received a Distinguished Flying Cross and the French Croix de Guerre for his actions under fire.

38   *The Vietnam War: The Illustrated History of the Conflict in Southeast Asia*, edited by Ray Bonds. (Crown Publishers Inc., New York 1979) p. 212.

39   Vietnam Studies, *Law At War: Vietnam 1964-1973* (Department of the Army, 1975), pp. 106–107.

40   Fussell, *Wartime*, pp. 96–104.

41   *The Vietnam War: The Illustrated History of the Conflict in Southeast Asia* (Crown Publishers, 1979), p. 212.

42   Lee N. Robins, "Lessons From the Vietnam Heroin Experience," *The Harvard Mental Health Newsletter*, December 1994, pp. 5–6.

43   *Dow Theory Letters*, 994, June 29, 1988, quoting Francis Keating, assistant secretary for drug enforcement for the U.S. Treasury Department. " 'Any industry with twenty-five million American consumers can support an enormous empire.' The empire Keating is referring to, of course, is the drug empire centered in Medellin, Columbia."

44   *Retired Officer* magazine, October 1987, p. 20.

45   Paul J. Mulloy, "War on Drugs Needs More Ammunition," *The Wall Street Journal*, January 11, 1989. Mulloy, a retired rear admiral, directed the Navy's anti-drug abuse campaign.

46   *World War II Super Facts*, Don McCombs, Fred L. Worth, (Warner Books, 1983), p. 382. Martin James Monti, an Army Air Corps lieutenant, defected to the Germans in October 1944 by flying his P-38 to Vienna. He was placed in command of an SS unit manned by several hundred other U.S. Army defectors. In January 1948 Monti was tried in Brooklyn Federal Court for treason, theft of U.S. Government property, and being an agent of the enemy. He was sentenced to 25 years in prison and given a $10,000 fine.

47   Benedict B. Kimmelman, "The Example of Private Slovik," *American Heritage*, September-October 1987, pp. 97–104.

48   Summers, *Vietnam War Almanac*, p. 140.

49   The lower death ratio of Vietnam was indicative of better medical care, hygiene, and disease prevention techniques rather than a lighter combat environment. In addition, weather conditions were generally more severe in Korea and World War II than in Vietnam. This was particularly true in the winter. Frostbite and death by freezing did not occur in Vietnam.

50 These figures connote the total time from the casualty event to a postoperative admittance to a convalescence hospital. In Vietnam the advent of the helicopter helped to transport casualties rapidly. In addition, hospitals were modern and well-equipped in Vietnam. They were also strategically well-placed to handle casualties. In Korea and World War II, the front lines changed rapidly, causing most casualty care to be at mobile medical units, which were often understaffed, ill-equipped, and located inconveniently.

51 "Vietnam Warriors: A Statistical Profile," *VFW Magazine*, March 1993.

52 Bill Mauldin, *Back Home* (New York: William Sloane Associates, 1947), p. 54.

53 Ibid., p. 55.

54 Correctional Populations, 1992, Bureau of Justice Statistics. Bernard Gavzer, "Life Behind Bars," *Parade Magazine*, August 13, 1995.

55 Dane Archer and Rosemary Gartner, "The Myth of the Violent Veteran," *Psychology Today*, December 1976.

56 Martin Seymour Blaustein, "Veterans in Prison," *Bravo Veterans Outlook*, February 1991.

57 "C'Mon America," VietNow pamphlet, Washington, D.C. The pamphlet lists the organization's ten committees. Four involve "problem areas": Agent Orange, Drug Abuse, Delayed Stress, Employment.

58 Gary Burdick, "From the Military to Mayhem," *High Society*, January 1995, pp. 118–121.

59 Marc Leepson, "Why American Vets Have Gone From Jungle to Jail," *Texas VVA Monthly*, pp. 3, 12. June 1990.

60 News release, Bureau of Labor Statistics, United States Department of Labor, Washington, D.C., October 21, 1994.

61 James W. Hall-Sheehy, "The Unknown Vietnam Vet Manager," *Harvard Business Review*, May/June, 1986.

62 Guy Gugliotta, "Master of the Game," *VVA Veteran*, April 1990, pp. 13–16. Orginally appeared in *Tropic*, the *Miami Herald* magazine.

63 Louis Harris and Associates, Inc., *Myths and Realities: A Study of Attitudes Toward Vietnam Era Veterans*, (Washington: Veterans Administration), 1980.

64 Barry Sussman and Kenneth E. John, "Poll Finds Veterans Are at Home Again," *Washington Post*, April 11, 1985, pp. A-1, 11.

65 Ibid., p. A-11.

66 Vietnam Experience Study, "Health Status of Vietnam Veterans: Psychosocial Characteristics," *Journal of the American Medical Association*, Vol. 259, No. 18, May 13, 1988, p. 2701.

67 "Fresh Light on a Group Portrait," *U.S. News and World Report*, May 23, 1988, p. 12.

Chapter Four: The Ragtag Brigade

68 Lori Montgomery, "Officer's Killer Changed From Person Friends Knew," *Dallas Times Herald*, January 26, 1988.

69 Dick Hitt, "Did We Learn Nothing From 'Hill Street'?" *Dallas Times Herald*, January 30, 1988.

70 Military record of Carl Dudley Williams, National Personnel Records Center, FOIA request by B. G. Burkett.

71 Letter to Arthur E. Wible, publisher and chief executive officer, *Dallas Times Herald*, from B. G. Burkett, March 8, 1988.

72 Letter to B. G. Burkett from Arthur E. Wible, publisher and chief executive officer, *Dallas Times Herald*, April 5, 1988.

73 Associated Press photo, *Houston Chronicle*, November 11, 1987.

74 Military record of J. W. Duckworth, National Personnel Records Center, FOIA request by B. G. Burkett.

75 Military record of Roque "Rocky" Manrique, National Personnel Records Center, FOIA request by B. G. Burkett.

76 KXAS-Channel 5, Dallas/Fort Worth NBC affiliate, 10 P.M. newscast, May 9, 1989.

77 Military record of Joseph Testa Jr., National Personnel Records Center, FOIA request by B. G. Burkett, April 14, 1889.

78 Jeff South, "Dallas Vietnam Veterans Unmask a Pretender," *Dallas Times Herald*, May 7, 1989, p. A-1.

79 Military record for Timothy Honsinger, National Personnel Records Center, FOIA request by B. G. Burkett.

80 Jeff South, "Vet Believed Slain Is Found Alive, Thriving," *Dallas Times Herald*, October 1, 1968, p. B-2. And, Jan H. McQueary, "Vietnam Vet: 'I'm Very Much Alive," *Mineral Wells Index*, December 14, 1988, p.1.

81 Letter to B. G. Burkett from Ray Kline, president of the National Academy of Public Administration, July 24, 1991. The study, begun in 1991 for the National Academy of Public Administration, a Congressionally chartered, nonpartisan, nonprofit organization of elected fellows, reviewed federal electronic databases for the National Archives and Records Administration (NARA). Phase I identified the databases. I was asked to participate in Phase II, which developed criteria to appraise existing and future databases for inclusion in the National Archives. My panel was chaired by Cynthia Kendall, deputy assistant secretary of Defense (Information Systems,) and included Charles McClure, Center for Science and Technology, School of Information Studies, Syracuse University; Kenneth Scheflen, director of the Defense Manpower Data Center; Dr. Brady Foust, Department of Geography, University of St. Thomas; and Dr. Dean Allard, director of Naval History, Naval Historical Center.

82 John MacCormack, "Vietnam War Museum Has Own Message," *Dallas Times Herald*, July 9, 1989, p. B-1.

83 Military record of Gaylord O. Stevens, National Personnel Records Center, FOIA request by B. G. Burkett, September 12, 1989.

84 Military record of Kenneth M. Bonner, National Personnel Records Center, FOIA request by B. G. Burkett, October 17, 1989.

85 John MacCormack, "Museum Founders Caught In Lie," *Dallas Times Herald*, October 22, 1989, p. A-1.

86 Roberto Suro, "A Vietnam War Legacy: Museum Based on a Lie," *The New York Times*, November 6, 1989.

Chapter Five: Cbs Hits "The Wall Within"

87 Transcript, produced and directed by Holly K. Fine and Paul R. Fine, written by Perry Wolf, with CBS News correspondent Dan Rather, *CBS Reports: The Wall Within* (CBS News, 524 West 57th Street, New York, N.Y.) June 2, 1988. It was followed by

"P.T.S.D.," produced and directed by Holly K. Fine and Paul R. Fine, written with Perry Wolf, transcript of 60 *Minutes*, June 5, 1988.

88   Jay Sharbutt, "Does CBS Vietnam Show Mean Return of Documentaries?," *Los Angeles Times*, June 2, 1988, p. VI-1.

89   Kenneth R. Clark, "CBS Documents War Within the Vets," *Chicago Tribune*, June 2, 1988, Sect. 5, p. 12.

90   Tom Shales, "'Wall Within': A Vietnam Exorcism on CBS," *Washington Post*, June 2, 1988, p. C-1.

91   Clark, "CBS Documents War Within the Vets."

92   "The Vietnam War with Walter Cronkite," CBS Video Library.

93   Military record of Elvis G. Iredale, National Personnel Records Center, FOIA request by B. G. Burkett, August 23, 1990.

94   Military record of John Allan Michaelson, National Personnel Records Center, FOIA request by B. G. Burkett, August 23, 1990.

95   Military record of Mikal C. Rice, National Personnel Records Center, FOIA request by B. G. Burkett, August 23, 1990.

96   Military record of Richard Joseph Call, National Personnel Records Center, FOIA request by B. G. Burkett, August 23, 1990.

97   Reed Irvine, "Notes From the Editor's Cuff," *AIM Report*, June 1988.

98   Julie McCormick, "A Veteran Struggles to Live After Vietnam," *Bremerton Sun*, Bremerton, Washington, June 1, 1988.

99   Correspondence from Janice Jaman, Port Townsend, Washington, to B. G. Burkett, October 4, 1990.

100 Military record of Steven Ernest Southards, National Personnel Records Center, FOIA request by B. G. Burkett.

101 Letter from Andrew Weir, BBC Television Features, Broadcasting House, Bristol, UK, to B. G. Burkett, June 24, 1991.

102 Eric Bergerud, *Red Thunder, Tropic Lightning* (New York: Penguin, 1993).

103 Military record of Terry Bradley, National Personnel Records Center, FOIA request by B. G. Burkett, August 23, 1990.

104 Doug Clark, "'The Wall Within' Blocks Impartiality," Spokane *Spokesman-Review*, June 9, 1988.

105 Report from Cmdr. Arthur S. Fusco, USN, to commanding officer, USS *Ticonderoga*, "Formal Board of Investigation to inquire into the circumstances surrounding the death of AMH3 James Leroy Rush, USN."

106 Military Record of George Greul, National Personnel Records Center, FOIA request by B. G. Burkett.

107 Telephone interview of George Greul by Malcolm McConnell, October 22, 1993.

108 According to the Vietnam Veterans' Readjustment Act, the trauma triggering PTSD did not have to occur in combat or in Vietnam. To be eligible for compensation, the veteran needs only to have one day of service during the Vietnam era and be certified by a VA psychiatrist as traumatized by an event during military service, not necessarily during combat. Someone may qualify for PTSD compensation if they claim the trauma resulted from a stateside incident.

109 Official U.S. Navy ship log, USS *Ticonderoga*, 1971.

110 *Manual of the Judge Advocate General*, Final Investigative Report on the death of Seaman Ronald J. Becker, U.S. Navy, aboard the USS *Ticonderoga*, October 18, 1971. Obtained through FOIA request by B. G. Burkett, January 14, 1995.

III   Telephone conversation with George Greul by David Levy for *Reader's Digest*.

II2   Military record of Kenton Franklin Gleason, National Personnel Records Center, FOIA request by B. G. Burkett, May 18, 1995.

II3   Phone interview by Glenna Whitley with Kenton Gleason, April 27, 1995.

II4   Letter from Thomas K. Turnage, VA Administrator, to Howard Stringer, President of CBS Inc., June 17, 1988.

II5   Letter from Howard Stringer, president of CBS Inc., to Thomas K. Turnage, June 30, 1988. After the documentary aired, Reed Irvine of Accuracy in Media ran a two-line ad on the front page of the *The New York Times*: "Are you mad at Dan Rather? Call 1–800–825–2286." Callers heard a message about The Wall Within, giving them the anchorman's number at CBS and encouraging them to register their disapproval of its "slander" of Vietnam vets. After his office was inundated with hundreds of calls, Rather hooked his answering machine up to blast the Star Spangled Banner at his critics. Four angry Vietnam veterans appeared at a press conference organized by Irvine to condemn CBS: Barry Caron of the Vietnam Veterans Institute, Pete Joannides of the VFW, John Fales of the Blind Veterans, and "Red" McDaniel, former POW and president of the American Defense Institute. "There are an awful lot of individuals whose names are on that wall (the Vietnam Memorial) who gave their lives instead of hurting women and children," said Fales, who lost his sight in Vietnam. Rather and the Fines continued to defend their work. Perry Wolff, executive producer and writer of the documentary, told the *New York Daily News* that AIM's charges were inaccurate. "We stated very clearly that these problems don't affect all veterans. No one has attacked us on the facts." They clearly did not want to look too closely.

II6   Reed Irvine, "Rather's Anthem Abuse," *AIM Report*, September 1988, p. 2.

II7   Phone interview with Marlowe Churchill by Glenna Whitley, April 24, 1995. Also letter from Marlowe Churchill, March 14, 1994.

II8   Marlowe Churchill, "Lost in the Woods," *News Tribune*, Tacoma, Washington, December 28, 1983, p. B-1.

II9   Marlowe Churchill, "Getting Well," *News Tribune*, December 30, 1983, p. B-1. Photograph by Russ Carmack. Also letter from Marlowe Churchill to author T. Michael Booth and B. G. Burkett, March 14, 1994.

I20   Associated Press, "U.S. Wilds Hide Scars of Vietnam," *The New York Times*, December 31, 1983.

I2I   Marlowe Churchill, "Anonymous Threats Frighten Trip-wire Vet Back to Wilderness," Tacoma *News Tribune*, January 12, 1984, p. A-1.

I22   Doug Clark, "CBS Visit Heaped More Pain on Hurting Vietnam Vets," Spokane *Spokesman-Review*, August 7, 1987.

I23   Ibid.

I24   Doug Clark, "'The Wall Within' Blocks Impartiality," Spokane *Spokesman-Review*, June 9, 1988.

I25   Rob Wallace, producer, Tom Jarriel, correspondent, transcript of "Lost in the Jungle," 20/20, ABC Television, Inc., June 14, 1991 and May 22, 1992.

I26   Paul A. Witteman, "Lost in America," *Time*, February 11, 1991, p. 76.

I27   Ironically, in 1994, Tom Jarriel came to interview me for 20/20 about phony vets. We quickly connected after discovering we had graduated from the same high school in Shreveport, Louisiana. "By the way, Jug got all the records on the show you did about the bush vets," one of the producers needled Jarriel, who winced. "Were any of those phonies?," Jarriel asked.

128 Telephone interview with Kim Akhtar, CBS spokesman, by Glenna Whitley, for *Texas Monthly.*

129 Walter Goodman, "What Parson Rather Left Out of His Sermon," *The New York Times*, October 17, 1993, p. H-33.

130 Staff, "CBS's Rather Faults State of TV News Programming," *The Wall Street Journal*, October 1, 1993.

131 Military record of Dan Irvin Rather, National Personnel Records Center, FOIA request by B. G. Burkett, August 23, 1990.

132 Mark Lane, *Conversations With Americans* (New York: Simon & Schuster, 1970), p. 1.

Chapter Six: Atrocities: The Good War Versus the Bad War

133 Antiwar pamphlet, "Out of the Depths Do I Cry Unto Thee," No. 1108, Indochina Archive, History of the Vietnam War on Microfilm, University of California.

134 "Police Guard Rites for Vietnam Hero," *The New York Times*, June 10, 1965.

135 John Wheeler, "Anti-Vietnam War Logic Is Being Ignored for Somalia," *The Dallas Morning News*, December 30, 1992, p. A-21.

136 "Circular on Antiwar Movements in the U.S.," Document captured on May 12, 1971 in South Vietnam, according to COMUSMACV report dated 30 June 1971. "This report contains information obtained from an enemy document and concerns a directive, with the signature block of Phuoc," says the report cover. "The directive, dated 28 April 1971, urges the addressees to motivate discussions among the people on recent antiwar demonstrations in the United States." Obtained from the Indochina Archive, History of the Vietnam War on Microfilm, University of California.

137 Chester A. Bain, "Vietcong Propaganda Abroad," *Foreign Service Journal*, Congressional Record, U.S. Senate, February 25, 1969.

138 Todd L. Newmark, "A Parade Won't Heal the Divisions Over Vietnam," *The Wall Street Journal*, November 12, 1982.

139 Robert W. Kagan, "Realities and Myths of the Vietnam War," *The Wall Street Journal*, April 1, 1982.

140 *The Winter Soldier Investigation: An Inquiry into American War Crimes*, Copyright 1972 by the Vietnam Veterans Against the War, Inc. (Beacon Press).

141 Norman Podhoretz, *Why We Were In Vietnam* (New York: Simon & Schuster, 1982), p. 197.

142 Pamphlet from Indochina Archive, History of the Vietnam War on Microfilm, University of California.

143 Douglas C. Waller, *The Inside Story of America's Secret Soldiers* (New York: Simon & Schuster, 1994).

144 Paul Fussell, "The Real War 1939–1945," *The Atlantic Monthly*, August 1989, pp. 32–39.

145 Lt. Gen. W. R. Peers, USA (Ret.), *The My Lai Inquiry* (New York: W. W. Norton, 1979).

146 Although Calley's unit was found to be above average in test scores and education by the Peers Report, many in the Americal Division had discipline problems previous to their assignment to the division.

147 William Wilson, "I Had Prayed to God That This Thing Was Fiction," *Battles and Leaders*, supplement to *American Heritage Magazine*, June 1997.

148 Usually these units initially suffer an extremely high level of casualties among the troops. Once such a unit gets into combat and becomes experienced and seasoned, its performance tends to improve. Attrition due to casualties and rotations allow

replacements who are typically of a higher caliber to upgrade the unit. Both Norman Schwarzkopf and Colin Powell, young captains regarded as up-and-coming officers, were brought into the Americal Division during the Vietnam War. The military often gives its best daunting tasks to test them.

One of the units that comprised the Americal was the 198th Infantry, which I saw formed and trained through this selection process at Fort Hood in 1967. From its inception, the 198th Infantry had been a disciplinary problem, with constant fighting, insubordination, and general unruliness. The ultimate illustration of their lack of military discipline occurred only hours before they were to ship out. That night, many of the men of the new 198th Infantry packed the various beer gardens that catered to enlisted men. When the duty officer came to shut down the main beer hall for the evening, standard procedure, he was met by an unruly mob of drunks. Men started throwing rocks through the windows of buildings on the main street at Fort Hood. Progressing down the street, they attacked parked cars, trying to overturn them or smash the windshields. What started as a rowdy band of intoxicated soldiers rapidly turned into a riot.

The Army is confronted with a dilemma in such circumstances. A soldier cannot be allowed to wreak havoc in order to avoid being sent to the combat zone. Therefore, all those charged with committing crimes during the rioting deployed with their units at dawn. During the 198th Infantry's ship transit of the Pacific about two dozen soldiers involved faced court-martial proceedings. Anyone who did not know that the Americal Division was a disaster looking for a place to happen was not paying attention. Lt. Calley was a platoon leader in the 11th Infantry Brigade of the Americal, which was formed exactly like the 198th Infantry.

149 Marc Leepson, "Those Who Forget the Past," *VVA Veteran*, January 1995, pp. 15–16, 34–35.

150 Ibid., p. 16.

151 Marc Leepson, "Some Like It Hot," *VVA Veteran*, May/June 1994.

152 Morley Safer, *Flashbacks* (New York: Random House, 1990), pp. 103–104.

153 Leepson, "Those Who Forget the Past," pp. 15–16, 34–35.

154 Ibid.

155 "The Legacy of Vietnam," *Newsweek*, April 15, 1985, p. 65.

156 Maj. Gen. John K. Singlaub, U.S. Army (Ret.) with Malcolm McConnell, *Hazardous Duty: An American Soldier in the Twentieth Century* (New York: Summit Books, 1991) p. 322.

157 McConnell, *Hazardous Duty*, p. 317.

158 Peter Braestrup, *The Big Story: How the American Press and Television Reported and Interpreted the Crisis of Tet 1968 in Vietnam and Washington* (New Haven and Longon: Yale University Press, 1978, Abridged Edition), pp. 193–197.

159 Letter from Phil Cannella to B. G. Burkett, March 10, 1992.

160 Susan Reed, "A Marine's Reparation," *People Weekly*, December 11, 1995, pp. 103–104. The phrase continues to pop up in odd ways. In January 1996, Tony Auth of the *Philadelphia Inquirer* ran a cartoon depicting a factory maximizing profits by "cutting the work force and making fewer widgets." The logic is that unemployed people can't afford to buy widgets anyway. The punch line: "We had to destroy the company in order to save it."

161 Thousands of Confederate soldiers died in Union prisons under similar conditions, but no one was ever charged. The victors made the rules.

162   J. B. McCraw, "Civil War's Andersonville Commandant Remembered," *The Stars and Stripes*, February 18, 1991, p. 8.

163   Douglas Holt, "Two Accused of Trying to Sell Art that Brother Looted From Nazis," *The Dallas Morning News*, January 5, 1996, pp. A-1, 32.

164   Hanson W. Baldwin, "The Critics Have Lost Their Cool," *The New York Times*, May 31, 1971. Obtained from the Indochina Archive, History of the Vietnam War on Microfilm, University of California.

165   Guenter Lewy, *America in Vietnam,*(New York: Oxford University Press 1978), Appendix I, p.42

166   A. Francis Hatch, "One Despicable Legacy of the Vietnam War is the False Portrayal of American Soldiers as Bloodthirsty Barbarians," *Vietnam*, August 1995, pp. 58–62.

167   Ibid., p. 59.

168   Daniel Lang, *Casualties of War* (New York: Pocket Books, 1989). This was first published in the October 18, 1969, issue of the *New Yorker*.

169   George Szamuely, "The Casualty of a Director's Whim," *Insight*, September 4, 1989, p. 63.

170   Leepson, "Those Who Forget the Past," p. 16.

171   *Listing of Army Personnel Who Died by Suicide or Execution, 7 December 1941 through 30 June 1946*, National Archives. And *Statistical Survey: General Courts-Martial In the European Theater of Operations*, History Branch Office of the Judge Advocate General with the United States Forces European Theater, 18 July 1942–1 November 1945, Vol. 1. The Center of Military History, Department of the Army, FOIA request by B. G. Burkett, July 25, 1990.

172   Record of Trial by General Court-Martial for Pvt. Armstead White, II Corps, Caltanissetta, Sicily, 21 July, 1943, National Archives. In approving the sentence, Theater Judge Advocate Brig. Gen. Adam Richmond pointed out that the severe punishment was warranted: "The act was committed on the soil of Sicily within a week after our first troops had set foot thereon and while our forces were still engaged with the enemy." And the attack happened in the presence of her husband and small child. "The act not only violates individual concepts of morality but also reflects upon our national honor."

173   Record of Trial by General Court-Martial for Pvt. William D. Pennyfeather, Cherbourg, France, 2 September, 1944, National Archives.

174   Hatch, "One Despicable Legacy of the Vietnam War is the False Portrayal of American Soldiers as Bloodthirsty Barbarians," p. 61.

175   Ibid.

176   During World War II, when the Japanese attacked Pearl Harbor, it was later determined that not a single Japanese bomb had fallen outside a military target. All of the civilian casualties in Honolulu and surrounding areas were caused by the defensive fire of the United States Navy falling back to earth.

177   Edited by Winston G. Ramsey, "The Ruhr Dams Raid 1943," *After the Battle*, Vol. 3, 1973, pp. 1–12. *After the Battle* is a British military history magazine.

178   Patrick Buchanan, "Hypocrisy of the Nuremberg Trials About to be Revealed," *Dallas Times Herald*, April 18, 1990.

179   James Webb, "Was it Necessary?," *Parade Magazine*, July 30, 1995, pp. 4–5.

180   Christopher Lew, "Trial By Fire," *World War II*, September 1995, pp. 26–32.

181   Charles W. Sweeney, "'The Sky Was Bleached a Bright White,'" *The Wall Street Journal*, July 19, 1995, p. A-12.

182 Bilton and Sim, *Four Hours in My Lai*, p. 367.

183 Charles W. Sasser and Craig Roberts, *One Shot—One Kill* (New York: Pocket Books, 1990).

184 E.B. Sledge, *With the Old Breed* (Oxford University Press, N.Y., 1990).

185 Herman Wouk, *Winds of War* (New York: Pocket Books, 1973).

186 Lt. Col. H. Ross Miller, USAF (Ret.), "Bismarck Sea Triumph," letter to the editor, *Air Force* magazine, October 1996, p. 7.

187 Edwin Hoyt, *Submarines at War: The History of the American Silent Service* (Stein and day, 1983), p. 183. Third War Patrol Report of USS *Wahoo*, January 16, 1943, to February 7, 1943, National Archives, request by B.G. Burkett.

188 Directive, Order of Investigation into Mistreatment of Prisoners of War, Headquarters, U.S. Forces, European Theater, signed by Commanding General Dwight David Eisenhower, July 18, 1945. Declassified May 29, 1980. "Summary of Reports of Investigation, Pursuant to Direction of the Theater Commander, dated July 18, 1945, into compliance with the provisions of the Geneva Prisoners of War Convention by United States Forces," no date, declassified May 29, 1980. National Archives.

189 Edited by Winston G. Ramsey, "The Webling Incident," *After the Battle*, Vol. 27, 1980, p. 30.

190 Edited by Winston G. Ramsey, "Dauchau," *After the Battle*, Vol. 31, 1981, p. 46.

191 Marjorie Miller, "Retired Israeli General Describes Killing Prisoners," *The Dallas Morning News*, August 16, 1995, pp. A:1, 18. (Distributed by *Los Angeles Times-Washington Post* News Service.)

192 *Los Angeles Times-Washington Post* News Service, "Israel in Turmoil Over POW Deaths," *The Dallas Morning News*, August 17, 1995, p. A-18.

193 Paul Solotaroff, "Exile on Main Street," *Rolling Stone*, June 24, 1993, pp. 62–68.

194 Ibid., p. 64.

195 Mark Lane, *Conversations With Americans*, (New York: Simon & Schuster, 1970).

196 James Reston Jr., *Saturday Review*, January 9, 1971, p. 26. A battalion is actually 800 to 850 men.

197 Neil Sheehan, Review, "Conversations with Americans," the *New York Times Book Review*, December 27, 1970, p. 5.

198 Lane, *Conversations With Americans*, pp. 25–30.

199 Sheehan, Review, "Conversations with Americans."

200 Lane, *Conversations With Americans*, pp. 110–116.

201 Sheehan, Review, "Conversations with Americans."

202 Lane, *Conversations With Americans*, pp. 31–35.

203 Sheehan, Review, "Conversations with Americans."

204 Ibid.

205 Lewy, *America in Vietnam*, (New York: Oxford University Press, 1978), p. 317.

206 Ibid., p. 317.

207 Susan Brownmiller, "Making Female Bodies the Battlefield," *Newsweek*, January 4, 1993, p. 37.

208 United Press International, "Antiwar Ad Unread by 49 GIs," *The Stars and Stripes*, April 19, 1971. Indochina Archive, History of the Vietnam War on Microfilm, University of California.

209 Phil Duncan, editor, "Congressional Quarterly's Politics in America," 102nd Congress, 1992, p. 678.

210 J. F. Ter Horst, "A Soldier and a Socialite," *Human Events*, May 22, 1971, p. 6.

211 *The Winter Soldier Investigation* (New York: Beacon Press, 1972).

212 William Overend, "Who is Al Hubbard?," *National Review*, June 1, 1971, p. 589.

213 Military Record of Michael R. Harbert, National Personnel Records Center, FOIA request by Daniel J. Cragg, May 14, 1982.

214 Erwin Knoll and Judith Nies McFadden, editors, *War Crimes and the American Conscience* (New York: Holt, Rinehart and Winston, Inc., 1970), p.106.

215 Robert Jay Lifton, M.D., *Home From the War* (New York: Basic Books, 1985). The book was reprinted, with a new introduction about the Gulf War, (Boston: Beacon, 1992).

Chapter Seven: The Creation of Posttraumatic Stress Disorder

216 Steve Bentley, "A Short History of PTSD," *VVA Veteran* magazine, January 1991, p. 13.

217 *Forbes* magazine, July 13, 1987, p. 327. This item appeared in a retrospective of *Forbes* from 1917.

218 Wilbur J. Scott, *The Politics of Readjustment* (New York: Walter de Gruyter, Inc., 1993), p. 30.

219 Ibid., p. 32.

220 Ibid., p. 33.

221 Dr. Phoebe S. Spinrad, "Patriotism as Pathology: Antiveteran Activism and the VA," *Journal of the Vietnam Veterans Institute*, Vol. 3, Number 1, 1994, p. 47.

222 Dr. Norman Camp, "The Vietnam War and the Ethics of Combat Psychiatry," *American Journal of Psychiatry*, July 1993, p. 1002.

223 Spinrad, "Patriotism as Pathology: Anti-Veteran Activism and the VA," p. 47.

224 Stuart Auerbach, "Added Stress on Vietnam Veterans Seen," *Washington Post*, as published in the *Los Angeles Times* on January 28, 1970. Indochina Archive, History of the Vietnam War on Microfilm, University of California.

225 Fussell, "The Real War 1939–1945," p. 36.

226 Ibid., p. 37.

227 Anthony Cave Brown, *Bodyguard of Lies* (New York: Harper & Row, 1975), p. 713.

228 Fussell, "The Real War 1939–1945," p. 38.

229 John McDonough, "They Were There to Win a War," *The Wall Street Journal*, August 11, 1995.

230 "The Military Psychiatrist," *New York Daily News*, July 27, 1971. Obtained from the Indochina Archive, History of the Vietnam War on Microfilm, University of California.

231 Lifton, *Home From the War*, p. 19.

232 Ibid., pp. 31, 69, 81.

233 Richard Homan, "Guilt Feelings Seen for Returning GIs," *Washington Post*, May 3, 1969.

234 Spinrad, "Patriotism as Pathology." p. 51.

235 John Del Vecchio, Foreword to Joel Osler Brende and Erwin Randolph Parson, *Vietnam Veterans: The Road to Recovery* (New York: Plenum, 1985), p. xii.

236 MacPherson, *Long Time Passing*, p. 168.

237 Camp, "The Vietnam War and the Ethics of Combat Psychiatry," p. 1003.

238 Associated Press, "Doctor Raps Tale of Viet Vets Adjustment Woes," *The Stars and Stripes*, April 1974. Indochina Archive, History of the Vietnam War on Microfilm, University of California.

239 Bruce Winters, "Viet Veterans Called 'Time Bombs,'" *Baltimore Sun*, January 15, 1975. Indochina Archive, History of the Vietnam War on Microfilm, University of California.

240 Tom Wicker, "The Vietnam Disease," *The New York Times*, May 27, 1975. Indochina Archive, History of the Vietnam War on Microfilm, University of California.

241 David Lamb, "Viet Veterans Melting Into Society," *Los Angeles Times*, November 3, 1975. Indochina Archive, History of the Vietnam War on Microfilm, University of California.

242 Spinrad, "Patriotism as Pathology," p. 63. Citing Melvin R. Jacob, *A Pastoral Response to the Troubled Vietnam Veteran* (Cincinnati: DAV Press, 1987), pp. 51–74. As Spinrad shows, most of Jacob's evidence comes from Lifton.

243 Judith Lewis Herman, *Trauma and Recovery* (New York: Basic Books, 1992), pp. 9, 27.

244 Jacob, *A Pastoral Response to the Troubled Vietnam Veteran*, p. 61.

245 Spinrad, "Patriotism as Pathology," p. 65.

246 Louis Harris and Associates, Inc., *Myths and Realities: A Study of Attitudes Toward Vietnam Era Veterans*, (Washington: Veterans Administration), 1980.

247 MacPherson, *Long Time Passing: Vietnam and the Haunted Generation* (Garden City, New York: Doubleday and Company), p. 232.

248 Scott, *The Politics of Readjustment*, pp. 35–37, 63–64.

249 Military record of Floyd G. "Shad" Meshad, National Personnel Record Center, FOIA request by B. G. Burkett, October 14, 1992.

250 Scott, *The Politics of Readjustment*, p. 37.

251 Wilbur J. Scott, "PTSD in DSM-III: A Case in the Politics of Diagnosis and Disease," *Social Problems*, Vol. 37, Number 3, August 1990, p. 307.

252 Scott, *The Politics of Readjustment*, p. 4.

253 Ibid., p. 5.

254 Lifton, *Home From the War*, pp. 36–37.

255 Sarah A. Haley, MSW, "When the Patient Reports Atrocities," *Archives of General Psychiatry*, Vol. 30, February 1974, pp. 191–196.

256 Al Hubbard. The poem first appeared in *The New Soldier* by John Kerry (New York: Collier Books, 1971) p. 92. Original emphasis.

257 Haley, "When the Patient Reports Atrocities," *Archives of General Psychiatry*, p. 192.

258 Ibid., p. 196.

259 Tom Wicker, "The Vietnam Disease," *The New York Times*, May 27, 1975.

260 Scott, "PTSD in DSM-III: A Case in the Politics of Diagnosis and Disease," *Social Problems*, p. 307.

261 *Diagnostic and Statistical Manual of Mental Disorders, Third Edition-Revised* (Washington, D.C., American Psychiatric Association, 1987). The diagnostic criteria for 309.89 Posttraumatic Stress Disorder:

A. "The person has experienced an event that is outside the range of usual human experience and that would be markedly distressing to almost anyone, e.g., serious threat to one's life or physical integrity; serious threat or harm to one's children, spouse, or other close relatives and friends; sudden destruction of one's home or community; or seeing another person who has recently been, or is being, seriously injured or killed as the result of an accident or physical violence."

B. The traumatic event is persistently reexperienced in at least one of the following ways:

(1) recurrent and intrusive distressing recollections of the event (in young chil-

dren, repetitive play in which themes or aspects of the trauma are expressed)

(2) recurrent distressing dreams of the event

(3) sudden acting or feeling as if the traumatic event were recurring (includes a sense of reliving the experience, illusions, hallucinations, and dissociative [flashback] episodes, even those that occur upon awakening or when intoxicated)

(4) intense psychological distress at exposure to events that symbolize or resemble an aspect of the traumatic event, including anniversaries of the trauma

C. Persistent avoidance of stimuli associated with the trauma or numbing of general responsiveness (not present before the trauma), as indicated by at least three of the following:

(1) efforts to avoid thoughts or feelings associated with the trauma

(2) efforts to avoid activities or situations that arouse recollection of the trauma

(3) inability to recall an important aspect of the trauma (psychogenic amnesia)

(4) markedly diminished interest in significant activities (in young children, loss of recently acquired developmental skills such as toilet training or language skills)

(5) feeling of detachment or estrangement from others

(6) restricted range of affect, e.g., unable to have loving feelings

(7) sense of a foreshortened future, e.g., does not expect to have a career, marriage, or children, or a long life

D. Persistent symptoms of increased arousal (not present before the trauma), as indicated by at least two of the following:

(1) difficulty falling or staying asleep

(2) irritability or outbursts of anger

(3) difficulty concentrating

(4) hypervigilance

(5) exaggerated startle response

(6) physiologic reactivity upon exposure to events that symbolize or resemble an aspect of the traumatic event (e.g., a woman who was raped in an elevator breaks out in a sweat when entering any elevator.)

262   Christopher Buckley, "Viet Guilt," *Esquire*, September 1983, pp. 68–72.

263   Tom Morganthau, etc., "The Troubled Vietnam Vet," *Newsweek*, March 30, 1981, pp. 28–29.

264   Military record of Daniel Spranger, National Personnel Records Center, FOIA request by B. G. Burkett, March 12, 1993.

265   Military record of Steven Cytryszewski, National Personnel Records Center, FOIA request by B. G. Burkett, April 5, 1993.

Chapter Eight: Rambo: An American Hero

266   "What They Did In the War," *People Weekly*, October 5, 1992, p. 54. Ironically, a man named Arthur John Rambo did die in Vietnam. He was a married twenty-four-year-old soldier who was killed in combat on November 26, 1969 in Tay Ninh Province. His name is listed on the Wall, 16W, 126. Stallone rode to fame and fortune on the name of a man who is all but forgotten except by his family.

267   Aljean Harmetz, "For Brian Dennehy, Character Tells All," *The New York Times*, April 23, 1989, Arts and Leisure, pp. 13, 21.

268   David Rensin, "20 Questions: Brian Dennehy," *Playboy*, November 1993, pp. 119, 164–166.

269   Military Record of Brian Manion Dennehy, National Personnel Records Center, FOIA request by B. G. Burkett, May 17, 1991.

270   M. K. Guzda, "Pretenders to Pain," *Baltimore Sun*, June 12, 1988.

271   William Marvel, "The Great Impostors," *Blue & Gray*, February 1991, pp. 32–33.

272   Brendan Gill, "Western Star Tom Mix," *Architectural Digest*, April 1994, p. 276.

273   S. Joseph Hagenmayer, "Records Say Beloved Ace's WW I Stories Just Won't Fly," *Philadelphia Inquirer*, March 10, 1995.

274   Frank H. Jonas, *The Story of a Political Hoax*, Research Monograph No. 8, The Institute of Government, University of Utah, Salt Lake City, 1966.

275   *The New York Times* Wire Service, "Veteran Rebuts Army's Finding Against Claim of Heroic Deeds," the *Orange County Register*, December 17, 1989, p. A-10.

276   *Charles Gordon Vick v. the United States*, 231 Ct. Claims 909, No. 18–82. August 20, 1982, pp. 909–910.

277   Susan Katz Keating, "Phony GIs Exposed: From Navy SEALs to the 'Marshal of France,'" *The American Legion*, June 1993, pp. 32, 55.

278   Ione Oliver, "Veteran Isn't Resting on his Laurels," *San Bernardino Sun*, November 1993.

279   Walter W. Stender and Evans Walker, "The National Personnel Records Center Fire: A Study in Disaster," *The American Archivist*, Volume 37, Number 4, October 1974, p. 528.

280   Military record of William C. Gehris, National Personnel Records Center, FOIA request by B. G. Burkett, December 29, 1993.

281   Marlowe Churchill, "He Says Fifty-four Decorations But the Army Lists 15," the Riverside, CA, *Press-Enterprise*, April 17, 1994, B-1.

282   Julie Bird, "Award's Namesake Revealed as a Fraud," *Air Force Times*, January 20, 1997, p. 4.

283   Jim O'Connell, "Rep. Cooley Remembers Korean War," Medford, Oregon, *Mail Tribune*, July 28, 1995, p. A-3.

284   That reporter left the paper and passed the report I obtained on to the journalists who replaced him.

285   Mark Wigfield, "Morning Reports are Indisputable," Medford, Oregon, *Mail Tribune*, April 30, 1996, p. A-7. Morning reports and duty rosters are the ultimate authority, the documents which the Pentagon uses to investigate fraud. These documents were required to be letter perfect. The company clerk was required to make six copies. The reports were reviewed by the first sergeant and signed by the unit commander. Any errors or strikeovers and the commander sent it back to be redone. In the case of the Oregon congressman, Wigfield was the third reporter to investigate Cooley. The first Ottaway News Service writer called me in 1994. I filed an FOIA request for Cooley's record and gave it to the first reporter. When that reporter left, another journalist took on the assignment. In April 1996, Wigfield published the results of his investigation, revealing Cooley's many prevarications.

286   Richard Reeves, "Masking the Past," *The Dallas Morning News*, May 7, 1996, p. A-19.

287   Tom Barnes, "Representative Caught in a Lie; Isn't a Veteran," *Hartford Courant*, September 19, 1984.

Chapter Nine: Would I Lie to You?

288 M. K. Guzda, "Pretenders to Pain," *Baltimore Sun*, June 12, 1988.

289 Dana Priest, "Suspected D.C. Terrorist Sought by U.S. in Bosnia," *Washington Post*, January 25, 1996, p. A-20.

290 Terry Carter, "Suspect Succumbs to Wounds," Newport News-Hampton, VA, *Times-Herald*, August 15, 1979.

291 Terry Carter, "Motive Sought in Hotel Murder," Newport News-Hampton, VA, *Times-Herald*, August 9, 1979, p. 1.

292 J. Lynn Lunsford and Alexei Barrioneuvo, "Arlington Officer Kills Man Armed with Knife," *The Dallas Morning News*, October 18, 1993, pp. A-17–19.

293 Military record of Richard Dale Moore, National Personnel Records Center, FOIA request, December 8, 1993, by B. G. Burkett.

294 Jeff South, "Youth Who Shot His Father Recalls Chronic Abuse, Fear," *Dallas Times Herald*, October 5, 1988, pp. A-1, 12.

295 McClatchy News Service, "Chaplain Lied About Past, Army Says," *The Herald*, July 22, 1990, p. B-4.

296 Lincoln Caplan, "The Jagged Edge," *ABA Journal*, March 1995, pp. 52–100.

297 Larry Reibstein, "The 'Zelig' of Wall Street," *Newsweek*, February 25, 1991, p. 68.

298 Chuck Hawkins, with Leah Nathans Spiro, "The Mess At Pru-Bache," *Business Week*, March 4, 1991, p. 66–72. Also see *Serpent on the Rock*, Kurt Ichenwald (Harper Business, 1995).

299 Don Oldenburg, "Impostors Usually Acting Out Deep-Seated Need to Succeed," *Houston Chronicle*, October 11, 1987, p. B-3.

300 Susan Katz Keating, "Phony Heroes of Conjured Combat," *Insight Magazine*, the *Washington Times*, June 4, 1990, pp. 50–51.

301 James M. Perry, "Harkin Presidential Bid Marred by Instances in Which Candidate Appears to Stretch Truth," *The Wall Street Journal*, December 26, 1991, p. 32.

302 Associated Press, "Vietnam Vets Protest Duke Statements," *The Dallas Morning News*, September 7, 1990.

303 Sally Jean Peck, "Wartime Memories Only Beginning to Fade," *Lewisville News*, November 10, 1991, pp. A-1, 7.

304 Military record of Michael D. Donley, National Personnel Records Center, FOIA request by B. G. Burkett, December 9, 1991.

305 Military record of William Archie Akin, National Personnel Records Center, FOIA request by B. G. Burkett, March 17, 1992.

306 Bronson Havard and Kevin J. Shay, "Addison Councilman Leads Impostor Life," Addison, Tex. *Register*, February 6, 1992. A-1.

307 Malcolm McConnell, *Stepping Over: Personal Encounters with Young Extremists* (New York: Reader's Digest Press, 1984) pp. 290–311.

308 Medal of Honor citation, Fred William Zabitosky, *Vietnam Era Medal of Honor Recipients 1964-1972*, Committee on Veterans' Affairs, United States Senate, April 15, 1973, p. 156.

309 Sally Giddens, "The Edelman File," Dallas, Texas, *D Magazine*, May 1988, pp. 54–82.

310 Edmund Pankau, *Check It Out: Everyone's Guide to Investigation* (Houston: Cloak and Data Press, 1990).

311 Steve Lohr, "A New Breed of Sam Spade," *The New York Times*, February 20, 1992.

312 Unpublished manuscript, Edmund Pankau, *Easy Money*, p. 4.

313 Laura Johannes, "Pankau, P.I.: Less Than Meets the Eye," *The Wall Street Journal*, January 12, 1994, p. T-1.

314 Military record of Edmund J. Pankau, National Personnel Records Center, FOIA request by B. G. Burkett, December 9, 1991.

315 *CFE News*, A Publication of the Association of Certified Fraud Examiners, March/April 1994, p. 3.

316 Johannes, "Pankau, P.I.: Less Than Meets the Eye," p. T-1.

317 Cary Spivak, "War service of memorial's top executive in doubt," *Milwaukee Sentinel*, November 18, 1993.

318 Cary Spivak, "Ouster of memorial chief sought," *Milwaukee Sentinel*, February 26, 1994, p. 7A.

319 Christine Wicker, "Violation of Trust," *Dallas Life* magazine, *The Dallas Morning News*, January 26, 1992, pp. 8–14.

320 Keating, *The American Legion*, June 1993, pp. 55–56.

321 Ian H. Fennell, "Pride In The Flag," *The Cranbury* (New Jersey) *Press*, May 31, 1995, p. A-1.

322 Tom Dammann, "Military Accidents?," *The New York Times*, December 31, 1984, p. I-23.

323 Military record of Thomas L. Dammann, National Personnel Records Center, FOIA request on November 30, 1990, by B. G. Burkett.

324 David Margolik, "15 Vials of Sperm: The Unusual Behest of an Even More Unusual Man," *The New York Times*, April 29, 1994, p. C-16. Kane may have had the last laugh. His will left frozen specimens he had deposited in a sperm bank to his girlfriend. The family filed suit to block her from obtaining the sperm and becoming pregnant with his child, thus producing another heir long after his death.

325 Hal Spence, "Homer Man Played 'Taps' in Last Goodbye to JFK," *Homer News*, November 18, 1993, p. A-7.

326 *Homer News* staff, "'Taps' Story Was a Hoax," *Homer News*, December 23, 1993, pp. A-1, 6.

327 Mark Turner, "'Taps' Hoax Shows Lack of Attention to Newsgathering Basics," *Homer News*, December 23, 1993, p. A-13.

328 Wayne A. Hall, "Purloined Glory Exposed," Newburgh, N.Y. *Sunday Record*, November 13, 1994, p. 5, 58. Hall interviewed B. G. Burkett for this story.

329 Military Record of John G. Osterhout, National Personnel Records Center, FOIA request by B. G. Burkett, October 14, 1994.

330 Bruce Jackson, "The Perfect Informant," *Journal of American Folklore*, October/December 1990, Vol. 103, No. 410, pp. 400–416.

331 173rd Airborne [Sep] Sky Soldiers, (Paduchah, Kentucky: Turner Publishing, 1993).

332 Military record of Lowell W. Olds, National Personnel Records Center, FOIA request by B. G. Burkett.

333 JoAnn Jacobsen-Wells, "'Fallen comrade' hailed by veterans after his tragic life and death," *Deseret News*, Salt Lake City, September 29, 1989, p. A-1.

334 Lew Ross, "Another Vietnam 'Unknown' KIA—'Killed in America,'" *BRAVO Veterans Outlook*, November 1989, p. 21.

335 Military record of Jerry W. Graham, National Personnel Records Center, FOIA request, August 28, 1991, by B. G. Burkett.

336 Larry Bailey, "The Preacher Is a SEAL," *Soldier of Fortune*, November 1994, pp. 58–70.

337 Bailey, *Soldier of Fortune*, p. 68. Bailey asked readers with information regarding the whereabouts of Wright to contact Soldier of Fortune, Attn: Phony Vets, P.O. Box 693, Boulder, CO 80306.

338 Jim Tunstall, "Vietnam Veteran Plans Run to Remember Fallen Comrades," *Tampa Tribune*, October 10, 1984, pp. A-1, 4.

339 Jim Tunstall and Glen Stubbe, "Former Green Beret From Florida an Instant Celebrity in New York," *Tampa Tribune*, May 8, 1985, pp. A-1, 4.

340 Jim Tunstall, "Vietnam Veterans Leave Florida on Commemorative March," *Tampa Tribune*, August 18, 1985, A-1.

341 Tunstall, *Tampa Tribune*, October 10, 1984, pp. A-1, 4.

342 Military record of William Francis Callahan, National Personnel Records Center, FOIA request by B. G. Burkett, March 9, 1990.

343 Jim Tunstall, "Army Disputes Veteran's Story," *Tampa Tribune*, October 24, 1985, pp. A-1, 6.

344 Megan Doren, "Repaying an Old Debt," *The Dallas Morning News*, May 18, 1991, pp. A-1, 15.

345 Megan Doren, "Vietnam Veteran Gets More Money For Trip," *The Dallas Morning News*, May 29, 1991.

346 Military record of Reggie A. Gutierrez, National Personnel Records Center, obtained through FOIA request by B. G. Burkett, June 27, 1991.

347 Military Record of Albert Wayne "Bud" Porter, National Personnel Records Center, FOIA request by B. G. Burkett, August 10, 1993.

348 Patrick J. Sullivan, "VFW Revokes Ex-Commander's Membership," *The Leader*, Port Townsend, Washington, November 29, 1995.

349 Charges and Specifications, Veterans of Foreign Wars of the United States, Department of the District of Columbia, in the court-martial of Gerard Patrick Miserandino, May 19, 1988.

350 Transcript of proceedings before the department of the District of Columbia, Veterans of Foreign Wars of the United States, in the matter of: a court-martial, Gerard Patrick Miserandino, June 13, 1998, pp. 84–86.

351 A confidential source provided copies of the DD-214 used by Edward A. Harrelson to obtain financial assistance from Operation We Remember, as well as copies of citations "awarding" him the Navy Cross and other medals.

352 Agreement To Participate in "Viet Nam: An Inner-View," (a video documentary and companion book) by Marc C. Waszkiewicz, May 28, 1991.

353 Military record of Edward A. Harrelson, National Personnel Records Center, obtained by confidential source.

354 *The State of North Carolina vs. Edward Allen Harrelson*, Judgment and Commitment, Robeson County Superior Court, June 10, 1971.

355 *State of Washington vs. Edward Harrelson*, Order, Judgment and Sentence (Special Sexual Offender Sentencing Alternative), Thurston County Superior Court, December 21, 1988.

356 Bruce Porter, "Terror On An Eight-Hour Shift" *The New York Times Sunday Magazine*, November 26, 1995, pp. 43–72.

357 Prosecuting attorney Mike Miller, phone interview with B. G. Burkett.

358 Military record of Lee Edward Seiber, National Personnel Records Center, FOIA request by Malcolm McConnell, January 29, 1996.

359 Associated Press, "Veteran Offers School Another View," *The Dallas Morning News*, March 14, 1991.

360 Linda Ellerbee, "Equal Time: Vietnam Vet Raises Voice to Give Peace a Chance," King Features Syndicate, *Dallas Times Herald*, March 24, 1991, p. F-8.

361 Military record of Michael R. Gayler, National Personnel Records Center, FOIA request by B. G. Burkett, June 14, 1991.

362 Doug Clark, "Desertions Put Black Eye on Peacenik's File," Spokane *Spokesman-Review*, July 14, 1991.

363 United Press International, "Schwarzkopf Splattered with Simulated Blood by Vietnam Vet," *The Stars and Stripes*, October 12–18, 1992, p. 2.

364 Dewey Webb, "Switch Blader," *New Times*, Phoenix, Arizona, August 18–24, 1994, pp. 17–20.

365 Military record of Robert G. Abbott, National Personnel Records Center, FOIA request by B. G. Burkett, October 31, 1994.

366 Letter, James R. Reckner, director of the Center for the Study of the Vietnam Conflict, Texas Tech University, to B.G. Burkett, June 29, 1995.

Chapter Ten: The VA and the PTSD "Epidemic"

367 "Bend Man Hit in Police Shootout," the *Bulletin*, Bend, Oregon, October 25, 1979, p. 1.

368 "NBC Magazine" with David Brinkley, December 5, 1980.

369 Jim Hill, "Viet Vet Loses; Judge Rejects Stress Trauma Argument," *The Oregonian*, Portland, Oregon, June 21, 1984, p. M-3. Despite Pard's claim that he had a patient-therapist relationship with the VA, the evidence showed that, although Pard on several occasions visited a Vet Center in Bend, he had not attended therapy regularly. In fact, he had not been to the clinic between April and October 1979, when the shooting took place, except for one visit six days before the shoot-out. The VA was not negligent, the judge ruled.

370 Bob St. John, "Vietnam Vet Tries to Keep Life in Order," *The Dallas Morning News*, March 5, 1991, p. A-15.

371 Military Record of Byron Norman, National Personnel Records Center, FOIA request by B. G. Burkett.

372 Interview with C. W. Gaffney by B. G. Burkett, March 20, 1991.

373 Barry Levin, J.D. and David Ferrier, *Defending The Vietnam Combat Veteran* (Los Angeles: Vietnam Veterans Legal Assistance Project, 1989).

374 Vietnam Experience Study, "Health Status of Vietnam Veterans: Psychosocial Characteristics," *Journal of the American Medical Association*, Vol. 259, No. 18, May 13, 1988, p. 2701.

375 Robert K. Ressler and Tom Shachtman, *Whoever Fights Monsters* (New York: St. Martin's Press, 1992), pp. 177–191.

376 Ibid., pp. 183–184.

377 Military Record of Duane Edward Samples, National Personnel Records Center, provided by Robert K. Ressler.

378 Bob Smith, "Samples' Vietnam C.O. Calls Syndrome 'Bull,'" *Silverton Appeal-Tribune*, August 27, 1981.

379 Mike Wallace, "Soldier of Misfortune," Transcript of 60 *Minutes*, televised February 13, 1983. (The program later was aired on June 2, 1985.)

380 Gary Burdick, "From the Military to Mayhem," *High Society*, January 1995, p. 120.

381 Jack Olsen, *The Misbegotten Son* (New York: Island Books, Dell Publishing, 1993), p. 213.

382 Military Record of Arthur John Shawcross, National Personnel Records, provided by Robert K. Ressler.

383 Olsen, *The Misbegotten Son*, p. 496.

384 Ressler, *Whoever Fights Monsters*, pp. 233–235.

385 Richard A. Kulka, Ph.D., William E. Schlenger, Ph.D., John A. Fairbank, Ph.D., Richard L. Hough, Ph.D., B. Kathleen Jordan, Ph.D., Charles R. Marmar, M.D., Daniel S. Weiss, Ph.D., *Trauma and the Vietnam War Generation* (New York: Brunner/Mazel, 1990).

386 Ibid., p. xxviii.

387 *Journal of the American Medical Association*, Vol. 259, No. 18, May 13, 1988, p. 2701.

388 Ibid., p. 2704.

389 Richard A. Kulka, Ph.D., et al, *"Trauma and the Vietnam War Generation: Report of Findings from the National Vietnam Veterans Readjustment Study,"* (New York: Burnner/Mazel, 1990), p. 11.

390 Commander, U.S. Military Assistance Command Vietnam (COMUSMACV), report, "Award of Purple Heart, Southeast Asia, 1962–1973."

391 Kulka, et al, *"Trauma and the Vietnam War Generation."*

392 Interview with Dr. Arthur Blank, National Director, War Veteran Counseling Service, Department of Veterans Affairs, by Malcolm McConnell for *Reader's Digest*, September 17, 1993.

393 Peter T. Kilborn, "Veterans Expand Hospital System in Face of Cuts," *The New York Times*, January 14, 1996, pp. Y-1, 13.

394 William Safire, "Most Sacred Cow," *The New York Times*, January 12, 1995. And "Sacred Cow, II," *The New York Times*, January 19, 1995.

395 Kilborn, "Veterans Expand Hospital System in Face of Cuts."

396 I asked Dr. Loren Pankratz to examine the NVVRS and my comments regarding it. Pankratz does peer reviews for the *America Journal of Psychiatry* of articles on PTSD and is a member of the scientific advisory board of the American Council on Science and Health. He concurred with my analysis. "I found your comments deadly perceptive," Pankratz wrote me on June 4, 1996. "It seems that you may not be a statistician or epidemiologist, but you know how to read. In fact, you may be one of the few who ever bothered to read it. After six of the 738 women claimed POW status, someone should have sent the study to the *Journal of Irreproducible Results*. I conclude that you also know how to read between the lines. No sober social scientist gives subjects multiple opportunities to come up with the 'correct' answer. These guys should work for a political party."

397 Press Release, Veterans Administration Public Affairs Office, FAX on September 14, 1993.

Chapter Eleven: The Vietnam Veterans' Guide to Tax-Free Living

398 John Ferraro and Josh Kovner, "Vet Holds Police at Bay for 3 1/2 Hours," *New Haven Register*, April 15, 1995.

399 Application for Arrest Warrant, Affidavit by Officer Jeffrey Mills, State of Connecticut, March 14, 1995.

400 Military record of Kenley Barker, National Personnel Records Center, FOIA request by B. G. Burkett.

401 Military record of Joseph Patrick Coyle, National Personnel Records Center, FOIA request by Malcolm McConnell, December 6, 1995.

402 Douglas Mossman, M.D., "At the VA, It Pays to be Sick," *The Public Interest*, Winter 1994, pp. 35–47.

403 Stephen Berman, MSW, and Dr. Robert Fowler, M.D., cochairs, *First Annual Report to the Under Secretary of Health by the Special Committee for Seriously Mentally Ill Veterans*, 1995.

404 Tutsie Silapalikitporn, Ph.D., *Cutting Ties* (Phoenix: Emotional & Behavioral Consultants, Inc., 1993), p. 149.

405 Philip Gold, "Sufferings of the Survivors," *Insight Magazine*, the *Washington Times*, October 23, 1989, pp. 14–15.

406 Deposition of David F. Hollingsworth III, February 6, 1991, pp. 16–17, taken in *Hollingsworth vs. American General Fire & Casualty Company*, 17th Judicial District Court, Parish of LaFourche, State of Louisiana.

407 Ibid., p. 21.

408 Hollingsworth deposition, taken July 23, 1992.

409 Ibid., pp. 22–25.

410 Ibid., p. 48.

411 Hollingsworth deposition, February 6, 1991, pp. 95–96.

412 Ibid., pp. 33–34.

413 Ibid., p. 35.

414 Ibid., pp. 32–33.

415 Ibid., p. 57.

416 Military service record of David F. Hollingsworth III, obtained from the National Personnel Records Center through FOIA, B.G. Burkett.

417 Hollingsworth deposition, July 23, 1992, pp. 13–14.

418 Report of Dr. Richard R. Roniger, assessment of David F. Hollingsworth III, July 18, 1992.

419 Telephone interview of Dennis Latham by Glenna Whitley, February 2, 1996.

420 Dennis Latham, *How to Receive Disability for PTSD* (Aurora, Indiana: Latham Publishing, 1992).

421 Telephone interview with Dennis C. Latham by Glenna Whitley, February 2, 1996.

422 Roxanne Hill, *Posttraumatic Stress Disorder: How to Apply for 100 Percent Total Disability Rating* (Vietnam Doorgunners Association, 1400 West First Street, Lee's Summit, Missouri, 1993). All emphasis in the original.

423 Ibid., p. 11.

424 Ibid., p. 12.

425 Ibid., p. 41.

426 Ibid., p. 30.

427 Ibid., p. 10. This inch-thick booklet includes copies of forms and stressor letters that led to a Vietnam veteran, a doorgunner, successfully obtaining a 100 percent disability rating. Although his name is redacted, one letter says he was a former crew chief aboard a UH-IH helicopter. It describes an action that occurred 28 July 1971. The veteran claimed he was in one of two OH-6A Loches flying at tree top level blowing up hooches. "I used my 50 cal to try to shot (sic) off the tree tops." [Improbable.] "The communication control ship reported we were in the middle of about a division of NVA." [A division is ten thousand enemy soldiers.] He described, between shooting "gooks" and trees, trying to hook seat belts together to make a life line to rescue Americans on the ground. [Impossible.] Using a hand-held M-60, "I loaded a two thousand round belt of ammo and never let up." [This type of ammunition doesn't come in two thousand-round belts and if he "never let up" he would

have burned out the barrel.] In another letter, he described a traumatic incident that occurred on February 5, 1971: the midair collision at an Army Air Field of an Air America fixed-wing craft and a Cobra helicopter. After witnessing the terrible crash, in which a female passenger's body was sliced in half and flung at his feet, he ran to the burning Cobra. He saw a man in the front seat try to escape but was unable to rescue him. "I watched him die, unable to help save his life." A hand-written notation on the letter, reproduced in the book, says that the dead man was "WO James Lee Paul, died Feb-05–1971." Army CWO James Lee Paul did die on February 5, 1971, but not in a midair collision at an Army air field. Casualty records show copilot Paul and pilot Carl M. Wood, flying a Cobra gunship on an extraction mission near Khe Sanh, were killed when they entered a heavy cloud cover and impacted on a mountainside. Wood's remains were recovered, but little could be found of Paul save his baseball cap, a watch, part of a ring, and a chinstrap. He is listed as missing in action, but he is presumed dead. (Thanks to the P.O.W. Network for the information on Paul.) This letter was used to obtain a 100 percent PTSD disability rating.

428 Guzda, "Pretenders to Pain: Fake Vietnam Vets," *Minneapolis Star Tribune* June 12, 1988, p. A-19.

Chapter Twelve: PTSD Made Easy

429 Interview with Richard R. "Richie" Burns by Glenna Whitley, Gainesville, Florida, September 16–18, 1995. Burns' DD-214 shows an impressive twenty-six-year career with the U.S. Army. His medals and decorations include: National Defense Service Medal, Vietnam Service Medal, Combat Infantryman Badge, Meritorious Unit Commendation, Overseas Service Ribbon, Bronze Star Medal with third Oak Leaf Cluster with Valor Device, Air Medal-2, Master Parachutist Badge, Silver Star, Pathfinder Badge, Purple Heart with Oak Leaf Cluster, Republic of Vietnam Honor Medal, Republic of Vietnam Civil Actions Medal Unit Citation Badge with Palm (two), Valorous Unit Award, German Parachute Badge, German Rifle Award, Jungle Expert Badge, Army Good Conduct Medal (sixth award), Army Service Ribbon, Army Achievement Medal, NCO Professional Development Ribbon (five), Special Forces Tab, Belgian Parachute Badge, Belgian Commando Badge "A" Brevet, German Army Efficiency Badge Gold, German Mountain Warfare Badge, Aircraft Crewman Badge, Republic of Vietnam Campaign Medal with Device, Recruiter Badge, RECONDO Badge, Republic of Vietnam Senior Parachutist Badge, Vietnam Service Medal with 8 Campaign Stars, Army Commendation Medal with 5th OLC, Republic of Vietnam Cross of Gallantry with Palm (Individual Award), Republic of Vietnam Cross of Gallantry with Palm (Unit Award 2), and Meritorious Service Medal.

430 Management Implications Report, Inspector General, April 4, 1990.

431 Loren Pankratz, Ph.D., Letters, "Munchhausen versus Munchausen," *Medical Journal of Australia*, 1986; 145, p. 301. This letter describes why the Munchausen syndrome is named after the storybook character and not the historic baron.

432 Loren Pankratz, Ph.D., and Greg McCarthy, M.D., "The Ten Least Wanted Patients," *Southern Medical Journal*, May 1986, pp. 613–620.

433 Loren Pankratz, Ph.D., "Geezers," *Journal of the American Medical Association*, 1988, Vol. 259, pp. 1228–1229.

434 L. Kofed, Loren Pankratz, Ph.D., and John Lipkin, M.D., "The Transient Patient in a

Psychiatric War: Summering in Oregon," *Journal of Operational Psychiatry*, Vol. 9, No. 1, 1978, pp. 42–47.

435 Landy Sparr, M.D., and Loren D. Pankratz, Ph.D., "Factitious Posttraumatic Stress Disorder," *American Journal of Psychiatry*, 140:8, August 1983, pp. 1016–1019.

436 Ibid., p. 1018.

437 L. Kofoed and Loren D. Pankratz, Ph.D., Letter, "Continued Appearance of Factitious Posttraumatic Stress Disorder," *American Journal of Psychiatry*, 1990, 147:pp. 811–812.

438 J. DeVance Hamilton, M.D., "Pseudo-Posttraumatic Stress Disorder," *Military Medicine*, Vol. 150, July 1985, pp. 353–356.

439 Jeff South, "Dallas Vietnam Veterans Unmask a Pretender," *Dallas Times Herald*, May 7, 1989. This story was triggered by my exposé of Joseph Testa, president of the Dallas Chapter of the Vietnam Veterans of America.

440 Loren Pankratz, Ph.D., and James Jackson, B.B.A., B.S.N., "Habitually Wandering Patients," *The New England Journal of Medicine*, December 29, 1994, pp. 1752–1772. Using very conservative cost estimates, Pankratz calculated that these 810 patients consumed $26.5 million of care in one year. They had a considerable impact on the whole of the VA system, being responsible for 2.8 percent of all admissions for acute psychiatric care. At the Waco, Texas, VAMC they were responsible for 3.7 percent of the entire workload in 1991. Twelve large hospitals had more than one hundred admissions by these 810 patients, and some small hospitals admitted unexpectedly high percentages of these patients. Smaller hospitals were probably eager to keep their census high to justify their existence.

441 Interview with Dr. Dennis Charney, Chief of Psychiatry, West Haven VA Medical Center, by Malcolm McConnell for *Reader's Digest*, September 17, 1993.

442 Steven M. Southwick, M.D., Rachel Yehuda, Ph.D., and Earl L. Giller Jr., M.D., Ph.D., "Personality Disorders in Treatment-Seeking Combat Veterans With Posttraumatic Stress Disorder," *American Journal of Psychiatry*, 150:7, July 1993, pp. 1020–1023.

443 Dr. Sally Satel, "Apocalypse Soon?," *The Psychiatric Times*, May 1994.

444 Lee Hyer, Ralph Bruno, Marilyn G. Woods, Patrick Boudewyns, "Treatment Outcomes of Vietnam Veterans with PTSD and the Consistency of the MCMI," *Journal of Clinical Psychology*, July 1989, Vol. 45, pp. 547–552.

445 Arieh Y. Shalev, M.D., Omer Bonne, M.D., and Spencer Eth, M.D., "Treatment of Posttraumatic Stress Disorder: A Review," *Psychosomatic Medicine*, 58: 165–182 (1996).

446 Lee Hyer, Patrick Boudewyns, William R. Harrison, William C. O'Leary, Ralph D. Bruno, Rayford T. Saucer, and John B. Blount, VAMC, Augusta, Georgia, "Vietnam Veterans: Overreporting Versus Acceptable Reporting of Symptoms," *Journal of Personality Assessment*, 1988, 52 (3), 475–486.

447 Dr. Douglas Mossman, "At the VA, It Pays to be Sick," *The Public Interest*, Winter 1994, pp. 35–47.

448 Personal interview Kenneth R. Atkins, Special Agent-In-Charge, Department of Veterans Affairs Inspector General, by B. G. Burkett, May 18, 1995.

449 Tom Zucco, "Aftereffects to Touch Soldiers for Long Time," *St. Petersburg Times*, subsequently appeared in the *Washington Times*, March 1, 1991.

450 Phoebe S. Spinrad, "Hotspur in Massachusetts: The Problem with *Achilles in Vietnam*," Review, *Vietnam Generation*, Vol. 6, 1995, pp. 192–196. Also, *The Ohio Scholar*, Spring 1995, pp. 7–11.

451 Telephone conversation with Jonathan Shay by B. G. Burkett, June 21, 1995.

452 Maxine Waters and Jonathan Shay, "Heal the 'Bad Paper' Vets," *The New York Times*, July 30, 1995.

453 Marie Villari, "From Hell to Help for Viet War Vet," *Syracuse Post-Standard*, November 12, 1989, pp. 4, 8. Also appeared as "Ex-Member of Assassin Team Turns to Helping Veterans," Newhouse News Service, *Dallas Times Herald*. Villari is married to Al Campani, past president of VVA Chapter 293 in Morrisville, N.Y.

454 Melanie Hirsch, "Exorcising a Demon Called Trauma," *Syracuse Post-Standard*, November 5, 1993, pp. B-1, 3.

455 Villari, "From Hell to Help for Viet War Vet," pp. 1-8.

456 Ibid., pp. 1-8.

457 Laura Palmer, "Vietnam Vet Finds Peace in Truth," *Dallas Times Herald*, March 12, 1990, p. C-4. Her column on David Goff Jr., appeared in the *El Paso Times* as "Trained Killer Breaks Through Calluses," on March 11, 1990.

458 Military Record of David Jerome Goff Jr., National Personnel Records Center, FOIA request by B. G. Burkett, November 28, 1989.

459 Telephone interview with David J. Goff, Jr. by Malcolm McConnell for *Reader's Digest*, September 24, 1993.

460 Telephone interview with Maj. Michael Wawrzyniak, USA Military Awards Office, by Malcolm McConnell for *Reader's Digest*, September 29, 1994.

461 David Tobin, "Vet Admits Lies About Serving in Vietnam," *Syracuse Post-Standard*, April 9, 1994, pp. A-1, 5.

462 Letter to Gary L. Sharpe, Acting U.S. Attorney, Department of Justice, from James T. Walsh, Member of Congress, 25th District, New York, January 26, 1994.

463 David Tobin, "Veteran Lied about Viet Heroism, U.S. Charges," *Syracuse Herald-Journal*, March 30, 1994, pp. A-1,8.

464 Statement to the FBI, signed by David Jerome Goff Jr., March 14, 1994.

465 David Tobin, "'I'm Very Sorry for What I Have Done,' Vet Says," *Syracuse Herald-Journal*, June 10, 1994.

466 Mark Allen Peterson, "Report: Most Seriously Mentally Ill Veterans Saw Combat," the *Stars and Stripes*, September 11–17, 1995.

467 Bremner, J.D.; Randall, P., Scott; T.M.; Brobebm R.A.; Seibyl, J.P.; Southwick, S.M.; Delaney, R.C.; McCarthy, G.; Charney, D.S.; and Innis, R.B. MRI-based measurement of hippocampal volume in patients with combat-related posttraumatic stress disorder, *American Journal of Psychiatry*, 152 (7), pp. 973–981 (1995).

468 Steven M. Southwick, M.D., C. Andrew Morgan III, M.D., Andreas L. Nicolaou, Ph.D., and Dennis S. Charney, M.D., "Consistency of Memory for Combat-Related Traumatic Events in Veterans of Operation Desert Storm," *American Journal of Psychiatry*, 154:2, February 1997, pp. 173–176. In addition to remembering things they hadn't noted one month after the war, 46 percent remembered one or more events that they didn't recall two years later. In other words, they forgot war trauma.

469 Robert E. Hales, M.D., M.B.A., and Douglas F. Zatzick, M.D., "What is PTSD?," *American Journal of Psychiatry*, 154:2, February 1997, pp. 143–145.

Chapter Thirteen: "Vietnam Killed Him": Suicide

470 Vern Anderson, Associated Press, "Dead 'War Hero' Unmasked: A Life of Lies to Hide Failures," *The New York Times*, October 10, 1989.

471   Laura Palmer, Syndicated Column, "Long-Awaited Requiem for Lost Souls of Vietnam," *Dallas Times Herald*, January 1, 1990, p. C-4.

472   Michael Lee Lanning, *Vietnam at the Movies* (New York: Ballantine, 1994), p. 81.

473   Evan Moore, "'Tunnel Rat' Who Died Unknown to Receive Memorial," *Houston Chronicle*, October 27, 1989, pp. A-1, 28.

474   Evan Moore, "In Death, as in Life, Vet Left Few Traces," *Houston Chronicle*, October 21, 1989, pp. A-1, 12.

475   Military record of John Kolosowski, National Personnel Records Center, FOIA request by B. G. Burkett, January 2, 1990.

476   Military record of Johnny Lapeere Bacot Jr., National Personnel Records Center, FOIA request by B. G. Burkett, January 2, 1990.

477   MacPherson, *Long Time Passing*, p. 239.

478   Ibid., p. 238.

479   Military record of Gerald Wayne Highman, National Personnel Records Center, FOIA request by B. G. Burkett, April 1, 1995.

480   Adrian Peracchio, "For Many Veterans, the War Never Ended," *Newsday*, September 25, 1979, pp. II-4–5.

481   MacPherson, *Long Time Passing*, p. 239.

482   Ibid., p. 239.

483   Military record of Edward R. Erickson, National Personnel Records Center, FOIA request by Malcolm McConnell, January 29, 1996.

484   Department of Defense casualty records. Two other Murphys who died in Vietnam had the middle name Michael; they were both Marines and both were single.

485   Steven J. Bentley, "VA Budget Cuts Add Insult to Injury," *Daily News*, Bangor, Maine, April 4, 1992.

486   Military record of William Harrington, National Personnel Records Center, FOIA request by B. G. Burkett, October 13, 1992.

487   Military record of Bruce H. Allen, National Personnel Records Center, FOIA request by B. G. Burkett, October 15, 1992.

488   Military record of Robert A. Daigneau, National Personnel Records Center, FOIA request by B. G. Burkett, September 28, 1992.

489   Military record of David Everett Garland, National Personnel Records Center, FOIA request by B. G. Burkett, November 30, 1992. Military record of Michael Floyd Obrin, National Personnel Records Center, FOIA request by B. G. Burkett, October 15, 1992.

490   Department of Defense casualty records.

491   *Listing of Army Personnel Who Died by Suicide or Execution, 7 December 1941 through 30 June 1946*, National Archives.

492   Jeff Zaslow, "Nurse Disputes Rate of Vietnam Vets' Suicide," syndicated column, *Dallas Times Herald*, September 2, 1990.

493   Peracchio, "For Many Veterans, the War Never Ended."

494   Richard K. Kolb, Letter to the Editor, "Real Figures vs. Myths on Vietnam Veterans," *The Wall Street Journal*, March 4, 1991.

495   Norman Hearst, M.D., M.P.H., Thomas B. Newman, M.D., M.P.H., and Stephen B. Hulley, M.D., M.P.H., "Delayed Effects of the Military Draft on Mortality," *New England Journal of Medicine*, Vol. 314, No. 10, March 6, 1986, pp. 620–624.

496   Lawrence Kolb, "Posttraumatic Stress Disorder in Vietnam Veterans," *New England Journal of Medicine*, Vol. 314, No. 10, March 6, 1986.

497 Cristine Russell, "Viet-Era Draftees' Suicide Rate High," *Washington Post*, March 6, 1986, p. A-4.

498 James Webb, "Viet Vets Didn't Kill Babies and They Aren't Suicidal," *Washington Post*, April 6, 1986.

499 Daniel A. Pollock, M.D., Philip Rhodes, M.S., Coleen A. Boyle, Ph.D., Pierre Decoufle, Sc.D., and Daniel L. McGee, "Estimating the Number of Suicides Among Vietnam Veterans," *American Journal of Psychiatry* 147:6, June 1990, pp. 772–776.

500 Ibid., p. 775.

501 Bill Ordine, "Suicide Looms Most Heavily Over Older White Men," *The Dallas Morning News*, May 4, 1995, p. C-2.

502 Vietnam Experience Study, "Health Status of Vietnam Veterans," *Journal of the American Medical Association*, Vol. 259, No. 18, May 13, 1988, p. 2701.

503 Norman L. Farberow, Ph.D., Han K. Kang, Ph.D., and Tim A. Bullman, M.A., "Combat Experience and Postservice Psychosocial Status as Predictors of Suicide in Vietnam Veterans," *Journal of Nervous and Mental Disease*, 1990, Vol. 178., No., pp. 32–37.

504 Tom Zucco, "Aftereffects to Touch Soldiers for a Long Time," *St. Petersburg Times*, subsequently appeared in the *Washington Times*, March 1, 1991.

505 Nadine Smith, "Vet Kills Self At Memorial," *Tampa Tribune*, October 12, 1989, p. B-1.

Chapter 14: An Army on the Streets: Homelessness

506 Lesley Stahl, Transcript, "Wild Man of West 96th Street," *60 Minutes*, CBS News, December 12, 1992.

507 Mary B. W. Tabor, "Man Who Attacked Pedestrians to Stay in Hospital Until Hearing," *The New York Times*, February 9, 1993. Editorial, "Down the Drain," *The Wall Street Journal*, February 9, 1993.

508 Peter Marin, "Helping and Hating the Homeless," *The World*, January 25, 1987, pp. 7–9, 20.

509 Laura Palmer, Syndicated Column, "Veteran Fights the Other Foe—Drugs," *The Dallas Morning News*, February 13, 1989, p. E-3.

510 Karen Franklin, "Gimme Shelter," *VVA Veteran*, February 1989, pp. 11–14

511 Ibid., p. 12.

512 Solotaroff, "Exiles on Main Street," *Rolling Stone*, June 24, 1993, pp. 63–68.

513 Associated Press Photo by Lynn Sledki, "Making a Statement," *Wichita Falls Times*, Wichita Falls, Texas, May 28, 1991.

514 *The VVA Veteran*, March 1991, p. 12, quoting Laurie Goodstein of the *Washington Post*.

515 John Bryant, "Vet's Timely Rescue from Garbage Truck Tops Combat Tales," *Austin American-Statesman*, April 21, 1989, p. A-1.

516 William C. Lhotka, "Panhandler with 'Vietnam' Ruse Convicted of Robbing Gas Station," *St. Louis Post-Dispatch*, May 1993.

517 Military record of Larry G. Hogue, National Personnel Records Center, FOIA request by B. G. Burkett, February 19, 1993.

518 John Carmody, "Report on a Controversy," *Washington Post*, September 8, 1993, p. D-6.

519 Christopher Ruddy, "What's the Vietnam Connection," *New York Guardian*, July 23, 1993.

520 Eric Breindel, "Tall Tales and Lies About Larry Hogue," *New York Post*, August 5, 1993.

521 Stahl, "Wild Man of West 96th Street," *60 Minutes*, aired again on August 15, 1993.

522 United Press International, "'Wild Man of 96th Street' Arrested Again," *Stars and Stripes*, July 25–31, 1994.

523 Gary S. Becker, "How the Homeless 'Crisis' Was Hyped," *Business Week*, September 12, 1994, p. 22.

524 U.S. Scene, "Study Says 600,000 Homeless," *Dallas Times Herald*, November 4, 1988, p. A-8.

525 Wire Report, "Homeless Suffer From a Variety of Ills," *The Dallas Morning News*, October 11, 1989.

526 Peter H. Rossi, *Down and Out in America: The Origins of Homelessness* (University of Chicago Press, 1989).

527 Associated Press, "Homeless Count Put at 228,621," *The Dallas Morning News*, April 13, 1991.

528 Becker, "How the Homeless 'Crisis' Was Hyped."

529 Alice S. Baum and Donald W. Burnes, *A Nation in Denial* (Westview Press, 1993).

530 Randall K. Filer, "What We Really Know About the Homeless," *The Wall Street Journal*, April 10, 1990.

531 *Review and Comments Upon the Missouri House of Representatives' Interim Committee Report on Homeless Veterans*, December 1, 1993.

532 News release, Bureau of Labor Statistics, United States Department of Labor, Washington, D.C., October 21, 1994.

533 Military record of Donald Richard Cederberg, National Personnel Records Center, FOIA request by Bill Marvel.

534 Bill Marvel, "On the Street: Jobless, Homeless and Living to Drink," *The Dallas Morning News*, May 25, 1993, pp. C-1, 7.

535 *Eye to Eye with Connie Chung*, Transcript, April 14, 1994.

536 Joseph Cerquone, "Lost Army of the Street," *VVA Veteran*, March/April 1992, pp. 11–13.

537 "A Task Force with a Mission," *VVA Veteran*.

538 Transcript of "Geraldo," The Investigative News Group, New York, May 27, 1988.

539 Paul Solotaroff, *The House of Purple Hearts* (New York: Harper Collins, 1995).

540 Ibid., p. 34.

541 Military record of Kenneth Leslie Smith, National Personnel Records Center, FOIA request by B. G. Burkett, September 10, 1993.

542 Department of Defense casualty records.

543 *U.S. vs. Kenneth Leslie Smith*, 81–0108, U.S. District Court, District of Maryland.

544 Brian C. Mooney, "Vets' Shelter Loses Some Luster," *Boston Globe*, June 25, 1995, pp. 1, 6.

545 Ken Smith arranged with the VA to pay some homeless veterans their disability and pension benefits through the shelter. Because of system overload, government agencies typically wait up to three months to have their requests fulfilled. A source at the National Archives says that when Smith wasn't able to obtain DD-214s and other documents fast enough to suit him, he complained to Rep. Joe Kennedy (D-Mass.), who wrote a scathing letter to the Archivist of the United States, demanding that improvements in the system be made for Smith's benefit. In response, the Archives instituted an FOIA fax system, which allowed "homeless vet advocates" to receive records in a few days. Archive officials had no way to verify that the request was really for a homeless veteran. Other veterans' agencies figured out that the way to get their requests for veterans' records filled fast was to label them "homeless," thus further flooding the system.

546   Solotaroff, *House of Purple Hearts*, pp. 181–184.

547   Eric Schmitt, "Victorious in War, Not Yet at Peace," *The New York Times*, May 28, 1995.

548   Photo by Sam Morris, "Veterans of Conflict," *The Dallas Morning News*, April 26, 1995, p. 1.

549   Associated Press, "One-Third of Homeless Men in Shelter Network Found to be Veterans," *Washington Post*, November 10, 1996, p. A-10.

Chapter Fifteen: The Purple Heart Flea Market

550   Consolidated Brief and Argument of Plaintiffs as Appellees and Cross-Appellants, in *Cartwright vs. Goodyear Tire Company*, 94–0700 and 94–0938, Appellate Court of Illinois, first Judicial District, 6th Division.

551   Ibid., Plaintiffs' Exhibit 73.

552   Ibid., Plaintiffs' Exhibit 73B, communication from Major Michael J. Wawrzyniak, Chief, Special Actions Military Awards Branch.

553   Ibid., Exhibit 73C, Gary Cartwright's DD-214.

554   Ibid., Deposition of Gary Cartwright, in *Cartwright vs. Goodyear Tire Co.*, Circuit Court of Cook County No. 88 L 6458, Illinois Appellate Court, first District 6th Division No. 94–0700.

555   Dale Andradé, *Ashes to Ashes: The Phoenix Program and the Vietnam War* (Lexington, Massachusetts: Lexington Books, 1990).

556   William B. Thayer, "Perspectives," *Vietnam* magazine, October 1991, pp. 58–61.

557   George "Bud" Day later became a lawyer. He has filed a class-action suit on behalf of military retirees, alleging breach of contract by the government in denying them and their families access to free military care.

558   Mary Jane Fine, "Sale of Purple Hearts Angers Veterans; Manufacturers, Others Defend Practice," *The Dallas Morning News*, November 24, 1995, p. A-52.

559   "Firm Plans Guilty Plea in Illegal Medal of Honor Sales," *The New York Times* News Service, October 19, 1996.

560   Marion Callahan, "Dishonoring the Medal of Honor," *Houston Chronicle,* December 4, 1996, p. A-4.

561   Davan Maharaj, "Man Accused of Posing as Army General," *Los Angeles Times*, August 18, 1995, p. B-1.

562   Letter from Allen Kirkendall to U.S. District Court.

563   Nina Bernardi, "Dishonoring the Medal of Honor," *State Journal-Register*, Springfield, Illinois, Copley News Service, October 21, 1994, pp. A-1, 7.

564   Peter Kendall and Linda Young, "Medal of Honor Winners Fight to Expose the Fakes," *Chicago Tribune*, July 4, 1995, pp. 1, 9.

565   Jason DaPonte, "Judge Decides Own Fate, Resigns Over Medal Hoax," *The Stars and Stripes*, 9–15 October 1995, p. 1.

566   Military record of David Wilk, National Personal Records Center, FOIA request by B.G. Burkett.

Chapter Sixteen: Fudging the Records

567   Army Investigative File of Awards to Sgt. Boyer N. Westover. The file includes a letter dated 5 February 1969 to the Commanding General, US Army Vietnam; copies

of a letter to President Lyndon B. Johnson from Mrs. Kenneth Wills; copies of altered records awarding Westover the DSC, Silver Star with one OLC, Bronze Star with 1 OLC for valor, Army Commendation Medal, and Purple Heart with two OLC; a press release announcing the awards to Westover; a copy of *Stars and Stripes* edition in which Westover's photograph appeared; a newspaper story extolling Westover's achievements; and correspondence with his superior officer. The Adjutant General in charge of the case concluded: "Request that an investigation be made to determine Sgt Westover's exact duties during his last tour in Vietnam, and that an attempt be made to determine how it was possible for him to prepare what appears to be bogus general orders, a bogus Hometown News Release and to falsify his DA Form 20." But the investigation failed to reveal collusion between Westover and anyone else.

568 Interview with CWO William Thayer by B. G. Burkett.

569 Military Record of Jack H. Maslin, National Personnel Records Center, FOIA request by B. G. Burkett, May 17, 1994.

570 Letter from B. G. Burkett to Major General George K. Hastings, December 3, 1994.

571 Memorandum to File, Re: Interview with SGT. Maslin held at ANG Headquarters on September 25, 1989, signed James F. Waehler, LTC, DE ANG, staff advocate general.

572 Jackie Cipriano, "Vietnam Veteran Decorated twenty Years Late," *The Flash*, Fort Dix, Winter 1990, Vol. 71, No. 1.

573 Psychological report regarding Benjamin V. Ricciardi by Clinical Psychologist Sandra Shoeneman, Ph.D., September 25, 1990.

574 Army Inspector General investigation regarding Benjamin V. Ricciardi, FOIA request by B. G. Burkett, January 14, 1995.

575 Memorandum for commander by Maj. General Frederick W. Roder, 4 November 1990, Headquarters 78th Division (Training), Sgt. Joyce Kilmer USAR Center, Edison, New Jersey.

576 Membership application of CSM Benjamin V. Ricciardi, 6 December 1990, Legion of Valor.

577 Letter from Albert F. Gleim to B. G. Burkett, October 26, 1992.

578 Military Records of Benjamin V. Ricciardi, National Personnel Records Center, FOIA request by B. G. Burkett, October 30, 1992 and August 5, 1993. In order to fully document Ricciardi's many claims, I filed numerous other FOIAs, including: General orders and decorations of the Bronze Star for Benjamin V. Ricciardi, Personnel and Logistics, Department of the U.S. Army, U.S. Total Army Personnel Command, Alexandria, Virginia, FOIA request by B. G. Burkett, November 3, 1993; General order 2290 for 1970, United States Military Assistance Command (MACV), and all general orders issued by MACV on March 23, 1970, Personnel and Logistics, Department of the U.S. Army, U.S. Total Army Personnel Command, Alexandria, Virginia, FOIA request by B. G. Burkett, December 3, 1993; general order 1122 from 1969 and all General orders issued December 12 1969 for the 101st Airborne Division, Personnel and Logistics, Department of the U.S. Army, U.S. Total Army Personnel Command, FOIA request November 16, 1993; Record of attendance, U.S. Army Special Forces Medical Course, U.S. Army Medical Department Center and School, Fort Sam Houston, Texas, FOIA request by B. G. Burkett December 16, 1993; New Jersey Army National Guard Military record of Benjamin V. Ricciardi, New Jersey Department of Military and Veterans Affairs, FOIA request by B. G. Burkett, December 17, 1993.

579 Civil service file of Benjamin V. Ricciardi, Department of Personnel, State of New Jersey, FOIA request by B. G. Burkett, December 30, 1993.

580 Letter from Enrique B. Mendez, major, U.S. Army, deputy staff judge advocate, to B. G. Burkett, December 19, 1994.

581 The judge dismissed the lawsuit, saying that I had not exhausted all administrative remedies. After filing additional FOIA requests, I still have not received the information.

582 Letter from Capt. T. J. Connelly to B. G. Burkett, February 5, 1996.

583 Letter from B. G. Burkett to Adm. Jeremy Boorda, January 5, 1996.

584 A journalist for *Newsweek*, alerted by a military researcher, was scheduled to interview Adm. Boorda about his medals. Instead, Adm. Boorda went home and shot himself.

585 Military Record of Clyde R. Bonner, National Personnel Records Center, FOIA request by B. G. Burkett, March 12, 1993.

586 Associated Press, "Baader and Two in West German Gang Sentenced to Life," *The New York Times*, April 29, 1977, p. A-3.

587 Associated Press, "Terrorist Killer of Three U.S. Soldiers to be Freed," *Las Vegas Review Journal*, November 25, 1994.

588 Interview with the late Col. Al Gleim, USA (Ret.), by B. G. Burkett.

589 Military Record of Fred N. Ranck, National Personnel Records Center, FOIA request by B. G. Burkett.

590 Resume of Stephen T. Banko III, sent to B. G. Burkett by Banko.

591 Annemarie Franczyk, "A Veteran of Veterans' Feelings," *Business First of Buffalo*, Week of June 17, 1991, pp. 10, 11.

592 Stephen T. Banko III, "The Week I Lost Two Cherries," *Eagle* magazine, pp. 64–69.

593 Stephen T. Banko III, "Do Widzenia," *BFLO Journal*, Spring 1991, p. 60.

594 Correspondence to "CG USARV LB RVN," from "CG USATCI FT DIX NJ," dated 25 July 1969. "A thorough check of records at this headquarters has been made, and no record of a Distinguished Service Cross to SGT Stephen T. Banko III could be found."

595 Military Record of Stephen T. Banko III, National Personnel Records Center, FOIA requests by B. G. Burkett, December 18, 1992, July 27, 1993, and August 20, 1993.

596 General order Number 1140, Award of the Distinguished Service Cross, Walter T. Bahl, Department of the Army, Headquarters, United States Army Vietnam, 2 April 1969.

Chapter Seventeen: War Stories and Other Lies: Writers Go to Vietnam

597 Dannion Brinkley, *Saved by the Light* (New York: Villard Books, 1994), p. 16.

598 Dannion Brinkley, *At Peace in the Light* (New York, HarperCollins, 1995), p. xii.

599 Military record of Dannion Brinkley, National Personnel Records Center, FOIA request by B. G. Burkett, June 14, 1995.

600 Roy Rivenburg, "No dearth of Near-Death Tales," *The Dallas Morning News*, March 31, 1995.

601 "Cincinnatus," *Self Destruction: The Disintegration and Decay of the U.S. Army During the Vietnam Era* (New York: Norton, 1981).

602 Michael Getler, "Army Critic Unmasked," May 2, 1981, p. A-1, *Washington Post*.

603 Mark Baker, *'Nam* (New York: William Morrow, 1981), p. xv.

604 Department of Defense casualty records.

605 Baker, *'Nam*, p. 183.

606 Bergerud, *Red Thunder, Tropic Lightning*, (1993), p. xii.

607   Military record of Charles W. Bowman Jr., National Personnel Records Center, FOIA request by B. G. Burkett, February 3, 1994.

608   Al Santoli, *Everything We Had* (New York: Random House, 1981).

609   Santoli, pp. 35–41.

610   Military record of Thomas A. Bird, National Personnel Records Center, FOIA request by B. G. Burkett, March 11, 1992.

611   Department of Defense casualty records.

612   Dan Cragg, "The Hanoi Connection—It's Time to Unplug It," *The Stars and Stripes*, May 27, 1982.

613   Santoli, *Everything We Had*, pp. 203–205.

614   Ibid, pp. 255–260.

615   Lou Drendel, *Huey: Modern Military Aircraft* (Squadron/Signal Publications), p. 61.

616   Military record of Stephen Phillip Klinkhammer, National Personnel Records Center, FOIA request by B. G. Burkett.

617   Michael Badamo, "A Century Separated the Unforgettable Battles at Shiloh and the Ia Drang Valley, Yet the Similarities are Striking," *Vietnam*, June 1992, pp. 58–63.

618   Eric Lee, *Saigon to Jerusalem* (Jefferson, North Carolina: McFarland & Company, Inc., 1992), p. 5.

619   Eric Lee, "Some of the Jewish Soldiers in Vietnam Thought How Nice It Would Be to Win a War in Six Days," *Vietnam*, June 1994, pp. 62–67.

620   U.S. Army Register of Officers for 1966, 1967, 1968, and 1969.

621   John Barry, "Women of War," *The Dallas Morning News*, July 17, 1996, pp. C-5–6. (This was a Knight-Ridder Newspapers wire story.)

622   Ron Kovic, *Born on the Fourth of July* (New York: Pocket Books, 1976).

623   Military record of Ronald L. Kovic, National Personnel Records Center, FOIA request by B. G. Burkett.

624   Letter from Cpl. Ronald L. Kovic to commandant of the Marine Corps, May 18, 1967, FOIA request by B.G. Burkett.

625   Diana West, "A 'True Story' That's Not So True," *Insight*, the *Washington Times* magazine, April 2, 1990, p. 58.

626   Richard Eilert, *For Self and Country* (New York: William Morrow & Company Inc., 1983), pp. 9–13.

627   Richard Eilert, "'Born on the Fourth': It's a Lie," *Washington Post*, February 6, 1990.

628   Dennis J. Marvicsin and Jerold Greenfield, *Maverick: The Personal War of a Vietnam Cobra Pilot* (New York: G. P. Putnam's Sons, 1990, Jove Books edition, September 1991).

629   Ibid., p. 302.

630   Military record of Dennis J. Marvicsin, National Personnel Records Center, FOIA request by B. G. Burkett, March 25, 1992.

631   Mickey Block, *Before the Dawn* (Pocket Books, 1989).

632   Military record of Mickey Block, National Personnel Records Center, FOIA request by B. G. Burkett.

633   Joel M. Hutchins, *Swimmers Among the Trees* (Novato, CA: Presidio Press, 1996).

634   Military record of Joel M. Hutchins, National Personnel Records Center, FOIA request by B. G. Burkett, 1996.

635   Larry Bailey, "'Swimmer' Up A Tree," *Soldier of Fortune*, November 1996, pp. 40–41.

636   Warner Smith, "*Covert Warrior: Fighting the CIA's Secret War in Southeast Asia and China, 1965-1967*" (Presidio Press, 1996). Even six months after I alerted Presidio and the Military Book Club that *Covert Warrior* was a bogus book, it was still being listed in new catalogs.

637 Jerry Carroll, *North SAR* (New York: Pocket Books, 1991).

638 Ibid., p. x.

639 Jerry Carroll, *No Place to Hide* (New York: Pocket Books, 1995), pp. 415–417.

640 Military record of Jerry Carroll, National Personnel Records Center, FOIA request by B. G. Burkett.

641 Major Bruce H. Norton, *One Tough Marine* (New York: Ballantine Books, 1993).

642 Charles F. Reske, "Operation Footboy: Undercover in the North," *Vietnam*, October 1995, pp. 30–36. Reske was a member of the top-secret U.S. Naval Security Group during the Vietnam War. He also wrote *MACV-SOG Command History Annex B: The Last Secret of the Vietnam War* (Alpha Press).

643 Letter to Harve Saal from John K. Singlaub, major general, U.S. Army (Ret.), July 4, 1994.

644 Letter to B. G. Burkett from Lt. General Bernard E. Trainor, USMC (Ret.), director of the National Security Program at the John F. Kennedy School of Government at Harvard University, December 21, 1994.

645 Letter to B. G. Burkett from J. H. "Pat" Carothers Jr., November 9, 1994.

646 Letter to B. G. Burkett from Maj. Gen. W. H. Rice, USMC (Ret.), October 5,1994.

647 Military record of Donald Nathan Hamblen, National Personnel Records Center, FOIA request by B. G. Burkett, October 3, 1994.

648 William R. Kimball, *Vietnam: The Other Side of Glory* (New York: Ballantine Books, 1987), pp. 189–209.

649 Ibid., p. 207.

650 Ibid., p. 209.

651 *Soldiers: A History of Men in Battle*, "The Irregulars," aired San Francisco KQED, January 29, 1991.

652 Editors, "Special Forces and Missions," *The New Face of War* (New York: *Time-Life Books*), p. 35.

653 Edward Doyle, Terrence Maitland, and editors, *The Vietnam Experience: the Aftermath* (Boston, MA: Boston Publishing Co., 1985), p. 145.

654 Membership application of John C. Gallagher for Special Operations Association, November 16, 1985.

655 Military record of John Charles Gallagher, National Personnel Records Center, FOIA request by G. A. Blakey Jr., Special Operations Association, August 20, 1990. Also, Letter from Special Forces Association to John C. Gallagher, terminating his membership, December 26, 1990. "Your wearing of unauthorized awards and decorations and your claim to have been a prisoner of war are considered an affront and an extreme insult to those personnel who are duly entitled to such status," said Cliff Newman, president of the SOA.

656 Letter to B. G. Burkett from Clayton S. Scott, membership chairman, Special Operations Association, August 30, 1994.

657 Henry Maurer *Strange Ground: An Oral History of Americans in Vietnam 1945-1975* (New York: Avon Books, 1989,) pp. 351–364.

658 Ibid., p. 353.

659 Ibid., p. 355.

660 Department of Defense casualty records.

661 Flyer for Shidoshi Dux Martial Arts Studios.

662 John Johnson, "Ninja Hero or Master Fake?" *Los Angeles Times*, May 1, 1988.

663 Military record of Frank William Dux, National Personnel Records Center, FOIA request July 13, 1995.

664 Military record of Frank William Dux, psychiatric report, January 22, 1978.

665 Frank W. Dux, *The Secret Man: An American Warrior's Uncensored Story* (New York: Regan Books [HarperCollins], 1996).

666 Letter from Larry Simmons, Commander, USN (Ret.), to Harper Collins Publishers Inc., April 4, 1996.

667 Fax from Gen. H. Norman Schwarzkopf to Robert Brown, editor, *Soldier of Fortune*, May 24, 1996.

668 Letter from Thomas R. Spencer Jr., Spencer & Klein, Washington, D.C., to Judith Regan, Regan Books, Harper Collins Publishers, April 17, 1996.

669 Anthony Herbert, *Soldier*, pp. 103–104.

670 Pete Billac, *The Last Medal of Honor* (Houston: Swan Publishing Co., 1990).

671 Profile, Pete Billac, mailed to B. G. Burkett, July 2, 1991.

672 Military record of Peter Samuel Billac Jr., National Personnel Records Center, FOIA request by B. G. Burkett, June 28, 1991.

673 Lenox Cramer, *Slow Dance On the Killing Ground* (Sharon Center, Ohio: Alpha Publications, 1990).

674 Letter to Jack Abraham, Special Operations Association, from John Staub, director of Alpha Publications, February 23, 1991.

675 Letter to Jack Abraham, Special Operations Association, from Lenox Cramer, Eddyville, Kentucky, February 27, 1991.

676 Military record of Lenox Barnes Cramer, National Personnel Records Center, FOIA request by B. G. Burkett, December 16, 1992.

677 Doug Valentine, *The Phoenix Program: A Shattering Account of the Most Ambitious and Closely-Guarded Operation of the Vietnam War* (New York, William Morrow and Company, 1990).

678 Military record of Elton Manzione, National Personnel Records Center, FOIA request by B. G. Burkett. Manzione popped up again in *VVA Veteran* magazine July 1991, in a story by Tim Wells called "The Assault on Hon Me." He was described as one of the U.S. advisors in the assault on Hon Me Island in the Tonkin Gulf, and was quoted as saying: "To say that the North Vietnamese attack on the Maddox was unprovoked just isn't true, and to say that no Americans participated in the raids on Hon Me and Hon Ngu is also untrue. I was there. I know what happened. Our job was to provoke a response. And looking back now, history points to the Gulf of Tonkin episode and the congressional resolution that followed as the start of that war. I mean, Jesus, what happened out there was the beginning of a war that cost over fifty-seven thousand American lives. Morally, I feel responsible for having been a part of that. I know it sounds crazy, but sometimes I was up at night with this ridiculous notion that, 'My God, I was the one who started it all.' Of course, in my saner, more rational moments, I know that's not true—but Hon Me happened, and because of the way it went down, there's this bitterness in my gut that tells me that I'm the guy responsible for all those names on The Wall." And I'm sure any suggestion that records show it never happened would be met with this Manzione quote from the same story: "This was strictly a 'black bag' mission."

Manzione seems to have a flair for fiction. In 1988, Elton Manzione Jr. submitted a creative writing project called "Shadow People," about a covert operative in Vietnam who likes to patrol while listening to the Rolling Stones, as a thesis to the graduate faculty of the University of Georgia in partial fulfillment of the requirements for the degree of Master of Arts.

679 John B. Dwyer, "Arsenal," *Vietnam*, October 1994, pp. 12, 16, 57.

680 Valentine, *The Phoenix Program*, p. 207.

681 F. C. Brown, "Limited Sources: The Phoenix Program," Review, *Foreign Intelligence Literary Scene*, pp. 9–10.

682 Postcard to F. C. Brown, from Doug Valentine, July 23, 1993.

683 Dale Andradé, *Ashes to Ashes: The Phoenix Program and the Vietnam War* (Lexington, Massachusetts: Lexington Books, 1990).

684 *Fact Sheet* on Scott Barnes, National League of Families of American Prisoners and Missing in Southeast Asia, Washington, D.C., July 15, 1988.

685 Scott Barnes with Melva Libb, *BOHICA: A True Account of One Man's Battle to Expose the Most Heinous Cover-Up of the Vietnam Saga!* (Canton, Ohio: BOHICA Corporation, 1987).

686 *BOHICA: The Facts Behind the Fantasies of the Author, Scott Barnes*, A Research Paper Published by the National League of Families of American Prisoners and Missing in Southeast Asia, Washington, D.C., 1988.

687 Military record of Scott Tracy Barnes, National Personnel Records Center, FOIA request by B. G. Burkett, January 2, 1990.

688 Letter from Col. Joseph A. Schlatter to the National League of Families, July 26, 1988.

689 Gene Mustain and Jerry Capeci, *Murder Machine: A True Story of Murder, Madness, and the Mafia* (New York: Penguin Books, 1992).

690 Edward F. Murphy, *Dak To* (Novato, California: Presidio Press, 1993), pp. 233–321.

691 173rd LRRP, 74th LRP, N/75 Ranger Alpha Roster. 75th Ranger Regiment.

692 Interview of Gene Mustain by Glenna Whitley.

693 Mark Moyar, *Phoenix and the Birds of Prey* (Naval Institute, 1997). I had researched Cable and had determined that his military career was fabricated. When author Mark Moyar contacted me about the impostor Yoshia Chee, we also swapped information on Cable. Moyar later interviewed Cable for his book on the Phoenix Program.

694 Letter of May 17, 1996. "Dear Mr. Burkett: As I informed you on the telephone Wednesday, Larry E. Cable did not graduate from Shimer College. Our records show that he attended from the Fall 1960 semester until the Spring 1962 semester. Sincerely, Ian Crump, Associate Dean."

695 Letter from B. G. Burkett to Dr. James R. Leutze Chancellor, University of North Carolina-Willmington, dated October 9, 1997.

696 Transcript, Volume XXIII, Number 37, "Vietnam 101," *60 Minutes*, CBS, May 26, 1991. First aired October 4, 1987.

697 Ken Stephens, "New Look at the '60s," *The Dallas Morning News*, May 29, 1988, p. A-1.

698 Military record of Dan Morris Gisel, National Personnel Records Center, FOIA request by B. G. Burkett, May 25, 1994.

699 Letter from William M. Stokes, III, Colonel, USA (Ret.), to B. G. Burkett, July 19, 1994. James T. Taylor, Jr., 5th Sp. Forces Gp., was awarded the Distinguished Service Cross for his actions at Doug Xoai. (US Army/Vietnam, General Order 737/1967.)

700 Walter Capps died in October 1997 at Dulles International Airport of a heart attack.

Chapter Eighteen: The Military Historian and the "Gay Beret"

701 Shelby Stanton, *Vietnam Order of Battle*, U.S. News, 1981. His other Vietnam history books include: *Green Berets at War*, Presidio Press, 1985, the story of Special Forces in

Vietnam; *Anatomy of a Division* (Warner Books, 1987), a portrait of the 1st Cav; *The Rise and Fall of An American Army*, Presidio Press, 1985, an analytical battlefield history; and *Rangers at War: LRRPs In Vietnam* (New York: Ivy Books, 1992). Stanton was also a major advisor to *The Vietnam Experience*, the *Time-Life* historical series about the war.

702   Shelby Stanton, *U.S. Army Uniforms of the Vietnam War* (Stackpole Books), 1989, book jacket.

703   Shelby Stanton, "With Project 404," *The Vietnam Experience: War in the Shadows* (Boston: Boston Publishing Co., 1988), p.93.

704   Military record of Shelby L. Stanton, National Personnel Records Center, FOIA request by B. G. Burkett, June 26, 1992.

705   Personal interview with Henry "Hank" Newkirk by B. G. Burkett, July 1, 1992.

706   Harry G. Summers Jr., Col., USA (Ret.), *Vietnam*, August 1992, p. 6.

707   Letter to William P. Barr, Attorney General, from Gary L. Brooks, general counsel, National Archives, July 23, 1992, with copies to Dick Cheney, secretary of defense, and Dr. Don W. Wilson, archivist of the United States.

708   Susan Katz Keating, "Tin Soldier? Shelby Stanton's War," *Washington Times*, July 23, 1992, pp. E-1, 2. Stories by Keating that followed: "Did Historian Steal Secret MIA Files?," July 30, 1992; "MIAs' Kin Angry at Delay in Probe of Secret Papers," July 31, 1992; "Secret Files on MIAs Returned by Historian," August 8, 1992, and "Families Look to Secret Files," August 8, 1992.

709   Shelby Stanton, *Rangers at War*, introduction.

710   Unawarded Contract MDA903–92–C-0122, Defense Supply Service, Office of the Chief Attorney, Pentagon, FOIA request by B. G. Burkett, February 9, 1995. Keating touched on the issue of the files. In 1985, an officer at the Pentagon had been contacted by Stanton. Stanton offered to sell the Pentagon sensitive original files on almost a thousand men still listed as MIA in Vietnam. Some contained delicate information, such as photos of American servicemen with their Asian girlfriends.

The files had belonged to the 525th Military Intelligence Group in Vietnam. (When many units were being shipped home, often the records were sent to Bangkok rather than the United States because there were still active Army commands in Thailand. Anything that involved intelligence was particularly likely to remain in Southeast Asia.) As the war ended, did the incipient historian Stanton acquire them by slapping shipping labels on the boxes and sending them to his home? The Pentagon officer wrote a memo about the files and Stanton's offer to sell them, but the memo apparently disappeared into the maw of the military bureaucracy.

711   The U.S. Army Central Identification Laboratory in Camp Kamehameha, Hawaii, responsible for resolving POW-MIA cases by conducting on-site evaluations, recovering remains and artifacts, and comparing them to pertinent information in the POW-MIA file, completed a review of the material recovered from Stanton on December 2, 1993. No information that changed the outcome of an unresolved POW-MIA case was discovered in the files. But MIA families were outraged that Stanton had kept the files to himself for twenty years.

712   U.S. Army Criminal Investigation Command Report of Investigation on Shelby L. Stanton, Number 92–CID201–10014–7F1, obtained through FOIA requests by B. G. Burkett, February 9, 1995 and March 23, 1995.

713   Random House has published several phony books. After the publication of *One Tough Marine*, I wrote editor Owen Lock a letter: "It looks like you have published yet

another bogus book. You keep calling these books nonfiction. Maybe a better term would be 'random fiction from Random House.'"

714   After I notified the National Archives, three different agencies began investigating Stanton: U.S. Army Criminal Investigation Division, the Defense Criminal Investigative Service, and the FBI. According to the investigative report of the CID (which I obtained in March 1995), on the day before Keating's "Tin Soldier" story ran, an apprehensive Stanton showed up at the office of the commander of the U.S. Army POW-MIA Affairs Section of TAPC. Stanton wanted to turn over some POW-MIA files.

The commander was skeptical. A lot of people claim to have sensitive POW-MIA files that turn out to be fraudulent. But Stanton identified himself as a retired Army captain with Special Forces in Vietnam and said a reporter was "harassing" him and his family about the files. Indicating they were "hot" and he didn't want to keep them any more, Stanton turned over seven boxes containing 476 classified POW-MIA files, which included original medical and dental records and sworn statements taken from witnesses with the casualties at the time of their capture or loss. Many documents were marked "SECRET," "OFFICIAL USE ONLY," and "CONFIDENTIAL."

Initially, the government wasn't sure how to handle Stanton's sudden "gift." They determined the files were authentic. They compared the files to Stanton's book *Green Berets at War*. He had listed the U.S. Army Special Forces soldiers who were POWs or MIAs of the Vietnam War. Following each was a brief paragraph describing the circumstances in which they were lost. The descriptions in Stanton's book matched that in the files almost verbatim.

Involved with the Kerrey Commission on MIAs, only days before, on July 17, 1992, Stanton had ironed out the details of a contract with the Office of the Secretary of Defense to write a study called "U.S. Laotian Operations and Casualty Accountability."

Stanton had been trying to get a consulting job as a POW-MIA expert with TAPC since November 1991, based on his vast depth of knowledge in the field and his extensive collection of documents on the subject. He said he obtained them while serving with Special Forces in Vietnam. When he heard the records were going to be thrown out, he asked if he could have them. He led the commander of the POW-MIA Affairs Office to think the documents were duplicates, of little or no value. Certainly nothing original or classified.

Told no job was available, Stanton went to the secretary of defense with another proposal. He would provide a study of the U.S. military servicemen lost in Southeast Asia during the Vietnam War to the POW-MIA Affairs Office. The OSD agreed to pay $59,400, based on Stanton's "unique ability" to perform the study, based on his personal archives. When asked where he got the files, he said only that he had access to them while he was "in-country" in Thailand. The proposal, which Stanton had been negotiating for months, didn't include acquisition of the files. The fee for that was to be addressed separately.

But abruptly, on July 18 Stanton withdrew his proposal saying that the six-month deadline was unrealistic. The government agent thought it was odd because Stanton had proposed the deadline himself. But it's obvious that Stanton, during interviews with Keating, realized her story was not going to be favorable and decided he had to return the documents.

Some of the names on the files were listed in the study proposal. While many of the files Stanton possessed would have been declassified in the intervening years, ninety-eight remained classified at the "CONFIDENTIAL" level.

715 Bill Hewitt, "They Also Serve," *People Weekly*, February 15, 1993, pp. 40–42.

716 Randy Shilts, *Conduct Unbecoming: Gays and Lesbians in the U.S. Military* (New York: St. Martin's Press, 1993).

717 Sam Donaldson, "Conduct Unbecoming," *ABC News Prime Time Live*, April 15, 1993.

718 Department of Defense casualty records.

719 Military record of Gerald Rosanbalm, National Personnel Records Center, FOIA request by Christopher Ruddy, July 16, 1993.

720 Military record of Donald Dean Winn, National Personnel Records Center, FOIA request by Christopher Ruddy, July 16, 1993.

721 Letter from Robert B. Annenberg, LTC, USA (Ret), to B. G. Burkett, August 30, 1993. Annenberg wrote me after receiving a call from Rosenbalm's lawyer, Mark Scherzer. "Since we now have a lawyer questioning me, and the possibility being raised that I have been misquoted, maybe it is time I got down on paper—in my own words—my recollections as to what did and did not happen," Annenberg wrote.

722 Officer Efficiency Report for Gerald L. Rosanbalm, signed Robert B. Annenberg, MAJ, Military Intelligence, March 6, 1968.

723 Letter from Brig. Gen. Robert W. Williams, USA (Ret.) to B. G. Burkett, January 25, 1994.

724 Christopher Ruddy, "Total Misconduct," *New York Guardian*, July 23, 1993, p.1.

725 Richard Johnson, "Decorating the Hero's Record," the *New York Post*, August 5, 1993, p. 1; "Smearing a Name on The Wall," *AIM Report*, September-B, 1993; Reginald Fitz and David Wright, "Gay War Hero is a Fake!," *National Enquirer*, p. 5.

726 John Lehman, "Sad Story of Gays in Military," *The Wall Street Journal*, May 18, 1993.

Chapter Nineteen: The Minority Myth: Blacks in Vietnam

727 Transcript, "The Bloods of 'Nam," Frontline, #414, 1986, WGBH Educational Foundation, Boston, MA.

728 Wallace Terry, *Bloods: An Oral History of the Vietnam War by Black Veterans* (New York: Random House, 1984).

729 Telephone Interview with Ronald Kender, Thomas Alva Edison High School, The School District of Philadelphia, by B. G. Burkett, July 1991.

730 John Roman, "Edison High: Blackboard Jungle," Delaware County *Daily Times*, September 8, 1985, p. 27.

731 Military records of James Joseph Allen Jr., Charles Joseph Antonelly, Samuel Nurrell Burton, Glenn Carter, Richard Albert Carter, William Chapman Jr., Milton Gay Clayborne, Deighton Alonzo Danielles, Charles Joseph Glenn III, Rocco Renell Isaac, Randolph Thomas Jefferson, Joseph Johnson Jr., Richard Francis McNichols, Adolfo Martinez, Joseph Mieczkowski, Kenneth Pettus, Alfred Alexander Purvis, Samuel Rodriguez, Joseph Alan Weber, Michael Matthew White, Bernard Richard Woehlcke, Robert Joseph Campbell, William B. Blackmon Jr., Lural Lee Blevins III, Zachrie Brookins Jr., Hector Warren Bryan, Louis Antonio Cobarrubio, Wayne Thomas Dilliman, Harold Arthur Doman, Roscoe Glover Jr., Irvin James Hopkins, Joe Thomas Johnson Jr., Dennis Kuzer, Kenney Earl Lassiter, Joseph Francis Lodise Jr., Gerald Joseph Maguire, John Gerome Miller Jr., Leroy W. Peagler, Lawrence John

Reichert Jr., Angelo Carmelo Santiago, Harry Baton Seedes III, Neely James Singletary, James Thealbeart Swift Jr., Aaron Leon Thomas, Henry Benny Thomas, John Joseph Thomas, Robert Torres, Nathaniel Washington, General White, Duane Gregory Williams, Francis Albert Zerggen, National Personnel Records Center, FOIA request by B. G. Burkett, February 12, 1991.

732   Department of Defense casualty records. In the years since the plaque was mounted, the school has discovered other casualties, bringing the total to 66. One, Sgt. Robert Joseph Campbell, a Caucasian graduate, was listed as KIA on December 21, 1965, but he actually died in Philadelphia several months after leaving Vietnam of malaria contracted in Southeast Asia.

733   The percentage of black casualties to total casualties in the war years: 1962 (1.8 percent); 1963 (4.2 percent); 1964 (5.8 percent) ; 1965 (14.4 percent); 1966 (16.3 percent); 1967 (12.5 percent); 1968 (13.2 percent); 1969 (11.4 percent); 1970 (11.04 percent); 1971 (11.4 percent); 1972 (10.1 percent); 1973 (2.4 percent); 1974 (1.6 percent); 1975 (4.4 percent). There were none before 1962.

734   Department of Defense casualty records.

735   Military record of Haywood Thomas Kirkland, National Personnel Records Center, FOIA request by B. G. Burkett, September 21, 1990.

736   Terry, *Bloods*, pp. 18–32.

737   Military Record of Harold Bryant, National Personnel Records Center, FOIA request by B. G. Burkett, September 21, 1990.

738   Department of Defense casualty records.

739   Terry, *Bloods*, pp. 33–55.

740   Military record of Richard James Ford III, National Personnel Records Center, FOIA request by B. G. Burkett, September 21, 1990.

741   Department of Defense casualty records.

742   Terry, *Bloods*, pp. 160–175.

743   Military record of Don F. Browne, National Personnel Records Center, FOIA request by B. G. Burkett, September 21, 1990.

744   Telephone interviews with LTC Hillel Schwartz, USA (Ret.), by B. G. Burkett, January 28, 1993 and February 23, 1993. Here's what really happened at the embassy: Under orders from General Westmoreland, former Army Maj. Hillel Schwartz, deputy G-2 for the 101st Airborne, took a platoon of riflemen to secure the embassy and the grounds during the early morning of the first day of the Tet Offensive. Under heavy fire from small arms and automatic weapons, Major Schwartz, a first lieutenant, and the better part of a platoon landed on the rooftop heliport of the embassy. Starting at the top, Schwartz and his team worked their way down through the building, systematically searching it floor by floor. Despite the gunfire outside the compound, the only "combat" occurred when a startled Major Schwartz saw himself in the mirror of the ambassador's liquor cabinet and blasted away at the reflection with his sidearm. (Embarrassed, Schwartz later profusely apologized to the ambassador for demolishing his liquor supply.)

745   Schwartz and his men removed all important documents, thousands of piasters, and gold dust from the embassy and took the valuables to Bien Hoa. A highly decorated career soldier, Schwartz received an Air Medal for valor for his actions during the embassy operation. His comments are supported by his military record; by General Order 127, 3 March 1968, by the Headquarters 101st Airborne Division, awarding Schwartz a Bronze Star Medal with V device; and General Order 7645, 17 October

1968, awarding him an Air Medal with V Device (Second Oak Leaf Cluster), all obtained from the National Personnel Records Center, FOIA request by B. G. Burkett, August 27, 1993. Another good source of information on the attack on the U.S. Embassy is the book *Tet!*, by Don Oberdorfer (Garden City, New York: Doubleday & Company, 1971).

746 Terry, *Bloods*, pp. 236–265.

747 Military record of Arthur Eugene Woodley, National Personnel Records Center, FOIA request by B. G. Burkett, September 21, 1990.

748 Marc Leepson, "*Dead Presidents*: Turning a Robin Hood Tale of Redemption into "*'Nam* In the Hood,'" *VVA Veteran*, November 1995, p. 23.

749 Robert W. Mullen, *Blacks in America's War*, Pathfinder Press.

750 Dr. Ken Werrell, "The Mutiny at Bamber Bridge," *After the Battle*, vol. 22, 1978, pp. 1–11.

751 Cynthia Gimbel and Alan Booth, "Who Fought in Vietnam?" *Social Forces*, The University of North Carolina Press, June 1996, 74(4):1137–1157.

752 David Halberstam, "There is Something Noble to It," *Parade Magazine*, September 17, 1995, p. 5.

753 Wallace Terry, "Life After Bloods," *VVA Veteran*, February 1994, pp. 15–17.

754 Michael Holmes, "Texas Guard Leader Appointed," *The Dallas Morning News*, November 19, 1995.

Chapter Twenty: Baby You Looked Like the Cong

755 M Sgt. Ray A. Bows, *Vietnam Lore* (Bows & Son Publishing: 1988), pp. 224–227.

756 George Esper, Associated Press, "Nurse First Woman Killed in Conflict," *Las Vegas Review-Journal*, July 3, 1988.

757 Department of Defense casualty records.

758 Lydia Fish, *The Last Firebase* (White Mane Publishing Co., Inc.) 1987, p. 46.

759 Col. Harry G. Summers, USA (Ret.) "Nurses Have Served Officially in Wartime Since 1961; Vietnam Proved Women Could Serve in Other Roles, Too," *Vietnam*, pp. 8–68–71.

760 Marianne Jacobs, RN, Ph.D., letter to the editor, *VVA Veteran*, March 1991, pp. 5, 32. Jacobs was writing to give the results of research she had done involving 257 nurses who had served in Vietnam. However, whether she identified the nurses through military records is not explained. According to Dr. Gail Watson, R.N., associate professor at Texas Woman's University College of Nursing, there are no known accurate lists of women who served in Vietnam. For her own research, Watson resorted to advertising for participants in various veteran publications and newsletters. The participants were then mailed a packet with a pre-paid envelope for return of the anonymous questionnaire. Unfortunately, there is no way to verify the validity of studies performed in this manner.

761 As told by Kathy Emanuelsen, "Something to Give," *Vietnam*, June 1991, pp. 27–32.

762 Laura Palmer, "How to Bandage a War," *The New York Times Sunday* magazine, November 7, 1993, pp. 36–43, 68.

763 Department of Defense casualty records.

764 Lynda Van Devanter, *Home Before Morning: The Story of an Army Nurse in Vietnam* (New York: Beaufort Books, 1983).

765 Dan Cragg, "Telling 'War Stories' on America's Campuses," *Washington Times*, December 14, 1982, p. A-10.

766 Carol Shevis, "Vietnam From a Woman's View," the Herndon *Observer*, November 12, 1982.

767 Sandra G. Boodman, "War Story," *Washington Post*, May 23, 1983, pp. C-1, 7.

768 Robb Ruyle, letter to Al Hemingway, senior editor of *Vietnam* magazine, December 21, 1996. Ruyle was the air evac and patient administration officer at the 71st Evacuation Hospital in Pleiku; Lynne was an emergency/triage nurse.

Lynda Van Devanter makes herself out to be a hero who rescues a seriously injured doorgunner from a helicopter only moments before it explodes on the 71st helipad. After saving the man's life, she's put in for a Bronze Star Medal with Valor; it comes back as a BSM with no V device because "they didn't award things like that to nurses." (Chapter 16 of *Home Before Morning*.)

Ruyle explained that the incident occurred after Van Devanter had been transferred to another unit. "Here is what really happened: A Huey slick radioed in to our ER that it was inbound, ETA one minute, shot up and leaking fuel and with a seriously injured doorgunner. When the chopper touched down on our helipad, the pilot and copilot jumped out and ran toward the ER entrance, yelling, 'Get back! Get back! It's gonna blow!' A litter team and a nurse passed them, heading for the chopper. The Huey was still winding down, it was *full* of holes, and leaking fuel and hydraulic fluid all over the place.

"The nurse jumped up into the waist, popped the unconscious doorgunner out of his safety harness, and helped the litter team get him onto the litter. The litter team ran him the fifty yards or so to the ER, where the nurse began immediate resuscitation, joined within seconds by two physicians and another nurse. They did cutdowns and pushed blood, bagged him with oxygen, and shocked his heart to try to get it started, but the gunner had lost too much blood and too much time. He died in the ER.

"The Huey stayed on the pad for hours before it was considered safe to approach. Toward dusk, a Chinook came in and hauled it away. It did not explode.

"How do I know this incident in such detail? Lynne was the nurse, and I had one end of the litter. (Not my usual job, but I just happened to be one of the two guys nearest the door when Lynne yelled for a litter team to go with her).

"Lynne was never put in for an award. Lynda's tripe about the BSM with V device just shows her ignorance of the criteria for the various awards. I've always thought that Lynne deserved to be put in for the Soldier's Medal for her work that day, but that didn't happen, and it was a long time ago."

769 Boodman, *War Story*, p. C-7.

770 Joanne Webb, Review, "Another Vietnam Story That Isn't True," *Washington Times*, June 15, 1983.

771 Operational Report, Headquarters, 71st Evacuation Hospital, Department of the Army, Period Ending 31 Jan 1970, 14 February 1970, p. 3. The same report cited the "John Turkey Movement," in which Van Devanter and a handful of other hospital personnel sent a letter to President Richard M. Nixon announcing a Thanksgiving fast to symbolize their protest of the war: "The news media picked up the story, and soon representatives from major national and international news agencies and three television networks were covering the planned fast. The hospital commander made it clear the fast would be acceptable as long as their protest remained within the Department of Defense guidelines for dissent in the Army. Only a few people actually participated in the fast. No observable adverse effects on morale or duty performance were observed."

772 Military Record of Lynda Van Devanter, National Personnel Records Center, FOIA request by B.G. Burkett.

773 As Told by Kathy Emanuelsen, "Something to Give," *Vietnam* Magazine, June 1991, p. 32.

774 Letter from Edward J. Drea, chief, Staff Support Branch, Center of Military History, Department of the Army, to B. G. Burkett, September 17, 1987.

775 Steve Chawkins, "Viet War Often Goes Unstudied," *Rocky Mountain News*, April 1, 1995, pp. 8, 24.

776 Ann Zimmerman, "War Tribute Incomplete, Veterans Say," *Dallas Times Herald*, April 21, 1988. The name of Ann Funck was spelled "Funk" in this story.

777 Military Record of Karen Ann Cowles (Ann Funck) National Personnel Records Center, FOIA request by B. G. Burkett.

778 Melissa Morrison, "TWU Indian Group Sends Old School Texts to Reservation," *The Dallas Morning News*, July 9, 1993, pp. A-23,24.

779 Joe Treen, Kent Demaret, Joseph Harmes, Bob Stewart, Rosie Carbo, "Epidemic or Hoax?," *People Weekly*, March 2, 1992, pp. 32–35.

780 Bruce Tomaso, "Town Glad for Quiet Year After AIDS Scare," *The Dallas Morning News*, February 15, 1991, pp. A-1, 7.

781 Military Record of Dona Kay Spence, National Personnel Records Center, FOIA request by B. G. Burkett.

782 News Release, Hopes and Holidays Christmas Card Program, The American Legion Department of Texas, Jacksboro, Texas.

783 Maggie Kennedy, "Artistic Veterans Lend Color to Christmas," *Dallas Times Herald*, November 22, 1991.

784 Military Record of Juanita Olvera (Johnnie Rainwater), National Personnel Records Center, FOIA request by B. G. Burkett, February 20, 1992.

785 Richard A. Serrano, "A Quest for Truth," *Los Angeles Times*, December 20, 1994, p. E-1.

786 Military Record of Anne Cecilia Caro and Anne Cecilia Dulaney (Anne Label), National Personnel Records Center. FOIA request by B.G. Burkett.

787 Patience H.C. Mason, *Recovering From the War: A Woman's Guide to Helping Your Vietnam Vet, Your Family, and Yourself* (New York: Penguin Books, 1990). Mason is married to Robert Mason, a Vietnam vet who wrote the best-selling book *Chickenhawk* (New York: The Viking Press, 1983).

788 Ken Scharnberg, "They Aren't Just Rap Centers Any More," *The American Legion*, p. 30.

789 Charles R. Figley, *Compassion Fatigue* (New York: Brunner/Mazel, Inc., 1995).

790 Aphrodite Matsakis, *Vietnam Wives* (Kensington, Maryland: Woodbine House, 1988).

791 Telephone Interview of Col. Joseph A. Schlatter, Director, Department of Defense POW-MIA Office, by Malcolm McConnell, September 15, 1993. Also confirmed by MG J. K. Singlaub, USA (Ret.), commander MACV-SOG 1966–1968.

792 Letter from Malcolm McConnell to Aphrodite Matsakis, Silver Springs Maryland, September 2, 1993. Letter from Matsakis to McConnell, October 1, 1993.

793 Ann Rule, *A Rose for Her Grave* (New York: Pocket Books, 1993).

794 Sally Randall is not her real name. Although my policy is not to use pseudonyms, I agreed to her request in this case because the woman was afraid of Crawford.

795 *United States vs. SSG Travis D. Crawford*, General Court-Martial Order, Headquarters, 32d Army Air Defense Command, Department of the Army, October 21, 1985.

796   *United States of America v. Travis Dean Crawford*, Judgment in a Criminal Case, October 26, 1993. Case number 3:93–CR-271–D, U.S. District Court, Northern District of Texas.

797   Petition for Offender Under Supervision, United States District Court, February 23, 1995.

798   _____ *v. Great Southern Video, Inc., d/b/a Great Expectations*, Cause No. 94–12742–J, 191st Judicial District, State District Court, Texas. Attorneys for the company filed a general denial in the lawsuit, which was still pending at press time.

799   The name Barbara Harris is a pseudonym to protect her children.

800   Military record of Louis Paul Rolofson Jr., National Personnel Records Center, obtained by Teresa D. Brown, assistant state's attorney, Madison County, Illinois.

801   Telephone interview with Terri Stout by Glenna Whitley. Also: Correspondence from Terri Stout, June 19, 1995. Extensive documents from *Kullman V. Kullman*, Superior Court of California, County of Lassen, Case number 23592.

802   Letter from Terri E. Stout to Malcolm McConnell, *Reader's Digest*, May 5, 1994. She wrote to *Reader's Digest*: "After finishing your article. I began to experience a sort of relief," Terri wrote, "almost a lifting of shame. Your article made me realize it really wasn't only me that had been fooled all these years."

803   Military Record of Gerard Joseph Kullman, National Personnel Records Center, FOIA request by B. G. Burkett, June 9, 1994.

Chapter Twenty-One: Bogus Guests at the Hanoi Hilton

804   Correspondence with David W. Fletcher, Desert Dust Press, Stanfield, Arizona, September 28, 1995.

805   *The Ballad of Don Liston,* Music and Lyrics by Jim Walktendonk, Recorded on the BooneyTunes Label, Copyright 1989. Here are a couple of verses:

> *On Christmas Eve it all comes back into view.*
> *He was captured*
> *by the V.C. and thrown into a bamboo cage*
> *lowered into a river*
> *his broken bones and body raged.*
> *Seventeen days of torture. Seventeen nights of Hell.*
> *By night he chewed his bamboo lashings and escaped*
> *down river to tell*
> *how he was naked in the jungle.*

806   David W. Fletcher, *Chieu-Hoi: Surrender with Open Arms*, Unpublished manuscript, Copyright 1992, Desert Dust Press, Stanfield, Arizona. Used by permission.

807   Letter to David W. Fletcher from author John M. Del Vecchio, December 12, 1992.

808   Geoffrey Norman, "Wine Tasting at the Hanoi Hilton," *Forbes*, November 26, 1990, pp. 68–73.

809   Michael Gunstanson, "Former POWs' Haunting Memories Resurface," *Fort Worth Star-Telegram*, January 22, 1991.

810   "Captured U.S. Military Personnel Returned at Operation Homecoming, 1973, Plus Earlier Returnees and Escapees, Vietnam War Era," Department of Defense.

811   Military Record of John Texas Kennelly, National Personnel Records Center, FOIA request by B. G. Burkett, February 1, 1991.

812 Military Record of Roger D. Dinsmore, National Personnel Records Center, FOIA request by B. G. Burkett, March 26, 1991.

813 Military Record of Jerry W. McCall, National Personnel Records Center, FOIA request by B. G. Burkett, March 26, 1991.

814 Linda B. Farris, "Korea or 'Nam: Which Was Worse?," *Orange* (Texas) *Leader*, July 3, 1991.

815 Linda B. Farris, "Launey's Vietnam Tours Took Him 'All Over' Nation," *Orange* (Texas) *Leader*, July 3, 1991.

816 "Escape from Camp 8 North Korea," Interview by Theo Baudoin of Archie Launey, junior vice commander of the American Ex-POW Department of Texas, *EX-POW Bulletin*, November 1990, p. 38.

817 Military Record of Archie Launey, National Personnel Records Center, FOIA request by B. G. Burkett, August 9, 1991.

818 Analysis by CWO William B. Thayer, November 15, 1993.

819 Military record of Sidney R. LaFleur, National Personnel Records Center, FOIA request by B. G. Burkett, March 12, 1991.

820 Telephone interview of Sally Morgan, American Ex-POW Association, by B. G. Burkett, August 7, 1991.

821 National League of Families of American Prisoners and Missing in Southeast Asia, Washington, D.C.

822 Susan Katz Keating, *Prisoners of Hope* (New York: Random House 1994).

823 Malcolm McConnell, *Inside Hanoi's Secret Archives: Solving the MIA Mystery* (New York: Simon & Schuster, 1995). I am mentioned in the foreword to both McConnell and Keating books for providing information and records about phony POWs.

824 James D. Sanders, Mark A. Sauter, and R. Cort Kirkwood, *Soldiers of Misfortune: Washington's Secret Betrayal of American POWs in the Soviet Union*, (Washington, D.C.: National Press Books, Inc., 1992).

825 Ibid., pp. 242–243.

826 Letter from F. Kimball Efird, archivist, Illinois State Archives, to B. G. Burkett, June 28, 1991.

827 Military record of Larry S. Pistilli, National Personnel Records Center, FOIA request by B. G. Burkett, May 20, 1991.

828 Keating, "Phony Vets of Conjured Combat," p. 51.

829 Associated Press, "Man Posing as Former POW is a Fake, Veterans Groups Warn," *The Dallas Morning News*, January 21, 1988, pp. A-15.

830 Shirley McLellan, "POW-MIA Vigil Continues," Royal Oak, Michigan, the *Daily Tribune*, September 16, 1988.

831 Letter from Charles F. Trowbridge Jr., deputy chief, Special Office for Prisoners of War and Missing in Action, Defense Intelligence Agency, August 28, 1990.

832 Deborah Kades, "Vets Escape Vietnam Through Therapy," *Daily News*, Beloit, Wisconsin, February 22, 1984.

833 Bill Barth, "Commitment To Truth Can Be Painful," *Daily News*, Beloit, Wisconsin, March 1984.

834 State of Minnesota Proclamation, Thomas Curtis Week, May 2, 1987. State of Minnesota proclamation, David Weiss Week, May 2, 1987.

835 Robert T. Smith, Column, *Minneapolis Star Tribune*, May 10, 1987.

836 Military record Of Thomas Charles Curtis, National Personnel Records Center, FOIA request by B. G. Burkett, October 21, 1990.

837 Military record of David William Weiss, National Personnel Records Center, FOIA request by B. G. Burkett, November 9, 1990.

838 Wes Hills, "Fake Hero Faces Prison For Telling War Stories," *Detroit Free Press*, January 28, 1993.

839 Joe Manuelli, "Former Elmwood Park Man is Profile in Courage," Fairborn *Shopper News*, August 1989.

840 Military Record of Gary L. Locks, National Personnel Records Center, FOIA request by B. G. Burkett, March 26, 1991.

841 Roy J. Horner, "A Brotherly Hand," *Louisville* (Kentucky) *Record*, September 18, 1986.

842 Military Record of John E. Reed, National Personnel Records Center, FOIA request by B. G. Burkett, November 13, 1995.

843 Jim Camden, "Veteran Takes Kids on Trip From Reality," Spokane *Spokesman-Review*, May 8, 1993, pp. B-1, 3.

844 Military Record of Joel Jay Furlett, National Personnel Records Center, FOIA request by Jim Camden.

845 Karine Schomer, "Viet Vets Walk Point," *VVA Veteran*, June 1986, p. 14.

846 Letter from Dan Cragg to Jeff Stein, editor of *VVA Veteran*, July 28, 1986.

847 Doug Pokorski, "Prisoner of War Stories," *State Journal-Register*, Springfield, Illinois, November 5, 1994, pp. 1, 6.

848 "Vets Mark Holiday," *Westland* (Michigan) *Observer*, June 2, 1988.

849 Telephone Interview with Stanley J. Bozich, Michigan's Own, Inc., Military and Space Museum, by Glenna Whitley, May 23, 1995.

850 Letter from Robert A. Slivatz, chairman, Special Forces Association, Chapter LV, to Stanley J. Bozich, director, Michigan's Own, Inc., Military and Space Museum, March 19, 1992.

851 Military Record of Randy G. Brock, National Personnel Records Center, FOIA request by B. G. Burkett, December 16, 1992. Also, correspondence from Lt. Col. J.G. Cele, Chief of U.S. Army POW-MIA Affairs, to B. G. Burkett, November 6, 1991.

852 Letter to Stan Bozich, Michigan's Own, Inc., Military and Space Museum, from Randy G. Brock Sr., February 28, 1992.

853 David Riley, "Vietnam Vets Finding a New Understanding," *Kentucky New Era*, November 12, 1984, pp. A-1, 2.

854 Military Record of Roger E. Watson, National Personnel Records Center, FOIA request by B. G. Burkett, November 23, 1993.

855 I obtained a general order awarding Roger E. Watson the Medal of Honor through a confidential source, who had obtained it from Watson. The late Col. Albert F. Gleim, USA (Ret.) confirmed that it was a real citation with Watson's name inserted instead of Lt. Charles Q. Williams.

856 Tara Gravel, "Vet Passes on Symbol of Courage," *Pocono* (N.Y.) *Record*, September 18, 1994, p. A-5.

857 Virginia S. Wiegand, "Fake Veteran Created Real Hurt Feelings," *Philadelphia Inquirer*, November 22, 1994, pp. B-1, 7.

858 Mark Wigfield, "General Was 'Suspicious' of Fraud," *Pocono* (N.Y.) *Record*, November 2, 1994, pp. A-1, 2.

859 Jane Ann Morrison, "Vegan Invited to Clinton Inauguration," Las Vegas *Review-Journal*, December 30, 1992, pp. A-1, 2.

860 Telephone Interview with Ronald Patrick Murphy by B. G. Burkett, February 28, 1995.

861 Morrison, "Vegan Invited to Clinton Inauguration," p. 2.

862 Jane Ann Morrison, "Vietnam Vet Gets Good News," *Las Vegas Review-Journal*, July 23, 1993, p. B-1. The story repeated Murphy's assertion that he spent twenty-seven days in 1971 as a POW.

863 Telephone interview with Don Rakoskie, Office of Under Secretary, Veterans Administration, March 16, 1995.

864 Military Record of Ronald Patrick Murphy, National Personnel Records Center, FOIA request by Rich Greenberg, producer, ABC News 20/20.

Chapter Twenty-Two: The Myth of Agent Orange

865 Telephone Interview of Jon Franklin by Glenna Whitley, December 10, 1995.

866 Scott, *The Politics of Readjustment*, pp. 87–88.

867 Jon Franklin, Column, *Baltimore Evening Sun*, 1985.

868 Ibid.

869 Ibid.

870 Richard Harwood, "Agent Orange: Just Another Hoax Sneaked Past the Media," *Washington Post*, October 3, 1990. Harwood wrote this column in his capacity as Ombudsman of the *Washington Post*.

871 Anthony L. Kimery, "'Ranch Hand,' The Use of Defoliants to Clear Ambush Sites, Was One of the Most Controversial Operations of the War," *Vietnam*, December 1991, pp. 8, 14–16.

872 Paul Cecil, *Herbicidal Warfare* (New York: Praeger Publishers, 1986), p. 168.

873 Scott, *The Politics of Readjustment*.

874 Carol Cooper, "Sympathy for the Devil," the *Village Voice*, October 25, 1983.

875 Fred A. Wilcox, *Waiting for an Army to Die* (Washington, DC: Seven Locks Press, 1989). First published in 1982.

876 Cecil, *Herbicidal Warfare*, p. 168.

877 Wilcox, *Waiting for an Army to Die*, p. 99.

878 Military record of Paul Reutershan, National Personnel Records Center, FOIA request by B. G. Burkett, August 5, 1992.

879 Wilcox, *Waiting for an Army to Die*, p. 14.

880 Military Record of Edmund P. Juteau, National Personnel Records Center, FOIA request by B. G. Burkett, July 28, 1992.

881 Wilcox, *Waiting for an Army to Die*, p. 39.

882 Military Record of Joseph C. Naples, National Personnel Records Center, FOIA request by B. G. Burkett, August 11, 1992.

883 Cecil, *Herbicidal Warfare*, p. 168.

884 Jeff Collins, "Vietnam Was What Ailed Him," *Dallas Times Herald*, March 6, 1990, pp. A-1, 12.

885 Anne Belli, "Court-at-Law Judge Nick Lundy Dies," *The Dallas Morning News*, November 7, 1991, p. A-38.

886 Military Record of Charles Nicholas "Nick" Lundy, National Personnel Records Center, FOIA request by B. G. Burkett, June 20, 1990.

887 Military Record of Henry Edwin Kinsey III, National Personnel Records Center, FOIA request by B. G. Burkett, June 14, 1990.

888 David Morris, "Man Makes Appeal for Veterans' Needs," Midland, Texas, *Reporter Telegram*, February 2, 1990. Also Steve Miller, "Wheelchair Traveler on Journey for

Better Care for Veterans," *Rapid City* (South Dakota) *Journal*, August 27, 1990.

889 Steve Miller, "Wheelchair Veteran Accused of Deception," *Rapid City Journal*, September 8, 1990. Also Steve Miller, "Wheelchair Veteran Denies Leaving False Impression," *Rapid City Journal*, September 9, 1990.

890 Cecil, *Herbicidal Warfare*, p. 168.

891 Michael Gough, *Dioxin, Agent Orange: The Facts* (Plenum, 1986).

892 Reuters, "Study Finds Dioxin Caused No Increase in Defects at Birth," *The New York Times*, March 18, 1988.

893 Associated Press, "Limited Health Risks From Dioxin Reported," *The New York Times*, May 12, 1984, p. 29.

894 Marilyn A. Fingerhut, Ph.D., et al, "Cancer Mortality in Workers Exposed to 2,3,7,8–Tetrachlorodibenzo-p-Dioxin," *The New England Journal of Medicine*, January 24, 1991.

895 Eric Felten, "Groundless Zero," *Insight*, the *Washington Times* magazine, August 12, 1991, p. 14.

896 Elizabeth M. Whelan, Sc.D., M.P.H., *Toxic Terror: The Truth Behind the Cancer Scares* (Buffalo, New York: Prometheus Books, 1993), p. 280. The American Council on Science and Health considers the 2, 4, 5–T scare one of the twenty greatest "unfounded" health fears in recent times, according to a 1997 book called *Facts vs. Fears,* by Adam J. Lieberman, published by ACSH.

897 Philip M. Boffey, "Lack of Military Data Halts Agent Orange Study," *The New York Times*, September 1, 1987, pp. C-1, 5.

898 Vietnam Experience Study, "Health Status of Vietnam Veterans," *Journal of the American Medical Association*, Vol. 259, No. 18, May 13, 1988, pp. 2701.

899 Felten, "Groundless Zero."

900 William H. Wolfe, M.D., et al, "Health Status of Air Force Veterans Occupationally Exposed to Herbicides in Vietnam," *Journal of the American Medical Association*, Vol. 264, No. 14, October 10, 1990, pp. 1824–1831. Also Joel E. Michalek, Ph.D., et al, "Health Status of Air Force Veterans Occupationally Exposed to Herbicides in Vietnam," *JAMA*, Vol. 264, No. 14, October 10, 1990, pp. 1832–1836.

901 Thomas M. Burton, "How Stanley Chesley Settles Things Quickly in Mass-Injury Suits," *The Wall Street Journal*, June 26, 1992. Chesley said that Yannacone's statement was "just not true."

902 L. Gordon Crovitz, "Contingency Fees and the Common Good," *The Wall Street Journal*, July 21, 1989.

903 "Agent Orange: Resolving a Painful Vietnam War Legacy," *Backgrounder*, the Heritage Foundation, Washington, D.C., May 22, 1984, p. 2.

904 Committee to Review the Health Effects in Vietnam Veterans of Exposure to Herbicides, *Veterans and Agent Orange: Health Effects of Herbicides Used in Vietnam* (Washington, D.C.: National Academy Press, 1993).

905 Ibid., p. 224.

906 "Dioxin Use Banned at VA Medical Facilities," *VVA Veteran*, March 1995, p. 9.

907 Jon Franklin, Speech to Toxicologists, Copyright (c) 1994 by Jon Franklin, University of Oregon, School of Journalism and Communication.

908 Editorial, "A Bad Agent Orange Decision," *Washington Post*, May 31, 1996, p. A-22.

909 Michael Fumento, "Gulf War Syndrome and the Press," *The Wall Street Journal*, March 4, 1997. Hanchette declined to comment for Fumento's story.

910 Jim Schnable, "The Real Causes of 'Gulf War Syndrome,'" *Washington Post*, November 15, 1996, p. A-30.

Chapter Twenty-Three: The VVA: Vietnam Victims of America

911 Mike Barnicle, "Incarceration and Good Sense," *Boston Sunday Globe*, February 20, 1994.

912 Joseph Cerquone, "Joe Yandle's Window of Opportunity," *VVA Veteran*, August 1994.

913 Kevin Cullen, "DA to Argue Against Yandle's Commutation," *Boston Globe*, June 7, 1995, pp. 1, 32.

914 Connie Paige, "Lifer Begs For Freedom at Emotional Hearing," *Boston Herald*, June 8, 1994.

915 Mike Wallace, "The Get Away Drivers," 60 *Minutes*, CBS News, February 6, 1994.

916 Cerquone, "Joe Yandle's Window of Opportunity," p. 6.

917 Kevin Cullen, "Release is Backed," *Boston Globe*, May 4, 1995, pp. 1, 27.

918 Military Record of Joseph Yandle, National Personnel Records Center, FOIA request by B. G. Burkett.

919 Nancy Zaroulis, Gerald Sullivan, *Who Spoke Up: American Protest Against the War in Vietnam, 1963-1975.* (Holt Rinehart and Winston, N.Y., 1984), p. 354.

920 Ibid., p. 355.

921 Military record of Jan Barry Crumb, National Personnel Records Center, FOIA request by B. G. Burkett, June 9, 1992.

922 Scott, *The Politics of Readjustment*, p. 22.

923 Military Record of Robert Muller, National Personnel Records Center, FOIA request by B. G. Burkett. Muller's record shows he received two Purple Hearts, a Combat Action Ribbon, a National Defense Service Medal, a Vietnam Service Medal with three bronze stars, a Republic of Vietnam Meritorious Unit Citation, and a Republic of Vietnam Campaign Medal.

924 Dan Cragg, "The Anatomy of Betrayal," *The National Vietnam Veterans Review*, August 1982, p. 8.

925 John Kerry and Vietnam Veterans Against the War, *The New Soldier* (New York: McMillan, 1971), p. 102.

926 Transcript #01104, *Phil Donahue Show*, pp. 11–12.

927 Cragg, "The Anatomy of Betrayal."

928 "An Angry Young Veteran," *V.F.W. Magazine*, April 1979, pp. 34–35.

929 A. D. Horne, *The Wounded Generation* (New York: Prentice-Hall, Inc., 1981), p. 119.

930 Cragg, "The Anatomy of Betrayal."

931 Ibid.

932 VVA Master Plan, 1979.

933 Dan Cragg, "Prominent Vietnam Vets Group is Returning to Hanoi," *The Wall Street Journal*, May 24, 1982.

934 Vietnam Veterans of America, Consolidated Financial Statement of VVA Foundation and seventeen Vietnam Veterans of America Chapters for the Fiscal Year Ending April 30, 1982.

935 "Veterans Revolt," *The Village Voice*, November 8, 1983.

936 Cragg, "The Anatomy of Betrayal."

937 Transcript, interview of Bobby Muller, by Paul Howse, ABC-TV, July 13, 1982.

938 Jean Seligman et al, "A Good Year for Vietnam Vets," *Newsweek*, May 17, 1982.

939 Louis Harris and Associates, Inc., *Myths and Realities*, 1980.

940 Translation, *Quan Doi Nhan Dan (People's Army)*, Vietnam, December 20, 1981.

941 James Coates, "Vietnam Vets Group Fighting for Its Life," *Chicago Tribune*, May 23, 1982.

942 Ibid.

943 Letter from Clifford G. Olsen, VFW National Commander, to Robert Muller, Executive Director of the VVA, March 20, 1984.

944 Letter from Clifford G. Olsen, VFW National Commander, to Members of Congress, April 28, 1984.

945 Records from *State of Rhode Island v. Wayne Smith*, Case #72–288, January 17, 1973. Smith was indicted for the December 6, 1971 murder of Kenneth Donnelly. Convicted of manslaughter, Smith was sentenced to 10 years in prison on January 3, 1973.

946 Military Record of Wayne F. Smith, National Personnel Records Center, FOIA request by B. G. Burkett, January 2, 1992.

947 Remarks by Robert O. Muller, Sonoma, CA, 1979, transcribed by Dan Cragg and Peter Joannides.

948 Letter "Brothers, Veterans, and Former Prisoners of War," signed by "Former Captain L.E. Mitchell," on Vietnam Veterans of America letterhead, December 13, 1981. It was signed by two others; one was Col. Fred Cherry, USAF (Ret.), and former Gunnery Sergeant John Deering, both legitimate POWs.

949 *Time*, July 13, 1983, pp. 21–22.

950 Rick Weidman, "VVA Responds to Critics," *Stars and Stripes*, July 22, 1982. I was never able to locate a military record for Larry E. Mitchell.

951 Dan Cragg, "The Dark at the End of the Tunnel," *National Vietnam Veterans Review*, Jan/Feb 1983, p. 9.

952 Terry McDonell, "The War Goes On," *Rolling Stone*, March 18, 1982, p. 11.

953 Weidman, "VVA Responds to Critics."

954 Cragg, "The Anatomy of Betrayal."

955 Steve Levin, "Overt Action," *The Dallas Morning News*, December 14, 1989, pp. C-1, 6.

956 Texas Department of Public Safety Computerized Criminal History Summary for Arthur John Woods Jr., October 11, 1995.

957 Military record of Arthur John Woods Jr., National Personnel Records Center, FOIA request by B. G. Burkett, January 2, 1990.

958 Bruce Tomaso, "A Would-Be Hero," *The Dallas Morning News*, August 25, 1990, p. A-1.

959 Bridgette Y. Rose, "Center May Suffer From Director's Claim He was a Vietnam Vet," *The Dallas Morning News*, August 26, 1990.

960 Military Record of James Louis Brazee Jr., National Personnel Records Center, FOIA request by B. G. Burkett, October 8, 1991.

961 "VVA Challenger Disqualified as Candidate," *Washington Post*, August 6, 1993.

962 Internal politics forced Jim Brazee's resignation from his post as VVA president in early 1997.

963 There now are four types of discharges: Honorable, General, Discharge Under Other Than Honorable Conditions, and Dishonorable.

964 Myra MacPherson, *VVA Veteran*, May 1985.

965 "Bringing Benefits Inside," *VVA Veteran*, May/June 1994, p. 10.

966 1995 Convention Issue, *VVA Veteran*, October 1995.

967 Letter from Dr. Tom Williams to Lester Bernstein, editor, *Newsweek*, May 20, 1982.

Chapter Twenty-Four: America's Wailing Wall

968 Although Buis' name was initially first on the wall, the name of Army Captain Harry G. Cramer, an advisor to the South Vietnamese who died two years earlier in 1957,

was later added. But some consider the first U.S. casualty of the Communists in Vietnam to be Maj. A. Peter Dewey, an OSS operative who arrived in Saigon on September 4, 1945 to arrange for the repatriation of 214 American POWs held by the Japanese. Dewey, his mission accomplished and scheduled to fly out that day, was killed by a burst of automatic rifle fire while riding in a jeep near the airport on September 26, 1945. His body was never recovered. In 1981, a Vietnamese refugee who had escaped communist Vietnam revealed that Dewey had been ambushed by a group of Advance Guard Youth, a military arm of the Viet Minh.

969   Although the United States military had a presence in South Vietnam beginning in 1959, fewer than two hundred American military troops died in Vietnam each year from 1960 until 1965, when the war began to pick up. The peak of the war casualties was 1968, the year of the Tet Offensive, when more than sixteen thousand died. American troops began to withdraw in 1970, and the deaths dropped to 6,084. By 1972, when most troops were withdrawn, only 640 casualties were reported. But there remained an American military presence, primarily embassy employees, CIA, and other intelligence operatives, until 1975, when the North invaded the South and 158 Americans were killed. Well after the war ended, even as late as 1989, the casualties continued, as men who were severely injured succumbed to complications arising from their wounds. And some who were listed as missing have been confirmed dead.

Many don't realize that about 17 percent of those whose names are on The Wall were not killed by the enemy. Altogether, 47,358 died as a result of hostile action. Of those, at least sixty-four men died in captivity; some were starved to death, others tortured and executed. The rest (10,355) died of other causes, including: accident, heart attack/stroke, suicide, disease, drowned or suffocated, accidental homicide, intentional homicide, and "misadventure," which was used most often to connote a drug overdose.

The Army took the heaviest toll, with 65 percent of the dead. Next was the Marine Corps, with 25 percent. (The 25th Infantry Division and the first Marine Division lost more men in Vietnam than they did in either World War II or Korea.) The Air Force accounted for about 5 percent of the casualties, and another 5 percent were in the Navy or Coast Guard.

The states with the highest percentage of casualties include California, with 9.58 percent, New York, with 7.08 percent, and Texas, with 5.87 percent. A significant number came from Puerto Rico, Guam, and other U.S. territories. About 120 of those who died were citizens of other countries who had enlisted in the U.S. military. Nations represented include England, Ireland, France, Germany, Switzerland, Italy, Bahamas, Jamaica, Mexico, Brazil, Panama, Colombia, Bolivia, Costa Rica, Peru, Japan, Australia, New Zealand, and the Philippines.

But the country that suffered the most casualties alongside Americans were from Canada. While about 20,000 Americans fled to Canada to escape the draft, somewhere between 30,000 and 40,000 Canadians joined the American military during the Vietnam era and an estimated 12,000 served in Vietnam itself. Seventy-four Canadians' names are on the wall as KIA, along with five listed as missing in action. Peter C. Lemon of Norwich, Ontario, was awarded the Medal of Honor for heroism in Vietnam.

970   "Flogging The Wall," *VVA Veteran*, April 1985, p. 7.

971   Allen Richards, "Court Bans Regulations on Mall T-shirt Sales," *Stars and Stripes*, September 18–24, 1995, p. 1.

972   Peter Meyer and the Editors of LIFE, *The Wall: A Day at the Vietnam Veterans Memorial* (New York: St. Martin's Press, 1993), p. 38.

973   Sal Lopes, *The Wall: Images and Offerings from the Vietnam Veterans Memorial* (New York: Collins Publishers Inc., 1987).

974   Laura Palmer, *Shrapnel in the Heart*, (New York: Random House, 1987).

975   Lopes, *The Wall*, p. 44.

976   Obituary, "Lt. Col. Charles Eatley, backed POW-MIA Issues," *Washington Times*, September 5, 1989. Also, Tom Wieber, "CSM Chuck 'Top' Eatley," *BRAVO Veterans Outlook*, October 1989.

977   Michael Katakis, *The Vietnam Veterans Memorial* (New York: Crown Publishers, Inc., 1988), pp. 22–23.

978   Military record of Charles M. Eatley, National Personnel Records Center, FOIA request by B. G. Burkett, August 25, 1989.

979   Duncan Spencer and Lloyd Wolf, *Facing The Wall: Americans at the Vietnam Veterans Memorial* (New York: Collier Books, 1986), p. 36.

980   Military record of Anatol Kononenko, National Personnel Records Center, FOIA request by B.G. Burkett, April 8, 1998.

981   After I notified a *The Dallas Morning News* reporter of DeJoseph's misrepresentation, he confirmed my information, and notified the Associated Press. The AP refused to run a retraction or notify the subscribers who ran the photo. They simply changed the caption for future users to read, "Roni DeJoseph, who says he is a Vietnam veteran. . . ."

982   "Making Amends," *People Weekly*, November 27, 1995, p. 146.

983   I found a total of twenty-five men who survived the war, but whose names are etched on the granite. Those men are: Robert Lee Bedker (10E-69), Robert M. Bennett (20E-127), Clark T. Bootz (7W-112), Stanley E. Bowen (22E-90), Peter H. Brown (11E-64), Carl Cox (17E-34), Willard D. Craig (12E-87), Marian J. Dominiak Jr. (32E-43), David R. Edwardson (22E-77), James R. Gilbreath (11W-73), Keith L. Hardy (18E-4), Larry G. Hatch (17E-122), Andrew J. Hilden (14E-108), Timothy L. Honsinger (10E-86), Dennis C. Huckaby (19W-101; his name is really Huckabay), Clifford W. James (18–E), Allan H. Jordan (10E-83), Louis D. Kimes (12E-89), Christopher G. Miraclia (7W-36), Rockney D. Monroe (18E-6), Alexander Manzanares Morales (19W-103), Frankie Northern (7W-47), Daniel P. Ovellette (11W-17), and Eugene J. Toni (7W-121).

Most of these men were decorated combat soldiers. Almost all had been seriously wounded and, after being stabilized, had been medevacked out of Vietnam. In most cases the units, believing that the men had been killed in action, listed them as such. Meanwhile, another record was opened to follow them through the medical process. Bowen served two tours and has three Purple Hearts. Army Capt. Peter Brown received the Silver Star, Bronze Star Medal, and a Purple Heart. Army Sgt. Eugene Toni lost part of both legs in Vietnam when he tripped a land mine on a reconnaissance patrol. Seeing his name on The Wall was unsettling. "It's kind of scary," he said when a reporter called him. "It's like seeing your name on a gravestone."

With such an ambitious project—listing more than fifty-eight thousand casualties—it was inevitable there would be some mistakes. Their names remain on The Wall; the only way a name can be removed is if a panel cracks and must be replaced.

In the process of locating these men alive, I found another peculiarity—a man who had never served in the military at all. In fact, he was completely fictitious.

Altogether, I found seven nonexistent people on The Wall: David A. Grilly (23W-100), Paul A. Froehl (65E- 8), James G. Griener (22W-52), Kris Bilmer (22W-116), Curtis E. Dandy (56E-5), Rodney G. Heisel (13W-111), and Douglas C. Rustine (47E-54).

These names are all variations on the names of real casualties, who are on The Wall as well: David A. Crilly (23W-98), Paul A. Proehl (66E-1), James G. Griner (22W-53), Kris Blumer (21W-53), Curtis E. Bandy (55E-39), Rodney G. Helsel (13W-112), and Douglas C. Ristine (47E-42).

The names of twelve deserters are engraved on the granite, including Michael John Kustigian of Worcester, Massachusetts, and Harry E. Mitchell, of Marion, Indiana. These two twenty-one-year-old seamen were reported to have disappeared from their ship, a light missile cruiser named the USS *Long Beach*, on May 5 or 6, 1968, when it was within sight of the coast of North Vietnam.

When the lockers of the two friends, who shared an apartment in Long Beach, were searched, it was discovered that their wallets and money were gone. In Kustigian's personal effects investigators found a color photo of a slain Viet Cong and a book titled *American War Crimes in Vietnam*, published by something called the Democratic Republic of Vietnam Commission for Investigation of the American Imperialistic War Crimes in Vietnam.

Friends told authorities that Kustigian had expressed some misgivings about his forthcoming nuptials and Mitchell had been despondent over an imminent break-up with a girlfriend. He had frequently talked about wanting to get out of the Navy. A friend's scuba gear, on loan to Mitchell, was missing. Both Kustigian and Mitchell were good swimmers. There was no evidence of foul play, no life boats were missing, and the safety lines were intact. The seas that night had been calm, with a bright moon and good visibility. After a search of the area, authorities concluded the two seamen deliberately disappeared over the side of the ship together and declared them missing. Since there was no evidence that they had died, on May 16, they were declared AWOL, and later listed as deserters. They were finally registered as casualties—missing, presumed dead.

In the midseventies, a review of Kustigian and Mitchell's disappearance resulted in them being declared missing in action. They were promoted retroactively to E-9. (In such cases, the next of kin is usually awarded back pay and death benefits.) In March 1980, Kustigian and Mitchell were declared KIA. Did they attempt to swim to shore and drown or did they make it to North Vietnam? The mystery may never be solved, but the names Michael John Kustigian and Harry E. Mitchell, with the date of death May 6, 1968, are on The Wall, at panel 56E, lines 11 and 12.

One deserter whose name is on The Wall turned up alive more than twenty-five years after his disappearance. In 1996, a frail seventy-three-year-old man named Mateo Sabog walked into a Social Security office in Chattanooga, Tennessee, and applied for benefits. But officials suspected he was an impostor using Sabog's name and Social Security number. After all, MSgt. Mateo Sabog had been declared dead, and his name was listed on the memorial.

A native of Waipahu, Hawaii, Sabog had been assigned to the 507th Transportation Group in Binh Dinh, South Vietnam. On February 25, 1970, at the end of his tour of duty, Sabog went through the outprocessing procedure at the Headquarters of the 507th in Saigon, en route to his new assignment at Fort Bragg, North Carolina. But he never arrived at his new post. He simply disappeared.

Fort Bragg had not been notified of Sabog's arrival, so it wasn't until 1973, when his brother Kenneth Sabog wrote the Army, that the military was aware he was missing. Mateo Sabog was listed as a deserter, but in 1979 Kenneth challenged that designation in a letter to President Jimmy Carter. The Army convened a board of officers and his status was changed to "missing, presumed dead." After all, Sabog had twenty-four years of honorable service and was eligible for retirement. Why would he have deserted returning *from* Vietnam? Kenneth Sabog wrote to the governments of Vietnam, Laos and Cambodia, trying to locate his brother's remains. At one point, the Army's Central Identification Laboratory in Hawaii indicated that some bones recovered in Vietnam might have been Sabog's.

Kenneth was astonished to hear that a wraith in a Tennessee government office was claiming to be his long-lost brother but confirmed that the man was Mateo. Army officials said it appeared that Sabog simply walked away from the military at some point. Using the name Robert Fernandez, he lived with a woman in California. He later moved to Rossville, Georgia, to take care of an elderly woman.

The Army returned Sabog to active duty but declined to "hardball" his case. Nobody wanted to beat up on a sickly old man. In fact, it appeared that Sabog might be eligible for a sizable windfall: retirement pay for six years, or about $117,000, plus other military benefits. His name remains on the black granite.

Index

NOTE: Page numbers in boldface type indicate photographs. Page numbers containing a subscript indicate an endnote; for example, 629₁₁₅ is endnote number 115 on page 629.